MANUFACTURING

MANUFACTURING

A Historiographical and Bibliographical Guide

DAVID O. WHITTEN,
EDITOR

BESSIE E. WHITTEN,
ASSISTANT EDITOR

**HANDBOOK OF AMERICAN BUSINESS HISTORY,
VOLUME I**

GREENWOOD PRESS
New York • Westport, Connecticut • London

Library of Congress Cataloging-in-Publication Data

Handbook of American business history / David O. Whitten, editor,
  Bessie E. Whitten, assistant editor.
    p. cm.
  Includes bibliographical references.
  Contents: v. 1. Manufacturing.
  ISBN 0-313-25198-3 (v. 1 : alk. paper)
  1. United States—Industries—History—Handbooks, manuals, etc.
I. Whitten, David O. II. Whitten, Bessie E. (Bessie Emrick)
HC103.H19 1990
338.0973—dc20   89-25921

British Library Cataloguing in Publication Data is available.

Library of Congress Catalog Card Number: 89-25921
ISBN: 0-313-25198-3

First published in 1990

Greenwood Press, Inc.
88 Post Road West, Westport, Connecticut 06881

Printed in the United States of America

The paper used in this book complies with the
Permanent Paper Standard issued by the National
Information Standards Organization (Z39.48-1984).

10 9 8 7 6 5 4 3 2 1

For Eleanor Craig Emrick and Verl Roy Emrick

CONTENTS

PREFACE

The idea for the *Handbook of American Business History* series originated with Greenwood Press. The Press invited me to construct a framework for the project, contract scholars to prepare the essays and bibliographies, and edit the final work. I accepted the challenge and chose the Enterprise Standard Industrial Classification (ESIC) as the structure around which I would organize the work. It was Greenwood's decision to begin the series with *Manufacturing*.

I invited hundreds of economic and business historians to participate in the Handbook of American Business History project. The membership lists of the Business History Conference, the Economic and Business Historical Society, and the Cliometrics Society were used to generate the invitation list. Furthermore, the names of economists belonging to the American Economic Association who declared economic history as one of their fields of interest were also invited to participate. The response was hearty. Contracts were drawn and work began.

My years of experience as editor of the *Wall Street Review of Books* taught me that overbooking was not the exclusive province of the scheduled airlines. Academics are more willing to sign contracts than they are to complete projects. Only by overbooking could I have gotten enough material to produce this volume. Some material contracted for it arrived too late for press, but will appear in later volumes. Iron and Steel Foundries, ESIC 33.2, for example, will appear in the next volume. Several important industries attracted no contract: Paper and Allied Products, ESIC 26.0, and Fabricated Metal Products, ESIC 34.0, are examples of industries not assigned. Some classifications were assigned to volunteers who did not complete their work:

Furniture and Fixtures, ESIC 25.0, and Printing and Publishing, ESIC 27.0, are examples. I will continue to prod current contract holders and recruit new ones to fill important gaps in our offerings. Future volumes of the Handbook will add to the material offered here as well as expand our investigations into additional ESIC classifications.

The Handbook of American Business History series is intended to supplement, not supplant, bibliographic materials available in business history. Contributors were asked to prepare concise histories of their industries or subindustries and support them with a bibliographic essay and a bibliography. The histories begin with the industries' rise to importance in the United States and continue to the present. The bibliographic essays present a narrative outline of the leading sources published (and sometimes not published, but available in an archives, library, or museum collection) since Robert W. Lovett's *American Economic and Business History Information Sources* (1971) and Henrietta M. Larson's *Guide to Business History* (1948). The essays are followed by bibliographic checklists of the titles mentioned in the narrative as well as others.

Some contributors prepared three distinct segments for their industries; others combined their work into one or two segments. I did not strive for uniformity, but encouraged contributors to prepare their material as they thought best. Source material is not homogeneous from industry to industry, and that heterogeneity is evident in the essays and bibliographies presented here. The contributors include business historians, economic historians, social historians, engineers, and lawyers. Most are academics, but not all. The chapters and subchapters reflect the differences in approach and interest of the contributors and the differences in the materials available on the various industries and subindustries. Jack Blicksilver, an economic historian, prepared a striking narrative economic history of the apparel industry complete with empirical support. Carol J. Miller, an attorney, imparts her legal point of view to her study and bibliography of the tobacco industry.

Every contributor to *Manufacturing* is deserving of praise, and I offer it here. Some require additional credit. Spiro G. Patton submitted our first segment; his work became our example for other contributors. Mira Wilkins wrote the introduction, but she did much more than that. She kept up with the progress of the work and offered encouragement. She also provided material on international business that was worked into many of the chapters. Cynthia Harris, my Greenwood editor, showed patience beyond expectations and gave me direction when I asked for it. Barbara K. Nelson, Kevin L. Cook, and Glenn A. Anderson of the Auburn University Library consulted the Online Computer Library Center (OCLC) to untangle many bibliographic riddles. Bessie Emrick Whitten, my wife and assistant editor, has done yeoman duty on the Handbook—no one has more time invested in this work. And no one has placed so indelible a mark on it.

Manuscript preparation was done repeatedly. Most segments were typed at least five times, accurately, conscientiously, and cheerfully by Loraine M. Hyde, Linda H. Mathis, and Margie D. Wright. They deserve special thanks.

MANUFACTURING

INTRODUCTION

MIRA WILKINS

This introductory chapter is on general works in U.S. business history, books, articles, and other items that do not fit under a single or even under two or three industry rubrics. The chapters that follow in this volume will cover contributions specific to a particular industry. This introduction is confined not only to the general literature but also to those historical studies that focus on business as an actor. Overall histories of the American economy and of the U.S. role in the world economy have been omitted. On occasion, however, influential books, articles, and information sources have been included that (1) give background data, (2) are not historical yet have had major impact on American business historians, and (3) cast special light on problems central to business history.

I start with the most general synoptic contributions, adding the principal business history textbooks and bibliographical sources. The first section also contains basic source material essential to the business historian. The second section turns to themes addressed by business historians (always leaving out studies on individual companies or industries since these will be covered in the industry chapters of this handbook). The themes, considered in sequence, are entrepreneurship and business biography; business organization, including mergers and acquisitions; technological change; government and business; business and labor relations; distribution of wealth; the regional dimensions of business history; and finally, U.S. business and international cartels. The third section contains a brief discussion of certain theoretical works that provide beacons for students of the history of American business. Since Volume 1 of this handbook is on manufacturing, a concluding part of this introduction contains books and articles related to the business history of manufacturing per se.

GENERAL STUDIES (INCLUDING TEXTBOOKS AND BASIC SOURCE MATERIALS)

The classic in American business history is Alfred D. Chandler, Jr.'s *The Visible Hand* (1977). Chandler's magisterial study of managerial capitalism—on the history of U.S., British, and German business in modern times, entitled *Scale and Scope* (forthcoming 1990)—does not replace *The Visible Hand*, but rather, through the comparative method, adds new and profound insights into what was uniquely American in business development. Chandler's contributions to the business history discipline have been legion. His 1962 *Strategy and Structure* had and continues to have enormous influence. His still earlier, and often reprinted, "The Beginnings of Big Business in American Industry" (1959) remains basic reading. Thomas K. McCraw (1988) has put together a highly useful tribute volume, comprising some of Chandler's principal contributions. Chandler revolutionized the business history discipline by seeking patterns in the rise of the large-scale, multiplant, multifunctional, multiproduct, and multiregional, multinational enterprise. He insisted that such modern, giant businesses presented managerial challenges not evident in single plant, single function, single product, local business enterprises and that the administration of these firms was a crucial subject for business historians. Chandler turned the attention of business historians from a focus on the individual entrepreneur to the nature of managerial strategies and structures of the major modern corporations. From *The Visible Hand* onward, Chandler has emphasized the technological "underpinnings" (his word in Chandler 1986) in the rise of modern business enterprise. His contributions to the discipline are without peer.

The history of American-headquartered multinational enterprise is covered in Mira Wilkins, *The Emergence of Multinational Enterprise: American Business Abroad from the Colonial Era to 1914* (1970), and in her *Maturing of Multinational Enterprise: American Business Abroad from 1914 to 1970* (1974a), while the history of foreign business in the United States is documented in her *History of Foreign Investment in the United States to 1914* (1989). She is now in the process of preparing a sequel to that volume, which will consider foreign investment, and specifically foreign business, in the United States from 1914 to the present. Both Chandler and Wilkins have recognized that it is impossible to understand U.S. business history without including the international dimension.

Textbooks on American business history are now numerous. As we view this literature, it is interesting how cognizant many American business historians were of the international context. This was certainly always true of business history at Harvard. One of the earliest textbooks was N.S.B. Gras and Henrietta M. Larson, eds., *Casebook in American Business History* (1939). This has been superseded by Alfred D. Chandler, Jr., and Richard Tedlow, eds., *The Coming of Managerial Capitalism: A Casebook on the*

History of American Economic Institutions (1985). The Gras and Larson casebook was designed to supplement Gras, *Business and Capitalism: An Introduction to Business History* (1939). Both the 1939 *Casebook* and the Gras history were far broader in scope than merely domestic U.S. business history.

In 1941 Thomas C. Cochran and William Miller published *The Age of Enterprise*, a revised paperback edition of which appeared in 1961. Meanwhile, Cochran offered students of business history his short but splendid *The American Business System: A Historical Perspective, 1900–1955* (1957) and also an equally brief *Basic History of American Business* (1959). In 1959 Arthur H. Cole, *Business Enterprise in Its Social Setting*, also appeared.

Students of U.S. business history in the 1960s read these general works plus the newly published ones of Chandler. In the 1970s and 1980s, a flood of business histories appeared. Herman E. Krooss and Charles Gilbert, *American Business History* (1972), remains useful. Likewise, Cochran published *Business in American Life: A History* (1972) and his excellent *200 Years of American Business* (1977). Newer well-done textbooks include Keith L. Bryant, Jr., and Henry C. Dethloff, *A History of American Business* (1983); James Oliver Robertson, *America's Business* (1985); Mansel G. Blackford and K. Austin Kerr, *Business Enterprise in American History* (1986); and C. Joseph Pusateri, *A History of American Business* (2d ed., 1988). Blackford, in his *Rise of Modern Business* (1988), compares the growth of U.S., British, and Japanese business.

Business historians for years relied on Larson's *Guide to Business History* (1948), which was updated by Lorna M. Daniells, *Studies in Enterprise: A Selected Bibliography of American and Canadian Company Histories and Biographies of Businessmen* (1957). Annual supplements to this volume appeared in *Business History Review* issues each summer 1959–62 and in the fall of 1963 and 1964. In 1971 Robert W. Lovett published *American Economic and Business History Information Sources*. At the close of 1987, the Center for the History of Business, Technology, and Society, at the Hagley Museum and Library, Wilmington, Delaware, became the American participant in an international venture to create a bibliography of business history.

Business History Review, the antecedents of which date back to 1926, is the journal of the discipline. *Business and Economic History* is issued annually covering the proceedings of the Business History Conference, the professional society of American business historians. The Economic and Business Historical Society publishes an annual volume entitled *Essays in Economic and Business History*. *Business History*, the British journal of business historians, often carries articles useful for American business historians.

Beginning in January, 1974, the Japanese have had once-a-year conferences on comparative business history, held at the Fuji Education Center,

Susono, Shizuoka; American business historians have participated, and the proceedings of each conference have been published (in English) by the University of Tokyo Press. These conferences have assisted business historians in placing American business history in an international context. While many have been industry-specific, some have been more general, for example, the first one on business strategy and structure (Nakagawa [1976]) and the most recent one on foreign business (including American business) in Japan (Yuzawa and Udagawa, forthcoming 1990).

The proceedings of other international conferences have in various ways helped American business historians discover more about American business history; see, for example, Harold Williamson, ed., *Evolution of International Management Structures* (1972); Herman Daems and Herman van der Wee, eds., *The Rise of Managerial Capitalism* (1974); Alfred D. Chandler, Jr., and Herman Daems, eds., *Managerial Hierarchies* (1980); Alice Teichova, Maurice Lévy-Leboyer, and Helga Nussbaum, eds., *Multinational Enterprise in Historical Perspective* (1986); and Ernest R. May and John K. Fairbank, eds., *America's China Trade in Historical Perspective* (1986).

Business historians must use corporate archives in their basic research. On such archives, see Karen Benedict, *A Select Bibliography on Business Archives and Record Management* (1981), updated in 1984 and 1986 by the Business Archives Section of the Society of American Archivists. The society also prepared a 1987 "Directory of Business Archives in the United States and Canada."

Universities, such as Harvard and Columbia, and institutions, such as the Hagley Museum and Library, are important depositories of business records. Robert W. Lovett and Eleanor Bishop compiled a guide to manuscripts in the Baker Library, Graduate School of Business Administration, Harvard University, subtitled "a guide to sources for business, economic, and social history" (1978). The Scudder Collection at the Business School Library, Columbia University, is very valuable. Michael Nash, "Business History at the Hagley Museum and Library" (1986), gives an introduction to that significant collection. Earlier Lovett had written on business records in libraries (1957) and the status of business archives (1969); see also Benedict's 1982 article on business archives literature. In the main, most business historians still follow others' footnotes (and their own contacts) in locating relevant collections. A general guide to business records in the United States (inside and outside corporate archives) is sorely needed. In addition to a business archive, every large company in the United States has at least one library (which often is *not* the same as its archives); such business libraries are invaluable in locating published background information relevant to the particular company's history. Likewise, public libraries in towns where a manufacturer is or was of significance have substantial published (and occasionally unpublished) data.

A number of "oral history collections" exist, containing interviews of business leaders. Some are located within business archives (usually done by the business itself). The most accessible oral history collection is in the Columbia University Library. The idea of oral history was that of Columbia University historian Allan Nevins, who had special interests in business history.

Every student of U.S. business history has at one time or another consulted *Moody's Manuals* and *Standard and Poor's*. Corporate annual reports, while lean as sources for the early histories of American business, have become richer over time. New York Stock Exchange Listing Statements have been helpful to some business historians, and "10K submissions" to the U.S. Securities and Exchange Commission (S.E.C.) offer invaluable data for the historian of post–World War II American business.

S.E.C. records are not the only U.S. government source employed by business historians. Reports of the U.S. Industrial Commission, the Bureau of Corporations, the Federal Trade Commission, the Temporary National Economic Committee, and the U.S. Tariff Commission, for example, as well as numerous House and Senate committee reports and hearings are highly informative. Likewise, publications of the League of Nations and the United Nations and their specialized agencies often offer good comparative data for the student of American business history.

Business historians have found in U.S. court records and reports on court decisions evidence on business behavior. "Lexis," an on-line computer service, now provides court decisions easily and quickly, serving as an invaluable source for research. Briefs and transcripts on major cases are available in the nation's best law libraries.

Industry publications, such as yearbooks, bulletins, and trade association serials, contain details about companies within an industry. Business historians have also used *Fortune's* and *Forbes's* annual lists of company rankings. Chandler (1962, 1977, 1990) has presented similar lists, accompanied by industry designations and other analyses. Back issues of business magazines and newspapers—*Fortune* and *Forbes* as well as the *Commercial and Financial Chronicle, Business Week,* and the *Wall Street Journal,* for example—all assist the business historian.

Basic statistics on business formations are in George Heberton Evans, Jr.,'s *Business Incorporations in the United States, 1800–1943* (1948). For more general statistical information, business historians rely heavily on the U.S. Bureau of the Census, *Historical Statistics of the United States, Colonial Times to 1970* (1975); annual issues of the U.S. Bureau of the Census, *Statistical Abstract of the United States*; and the annual *Economic Report of the President. Historical Statistics of the United States* contains references on specific sources. These U.S. government publications offer only aggregate statistics. Company records, business manuals, industry- or company-specific government reports, and trade association publications (for example) must be turned to for material on individual companies:

profit and loss statements, balance sheets, production and sales data, and so forth.

THEMES

Entrepreneurship and Business Biography

For many years, studies of entrepreneurs and entrepreneurship dominated the field of business history. The Research Center in Entrepreneurial History (1948–58) at Harvard University had a journal, *Explorations in Entrepreneurial History*, which under the direction of the center explored all facets of entrepreneurial behavior, domestically and internationally. In a first-rate Ph.D. dissertation in 1977 (published in 1986), Steven A. Sass has written a historiographical work on entrepreneurial historians and history, 1940–60.

Before the center was organized, there had been many studies of businessmen, often representing them as predatory individuals. Works such as Gustavus Myers, *The History of Great American Fortunes* (first published in 1909 and in a Modern Library edition in 1936), Matthew Josephson, *Robber Barons* (1934), and Miriam Beard, *A History of the Business Man* (1938), presented images of greedy men with few favorable attributes. By contrast, Joseph Schumpeter, *The Theory of Economic Development*, first published in German in 1911 and translated into English in 1934, described (some say romanticized) the business entrepreneur as the force for positive economic advance. In 1932 Frank W. Taussig and C. S. Joslyn published an influential volume on American business leaders subtitled "a study in social origins and stratification."

From the 1940s onward, there came to be two streams of responses to the earlier literature on business biography and entrepreneurship. At the Harvard Business School, a group under the auspices of Gras and his immediate successors published business histories and business biographies that sought to counter the image of the "bad businessman." At Columbia University, Nevins wrote sympathetically the biographies of several giants in American business history. The issue arose, were businessmen "robber barons," to use Josephson's title *and* viewpoint, or were they "industrial statesmen"? Larson, Ralph Hidy, Nevins, and others painted portraits of industrial statesmen, men who had built America. This group of scholars produced an outflow of business histories and business biographies dealing with specific men and their companies.

The second stream of reactions took place within the Research Center in Entrepreneurial History. Here the scholars were less concerned with businessmen as heroes or villains and more with what constituted entrepreneurial behavior and what the social origins of entrepreneurs were. In books and journal articles (especially, but not exclusively, in *Explorations in En-*

trepreneurial History), these men and women explored the meaning of entrepreneurship and the applicability of Schumpeter's views (Schumpeter himself was at Harvard University and was involved in the center until his death in 1950). Robert Aaron Gordon had published *Business Leadership in the Large Corporation* in 1945, and business historians at the center discussed the relationships between rational and cognitive entrepreneurship and matters of "multiple leadership" posed by Gordon (Cole 1946). The group at the center was very influenced by developments in the field of sociology. The individuals participating included Cole (the founder), Leland H. Jenks, Cochran, Hugh G. J. Aitken, Miller, Sigmund O. Diamond, Fritz Redlich, Harold Passer, Frances Gregory, Irene Neu, Mabel Newcomer, Douglass C. North, and Alfred D. Chandler, Jr., all of whom made major contributions to the field of American business history. Others at the center (whom I have not mentioned) were involved exclusively in European, Canadian, Australian, or Latin American business history, so articles and discussions were often comparative. Despite the international character of the publications, rarely did the group look at business over borders (Jenks, who in 1927 had published a significant work on British capital overseas before 1875, was one exception, and occasionally Redlich dealt with the subject). Those at the center who specialized on American topics wrote on the social history of American elites (for example, Newcomer 1952, 1955) and on the reputation of American businessmen (Diamond 1955). William Miller, ed., *Men in Business: Essays on the Historical Role of the Entrepreneur* (1962), included a number of contributions by members of the center, as did Aitken, ed., *Explorations in Enterprise* (1965), a splendid compilation, with articles by Aitken himself, Cole, Schumpeter, W. T. Easterbrook, Jenks, and Cochran; it is particularly valuable in capturing the mood at the center. Redlich (1971) later republished a number of his own essays on entrepreneurship.

Thus, although the center came to an end in 1958, publications by its participants continued, as did its influence. Every business historian who started his or her career in the 1950s, 1960s, and early 1970s was influenced by the center. Likewise, the debate over robber barons versus industrial statesmen persisted well into the 1960s, and even a little beyond. John Chamberlain, *The Enterprising Americans* (1963), looked kindly on businessmen, while Ben B. Seligman's *The Potentates: Business and Businessmen in American History* (1971) was more in the robber barons tradition. In 1968, in the D. C. Heath Series, which was frequently assigned as required reading in standard American history courses, Peter d'A. Jones edited a collection entitled *The Robber Barons Revisited*.

Meanwhile, in 1961, an influential textbook in American economic history was issued that ignored key American businessmen as forces in economic change. Surely in part in response to the uproar, one of its three authors, Jonathan Hughes, wrote *The Vital Few* (1966, 2d ed. 1986); later, Hughes would describe the book as his "attempt to contribute to the *genre*

Professor Cole and his Center had developed" (Hughes 1983, 135). While Hughes arranged his entrepreneurs according to periods, or stages if you like, his biographical approach was traditional.

In the 1970s and 1980s, as the main direction of studies in business history, under the influence of Chandler, turned more toward the nature and characteristics of business institutions and business leaders as managers, business biography and studies of individual entrepreneurs have persisted. When some authors looked at small businesses (see next subsection of this essay), once again attention turned to the individual-owner-manager (the entrepreneur).

Some of the more recent contributions to entrepreneurial research deal with the role of minority groups. Juliet E. K. Walker, "Racism, Slavery, and Free Enterprise: Black Entrepreneurship in the United States Before the Civil War," in *Business History Review* (1986), is an excellent article, the notes to which contain a fine bibliography on early black business entrepreneurs in the United States.

There also continue to be numerous volumes of business biography, for example, Robert Sobel, *The Entrepreneurs* (1974); in 1987 Thomas V. DiBacco published *Made in the U.S.A.: The History of American Business*, which seems part of the literature of three decades past. Who would believe it possible to write a book on business history in 1987 that never mentions Chandler?

Business Organization, Including Mergers and Acquisitions

At the same time as the research went forth on entrepreneurship and business leadership, there came to be a recognition that in the late nineteenth and twentieth centuries, the owner-managed firm was increasingly being replaced by impersonal shareholder ownership of large-scale managerial enterprises. Businesses had grown, sometimes by mergers and acquisitions, sometimes by internal growth; sometimes through horizontal integration, sometimes through vertical integration; sometimes through diversification; and sometimes through unrelated mergers.

In 1932 Adolf A. Berle and Gardiner C. Means published *The Modern Corporation and Private Property* (rev. ed., 1967). Berle and Means pointed out that with the modern corporation there had arisen a separation of ownership and control. Thousands of stockholders "owned" the modern corporation that was administered by managers, who held a bare fraction (if any) of the corporate shares. Berle and Means asked, "Must we not, therefore, recognize that we are not dealing with property in the old sense?" (1967, viii) In an introduction to the 1967 edition of their work, Berle noted that the modern corporation with its managerial organization had resulted in immense increases in productivity (xxv). The divorce between ownership and control had accelerated and fueled a corporate revolution (xxx, xxix-xxxviii). Clearly, a business historian studying the nature of modern American business developments had to consider the managerial enterprise.

And business historians did, dealing specifically with the consequences of the growth of large-scale enterprises. Most conspicuous were the giants that came into being through mergers and acquisitions. There had been a long literature on business mergers, inaugurated perhaps with the multivolume report of the U.S. Industrial Commission at the turn of the century. Ralph L. Nelson, *Merger Movements in American Industry, 1895–1956* (1959), tracked the pace of mergers and identified periods of the most intense merger activity. Glenn Porter's *The Rise of Big Business, 1860–1910* (1973) was a useful contribution on the first era of giant enterprise, separating out mergers and acquisitions from internal growth. Naomi R. Lamoreaux, *The Great Merger Movement in American Business, 1895–1904* (1985), provides a major advance.

Anthony Patrick O'Brien, in a *Journal of Economic History* article, "Factory Size, Economies of Scale, and the Great Merger Wave of 1892–1902" (1988), highlighted some of the principal issues that have been debated over the years. Chandler had earlier argued (1959, 1962, 1977; see also G. Porter 1973) that the growth of big business was frequently by forward vertical integration (usually part of the business's internal growth) rather than by horizontal integration (most typically mergers and acquisitions). Chandler had stressed that *in both cases* unless there was integration and rationalization of the new large enterprises, inefficiencies would result. But *with integration* and appropriate managerial structures, Chandler believed, efficiencies were a consequence. Earlier critics had paid little attention to internal growth and maintained that mergers were basically to suppress competition and thus always resulted in inefficiencies. Could large-scale business, whether grown large by virtue of mergers and acquisition or by internal growth, actually be more efficient than smaller ones? "Yes," had been the reply of Berle and Means and of Chandler.

Recently, there have been suggestions among economists—in the spirit of Chandler and Berle and Means—that since one firm may have superior management to that of many small enterprises, placing the assets of merged units under a single management would mean higher asset value of the unified group; mergers could lead to cost savings (Posner 1986, 278, for example). O'Brien's 1988 article explores a more limited proposition: in the great merger movement at the turn of the century, were there "unexploited economies of scale" that were finally realized? Did the rise of the large factory date from the merger movement? O'Brien concludes that the principal innovations in factory size and the scale economies that created efficiencies took place in the 1870s and 1880s and that the turn-of-the-century merger movement was motivated more by desires to reduce price competition than to exploit economies of scale. O'Brien deals exclusively with matters related to *factory size*, rather than the broader issue posed by

Chandler (and Berle and Means), of whether unified managerial coordination of the entire enterprise offered potential efficiencies. Thus, while O'Brien adds fuel to the discussion on the efficiencies of mergers, he does not get to the heart of the important question: Under what circumstances does growth through mergers create efficiency, and under what circumstances does it hamper efficiency by suppressing competition? O'Brien does, however, push us to focus on what has become a crucial source of confusion: should "industrial structure" be discussed at a factory (plant) level or at a "firm" level? If the attention is to the firm (rather than to the plant), then the nature of the controversy changes and the cost issues deal with—as John Joseph Wallis and Douglass C. North (1988, 654; see also, more important, North 1985) have put it—"coordinating and monitoring" the cost of "inter-firm transactions" (market) versus the costs of intra-firm transactions (hierarchy).

The business history controversies and discussions thus revolve around whether the rise of big business (through mergers *or* through internal growth) does (or can) result in efficiencies (better use of assets, cost savings; more monies available for research and development), or whether the growth inevitably creates inefficiencies through the introduction of unwieldy size and the suppression of competition. The question for business historiansmoves beyond that of economies of scale to economies of scope (the economies of managing *different* kinds of activities under a single managerial structure). The arguments look to the nature of business organization and the kinds of efficiencies that can arise when (and if) managerial structures are appropriate. The debate also pushes the discussion to a consideration of types of managerial structures.

The topic, stimulated in large part by the work of Chandler, has enormous public policy implications. If mergers and the creation of "monopoly power" result by their very nature in inefficiencies (high costs) and higher prices, then forbidding combination or breaking up large business, or regulation (in the case of natural monopolies) is appropriate. If, however, through the adoption of new managerial methods (multidivisional organizations, for example), large business enterprises can through growth introduce cost reductions that provide for greater efficiencies and lower prices for the consumer (Chandler 1962; O. Williamson 1975, 1981), then the public policy prescriptions are different. Essential to the argument of Chandler and Oliver E. Williamson—and the contribution they make to the business history literature—is that the cost reductions lie in *the management of the entire firm*, not merely in the rationalization of production and the economies of scale of individual factories.

In the 1950s and, more important, in the 1960s, many American businesses became conglomerates, mergers of unrelated business enterprises (Didrichsen 1972 considers conglomerates in the context of the development of diversified firms). In the initial drafts of Chandler's *Scale and Scope* (forthcoming 1990), he had intended to extend his arguments on managerial efficiencies to these enterprises and discuss how conglomerates were unable to take advantage of the organizational efficiencies of related business activities. In the end he decided not to include this, but one can expect subsequent work from Chandler on this subject.

Undoubtedly, the leveraged buyouts of the 1980s and the massive mergers and acquisitions that include not only domestic but foreign firms as acquirers will be considered in the future by business historians in the context of their studies of business growth, mergers, efficiency, and the ability of managerial structures to affect costs, prices, and profits. Also on future agendas will be the question, Do divestments provide for more efficient use of assets, or are they wasteful manipulations of a new generation of robber barons?

The command post for business enterprise has been the office with its typewriters, duplicators, and filing systems. JoAnne Yates, in *Control Through Communication: The Rise of System in American Management* (1989), sets out the growing importance of written communication from 1850 to 1920. In today's world of expanding electronic communications, this volume is a timely reminder of how much has changed in recent years.

As business historians have studied giant enterprises, they also have paid attention to the persistence of small businesses, so-called peripheral firms. On this see Stuart W. Bruchey, ed., *Small Business in American Life* (1980). Blackford has done fine work on several small businesses. There has been a recognition that small businesses continue to coexist with giant enterprises (Averitt 1968; Galbraith 1972). A number of small businesses are "independent," yet only survive by supplying giant enterprises with goods or services. Students of the history of multinational enterprise have often asked questions about when the "market" (independent firms) and when "hierarchy" (internalization of one firm) is used in the extension of business abroad. In a sense, the questions related to domestic business are identical, and the business historian needs to study not only small business, but its relationships with giant enterprise. How much of small business is truly independent, and how much satellites of larger firms?

In discussions of large and small businesses, the question of "family"— of family businesses—has arisen. Wayne Broehl (1989) notes the special issues and topics that relate to this subject.

Technological Change

Stimulating general works on American technology include W. P. Strassmann, *Risk and Technological Innovation* (1959); H. J. Habakkuk, *American and British Technology in the Nineteenth Century* (1962); Melvin Kranzberg and Carroll W. Pursell, Jr., eds., *Technology in Western Civilization* (1967; volume 2 of this two-volume work is almost exclusively devoted to U.S. technology); Nathan Rosenberg, ed., *The American System of Manufactures* (1969); John Jewkes, David Sawers, and Richard Stiller-man, *The Sources of Invention* (1969); David F. Noble, *America by Design: Science, Technology, and the Rise of Corporate Capitalism* (1977); Otto Mayr and R. C. Post, eds., *Yankee Enterprise* (1981); and David Hounshell, *From the American System to Mass Production 1800–1932* (1984). Houn-shell is currently preparing a two-hundred-year history of science, technol-ogy, and business in the United States (from 1776 to 1986).

A most provocative contribution on technology and American business history is the far-ranging study by Michael J. Piore and Charles F. Sabel, *The Second Industrial Divide* (1984), which discusses the emergence of mass production technologies (the first industrial divide) and then the role of "flexible specialization" (the second industrial divide).

Likewise exciting is the work of Paul David on technology generation and diffusion and the ramifications of technology, and especially "gateway technologies" (David 1975; David and Bunn 1988). David has been con-sidering path-dependence in technological developments (David forthcom-ing 1990).

Missing from many of the new general works on business history and technological change is the role of multinational corporations. Every student of contemporary multinational corporations and the history of multina-tional enterprises writes on the technological advantages that move with the expansion of business over borders (Gruber, Mehta, and Vernon 1967; Kindleberger 1969; Teece 1977; Wilkins 1970, 1974a, 1989); yet with a few notable exceptions that are industry-specific or out of the mainstream, for example, Wilkins's *Journal of Economic History* article, "The Role of Private Business in the International Diffusion of Technology" (1974b), American business historians have paid inadequate attention to the tech-nological transfers associated with corporations' international investments and international licensing accords.

Government and Business

The American government (federal, state, local) has had numerous and complex relations to business, and business historians have long been in-terested in the effects of these relationships on business development. Thus, the authority to incorporate is a governmental function, and business his-torians have found useful Oscar Handlin and Mary F. Handlin, "Origins of the American Business Corporation" (1945). While most of the literature on government and business covers the federal government's activities, the authority to incorporate was an early function of state governments. His-torians have not neglected state government policies, and Henry W. Broude, "The Role of the State in American Economic Development" (1964), dealt with this subject, as did studies of Pennsylvania, Georgia, California, Ohio, and Massachusetts (Hartz 1948; Heath 1954; G. Nash 1964; Handlin and Handlin 1969).

An early and significant role of the federal government in relation to business was tariff policy; it is best treated in the classic by Taussig, *The Tariff History of the United States* ([1931] 1964). Every business and government textbook has historical sections on antitrust legislation, enforcement, and regulation. American history textbooks consider the U.S. government's policies vis-à-vis business enterprise; there are, in addition, numerous studies by historians that cover particular periods in American history, the Progressive Era, the New Deal, and so forth, along with the specifics of business and government interactions. So, too, historians have been concerned with business and diplomacy and the relationships between government and business in the expansion of U.S. business abroad and business in the United States. Economists have written at great length on issues of "public choice," and some small part of that literature is historical in its orientation. Likewise, the contributions of lawyers on the subject of government and business are prolific. Regrettably, it is impossible to do justice to this immense topic in this short introduction. Accordingly, I will confine myself to the work of business historians.

Among business historians, the contributions of McCraw have been especially outstanding. In 1975 he published in *Business History Review* "Regulation in America: A Review Article." Subsequently he has edited *Regulation in Perspective* (1981) and written the important *Prophets of Regulation* (1984). A recent work on business and government, from FDR to Ronald Reagan, is Kim McQuaid, *Big Business and Presidential Power* (1982). Louis Galambos and Joseph Pratt have provided a fine overview of U.S. business and public policy in the twentieth century in their *Rise of the Corporate Commonwealth: U.S. Business and Public Policy in the Twentieth Century* (1988). William H. Becker (1973, 1982) gives a business historian's view on governments' role in relation to export markets in the late nineteenth and early twentieth centuries. A number of business historians have dealt with multinationals and the responses of American and foreign governments (see, for example, Wilkins 1970, 1974a, 1989; Mason 1988). Most such studies of multinationals are, however, company- and industry-specific and thus cannot be included in this introductory essay.

Business and Labor Relations

Until very recently, business historians have tended to shortchange labor relations—business history from "below," as Dan Raff puts it. Studies of business and labor relationships still are for the most part specific to particular industries. There have been, to be sure, many contributions on shop management and the application of scientific management in the factory. These have dealt with how labor is managed rather than with management-labor relationships. Josepha M. Perry, "Selections on Scientific Management" (1960), provides a splendid introduction to the field. Textbooks on labor-management relations usually have historical sections. Labor histories abound, where the focus is principally on labor and only secondarily (and superficially) on managerial strategies in labor relations. Three recent contributions to the general business history of labor-business relationships are Howell John Harris, *The Right to Manage: Industrial Relations Policies of American Business in the 1940s* (1982); Sanford M. Jacoby, *Employing Bureaucracy: Managers, Unions and the Transformation of Work in American Industry* (1987); and David Montgomery, *The Fall of the House of Labor: The Workplace, the State and Labor Activism 1865–1925* (1987).

Distribution of Wealth

Almost by definition, businessmen are wealthier than nonbusinessmen, and business historians have often used as source materials books such as Moses Yale Beach, *Wealth and Biography of the Wealthy Citizens of New York* ([1855] 1973). More recent studies on income inequality by Simon Kuznets (1953, 1955), Edward Pessen (1973), and Jeffrey G. Williamson and Peter H. Lindert (1980) and on *Men of Wealth in the United States 1850–1870* (Soltow 1975) have been used by business historians. The evidence on income distribution and, more important, its impact on business development have been conflicting and inconclusive.

Regional Dimensions of Business History

The immense size of the United States would suggest that there should be numerous studies on regional aspects of business history. There are, indeed, many industry-specific works that handle considerations associated with business location. There have been studies of cities, such as Chicago, that contain much of use to the business historian (Pierce 1957, for example). Fred Bateman, James D. Foust, and Thomas Weiss (1971) have dealt with large-scale manufacturing in the South and West, 1850–1860. So, too, Bateman and Weiss have done comparisons by regions (see Atack 1986, 465, for a list of their publications). Likewise, a number of books on foreign business in the United States have been devoted to particular regions, principally the American West (Ostrye 1986; Jackson 1968; Kerr 1976). There have been popular volumes on the movement of industry south in the post-World War II years, but this change has not been reflected in the scholarly publications of business historians.

U.S. Business and International Cartels

There is a sizable literature on U.S. business involvement in international cartels. Antitrust laws made domestic cartels illegal in the United States. By contrast, for many years the law was not clear on international agreements. in the 1930s, 1940s, and 1950s, economists paid considerable attention to the participation by American businesses in these cartels and much was written on the subject. A large part of this literature is now quite old (Plummer [1938] 1971; Hexner 1946; Stocking and Watkins 1946), yet has not been superseded. Also valuable in this connection is the work of two lawyers, Kingman Brewster (1958) and Wilbur Lindsay Fugate (1958). These materials have often been consulted by business historians.

THEORETICAL CONTRIBUTIONS

Business historians have, in general, not paid much attention to theory, with the exception of their long-standing "love affair" with Schumpeter. Schumpeter's entrepreneur, who "made things happen," was an attractive paradigm for business biographers. In the 1960s, David C. McClelland's *The Achieving Society* (1961) and Everett E. Hagen's *On the Theory of Social Change* (1962) sharpened the thinking of a generation of business historians. So, too, the work of Berle and Means (1932, 1967) had, as we have seen, major impact on business historians. In this tradition, John Kenneth Galbraith's *The New Industrial State* (1967), with its emphasis on the technostructure of business, fits into the new directions being undertaken by business historians.

Business historians are, by definition, interested in the growth of the firm, and some have been influenced by Edith Penrose, *The Theory of the Growth of the Firm* (1959), and R. H. Coase, "The Nature of the Firm" (1937). In recent years particularly, the writings of Oliver E. Williamson (1975, 1979, 1981, 1985) have had profound impact. Likewise, Kenneth Arrow, *The Limits of Organization* (1974), and Armen Alchian and Harold Demsetz, "Production, Information Costs, and Economic Organization" (1972), have had influence.

Business historians who have written on multinational enterprise have drawn on the work of Raymond Vernon (for example, 1966), Richard E. Caves (for example, 1982), Mark Casson (for example, 1987), and John H. Dunning (for example, 1988). It was students of multinational enterprise who first recognized the relevance of Coase (1937) to business history (see Wilkins 1988, 45, for some historiography); Chandler (1977) found Coase's insights on internalization highly relevant. Peter Hertner and Geoffrey Jones have edited *Multinationals: Theory and History* (1986), which has essays that explore the application of theory to the history of multinational enterprise.

Business historians have become aware of the role of transaction costs in the growth of the firm, using the insights of Coase (1937), Oliver E. Williamson (1975, 1979, 1981, 1985), and to a lesser extent, John C. McManus (1975). Questions being asked concern why and how a firm grows in one direction or another and whether transaction costs make the difference. What are the limits on the efficient growth of the firm?

William J. Baumol, John C. Panzar, and Robert D. Willig's work on *Contestable Markets and the Theory of Industry Structure* (1982) is bound to have impact. A splendid summary of the importance of this work for an understanding of multiproduct cost structures is in Michael Spence, "*Contestable Markets and the Theory of Industry Structure*: A Review Article" (1983). Michael E. Porter, *Competitive Advantage: Creating and Sustaining Superior Performance* (1985), contains valuable insights for the business historian. Undoubtedly, Giovanni Dosi's recent work will also prove stimulating. Dosi, "Sources, Procedures, and Microeconomic Effects of Innovation" (1988), has summarized the research being done on "determinants and effects of innovative activities in contemporary market economies." His essay offers bibliography and perceptions that should shape future business historians' endeavors. In short, new work in microeconomic theory and in industrial organization has become increasingly useful for business historians.

MANUFACTURING

Specifically on the business history of manufacturing, Victor S. Clark's three-volume study, *The History of Manufactures in the United States* (1929), is superb. James Leander Bishop, *A History of American Manufactures from 1608 to 1860* (1864), is less satisfactory. Its title notwithstanding, Chauncey Depew, ed., *1795–1895: One Hundred Years of American Commerce* (1895), is a fine introduction to the development of American manufacturing. While more on selling than on manufacturing, Glenn Porter and Harold G. Livesay's *Merchants and Manufacturers* (1971) casts new light on the relationships between manufacturing and marketing.

A useful contribution to the business history of early nineteenth-century manufacturing is Howard B. Rock, *Artisans of the New Republic: The Tradesmen of New York City in the Age of Jefferson* (1979); he shows the unity between the manufacturer and the skilled craftsman (and the early ambiguity between the businessman and the skilled worker). Chandler, "Anthracite Coal and the Beginnings of the Industrial Revolution in the United States" (1972), points out the connections between the development of coal supplies and the transformation of manufacturing in America. Jeremy Atack, "Firm Size and Industrial Structure in the United States During the Nineteenth Century" (1986), takes on the issue of the size of firms in the United States between 1820 and 1870 and, like O'Brien (1988), concentrates on plants and production economies. Atack's exciting essay directs the reader to a number of contributions that he and others have made on this subject. The issue of the optimum size of a manufacturing unit (the minimum efficient scale) and the size of the firm, as noted earlier, is important; Atack emphasizes that, in the years 1820–70, in most industries the small plant remained the typical producing unit. He poses questions on the survival of the less than optimum efficient scale plants. Hounshell, *From the American System to Mass Production 1800–1932* (1984), is a fascinating contribution on the rise of the modern American factory.

Manufacturing is only one aspect of the multifunctional twentieth-century firm. While contributions on manufacturing are important, from the late nineteenth century onward, to study the history of most businesses exclusively in terms of plant size (and economies in manufacturing) fails to capture the history of the multifunctional (and multiplant, multiregional, multinational) business firm per se. Studies of manufacturing certainly, however, add insights into the nature and characteristics of business efficiency and business growth.

In short, and in conclusion, while many business historians have confined themselves to a particular company or industry, there is, in addition, a large literature that provides a framework of industry- and company-specific works. The contributions covered above are of relevance to all the business histories that are included in the subsequent chapters in this handbook.

BIBLIOGRAPHY

Aitken, Hugh G. J., ed. *Explorations in Enterprise.* Cambridge, MA: Harvard University Press, 1965.

Alchian, Armen, and Harold Demsetz. "Production, Information Costs, and Economic Organization." *American Economic Review* 62 (December 1972): 777–95.

Arrow, Kenneth. *The Limits of Organization.* New York: W. W. Norton, 1974.

Atack, Jeremy. "Firm Size and Industrial Structure in the United States During the Nineteenth Century." *Journal of Economic History* 46 (June 1986): 463–75.

Averitt, Robert T. *The Dual Economy.* New York: W. W. Norton, 1968.

Bateman, Fred, James D. Foust, and Thomas Weiss. "Large Scale Manufacturing in the South and West, 1850–1860." *Business History Review* 45 (Spring 1971): 1–17.

Baumol, William J., John C. Panzar, and Robert D. Willig. *Contestable Markets and the Theory of Industry Structure.* New York: Harcourt Brace Jovanovich, 1982.

Beach, Moses Yale. *Wealth and Biography of the Wealthy Citizens of New York.* 1855. Reprint. New York: Arno Press, 1973.

Beard, Miriam. *A History of the Business Man.* New York: Macmillan, 1938.

Becker, William H. "American Manufacturers and Foreign Markets, 1870–1900: Business Historians and the 'New Economic Determinists.' " *Business History Review* 47 (Winter 1973): 466–81.

———. *The Dynamics of Business-Government Relations: Industry and Exports 1893–1921.* Chicago: University of Chicago Press, 1982.

Benedict, Karen. *A Select Bibliography on Business Archives and Record Management*. Chicago: Society of American Archivists, 1981.

——. "Business Archives Literature." *American Archivist* 45 (Summer 1982): 312–14.

Berle, Adolf A., and Gardiner C. Means. *The Modern Corporation and Private Property*. 1st ed. 1932. Rev. ed. New York: Harcourt, Brace & World, 1967.

Bishop, James Leander. *A History of American Manufactures from 1608 to 1860*. Philadelphia: E. Young, 1864.

Blackford, Mansel G. *The Rise of Modern Business*. Chapel Hill: University of North Carolina Press, 1988.

Blackford, Mansel G., and K. Austin Kerr. *Business Enterprise in American History*. New York: Houghton Mifflin, 1986.

Brewster, Kingman. *Antitrust and American Business Abroad*. New York: McGraw-Hill, 1958.

Broehl, Wayne. "Family Business." *Business and Economic History* 2d ser., 18 (1989): 1–10.

Broude, Henry W. "The Role of the State in American Economic Development." In *United States Economic History, Selected Readings*, edited by Harry N. Scheiber. New York: Knopf, 1964.

Bruchey, Stuart W., ed. *Small Business in American Life*. New York: Columbia University Press, 1980.

Bryant, Keith L., Jr., and Henry C. Dethloff. *A History of American Business*. Englewood Cliffs, NJ: Prentice-Hall, 1983.

Business Archives Section, Society of American Archivists. "Directory of Business Archives in the United States and Canada." Unpublished, 1987.

Casson, Mark. *The Firm and the Market*. Cambridge, MA: MIT Press, 1987.

Caves, Richard E. *Multinational Enterprise and Economic Analysis*. Cambridge, Eng.: Cambridge University Press, 1982.

Chamberlain, John. *The Enterprising Americans*. New York: Harper & Row, 1963.

Chandler, Alfred D., Jr. "The Beginnings of Big Business in American Industry." *Business History Review* 33 (Spring 1959): 1–31.

——. *Strategy and Structure*. Cambridge, MA: MIT Press, 1962.

——. "Anthracite Coal and the Beginnings of the Industrial Revolution in the United States." *Business History Review* 46 (Summer 1972): 141–81.

——. *The Visible Hand*. Cambridge, MA: Harvard University Press, 1977.

——. "Technological and Organizational Underpinnings of Modern Industrial Multinational Enterprise." In *Multinational Enterprise in Historical Perspective*, edited by Alice Teichova, Maurice Lévy-Leboyer, and Helga Nussbaum, 30–54. Cambridge, Eng.: Cambridge University Press, 1986.

——. *Scale and Scope*. Cambridge, MA: Harvard University Press, forthcoming, 1990.

Chandler, Alfred D., Jr., and Herman Daems, eds. *Managerial Hierarchies*. Cambridge, MA: Harvard University Press, 1980.

Chandler, Alfred D., Jr., and Richard Tedlow, eds. *The Coming of Managerial Capitalism: A Casebook on the History of American Economic Institutions*. Homewood, IL: Richard D. Irwin, 1985.

Clark, Victor S. *The History of Manufactures in the United States*. 3 vols. New York: Carnegie Institution, 1929.

Coase, R. H. "The Nature of the Firm." *Economica* n.s. 4 (1937): 386–405.

Cochran, Thomas C. *The American Business System: A Historical Perspective, 1900–1955*. New York: Harper & Row, 1957.

————. *Basic History of American Business*. Princeton, NJ: D. Van Nostrand, 1959.

————. *Business in American Life: A History*. New York: McGraw-Hill, 1972.

————. *200 Years of American Business*. New York: Basic Books, 1977.

Cochran, Thomas C., and William Miller. *The Age of Enterprise*. 1st ed. 1941. Rev. ed. New York: Harper & Bros., 1961.

Cole, Arthur H. "An Approach to the Study of Entrepreneurship." *Journal of Economic History* Supplement 6 (1946): 1–15.

————. *Business Enterprise in Its Social Setting*. Cambridge, MA: Harvard University Press, 1959.

Daems, Herman, and Herman van der Wee, eds. *The Rise of Managerial Capitalism*. Louvain: Leuven University Press, 1974.

Daniells, Lorna M. *Studies in Enterprise: A Selected Bibliography of American and Canadian Company Histories and Biographies of Businessmen*. Boston: Baker Library, Harvard University, Graduate School of Business Administration, 1957.

David, Paul A. *Technical Choice, Innovation and Economic Growth*. New York: Cambridge University Press, 1975.

————. "Path-Dependence: Putting the Past into the Future of Economics." *Journal of Economic Literature* (forthcoming 1990).

David, Paul A., and Julie Ann Bunn. "The Economics of Gateway Technologies and Network Evolution." *Information Economics and Policy* 3 (1988): 165–202.

Depew, Chauncey, ed. *1795–1895: One Hundred Years of American Commerce*. New York: D. O. Haynes, 1895.

Diamond, Sigmund O. *The Reputation of the American Businessman*. Cambridge, MA: Harvard University Press, 1955.

DiBacco, Thomas V. *Made in the U.S.A.: The History of American Business*. New York: Harper & Row, 1987.

Didrichsen, Jon. "The Development of Diversified and Conglomerate Firms in the United States, 1920–1970." *Business History Review* 46 (Summer 1972): 202–19.

Dosi, Giovanni. "Sources, Procedures, and Microeconomic Effects of Innovation." *Journal of Economic Literature* 26 (September 1988): 1120–71.

Dunning, John H. *Explaining International Production*. London: Unwin Hyman, 1988.

Evans, George Heberton, Jr. *Business Incorporations in the United States 1800–1943*. New York: National Bureau of Economic Research, 1948.

Fugate, Wilbur Lindsay. *Foreign Commerce and the Antitrust Laws*. Boston: Little, Brown, 1958.

Galambos, Louis, and Joseph Pratt. *The Rise of the Corporate Commonwealth: U.S. Business and Public Policy in the Twentieth Century*. New York: Basic Books, 1988.

Galbraith, John Kenneth. *The New Industrial State*. Boston: Houghton Mifflin, 1967.

————. "The Structure of the Firm and the Structure of the Industry: A Study in Industrial Development." In *Evolution of International Management Struc-*

tures, edited by Harold Williamson, 3–12. Newark: University of Delaware Press, 1972.

Gordon, Robert Aaron. *Business Leadership in the Large Corporation*. Washington, DC: Brookings Institution, 1945.

Gras, N.S.B. *Business and Capitalism: An Introduction to Business History*. New York: F. S. Crofts, 1939.

Gras, N.S.B., and Henrietta M. Larson, eds. *Casebook in American Business History*. New York: Appleton-Century-Crofts, 1939.

Gruber, W. D., D. Mehta, and R. Vernon. "The R&D Factor in International Trade and Investment of U.S. Industries." *Journal of Political Economy* 75 (February 1967): 20–37.

Habakkuk, H. J. *American and British Technology in the Nineteenth Century*. Cambridge, Eng.: Cambridge University Press, 1962.

Hagen, Everett E. *On the Theory of Social Change*. Homewood, IL: Dorsey Press, 1962.

Hagley Museum and Library. *1987 Annual Report*.

Handlin, Oscar, and Mary F. Handlin. "Origins of the American Business Corporation." *Journal of Economic History* 5 (May 1945): 3–23.

———. *Commonwealth: A Study of the Role of Government in the American Economy—Massachusetts*. Cambridge, MA: Harvard University Press, 1969.

Harris, Howell John. *The Right to Manage: Industrial Relations Policies of American Business in the 1940s*. Madison: University of Wisconsin Press, 1982.

Hartz, Louis. *Economic Policy and Democratic Thought: Pennsylvania, 1776–1860*. Cambridge, MA: Harvard University Press, 1948.

Heath, Milton. *Constructive Liberalism: The Role of the State in the Economic Development of Georgia to 1860*. Cambridge, MA: Harvard University Press, 1954.

Hertner, Peter, and Geoffrey Jones, eds. *Multinationals: Theory and History*. Aldershot: Gower, 1986.

Hexner, Erwin. *International Cartels*. Chapel Hill: University of North Carolina Press, 1946.

Hounshell, David. *From the American System to Mass Production 1800–1932*. Baltimore: Johns Hopkins University Press, 1984.

Hughes, Jonathan. "Arthur Cole and Entrepreneurial History." *Business and Economic History* 2d ser., 12 (1983): 133–44.

———. *The Vital Few*. 1st ed. 1966. 2d ed. Boston: Houghton Mifflin, 1986.

Jackson, W. Turentine. *The Enterprising Scot: Investors in the American West After 1873*. Edinburgh: Edinburgh University Press, 1968.

Jacoby, Sanford M. *Employing Bureaucracy: Managers, Unions and the Transformation of Work in American Industry*. New York: Columbia University Press, 1987.

Jenks, Leland H. *The Migration of British Capital to 1875*. 1927. Reprint. New York: Harper & Row, 1973.

Jewkes, John, David Sawers, and Richard Stillerman. *The Sources of Invention*. 2d ed. New York: W. W. Norton, 1969.

Jones, Peter d'A., ed. *The Robber Barons Revisited*. Boston: D. C. Heath, 1968.

Josephson, Matthew. *Robber Barons*. New York: Harcourt, Brace & World, 1934.

Kerr, W. G. *Scottish Capital on the American Credit Frontier*. Austin: Texas State Historical Association, 1976.

Kindleberger, Charles P. *American Business Abroad*. New Haven: Yale University Press, 1969.

Kranzberg, Melvin, and Carroll W. Pursell, Jr., eds. *Technology in Western Civilization*. 2 vols. New York: Oxford University Press, 1967.

Krooss, Herman E., and Charles Gilbert. *American Business History*. Englewood Cliffs, NJ: Prentice-Hall, 1972.

Kuznets, Simon. *Shares of Upper Income Groups in Income and Saving*. New York: National Bureau of Economic Research, 1953.

———. "Economic Growth and Income Inequality." *American Economic Review* 45 (March 1955): 1–28.

Lamoreaux, Naomi R. *The Great Merger Movement in American Business, 1895–1904*. New York: Cambridge University Press, 1985.

Larson, Henrietta. *Guide to Business History*. Cambridge, MA: Harvard University Press, 1948.

Lovett, Robert W. "Business Records in Libraries." *American Archivist* 20 (July 1957): 253–61.

———. "The Status of Business Archives." *American Archivist* 32 (July 1969): 247–50.

———. *American Economic and Business History Information Sources*. Detroit: Gale Research, 1971.

Lovett, Robert W., and Eleanor Bishop, comps. *Manuscripts in Baker Library: A Guide to Sources for Business, Economic, and Social History*. 4th ed. Boston: Baker Library, 1978. Earlier editions of this work were published under the title *List of Business Manuscripts in Baker Library*.

McClelland, David C. *The Achieving Society*. Princeton, NJ: D. Van Nostrand, 1961.

McCraw, Thomas K. "Regulation in America: A Review Article." *Business History Review* 59 (Summer 1975): 159–83.

———, ed. *Regulation in Perspective*. Boston: Harvard Business School Press, 1981.

———. *Prophets of Regulation*. Cambridge, MA: Harvard University Press, 1984.

———, ed. *The Essential Alfred Chandler*. Boston: Harvard Business School Press, 1988.

McManus, John C. "The Costs of Alternative Economic Organizations." *Canadian Journal* 7 (August 1975): 334–50.

McQuaid, Kim. *Big Business and Presidential Power*. New York: William Morrow, 1982.

Mason, Mark. "The Development of United States Enterprise in Japan: Studies in Government Policy and Corporate Strategy." Ph.D. diss., Harvard University, 1988.

May, Ernest R., and John K. Fairbank, eds. *America's China Trade in Historical Perspective*. Cambridge, MA: Harvard University Press, 1986.

Mayr, Otto, and R. C. Post, eds. *Yankee Enterprise*. Washington, DC: Smithsonian Institution Press, 1981.

Miller, William, ed. *Men in Business: Essays on the Historical Role of the Entrepreneur*. New York: Harper & Row, 1962.

Montgomery, David. *The Fall of the House of Labor: The Workplace, the State and Labor Activism 1865–1925.* Cambridge, Eng.: Cambridge University Press, 1987.

Myers, Gustavus. *The History of Great American Fortunes.* New York: Modern Library, 1936.

Nakagawa, Keiichiro, ed. *Strategy and Structure of Big Business.* Tokyo: University of Tokyo Press, [1976?].

Nash, Gerald D. *State Government and Economic Development in California, 1849–1933.* Berkeley: University of California Press, 1964.

Nash, Michael. "Business History at the Hagley Museum and Library." *Business History Review* 60 (Spring 1986): 104–24.

Nelson, Ralph L. *Merger Movements in American Industry, 1895–1956.* Princeton, NJ: Princeton University Press, 1959.

Newcomer, Mabel. "The Chief Executive of Large Business Corporations." *Explorations in Entrepreneurial History* 5 (October 15, 1952): 1–33.

———. *The Big Business Executive: The Factors that Made Him, 1900–1955.* New York: Columbia University Press, 1955.

Noble, David F. *America by Design: Science, Technology, and the Rise of Corporate Capitalism.* Oxford: Oxford University Press, 1977.

North, Douglass C. "Transaction Costs in History." *Journal of European Economic History* 14 (Winter 1985): 557–72.

O'Brien, Anthony Patrick. "Factory Size, Economies of Scale, and the Great Merger Wave of 1898–1902." *Journal of Economic History* 48 (September 1988): 639–49.

Ostrye, Anne T. *Foreign Investment in the American and Canadian West, 1870–1914: An Annotated Bibliography.* Metuchen, NJ: Scarecrow Press, 1986.

Penrose, Edith. *The Theory of the Growth of the Firm.* New York: Wiley, 1959.

Perry, Josepha M. "Selections on Scientific Management." Harvard Business School Case No. BH118, 1960.

Pessen, Edward. *Riches, Class and Power Before the Civil War.* Lexington, MA: D. C. Heath, 1973.

Pierce, Bessie Louise. *A History of Chicago, 1871–1893.* Chicago: University of Chicago Press, 1957.

Piore, Michael J., and Charles F. Sabel. *The Second Industrial Divide.* New York: Basic Books, 1984.

Plummer, Alfred. *International Combines in Modern Industry.* 1938. Reprint. Freeport, NY: Books for Libraries Press, 1971.

Porter, Glenn. *The Rise of Big Business, 1860–1910.* Arlington Heights, IL: Harlan Davidson, 1973.

Porter, Glenn, and Harold G. Livesay. *Merchants and Manufacturers.* Baltimore: Johns Hopkins University Press, 1971.

Porter, Michael E. *Competitive Advantage: Creating and Sustaining Superior Performance.* New York: Free Press, 1985.

Posner, Richard A. *Economic Analysis of the Law.* 3d ed. Boston: Little, Brown, 1986.

Pusateri, C. Joseph. *A History of American Business.* 2d ed. Arlington Heights, IL: Harlan Davidson, 1988.

Redlich, Fritz. *Steeped in Two Cultures.* New York: Harper Torchbook, 1971.

Robertson, James Oliver. *America's Business.* New York: Hill & Wang, 1985.

Rock, Howard B. *Artisans of the New Republic: The Tradesmen of New York City in the Age of Jefferson*. New York: New York University Press, 1979.

Rosenberg, Nathan, ed. *The American System of Manufactures*. Edinburgh: Edinburgh University Press, 1969.

Sass, Steven A. *Entrepreneurial Historians and History: Leadership and Rationality in American Economic Historiography, 1940–1960*. New York: Garland, 1986.

Schumpeter, Joseph. *The Theory of Economic Development*. Cambridge, MA: Harvard University Press, 1934.

Seligman, Ben B. *The Potentates: Business and Businessmen in American History*. New York: Dial Press, 1971.

Sobel, Robert. *The Entrepreneurs*. New York: Weybright & Talley, 1974.

Soltow, Lee. *Men of Wealth in the United States 1850–1870*. New Haven: Yale University Press, 1975.

Spence, Michael. "*Contestable Markets and the Theory of Industry Structure*: A Review Article." *Journal of Economic Literature* 21 (September 1983): 981–90.

Stocking, George W., and Myron W. Watkins. *Cartels in Action*. New York: Twentieth Century Fund, 1946.

Strassmann, W. P. *Risk and Technological Innovation*. Ithaca: Cornell University Press, 1959.

Taussig, Frank W. *The Tariff History of the United States*. 8th rev. ed. 1931. Reprint. New York: Capricorn Books, 1964.

Taussig, Frank W., and C. S. Joslyn. *American Business Leaders: A Study in Social Origins and Stratification*. New York: Macmillan, 1932.

Teece, David J. "Technology Transfer by Multinational Firms: The Resource Cost of Transferring Technological Know-how." *Economic Journal* 87 (June 1977): 242–61.

Teichova, Alice, Maurice Lévy-Leboyer, and Helga Nussbaum, eds. *Multinational Enterprise in Historical Perspective*. New York: Cambridge University Press, 1986.

U.S. Bureau of the Census. *Historical Statistics of the United States, Colonial Times to 1970*. Washington, DC: U.S. Government Printing Office, 1975.

Vernon, Raymond. "International Investment and International Trade in the Product Cycle." *Quarterly Journal of Economics* 80 (May 1966): 190–207.

Walker, Juliet E. K. "Racism, Slavery, and Free Enterprise: Black Entrepreneurship in the United States Before the Civil War." *Business History Review* 60 (Autumn 1986): 343–82.

Wallis, John Joseph, and Douglass C. North. "Should Transaction Costs Be Subtracted from Gross National Product?" *Journal of Economic History* 48 (September 1988): 651–54.

Wilkins, Mira. *The Emergence of Multinational Enterprise: American Business Abroad from the Colonial Era to 1914*. Cambridge, MA: Harvard University Press, 1970.

———. *The Maturing of Multinational Enterprise: American Business Abroad from 1914 to 1970*. Cambridge, MA: Harvard University Press, 1974a.

———. "The Role of Private Business in the International Diffusion of Technology." *Journal of Economic History* 34 (March 1974b): 166–88.

———. "European and North American Multinationals 1870–1914: Comparisons and Contrasts." *Business History* 30 (January 1988): 8–45.

———. *The History of Foreign Investment in the United States to 1914.* Cambridge, MA: Harvard University Press, 1989.

Williamson, Harold, ed. *Evolution of International Management Structures.* Newark: University of Delaware Press, 1972.

Williamson, Jeffrey G., and Peter H. Lindert. *American Inequality: A Macroeconomic History.* New York: Academic Press, 1980.

Williamson, Oliver E. *Markets and Hierarchies: Analysis and Anti-trust Implications. A Study in the Economics of Internal Organization.* New York: Free Press, 1975.

———. "Transaction-Cost Economics: The Governance of Contractual Relations." *Journal of Law and Economics* 22 (October 1979): 233–61.

———. "The Modern Corporation: Origins, Evolution, Attributes." *Journal of Economic Literature* 19 (December 1981): 1537–68.

———. *The Economic Institutions of Capitalism.* New York: Free Press, 1985.

Yates, JoAnne. *Control Through Communication: The Rise of System in American Management.* Baltimore: Johns Hopkins University Press, 1989.

Yuzawa, T., and M. Udagawa, eds. *Foreign Business in Japan.* Tokyo: University of Tokyo Press, forthcoming.

Serials

Business and Economic History

Business History

Business History Review

Business Week

Commercial and Financial Chronicle

Economic Report of the President

Essays in Economic and Business History

Explorations in Entrepreneurial History

Forbes

Fortune

Moody's Manuals

Standard and Poor's

Statistical Abstract of the United States

Wall Street Journal

Part I

Food and Kindred Products
ESIC 20.0

CHAPTER 1 _____

MEAT AND MEAT PRODUCTS, 20.1

_____ ROBERT M. ADUDDELL AND LOUIS P. CAIN

Although some segments of the meat industry have been studied intensively, others have been neglected. Meat and meat products account for a substantial proportion of consumers' expenditures on food. During the great merger movement at the turn of the twentieth century, the meat industry was described as the greatest trust in the world and reputedly had the power to monopolize the nation's food supply. Such trepidations account for the history of governmental investigations of the industry. Studies of the interconnections between the livestock, railroad, and meat industries constitute several linear yards of government documents. The living and working conditions of the industry's labor force have been investigated by economists, sociologists, and muckrakers. In contrast, the technology of this industry and the personalities of its leading entrepreneurs have rarely been scrutinized. Few studies have focused on firms producing meat from animals other than cattle and hogs. Some were undertaken by the U.S. Department of Agriculture and by university extension programs. Their contribution is a snapshot of contemporary conditions.

This bibliography is divided into eight sections. The first lists general industry titles and is followed by specific studies of the beef, pork, and poultry industries in the second through fourth sections. The fifth section lists corporate and entrepreneurial biographies. The sixth section, public policy studies, concentrates on the industry's antitrust history and governmental inspection and grading. Consumption and marketing studies are the subject of the seventh section. The eighth section, labeled miscellaneous studies, lists works relating to the industry's labor force and technology—labor force and technology issues that were not involved in the two principal public policy controversies. The following paragraphs review the important entries in each section.

INDUSTRY STUDIES

The five most accessible general studies of the meat-packing industry, including discussions of public policy as well as production, were written by Rudolf Alexander Clemen (1923), J. Russell Ives (1966), Jimmy M. Skaggs (1986), Willard F. Williams and Thomas T. Stout (1964), and Mary Yeager (1981). Clemen was one of the first scholars to write a comprehensive, objective history of the industry that discusses the production flow from feedlot to retail outlet. It remains the primary source for investigations of the turn-of-the-century "Big Five" meat-packing firms. Ives's work is a much shorter, more recent treatment of the industry, written under the auspices of the American Meat Institute as part of its home study program. It provides a careful statistical analysis of the trends in the industry. Skaggs's overview is a good place to begin a study of the industry. Williams and Stout provide a textbook-like treatment of the business and economics of the industry. They integrate material on the livestock business into their discussion of the meat industry. Yeager adds insight into the turn-of-the-century Big Five. Using corporate records and modern economic analysis, she creates a business historian's view of the industry. Her work contrasts with that of industry insiders like Clemen and Ives.

The industry in the pre-refrigeration era is discussed by Charles Leavitt (1931, 1934), Allen B. Paul (1953), J. F. Rusling (1878), Clemen, and Yeager. Rusling, Herman Hirschauer (1905), Charles Edward Russell (1905), Upton Sinclair (1906), and Algie Martin Simons (1899) discuss the emergence of the modern meat-packing industry and dramatically illustrate contemporary issues. In many respects the *Report on the Meat-Packing Industry* from the U.S. Federal Trade Commission (1919) was a response to issues raised by Sinclair and others. John M. Connor and his coauthors (1985) and Bruce W. Marion (1986) have written the most recent comprehensive studies of the meat industry. Their works integrate discussions of structural performance and public policy over the life of the American meat-packing industry.

THE BEEF INDUSTRY

Until about 1960 firms in the meat-packing industry did not specialize in particular animal species. Willard F. Williams, Earl K. Bowen, and Frank C. Genovese (1959) carefully document how federal grade standards eliminated the product differentiation of fresh beef by packers and made the industry more competitive. In the first half of the twentieth century, differentiating consumer products was important to the large, integrated packers who processed more than one species. Today's meat-packing industry, dominated by such firms as Iowa Beef and Missouri Beef, specializes by species, but firm names do not appear in the supermarket.

The literature on the beef industry is, for the most part, small and recent. Four notable exceptions are articles by Fred Croxton (1905) and Mary Yeager Kujovich (1970), a report on the industry from the Commissioner of Corporations (U.S. Bureau of Corporations 1905), and a Senate Select Committee's report on meat products (U.S. Senate 1890). The latter two are the famous Garfield and Vest reports that, like Upton Sinclair's book, influenced public policy. Of the literature on the recent period, works by Herrell DeGraff (1960) and James R. Simpson and Donald E. Farris (1982) are comprehensive. Simpson and Farris examine the industry worldwide.

THE PORK INDUSTRY

The pork industry is important because only 30 percent of its output is sold fresh. The balance is processed into bacon, ham, sausage, and other products. Processed pork has always been more popular with consumers than processed beef. Furthermore, processed pork products are easily differentiated, so small, specialized producers can compete with large, integrated ones. The pork industry is in many respects older than the beef industry. Its principal modern historian is Margaret Walsh (1977, 1978, and 1982b). Marvin L. Hayenga, James V. Rhodes, Jon A. Brandt, and Ronald E. Deiter (1985) have written the most comprehensive study of the current production and distribution system in the industry. Robert E. Schneidau and Lawrence A. Duewer (1972) show how price changes affect the structure of the industry.

THE POULTRY INDUSTRY

The poultry industry as its exists today is of recent origin. The sale of chicken by fast-food restaurants has encouraged the production of animals in factories instead of on farms. Floyd Lasley (1983) and K. E. Nelson (1980) document the emergence of this highly concentrated, integrated industry in the years since 1950. Hiroshi Nakamura and Thomas Hieronymous (1966) discuss the same topics at a much earlier point in the evolution of the industry.

BIOGRAPHY AND COMPANY HISTORY

A good description of the meat industry a century ago can be found in works by Lawrence Oakley Cheever (1948) and Rudolf Alexander Clemen (1964). Dale C. Tinstman and Robert L. Peterson (1981) offer similar descriptions of the contemporary industry. None of the biographies is analytical or objective. They stress management style and personalities. J. Ogden Armour (1906), Helen Swift (1937), and Louis F. Swift and Arthur Van Vlissingen, Jr. (1927), have added familiar names to books about the industry. Thomas W. Goodspeed (1922), Harper Leech and John Charles Carroll (1938), and Louise A. Neyhart (1952) have authored biographies that are more self-serving than the autobiographies.

PUBLIC POLICY STUDIES

There are four primary policy issues in the meat-packing industry. First and foremost is compliance with antitrust laws. Second is inspection at stockyards and packing houses, initiated to eliminate the sale of diseased animals and meat. (Only interstate shipments are federally inspected—not all packing houses produce federally inspected and graded products.) The third issue is the production of meat products with additives and preservatives and its regulation under the federal Pure Food and Drug Act. The fourth is the flow of information on livestock prices and shipping charges and the provisions of the Packers and Stockyards Act that regulate them.

The most intensive antitrust action was concentrated in the first two decades of the twentieth century. The three government documents that provide the most illuminating background on this era are the Vest, Garfield, and Federal Trade Commission reports, which are included in the section on industry studies. The two most important public policy statements to emerge from this era are the Packer Consent Decree (U.S. Federal Trade Commission 1924–25), which addressed antitrust questions, and the Packers and Stockyards Act (U.S. Congress 1971).

Robert M. Aduddell and Louis P. Cain (1981a, 1981b) address the conditions that led to the signing of the Consent Decree and its subsequent effects on the industry. In other essays they investigate antitrust issues in the nineteenth century (Aduddell and Cain 1973) and trace the effects of the Consent Decree into the post–World War II period (Aduddell and Cain 1982). Several articles expressing a variety of opinions about the Federal Trade Commission investigation and the legitimacy of the commission's conclusions were published shortly after its report was released. These include papers by William Camp (1921), William B. Colver (1919), Henry Veeder (1921), G. O. Virtue (1920), and L.D.H. Weld (1921). George B. Fife (1902), who wrote for a popular magazine, and William Hill (1908) and Francis Walker (1906), who published in economics journals, reflect on similar issues at an earlier date.

Federal inspection and grading is not addressed directly but is covered in books by Herrell DeGraff (1960), Willard F. Williams, Earl K. Bowen, and Frank C. Genovese (1959) (listed with beef industry), and Willard F. Williams and Thomas T. Stout (1964) (listed with industry studies), and in many of the books on meat marketing discussed in the next section.

The application of the pure food and drug laws to the meat-packing industry is discussed by Oscar E. Anderson, Jr. (1958), Thomas A. Bailey (1930), C. W. Crawford (1933), Herman Hirschauer (1905), Kathleen Hughes (1983), R. James Kane (1964), and C. C. Regier (1933), and in the Dodge Commission's report (U.S. Senate 1901–2), the release of which marked the beginning of public concern over adulteration. In popular parlance, the Dodge report is the saga of the embalmed beef controversy during the Spanish-American War. Books by Hirschauer, Upton Sinclair, and others inflamed public opinion and led to the passage of the Pure Food and Drug Act, and the first Meat Inspection Act in 1906. Bailety investigates the social milieu in which these laws were passed; Crawford, Hughes, and Regier discuss the continuous attempts to enforce them. Anderson has written a biography of one of the leading proponents of the legislation.

The Packers and Stockyards Act was an attempt to correct many of the problems uncovered by the Federal Trade Commission investigations. Some sections, for example, addressed conditions upstream and downstream from meat packers. Overall, however, the act deals less with antitrust than the drafters had intended. Writing shortly after passage of the act, Camp (1921) tried to anticipate its impact. Wilford White (1930) published an inquiry into one provision of the act roughly a decade after its acceptance by the industry. M. L. Hayenga and his coauthors (1979, 1980) dealt with the necessity of accurate information for the efficient operation of auction markets for livestock and meat. They examine the provisions and amendments of the Packers and Stockyards Act and analyze their influence on the meat-packing industry.

After the mergers in recent years between food companies and packers (U.S. Federal Trade Commission 1968), the industry is as concentrated today as it was at the time of the Consent Decree and the Packers and Stockyards Act. Only one of the Big Five remains one of the five leading firms today, and even that company has changed. This new concentration is the focus of the work of Bruce W. Marion and his numerous coauthors in the North Central Regional Research Project 117—NC 117—investigation (see, for example, his 1976 and 1979 articles). An equally forceful study of concentration can be found in the work of Willard F. Mueller, in particular his monograph with John Culbertson and Brian Peckham (1982).

CONSUMPTION AND MARKETING STUDIES

Jean-Paul Chavas (1983) has written a widely cited study on changes in the demand for meat in local, regional, national, and international markets. Richard C. Haidacher et al. (1982) detail the gradual reduction in the demand for beef and pork and the relative increase in the demand for poultry and fish. David Smallwood and James Blaylock (1981) set out household budget studies that underlie consumers' demand for meat products. Faith

M. Williams (1929) made an early attempt at demand estimation. M. D. Etheridge (1975) describes packinghouse products of the future.

Steward H. Fowler (1961) and John H. McCoy (1979) have written standard marketing textbooks for this industry. Fowler and coauthor Karen J. Friedmann (1980) discuss marketing in the pre-refrigeration era. As part of the original American Meat Institute series, E. L. Rhoades (1929) describes marketing in the years of the peddlar car and butcher shop, before the supermarket became the primary merchandiser of meat to the consumer. The current meat retailing market is discussed by J. M. Connor (1981), Bruce W. Marion et al. (1979), and Hiroshi Nakamura and Thomas Hieronymous (1966). The prospect of livestock cooperatives selling direct to supermarkets, thereby bypassing the packing industry, is the subject of a report from the U.S. Department of Agriculture (1978). Cooperatives are being considered because of the slow growth in demand for food, particularly for red meat.

MISCELLANEOUS STUDIES

David Brody's (1964) widely quoted labor history is the primary source on labor in the meat-packing industry. John R. Commons's (1904) work is an article by one of the leading labor economists of the turn of the century. Charles Joseph Bushnell's (1902) book helped establish the Chicago School of Sociology. Daniel J. Elazar (1969) discusses many of the issues that plagued the industry, emphasizing those that affected Jewish workers. Women and blacks in the packing industry are discussed by Edith Abbott and S. P. Breckinridge (1911), Mary Elizabeth Pidgeon (1932), and Walter Fogel (1971).

Economic measures of technological change and production conditions in the industry are discussed in works by G. F. Bloom (1972), James H. Cothern, R. Mark Peard, and John L. Weeks (1978), S. H. Logan (1966), and S. H. Logan and Gordon A. King (1962). Oscar E. Anderson (1953) discusses refrigeration, a development that gave rise to the initial concentration in meat packing. George E. Putnam's (1921) article is an early discussion of joint costs—a continuing problem in the industry.

H. C. Hill (1923) argues that transportation routes explain Chicago's emergence as the center of the packing industry. Jack Wing (1865) paints a picture of the newly opened Chicago Union Stockyards before they became "hog butcher to the world."

In addition to the statistics produced by the federal government, the American Meat Institute is an excellent source for annual industry data and for the odd collection of historical statistics (1982).

Thomas Horst (1974) deals with American food processing companies in their domestic and international operations—before and after 1950. He focuses on the twenty largest American-owned food processing enterprises (meatpackers, dairy products producers, soft drink companies, and a range of others).

BIBLIOGRAPHY

Industry Studies

American Meat Institute. *The Packing Industry*. Chicago: University of Chicago, Press, 1924.

Bergman, Arvid Mathias. *A Review of the Frozen and Chilled Trans-oceanic Meat Industry*. Stockholm: Almqvist & Wiksell, 1916.

Brandow, George E. "Appraising the Economic Performance of the Food Industry." In *Lectures in Agricultural Economics*, edited by Clark Edwards. Washington, DC: U.S. Department of Agriculture, Economic Research Service, 1977.

Butz, Dale E., and George L. Baker, Jr. *The Changing Structure of the Meat Economy*. Cambridge, MA: Harvard University Graduate School of Business Administration, 1960.

Clemen, Rudolf Alexander. *The American Livestock and Meat Industry*. New York: Ronald Press, 1923.

———. *By-products in the Packing Industry*. Chicago: University of Chicago Press, 1927.

Collins, Norman, and Lee Preston. "The U.S. Food and Tobacco Industries: Market Structure, Structural Change, and Economic Performance." AER451. Washington, DC: U.S. Department of Agriculture, Economics, Statistics, and Cooperative Services, 1980.

Connor, John M., Richard T. Rogers, Bruce W. Marion, and Willard F. Mueller. *The Food Manufacturing Industries: Structure, Strategies, Performance, and Policies*. Lexington, MA: Lexington Books, D. C. Heath, 1985.

Critchell, James Troubridge, and Joseph Raymond. *A History of the Frozen Meat Trade: An Account of the Development and Present Day Methods of Preparation, Transportation, and Marketing of Frozen and Chilled Meats*. London: Constable, 1912.

David, John H., and Ray A. Goldberg. *A Concept of Agribusiness*. Boston: Harvard University Graduate School of Business Administration, 1957.

Fowler, Bertram B. *Men, Meat and Miracles*. New York: Julian Messner, 1952.

Greig, W. Smith. *The Economics of Food Processing*. Westport, CT: AVI, 1971.

Hampe, Edward C., and Merle Wittenberg. *The Lifeline of America: Development of the Food Industry*. New York: McGraw-Hill, 1964.

Hinman, Robert Byron, and Robert B. Harris. *The Story of Meat*. Chicago: Swift, 1939.

Hirschauer, Herman. *The Dark Side of the Beef Trust: A Treatise Concerning the "Canner" Cow, the Cold Storage Fowl, the Diseased Meats, the Dopes and Preservatives*. Jamestown, NY: Theodore Z. Root, 1905.

Hoffman, A. C. *Large-Scale Organization in the Food Industries*. U.S. Temporary National Economic Committee Monograph 35. Washington, DC: U.S. Government Printing Office, 1940.

Ives, J. Russell. *The Livestock and Meat Economy of the United States*. Washington, DC: American Meat Institute, 1966.

James, Clifford L., Edward C. Welsh, and Gordon Arneson. *Industrial Concentration and Tariffs*. U.S. Temporary National Economic Committee Monograph 10. Washington, DC: U.S. Government Printing Office, 1941.

Leavitt, Charles. "Some Economic Aspects of the Western Meat Packing Industry, 1830–1860." *Journal of Business of the University of Chicago* 4 (January 1931): 68–90.

———. "Transportation and the Livestock Industry of the Middle West to 1860." *Agricultural History* 8 (January 1934): 20–33.

McFall, Robert James. *The World's Meat*. New York: Appleton-Century-Crofts, 1927.

Marion, Bruce W. *The Organization and Performance of the U.S. Food System*. NC 117 Committee. Lexington, MA: Lexington Books, D. C. Heath, 1986.

Markham, Jesse W., and David MacFarland. "Organization and Performance in Food Manufacturing." In *Competition in Food Marketing*, edited by Leigh H. Hammond. Raleigh, NC: Agricultural Policy Institute, 1967.

Marple, Gary A., and Harry B. Wissman, eds. *Grocery Manufacturing in the United States*. New York: Praeger, 1968.

Mueller, Willard F., John Culbertson, and Brian Peckham. *Market Structure and Technological Performance in the Food Manufacturing Industry*. NC 117 Monograph 11. Madison: University of Wisconsin Press, 1982.

Mullendore, William Clinton. *History of the United States Food Administration, 1917–1919*. Stanford: Stanford University Press, 1941.

National Commission on Food Marketing. *The Structure of Food Manufacturing*. Technical Study 8. Washington, DC: U.S. Government Printing Office, 1966.

Nicholls, William H. "Market Sharing in the Meat Packing Industry." *Journal of Farm Economics* 22 (1940): 225–31.

———. *Imperfect Competition in the Agricultural Industries*. Ames: Iowa State University Press, 1941.

Orear, Leslie F., and Stephen H. Diamond. *Out of the Jungle*. Chicago: Hyde Park Press, 1968.

Paul, Allen B. *Growth of the Food Processing Industries in Illinois from 1849 to 1947*. Chicago: University of Illinois Press, 1953.

Rusling, J. F. *The Railroads, the Stock-Yards, the Eveners Expose of the Great Railroad that Robs the Laborer of the East and Producer of the West of $5,000,000 a Year*. Washington, DC: Polkinhorn Printers, 1878.

Russell, Charles Edward. *The Greatest Trust in the World*. New York: Ridgway-Thayer, 1905.

Simons, Algie Martin. *Packingtown*. Chicago: Kerr, 1899.

Sinclair, Upton. *The Jungle*. New York: Doubleday, Page, 1906.

Skaggs, Jimmy M. *Prime Cut: Livestock Raising and Meatpacking in the United States, 1607–1983*. College Station: Texas A&M University Press, 1986.

Swem, Edward R. *The Significant Sixty: A Historical Report of the Progress and Development of the Meat Packing Industry, 1891–1951*. Chicago: National Provisioner, 1952.

U.S. Federal Trade Commission. *Report on the Meat-Packing Industry*. 6 vols. Washington, DC: U.S. Government Printing Office, 1919.

————. *Report on the Private Car Lines*. 3 vols. Washington, DC: U.S. Government Printing Office, 1920.

Walsh, Margaret. *The Rise of the Midwestern Meat Packing Industry*. Lexington: University Press of Kentucky, 1982a.

Weld, L.D.H. *Private Freight Cars and American Railways*. New York: Columbia University Press, 1908.

Weld, L.D.H., A. T. Kearney, and F. H. Sidney. *Economics of the Packing Industry*. Chicago: University of Chicago Press, 1925.

Williams, Willard F., and Thomas T. Stout. *Economics of the Livestock-Meat Industry*. New York: Macmillan, 1964.

Yeager, Mary. *Competition and Regulation: The Development of Oligopoly in the Meat Packing Industry*. Greenwich, CT: JAI Press, 1981.

The Beef Industry

Croxton, Fred. "Beef Prices." *Journal of Political Economy* 13 (March 1905): 201–16.

DeGraff, Herrell. *Beef Production and Distribution*. Norman: University of Oklahoma Press, 1960.

Faminow, M. D., and M. E. Sarhan. "Economic Analysis of the Location of Fed Cattle Slaughtering and Processing in the United States." AERR189. Urbana: University of Illinois, 1983.

Fowler, Steward H. *Beef Production in the South*. Danville, IL: Interstate Printers & Publishers, 1957.

Hall, Lana, Andrew Schmitz, and James Cothern. "Beef Wholesale Retail Marketing Margins and Concentration." *Economica* 46 (1979): 295–300.

Kujovich, Mary Yeager. "The Refrigerator Car and the Growth of the American Dressed Beef Industry." *Business History Review* 44 (Winter 1970): 460–82.

Nelson, K. E. "Market Information and Pricing Mechanisms in Livestock and Meat Industry: Issues and Alternatives." In *Market Information and Price Reporting in the Food and Agricultural Sector*. NC 117 Monograph 9. Madison: University of Wisconsin Press, 1980.

Simpson, James R., and Donald E. Farris. *The World's Beef Business*. Ames: Iowa State University Press, 1982.

Structure, Performance and Prospects of the Beef Chain. Paris: Organization for Economic Development, 1978.

Towards a More Efficient Beef Chain: Documentation Assembled for the Symposium Organized in Paris from 10th–13th January, 1977. Paris: Organization for Economic Development, 1977.

U.S. Bureau of Corporations. *Report of the Commissioner of Corporations on the Beef Industry, 1905* [the Garfield Report]. 59th Cong., Special Sess., 1905. Sen. Doc. 3. Washington, DC: U.S. Government Printing Office, 1905.

U.S. Senate. *Report of the Senate Select Committee on Meat Products* [the Vest Report]. 51st Cong., 1st Sess. Senate Report No. 829, 4 vols. Washington, DC: U.S. Government Printing Office, 1980.

Williams, Willard F., Earl K. Bowen, and Frank C. Genovese. *Economic Effects of U.S. Grades for Beef*. U.S. Department of Agriculture, Agricultural Marketing

Service, Marketing Research Report No. 298. Washington, DC: U.S. Government Printing Office, January 1959.

The Pork Industry

Cuff, Robert D. "The Dilemma of Voluntarism: Hoover and the Pork-Packing Agreement, 1917–1919." *Agricultural History* 53 (1979): 727–47.

Gignilliant, John L. "Pigs, Politics and Protectionism: The European Boycott of American Pork, 1879–1891." *Agricultural History* 35 (1961): 3–12.

Hayenga, Marvin, James V. Rhodes, Jon A. Brandt, and Ronald E. Deiter. *The U.S. Pork Sector: Changing Structure and Organization*. Ames: Iowa State University Press, 1985.

Hilliard, Sam Bowers. *Hog Meat and Hoecake: Food Supply in the Old South, 1840–1860*. Carbondale: Southern Illinois University Press, 1972.

Laidler, Harry W. " 'Slaughter of Innocents' in Oklahoma: The Emergency Hog Slaughter of 1933." *Red River Valley Historical Review* 7 (1982): 42–49.

Schneidau, Robert E., and Lawrence A. Duewer. *Symposium: Vertical Coordination in the Pork Industry*. Westport, CT: AVI, 1972.

Walsh, Margaret. "Pork Packing as a Leading Edge of Midwestern Industry." *Agricultural History* 11 (October 1977): 702–17.

———. "The Spatial Evolution of the Midwestern Pork Industry, 1835–1873." *Journal of Historical Geography* 1 (1978): 1–22.

———. "From Pork Merchant to Meat Packer: The Midwestern Meat Industry in the Mid-Nineteenth Century." *Agricultural History* 56 (1982b): 127–37.

The Poultry Industry

Broiler Industry. *Nation's Top Broiler Firms*. Mt. Morris, IL: Watt, December 1982 and December 1984.

Lasley, Floyd. "The U.S. Poultry Industry: Changing Economics and Structure." AER502. Washington, DC: U.S. Department of Agriculture, Economic Research Service, July 1983.

Nakamura, Hiroshi, and Thomas Hieronymous. *Organization and Competition in the Poultry and Egg Industries*. Technical Study No. 2. Washington, DC: U.S. Government Printing Office, 1966.

Nelson, K. E. "Market Information and Pricing Mechanisms in Livestock and Meat Industry: Issues and Alternatives." In *Market Information and Price Reporting in the Food and Agricultural Sector*. NC 117 Monograph 9. Madison: University of Wisconsin Press, 1980.

Biography and Company History

Armour, J. Ogden. *The Packers, the Private Car Lines and the People*. Philadelphia: Henry Altemus, 1906.

Cheever, Lawrence Oakley. *The House of Morrell*. Cedar Rapids, IA: Torch Press, 1948.

Clemen, Rudolf Alexander. *George Hammond, 1838–1886: Pioneer in Refrigerator Transportation*. New York: Newcomen Society in North America, 1964.

Drury, John. *Rare and Well Done: Some Historical Notes on Meat and Meat Men*. Chicago: Quadrangle Books, 1966.

Eddy, Arthur J. *Ganton and Company*. Chicago: McClurg, 1908.

Goodspeed, Thomas W. *Gustavus Franklin Swift*. Chicago: University of Chicago Press, 1922.

Leech, Harper, and John Charles Carroll. *Armour and His Times*. New York: Appleton-Century-Crofts, 1938.

Mallman, Sharon M. "Milwaukee's John Cudahy." *Historical Messenger of the Milwaukee County Historical Society* 32 (Autumn 1976): 70–87.

Neyhart, Louise A. *Giant of the Yards*. Boston: Houghton Mifflin, 1952.

Swift, Helen. *My Father and My Mother*. Chicago. N.P., 1937.

Swift, Louis F., and Arthur Van Vlissingen, Jr. *The Yankee of the Yards: The Biography of Gustavus Franklin Swift*. Chicago: A. W. Shaw, 1927.

Tinstman, Dale C., and Robert L. Peterson. *Iowa Beef Processors, Inc.: An Entire Industry Revitalized*. New York: Newcomen Society in North America, 1981.

Public Policy Studies

Aduddell, Robert M., and Louis P. Cain. "Location and Collusion in the Meat Packing Industry." In *Business Enterprise and Economic Change*, edited by Louis P. Cain and Paul J. Uselding. Kent, OH: Kent State University Press, 1973.

———. "The Consent Decree in the Meatpacking Industry, 1920–1956." *Business History Review* 55 (1981a): 359–78.

———. "Public Policy Toward 'The Greatest Trust in the World.' " *Business History Review* 55 (1981b): 217–42.

———. "A Strange Sense of Deja Vu: The Packers and the Feds, 1915–82." *Business and Economic History* 2d ser., 11 (1982): 49–60.

Anderson, Oscar E., Jr. *The Health of a Nation: Harvey W. Wiley and the Fight for Pure Food*. Chicago: University of Chicago Press for the University of Cincinnati, 1958.

Arant, Willard D. "Wartime Meat Policies." *Journal of Farm Economics* 28 (1946): 903–19.

Arnould, Richard J. "Changing Patterns of Concentration in American Meat Packing, 1880–1963." *Business History Review* 45 (Spring 1971): 19–34.

Bailey, Thomas A. "Congressional Opposition to Pure Food Legislation, 1879–1906." *American Journal of Sociology* 36 (July 1930): 52–65.

Camp, William. "Reforms in the System of Food Distribution." *Journal of Political Economy* 29 (December 1921): 824–25.

Collins, Norman, and Lee Preston. "Concentration and Price-Cost Margins in Food Manufacturing Industries." *Journal of Industrial Economics* 14 (1966): 226–42.

Colver, William B. "The Federal Trade Commission and the Meat Packing Industry." *Annals of the American Academy of Political Science* 82 (1919): 218–22.

Connor, J. M. "Advertising, Promotion and Competition: A Survey with Special

Reference to Food." *Agricultural Economic Research* 33 (January 1981): 19–27.

Cotterill, R. W., and W. F. Mueller. "The Impact of Firm Conglomeration on Market Structure: Evidence for the U.S. Food Retailing Industry." *Antitrust Bulletin* 25 (Fall 1980): 557–82.

Crawford, C. W. "Technical Problems in Food and Drug Law Enforcement." *Law and Contemporary Problems* 1 (1933): 36–43.

Dahl, D. C., and W. W. Grant, eds. *Antitrust and Agriculture*. Miscellaneous Report 137. Minneapolis: Minnesota Agricultural Station, 1975.

———. *Bibliography of Agriculture and Food Law: 1960–1978*. NC 117 Special Report. Madison: University of Wisconsin Press, August 1978.

Dahl, D. C., W. W. Grant, and L. Geyer. *Federal Antitrust Policy and the U.S. Food System*. NC 117 Monograph. Madison: University of Wisconsin Press, August 1983.

Fife, George B. "The Great Business Combination of Today: The So-Called Beef Trust." *Century Magazine* 65 (November 1902): 148–58.

Garoyan, Leon, ed. *Economics of Conglomerate Growth*. Corvallis: Oregon State University Press, 1969.

Geithman, F. E., H. P. Marvel, and L. W. Weiss. "Concentration, Price and Critical Concentration Ratios." *Review of Economics and Statistics* 58 (August 1981): 346–53.

Gisser, Micha. "Welfare Implications of Oligopoly in U.S. Food Manufacturing." *American Journal of Agricultural Economics* 64 (1982): 616–24.

Hall, Lana, Andrew Schmitz, and James Cothern. "Beef Wholesale-Retail Marketing Margins and Concentration." *Economica* 46 (1979): 295–300.

Hamilton, Walton, and Irene Hill. *Antitrust in Action*. Temporary National Economic Committee Monograph 16. Washington, DC: U.S. Government Printing Office, 1940.

Hayenga, M. L., ed. *Pricing Problems in the Food Industry (with Emphasis on Thin Markets)*. NC 117 Monograph. Madison: University of Wisconsin Press, February 1979.

Hayenga, M. L., and L. F. Schrader. "Formula Pricing in Five Commodity Marketing Systems." *American Journal of Agricultural Economics* 62 (November 1980): 753–59.

Herrick, Arthur D. *Food Regulation and Compliance*. 2 vols. New York: Revere, 1948.

Hill, William. "Relations of Packer's Credit to Panic and Prices." *Journal of Political Economy* 16 (1908): 87–102.

Hirschauer, Herman. *The Dark Side of the Beef Trust: A Treatise Concerning the "Canner" Cow, the Cold Storage Fowl, the Diseased Meats, the Dopes and Preservatives*. Jamestown, NY: Theodore Z. Root, 1905.

Hughes, Kathleen. *Return to the Jungle: How the Reagan Administration Is Imperiling the Nation's Meat and Poultry Inspection Programs*. Washington, DC: Center for the Study of Responsive Law, 1983.

Jones, Eliot. *The Trust Problem in the United States*. New York: Macmillan, 1921.

Kane, R. James. "Populism, Progressivism, and Pure Food." *Agricultural History* 38 (1964): 161–66.

Laidler, Harry W. *Concentration of Control in American Industry.* New York: Thomas Y. Crowell, 1931.

Letwin, William. *Law and Economic Policy in America: The Evolution of the Sherman Antitrust Act.* New York: Random House, 1965.

Marion, Bruce W. "Government Regulation of Competition in the Food Industry." *American Journal of Agricultural Economics* 61 (February 1979): 178–85.

Marion, Bruce W., and T. L. Sporleder. "An Evaluation of the Economic Basis for Antitrust Policy in the Food Industry." *American Journal of Agricultural Economics* 58 (December 1976): 867–73.

Masson, Alison, and Russell C. Parker. *Price and Profit Trends in Four Food Manufacturing Industries.* Staff report to the Federal Trade Commission. Washington, DC: U.S. Government Printing Office, 1975.

Mueller, Willard F., John Culbertson, and Brian Peckham. *Market Structure and Technological Performance in the Food Manufacturing Industry.* NC 117 Monograph 11. Madison: University of Wisconsin Press, 1982.

Mueller, Willard F., and L. Hamm. "Trends in Industrial Market Concentration: 1947 to 1970." *Review of Economics and Statistics* 56 (November 1974): 511–20.

Mueller, Willard F., and R. T. Rogers. "Changes in Market Concentration of Manufacturing Industries, 1947–1977." *Review of Industrial Organization* 1 (Spring 1984): 1–14.

Nakamura, Hiroshi, and Thomas Hieronymous. *Organization and Competition in the Livestock and Meat Industry.* Technical Study No. 1. Washington, DC: U.S. Government Printing Office, 1966.

Parker, Russell C. "Antitrust Issues in the Food Industries." *American Journal of Agricultural Economics* 58 (December 1976): 854–60.

Regier, C. C. "The Struggle for Food and Drug Legislation." *Law and Contemporary Problems* 1 (1933): 3–15.

U.S. Congress. *Packers and Stockyards Act, 1921, as Amended: Regulations, Statement of General Policy.* Washington, DC: U.S. Government Printing Office, 1971.

———. Subcommittee on Antitrust. *Impact of Market Concentration on Rising Food Prices.* Hearings before the Subcommittee on Antitrust, Monopoly, and Business Rights of the Senate Committee on the Judiciary. Washington, DC: U.S. Government Printing Office, 1979a.

———. Subcommittee on Small Business. *Hearings: Small Business Problems in the Marketing of Meat and Other Commodities: Anticompetitive Practices in the Marketing of Meat and Other Commodities.* 96th Cong., 1st Sess. Washington, DC: U.S. Government Printing Office, 1979b.

U.S. Federal Trade Commission. *Packer Consent Decree: Report Concerning the Present Status of the Consent Decree in the Case of the United States vs. Swift & Co. et al., Entered in the Supreme Court of the District of Columbia, February 17, 1920.* 68th Cong., 2d Sess. 1924–25. Sen. Doc. 219. Serial 8413.

———. *Enforcement Policy with Respect to Product Extension Mergers in Grocery Products Manufacturing.* Washington, DC: U.S. Government Printing Office, 1968.

———. *Economic Report on the Influence of Market Structure on the Profit Per-*

formance of Food Manufacturing Companies. Washington, DC: U.S. Government Printing Office, 1969.

U.S. Senate. Report of the Commission Appointed by the President to Investigate the Conduct of the War Department in the War with Spain [the Dodge Commission]. 8 vols. Sen. Ex. Doc. 221. 56th Cong., 1st Sess. Washington, DC: U.S. Government Printing Office, 1901–2.

Veeder, Henry. "The Federal Trade Commission and the Packers." Illinois Law Review 15 (March 1921): 485–503.

Virtue, G. O. "The Meat Packing Investigation." Quarterly Journal of Economics 34 (August 1920): 626–85.

Walker, Francis. "The Beef Trust and the United States Government." Economic Journal 16 (December 1906): 491–514.

Weld, L.D.H. "The Meat Packing Investigation: A Reply." Quarterly Journal of Economics 35 (May 1921): 412–30.

White, Wilford. "The Refrigerator Car and the Effects upon the Public of Packer Control of Refrigerator Car Lines." Southwestern Political and Social Science Quarterly 10 (March 1930): 388–400.

Whitney, Simon. Antitrust Policies: American Experience in Twenty Industries. 2 vols. New York: Twentieth Century Fund, 1958.

Wilcox, Clair. Competition and Monopoly in American Industry. Temporary National Economic Committee Monograph 21. Washington, DC: U.S. Government Printing Office, 1940.

Consumption and Marketing Studies

Capie, Forrest, and Richard Perren. "The British Market for Meat, 1850–1914." Agricultural History 54 (1980): 502–15.

Caswell, Julie A. "Direct and Network Control of Firms in the Agribusiness Sector." Ph.D. diss., University of Wisconsin-Madison, 1984.

Chavas, Jean-Paul. "Structural Change in the Demand for Meat." American Journal of Agricultural Economics 65 (1983): 148–53.

Connor, J. M. "Food Product Proliferation: A Market Structure Analysis." American Journal of Agricultural Economics 63 (November 1981): 607–17.

Duddy, E. E., and D. A. Revzan. The Changing Relative Importance of the Central Livestock Markets. Chicago: University of Chicago Press, 1938.

Etheridge, M. D. Competitive Potential of Synthetic Meat Products: Some Efficiency Implications of Nutritional Composition. Reno: Western Agricultural Economics Association, Proceedings 48th Annual Conference (July 1975): 191–95.

Fowler, Steward H. The Marketing of Livestock and Meat. 2d ed. Danville, IL: Interstate Printers & Publishers, 1961.

Fowler, Steward H., and Karen J. Friedmann. "Urban Food Marketing in Los Angeles, 1850–1885." Agriculture History 54 (1980): 433–45.

Haidacher, Richard C., et al. Consumer Demand for Red Meats, Poultry, and Fish. ERS Report No. AGES820818. Washington, DC: U.S. Department of Agriculture, Economic Research Service, 1982.

Hill, William. "Relation of Packer's Credit to Panic and Prices." Journal of Political Economy 16 (February 1908): 87–102.

Knight, Ewart B., Virginia W. Plummer, and Louis Johnson, Jr. *The Management and Marketing Practices of the Small Independent Meat Packers of Tennessee.* Cookeville, TN: Tennessee Polytechnic Institute, 1962.

McCoy, John H. *Livestock and Meat Marketing.* Westport, CT: AVI, 1979.

Manchester, Alden C., and Richard A. King. *U.S. Food Expenditures, 1954–78.* Agricultural Economic Report No. 431. Washington, DC: U.S. Department of Agriculture, Economics, Statistics, and Cooperative Service, 1979.

Marion, B. W., et al. *The Food Retailing Industry: Market Structure, Profits, and Prices.* New York: Praeger, 1979.

Nakamura, Hiroshi, and Thomas Hieronymous. *The Structure of Food Retailing.* Technical Study No. 7. Washington, DC: U.S. Government Printing Office, 1966.

Nicholls, William H. "Market Sharing in the Meat Packing Industry." *Journal of Farm Economics* 22 (April 1940): 225–31.

Packard, Vernal S., Jr. *Processed Foods and the Consumer.* Minneapolis: University of Minnesota Press, 1971.

Rhoades, E. L. *Merchandising Packinghouse Products.* Chicago: University of Chicago Press, 1929.

Smallwood, David, and James Blaylock. *Impact of Household Size and Income on Food Spending Patterns.* Technical Bulletin No. 1650. Washington, DC: U.S. Department of Agriculture, Economics and Statistics Service, 1981.

U.S. Congress. House. Committee on Small Business. Subcommittee on SBA. *Small Business Problems in the Marketing of Meat and Other Commodities. Part 7—Monopoly Effects on Producers and Consumers.* Hearings before the Subcommittee on SBA. Washington, DC: U.S. Government Printing Office, 1979.

U.S. Department of Agriculture. *The Future Role of Cooperatives in the Red Meat Industry.* Washington, DC: U.S. Department of Agriculture, Economics, Statistics, and Cooperatives Service, Marketing Research Report 1089, April 1978.

U.S. Federal Trade Commission. *Economic Inquiry into Food Marketing. Part 1, Concentration and Integration in Retailing.* Staff Report. Washington, DC: U.S. Government Printing Office, January 1960.

Wentworth, Edward N. "Livestock Products and the Tariff." *Journal of Farm Economics* 7 (July 1925): 319–45.

Williams, Faith M. "The Measurement of the Demand for Food." *Journal of the American Statistical Association* 24 (September 1929): 288–95.

Miscellaneous Studies

Abbott, Edith, and S. P. Breckinridge. "Women in Industry: The Chicago Stockyards." *Journal of Political Economy* 19 (October 1911): 632–54.

American Meat Institute. *Financial Facts About the Meat Packing Industry 1925–1981.* Chicago: American Meat Institute, 1982.

———. *Financial Review of the Meatpacking Industry.* Washington, DC: American Meat Institute. Annual.

———. *Meatfacts: A Statistical Summary About America's Largest Food Industry.* Chicago: American Meat Institute. Annual.

Anderson, Oscar E. *Refrigeration in America*. Princeton: Princeton University Press, 1953.

Arnould, Richard J. *Diversification and Profitability Among Large Food Processing Firms*. Agricultural Economic Report No. 171. Washington, DC: U.S. Department of Agriculture, Economic Research Service, 1970.

Bloom, G. F. *Productivity in the Food Industry: Problems and Potential*. Cambridge, MA: MIT Press, 1972.

Brody, David. *The Butcher Workmen: A Study of Unionization*. Cambridge, MA: Harvard University Press, 1964.

Bushnell, Charles Joseph. *The Social Problem at the Chicago Stockyards*. Chicago: University of Chicago Press, 1902.

Commons, John R. "Labor Conditions in Meat Packing and the Recent Strike." *Quarterly Journal of Economics* 19 (November 1904): 1–32.

Cothern, James H., R. Mark Peard, and John L. Weeks. "Economies of Scale in Beef Processing and Portion Control Operations: Northern California—1976." Leaflet 21017. Division of Agriculture Sciences, University of California-Davis, 1978.

Elazar, Daniel J., ed. "Working Conditions in Chicago in the Early Twentieth Century: Testimony Before the Illinois Senatorial Vice Committee, 1913." *American Jewish Archives* 21 (1969): 149–71.

Fogel, Walter. "Union Impact on the Retail Food Wages in California." *Industrial Relations* 6 (1966): 79–94.

————. "Blacks in Meatpacking: Another View of the Jungle." *Industrial Relations* 10 (1971): 338–53.

Hill, H. C. "The Development of Chicago as a Center for the Packing Industry." *Mississippi Valley Historical Review* 10 (December 1923): 153–73.

Horst, Thomas. *At Home Abroad: A Study of the Domestic and Foreign Operations of the American Food-Processing Industry*. Cambridge, MA: Ballinger, 1974.

Logan, S. H. *Economies of Scale in Cattle Slaughtering Plants*. National Commission on Food Marketing. Technical Study No. 1. Supplement No. 2. Washington, DC: U.S. Government Printing Office, 1966.

Logan, S. H., and Gordon A. King. *Economies of Scale in Beef Slaughtering Plants*. Gianini Foundation Research Report 260. Berkeley: University of California Agricultural Experiment Station, 1962.

Pidgeon, Mary Elizabeth. *The Employment and Growth of Women in Slaughter and Meat Packing*. Washington, DC: U.S. Government Printing Office, 1932.

Putnam, George E. "Joint Costs in the Packing Industry." *Journal of Political Economy* 29 (April 1921): 292–303.

Rust, Charles H., and Clive R. Harston. *The Survival and Growth Potential of Small Meatpacking Businesses in Montana*. Helena: Montana State Planning Board, 1963.

Sims, Grover J. *Meat and Meat Animals in World War II*. Monograph 9. Washington, DC: U.S. Department of Agriculture, 1951.

U.S. Congress. Office of Technology Assessment. *Emerging Food Marketing Technologies*. Washington, DC: U.S. Government Printing Office, 1978.

Wing, Jack. *The Great Union Stockyards of Chicago*. Chicago: Religio-Philosophical Publishing Association, 1865.

CHAPTER 2

BAKERY PRODUCTS, 20.5

DONALD R. STABILE

THE PRE-INDUSTRIAL ERA

Prior to the Civil War, small bakeries employed technology essentially unchanged from that of the Romans and produced bread for local customers. These bakeries were the prevalent units of commercial output, but they did not dominate the production of bakery goods: home baking was the major form of production. Although the growth of the industry paralleled urbanization in the United States from 1800 to 1850, only about 10 percent of the bread consumed was provided by bakeries. According to the U.S. Census of Manufactures of 1850, 2,027 bakeries employed 6,727 workers and produced $13 million worth of bakery products annually; 95 percent of those bakeries, however, earned less than $5,000 per year. The distribution of perishable bread and baked goods was limited to retail outlets (Panschar 1956).

The baking of crackers and biscuits was more advanced industrially than bread production in the pre–Civil War era. The requirements of provisioning ocean-going ships had fostered the development of a nonperishable, unleavened bread that would not spoil during long voyages. The first cracker bakery in the United States was established in 1792 at Newburyport, Massachusetts (Cahn 1969). By 1801 Joshua Bent of Massachusetts had transformed his ship's bread into an easily handled product, Bent's Water-Cracker. In 1813 a patent on a manufacturing process for ship's bread was awarded to Jehoshaphat Starr of Middletown, Connecticut, and in 1815 a biscuit-making machine was patented by William Liddle of New York (Alsberg [1926] 1973). By 1840 three varieties of crackers—butter crackers, soda crackers, and sugar biscuits—had appeared on the market. Because they were less perishable than bread, crackers could be more widely distributed. Furthermore, they were unleavened, so their production was simpler and easily mechanized. Wholesale distribution to general stores was initiated (Panschar 1956). In 1845 the Kennedy bakery of Arlington, Massachusetts, introduced steam power to run its machinery, and a fleet of wagons was soon delivering Kennedy crackers to the surrounding towns (Cahn 1969).

The Civil War did little to boost the sales of perishable bakery products. Crackers were an important food among the armies, so cracker manufacturers' profits rose. In the transportation revolution that followed the war, crackers were eliminated as a staple food item. During the period from 1850 to 1900, further urbanization and rising real incomes increased the demand for processed foods. Baking, however, was the last form of food processing to be removed from the home. Despite a sevenfold increase in the number of bakeries and a thirteenfold increase in the value of commercial bread production, 75 percent of the bread consumed in 1900 was still baked at home (Panschar 1956).

THE GROWTH OF MANUFACTURING

During the years of expansion in bakery production, technological change altered bread manufacturing. Bread was baked in peel ovens (named for the long-handled peels used to remove the hot loaves) that dated to Roman times. The oven was heated by a fire built directly inside it. After each use, the fire had to be extinguished and the oven cleaned before the process could be repeated. The first advance was a firebox added to the door. Further improvement brought a second firebox to provide uniform heat from both sides of the oven. In the 1870s the firebox was placed beneath the oven and the heat conducted to the oven by flues. There was no longer a need to extinguish the fire between batches. Continuous firing, coupled with draw plates and rotary trays to facilitate loading and unloading the bread, tripled the productivity of the peel ovens.

Advances in the techniques of baking were complemented by other technological changes. Machines for mixing and rolling dough appeared in the 1870s. In 1895 an automatic dough divider, which separated dough into the proper length for loaves, was introduced. A molding machine to form dough into loaves had been in use since 1888. The production of bread was advanced by the use of compressed yeast as a leavening agent, a product developed by Charles Fleischman in 1868. Earlier, bakeries had produced their own leavening agents, with uneven results. Baking with standard yeast eliminated losses from bread that did not rise. Despite these improvements, bakers resisted technological change, and units of production remained small. In 1899, 78 percent of the bakeries in the United States employed fewer than four workers, and only 1 percent employed more than one hundred (Panschar 1956).

Many ill effects of such small-scale, highly competitive units were felt in the industry. Bakery proprietors cut costs by scrimping on wages and sanitation. In New York City, for example, many bakeshops were located in cellars that were more suitable for the storage of coal. Workers put in fourteen-hour days and were compelled to lodge with their employers. Night and weekend work was common because bakers tried to have fresh bread available when consumers desired it. Workers endured these conditions in the hope that they, too, would eventually own their own shops. Insalubrious conditions led several states—New York and Minnesota were in the forefront—to establish sanitation regulations and health inspections for bakeries. Mechanized bread production mitigated these harsh conditions, even as it dashed the workers' dreams of ownership by placing the cost of a plant beyond their reach (Kaufman 1987).

Large-scale plants producing bread for wholesale consistently attempted to operate union-free. The Ward bakeries set up a Department of Employee Welfare in 1913 and allocated a portion of the company's profits to a benefit fund. Other companies provided dances and free refreshments for their employees (Kaufman 1987).

The technology of cracker production improved in the 1890s with the National Biscuit Company's development of automatic wrapping machinery. Biscuit and cracker bakers expanded into wholesale distribution of their products over a wide area in the 1870s and 1880s. They used jobbers and wholesalers to take advantage of improvements in rail transportation and to operate in a national market. Competition drove manufacturers toward merger and consolidation in the 1880s. In 1898, through the efforts of the Moore brothers (who would later be instrumental in the formation of United States Steel), the National Biscuit Company was formed through a merger of several regional consolidations.

The Moores had previously formed the New York Biscuit Company from more than twenty bakeries, including the Kennedy bakery, one of the largest and most up-to-date in the country. At the same time, Adolphus Green formed the American Biscuit Company in Chicago through other regional mergers. The two companies merged after a period of intense price competition (Cahn 1969). The new company immediately pursued an innovative marketing strategy: National Biscuit bypassed wholesalers for direct sales to retailers. As part of this strategy, National Biscuit combined small-unit packaging and a national advertising campaign for a new product, Uneeda Biscuit, whose freshness was insured by a patented inner seal wrapping (Cahn 1969). At the same time the company began selling to retail stores through route-salesmen. By 1900 sales by cracker and biscuit manufacturers constituted about 30 percent of the sales volume of crackers and bread products (Panschar 1956).

TRANSFORMATION TO AN INDUSTRY

Continued mechanization and innovations in marketing between 1900 and 1930 transformed the manufacture and distribution of bread and bakery products into a modern industry. During these years, housewives rapidly shifted from baking bread to purchasing it. New methods of production, especially with standard leavening agents, yielded an improved commercial bread whose quality was at least equal to that of home-baked. And more stringent industry-wide standards and automatic bread-wrapping machines to seal the bread had improved sanitation in the production line. As bakeries grew and competed over wider markets, they began advertising their products, not only to convince housewives of the improved quality and sanitary production of their bread but also to build brand loyalty.

During World War I there were food shortages, especially of flour and wheat. Substitution of other cereal grains was necessary (rye, oats, and barley were most commonly used), and bakeries were better equipped than housewives were to handle this substitution. The rise of specialized grocery stores also created greater demand. These stores were willing to handle bread products on consignment: unpurchased, stale bread could be returned to the wholesaler at no cost to the retailer (Panschar 1956).

As the market changed, bakeries became wholesale distributors of their products. Bread trucks delivered their products to ever wider areas. Mechanization continued to improve the baking process. Bakery workers learned that, in moving dough from dividing to molding, the product quality was improved if the dough was "rounded" and "proofed" to give it a slight skin, then allowed to recover. In 1906–7 this process was mechanized. During World War I, air conditioning was introduced to create the best atmospheric conditions for rounding and proofing. Stronger, safer mixing machines were also devised at this time. Around 1910 large ovens through which the bread was conveyed on a moving line greatly enhanced productivity, as bread could then be baked continuously rather than in batches. Bread-slicing machines were invented in 1928 and immediately put to use. By 1930 the technology of bread baking permitted the complete integration of production, with equipment available to mechanize each step in the baking process (Panschar 1956).

Bread companies began selling to chain-store groceries that appeared between 1900 and 1930. This new market required different methods of distribution and sales. The chain stores pursued a policy of selling bread at prices below standard retail in an area. In some areas wholesale bakeries responded by refusing to sell to the grocery chains. Several grocery chains introduced house brands: by 1930 Kroger had twelve bakeries and A & P thirty-five (Alsberg [1926] 1973). But the chain-store bakeries secured only about 10 percent of the market (Panschar 1956).

The entrance of grocery chains into baking was evidence of the widespread cutthroat competition that marked the bakery industry. The frequent mergers of bakery companies in the 1920s were not only a response to that competition, but also a means of securing the financial stability required by large-scale technology. Mergers established stability first in local areas, but soon spread to wider regions as the arena of competition expanded. National mergers were eventually effected, forming large companies such as Continental Baking Corporation, Ward Baking Corporation, Purity Baking Corporation, and General Baking Company.

The organizing genius behind the national merger movement, William B. Ward, possessed a unique combination of money, promotional talent, and bakery management experience. Ward's family had been in the baking business for two generations. He started his own bakery in Buffalo in 1912. In 1922 he formed United Bakeries Corporations as a holding company for nineteen operating plants in Buffalo, Rochester, and Kansas City. In 1923 he formed a second holding company, Ward Baking Company, to operate seventeen plants owned by his uncle. Then, in 1924, he set up the Continental Baking Company to manage United Bakeries and to purchase several other firms. By 1926 Continental held nearly 100 plants and was the largest producer in the country. But Ward was not finished; in 1925 he formed the General Baking Company, which soon owned forty-two bakeries.

Ward's overall scheme was revealed in 1926, when he created the Ward Food Products Corporation and attempted to control Continental, Ward, and General. This combination would have accounted for 20 percent of the bread production in the United States. Soon after his plans were announced, Ward was confronted with a federal suit for violation of the Sherman and Clayton Antitrust acts. A consent decree was negotiated that restrained Ward and his companies from any further control or acquisitions in the bread industry. Ward died shortly thereafter, and the companies he formed spent years restructuring (Panschar 1956).

As more bakeries shifted from retail sales to wholesaling, new marketing strategies emerged. In addition to price-cutting, product differentiation was employed. Ward, for example, marketed his bread under the Tip-Top brand and used the label to gain control over other companies (Kaufman 1987). In the early 1900s, as comic strip characters became popular, their creators licensed them as brand names for bakers. The comic strip "Buster Brown" was very successful; sixty-five bakeries were reportedly using it on their labeling in 1907. Coupons good for price discounts and bread wrappers redeemable for gifts won the housewife's favor, and small gifts were given to grocers to secure shelf space. Competition encouraged waste. Bakeries loaded large displays onto store shelves, and the amount of unsold bread returned to the bakeries increased from the usual 1 percent to as much as 25–30 percent. Some national companies such as Ward's practiced geographic price discrimination. As early as 1922 the American Bakers Association attempted to eliminate destructive competition through a voluntary code of ethics, but they were unsuccessful. By 1929 large bakeries (over $500,000 in sales) represented only 4.6 percent of the plants but accounted for 39.7 percent of sales. There was little concentration on the national level, however, because there were over 16,000 plants at the time. Half the bakery sales were to grocery stores in 1929 (Panschar 1956).

In the cookies and crackers branch of the industry, National Biscuit continued its domination of the national market. By 1920 the company had augmented its cracker production with cookies, including Lorna Doone and Oreo. Following the break industry, cookie and cracker producers mechanized delivery systems and replaced horse-drawn wagons with trucks. Competition brought price-cutting tactics by the Loose-Wiles Biscuit Company and the formation of the United Biscuit Company in 1927 (Cahn 1969). Together, National Biscuit and Loose-Wiles baked an estimated 65 percent of all biscuits and crackers (Alsberg [1926] 1973).

THE DEPRESSION

The Great Depression of 1929–33 brought an end to the long trend of rising demand for bread. Bread prices fell by 26 percent and production by 25 percent. Employment dropped to 88 percent of its former high, and wages were cut to 66 percent of the 1929 levels. Because bread is a staple product, the unexpected decline was attributed to the reduced waste of food and a return to home baking. These forces are especially powerful in explaining the 50 percent drop in the purchase of sweet baked goods.

When the National Recovery Administration (NRA) was formed, the bakery industry saw an opportunity to end ruinous competition. Under the leadership of the American Bakers Association, over 600 delegates met in Chicago in August 1933 to write a voluntary code for the industry. The committee formed at the meeting would ultimately produce an NRA code that eliminated price discounts, premiums, and so on. Disagreement erupted over consignment sales, which were favored by large wholesalers, but opposed in areas where wholesalers were weak. The code left consignment sales to the discretion of the companies in each state or region.

The framers of the "Code for Bakeries" paid scant attention to section 7(A), the labor code. While the harsh labor provisions set forth in the Chicago meeting were moderated in negotiations with government officials, the final code adopted was viewed unfavorably by the Bakery and Confectionery Workers' Union (AFL). The code did not provide wage and hour levels consistent with the union's call for reemployment.

The code proved difficult to administer: How was the NRA to define the designated market with any precision? The costs of administering the code were to be raised as a fixed percentage of sales from each industry member, but less than half the amount due was collected. Compliance with the code was poor. Many bakers continued discounts. The code authority had a file of over 5,500 complaints of code violations. Despite these problems, by the time the NRA was declared unconstitutional in 1935, there had been some diminution of open price wars.

The labor provision of the code barely improved working conditions. Hours were reduced slightly and a moderate amount of reemployment took place. Organization drives by the Bakery and Confectionery Workers' Union in mechanized bakeries were a failure, and, although union membership rose from 16,000 to 20,000 from 1932 to 1935, it was well below pre-Depression figures. After the passage of the National Labor Relations Act in 1935, organization drives by the Bakery Workers' Union and the Teamsters Union were more successful, and union membership rose to 30,000.

The industry began a slow recovery after 1933; bread prices had risen only 17 percent by 1935. Small-scale retail shops and home delivery companies, hardest hit by the Depression, did not regain their lost market shares. By the late 1930s, a change had also taken place in the industry's product mix, with bread showing some decline compared to sweets. A much higher portion of sales was being made through chains and supermarkets (Panschar 1956).

The cookie and cracker companies also suffered from the hard years of the Depression. In January 1935 National Biscuit was hit with the first strike ever by its employees, as over 7,500 workers in plants in New York, Philadelphia, and Atlanta walked off the job. Three months passed before an agreement was reached between management and workers represented by Federal Labor Union #19585 of the AFL (Cahn 1969).

The band oven, a major technological advance in cookie and cracker baking, was introduced in the 1930s. The oven operated like an assembly line. Dough was rolled in a continuous form, and specific products were cut from the dough and pulled through the oven; the speed of the conveyor determined the baking time. Because band ovens several hundred feet long required new factories to house them, established firms in the industry were slow to re-equip. Spurred by the need to merchandise its products for sale in self-service supermarkets, the industry also began using new packaging materials such as cellophane (Cahn 1969).

THE POSTWAR YEARS

The economic recovery of World War II extended to the bakery industry. Incomes rose and increasing numbers of women entered the labor market. Increased labor force participation by women ended the home baking of bread and limited the home baking of cakes and pies. By the end of the war, these changes were permanent; consumers had become accustomed to bakery products. At the behest of the government, bakers began to enrich bread during the war and continued the practice afterwards. By 1947 only 15.3 percent of the 22,483 bakeries in the United States sold primarily to grocery stores, but their sales amounted to 50.2 percent of all sales. Although nearly 75 percent of the bakeries sold retail, they made only 25 percent of the sales (Panschar 1956).

In 1950 the largest firm in the industry was Continental Baking Company, which marketed its products under the brand names Wonder Bread and Hostess Cakes. Continental operated seventy-five plants in twenty-eight states, and Wonder Bread was available for sale to about 80 percent of the American people. On a national level, however, Continental made only 5.2 percent of industry sales, with its share of local markets ranging from 5 to 30 percent. The next four largest companies were American Bakeries Company (sixty plants in fifty cities), General Baking Company (forty-three plants in thirty-nine cities), Campbell Taggart Associated Bakeries, Inc. (forty-seven plants in forty-seven cities), and Ward Baking Company (twenty-three plants in twenty-one cities) (Slater 1956).

The diffusion and size of bakeries makes any calculation of industry concentration difficult. One study made in the 1950s showed a much higher level of concentration at the local level than the national. Using data from an unidentified metropolitan area, Charles C. Slater (1956) found that the top four firms accounted for about 57 percent of the bread sales and about 95 percent of the packaged cake sales. In a medium-sized city, the top four firms sold 94.1 percent of the bread produced and 75 percent of the cakes. In a small city, the top four firms sold 90 percent of the bakery goods, and retail bake shops sold the rest.

The range in the scale of operations forced an unusual pattern of product diversity on individual bakers. Because grocers, in their efforts to provide a full product line to consumers, could provide products from a variety of sources, it was possible for bakeries to specialize. But because the sales volume at a store had to be large enough to warrant a driver's stopping there, bakeries pursued strategies pitched to the size of their plants. Large bakeries employed a strategy of high-volume sales for a few specialized products. Small ones provided a more complete line to make servicing a store profitable in terms of total sales. Small bakeries were able to survive by providing a wider array of high-cost specialty items (Slater 1956).

Unionization of bakery workers had greatly increased by the 1950s. As bakeries mechanized and expanded their distribution networks, the union shifted from organizing skilled workers in small shops to organizing all workers in the industry. Production workers inside the plant were organized by the Bakery and Confectionery Workers' International Union, which in the 1950s claimed to represent nearly all of the 75 percent of bakery production workers who were unionized. Outside workers, primarily delivery drivers and route salesmen, fell under the jurisdiction of the Teamsters Union (Slater 1956).

Through the 1940s and 1950s, National Biscuit remained the major company in the cookie and cracker industry. In 1945 there were about 165 companies with national or regional distribution of cookie or cracker lines. The other large national companies were Sunshine Biscuits (formerly Loose-Wiles) and United Biscuit Company. Because they were less entrenched in the industry, these two companies were more innovative than National Biscuit, especially in introducing band ovens (Cahn 1969).

In 1953 a continuous mix machine was introduced, which allowed for the automatic production of bread baking. The continuous mix machine, combined with a new process of liquid fermentation, made bread mixes feasible and introduced a high degree of automation to the bread industry. Mixing, developing, dividing, shaping, and panning the bread dough could now be done continuously (Chumley 1967). Despite the potential for reduced labor costs, the continuous mix process was not widely accepted, because it produced more than many firms could sell (*Technology and Labor in Five Industries* 1979).

RECENT DEVELOPMENTS

In 1979 it was estimated that technology in the baking industry had not improved significantly in twenty years. Productivity growth since 1959 had been moderate (*Technology and Labor* 1979). There had been important changes in industry structure and competition, however. Wholesale bakers faced increasing competition in bread production; vertically integrated grocery chain stores accounted for about 11 percent of production by the 1960s. Nationally, the four largest bakeries accounted for 23 percent of production in 1963, up from 20 percent in 1954. In terms of specific markets, the nine largest bakeries selling wholesale to grocery stores made 52 percent of the sales. Because of the perishability of bread, however, its distribution was still geographically limited. As a result, at a city level (based on a survey of seventeen cities) the top four bakeries sold an average of 63 percent in 1963. From 1947 to 1963 the number of baking companies declined from 6,000 to 4,300 (*Organization and Competition in the Milling and Baking Industries* 1966).

Frozen products, in the form of dough that can be baked into bread at home, and cakes and pies entered the market during the 1960s and accounted for about 5 percent of the industry volume. Over the next two decades the bread industry continued to face shifting demand patterns, as consumers' preferences moved from white bread toward specialty breads. Industry consolidation continued; 2,755 companies (representing 2,964 plants) disappeared between 1958 and 1977. By 1978 frozen bakery products accounted for 7.6 percent of baked goods sales (*SBI* 1982). In 1968 ITT, following a practice of conglomerate merger, purchased Continental Baking Company. ITT sold Continental to Ralston Purina in 1984. Continental remained the largest bakery company in the nation in 1984, with 11 percent of national sales. It was followed by Campbell Taggart (7 percent), Interstate Brands (5 percent), and Flowers Industries (4 percent) for a top-four concentration ratio of slightly over 27 percent (*A Profile of the Baking Industry* 1985).

In the cookies and crackers segment of the industry, recent decades have seen a continuation of product differentiation. The latest product innovation is soft cookies, produced with high-fructose syrup instead of sugar. Nabisco (formerly National Biscuit), which merged with R. J. Reynolds Tobacco in 1985, remains the dominant firm in the industry, with 32 percent of industry sales in 1984. Nabisco is followed by Keebler Company (formerly United Biscuit) with 17 percent, Sunshine Biscuits with 9 percent, and Lance, Inc., with 6 percent, for a top-four concentration ratio of 64 percent (*Profile* 1985).

About 230,000 people worked in the baking industry in the early 1970s, nearly 25 percent fewer than in the peak year 1956. Production workers accounted for almost 60 percent of that total. By comparison, production workers in all of manufacturing account for 75 percent of the labor force. The lower percentage in the baking industry is a reflection of a distribution system that relies on a driver-salesman to deliver bread and baked goods directly to a variety of stores (*Technology and Labor* 1979). In 1984 about half the bakery production workers belonged to unions. About 75 percent of the workers in bakeries were organized, the majority of whom were represented by the Bakery, Confectionery and Tobacco Workers International Union (see below) (*Profile* 1985).

BIBLIOGRAPHIC ANALYSIS

The bakery products industry remains virtually untouched by individual scholarship in economic and business history. The major sources on the industry were all commissioned by specific industry associations, companies, or unions. Additional studies have been made by government agencies, but these are characteristically broad, with few references to specific companies or individual practices. A large number of trade journals serve the industry, but rarely take a historical perspective. The industry remains too diffuse for historical research without the cooperation of the various firms and associations that make up the industry. No major journal articles have appeared in the last two decades.

Industrial History

The primary sources on the industrial history of bakery products are William G. Panschar's *Baking in America, Volume 1: Economic History* (1956) and Charles C. Slater's *Baking in America, Volume 2: Market Organization and Competition* (1956). Both authors were funded by a grant from the American Bakers Association and were able to draw upon industry executives as well as an advisory committee set up by the association for the project. Panschar's work is especially descriptive of pre-industrial baking, although his main focus is the economic history of the industry to 1950. This pre-industrial history is particularly useful, because the baking industry in the United States was built on marketing methods used during feudal times and production techniques developed by the Romans. Slater's companion volume provides a thorough analysis of the bakery industry circa 1950. Slater used an industrial organization approach to paint a complete picture of the structure of the industry and to analyze pricing, production, and distribution. He included a graphic account of bread baking that explains many of the technological innovations described by Panschar. Nevertheless, the industry has changed substantially over the last three decades, so Slater is mainly useful as a historical source.

Slater's approach is imitated in another volume that uses different data and a slightly later time frame. Richard G. Walsh and Bert M. Evans (1963) present engineering estimates of optimal plant sizes in the 1950s and a broad description of the contemporary technology of baking. They also discuss price leadership in local bread markets.

Company History

Few company histories have been written for the bakery products industry. The National Biscuit Company (Nabisco), a fully integrated company with a national distribution system, commissioned William Cahn (1969) to write its history. Cahn uses a popular style and devotes most of his writing to the personalities of the founders and successive top executives of the company. The book does contain background on many of Nabisco's better-known products (Uneeda Biscuits, Oreo Cookies, Premium Saltines, Ritz Crackers, and Shredded Wheat) and touches on some of the technological innovation within the industry. The company is traced through a product life cycle of innovation, production, and distribution improvements. It had stagnated as a mature company by the 1940s. A period of reinvigoration followed during the 1950s.

Labor History

The central force that pervades the industry is the labor union that represents its workers, the Bakery, Confectionery and Tobacco Workers International Union. A history of that union represents the most recent research effort on the industry. *A Vision of Unity: The History of the Bakery and Confectionery Workers International Union* (Kaufman 1987) was published by the union and is written in a popular style with no footnotes, references, or bibliography. Most of the material was drawn from union records, journals, and conversations with union officials, and highlights the union leadership.

Trade unionism in the bakery products industry began with the migration of German bakers to the United States; these workers brought with them a commitment to unionism and socialism that remained a part of their organizing strategy for several decades. In January, 1886, at a convention in Pittsburgh, delegates formed the Journeymen Bakers' National Union, headquartered in New York City. The new union found itself in direct conflict with the Knights of Labor, which already had several strong locals among bakers; so on February 22, 1887, it affiliated with the AFL. Dual unionism remained a problem for the next decade, however. The union's name was changed to Journeymen Bakers' and Confectioners' International Union in 1890 and to Bakery and Confectionery Workers International Union (B & C) in 1903. The union maintained a loose connection with the Socialist Labor Party, but gradually evolved toward business unionism. Membership in 1900 totalled 5,208. Most of its organizing efforts were concentrated in the bread bakeries. Attempts to organize the National Biscuit Company in 1903 were defeated by a well-planned lockout. Still, by 1911 the union had grown to 20,394 members. Membership peaked at 28,070 before declining to about 22,000 during the harsh open-shop era of the 1920s.

The union continued to decline during the Great Depression, bottoming out at 16,000 members in 1933. Spurred by section 7(A) of the National Industrial Recovery Act and the passage of the National Labor Relations Act, membership rose to 37,376 by 1936. Mechanization in the industry led the B & C to espouse the industrial unionism that would be promoted by the Congress of Industrial Organizations (CIO); nevertheless, the B & C remained loyal to the American Federation of Labor (AFL). Workers at National Biscuit, which had formed separate Federal Labor Unions, transferred to the B & C by the end of the 1930s. In 1941 the union had nearly 100,000 members: 62,581 in bread and pie shops and 8,568 in the biscuit and cracker industry. For the next two decades, the union continued to grow. Dissension over the corruption of the union's president, Jim Cross, culminated in a split and the expulsion of the Cross faction from the AFL on December 10, 1957. An alternate union, the American Bakery and Confectionery Workers International Union, was formed as an AFL affiliate, and soon secured the right to represent about two-thirds of the former members of the B & C. The B & C continued with some support from the Teamsters Union. In December, 1969, the two unions merged and retained the older name. Another merger in 1978 created the present Bakery, Confectionery and Tobacco Workers International Union, with a membership of about 167,000.

BIBLIOGRAPHY

Alsberg, Carl L. *Combination in the American Bread-Baking Industry.* 1926. Reprint. New York: Arno Press, 1973.
Cahn, William. *Out of the Cracker Barrel: The Nabisco Story from Animal Crackers to ZuZus.* New York: Simon & Schuster, 1969.

Chumley, Toledo W. *Adoption of the Continuous Mix Process in Bread Baking.* Washington, DC: U.S. Department of Agriculture, 1967.

Economic Report on the Baking Industry. Washington, DC: Federal Trade Commission, November 1967.

Kaufman, Stuart Bruce. *A Vision of Unity: The History of the Bakery and Confectionery Workers International Union.* Washington, DC: Bakery, Confectionery and Tobacco Workers International Union, 1987; distributed by the University of Illinois Press.

Organization and Competition in the Milling and Baking Industries. Washington, DC: National Commission on Food Marketing, June 1966.

Panschar, William G. *Baking in America, Volume 1: Economic History.* Evanston, IL: Northwestern University Press, 1956.

A Profile of the Baking Industry. Washington, DC: Food and Allied Service Trades Department, A.F.L.-C.I.O., October 1985.

The SBI Report on the Market and Economics of the Bakery Products Industry. Wantagh, NY: Specialists in Business Information, 1982.

Slater, Charles C. *Baking in America, Volume 2: Market Organization and Competition.* Evanston, IL: Northwestern University Press, 1956.

Technology and Labor in Five Industries. Washington, DC: U.S. Department of Labor, Bureau of Labor Statistics, 1979.

Walsh, Richard G., and Bert M. Evans. *Economics of Change in Market Structure, Conduct and Performance: The Baking Industry, 1947–1958,* n.s. 28. Lincoln: University of Nebraska Studies, December 1963.

CHAPTER 3 ———————————————————————

DISTILLED SPIRITS, 20.85

——————————————————— K. AUSTIN KERR

The beverage distilling industry in the United States has an unusual history. Along with vintners and brewers, distillers have been forced at various times by state prohibition laws and the Eighteenth Amendment to the Constitution to use their capital for other businesses. Since the repeal of Prohibition in 1933, the alcoholic beverage industries have been more stringently regulated than other businesses that make and sell products for human consumption. Because distillers manufacture a psychotropic drug whose misuse causes serious public health problems, the government limits their entrepreneurial freedom to package, label, and advertise spirits. Furthermore, the retail price of distilled beverages includes a tax share larger than that for any other consumer good.

Before and after national Prohibition, the American distilling industry was a vehicle for profitable investment. After 1890 it fell behind brewing as a supplier of beverage alcohol in the American market. Nevertheless, distilling remained a large-scale business. After 1937 the largest distilling firm operating in the United States was the Canadian-based Seagram Company Ltd., which in 1986 reported annual sales of $3,344,820,000 (the American subsidiary was Joseph E. Seagram & Sons, Inc.). That same year Seagram Company Ltd. employed about 14,400 people in distilleries and bottling plants in twenty-one nations. Its distilleries had a daily capacity of about 374,000 U.S. proof gallons (a proof gallon contains 50 percent alcohol). Led by this large firm, the distilling industry paid excise taxes in 1983 on spirits that generated $3,756,600,000 for the United States Treasury and $6,896,512,000 in combined federal, state, and local revenues.

The distilling industry began in antiquity as humans learned to ferment sugars from honey, grain, milk, and cane to produce ethyl alcohol. Water forms steam at a higher temperature than alcohol; so heat applied to the alcoholic brew in a distilling apparatus allows the concentration of alcohol by separating it from water. A variety of agricultural products may be fermented to produce an alcoholic "beer" for eventual distillation into spirituous liquors. The American beverage distilling industry that evolved in the nineteenth and twentieth centuries was distinctive for its use of corn (maize) to produce bourbon whiskey (Carson 1963).

Europeans who migrated to North America in the early seventeenth century brought familiarity with distilling and made the industry one of the most important in the thirteen British colonies that became the United States. The colonists imported sugar and molasses (a by-product of the manufacture of sugar from cane) and used the molasses as the raw material for the distillation of rum. Rum was widely consumed in the North American colonies and exported abroad. American merchants began to import West Indian molasses in the 1640s and erected distilleries to produce rum. The distilling industry thrived in the port towns of colonial America. A majority of the distilleries were in New England, operated by merchants as an adjunct to other businesses. Between 1768 and 1772 Americans consumed 8 million gallons of rum annually, 5 million of which were produced in 143 distilleries.

The distilling industry changed in the early nineteenth century as new technologies were introduced and the American population moved westward. Continuous process stills that allowed for a more efficient production of alcohol were invented in Europe. Americans, especially those located on the trans-Appalachian frontier, began to use rye and corn (maize) as the raw material for whiskey. The capital requirements for erecting a still were small, and the cost of transporting grain to distant markets was prohibitive. Farmers chose to convert their grain to less bulky, higher value alcohol, or whiskey, and the distilling industry proliferated. The market for distilled spirits was large: in 1825 the annual per capita consumption by adults was over nine gallons (Rorabaugh 1979; Whitten 1975).

After 1825 the grain trade flourished, transportation costs fell with the opening of the midwestern canal systems, and the distilling industry began to concentrate in Pittsburgh, Cincinnati, and southwestern Pennsylvania. The per capita consumption of whiskey began to shrink as Americans began to drink less, influenced perhaps by the mushrooming temperance movement. Nevertheless, the growing population maintained the distillers' market for processed agricultural products. The industry was organized into small firms that completed one step of the manufacturing or distribution process and sold the product to another firm. A distiller produced alcohol and sold it to a rectifier, who further purified and flavored it. Rectifiers sold their products to wholesalers who in turn distributed spirits to retail outlets, commonly called saloons before 1920. The most popular distilled spirits sold in the United States before 1920 were blended whiskeys, beverages in which rectifiers and wholesalers mixed aged whiskey with alcohol and coloring and flavoring agents. Unblended, or "straight," whiskeys were also sold, however, especially by small firms manufacturing bourbon in Kentucky and Tennessee.

Taxation policies of the federal government have had a profound impact on the trade in distilled spirits. During the Civil War the government increased the tax on distilled spirits on several occasions but did not impose the tax retroactively on liquors already in inventory. That policy encouraged an expansion in distilling as speculators rushed to invest in plants to produce and store liquor at what they expected to became an advantageous tax rate. After the Civil War the industry was beset with overcapacity and internecine competition.

The distilling industry in the post–Civil War period centered in Peoria, Illinois. There distillers enjoyed nearby supplies of grain and coal, plentiful water and good rail connections. One by-product of distilling was cattle feed (the discarded cooked grain mash), and Chicago provided the nation's largest single cattle market. Peoria-based firms led attempts to control competition. Foremost among these was the Distillers' and Cattle Feeders' Trust, which by 1889 held the stock of eighty-six firms. The trust was incorporated in 1890. In 1894 the Illinois Supreme Court declared the trust an illegal combination in restraint of trade and ordered it dissolved.

Efforts to concentrate control in the distilling industry were concluded in 1902 by the formation of the Distillers Securities Corporation. A holding company, it owned the stock of a variety of older firms and combined distilling, rectifying, distribution, and marketing in one vertically integrated business corporation that dominated the industry. The Distillers Securities Corporation had the advantage of efficiencies in production and distribution, and in brand identification among drinkers. Distillers, however, faced a shrinking share of the beverage alcohol market in the United States. Following its introduction in the 1840s, lager beer gradually replaced whiskey and other distilled spirits in Americans' liquor preferences. By 1890 Americans consumed more beer than any other beverage alcohol (Kerr 1985).

Prohibition was a reform movement that nearly destroyed the American distilling industry. Prohibitionists were convinced that distillers were part of an evil liquor trust that was encouraging more Americans to drink, and to drink more, of the dangerous drug alcohol. Rooted in the evangelical Protestant churches and an ethos that demanded sacrifices for the larger social good, the Prohibition movement waxed and waned after 1850; after 1900 it burgeoned. Prohibition reformers believed that if the manufacture, sale, and transportation of alcoholic beverages were made illegal, Americans would have less incentive to drink liquor and reformers would enjoy a superior opportunity to persuade their fellow men and women to lead abstemious lives. During national Prohibition (1920–33), consumption of beverage alcohol dropped substantially (Kerr 1985).

The distilling industry as it was organized before Prohibition nearly disappeared in the 1920s. To shift its resources to the yeast, vinegar, and cereal businesses, the Distillers Securities Corporation became the U.S. Food Products Corporation. Bankrupted in the depression of 1921, the firm reorganized as the National Distillers Products Corporation and began to earn modest profits. National Distillers reentered the distilled spirits business upon the repeal of Prohibition on December 5, 1933, but did not again dominate the industry.

After the repeal of Prohibition, the structure of the distilling industry changed. From the 1930s until the merger waves of the 1960s, the industry was dominated by an oligopoly of four firms: the National Distillers Products Corporation, Schenley Distillers Corporation, Distillers Corporation (Seagram), and Hiram Walker-Gooderham & Worts, Ltd. Both Seagram and Walker were Canadian-based firms that had prospered from the illicit liquor trade in the United States. Of the two, Seagram was the larger. After 1937 Seagram assumed leadership in the American distilling industry (Newman 1978; Denzin 1977; Haller 1985). The Brown-Forman Distilling Company of Louisville, Kentucky, was also prominent and, by the 1980s, had become the second largest firm in the industry.

With the repeal of Prohibition, the distilling industry was reestablished with the assistance of the federal government. Rejecting proposals for more stringent control through public ownership of liquor distribution facilities, the administration of Franklin D. Roosevelt turned to the provisions of the National Industrial Recovery Act (NIRA) to regulate the liquor industries. Under that 1933 law, each branch of the industry, save retailing, had a so-called code of fair competition. The Federal Alcohol Control Administration, which had been created by executive order on December 4, 1933, administered those codes (Laforge 1987).

The code for the distilling industry, signed by President Roosevelt on November 26, 1933, was part of the larger New Deal effort to help business recover from the Great Depression. The distillers' code restricted entry and abetted the formation of the oligopoly that came to dominate the industry after repeal. Leading figures in the industry organized a governing body—the Code Authority—that controlled plant capacity and production by granting or revoking permits. New Deal policy for distilling and other businesses included so-called open prices, a euphemism for price-fixing (O'Neil 1940). The government-industry partnership that the policy represented prevented the deception of consumers, the shipment of liquor in violation of state laws (some states retained prohibition measures), and unfair trade practices, such as the bribing of retailers. The supply of liquor was to be coordinated with the demand to stabilize prices and insure profits for the industry. There were no plans to regulate the advertising of liquor or the labeling of ingredients.

The Supreme Court's decision that the NIRA was unconstitutional brought no important changes in the federal partnership with the distilling industry. Cooperating with the distilling industry, Congress enacted the Federal Alcohol Administration Act on August 24, 1935. The new law adopted some of the policies of the Federal Alcohol Control Administration, including its exact language in advertising and labeling regulations, but it eliminated provisions for maintaining prices and limiting production. Because the distilling industry had stabilized so quickly after repeal, policy makers believed that regulating prices and production was no longer necessary. The Federal Alcohol Administration, an agency in the Treasury Department, was to administer the law.

Raising revenue by taxing distilled spirits had long been a policy of the federal government, and the Treasury Department helped shape the distilling industry. In 1934 the Alcohol Tax Unit was organized within the Bureau of Internal Revenue; the unit's staff of 1,400 agents also enforced the National Firearms Act of 1934. In 1940 Congress disbanded the Federal Alcohol Administration and assigned its duties to the Alcohol Tax Unit. In 1972 the Bureau of Alcohol, Tobacco, and Firearms in the Treasury Department replaced the Alcohol Tax Unit of the Bureau of Internal Revenue. The distilling industry and the tax agencies cooperate to guarantee stability for the distillers and substantial revenues for the government (Laforge 1987).

The policies of the federal government combined with the regulatory policies of state governments to shape the distribution of distilled spirits as well as ownership within the industry. Following repeal of Prohibition, some states retained a monopoly on the retail sales of packaged liquor. State governments usually prevented vertical integration from the manufacturing to the retail level, fearing that it might create incentives for large sales of dangerous spirits. Laws ordinarily required a three-tiered distribution system: the distiller sold to independent wholesalers who in turn supplied retailers—either private dealers or state agencies. Some states enacted so-called fair trade laws that prevented price competition in distilled spirits. Although those laws ostensibly controlled and even discouraged drinking, the distilling industry supported them, for they also safeguarded investments and ensured profitability.

The mobilization of the American economy during World War II had a long-term impact on the distilling industry. Industrial alcohol was used to produce synthetic rubber and smokeless powder, two goods vital to victory. In 1942, cooperating with mobilization officials, the beverage distillers converted their plants to the manufacture of industrial alcohol, and supplied the market for beverage alcohol from inventories. Shortages required some state liquor control agencies to ration the sale of spirits. The market for alcoholic beverages expanded during the prosperous war years to the advantage of the rival brewing industry, whose facilities were not suitable for the production of industrial alcohol. Many brewers were able to continue and even expand production (Rubin 1979). Moreover, continuing shortages of food grains immediately after the war prevented the distilling industry from resuming normal peacetime operations until 1948.

The postwar economy brought prosperity to the American distilling industry. With the general rise in the nation's standard of living, Americans spent a progressively smaller percentage of their disposable incomes on distilled spirits and other liquors, and their expenditures were increasingly for higher priced—more profitable to produce—brands. On average, individual consumption by adults increased from 1.8 gallons of spirits in 1948 to over 3 gallons in the first half of the 1970s. The demand for spirits declined thereafter, but remained larger than it had been in the 1940s and 1950s. In 1968, 129.3 million cases were sold. Sales rose to a peak of 166 million cases in 1979 and then fell to 156.4 million cases by 1984.

The organization of the distilling industry changed in the decades after World War II. Although distilling remained an oligopoly, mergers, investments in other industries, and foreign investments in American firms, along with changing consumer preferences, reshaped the industry (Cavanaugh and Claironte 1985). The National Distillers Products Corporation invested in the chemical industry in 1949, merged with U.S. Industrial Chemicals, Inc., and changed its name to National Distillers & Chemical Corporation in 1957. In 1987 the firm sold the last of its beverage alcohol operations. Seagram consolidated its position as the largest distilling firm by acquiring distilleries and wineries in the United States and abroad. In 1964 Seagram began to invest in American oil and gas properties, but sold its holdings in 1980. In 1981 Seagram acquired over 20 percent of the shares in E. I. du Pont de Nemours and Co. Rapid American absorbed Schenley Industries, which from 1934 to 1937 had been the nation's largest distilling firm. The conglomerate sold Schenley's Canadian subsidiary in 1981 and, in 1987, attempted to sell the remaining portion of Schenley. Hiram Walker-Gooderham & Worts slipped in the American market, and by 1986 was owned by the Canadian conglomerate, Olympia & York Developments Ltd. Brown-Forman maintained large investments in the distilling industry, becoming the second largest distilling firm conducting business in the United States, but also diversified into other businesses. Meanwhile, the British influence in the American distilling industry became more important. In 1983 the Distillers Company Ltd. began to purchase American firms.

The changing structure of the international distilling industry and developments in the distribution of spirits have influenced the business in America. After 1975 two contradictory governmental impulses held potential for change in the distilling industry. Responding to the gradual rise in per capita consumption of beverage alcohol that followed the repeal of Prohibition, public health officials encouraged Americans to moderate if not cease their consumption of alcoholic beverages and urged governmental authorities to regulate closely the packaging, labeling, and sales of liquor and to warn consumers of the dangers associated with drinking (Laforge 1987). Second, deregulation, abetted by the retail sale of alcoholic beverages by large chain stores and grocers, brought an end to the fair trade laws that had meant profitable price stability for distillers. Moreover, as the market for spirits began to decline some distillers began discounting, insofar as local laws allowed, in an attempt to sell larger volumes.

BIBLIOGRAPHY

Carson, Gerald. *The Social History of Bourbon.* New York: Dodd, Mead, 1963.

Cavanaugh, John, and Frederick F. Claironte. *Alcoholic Beverages: Dimensions of Corporate Power.* London and Sydney: Croom Helm, 1985.

Crowgey, Henry G. *Kentucky Bourbon: The Early Years of Whiskeymaking.* Lexington: University Press of Kentucky, 1971.

Denzin, Norman K. "Notes on the Criminogenic Hypothesis: A Case Study of the American Liquor Industry." *American Sociological Review* 42 (December 1977): 905–20.

Downard, William L. *Dictionary History of the American Brewing and Distilling Industries.* Westport, CT: Greenwood Press, 1980.

Getz, Oscar. *Whiskey: An American Pictorial History.* New York: David McKay, 1978.

Haller, Mark H. "Bootleggers as Businessmen: From City Slums to City Builders." In *Law, Alcohol, and Order: Perspectives on National Prohibition,* edited by David E. Kyvig, 159–76. Westport, CT: Greenwood Press, 1985.

Kerr, K. Austin. *Organized for Prohibition: A New History of the Anti-Saloon League.* New Haven: Yale University Press, 1985.

Laforge, Robert G. "Misplaced Priorities: A History of Federal Alcohol Regulation and Public Health Policy." Ph.D. diss., Johns Hopkins University, 1987.

Mittelman, Amy. "The Politics of Alcohol Production: The Liquor Industry and the Federal Government, 1862–1900." Ph.D. diss., Columbia University, 1986.

Newman, Peter C. *Bronfman Dynasty: The Rothschilds of the New World.* Toronto: McClelland & Stewart, 1978.

O'Neil, John E. "Federal Activity in Alcoholic Beverage Control." *Law and Contemporary Problems* 7 (Autumn 1940): 57.

Rorabaugh, W. J. *The Alcoholic Republic: An American Tradition.* New York: Oxford University Press, 1979.

Rubin, Jay L. "The Wet War: American Liquor Control, 1941–1945." In *Alcohol, Reform and Society: The Liquor Issue in Social Context,* edited by Jack S. Blocker, Jr., 235–58. Westport, CT: Greenwood Press, 1979.

Whitten, David O. "An Economic Inquiry into the Whiskey Rebellion of 1794." *Agricultural History* 49 (1975): 491–504.

Part II

Tobacco
ESIC 21.0

Chapter 4

TOBACCO MANUFACTURING, 21.0

Carol J. Miller

The Tobacco Institute estimates that in 1983 "tobacco core sectors and supplier industries accounted for $31.5 billion of GNP...and employed 710,000 workers to produce and deliver tobacco products and their associated goods and services" (Warner 1987, 2030). In addition, $13.5 billion in tax revenues were generated on local, state, and federal levels. The "Big Six" of the tobacco industry are Philip Morris, R. J. Reynolds, P. Lorillard, Liggett Group, Brown and Williamson, and American Brands.

Despite attacks from health and antismoking groups, the $35 billion tobacco industry is profitable. To maintain profits, tobacco companies combine advertising and government subsidies with strategic corporate adaptation, promotions to the Third World countries, and diversification. Although domestic per capita consumption of cigarettes has declined 10–12 percent since 1982, Asian consumption has increased at the annual rate of 2 percent, creating a $15 billion per year export market. Although Philip Morris has diversified into food lines by purchasing General Foods, it sells $14.5 billion in cigarettes a year and owes 72–80 percent of its $3 billion profit to its tobacco base (80 percent, NBC Nightly News, June 13, 1988; 72 percent, Flanigan 1987).

The economics of the tobacco industry extends beyond profits to an estimated $65–$81 billion in health hazards, medical expenses, reduced productivity, and property damages from firsthand and secondhand smoke. Costs include 350,000 smoking-related deaths per year (U.S. Congress, Hearings on H.R. 4972, 1986). As lawsuits against the tobacco industry increase, litigation costs must also be factored into the economic picture.

EARLY HISTORY

By the time of the Spanish conquest of South America in the 1500s, the use of tobacco was ingrained in local Indian culture and dated back to the classic Mayan period, A.D. 600–900. Ancient carvings in Chiapas, Mexico, illustrate a priest blowing smoke through a tube. It is believed that the Chiapanec cultivated *Nicotiana tabacum*, the tobacco in commercial use today. In 1492 Christopher Columbus noted the practice of natives who "drank smoke" in the Caribbean islands. Tobacco trade between Indian tribes was well established before Europeans discovered America; ornamental reed cigarettes were observed during Cortez's explorations of Mexico in 1519. By the mid–1500s the use of American tobacco had been assimilated into European culture (Wagner 1971). There is also historical evidence of a long-term practice of smoking various herbs and plants other than tobacco. In the eleventh century Arabian physicians prescribed smoking medicinal plants for asthma. Hippocrates, Pliny, and Galen recommended inhaling the smoke from burning substances like coltsfoot as treatment for asthma. Smoking devices were adaptations of Greek water pipes. The practice of smoking opium and hemp (marijuana) in the Far East has ancient origins, older than the practice of smoking tobacco. From relief of pain and anxiety to inducement of hallucination or pleasure, the practice of smoking various substances has a long-standing worldwide history (Wagner 1971).

Modern warnings about the health hazards of using tobacco contrast sharply with bygone medical myths that no doubt encouraged the early growth of the tobacco industry. Influenced in part by the American Indians' use of tobacco for medicinal and religious purposes, European physicians of the sixteenth and seventeenth centuries regarded tobacco as a remedy for countless ailments. Tobacco was initially sold in European apothecaries. From cancer to respiratory ailments to stomach cramps to female disorders, tobacco was prescribed for inhalation, chewing, and external application in combination with other herbs. Folklore and the accepted use of tobacco intertwined with the humorous theory of medicine, and tobacco continued to have a cultural impact in backwoods areas of America into the early twentieth century (Kell [1965] 1986).

Not all images of tobacco in the 1500s and 1600s were favorable, however. Religious condemnation of its use was strong. Spanish Inquisitions imprisoned practitioners of the "ungodly habit" of smoking. In Orthodox Russia under Tsar Michael's 1641 decree, exile was a punishment for tobacco trafficking. Snuffers could be tortured, their noses slit for partaking in the "abomination to God." A Chinese decree in 1638 forbade the tobacco trade under threat of decapitation, yet orientals freely smoked other substances.

At the time of the English colonization of Virginia, on the eve of the era in which the economic structure of this seventeenth-century colony would be built on the tobacco industry, King James I of England had grave reservations about encouraging tobacco cultivation in the New World, describing the use of tobacco as "a custom loathsome to the eye, hateful to the nose, harmful to the brain, dangerous to the lungs, and in the black stinking fume thereof, nearest resembling the horrible Stygian smoke of the pit [Hades] that is bottomless" (King James I 1604). Dr. Benjamin Rush, a signer of the Declaration of Independence, expressed similar reservations in a 1798 essay entitled "Observations upon the Influence of the Habitual Use of Tobacco upon Health, Morals, and Property."

Despite warnings and Christian condemnations, the social acceptability and economic marketability of tobacco grew in the sixteenth and seventeenth centuries. During the reign of Queen Elizabeth, Sir Francis Drake and Sir Walter Raleigh promoted smoking as an upper-class indulgence. Initially an expensive habit, tobacco sold for its weight in silver shillings in 1600, fostering its use at dances, hunts, and card games of the elite (Wagner 1971).

In 1531 the Spanish were growing tobacco in the West Indies. By 1580 commercial planting was promoted in Cuba and Venezuela. In the mid–1500s varieties of the plant were grown in Europe (Wagner 1971). The Netherlands became the foremost European cultivator of Oronoco tobacco, which later competed for British-American markets.

COLONIAL NORTH AMERICAN HISTORY

Tobacco was destined to become a cornerstone of mercantilism in colonial America. England needed an outlet for surplus population, sources of raw materials, and markets for its products. The American colonies accommodated.

Sugar and tobacco were the staple cash crops underwriting settlement in the British West Indies and the middle and southern British colonies by the mid–1600s. Virginia was founded by profit-seeking investors who formed successive joint stock companies from 1607 until Virginia became a royal colony in 1624. Tobacco production was profitable by the 1620s. Introduced at Jamestown by John Rolfe, N. tabacum (grown in the Caribbean) was planted on fertile lands along the James River and quickly became a source of profit and tax revenue.

Virginia, Maryland (which grew a subspecies of stronger flavor), and later North Carolina led British tobacco production. By 1627 the British were importing .5 million pounds of tobacco from Virginia, a figure that rose to 16 million pounds by the 1660s and 21 million pounds by 1682. Tobacco prices fluctuated widely. Prices peaked between 1648 and 1654 and began falling after Navigation Act restrictions in 1663 accounted for a drop from 48 to 10 shillings per pound. There were further declines from 1686 to 1696 and 1703 to 1716. Market saturation, competition from German and Dutch tobacco growers, and depletion of the soil were problems; crop rotation was not fully understood in the 1600s (Main 1982). By 1772 the price had fallen to three-fourths pence per pound (Wagner 1971).

Tobacco was marketed in the seventeenth century by consignment. There were long delays in return on investment and costly outlays for freight and duties. By the 1700s marketing through British agents was common. Planters exchanged tobacco for manufactured goods at local stores maintained by agents. Marketing costs fell as towns became central freight locations, and 400–pound capacity hogsheds replaced those that held 250 pounds. In the mid–1700s many of the well-established planters of the Virginia aristocracy (such as George Washington and Thomas Jefferson) were nonetheless frequently in debt (Wagner 1971).

Many immigrants to America came as indentured servants or slaves. Over one-third of the seventeenth-century immigrants bought their passage with returns on tobacco (Main 1982). Two-thirds to three-fourths of the early immigrants to Virginia came as indentured servants.

Tobacco planters shifted from white indentured servants to slaves in the final two decades of the 1600s. By 1690 slaves outnumbered indents for the first time in the tobacco colonies. In Maryland there were 1.75 servants and 0.25 slaves per estate in 1670 and 0.25 servants and two slaves per estate by 1710. Prior to 1684, less than half of the men with estates valued in excess of 150 pounds owned any slaves; by 1712 almost all men of that wealth owned slaves. Wealthy Virginians raising sweet-scented tobacco acquired slaves more readily than their less wealthy counterparts in Maryland, who raised primarily Oronoco tobacco. Owners of smaller estates relied on family members for labor (Main 1982).

Slaves cost two to two-and-a-half times the price of an indentured servant in the mid–1600s. From 1620 to the 1640s the average life expectancy for black imported slaves was seven years, with ten years necessary to recoup investment. As the life expectancy of blacks rose above ten years after the 1670s, a twenty-pound investment in a slave became attractive, especially since the slaves were less prone to rebellion than the lower-class whites (Main 1982).

A single worker could produce an average of 1,500 pounds of tobacco per year, an amount that fluctuated between 400 and 2,000 pounds. Tobacco was started in seed beds and transplanted to rich, moist soil in May (in Virginia) or June (in Maryland). Placed about four feet apart in tilled soil, plants would grow a foot high within a month. At that height they were topped—the leading stem pinched off—and primed—the lower leaves removed. Fully ripe leaves were cut and cured. Curing in the air was preferable to drying or curing by the smoke and heat of a fire, which left a residual taste in the leaves. An optimum level of drying prevented rotting (if too wet) or crumbling (if too dry). Once dried, the leaves were ready for "striking" and bundling into "hands" for packing into hogsheds for transportation to market. For some sweet Virginia varieties, stems were removed prior to the packing process. Maryland legislation set dates by which coopers were to have hogsheds completed for use (half by October 10, half by December 10) and established standards for production and shipping (Main 1982).

1800s TO WORLD WAR I

Tobacco continued to be the dominant American export crop until it was surpassed by cotton in 1803. There were 119 tobacco factories in Virginia and North Carolina in 1840 and 348 in 1860. On the eve of the Civil War, Richmond's more than 50 factories represented a $5 million enterprise that employed over 3,400 workers (Wagner 1971).

By 1830 Kentucky, Tennessee, Ohio, and Missouri accounted for one-third of the U.S. tobacco crop, a proportion that increased to one-half by the Civil War (Wagner 1971). Although North Carolina maintained a position of importance, the end of slavery shifted production away from Maryland and Virginia to Kentucky, Tennessee, and southern Ohio. Through land conservation, yields per acre were improved; North Carolina led with a 29 percent yield increase from 1880 to 1905 (Whitten 1983).

The plug market grew in the mid–1800s. Richmonder Robert A. Mayo marketed "Navy Tobacco," named for his monopoly of plug for the U.S. Navy. James Thomas, Jr., dominated the California plug market. Hoarding tobacco at the outbreak of the American Civil War proved profitable for Thomas, who had sufficient resources to outfit a Confederate artillery unit. By the Civil War, New York's plug factories were second only to those of Virginia (Wagner 1971). By 1880 Winston, North Carolina, firms dominated the plug industry (Whitten 1983).

New product lines emerged in the 1800s. Although the pipe was favored for smoking tobacco in the 1700s, cigars were imported from Cuba in 1810. The Caribbean dominated the cigar industry initially, but the U.S. cigar leaf production developed in Ohio and New England. By the end of the century cigarettes occupied a new and growing niche after overcoming an effeminate image and moralistic campaigns against the evils of smoking.

Cigarette smoking gained acceptance in the United States during the late nineteenth century. A poor man's by-product of Seville's cigar industry, cigarettes migrated from Portugal and Italy to Russia and Japan and eventually to France. The name cigarette was applied to this new portion of the French tobacco monopoly in 1843. After the Crimean War of 1854–56, British officers initiated them into British society. Despite Americans' early reluctance to accept an alternative to the masculine cigar, cigarettes manufactured by British merchants Philip Morris and Robert Gloag made inroads into the U.S. tobacco market. Few cigarettes were available in the United States before the Civil War, but expensive Turkish leaf cigarettes with "Russian tips" were introduced after the war. American Bright tobacco was used in some domestic cigarettes by 1870 (Wagner 1971).

Americans' adoption of the cigarette led to the proliferation of tobacco firms, and eventually the five leading producers of 1890 combined as the American Tobacco Company. Three Richmond tobacco firms manufactured cigarettes, and the Peerless Tobacco Works of Rochester, New York, dominated one-sixth of the 1885 market with brands such as Vanity Fair, Fragrant Vanity Fair, Cloth of Gold, Three Kings, Old Gold, and Orientals. The Baltimore firms of Marburg and Felgner sold Estrella, High Life, Melrose, and Golden Age. Other brand names included The People's Choice, Daniel Webster, and Cherry Ripe. Allen & Ginter, established in Richmond in 1875, marketed Bon Ton, Napoleons, Dubec, The Pet, and Opera Puffs. By 1888 the Durham, North Carolina, firm of James Buchanan (Buck) Duke was producing 744 million cigarettes per year (Wagner 1971).

WORLD WAR I TO 1950

The cigarette was the dominant tobacco industry product by 1930. In 1910 only 5 percent of U.S. tobacco leaves had been used for cigarettes, most of the leaves being purchased by Duke's American Tobacco trust. Between 1910 and 1930, however, the production of cigarettes rose 1300 percent. By 1929 cigarettes made up 53.6 percent of the value of tobacco products, up from 16.6 percent in 1914.

The court-ordered breakup of the American Tobacco Company in 1911 changed the industry from a monopoly to a oligopoly. From World War I to the 1930s, three domestic and two foreign tobacco companies controlled the industry and used their market power to hold leaf prices down. Foremost in American cigarettes were three of the companies created by the 1911 antitrust suit: R. J. Reynolds (Camels), American Tobacco Company (Lucky Strikes), and Liggett & Myers (Chesterfields). In the early 1930s these controlled 90 percent of the domestic market. Although it developed a 7 percent market share with Old Gold cigarettes in the 1920s, Lorillard, the fourth company created by the suit, did not fare as well as the others (Badger 1980).

British-American Tobacco Company (BAT), formed by American Tobacco and British Imperial Tobacco, dominated the world market. In the early 1930s, when 60 percent of North Carolina's tobacco crop was still being exported, Export Leaf Co. (a subsidiary of BAT) and Imperial Tobacco were the primary purchasers. Half of the exports went to the United Kingdom and one-fourth to China. In 1927 BAT purchased a Winston-Salem snuff firm, Brown & Williamson. By 1933 Brown & Williamson and Axton-Fisher had captured 20 percent of the market and forced the Big Three to cut cigarette prices (Badger 1980). (Sherman Cochran's book [1980] on

British-American Tobacco Company considers the role in China of a British-headquartered enterprise that was initially American-controlled).

In 1929 half of the U.S. acres in tobacco were devoted to Bright. North Carolina produced 70 percent of the U.S. flue-cured Bright tobacco crop in the 1930s. At the time of the Great Depression, four-tenths of the North Carolina workers still farmed, primarily growing tobacco or cotton. One-tenth of the North Carolina labor force was employed in tobacco plants in Reidsville (American Tobacco), Durham (American Tobacco and Liggett & Myers), and Winston-Salem (R. J. Reynolds). These plants were responsible for one-third of the state's manufacturing and 57 percent of the nation's cigarette production (Badger 1980).

Despite the economic impact the tobacco industry had in the Carolinas, Georgia, Kentucky, and Tennessee tobacco growers had little bargaining power, and leaf prices remained low. There were numerous unsuccessful attempts to establish grower cooperatives in the late 1920s and early 1930s, some with state or federal encouragement. Voluntary acreage reduction was equally unsuccessful, because individual tobacco growers were heavily in debt and had to produce as much as possible. Merchants often charged 25 percent interest to tobacco growers who purchased items on credit; fertilizer manufacturers' interest rates were frequently higher. The price for flue-cured tobacco, 20 cents per pound or higher in 1920–27, fell to 8.4 cents by 1931.

Similarly, a sharecropper's annual income of $593 in 1928 fell to $134–350 after farm expenses in 1932. Over 150,000 pieces of farm property were sold for delinquent property taxes, as ninety-three banks collapsed in North Carolina in 1930. Meanwhile, manufacturing profits rose from $115 million in 1927 to $145 million in 1930. Without bargaining power, growers were unable to share the tobacco manufacturers' increased profits (Badger 1980).

Until Congress established the federal Agricultural Adjustment Administration, acreage controls, and price supports, growers were without relief. New Deal legislation in 1933 allowed the Secretary of Agriculture to contract with basic commodities producers for reduced acreage in exchange for rent and benefits payment under a "Voluntary Domestic Allotment Plan." A processing tax on the commodity was to fund the program. Uncooperative growers were taxed under the Kerr-Smith Act, as were those producing in excess of the Secretary's established quotas. Tobacco was not one of the primary commodities for which the legislation was initially constructed; nevertheless, growers benefitted because they received a special, favorable base period for the establishment of parity prices. Acreage and poundage allotments were controlled in 1934–35. A poundage-only policy in 1938 was replaced with an acreage allotment program in 1939. Poundage quotas were reinstated in 1965, but acreage controls on tobacco crops have been used since 1940 (Badger 1980).

Financial support for the government's tobacco program centers around the Commodity Credit Corporation (CCC) and the Cooperative Stabilization Corporation (CSC). The CCC absorbs market fluctuations and has met its obligations every year except 1955–56. The CSC purchases and resells tobacco that does not reach support prices (Badger 1980).

New Deal regulatory oversight opened a new era for the tobacco industry: collective capitalism. "A virtual closed shop and guaranteed income were acceptable for the growing of tobacco, but they were not to be tolerated for industrial labor" (Badger 1980, 218). This difference in policy sprang from the dire need for price stability and price support for the powerless, unorganized tobacco growers. Without government support tobacco agricultural cooperatives never approached the success of industrial labor unions. Despite constitutional objections to compulsory quotas in the 1930s, the allotment and price support system for tobacco survived into the 1980s.

Government tobacco production quotas brought price increases for the growers. From 1934 to 1939 price increased threefold over the 1932 low. The tobacco growers achieved 97 percent parity with the 1920–29 prices; other farmers achieved 70 percent. During and after World War II prices for flue-cured tobacco rose steadily. Although higher prices hurt the export market, tobacco growers' incomes increased. Tenant farmers and small farmers, however, benefitted little (Badger 1980).

Tobacco growing and harvesting remained labor intensive until the 1970s, when a successful mechanized tobacco harvester reduced harvest labor by 85 percent. The warehouse auctioning system survived the government allotment controls. Although the 1935 Flanagan Act allowed for government grading if two-thirds of the growers desired it, grading by warehousemen is still common. The 1974 Growers Designation Plan coordinated the schedules of growers, graders, buyers, and warehousemen by crop maturity dates, so markets could open at optimum times (Badger 1980).

COMPONENTS OF THE TOBACCO INDUSTRY

Cigarettes

The cigarette industry boom in America can be traced to Duke's adoption of James Bonsack's cigarette rolling machine. Bonsack's machine could produce 120,000 cigarettes a day, about the output of sixty hand rollers. To sell his vast output, Duke used aggressive marketing practices: placing picture cards of famous actresses and sports figures in cigarette packages, sponsoring a national polo team tour, and cutting prices. In his drive to dominate the industry Duke spent $800,000 for advertising and promotion in 1880 (Wagner 1971).

Taxes on cigarettes influenced the growth of the cigarette industry. To help finance the Civil War, the Union levied a 0.1 cent per unit tax on cigarettes in 1864 and increased it to 0.5 cents in 1867. After an 1868 reduction to 0.15 cents, the tax was raised to 0.175 in 1874. The 1883 tax reduction from $1.75 to 50 cents per thousand cigarettes paved the way for mass production and price-cutting by the Duke family (Whitten 1983).

In 1890 the five leading tobacco firms combined into the American Tobacco Company, which controlled 90 percent of the U.S. market. This near monopoly corporation was the subject of an antitrust suit brought under the Sherman act. The courts divided the company in 1911 and created four of the firms that would dominate the cigarette industry in the second half of the century: American, Reynolds, Liggett & Myers, and Lorillard (Wagner 1971).

The U.S. cigarette industry of the 1980s is dominated by six companies. According to 1986 statistics, Philip Morris leads the industry with 36.8 percent (37.9 percent in 1987) of the market, followed by R. J. Reynolds with 32.4 (32.7 percent in 1987). Brown & Williamson maintained 11.9 percent of the cigarette market; Lorillard, 8.1 percent (8.2 percent in 1987); American Brands, 7.2 percent; and Liggett Group, 4 percent ("Cigarette Sales," Spring 1988, p. 3). Four of the five largest tobacco companies rank first and second among newspaper and magazine advertisers (U.S. Congress, Hearings on H.R. 4972, 1986).

Major brands marketed by the Big Six increased from eighteen in 1950 to forty-seven in 1962 to 100 by 1975 (Miles and Cameron 1982, 93, 103). Leading brands included Philip Morris's Marlboro; RJR's Winston, Salem, Camel, More, and Vantage; Loews' Kent and Newport; Liggett's Chesterfield and L&Ms; and American Brands' Pall Mall and Carlton. Dominant brands in 1987 were Marlboro (introduced in 1955), with 23.8 percent of the American cigarette market, and Winston (originated in 1954), with 11.3 percent ("Marlboro Increases Market Share" 1987; "Cigarette Sales," Spring 1988, p. 3).

The top five tobacco-growing states produced 1,057.5 million pounds in 1987. North Carolina (headquarters for R. J. Reynolds) led production with 468 million pounds, followed by Kentucky, with 326 million pounds; South Carolina, 94 million; Tennessee, 93.5 million; and Virginia, 76 million. Yet one-third of the tobacco used in American cigarettes is imported, under the regulation of the Department of Agriculture (U.S. Congress, Hearing, FTC Nicotine Program, 1987, p. 22).

U.S. domestic consumption of cigarettes peaked in 1981, but has declined at the rate of 2 percent per year since. Although total domestic consumption had exceeded 600 billion units by the mid–1970s, only 584 billion cigarettes were purchased in 1986 and 568 billion units in 1987, a 2.5 percent decline ("No Smoke," September 15, 1987, p. 12A; "Cigarette Sales," Spring 1988, p. 3).

The per capita consumption of cigarettes responds to publicity about the dangers of smoking. It fell to just over 3,500 in 1954 after the Sloan-Kettering Report established a serious link between smoking and health hazards. Ten years later, 1964, when the Surgeon General's report was released, per capita consumption was at an all time high of 4,300. The 1970 mass media cigarette advertising ban precipitated a decline to about 4,000. A 17 percent decline in per capita consumption was recorded over the years 1975–84 (Rogers et al. 1985). Although per capita consumption decreased, total domestic consumption increased until 1981, as population growth aided total sales. Since 1981 consumption has fallen 10–12 percent (Miles and Cameron 1982). Surveys reveal that New Hampshire, which has low tobacco taxes, leads the nation in sales—a 1986 average of 196 packs per adult. Hawaii sold 61 packs of cigarettes per adult for the national low.

Three times as many men as women smoked in the 1930s (Warner 1987). Smoking peaked in 1965 at 52.4 percent of the adult males and 34.1 percent of adult females. Percentages fell to 38.3 percent and 29.4 percent by 1980, and 29.5 percent and 23.8 percent by 1987. On the basis of these estimates, there were 47 million adult smokers in the United States in 1987 (Bailey 1987). Among teenagers, female smokers (20 percent) outnumber male smokers (16 percent) (U.S. Congress, Hearings on H.R. 4972, 1986).

In the 1980s marketing tactics targeted the upscale "Yumpie/Yuppie" market. Philip Morris marketed silver and gold decorated boxes for its Benson & Hedges De Luxe Ultra Lights and introduced Players brand in a black pinstriped box. Players boasted a "twist-type variable tar filter" adjustable to suit the smoker's taste preference. R. J. Reynolds introduced a "designer cigarette" named Ritz that carries the YSL logo of French designer Yves Saint Laurent. Aimed at the "fashion-conscious female smoker" between twenty and forty years of age, it is a 100mm "low-tar" cigarette with regular and menthol alternatives. Brown & Williamson's new brands, St. James Court and Eli Cutter, have targeted the Yumpie/Yuppie and male macho markets ("Epidemic of New Cigarette Brands," April 1985, p. 5; " 'Volvo Drivers' and 'Upscale Buyers' Targeted," January 1984, p. 4).

On the other end of the marketing scale, generic brands have been created as an alternative to name brands, and the ethnic markets have been targeted. Five of the Big Six are experimenting with twenty-five cigarettes per pack. R. J. Reynolds, for example, has introduced Century brand for the cost-conscious smoker. Century offers twenty-five cigarettes for about the same price as a regular pack of twenty. The generic market supplier is Brown & Williamson, which became the supplier for Generic Products Company in 1985. Hispanics are the target for the Liggett Group's Dorado and L&M Superior brands, and Philip Morris's "full-flavor" menthol Rio.

Cigars

After 1810, Cuban cigars became macho symbols for smokers. Social acceptability was enhanced by President John Quincy Adams, who smoked the imported Havanas. He later abandoned the habit for health reasons

(Wagner 1971). The popularity of the masculine image associated with cigars retarded the cigarette market at the turn of the century. More recently, however, cigar sales have shown a two-decade-long decline. Sales of 3.4 million, plus 1.2 million "little cigars," brought $705 million in 1984. In that year large and small cigar sales declined by 2.4 percent, while cigarillos—little cigars—declined 7.5 percent ("Cigar Sales Drop in 1984," October 1985, p. 7). Stock analyst John C. Maxwell of the Wall Street firm of Furman Sel Mager Diet & Birney reported an overall drop of 9 percent in 1986. Specifically, sales of little cigars plunged 20.3 percent, followed by a 5.5 percent decline in large cigars ("Cigar Sales Decline Continues," Fall 1987, p. 5). To reduce this downward trend cigar manufacturers are targeting the baby boomer generation and Yumpies/Yuppies, portraying cigars as a symbol of masculine success ("T.V. Hunks," April 1985, p. 5).

Culbro, Inc., owner of General Cigar Co., manufactures Garcia Y Vega, White Owl, Robt. Burns, Corina, Wm. Penn, Tiparillo, Tijuana Smalls, London Dock, Kentucky Club, and various chewing tobacco lines. Culbro also owns Snacktime Co. and Imperial Nurseries ("Tobacco Industry Conglomerates," July 1984, p. 11).

Smokeless Tobacco: Snuff and Plug

Snuffing was originally an upper-class practice fostered in France in the 1700s. The modern P. Lorillard Co., America's oldest tobacco manufacturer, traces its origins to the small American snuff mills established in New York City by French Huguenot emigré Pierre Lorillard (Wagner 1971).

Major markets today for dark, air- and fire-cured tobacco for chewing and snuff are centered around Lexington and Hopkinsville, Kentucky, and Springfield, Tennessee. When soldiers began rolling cigarettes during the Civil War, the Lexington area farmers switched from hemp (for ropes) to tobacco growing. Today the dark, air-cured tobacco for chewing as well as 80 percent of the tobacco used in snuff is grown in this region. Lexington claims to be the world's largest loose-leaf tobacco market, auctioning 100 million pounds of tobacco annually from December through February.

Chewing tobacco is produced by the Big Six and specialty companies. The U.S. Tobacco Company manufactures Skoal, Skoal Bandits, Copenhagen, Borkum Riff, Amphora, and Perfecto Garcia. This diversified company also owns Dr. Grabow pipes, Zig Zag cigarette papers, Cedar King pencils, and Chateau Ste. Michelle wines. Culbro, Inc.'s product lines include the Helme Tobacco Company's Gold River, Mail Pouch, Silver Creek, Redwood, and Chattanooga Chew. Traditional cigarette companies' chewing tobacco lines include the Liggett Group's Pinkerton Tobacco Company's Red Man Chew and Lorillard's Beech-nut Chewing Tobacco ("Tobacco Industry Conglomerates," July 1984, p. 11). R. J. Reynolds's chewing tobacco lines (Prince Albert and Work Horse chew) were sold to Alfred &

Christian Petersen, Ltd. (an American subsidiary of a Danish tobacco company), removing Reynolds from the chewing tobacco retail market ("Tobacco Industry Update," January 1986, p. 6).

The 6.2 percent decline in sales of smokeless tobacco products in 1986 represented declines of 3 percent in moist snuff, 6.4 percent in loose-leaf chewing tobacco, 13.7 percent in moist plug tobacco, and 14 percent in plug tobacco ("Snuff Sales Dip," Fall 1987, p. 5). The link between these products and oral cancer prompted the Sixth Annual World Conference on Smoking and Health (November 9–12, 1987, in Tokyo, Japan) to recommend banning smokeless tobacco where it was "not yet an established habit" and severely restricting its promotion elsewhere.

New Product Lines

Product innovation has been the response to regulations imposed on the tobacco industry. The late 1950s and 1960s witnessed a rise in sales of low-tar and filter-tipped cigarettes. At the beginning of the 1950s, filter-tipped brands occupied 1 percent of the cigarette market; by the end of the decade, 50 percent. The Sloan-Kettering Institute's 1953 report prompted R. J. Reynolds to introduce filter-tipped Winston; by 1985 Winston accounted for 11.3 percent of sales and was the second most popular cigarette brand in the American market. Though slower to innovate, American Brands, which controlled two of the top three nonfiltered brands in the 1950s (Lucky Strike and Pall Mall), made 12 percent of its sales in filtered brands by 1963 (Miles and Cameron 1982). Filtered cigarettes claim 93 percent of the American market, up from 53 percent in 1963. Furthermore, 57 percent of the cigarette advertising dollars are spent promoting low-tar cigarettes, which now constitute 51 percent of the market (U.S. Congress, Hearings on H.R. 1272 and H.R. 1532, 1987).

Foreign studies indicate that low-tar and filter-tipped cigarettes have greater market penetration in countries that still allow some forms of media advertising. Low-tar cigarettes hold 52 percent of the market in Sweden, which still allows some advertising, but 31 percent in Norway and 38 percent in Finland, two countries that ban advertising (U.S. Congress, Hearings on H.R. 1272 and H.R. 1532, 1987).

In 1988 Reynolds test marketed a "smokeless" steam cigarette called Premier. It does not burn tobacco or get shorter with use. A heat-producing mechanism in the end of the cigarette heats an "aerosol forming material" (such as water) that circulates through the cigarette. Charcoal heats a glycerin packet that emits a nicotine flavor. Advantages over traditional cigarettes include less sidestream smoke and rapid dissipation of smoke. Because tobacco is not actually burned, no ash is emitted, and health dangers associated with tar are eliminated. The smokeless cigarette extinguishes itself, reducing fire risks; however, certain dangers remain. Nicotine and carbon monoxide are present, and new risks may be associated with the heating element and the fumes from heating and burning plastics ("No Smoke," September 15, 1987, p. 12A; "Breath of Controversy," September 15, 1987, pp. 1A, 12A).

Reynolds is not alone in developing low-smoke and smokeless cigarettes. Rothmans of Pall Mall Canada is test marketing Passport, a tar cigarette with about half the normal sidestream smoke. Advanced Tobacco Products of San Antonio is patenting a smokeless tobacco product ("Epidemic of New Cigarette Brands," April 1985, p. 5).

Other companies have begun to market "quit-smoking" kits that include nicotine-flavored substances. Products such as Cigarrest are capitalizing on the health consciousness of Americans. Nicorette, nicotine chewing gum, is advertised as an alternative to smoking that supplies similar nicotine levels (McCusker 1984). "Quit Smoking" clinics, offered by the American Lung Association, and various private organizations, have increased in the 1980s.

Catering to the smoker who does not want to quit, but is concerned with fashion and hygiene, Jeffrey Martin, Inc., produces Topol tooth polish and mouthwash to reduce yellowing on teeth and bad breath. More than half of the mouthwash sold in the United States is sold to the 30 percent of the population who smoke; thus the $500 million mouthwash business has an ancillary connection to the tobacco industry ("New Help for 'Smoker's Breath,' " October 1985, p. 7).

Tobacco is regarded as a health hazard. Approximately 50,000 published studies have cited cigarette smoking as America's most preventable cause of illness and death. Studies discussed by Dr. Ronald M. Davis (American Medical Association) and Dr. Charles A. LeMaistre (President of the American Cancer Society) demonstrate that in the 1980s over 350,000 people die annually of smoking-related illnesses (U.S. Congress, Hearings on H.R. 4972, 1986). One out of every three to four smokers dies from tobacco-induced illness. Tobacco is linked to one-sixth of all American deaths (Warner 1987, 2081, 2083).

Although contemporary coverage concentrates on the new wave of anti-smoking legislation of the past twenty-five years, twelve states and several cities restricted the manufacture or sale of cigarettes as early as 1909. New Hampshire levied a fine for selling cigarettes; in Illinois a $100 fine or a thirty-day imprisonment were penalties for manufacturing or selling cigarettes; in Tennessee cigarettes were made nonlegitimate articles of commerce. An 1897 federal statute banned the use of coupons in cigarette packages, and federal taxes on cigarettes fluctuated with public outcries against smoking (Wagner 1971). Early twentieth-century legislation, however, was directed against cigarettes in particular, not against the tobacco industry as a whole. The effectiveness of the legislation is questionable, since national sales of cigarettes doubled from 1904 to 1909. By 1927 most of the anticigarette laws had been repealed (Wagner 1971).

The $35 billion tobacco industry of the 1980s is responsible for an estimated $65–81 billion in medical costs, loss of productivity, and property damage. Through Medicare and Medicaid payments, the government financed approximately $4.2 billion of the $22 billion spent in the eighties on treatment of diseases related to tobacco smoking. According to estimates from the Congressional Office of Technology Assessment, an additional $43 billion was lost in productivity and earnings in 1985 (U.S. Congress, Hearings on H.R. 4972, 1986).

Health care costs for smokers are higher than for nonsmokers. Nevertheless, what smokers add to health care system costs may not be great, because smokers tend to die younger than nonsmokers. Fewer smokers draw on the medical care system during typical retirement years, when nonsmokers suffer age-related ailments. One of the costs of a "smoke-free" society would be the expense of maintaining a longer-lived populace (Warner 1987).

In the 1970s and 1980s, Washington and other states passed laws requiring motels to maintain floors where smoking is prohibited. Such laws recognize that nonsmokers have rights and that businesses often spend 40 percent more for cleaning and repair on smoking floors. Beyond the cleaning bills is the fire hazard. Over half of residential fires are caused by careless smoking, and cigarettes are the leading cause of 2,000 burn deaths annually. Eighty-five percent of street litter is related to smoking and tobacco products, according to findings by FANS (Fresh Air for Nonsmokers). Some retailers of paper and cloth products, which absorb tobacco odor and are vulnerable to fire, are beginning to post no-smoking signs in their establishments. In some cities, Springfield, Missouri, for instance, the voluntary posting of such a sign by a retailer carries with it police enforcement and fines for violations.

ADVERTISING IN THE UNITED STATES

From $249.5 million in 1963 to $2648.6 million in 1983, cigarette advertising and promotional costs have continued to spiral despite partial media bans. In 1963 three-fourths of that year's cigarette advertising budget was spent on television and radio, media banned by 1971 ("Cigarette Advertising," October 1985). Despite an increase in city ordinances forbidding such activity, tobacco companies spent $148 million on cigarette sampling distributions in 1984—five times the amount spent for sampling in 1975.

The United States bans some tobacco advertising. Television and radio advertising bans were introduced for cigarettes in 1970, for little cigars in 1973, and for smokeless tobacco in 1986. Warning labels on cigarettes were initially legislated in 1965; stronger warnings were mandated in 1984. Warning labels on smokeless tobacco products have been required since 1986.

Though barred from television and radio since the Public Health Cigarette

Smoking Act of 1970, cigarette companies spent an estimated $2.7 billion on advertising and promoting in 1983. Cigarettes are the single most heavily advertised product in America. The tobacco industry has considerable impact on other industries. It accounts for approximately 50 percent of the outdoor billboard business and is the source of 10–15 percent of advertisements in newspapers and magazines (U.S. Congress, Hearings on H.R. 4972, 1986).

Authorities disagree on the goal of tobacco advertising—brand shifting or increasing consumption. Tobacco companies claim that advertising is not aimed at creating new demand, but only induces brand shifting in a large static market. Congressman Hal Rogers of Kentucky echoes this argument by emphasizing that "soap advertising doesn't cause bathing. Gasoline advertising doesn't cause driving. So cigarette advertising does not cause smoking" (U.S. Congress, Hearings on H.R. 1272 and H.R. 1532, 1987, 49).

Wharton School professor Scott Ward contrasts the effect of advertising in a new and a mature market. For a new product, video recorders, for example, advertising creates consumer awareness of the product and promotes demand for it. In a mature market, cigarettes, for example, consumers know about the product, so advertising creates brand shifting among an established clientele (U.S. Congress, Hearings on H.R. 1272 and H.R. 1532, 1987).

Tobacco subsidies, taxation, and warnings about tobacco products are ethical and economic problems for the U.S. government. The cigarette industry receives $90 million in price supports, and tobacco growers receive a greater percentage of income from federal subsidies than farmers in any other sector. Federal cigarette excise taxes remained at 8 cents per package from 1951 to 1982. The increase to 16 cents per pack in 1987 has been extended indefinitely under the Omnibus Reconciliation Act of 1986. The tax increase may account for the decrease in tobacco sales since 1982.

The Price Support Program of 1938 established acreage allotments and remains a prop for small tobacco farms. Each type of tobacco has a price support level established by the Secretary of Agriculture. If tobacco growers are unable to acquire the guaranteed price for their tobacco, they may receive cash advances upon consignment of their tobacco to marketing associations that are backed by government loans.

Until the No-Net-Cost Tobacco Act of 1983, federal loans backed the marketing, storage, and handling of surplus and below-market-priced tobacco. Sales proceeds were used to minimize loan balances. Changes in the 1983 act required the tobacco grower to bear the storage cost for below-market-priced tobacco. Assessments on growers rose from 3 cents a pound to 25 cents a pound. The Omnibus Reconciliation Act of 1986 reduced 1986 price support levels, gave tobacco manufacturers control over acreage allotments and quotas, and substantially discounted domestic sales of government inventories of tobacco. Despite surpluses of 740 million pounds in warehouses and projected sales of 692 million pounds, one-third of the tobacco used in U.S. cigarettes in 1986 was grown abroad.

Although tobacco consumption in America has decreased by 2 percent per year since 1981, consumption is on the rise internationally. In 1950 just over 15 million cigarettes were exported by U.S. firms (mainly to U.S. servicemen); 374 million were consumed domestically. In the eighties U.S. manufacturers are shifting their focus to overseas markets (Miles and Cameron 1982). Third World countries consume about one-third of the $200 billion international cigarette market. Antismoking forces have not acquired a stronghold in the Third World countries, where life expectancy is low (Mufson 1986).

BIBLIOGRAPHY

Abramson, J. "Battle Lines Drawn in Cigarette Ad Fight." *Legal Times* 9 (November 10, 1986): 1.

Alsop, Ronald, Alix Freedman, and Betsy Morris. "RJR Takeover Could Hurt Marketers and Consumers." *Wall Street Journal* (December 2, 1988): A10.

Ashley, R., C.W.J. Granger, and R. Schmalensee. "Advertising and Aggregate Consumption: An Analysis Causality."*Econometrica* 48 (1980): 1149–67.

Assmus, G., J. U. Farley, and D. R. Lehmann. "How Advertising Affects Sales: Meta Analysis of Econometric Results." *Journal of Marketing Research* 21 (1984): 65–74.

Badger, Anthony J. *Prosperity Road: The New Deal, Tobacco, and North Carolina.* Chapel Hill: University of North Carolina Press, 1980.

Bailey, William J. "New Surveys Show that Smoking Rates Continue to Drop!" *Tobacco-Free Young America Reporter* (Fall 1987): 1.

Bean, Ed. "Tobacco Industry's Court Victories Fail to Slow Product-Liability Suits." *Wall Street Journal* (January 30, 1986): 33.

Berkowitz, Peggy. "Canadian House Approves Curbs on Tobacco Ads." *Wall Street Journal* (June 1, 1988): 32.

Beverly, Robert. *The History and Present State of Virginia.* Edited by Louis B. Wright. Chapel Hill: University of North Carolina Press, 1947.

"Beyond Marlboro Country." *Business Week* (August 8, 1988): 54–58.

Biglan, A., and E. Lichtenstein. "A Behavior-Analytic Approach to Smoking Acquisition: Some Recent Findings." *Journal of Applied Social Psychology* 14 (1984): 207–23.

Billings, Warren M., ed. *The Old Dominion in the Seventeenth Century: A Documentary History of Virginia, 1606–1689.* Chapel Hill: University of North Carolina Press, 1975.

Bishop, John A., and Jang H. Yoo. " 'Health Scare,' Excise Taxes and Advertising Ban in the Cigarette Demand and Supply." *Southern Economic Journal* 52 (1985): 402.

Bordley, John Beale. *A Summary View of the Courses of Crops, in the Husbandry of England and Maryland*. Philadelphia: C. Cist, 1784. Reprint. Wilmington, DE: Scholarly Resources, 1973.

Bourgeois, J. C., and J. G. Barnes. "Does Advertising Increase Alcohol Consumption?" *Journal of Advertising Research* 19 (1979): 19–29.

"Breath of Controversy Touches Smokeless Smokes." (Springfield, MO) *News Leader* (September 15, 1987): 1A, 12A.

"Brown & Williamson Tobacco Shifts Target to Price/Value Market Segments." *Smoking and Health Reporter* (October 1985): 7.

Browne, William Hand, et al., eds. *Archives of Maryland*. 72 vols. to date. Baltimore, 1883– .

Byrd, William. *The Great American Gentlemen: The Secret Diary of William Byrd of Westover, 1709–1712*. Edited by Louis B. Wright and Marion Tinling. New York: Putnam, 1963.

Calvert Papers, 1889–1899. Baltimore: Maryland Historical Society.

Carrizosa, Philip. "Asbestos Firms Say Smoking Hurts Workers: Seek Market Share Recovery Against Tobacco Companies: Surprise Thrust." *New Jersey Law Journal* 9 (October 9, 1980): 106.

Carver, Jonathon. *A Treatise on the Culture of the Tobacco Plant*. London: Lake White, 1779.

Child, Sir Josiah. *A New Discourse of Trade*. London: S. Everingham, 1693.

"Cigarette Advertising and Promotion Outlays More Than Double in Three Years— Sales Fall, However." *Smoking and Health Reporter* 3 (October 1985): 8.

"Cigarette Companies Among Top Advertising Buyers." *Tobacco-Free Young America Reporter* (Fall 1987): 6.

"Cigarette Sales Continue Their Downward Spiral." *Tobacco-Free Young America Reporter* (Spring 1988): 3.

"Cigarette Tax Draws Fire, Support." (Springfield, MO) *Leader Press* (June 13, 1988): 1A.

"Cigar Sales Decline Continues." *Tobacco-Free Young America Reporter* (Fall 1987): 5.

"Cigar Sales Drop in 1984." *Smoking and Health Reporter* (October 1985): 7.

Clairmonte, Frederick F. "World Tobacco: A Study in Conglomerate Structures." *Journal of World Trade Law* 14 (January-February 1980): 23–38.

"Coalition on Smoking or Health Petitions FTC to Stop 'False and Deceptive' Ads by R. J. Reynolds Tobacco Company." *Smoking and Health Reporter* 2 (July 1985): 1, 5.

Cochran, Sherman. *Big Business in China: Sino-Foreign Rivalry in the Cigarette Industry, 1890–1930*. Cambridge, MA: Harvard University Press, 1980.

Cohen, Laurie P. "Decision on Bid Deemed Likely to Survive in Court." *Wall Street Journal* (December 2, 1988): A10.

Comanor, William S., and Thomas A. Wilson. *Advertising and Marketing Power*. Cambridge, MA: Harvard University Press, 1974.

Compion, Gerry. "Tobacco Lawyers' Economic Evidence Limited." *New Jersey Law Journal* 18 (October 2, 1986):11.

Cook, Ebenezer. *The Sot-Weed Factor; Or, a Voyage to Maryland*. London: A. Satyr, 1708.

Darmstadter, Ruth. "Snuff and Chew: The Tobacco Industry Plugs Nicotine by Osmosis." *Business and Society Review* (Fall 1983): 23–27.

Dickinson, Becky. "Infighting Marks FTC First Amendment Case." *Legal Times* 9 (December 15, 1986): 4.

"Epidemic of New Cigarette Brands Plagues U.S." *Smoking and Health Reporter* (April 1985): 5.

Finger, William R., ed. *The Tobacco Industry in Transition: Policies for the 1980s.* Lexington, MA: D. C. Heath, 1981.

Fishbein, Martin. "Consumer Beliefs and Behavior with Respect to Cigarette Smoking: A Critical Analysis of the Public Literature." A Report Prepared for the Staff of the FTC (Appendix A of FTC Report to Congress pursuant to the Public Health Cigarette Smoking Act for the Year 1976).

Flanigan, James. "Adversity, Diversity Boost Tobacco Stocks." *Kansas City Star* (August 31, 1987): A8.

Force, Peter. *Tracts and Other Papers, Relating Principally to the Origin, Settlement, and Progress of the Colonies in North America, from the Discovery of the Country to the Year 1776.* 4 vols. Washington, DC, 1837–46. Reprint. Gloucester, MA: 1963.

Friedman, Kenneth Michael. *Public Policy and the Smoking-Health Controversy.* Lexington, MA: D. C. Heath, 1976.

"FTC Reopens Deceptive Advertising Complaints Against R. J. Reynolds." *Tobacco-Free Young America Reporter* 5 (Spring 1988): 3.

"General Foods Sells Out to Philip Morris." *Smoking and Health Reporter* (January 1986): 6.

Grabowski, Henry G. "The Effects of Advertising on the Interindustry Distribution of Demand." *Explorations in Economic Research* 3 (1976): 21.

Gras, N.S.B., ed. *Harvard Studies in Business History XII.* Cambridge, MA: Harvard University Press, 1948.

Hall, Clayton Coleman, ed. *Narratives of Early Maryland, 1633–84.* New York: Charles Scribner's Sons, 1910. Reprint. New York: Barnes & Noble, 1946.

Hall, Trish. "Smoking of Cigarettes Seems to Be Becoming a Lower-Class Habit." *Wall Street Journal* (June 25, 1985): A1.

Hamilton, James L. "The Demand for Cigarettes: Advertising, the Health Scare, and the Cigarette Advertising Ban." *Review of Economics and Statistics* 54 (1972): 401.

Harrower, John. *The Journal of John Harrower, an Indentured Servant in the Colony of Virginia, 1773–1776.* Edited by Edward Miles Riley. Williamsburg, VA: Colonial Williamsburg, 1963.

Hartsook, Elizabeth, and Gust Skordas. *Land Office and Prerogative Court Records of Colonial Maryland.* Hall of Records Commission Publication No. 4. Annapolis: Hall of Records Commission, 1946.

"Hawaii Has Lowest Smoking Rates." *Tobacco-Free Young America Reporter* (Fall 1987): 6.

Helyar, John. "In Winston-Salem, Workers' Good Will Goes Up in Smoke." *Wall Street Journal* (November 30, 1988): A1, A12.

Helyar, John, and Bryan Burrough. "How Underdog KKR Won RJR Nabisco Without Highest Bid." *Wall Street Journal* (December 2, 1988): A1, A4.

Hening, W. W., ed. *The Statutes at Large, Being a Collection of All the Laws of Virginia.* 13 vols. Richmond: Samuel Pleasants, 1809–23.

Hirschman, R. S., H. Leventhal, and K. Glynn. "The Development of Smoking

Behavior: Conceptualizing and Supportive Cross-Sectional Survey Data." *Journal of Applied Social Psychology* 14 (1984): 184–206.

Huebner, Albert. "Tobacco's Lucrative Third World Invasion." *Business and Society Review* (Fall 1980): 49–53.

Ippolito, Pauline M., and David T. Scheffman, eds. *Empirical Approaches to Consumer Protection Economics.* Washington, DC: U.S. Federal Trade Commission, 1984.

Johnston, J. "Advertising and the Aggregate Demand for Cigarettes: A Comment." *European Economic Review* 14 (1980): 117–25.

Kell, Katharine. T. "Tobacco in Folk Cures in Western Society." *Journal of American Folklore* 78 (1965): 99–112. Reprint. Randy Roberts and James S. Olson, eds. *American Experiences.* Vol. 1, 1607–1877. Glenview, IL: Scott, Foresman, 1986.

Langley, Monica. "FTC Probe of Philip Morris-Kraft Merger Is Closed After Heavy Stock Trading." *Wall Street Journal* (December 1, 1988): A10.

Larson, Henrietta M., ed. *Guide to Business History.* Ann Arbor, MI: University Microfilms, 1960.

The Laws of the Province of Maryland, Collected into One Volume, by Order of the Governor and Assembly of the Said Province ... to the year 1719. Philadelphia, 1718. Reprint. Wilmington, DE: Michael Glazier, 1978.

Leventhal, H., and P. D. Cleary. "The Smoking Problem: A Review of the Research and Theory in Behavioral Risk Modification." *Psychological Bulletin* 88 (1980): 370–405.

"Lorillard Markets in Prisons." *Smoking and Health Reporter* (January 1986): 6.

"Low-Smoke Cigarette Proposed." *Smoking and Health Reporter* (April 1985): 5.

McCusker, Kevin T. "A Physician's View of Nicorette." *Smoking and Health Reporter* (April 1984): 5.

McGuinness, T., and K. Cowling. "Advertising and the Aggregate Demand for Cigarettes." *European Economic Review* 6 (1975): 311–28.

Main, Gloria L. *Tobacco Colony Life in Early Maryland, 1650–1720.* Princeton, NJ: Princeton University Press, 1982.

"Marlboro Increases Market Share." *Tobacco-Free Young America Reporter* 6 (Fall 1987): 5.

Miles, Robert H., and Kim S. Cameron. *Coffin Nails and Corporate Strategies.* Englewood Cliffs, NJ: Prentice-Hall, 1982.

Mufson, Steve. "Cigarette Companies Develop Third World as a Growth Market." *Wall Street Journal* (July 5, 1986): A1.

"New Help for 'Smoker's Breath.' " *Smoking and Health Reporter* (October 1985): 7.

"Next Year—The Excise Tax!!!" *Smoking and Health Reporter* (October 1984): 8.

"No Smoke, but There May Be Fire: New Cigarette Could Give Lift to Tobacco Industry." (Springfield, MO) *News Leader* (September 15, 1987): 12A.

Okie, Susan. "Smoking's Contribution to U.S. Deaths." *Washington Post* (October 30, 1987): A23.

"Park Avenue Tobacco Company." *Smoking and Health Reporter* (October 1985): 7.

"Park Avenue Tobacco Company '1776' Segments the Military Market." *Smoking and Health Reporter* (April 1985): 5.

Peles, Y. "Rates of Amortization of Advertising Expenditures." *Journal of Political Economy* 79 (September–October 1971): 1032–58.

"Philip Morris Plans to Counter-Attack." *Smoking and Health Reporter* (April 1986): 7.

Quinn, John F. "The Business Ethics of Cipollone v. Liggett Group: Moral Theory and Defective Tobacco Advertising and Warnings." Paper presented at the Midwest Business Law Association, Chicago, March 25, 1988.

"Reynolds Accused of Deceptive Tobacco Ads." *Kansas City Times* (June 17, 1986): A1, A12.

Riley, John. "Secret Tobacco Documents Stay Secret." *National Law Journal* 8 (March 24, 1986): 3.

" 'RIO' Cigarettes Targets Hispanics." *Smoking and Health Reporter* (April 1985): 5.

" 'RITZ' Designer Cigarettes." *Smoking and Health Reporter* (April 1985): 5.

"R. J. Reynolds and Nabisco Announce Merger." *Smoking and Health Reporter* (October 1985): 7.

R. J. Reynolds Tobacco Co., Inc.—FTC opinion, Dkt. 9206 (April 11, 1988), as reported in the *Trade Regulation Reporter* (CCH): Para. 22, 522.

"RJR-Nabisco Announces Plans for a 'Smokeless' Cigarette." *Tobacco-Free Young America Reporter* (Fall 1987): 4.

"RJR-Nabisco Fires Ad Agency that Created Northwest Airlines Ad About Smoking Ban." *Tobacco-Free Young America Reporter* (Spring 1988): 8.

"RJR Sells Chewing Tobacco Business." *Smoking and Health Reporter* (January 1986): 6.

Rogers, B., et al. "Trends in Tobacco Consumption in Seven Countries 1950–1984." Unpublished paper presented at the 34th International Congress on Alcoholism and Drug Dependence, Calgary, Canada, 1985. Cited in Health Protection Act of 1987, Hearings before the Subcommittee on Transportation, Tourism, and Hazardous Materials of the Committee on Energy and Commerce, House of Representatives (1987).

Sainsbury, W. Noel, et al., eds. *Calendar of State Papers, Colonial Series*. London: 1860– .

" 'St. James Court' and 'Eli Cutter.' " *Smoking and Health Reporter* (April 1985): 5.

"Sales Go Down, but . . . Cigarette Profits Up." *Smoking and Health Reporter* (January 1986): 6.

Schmalensee, Richard. *The Economics of Advertising*. Amsterdam: North-Holland, 1972.

Sherwood, Steve. "Tobacco Firms Share Asbestosis Liability: Attorney." *Business Insurance* 15 (December 7, 1981): 31.

Shuffett, D. Milton. "History of Farm Structure in the Production of Burley Tobacco 1940–1979." *Agricultural Law Journal* 2 (Fall 1980): 422–33.

Smith, Barney, Harris, Upton & Co. *Wall Street Journal* (December 2, 1988): A4.

Smith, Joseph H., and Philip A. Crowl, eds. *Court Records of Prince Georges County, Maryland 1696–1699*. American Legal Records, vol. 9. Washington, DC: American Historical Association, 1964.

[Snuff]. *Advertising Age* (July 13, 1987).

"Snuff Sales Dip." *Tobacco-Free Young America Reporter* (Fall 1987): 5.

Spotswood, Alexander. *The Official Letters of Alexander Spotswood*. Richmond: Virginia Historical Society, 1882–85.

Sticht, J. Paul. *The RJR Story: The Evolution of a Global Enterprise*. New York: Newcomen Society in North America, 1983.

Surgeon General's Advisory Committee on Smoking and Health. *Smoking and Health: Report of the Advisory Committee to the Surgeon General of Public Health Service*. Washington, DC: U.S. Department of Health, Education, and Welfare, Public Health Service, 1964.

"Teen-Age Smoking Declines Again." *Smoking and Health Reporter* (April 1985): 1.

Tilley, Nannie M. *The R. J. Reynolds Tobacco Company*. Chapel Hill: University of North Carolina Press, 1985.

"Tobacco $$$ to Congressional Candidates." *GASP of Massachusetts* (Winter 1987): 8.

"Tobacco Industry Conglomerates—Status Report on Diversification in the Tobacco Industry, 1984." *Smoking and Health Reporter* (July 1984): 11.

"Tobacco Industry Update." *Smoking and Health Reporter* (October 1985): 7.

"Tobacco Industry Update." *Smoking and Health Reporter* (January 1986): 6.

"Tobacco Industry Update." *Smoking and Health Reporter* (April 1986): 7.

"Tobacco Suit: Broad Discovery Snuffed Out." *American Bar Association Journal* 74 (June 1, 1986): 84.

"T.V. Hunks and 'Humpty Tumpie' Cigar Marketing Plan for 1985." *Smoking and Health Reporter* (April 1985): 5.

" 'Twist' Filter Cigarettes Finally Hit Market." *Smoking and Health Reporter* (October 1985): 7.

U.S. Bureau of the Census. *Historical Statistics of the United States, Colonial Times to 1970*. Washington, DC: U.S. Government Printing Office, 1975.

U.S. Congress. House, Committee on Agriculture. Subcommittee on Tobacco and Peanuts. Dark Air-Cured and Dark Fire-Cured Tobacco Quotas. 100th Cong., 1st sess., 1987.

———. Committee on Agriculture. Subcommittee on Tobacco and Peanuts. Economic Conditions Affecting Tobacco and Peanut Producers. Hearing. 100th Congress., 1st sess., 1987.

———. Committee on Energy and Commerce. Subcommittee on Health and the Environment. Advertising of Tobacco Products. Hearings on H.R. 4972. 99th Cong., 2d sess., 1986.

———. Committee on Energy and Commerce. Subcommittee on Health and the Environment. Designation of Smoking Areas in Federal Buildings. Hearings on H.R. 4488 and H.R. 4546. 99th Cong., 2d sess., 1986.

———. Committee on Energy and Commerce. Subcommittee on Transportation, Tourism, and Hazardous Materials. FTC Nicotine Program. Hearing. 100th Cong., 1st sess., 1987.

———. Committee on Energy and Commerce. Subcommittee on Transportation, Tourism, and Hazardous Materials. Health Protection Act of 1987. Hearings on H.R. 1272 and H.R. 1532. 100th Cong., 1st sess., 1987.

"Verdict Can Be Considered Victory for Industry, Experts Say." (Springfield, MO) *Leader-Press* (June 13, 1988): 10A.

" 'Volvo Drivers' and 'Upscale Buyers' Targeted by New Brands and Gimmicks."
    Smoking and Health Reporter (January 1984): 4.
Wagner, Susan. *Cigarette Country Tobacco in American History and Politics.* New
    York: Praeger, 1971.
Warner, Kenneth E. "Health and Economic Implications of a Tobacco-Free Society."
    Journal of the American Medical Association 258, no. 16 (October 1987):
    2081–86.
Weis, W. L. "A Smoke over Tobacco's Future." *Business and Society Review* (Winter
    1985): 37–40.
Whitten, David O. *The Emergence of Giant Enterprise, 1860–1914.* Westport, CT:
    Greenwood Press, 1983.
Wilder, Ronald P. "Advertising and Inter-Industry Competition: Testing a Gal-
    braithian Hypothesis." *Journal of Industrial Economics* 23 (1974): 215.

Part III

Textiles
ESIC 23.0

APPAREL AND OTHER TEXTILE PRODUCTS, 23.0

_____ JACK BLICKSILVER

A commercial, profit-driven apparel industry was slow to emerge in America. Industrial labor in the agrarian colonial economy was scarce and expensive. Backcountry farmers could not afford commercial clothing, and wealthy planters and seaport-based merchants preferred quality British-made garments to those fabricated by itinerant tailors or urban craftsmen. Well into the first half of the nineteenth century households manufactured their own apparel; family members, indentured servants, and slaves wore clothing made from wool, hemp, flax, skins, and Sea Island long-staple cotton. Homemade apparel worn by runaway slaves was often described in newspaper advertisements placed by owners seeking their return. In his *Report on Manufactures*, Alexander Hamilton noted that, in many of the fledgling nation's districts, local residents made as much as 80 percent of their own clothing (Ewen and Ewen 1982). As late as 1810, two-thirds of all garments worn in the United States were homemade. After 1815 dealers in New York City bought, cleaned, and refinished used garments, then sold them secondhand to immigrants and transients.

In the early nineteenth century ready-made apparel was first made commercially for sailors and merchant seaman. In "slop shops" women from nearby farms were paid by piecework to hand sew crude, ill-fitting garments cut from rough material of British or East Indian origin. Brooks Brothers, the illustrious haberdashery, started as a slop shop in the period prior to the War of 1812.

After the war, the domestic ready-to-wear clothing industry benefitted from protective tariffs and a growing market. Congress increased duties on imported ready-made clothing from 30 percent ad valorem in 1816 to 50 percent ad valorem in 1828 and imposed a comparable level of protection on woolen textiles. Nevertheless, lower labor costs overseas permitted the English to sell hand-tailored suits in the United States at prices below those for American-made garments. Furthermore, Americans were less critical of workmanship than European consumers were, and American males bought standardized clothing. Ambitious New York tailors recognized the potential of a growing middle-class market and reorganized their shops into separate departments for custom work and ready-to-wear production (Feldman 1960). Until the 1840s tailor's tools were simple, and shops remained unmechanized. As cutting rooms were enlarged, specialists in various garment-making categories worked side by side. Seamstresses were employed in great numbers, although many continued to work at home. At times of peak demand, work was subcontracted.

In 1846 Elias Howe, Jr., patented a practical sewing machine that reshaped the antebellum apparel industry. Isaac M. Singer devised a rocking treadle for Howe's machine and added a balance wheel on the upper shaft to increase momentum. Operating the machine by a heel and a toe motion on the rocking treadle freed the sewer's hands to guide the cloth being stitched. The improved sewing machine increased labor productivity twentyfold. Although lightweight family sewing machines priced at $125 and made available on an installment plan gained great popularity among American housewives during the 1850s, Singer's heavier industrial models, designed for use in tailor's shops and factories, had a greater impact on apparel making. A series of experiments conducted by the Wheeler and Wilson Company disclosed that a man's shirt required 14 hours, 26 minutes to fabricate by hand sewing, but only 1 hour and 16 minutes by sewing machine; frock coats, an average of 16 hours, 35 minutes by hand, but 2 hours and 38 minutes by machine (Cooper 1976). With the impetus provided by the industrial sewing machine, production of ready-to-wear men's clothing, centered in the Northeast, expanded rapidly. Custom tailoring was on the defensive.

Across the continent in the San Francisco Bay area, pioneer manufacturers Levi Strauss and J. H. Browning began producing ready-to-wear apparel during the 1850s for miners and lumbermen—a mobile male labor force far from home production. Overalls and trousers were fabricated from sailcloth and sturdy tent canvas. In filling Strauss's orders for rugged fabric, his brothers in New York turned to denim, a twill weave available from France. To meet the demands for rough outdoor wear, Strauss adopted rivets and multiple stitching, a technology borrowed from horse blanket construction.

During the 1850s capital invested in apparel making doubled, and the value of output grew by 51.5 percent. Industry employment, however, increased by only 2.4 percent, and the number of firms declined by 11 percent. The 1860 census report on manufactures attributed these changes to "a silent revolution...chiefly through the agency of the sewing machine, whereby many small shops have been merged into large wholesale establishments for the manufacture and sale of ready-made clothing" (U.S. Bureau of the Census, *Eighth Census, Manufactures*, 1x). A major stimulant to growth in the garment industry was the soaring demand by slave owners for clothing made of cheap, coarse fabric. The Singer Sewing Machine Company promoted its "new, improved sewing machine especially adapted to the making up of Negro clothing" (Ewen and Ewen 1982, 166).

On the eve of the Civil War apparel making was a major manufacturing industry. In 1859 the men's clothing sector employed 114,800 wage earners in 4,014 plants, produced $80.3 million worth of apparel, and ranked third among manufacturing industries in employment and value-added ($36.7 million) and fifth in value of product. At the same time the women's clothing sector was a fledgling. Ready-made women's cloaks were an established market item by 1853, when the sewing machine was first used in their manufacture. Machine sewing reduced the cost of constructing the garment by as much as 80 percent. Crinolines and hoopskirts, it was soon discovered, were easier to stitch by machine than by hand; nonetheless, progress in the machine manufacture of women's apparel was painfully slow (Cooper 1976). In 1859 the women's apparel sector employed 5,739 wage earners in 188 plants and contributed $7.2 million to the industry in value of product and $3.9 million in value-added by manufacture.

New York–based apparel makers were favorably located to take advantage of low-wage immigrant labor entering the city and were thus major beneficiaries of the surging market demand for ready-to-wear clothing. In 1860 New York State accounted for almost half of the nation's capital and employment in the apparel industry. Second- and third-ranked Pennsylvania and Connecticut lagged far behind. New York City merchants, moreover, aggressively marketed ready-made garments through effective advertising and lenient credit policies; they sold at auction and adopted a range of techniques to lure out-of-town retailers to purchase their inventory. Reluctant to rely on visiting jobbers and shopkeepers, a growing number of New York apparel wholesalers established sales outlets in regional centers throughout the nation.

The northern-based apparel industry burgeoned during the Civil War, profiting from extensive military orders and the expanding civilian demand for clothing. Before 1861 the U.S. Army manufactured its own uniforms and was reluctant to experiment with machine-made clothing, fearing that the product would be inadequate for combat duty, especially under rough frontier conditions. The sewing machine was initially confined, therefore, to stitching caps and chevrons. With the outbreak of war, the contracts signed for military clothing did not specify a method of manufacture. Suppliers soon turned increasingly to machine-made apparel to assure standard quality and to meet contract deadlines. Conscripts were measured and a range of sizes was established. For the first time standard uniform measurements were adopted. Most Civil War uniforms contained at least some machine stitching. The durability of machine stitching was seriously compromised, however, by the quality of the thread, a problem that was not resolved until after the war. In the mid–1860s a Scottish firm headed by George and William Clark set up a plant in Newark, New Jersey, to produce six-cord cabled thread, composed of three two-ply yarns. Clark's superior cabled thread solved the machine thread problem and enhanced the public's receptivity to ready-made apparel during the post–Civil War era.

For several decades after 1865 machine-made apparel remained concentrated in the men's and boys' segments of the clothing industry. The postwar generation of American women continued to rely on paper dress patterns and moderately priced sewing machines to make their own fashionable clothing inexpensively. Successful firms like Butterick and Company expanded the paper dress pattern industry by systematizing production, advertising extensively, and distributing their patterns through a strong national network. By the turn of the century such national magazines as *Godey's Lady's Book*, *Mirror of Fashion*, and *Ladies' Home Journal* published patterns for garments to be made at home (Seebohm 1982). Meanwhile, the burgeoning demand for mass-produced men's clothing sparked expansion of the ready-to-wear industry. Newly arrived male immigrants believed, correctly, that store-bought, factory-made apparel would facilitate their acceptance into American society. Farm-bred youths migrating to urban areas were likewise convinced that attractive and well-fitted, yet reasonably priced, ready-made shirts and double-breasted frock coats would ease their upward path in life. For those who remained on the farm or resided in small towns, a comparable range of garments was available at modest prices through mail-order catalogues and in small-town retail specialty shops stocked in part by the manufacturing and wholesale divisions of such large urban department stores as Marshall Field in Chicago. By the turn of the century, most American males were wearing ready-to-wear clothing.

From 1869 to 1899, the apparel industry's decennial rate of change in real manufacturing value-added grew faster than in the overall manufacturing sector. Its contribution to the nation's real manufacturing value-added increased from 6 percent in 1869 to 11.4 percent in 1899. By 1899 the apparel industry ranked first among all manufacturing industries as measured by real value-added. The apparel industry also outpaced most other manufacturing industries in labor productivity gains, particularly during the 1879–99 era. By 1880 shears were being replaced by the sword knife and the slotted table in the cutting room. Advances in electric motor construction led to great improvements in the small portable rotary and the reciprocating electric knives. After 1900 improvements in technology continued with the adoption of steam pressing irons in place of gas- or coal-heated irons and the electrification of the sewing machine (Rischin 1962). But, in all likelihood, the factor most responsible for the productivity gains of the late nineteenth century was the nefarious "sweating" system of production. During the 1880s, value-added per employee increased 75 percent for apparel but only 40 percent for all manufacturing; during the 1890s, 20 percent for apparel and 1 percent for all manufacturing.

The apparel industry's impressive growth and productivity gains were accompanied by structural changes. Such insightful contemporary novels as *The Rise of David Levinsky*, written by Abraham Cahan in 1917, depicted the spread of the jobber-contractor system. Jobbers, typically wholesalers, designed garments, bought cloth from the mills, often cut the fabric, and then farmed out the manufacture of the garments on consignment. Contractors, often skilled tailors turned businessmen, bought or rented sewing machines; recruited operators, basters, pressers, finishers, fitters, button-hole-makers, and other specialists; and supervised the making of the garment, dividing the labor into "section work." A task system was devised in which the ten to twenty members of the work group were assigned a production quota. When slack seasons and weak retail demand for the product dictated razor-thin margins, jobbers pitted contractors against each other. The pressure to increase production at reduced compensation was then transferred to the members of the contractor's team.

The intensely competitive and exploitive task system was especially well suited to the fashion-dictated, seasonal women's apparel industry that began to grow rapidly during the 1880s. At times of peak demand, first-generation East European Jewish and Italian workers labored as many as eighty-four hours a week to produce garments on schedule.

By the turn of the century, New York City had emerged as the nation's principal apparel spot market, to which buyers flocked for quick delivery, especially of less expensive grades of goods, modified fashions, and novelties. The flexibility inherent in the contract system allowed jobbers with orders for finished goods to turn to an unorganized reserve army of immigrants to meet production deadlines. In 1900 New York City accounted for 37.3 percent of the industry value of product for men's apparel, but other apparel producing centers had begun to specialize in specific subcategories of men's suits, coats, and furnishings. Chicago, soon to become the home base for Hart Schaffner & Marx, contributed 13 percent to industry value-added in men's apparel; Philadelphia accounted for 6.8 percent and Baltimore 6.3 percent. Women's apparel production, although beginning to grow rapidly, continued to lag behind men's: 83,739 employees in women's apparel compared to 120,927 in men's and $74.6 billion value-added compared to $131.5 million.

During the first decade of the twentieth century, production in the women's segment of the apparel industry surged. The growing employment of women in clerical and sales jobs, as well as in light manufacturing, drew many young women out of their homes and provided them with a personal source of purchasing power. By 1905 there were 5.3 million women in the labor force, including 100,000 secretaries, 17,000 milliners, and 413,000 nonfactory dressmakers. Upward-striving women for whom "the importance of the right clothes... cannot be overestimated" emulated the Gibson Girl, created by illustrator Charles Dana Gibson (Seebohm 1982, 36). An entire array of reasonably priced, machine-made Gibson Girl apparel—tailor-made suits, matching shirtwaists, skirts, corsets, and shoes—flourished as young women strove for the regal carriage, high collar, cinched-in waist appearance that Gibson's confident, unruffled model portrayed. The Sears catalogue in 1905 offered 150 versions of the shirtwaist (Greenwood and Murphy 1978).

More affluent Americans continued to be served by Paris couturiers and London tailors, but growing numbers of domestic dressmakers, milliners, and custom tailors proved competent in adapting European high fashion to the needs of their demanding clientele. Assisted by speedy distribution methods and special second-class mailing privileges, at least ten major fashion magazines reached a growing national audience of upper-middle-class and upward-striving women. Although rayon had been developed during the 1890s as an inexpensive substitute for silk, natural fibers predominated, and silk garments became much more commonplace. Rising disposable income and improved furriery spurred the popularity of fur garments. The effects of electrification, the migration of skilled furriers from Eastern Europe, a sewing machine that reliably produced an even seam and a strong, uniform stitch, and equalized tariffs on finished and unfinished furs snowballed: the number of fur workers jumped from 4,184 in 1899 to 10,271 in 1913.

By 1914 the women's clothing sector had pulled ahead of the men's in number of establishments (5,564) and value of product ($473.9 million). It trailed slightly in employment (168,907 wage earners) and value-added ($221.5 million). Between 1899 and 1914 the commercial manufacture of children's clothing, which dated from 1889, also grew rapidly.

On the eve of World War I the apparel industry was geographically concentrated. In 1914 New York City, with 28.2 percent of total apparel employment and accounting for 35.6 percent of the value of product, dominated eight of ten major clothing categories. It accounted for 71.7 percent of women's apparel, 62 percent of millinery and lace goods, 35.5 percent of the value of men's clothing, 40.9 percent of men's furnishings, and 30.5 percent of men's shirts. Troy, New York, accounted for nine-tenths of men's collars and cuffs; corsets were fabricated chiefly in Connecticut.

Most apparel establishments were small. In 1914 two-thirds of all plants employed no more than twenty wage earners; 27.7 percent, no more than five. At the other extreme, however, each of twenty-four establishments, most of them located outside New York City, employed more than 1,000 wage earners. Overall, 46.5 percent of apparel employment was concentrated in establishments of more than 100 workers. Women comprised 62.6 percent of all apparel wage earners. They accounted for slightly more than half of the workers employed in making men's clothing, 63.3 percent of those in women's clothing, and 80.8 percent in men's furnishings. At the outbreak of World War I the large pool of immigrant labor began to dry up, but black women migrating north to seek better job opportunities entered the garment trades in considerable numbers.

The period preceding World War I marks the beginning of a strong union movement in the apparel industry. To represent dressmakers primarily, the International Ladies Garment Workers Union (ILGWU) was launched, and spearheaded a number of strikes that wrested substantial concessions from employers. A walkout of Waist-Makers Local 25 of the ILGWU in September, 1909, triggered a three-month general strike that brought a settlement granting a fifty-two-hour workweek, four paid holidays, and recognition of the right of collective bargaining. This victory inspired 60,000 workers in cloak-making shops to embark on an industry-wide strike in July, 1910. Negotiations were hampered by bitter contention between groups of strikers and employers who were coreligionists from Russia and the Austro-Hungarian Empire. Banker Jacob Schiff and Louis Marshall, distinguished members of the close-knit German-Jewish community, intervened to help generate a historic agreement termed the Protocol of Peace. The landmark agreement provided for a fifty-hour workweek, ten paid holidays, time-and-a-half for overtime, and a minimum wage; abolished inside contracting, which dealt a severe blow to the operation of sweatshops; and established boards of arbitration and grievances.

Employers' continued resistance to unionization in the apparel industry was dramatically demonstrated in March, 1911, when the Asch Building in New York City caught fire and 850 persons working on an upper story for the Triangle Shirtwaist Company found escape doors locked against possible intrusion by labor organizers. One hundred and forty-six persons, mostly young female employees, but including one wife and two sons of company partners, died in the tragedy, and many more were maimed and disfigured. In 1913 New York State passed a workmen's compensation law to replace the 1910 law that had been declared unconstitutional.

In 1913 the International Fur Workers Union (IFWU) organized and affiliated with the American Federation of Labor (AFL). The creation of the IFWU followed a general strike of 10,000 furriers in 1912. Management refused to recognize the union, but acquiesced in a joint board to monitor sanitary conditions in the industry and a joint committee for the adjudication of disputes. In 1914 the Amalgamated Clothing Workers (ACW) was formed as an industrial union, largely to represent immigrant Jewish and Italian workers in men's clothing who were dissatisfied with the United Garment Workers, AFL, a craft union that represented only skilled workers. The ACW was headed by Sidney Hillman, who had led the nascent union in a successful strike in Chicago against Hart Schaffner & Marx. In 1920, 57.8 percent of the men and 46 percent of the women who worked in apparel production were organized; only 20.8 percent of all nonfarm workers were organized. One-fourth of the nation's female union membership were registered in New York State, and many were employed in the garment trades. The 1920s emerged as a watershed for the apparel industry, but the events of the preceding half-decade had presaged change. The outbreak of World War I in Europe sharply reduced migration to the United States. As labor shortages developed, large numbers of black men and women were drawn from the South to the industrial Northeast and Midwest, and growing numbers of black women were employed in textile mills and garment factories in the South and elsewhere. American participation in the conflict brought an influx of women into the labor force, some from the middle and upper middle classes. In the October, 1918, issue of Vogue magazine, an article entitled "What War Has Done to Clothes" stated, "Now that all women work, working clothes have acquired a new social status and chic." The article described practical women's clothing; informal loungewear to be worn after a hard day's work; long-sleeved dresses made of warm fabrics for heatless days; and uniforms, whose inclusion sanctioned, for the first time, women's donning male apparel (Seebohm 1982, 101). French couture was not dethroned, but its influence was challenged by American-born designers who showed their original creations under the charitable auspices of social arbiters like Mrs. Stuyvesant Fish and leading specialty shops like Henri Bendel and Bergdorf Goodman. The 1914–18 period has been termed "the beginning of America's stylistic coming-of-age" (Seebohm 1982, 102).

Perhaps more than anything else, the decade of the 1920s was dominated by what Frederick Lewis Allen termed the Revolution in Manners and Morals. The weight and kinds of material used in making women's clothing and the amount of clothing worn changed as the boyishly slender figure became popular, and the ready-to-wear industry devised production and merchandising techniques to reconcile individual tastes with mass production methods (Ewen and Ewen 1982, 228–29). The strength of consumer demands, unpredictable and at times beyond manipulation, is demonstrated by the changing height of skirt hems. The average distance above the ground was 6–7 inches in 1919; after rising considerably in 1920, the hemline dipped as Paris dressmakers forecast the return of longer skirts. American manufacturers accepted this premise, and shops stocked the longer skirts. Women buyers boycotted the longer skirts, however, and inventories piled up. Apparel producers finally bowed to their customers' preferences and resumed production of shorter skirts. By 1927 the hemline reached the knee and remained there until 1929. Women also favored silk or rayon stockings and underwear. Petticoat production virtually ceased. In 1928 the Journal of Commerce estimated that, during the preceding fifteen years, the amount of material required for a woman's complete costume (except for stockings) had dropped from more than nineteen yards to seven yards (Allen 1931, 103–5).

Apparel manufacturers and retailers followed the pulse of the changing marketplace, and young people under thirty became important customers. Market research disclosed that teenaged females were playing decisive roles in the selection of their clothing. Among families headed by immigrants, the second generation—children born in the United States—often set the clothing standards and persuaded parents to wear the fashions of the new country.

During a decade of growing affluence in urban America, an increasing share of disposable income shifted to such nonnecessities as personal transportation, entertainment, and travel. Clothing expenditures declined from 11 percent of total consumption in 1921 to 9 percent in 1930. Moreover, the trend toward shorter working hours and more leisure led to important changes in apparel usage. Fewer business suits and long-sleeved shirts were needed. Underwear consumption declined during the decade, and both men and women began wearing less and lighter apparel. Among the rising middle class, however, fur coats became de rigueur for members of both sexes.

Responding to powerful forces in the marketplace, the apparel industry altered its structure, shifted its geographic base of operations, and broadened its product mix. Standardized garments, such as men's shirts and trousers and boys' knee pants, required little skill to complete; makers of those garments began leaving New York City in search of lower rent and a plentiful labor supply and to escape restrictive union rules. Small towns in Pennsylvania, New Jersey, and upstate New York were the initial beneficiaries of this migration.

In New York City's garment district the manufacture of women's cloaks and suits in medium-sized, inside shops, where the garment was cut and fabricated in its entirety, gave way to the jobber-contractor system. The jobber purchased the fabrics, designed the garment, maintained cutting rooms, and stored and marketed the finished garment. The contractor, who was usually a former cutter and foreman with little or no capital, fabricated the garment and suggested design changes. Major forces propelling change included unpredictable shifts in fashion, which increased risk and intensified the seasonality of the business. Jobber-contractor arrangements reduced labor problems that some manufacturers associated with unionization but intensified competition among an increasing number of small contractors. In 1922, 77.1 percent of all plants producing women's apparel in the New York City area employed fewer than twenty workers. Only 48.4 percent of the shops would have fit the smallest size category at the turn of the century. By 1929 about three-fourths of all women's suits and cloaks made in New York City were produced in small contract shops. New York continued to provide the industry's largest pool of entrepreneurial talent in the high-fashion segment of the women's apparel industry.

The marketing of apparel changed extensively in the 1920s. Responding quickly to shifts in fashion, specialty shops such as Bergdorf Goodman and Saks Fifth Avenue in New York City, Neiman Marcus in Dallas, and Bullock Wilshire in Los Angeles surged in popularity. Department stores and chains began sending their buyers to New York apparel showrooms rather than waiting for salesmen to call. To reduce inventory losses, retailers placed orders more frequently but for smaller quantities. Apparel makers catered to out-of-town buyers and capitalized on the jobber-contractor system to process large orders quickly. New York City's role as the nation's foremost apparel spot market was enhanced by the availability of garment makers in other cities within a one-day delivery range of Manhattan.

A sharp cutback in apparel consumption during the Great Depression forced the apparel industry to retrench. Fashion reacted quickly to the stock market crash. Skirt lengths during the early 1930s plunged in tandem with stock prices. Fashionable evening dresses soon swept the ground. Ruffles, frills, and flounces were featured. Women once again took to wearing corsets. Milliners took heart as bobbed hair lost favor. Greater formality in evening wear was reflected in long white gloves, swallow-tail coats, and silk hats. Nonetheless, by 1933–34 clothing expenditures had plummeted to 8 percent of personal consumption and remained at that historically low level for the rest of the decade. With more and more women forced to sew their own garments at home, the pattern business thrived. When the readership of *Vogue* and *Vanity Fair* stagnated, publisher Condé Nast was persuaded to introduce a low-priced line of patterns modeled after clothes worn by Hollywood motion-picture stars. The highly successful *Hollywood Pattern Book* was distributed to leading middle-income chain stores rather than to exclusive *Vogue* assigned outlets. Nast's most successful magazine during the 1930s was *Glamour*, which was patterned after Street & Smith's *Mademoiselle* and aimed at ambitious career women. Nast's popular magazines featured smart yet inexpensive apparel and reflected his conviction that "style is as important in less expensive clothes as it is in those in the higher price level" (Seebohm 1982, 335).

The 1930s brought a few bright spots to penetrate the gloom surrounding the apparel industry. Seersucker and Palm Beach cloth, developed during the preceding decade, became popular for summer-weight clothing. Beginning in 1928 Sanforized fabric, cotton treated to control shrinkage, was used in a wide range of apparel. The Du Pont chemical company developed nylon and presaged the growing role of synthetic fibers and multifiber fabrics in the postwar era. In a generation starved for admirable role models, professional athletes and motion-picture stars exerted a profound impact on fashion. Knit polo shirts, tennis dresses, and riding breeches were purchased by those who could afford them. Clark Gable popularized the sport shirt, and, in 1933, Marlene Dietrich introduced women's trouser suits. Heiress Brenda

Duff Frazier debuted the strapless evening gown at her own dazzling entrance into society.

Some apparel firms were launched during the most dismal years of the 1930s and survived the decade. Beginning in July, 1933, with eight sewing machines and five female employees, the Stone Manufacturing Company in Greenville, South Carolina, made cotton bloomers of knit jersey that sold for $1.25 a dozen. The firm subsequently broadened its product line to include slips, aprons, housedresses, dustcaps, and children's sunsuits that sold for ten cents at Woolworth. In 1939 the U.S. National Resources Committee forecast that, with any sizable expansion of national income in the next decade, purchases of apparel and furnishings, medical care, and recreation would post a more than proportionate rate of gain. The war years validated this hypothesis; by 1945 apparel's share of consumer expenditures was 12 percent. A strong civilian demand combined with the extensive clothing requirements of the Allied military establishment to increase apparel producers' profits. Profits averaged 2.6 percent of net worth in 1938 and ranged from 9.8 percent to 11.8 percent of net worth during 1941–45. The emergence of teenagers as a salient market segment during the war years foreshadowed the impact of the baby boom generation. Bulky jeans, ribbed white ankle socks, and Sloppy Joe sweaters presaged the vast potential for junior fashions as purchasing power expanded.

Wartime also witnessed a sustained surge in union membership among apparel workers, a growth spurred by favorable New Deal legislation. The International Ladies Garment Workers Union grew from a low of 40,000 members in 1931–32 to 250,000 members in 1938 and continued to expand as apparel employment burgeoned. Led by David Dubinsky, ILGWU president from 1932 until 1966, the union assumed a major role in assisting cash-poor apparel firms to operate more efficiently, to initiate modernization programs, and to engage more extensively in advertising. These efforts, as well as a program promoting New York City as the fashion capital of the world, were sustained during the postwar period. A milestone in collective bargaining was reached in 1941 when the ILGWU signed a three-year agreement with firms employing 85,000 dressmakers. The Amalgamated Clothing Workers pursued a comparable path in fostering harmonious relations with firms in a fragmented, intensely competitive industry. The ACW encouraged increased productivity through time and motion studies, advocated the adoption of scientific management methods, and favored reliance on full-time arbitrators to maintain labor-management harmony and avoid strikes.

As the United States entered the post–World War II period the characteristics of the apparel industry remained molding forces: small scale, price competition, sensitivity to labor supply and cost, and dependence on surprisingly elastic consumer demand. These were influenced, however, by a number of new developments. The most notable began in the 1970s as the acceleration of imports from low-wage producers overseas forced the industry to adopt a broad range of response strategies. Apparel firms became larger and more diversified despite evidence that, in many industry subsectors, the optimum level of efficiency can be attained in small plants. Moreover, many firms began production overseas. Overall, the garment trades remained intensely competitive, and the attrition rate climbed as the industry continued to be buffeted by sudden shifts in fashion. By the 1980s, an inherent industry volatility, low returns on capital, and a high turnover rate had been intensified by market erosions associated with apparel imports.

The postwar apparel industry was favorably affected by an unanticipated baby boom from 1945 through 1958, whose effects reverberated through older age groupings for three decades. From 1950 to 1960 the 5–to–15–year cohort increased from 26.7 to 38.5 million and by 1970 to 45.3 million. During the 1960s the 20–to–24–year cohort increased 55 percent. During the 1970s the 25–to–44–year cohort increased from 48.4 million to 62.3 million, or 28.7 percent. During the first half of the 1980s the 35–to–44–year cohort grew by 22.2 percent. Despite favorable demographic trends, apparel prices in the postwar period rose far less than prices for most other goods and services. Nonetheless, consumer purchases of clothing as a percentage of overall consumption fell from a high of 12.6 percent in 1947–49 to 8.1 percent in 1960 and into the 7 percent range during the 1970s. Owing in part to the favorable shift in age distribution and the large increase in female employment, real disposable personal income rose 25 percent between 1974 and 1985, but per capita consumption of apparel (in stable dollars) rose 52 percent (Chmura 1987).

Apparel's declining share in aggregate consumer expenditures during much of the post–World War II period can be partly attributed to its decline as a status symbol. Casual, lightweight clothing gained popularity, a trend furthered by improvements in heating and air conditioning. All-weather topcoats, sports jackets and slacks, and separate blouses and skirts increased market shares at the expense of heavy winter overcoats, two- and three-piece suits, and dresses for business and evening wear. Only in the 1980s did increased female employment at the supervisory and managerial levels lead to some resurgence in the women's suit industry. The men's suit segment continued to slump, with only activewear and leisure clothing stimulating the dormant men's wear market. Fashion-oriented retailers like Bloomingdale's democratized the high-fashion market by pioneering designer boutiques within the department store.

The general shift to more casual and often lower priced garments influenced some manufacturers to abandon specialization and diversify their product mixes. The mortality rate of small, specialized firms remained inordinately high; even during the relatively prosperous mid–1960s, one of every five apparel firms had a life span of five years or less. Nonetheless, these firms continued to dominate as apparel producers sought niches secure from cutthroat foreign competition. In the mid–1970s, one-half of all apparel manufacturing establishments employed fewer than 20 persons; only 4 percent employed more than 250 persons. In general, value-added per manufacturing man-hour did not increase with plant size. For contractors in every product subsector, economies of scale were highest in plants with fewer than 20 employees; for manufacturers of men's and boy's nightwear and shirts, in plants up to 99 employees. Only in men's and boys' suits and coats did value-added per worker continue to increase until as many as 500 persons were employed.

The jobber-contractor system remained entrenched, especially in the women's segment of the industry. Nonetheless, by the mid–1950s its dominance began to wane in such industry subsectors as intimate apparel, where infrequent style changes enhanced the advantages of mass production. Some contractors became captive producers for department stores, apparel retail chains, and mail order houses because large retail outlets found it feasible to purchase directly from the manufacturer. For many specialty shops, however, wholesalers continued to help assemble goods, provide short-term credit, and alert retail merchants to mercurial market changes. A host of regional apparel marts in Chicago, Los Angeles, Dallas, Denver, Miami, and Atlanta benefitted small retailers and regional chains by conducting periodic trade shows that featured the latest Parisian and New York fashions.

Measurements of apparel industry profitability in the post–World War II era reveal that, on average, producers with annual sales over $20 million were more profitable than were smaller firms. The difference in favor of large firms was greatest in the men's apparel sector. There were marked variations in profitability, however, among the industry's diverse product lines. The most profitable lines consistently were men's suits and shirts and women's sportswear, foundation garments, and nightwear. Product lines with below average earnings included girls' apparel, boys' and youth's apparel, and, in some years, men's casual pants and jeans. These product lines were most subject to competitive pressure from domestic and foreign producers.

Low profit margins as well as low wages paid to production workers have been linked historically with the apparel industry's ease of entry, limited capital requirements, and labor intensiveness. These industry characteristics were not altered during the post–World War II era. Some producers were quick to adopt the latest technology, but the small size and low profitability of most apparel firms hampered the pace of modernization. By the early 1960s no more than 5 percent of the apparel industry had automated (Ghadar et al. 1987). Capital investment per employee more than doubled between 1960 and 1976, increasing from $2,800 to $6,100 per employee in 1972 dollars. Nonetheless, apparel remained among the lowest of all domestic manufacturing industries in capital invested per worker and in annual productivity gains.

Spurred by the rising threat of foreign competition, industry trade groups, major labor unions, and the U.S. Department of Commerce are trying to enhance productivity through cooperative research projects. The Textile Clothing Technology Corporation was established in 1980 to develop a system of robots, scanners, and automated sewing machines capable of sharply reducing the labor in assembling suits, shirts, and trousers. By mid-decade research efforts along these lines at Draper Laboratories, the Singer Company, and various universities appeared promising. Meanwhile, such large apparel producers as the Greif Company, a division of Genesco that markets eight lines of designer-label clothing, adopted computerized pattern making, grading, and cutting and improved quality and reduced labor costs considerably. In implementing this capital-intensive strategy, management discovered that organized labor was "a driving force supporting Greif's technology acquisitions to maintain competitiveness" (O'Rourke 1987, 37). Bill Loftin, founder of 240–employee Fashion Star, Inc., in rural Carroll County, Georgia, is representative of innovative, median-sized apparel producers. By extensively automating his sewing room and installing a Swiss-designed Eton system to convey fabric pieces from operator to operator, Loftin lowered the average cost per garment by as much as 43 percent. Technological advances such as these boosted productivity in the apparel industry 4 percent in 1984; the all-industry average that year was 2.8 percent. The high cost of laser-based cutting and stitching machines, microcomputer controls, and robots confines progress primarily to the largest, most financially secure, and innovative garment-producing firms.

Confidence in the future of the U.S. apparel industry has been sorely tried by the growing inroads of foreign-made garments into the domestic market. During the 1960s apparel imports increased from less than 2 percent of domestic consumption to about 5 percent; the markets most deeply penetrated were men's shirts, women's blouses, and children's wear. By the 1970s the styling and quality of apparel imports had improved and foreign marketers aggressively competed in a broadening range of higher-priced product lines. From 1972 to 1980 the apparel trade deficit increased at a compound annual rate of 14.1 percent; by the early 1980s apparel exports barely exceeded $1 billion, but imports exceeded $6.6 billion. By 1984, $19 worth of apparel was imported for every $1 exported. The trade deficit reached $11.4 billion, and imports represented one-fourth of the total wholesale value of apparel sold in the nation. Concern in the industry was accentuated by the growing importance of Far Eastern suppliers of apparel, whose labor costs are among the world's lowest. In 1984, 69 percent of all apparel imports came from Hong Kong, Taiwan, Korea, and China. Imports from Sri Lanka, although relatively slight, are increasing rapidly. Japan, which accounted for 35 percent of apparel imports in 1964, exported only 3 percent twenty years later. Although apparel consumption in the United States grew considerably from 1973 until the mid–1980s, imports accounted for the difference (Ghadar et al. 1987).

One response to declining industry profitability is "offshore sourcing": processing and assembling domestic-designed garment components beyond the nation's borders and shipping them back for final sale. Under item 807 of the tariff schedules, importers of semimanufactured and manufactured goods assembled overseas from domestic materials pay duties only on the value-added. An apparel firm using item 807 could buy an offshore facility, engage in a joint venture, use contractors, or enter an agreement with organizations that provide packages. Apparel imported under item 807 increased from less than 3 percent of the dollar value of total apparel imports in 1970 to 10 percent by 1974, and stabilized at about that level. Mexico, with sister plants in Southern California and along the Texas border, emerged as the dominant 807 source; considerable production was also concentrated in five Caribbean and Latin American nations. Although spokesmen for organized labor have sharply criticized these production arrangements, apparel industry leaders contend that jobs that would have been captured by foreign producers have been saved. Apparel producers have learned, however, that 807 sourcing ties up working capital and is beset by quality control problems and political instability.

In an effort to reverse the rising tide of foreign-made garments, apparel producers have joined forces with organized labor to effect rigid restraints, including tariffs and quotas, on imports. During the 1970s the negotiation of a Multifiber Arrangement (MFA) with a group of fifty nations, and its subsequent renewal through July, 1991, established an umbrella for a host of bilateral agreements. Apparel became the only U.S. manufacturing industry with worldwide import controls and provisions for orderly marketing agreements. With the domestic market during the 1970s expanding at an annual rate below 6 percent, the MFA envisioned a gradual, albeit controlled, enlargement of market shares by various imported apparel items. The bilateral agreements, however, varied widely in their capacity to control the growth of imports from individual countries. Only a limited number of apparel products were subject to specific restraints, so newly emerging apparel producers captured large segments of the U.S. market before joint negotiations to limit imports could be arranged.

President Ronald Reagan's veto of the Textile and Apparel Trade Enforcement Act of 1986 convinced industry leaders and trade associations that they could not rely on political agreements to stem the import tide. One proposal called for major segments of the industry to view themselves primarily as middlemen between overseas producers and domestic retailers, a strategy that implied a dramatic downsizing of domestic apparel production. One proponent of this strategy, the chairman of the board at Williamson-Dickie Manufacturing Company in Ft. Worth, Texas, envisioned "an intensely international apparel industry," under which "one could easily buy a garment made in Jamaica, from cloth woven in Italy, from cotton grown in Mexico, blended with polyester made in Korea from petrochemicals made in Louisiana from oil produced in Venezuela and shipped to the store from a warehouse in Fort Worth" (Williamson 1985, 20).

Other industry leaders, viewing C. Dickie Williamson's forecast as a worst-case last resort, renewed their efforts to capitalize on still potent domestic competitive edges. These include greater exploitation of the contributions of an expanding corps of native fashion designers, male and female, based in California as well as in New York City. "Crafted with Pride in the U.S.A.," a resort to chauvinism—especially when it includes a highly publicized tour by Miss America, garbed exclusively in U.S. designed and fabricated apparel—has in itself limited potential for success, but combined with "quick response" prospects brighten. Quick response schedules initiated by industry powerhouses Levi Strauss and Milliken & Company as part of their "partners-in-progress" program enabled Milliken to produce fabric to Levi's exacting standards in sizes that permitted the apparel maker to utilize every inch of material. Confident of Milliken's quality and reliable delivery record, Levi suspended inspection of the goods, enabling Milliken to ship directly to Levi's factory and avoid warehousing expenses. Furthermore, advanced data and telecommunications linkups saved Levi the time and expense of sorting the material at the plant. The result was a radical reduction of delivery time and inventory. In another quick-response linkup, Burlington Industries supplied fabric to the Lanier Clothes Division of Oxford Industries in time for Lanier to restock Penney's inventory in forty-eight to seventy-two hours. During a five-month pilot project, Penney stores that relied on the linkup enjoyed higher sales of men's suits and sports coats than the Penney stores that did not use quick response. Success with the pilot project enabled the three participating firms to extend the quick-response linkup. Perhaps such programs will smooth the path to sustained progress for the embattled apparel industry.

BIBLIOGRAPHIC ESSAY

An understanding of the historical development of the apparel industry can be gained by examining changing styles and the major forces promoting change. Douglas Gorsline (1952) uses chronologically dated pages and almost 1,800 detailed drawings in his encyclopedia of historical dress. An extensive section on U.S. dress for men and women covers the period 1840 to the early twentieth century. For more recent years, Gorsline's work should be supplemented with Catherine B. MacLaren's (1985) brief survey of fashion, 1900 to 1970, and Ellen Melinkoff's (1984) lively social history of women's clothing, 1950 to 1980. An excellent introduction to creating and marketing fashion is provided by Kathryn M. Greenwood and Mary Fox Murphy (1978). They include a section on fashion trends from 1900 to the 1970s as well as chapters on fashion makers, manufacturing, and merchandising. Jeannette A. Jarnow and Beatrice Judelle's text on the business of fashion has gone through four editions since 1965. It contains well-rounded sections on materials, apparel producers, couture, and retailers. The readings supplementing the text are well selected. Especially helpful are "What Were They Wearing? 1910–1960," taken from *Women's Wear Daily*; an essay by Virginia Pope, "The Development of American Creativity in Fashion"; and a biographical sketch of Norman Norell, acknowledged dean of American designers.

Within the American setting, themes dealing with immigrant assimilation, upward mobility, mass consumption, and the democratization of fashion are important. The role of apparel and the clothing industry in facilitating these developments is argued persuasively and at times brilliantly in Stuart and Elizabeth Ewen's *Channels of Desire: Mass Images and the Shaping of American Consciousness* (1982). In the literature of self-improvement there are scores of books stressing the importance of appropriate dress. John T. Molloy's *Dress for Success* (1976) and *The Woman's Dress for Success Book* (1978) are an adequate sample. Molloy, whose credentials include counseling companies "on problems of dress" and giving clothing advice to executives of a half-dozen Fortune 500 corporations, includes brief chapters on advice for minorities, especially blacks and Hispanics. In essence he advises, "Dress conservatively; wear only those garments that are considered upper-middle class symbols—pinstripe suits, end-on-end blue shirts, Ivy League ties" (1976, 152). For upward-striving males seeking positions of influence, Egon Von Furstenberg recommends apparel that conveys the "power look" (1979). Among those promoting social mobility during the first half of the twentieth century none was more influential than Condé Nast, publisher of *Vogue* and *Vanity Fair*. Caroline Seebohm's (1982) well-researched and sprightly life and times of Nast is indispensable in understanding the significant role of apparel in Nast's work. Also vital in assessing the impact of the World War I era on morals, manners, and clothing styles is the work of Frederick Lewis Allen (1931). A book on couture and the emergence of American designers is Caroline R. Milbank's (1985) survey of first-rank designers. It should be supplemented by the witty and gossipy memoirs of Diana Vreeland (1984), fashion editor of *Harper's Bazaar* and editor-in-chief of *Vogue*.

The apparel industry is assessed in any number of "structure of industry" texts. Particularly helpful for an introduction to the economics of the industry is E. B. Alderfer and H. E. Michl's *Economics of American Industry* (1957). Various sectors of the apparel industry have their own association and trade journals that contain useful information. In a class by itself is

Women's Wear Daily (WWD), dating from 1910. Katie Kelly's (1972) discursive assessment of the evolution of the industry through the pages of WWD is useful. The umbrella trade association for the industry, American Apparel Manufacturers Association, is its prolocutor on public policy issues and the source for an annual economic profile of the industry. The profile includes current and historical statistics on apparel industry employment, payrolls, capital expenditures on new plant and equipment, business failures, exports, and imports. It is a convenient source of data because it includes nearly all major economic series reported by the federal government as well as those by a number of private organizations.

Technology has, of course, been vital to the development of the ready-to-wear clothing industry. Grace R. Cooper (1976) provides an excellent, illustrated account of the invention and improvement of sewing machinery, and Ruth Brandon's (1977) carefully researched biography of Isaac Singer is entertaining as well as informative. The early history of Singer's international business has been told by Robert Bruce Davies, *Peacefully Working to Conquer the World: Singer Sewing Machines in Foreign Markets, 1854–1920* (1976), and in more detail for Imperial Russia by Fred V. Carstensen (1984). Not to be missed, however, is Ross Thomson's article in the *Journal of Economic History* (1987). Thomson's thesis that shifting sales are linked to technological innovation is based on a study of almost 2,000 sewing machine patents. Mary T. O'Rourke (1987) provides an interesting case study of recent technological advances in the men's high-quality apparel sector. At a more popular level, but insightful on a range of issues, is an article in *Business Week*, "Apparel's Last Stand: The Search for a Niche, New Technology, and Merger Partners" (1979). Joel Seidman's *Needle Trades* (1942) remains the best introduction to earlier trends in technology as well as other facets of the evolution of the apparel industry.

The historic small-scale, intensely competitive, high-turnover, noncorporate character of the garment industry largely explains the paucity of solidly researched company studies. Ed Cray's (1978) wide-ranging survey of Levi Strauss is illuminating. Much smaller in scale, but well done, is Richard H. Keehn's (1986) survey of Jockey International. In 1909 Jockey developed the closed-crotch union suit; in the mid–1930s, men's briefs; and, after World War II, bikini-style briefs. Roger Waldinger's (1986) study of immigrants and enterprise in the New York apparel trades casts light on the rise of ethnic entrepreneurs, as does Irving Howe's comprehensive *World of Our Fathers: The Journey of the East European Jews to America and the Life They Found and Made* (1976). The role of skilled, petty capitalist furriers is charmingly depicted in Sara Sandberg's memoir *Mama Made Minks* (1964). Nonetheless, the diverse motivations to succeed among apparel manufacturers of the 1890 to 1930 era—often first-generation Americans—are best described in a novel. Abraham Cahan (1917), a contemporary observer and longtime editor of the *Jewish Daily Forward*, brilliantly depicts the emergence of mass production in the women's garment industry. Of lesser quality, but based on reality, are Norman Bogner's *Seventh Avenue* (1966) and Lewis Orde's *Rag Trade* (1978), which deal with the men's clothing industry. James Traub's article in *Smithsonian* (1985) examines prospects for the industry from the vantage point of the producers. Egal Feldman, *Fit for Men: A Study of New York's Clothing Trade* (1960), contains much information on major firms in the industry. The speeches made by leading business executives at dinners sponsored by the Newcomen Society are not critical assessments of the firms discussed; nonetheless, useful information and insights are often conveyed, sometimes unintentionally. Talks by Eugene E. Stone III (1985) of Stone Manufacturing Company and C. Dickie Williamson (1985) of Williamson-Dickie Manufacturing Company make important contributions to the history of the apparel industry in the Southeast and Southwest during the twentieth century. The unpublished paper by Harry Kuniansky (1987) focuses on a southern apparel producer during the post–World War II period.

Geographic shifts in the location of the apparel industry are illuminated in the essays by T. Arnold Hill and Elizabeth L. Otey in the *Annals of the American Academy of Political and Social Science* (1931). The entire issue was devoted to the advent of industry in the South. The Fantas Company's (1966) study of Appalachia as a possible site for an expanding apparel industry assesses the pluses and minuses of the region. The articles by David Avery and Gene D. Sullivan (1985) and James C. Leonard III (1986) examine the status and prospects of the garment trades in the Southeast in the light of growing foreign competition. Emma L. Fundaburk (1966) offers a scholarly assessment of the apparel industry's prospects on Hawaiian islands other than Oahu. Her prognosis is pessimistic in the absence of government policies to directly encourage the relocation of plants. José de la Torre's (1986) work is an important contribution to the history of trends in the clothing industry in developed countries and is thus relevant to the industry's prospects within the continental United States.

More research has been directed to labor conditions and labor-management relations within the apparel industry than to the less dramatic internal operations of the firms. In addition to the splendid studies by Howe (1976) and Moses Rischin (1962), the serious student must consult a much earlier but still standard study on women's garment workers by Louis Levine (1924). Ande Manners's *Poor Cousins* (1972) is a well-written, useful supplement to Rischin's and Howe's accounts of East European Jews in the garment trades. In recent decades there has been a spate of research on the changing role of Italian immigrants in the clothing industry and the relations between Jewish and Italian workers in production as well as within the labor unions. Humbert S. Nelli's (1970) work on Italians in Chicago, 1880–1930, contains interesting information on garment workers as well as on the 1910 strike at the Hart Schaffner & Marx apparel plant. Nelli's *From*

Immigrant to Ethnic: The Italian Americans (1983) is a broad-based study that should also be consulted. Thomas Kessner (1977) looks at the interaction and diverse fortunes of Italian and Jewish immigrants in New York City from 1880 to 1915. Rosara L. Passero (1978) examines ethnicity in the men's clothing industry from 1880 to 1950, focusing on the Italian experience in Philadelphia. Barbara M. Wertheimer (1977) examines women's work in the men's clothing industry before World War I and their participation in the Amalgamated Clothing Workers of America. The work edited by Alfredo Mirande and Evangelina Enriquez, *La Chicana: The Mexican-American Woman* (1979), includes an excellent section on employment conditions in the apparel industry in the Southwest. George M. Green's (1971) article, "The ILGWU in Texas, 1930–1970," illuminates the growth of the industry in Texas, its labor force, working conditions, and unionization. Steven Fraser studies the interaction between ethnic groups of workers and between the groups and management. His "Landslayt and Paesani: Ethnic Conflict and Cooperation in the Amalgamated Clothing Workers of America" (1986) underscores the importance of the cultural legacies, seasonal unemployment, and periodic layoffs so characteristic of the industry. "Landslayt and Paesani" should be read in conjunction with Fraser's article in the *Business History Review* (1983) in which he examines the intense competition between small, marginal producers and large, prosperous producers that is based on the costs and conditions of labor.

Although of uneven quality, a large body of literature traces the rise of organized labor within the apparel industry and the shifting relationships between workers, management, and unions. James W. Kuhn's chapter in Ivar Berg's *The Business of America* (1968) is a brief, useful introduction. Jesse T. Carpenter's (1972) *Competition and Collective Bargaining in the Needle Trades, 1910–1967* is the basic work to be consulted, although Levine (1924) is still useful. The study by Edwin Fenton (1975) on Italian and American labor to 1920 contains information unavailable elsewhere. The well-researched articles by Maxine S. Seller (1986) and Alice Kessler-Harris (1976) bring to the forefront the role of women in the emergence of the International Ladies Garment Workers Union and the garment strikes of the early twentieth century. An interesting comparison is the study by Catherine Macleod (1974) on the Toronto, Canada, dressmakers' strike of 1931. Matthew Josephson's (1952) biography of Sidney Hillman and David Dubinsky's (1977) autobiography are indispensable. The unique relationship between the unions and management—antagonists dividing up the industry's profits, but cooperating to assure continued profitability—is detailed in both works.

The retail marketing of apparel has been more extensively researched than has its production. An excellent introduction to the development of the department store is Robert Hendrickson's lively and anecdotal *The Grand Emporiums: The Illustrated History of America's Great Department*

Stores (1979). His work highlights the treatment of women in the development of apparel retailing, including Mary Ann Magnin, founder in 1880 of San Francisco's I. Magnin, and Lena Himmelstein, an immigrant seamstress who launched Lane Bryant as a pioneer maker of maternity gowns. Among the large number of general studies of department stores, many of them "puff jobs," particularly useful in understanding the retailers' strategies for apparel are Ralph M. Hower's (1943) history of Macy's, 1858 to 1919 and Robert W. Twyman's (1954) study of Marshall Field, 1852–1906. Marshall Field was both producer and major wholesaler of a range of apparel. J. C. Penney's overview of a half-century career (1950) provides insights into the mass-marketing practices of a pioneer retailer, and includes a digression into the proper wrapping of men's shirts. Booton Herndon (1972) gives an insightful picture of the process of product upgrading as approached by Montgomery Ward. Mark Stevens's (1979) study of Bloomingdale's is valuable in showing how high-quality, designer-produced ready-to-wear replaced Parisian-inspired haute couture, at least among the upper middle class, during the post–1950 period. Jane Cahill's *Success on a Shoestring: Fifty-three Smaller Fashion Shops and How They Grew* (1953) is a series of case studies on entrepreneurship among small specialty retailers which were first published in *Women's Wear Daily*. Opinionated and insightful, Stanley Marcus's memoirs of his career with Neiman Marcus (1974), supplemented by his *Quest for the Best* (1979), is essential for an understanding of the strategies suitable to the successful specialty store. His discussions of changes in fashion and his views on American and foreign apparel designers are informative and thought-provoking.

The difficulties facing the apparel industry during the 1970s and 1980s have been the subject of numerous conferences and industry and academic studies. The best overall treatment is that by Fariborz Ghadar et al. (1987); but the work by Jeffrey S. Arpan et al. (1982) and W. Denney Freeston, Jr. (1983), on international competition and the influence of technology should not be overlooked. The publications by the International Labor Organization on the social and labor practices of multinational enterprises (1984) and the employment effects within the industry of profound shifts in apparel trade balances (1980a, 1980b) provide an international dimension to the industry's problems. In an article on the effect of exchange rate variations on apparel imports, Christine Chmura (1987) reports that a 1 percent increase in exchange rates is linked to a 1.4 percent increase in imports. She concludes that, although exchange rate variations do have a significant effect on apparel imports, changes in income have an even greater impact.

The apparel industry's search for greater security and assured profitability is detailed in a number of works. Donald W. Huffmire's (1971) unpublished dissertation provides interesting information on textile producers' growing interest in forward integration through the apparel stage, a strategy that has been pursued by a number of firms since his work was conducted. José de la Torre et al. (1978) examine a broad range of coping strategies, as do Avery and Sullivan (1985) in their study for the Federal Reserve Bank of Atlanta. The industry's prime trade association, the American Apparel Manufacturers Association, has also been active in this area and has produced a useful compendium for its members, *Apparel Manufacturing Strategies* (1984).

BIBLIOGRAPHY

Alderfer, E. B., and H. E. Michl. *Economics of American Industry.* 3d ed. New York: McGraw-Hill, 1957.

Allen, Frederick Lewis. *Only Yesterday: An Informal History of the Nineteen-Twenties.* New York: Harper & Bros., 1931.

American Apparel Manufacturers Association. *Apparel Manufacturing Strategies.* Arlington, VA: AAMA, 1984.

"Apparel's Last Stand: The Search for a Niche, New Technology, and Merger Partners." *Business Week* (May 14, 1979): 60–70.

Argensinger, Jo Ann E. "Struggle Without Triumph: Women Workers and the 1932 Garment Strike in Baltimore." Paper presented at the Southern Labor History Conference, Atlanta, GA, April 24–26, 1980.

Arpan, Jeffrey S., et al. *The U.S. Apparel Industry: International Challenge, Domestic Response.* Atlanta: Georgia State University, Business Publishing Division, 1982.

Avery, David, and Gene D. Sullivan. "Changing Patterns: Reshaping the Southeastern Textile-Apparel Complex." Federal Reserve Bank of Atlanta. *Economic Review* (November 1985): 34–44.

Bogner, Norman. *Seventh Avenue.* New York: Coward McCann, 1966.

Brandon, Ruth. *A Capitalist Romance: Singer and the Sewing Machine.* Philadelphia: J. B. Lippincott, 1977.

Cahan, Abraham. *The Rise of David Levinsky.* New York: Harper & Bros., 1917.

Cahill, Jane. *Success on a Shoestring: Fifty-three Smaller Fashion Shops and How They Grew.* New York: Fairchild Publications, 1953.

Carpenter, Jesse T. *Competition and Collective Bargaining in the Needle Trades, 1910–1967.* Ithaca, NY: Cornell University Press, 1972.

Carstensen, Fred V. *American Enterprise in Foreign Markets.* Chapel Hill: University of North Carolina Press, 1984.

Chmura, Christine. "The Effect of Exchange Rate Variation on U.S. Textile and Apparel Imports." Federal Reserve Bank of Richmond. *Economic Review* (May/June 1987).

Cooper, Grace R. *The Sewing Machine: Its Invention and Development.* 2d ed. Washington, DC: Smithsonian Institution Press, 1976.

Cray, Ed. *Levi's.* Boston: Houghton Mifflin, 1978.

Davies, Robert Bruce. *Peacefully Working to Conquer the World: Singer Sewing Machines in Foreign Markets, 1854–1920.* New York: Arno Press, 1976.

de la Torre, José. *Clothing-Industry Adjustment in Developed Countries.* New York: St. Martin's Press, 1986.

de la Torre, José, et al. *Corporate Responses to Import Competition in the U.S.*

Apparel Industry. Atlanta: Georgia State University, Business Publishing Division, 1978.

Dubinsky, David, with A. H. Raskin. *David Dubinsky: A Life with Labor*. New York: Simon & Schuster, 1977.

Ewen, Stuart, and Elizabeth Ewen. *Channels of Desire: Mass Images and the Shaping of American Consciousness*. New York: McGraw-Hill, 1982.

Fantas Company. *The Apparel Industry. Report No. 3. The Appalachian Location Research Studies Program*. Prepared for the Appalachian Regional Commission. New York: Fantas, 1966.

Feldman, Egal. *Fit for Men: A Study of New York's Clothing Trade*. Washington, DC: Public Affairs Press, 1960.

Fenton, Edwin. *Immigrants and Unions: A Case Study of Italians and American Labor, 1870–1920*. Reprint. New York: Arno Press, 1975.

Fraser, Steven. "Combined and Uneven Development in the Men's Clothing Industry." *Business History Review* 57 (Winter 1983): 522–47.

———. "Landslayt and Paesani: Ethnic Conflict and Cooperation in the Amalgamated Clothing Workers of America." In *"Struggle a Hard Battle": Essays on Working-Class Immigrants*, edited by Dirk Hoerder, 280–303. DeKalb: Northern Illinois State University Press, 1986.

Freeston, W. Denney, Jr. *The Competitive Status of the U.S. Fibers, Textiles, and Apparel Complex: A Study of the Influences of Technology in Determining Industrial Competitive Advantage*. Washington, DC: National Academy Press, 1983.

Fundaburk, Emma L. *Characteristics, Problems and Potentials of Apparel Manufacturing in the Neighbor Islands*. Honolulu: University of Hawaii, 1966.

Ghadar, Fariborz, et al. *U.S. Industrial Competitiveness: The Case of the Textile and Apparel Industries*. Lexington, MA: D. C. Heath, 1987.

Gorsline, Douglas. *What People Wore: A Visual History of Dress from Ancient Times to Twentieth Century America*. New York: Bonanza Books, 1952.

Green, George M. "The ILGWU in Texas, 1930–1970." *Journal of Mexican-American History* 1 (Spring 1971): 144–69.

Greenwood, Kathryn M., and Mary Fox Murphy. *Fashion Innovation and Marketing*. New York: Macmillan, 1978.

Hamilton, Alexander. "Report on Manufactures." Communicated to the House of Representatives, December 5, 1791. Reprinted in *Alexander Hamilton's Papers on Public Credit, Commerce, and Finance*, edited by Samuel McKee, Jr., 175–276. New York: Liberal Arts Press, 1957.

Helfgott, Roy B. "Women's and Children's Apparel." In *Made in New York: Case Studies in Metropolitan Manufacturing*, edited by Max Hall. Cambridge, MA: Harvard University Press, 1959.

Hendrickson, Robert. *The Grand Emporiums: The Illustrated History of America's Great Department Stores*. New York: Stein & Day, 1979.

Herndon, Booton. *Satisfaction Guaranteed: An Unconventional Report to Today's Consumers*. New York: McGraw-Hill, 1972.

Hill, T. Arnold. "Negroes in Southern Industry." *Annals of the American Academy of Political and Social Science* 153 (January 1931): 170–81.

Hix, Charles, and Brian Burdine. *Dressing Right: A Guide for Men*. New York: St. Martin's Press, 1978.

Howe, Irving, with Kenneth Libo. *World of Our Fathers: The Journey of the East European Jews to America and the Life They Found and Made.* New York: Harcourt Brace Jovanovich, 1976.

Hower, Ralph M. *History of Macy's of New York, 1858–1919.* Cambridge, MA: Harvard University Press, 1943.

Huffmire, Donald W. "An Analysis of the Strategies of the Textile Mill Products Industry in the Post World War II Period." Ph.D. diss., Atlanta, Georgia State University, 1971.

International Labor Organization. *The Employment Effects in the Clothing Industry of Changes in International Trade: Second Tripartite Technical Meeting for the Clothing Industry.* Geneva: ILO, 1980a.

———. *General Report: General Tripartite Technical Meeting for the Clothing Industry.* Geneva: ILO, 1980b.

———. *Social and Labour Practices of Multinational Enterprises in the Textile, Clothing and Footwear Industries.* Geneva: ILO, 1984.

Jarnow, Jeannette A., and Beatrice Judelle. *Inside the Fashion Business: Text and Readings.* New York: John Wiley, 1965.

———. *Inside the Fashion Business: Text and Readings.* 4th ed. New York: Macmillan, 1987.

Josephson, Matthew. *Sidney Hillman: Statesman of American Labor.* Garden City, NY: Doubleday, 1952.

Keehn, Richard H. "Jockey International: Product and Marketing Innovation in Underwear." In *Essays in Economic and Business History: Selected Papers from the Economic and Business Historical Society,* edited by Edwin J. Perkins, vol. 4 (1983–85), 121–32. Los Angeles: University of Southern California, History Department, 1986.

Kelly, Katie. *The Wonderful World of Women's Wear Daily.* New York: Saturday Review Press, 1972.

Kessler-Harris, Alice. "Organizing the Unorganizable: Three Jewish Women and Their Union." *Labor History* 17 (Winter 1976): 5–23.

Kessner, Thomas. *The Golden Door: Italian and Jewish Immigrant Mobility in New York City, 1880–1915.* New York: Oxford University Press, 1977.

Kuhn, James W. "Business Unionism in a Laboristic Society." In *The Business of America,* edited by Ivar Berg, 284–310. New York: Harcourt, Brace & World, 1968.

Kuniansky, Harry. "A Business History of MLM Company, 1966–1984." Paper presented at the annual meeting of the Economic and Business Historical Society, San Francisco, April 25, 1987.

Leonard, James C. III. "The Southeast's Textile/Apparel Trade and the Import Threat." Federal Reserve Bank of Atlanta. *Economic Review* (January 1986): 16–19.

Leuchtenburg, William Edward. *The Perils of Prosperity, 1914–32.* Chicago: University of Chicago Press, 1958.

Levine, Louis [Louis Lorwin, pseud.]. *The Women's Garment Workers: A History of the International Ladies Garment Workers.* New York: B. W. Huebach, 1924.

MacLaren, Catherine B. *Fashion: 1900 to 1970.* Cincinnati: Mosaic Press, 1985.

Macleod, Catherine. "Women in Production: The Toronto Dressmakers' Strike of

1931." In *Women at Work, Ontario, 1850–1930*, edited by Janice Acton et al., 309–29. Toronto, Canada: The Women's Press, 1974.

Manners, Ande. *Poor Cousins*. New York: Coward, McCann & Geoghegan, 1972.

Marcus, Stanley. *Minding the Store: A Memoir*. Boston: Little, Brown, 1974.

——. *Quest for the Best*. New York: Viking, 1979.

Melinkoff, Ellen. *What We Wore: An Offbeat Social History of Women's Clothing, 1950–1980*. New York: William Morrow, 1984.

Milbank, Caroline R. *Couture: The Great Designers*. New York: Stewart Tabori & Chang, 1985.

Mirande, Alfredo, and Evangelina Enriquez, eds. *La Chicana: The Mexican-American Woman*. Chicago: University of Chicago Press, 1979.

Molloy, John T. *Dress for Success*. New York: Warner Books, 1976.

——. *The Woman's Dress for Success Book*. New York: Warner Books, 1978.

Nelli, Humbert S. *The Italians in Chicago, 1880–1930: A Study in Ethnic Mobility*. New York: Oxford University Press, 1970.

——. *From Immigrant to Ethnic: The Italian Americans*. New York: Oxford University Press, 1983.

Orde, Lewis. *Rag Trade*. New York: St. Martin's Press, 1978.

O'Rourke, Mary T. "The Greif Company." *Retail Driven Technology* (September 1987): 35–42.

Otey, Elizabeth L. "Women and Children in Southern Industry." *Annals of the American Academy of Political and Social Science* 153 (January 1931): 163–69.

Passero, Rosara L. "Ethnicity in the Men's Ready-Made Clothing Industry, 1880–1950: The Italian Experience in Philadelphia." Ph.D. diss., University of Pennsylvania, 1978.

Penney, J. C. *Fifty Years with the Golden Rule*. New York: Harper & Bros., 1950.

Rischin, Moses. *The Promised City: New York's Jews, 1870–1914*. Cambridge, MA: Harvard University Press, 1962.

Sandberg, Sara. *Mama Made Minks*. New York: Doubleday, 1964.

Seebohm, Caroline. *The Man Who Was Vogue: The Life and Times of Condé Nast*. New York: Viking Press, 1982.

Seidman, Joel. *The Needle Trades*. New York: Farrar & Rinehart, 1942.

Selekman, B. M., et al. "The Clothing and Textile Industries." In *Food, Clothing and Textile Industries, Wholesale Markets and Retail Shopping and Financial Districts, Present Trends and Probable Future Developments*. Vol. IB. 1929. Reprint. New York: Arno Press, 1974.

Seller, Maxine S. "The Uprising of the Twenty Thousand: Sex, Class, and Ethnicity in the Shirtwaist Makers' Strike of 1909." In *"Struggle a Hard Battle": Essays on Working-Class Immigrants*, edited by Dirk Hoerder, 254–79. DeKalb: Northern Illinois State University Press, 1986.

Stevens, Mark. *"Like No Other Store in the World": The Inside Story of Bloomingdale's*. New York: Thomas Y. Crowell, 1979.

Stone, Eugene E. III. "Stone Manufacturing Company: The First Half Century of Clothing a Changing World." New York: Newcomen Society of the United States, 1985.

Tentler, Leslie W. *Wage-Earning Women: Industrial Work and Family Life in the United States, 1900–1930*. New York: Oxford University Press, 1979.

Thomson, Ross. "Learning by Selling and Invention: The Case of the Sewing Machine." *Journal of Economic History* 47 (June 1987): 433–45.

Traub, James. "Behind All of That Glitz and Glitter, the Garment District Means Business." *Smithsonian* (August 1985): 30–37.

Tryon, Rolla M. *Household Manufactures in the United States, 1640–1860.* Ph.D. diss., University of Chicago, 1915. Reprint. New York: Augustus M. Kelley, 1966.

Twyman, Robert W. *History of Marshall Field and Company, 1852–1906.* Philadelphia: University of Pennsylvania Press, 1954.

U.S. Bureau of the Census. *Manufactures of the United States in 1860: Compiled from the Original Returns of the Eighth Census.* Washington, DC: U.S. Government Printing Office, 1865.

U.S. Council on Wage and Price Stability. Textiles/Apparel. *A Study of the Textile and Apparel Industries.* Washington, DC: U.S. Government Printing Office, 1978.

U.S. National Resources Committee. *The Structure of the American Economy. Part I, Basic Characteristics.* A report prepared by the industrial section under the direction of Gardiner C. Means. Washington, DC: U.S. Government Printing Office, 1939.

Von Furstenberg, Egon. *The Power Look.* New York: Fawcett, 1979.

Vreeland, Diana. *D. V.* New York: Knopf, 1984.

Waldinger, Roger. *Through the Eye of the Needle: Immigrants and Enterprise in the New York Garment Trades.* New York: New York University Press, 1986.

Walsh, Margaret. "The Democratization of Fashion: The Emergence of the Women's Dress Pattern Industry." *Journal of American History* 66 (September 1979): 299–313.

Wells, David A. *Recent Economic Changes and Their Effect on the Production and Distribution of Wealth and Well-Being of Society.* New York: D. Appleton, 1890.

Wendt, Lloyd, and Herman Kogan. *Give the Lady What She Wants!* Chicago: Rand McNally, 1952.

Wertheimer, Barbara M. *We Were There: The Story of Working Women in America.* New York: Pantheon, 1977.

Williamson, C. Dickie. "Williamson-Dickie Manufacturing Company: A Partnership for Progress." New York: Newcomen Society of the United States, 1985.

Part IV

Lumber
ESIC 24.0

LUMBER AND WOOD PRODUCTS, 24.0

_____ MICHAEL V. NAMORATO

The lumber industry in the United States is distinguished by its longevity. Considering the usefulness of wood for construction and the United States' appetite for building, it is not surprising that the lumber industry dates from the colonial period. Its growth has fluctuated, but the industry has demonstrated a penchant for continuing development and interaction with forestry, conservation, public land law, tariffs, and westward migration. The availability of virgin timerlands and, in more recent decades, second-growth forests dictated the regional development of the lumber industry. Through scientific conservation and technology, the industry progressed from labor-intensive to capital-intensive. As a business enterprise, the lumber industry uniquely reflects general patterns of American business.

OVERVIEW

In the colonial era, lumbering was a means of clearing agricultural land and supplying England with raw materials. Before 1830 forests were regarded more as obstacles to agriculture than as valuable, exploitable resources. The northeastern United States dominated the industry, and Maine was the leading producer of lumber.

Between 1850 and 1870, the United States expanded westward, and the lumber industry followed. Timber was used for housing and railroads. New York, Pennsylvania, and the Mid-Atlantic states became lumbering centers for a short time before giving way to the Midwest, especially Michigan, Wisconsin, and Minnesota, which became the timber heartland of America. The river systems of the Midwest transported logs to market and supported the rise of distribution centers like Chicago.

Technology progressed, and the virgin forests in the Lake states disappeared; by 1900 new centers for lumber production had appeared. The Rocky Mountain states, the South, and the Far West became lumber producers as the country entered the so-called Age of Lumber. As the white pine species was depleted, other types of wood were used in America's workplace—yellow pine, Douglas fir, and ponderosa pine. From 1900 until World War I, the lumber industry prospered, but clear-cutting damaged America's forest lands and sparked a conservation movement. An industry slowdown followed the collapse of the housing market during the Great Depression.

Lumbering revived during World War II as the nation exploited wood products in its fight against the Axis. When brick, cement, and steel came into wide use, more specialized lumber applications appeared. With improved technology, better conservation and cutting practices, and new transportation methods, lumbering prospered after 1945. Since then, the industry has grown consistently because of better forestry practices, mechanization, and increased demand. In 1986, for example, the United States harvested $8.5 billion worth of timber, exported $1.3 billion worth, and produced 39,540 million board feet of lumber. The largest single consumer of lumber remained residential construction (U.S. Department of Commerce 1986). All in all, lumbering became more sophisticated in its exploitation of natural resources, less labor- and more capital-intensive, and increasingly committed to sustained-yield management practices.

REGIONAL DEVELOPMENT

The history of the lumber industry reveals a reliance on America's natural forests. The industry expanded from the Northeast to the Mid-Atlantic, the Lake states, the South, the Rocky Mountain states, and the Far West. Each regional development has a distinctive history.

The Northeast

The early history of the Northeast was characterized by land clearing and deforestation. White pine was the main species harvested. During the colonial period, lumber was used for a variety of purposes, including housing, buildings, and firewood. Lumbering complemented agriculture.

The colonies began exporting planks and masts to England circa 1630. Shipbuilding was particularly important to England, a country committed to maintaining naval superiority in Europe. The North American colonies geared their production accordingly and enjoyed a prosperous trade. The American Revolution brought changes. Lumber production slowed as European markets dried up, and American technology remained primitive. Sawmills were small and served local markets. Fortunately, the market for

American lumber returned when Europe entered the Napoleonic Wars (D. Smith 1983).

As Europe became entangled in war, the demand for American forest products intensified. Boston, New York, and Baltimore exported pine and oak to England and the West Indies. The eastern United States also bought lumber as its own industries began to grow. By the 1830s the lumber market was expanding, encouraging concentration. Bangor, Maine, on the Penobscot River and Albany, New York, on the Hudson River became centers of trade because they were well located for water transportation.

The first permanent boom was established across the Penobscot River near Bangor in 1832. Although booms would remain important throughout much of the nineteenth century, logging railroads began to appear in the 1850s. The lumbering industry thrived on improved transportation and technology. Better felling tools and on-site processing allowed expansion of production and sale of New England lumber. Logs were milled, sold to commission merchants, and marketed directly by mill owners (Wood 1935).

The 1880s brought change to New England's lumber industry. Boom drives declined, and new centers of production developed around portable sawmills. Forest depletion was so great in the Northeast that loggers were cutting second-growth forests. Lumbering was declining in the Northeast but accelerating in the Lake states, the South, and the West. Instead of abandoning the industry, the Northeast began to specialize in hardwood production. New England has survived as a lumber region by integrating the production of different types of lumber.

The Midwest

The Midwest includes the Lake states (Michigan, Wisconsin, and Minnesota) and the Central states (Illinois, Indiana, and Ohio). Large-scale production was stimulated by the growth of large urban centers, especially Chicago. The Northeast was also a market for western timber. These factors combined with the Lake states' excellent river system for log transportation to generate a rapidly expanding lumber industry that dominated the national market between 1870 and 1930 (Twining 1963–64, 1983). Michigan was the leading producer from 1860 to 1890, then Wisconsin and Minnesota dominated until the turn of the century. For the Central states of the Midwest, the story was somewhat different.

The output in Illinois, Indiana, and Ohio matched neither the tremendous rise and fall in lumber production in the Lake states nor the output in the Far West. In these states, lumber was used in industry, and sawmills were built concomitantly with farms. Production reached its zenith between 1899 and 1909; most of the timber lumbered was hardwood. One of the leading historians of the region attributed the deforestation of the Central states not to commercial lumbering but to clearing land for farming (Williams 1983).

The South

As in New England, the lumber industry in the South is rooted in the colonial era. In the seventeenth century, the South was a vast virgin forest land. Before tobacco became important, lumber was a leading export from Virginia and other Southern states. New England pine was in greater demand than southern yellow pine because the latter was harder to work and mold to different uses. Southern pine was used in the South for cooperage, fencing, and shipbuilding or was exported abroad. In the eighteenth century the growth of New Orleans, the development of the sugar industry, and the revival of European trade improved the market for southern pine. Before the Civil War, the South had developed several trade centers, including Norfolk, Charleston, Mobile, and New Orleans (T. D. Clark 1983, 1984; V. S. Clark 1929; Gray 1933).

Technology facilitated the further growth of southern lumber. Steam-driven sawmills stimulated production in the early nineteenth century. Railroads became a source of demand for lumber even as they improved the transportation of timber. The South also gained markets when white pine production began to decline in the Northeast and the Lake states.

The increased demand for southern timber in the years from 1865 to 1900 spurred a proliferation of southern sawmill towns and villages, such as Laurel and Hattiesburg, Mississippi, and Bogalusa, Louisiana (Goodyear 1950). By 1880 the South was producing a little over 10 percent of American lumber and by 1910 nearly 45 percent.

From 1890 to 1920, great sawmills turned out lumber production highs that depleted southern forests. By 1930 the stands of southern pine and hardwoods had been almost destroyed by the lumberer's cut-out-and-get-out policy. The residual was fuel for the worst fires seen in America. Flooding followed because the land no longer slowed runoff.

The South learned from its mistakes. As early as 1920 conservation proponents like Henry E. Hardtner had introduced scientific forestry, forest fire protection, and reforestation programs (Moore 1979). By the 1930s second-growth yellow pine covered the South, and large companies began to adopt sustained-yield policies. The Tennessee Valley Authority (TVA) also fostered scientific conservation measures. Today, the South leads in paper production, tree farms, and furniture making.

The West

The West comprises both the Rocky Mountain states and the Far West. In the Rocky Mountain states, Idaho and Montana produced lumber. The region has little forest growth, and that is found in high mountains. Timber species include Douglas fir, larch, and ponderosa pine (Hammond 1983).

The history of lumber production in these states is a sad story. In the 1860s and 1870s lumbermen mercilessly exploited the forest. Timber was used for a variety of purposes and especially for mining. Federal land policies, including the Homestead Act and the Timber and Stone Act, all but gave away the forest lands. Ultimately, large lumber companies like Weyerhaeuser acquired huge tracts of land. By 1900 sawmills had proliferated in Idaho and Montana, and lumber production increased. Lumberjacks from the East, moreover, flocked west when eastern forests could no longer employ them. Production soared, then dropped by the 1930s. Since World War II, both Idaho and Montana have increased lumber production, particularly in softwoods.

Farther west the lumber industry accelerated more rapidly. Washington, Oregon, and California were the three most important lumbering states on the Pacific Coast. As in the Northeast, lumbering there began early: in the 1770s the Spanish culled the forests in the territories they claimed (Cox 1975). Forest depletion was minimal before the California gold rush of 1849. Sawmills appeared everywhere and then disappeared with the rush. Nevertheless, the most important asset of the Pacific Coast remained its huge timber reserves, and the developing railroads enhanced accessibility. As the lumber industry of the Northeast and Midwest declined, logging companies moved west. By the end of the nineteenth century, the West led the industry. The Pacific Coast expansion, however, was limited by the Jones Act of 1920, which restricted the coastal and intercoastal trade of the United States to American-owned vessels. West Coast lumbermen were not permitted to ship their goods on cheaper, foreign-owned ships. By 1940 Pacific Coast lumbering was expanding again, and World War II increased demand for forest products. Since 1945 West Coast lumbering has become a technology-aware, capital-intensive industry made up of large, consolidated firms (Cox 1983a).

THE LUMBER INDUSTRY AS A BUSINESS ENTERPRISE

Although unique in some ways, the lumber industry was overall typical of American industry. The technological, transportation, and labor history of lumbering firms is much the same as for other American companies. The lumber industry grew, production increased, and technology became critical, especially after the first-growth forests had been exploited. As the industry moved west and forests became more difficult to access, the lumber industry created a new transportation system. Initially, the industry used waterways, then logging railroads, and later gasoline-powered and diesel-powered machines. By the 1920s and 1930s, tractors, logging railroads, and trucks were the mainstay of the industry's transport network. The lumber industry was like other American business enterprises in its handling of labor. Unions had difficulty penetrating the lumber camps. Violence and terror sometimes ruled, especially when the Wobblies began organizing (Dubofsky 1969; Tyler 1967). Yet, unlike other American workingmen, the lumberjack was and remained mobile and self-reliant. Southern mills, however, differed from those in the Midwest and the West. Owners ran company towns with strong overtones of paternalism.

Technology

Like all American industry, lumbering was circumscribed by its technology. Felling timber and cutting it up depended at first on labor-intensive techniques and later on capital-intensive machinery. Colonial Americans used European methods to cut their forests; not until 1789 was the felling ax developed. During the antebellum period lumbermen began using a double-bitted ax for felling and cutting. By the 1870s they had switched to cross saws, and by 1900 the saw had replaced the ax as the primary felling tool. Improvements followed: lumberjacks used bucksaws and eventually the gasoline-powered chain saw. Developed by Andreas Stihl in 1927, the chain saw revolutionized the industry (Lucia 1981). The 1940s brought hydraulic and tractor-mounted shears.

Lumbering includes felling trees, processing, and yarding. Tree-cutting technology developed quickly: the broadax, the goose-wing ax, and the on-site processing mill. Oxen and horses were used for yarding until the 1920s, when the internal combustion engine replaced animal power in hauling logs. In the 1930s diesel tractors came into use and, in the 1970s and 1980s, balloons and helicopters for skyline logging.

Transportation

Moving logs from the cutting site to the processing plant is difficult and expensive. Log transport is divided into two phases: skidding—moving logs to a collecting site—then moving the logs to a mill. Throughout the colonial and antebellum periods loggers relied on water and gravity to move their timber. Logging dams were authorized and used in Maine as early as the 1820s. A dam created an artificially high water level that facilitated the flow of logs to their destination. By 1835 the Kennebec Association was driving logs to a boom stretched across the Kennebec River. The boom stopped the logs for sorting, rafting, and identification. The most famous of the eastern booms was the Penobscot near Oldtown, Maine. By 1860 Maine had ten booms in operation.

After the Civil War, almost every major river in the Great Lakes area and beyond had a boom. In Michigan, Wisconsin, and Minnesota there were nearly thirty. Logging railroads displaced water transit and intensified the rate at which American forests were cleared. Between 1900 and 1940, the logging railroad was the heart of timber transport, but new technology was already on the scene—diesel-powered trucks and tractors. A fascinating consequence was the reappearance of small, family-owned logging companies. Decentralized lumber-moving equipment combined with the chain saw, higher lumber prices, and army surplus trucks to bring back the small operator (Rector 1953, 1983).

Labor

Lumber camp workers were usually strong-willed single men without family ties (Kilar 1983; Jensen 1945). In the South, the company-owned sawmill dominated workers' lives; in the Far West, bloody incidents at Everett, Seattle, and Centralia attested to labor unrest and violence (W. Smith 1920).

The first major union to appear in the lumber industry was the Knights of Labor. Recruiters for the Knights were hindered by the loggers' mobility. The American Federation of Labor (AFL) enjoyed a slightly larger membership. In 1903 the AFL formed the International Shingle Weavers Union of America (ISWUA); worker mobility was the primary reason for the union's collapse in 1911. The Industrial Workers of the World (IWW, or Wobblies) organized in the South and Pacific Northwest, fighting hard and violently for their goals. The AFL responded to IWW success by reorganizing the defunct ISWUA into the International Union of Shingle Weavers, Sawmill Workers, and Woodsmen (IUSWSWW). Rechartered in 1916, the IUSWSWW adopted its former name, the International Shingle Weavers Union of America.

In May, 1916, ISWUA called a strike in Everett, Washington. The IWW got involved, and violence followed its call for the workers to sabotage their mills. Responding to this threat, Colonel Bryce Disque organized the Loyal Legion of Loggers and Lumbermen. More violence ensued. The IWW grew until suppressed in the 1919 depression and the Red Scare. Since then, lumbering unions have gradually succumbed to company paternalism. In the 1930s the Congress of Industrial Organizations (CIO) formed the International Woodworkers of America (IWA). Although internal dissension created problems initially, the IWA became the principal union in the lumber industry. Heavy membership in the Midwest and South boosted its numbers to nearly 110,000 by 1980.

Land Laws and Conservation

Public land laws affect the lumber industry's development and growth. Early clear-cutting laid forests bare and wasted resources, but the mature industry gave an impetus to the conservation movement of the twentieth century (Wyant 1982). Before 1878 federal land laws did not distinguish timberland from agricultural lands. Furthermore, both the Timber Cutting Act and the Timber and Stone Act of 1878 allowed timberland to be appropriated directly in 160–acre tracts and thereby encouraged waste and fraudulent land claims by large lumber companies (Carstensen 1963; Gates and Swenson 1968; Rohrbough 1968). Fortunately, Theodore Roosevelt and Gifford Pinchot implemented a conservation program calling for scientific management of America's natural resources (Pinkett 1970). Their beginnings led to other conservation policies such as forest reserves, sustained-yield management, and scientific forestry.

Marketing

The lumber industry has developed its own marketing structures and techniques. The two most important elements in lumber products are quality and price. As markets expanded and new species of timber appeared, more sophisticated marketing techniques evolved. By the 1870s manufacturers and wholesalers had begun advertising and had introduced product differentiation. A national system of marketing and distribution followed (Kohlmeyer 1983a, 1983b).

During the colonial period, the small, local lumber markets were dependent on factors. The industry moved west, and Chicago became a principal distribution point for pine and hardwood. At the turn of the twentieth century, new timber species reached the market not by water but by rail. As southern yellow pine and western Douglas fir began to replace white pine, the railroads expanded the market for lumber products. James J. Hill established a special rate on timber shipments to the Midwest and East, thereby increasing production and promoting the Pacific Coast industry.

U.S. industry leaders often sought tariff protection against foreign competition, especially from Canada. Like so many other U.S. industries, lumber depended on governmental aid.

As lumbering developed, so did trade associations: the Mississippi Valley Lumbermen's Association in 1891, the National Wholesale Lumber Dealers Association in 1893. These and other organizations worked to influence grading, railroad prices, and tariffs. As lumber prices declined in the 1920s and 1930s, the associations resorted to trade promotion, advertising, and product development. During the New Deal, however, the industry's participation in the National Recovery Administration was clouded by charges of collusion among the largest producers. Since World War II, lumber marketing has progressed, and retail outlets today are building-materials centers.

Entrepreneurship

Lumbering has benefitted from entrepreneurial talent and expertise. Men like Henry H. Crapo, Henry W. Sage, Philetus Sawyer, and Frederick Weyerhaeuser were, in many respects, akin to the oil, railroad, and iron and steel tycoons of their time. They took a direct and personal interest in their companies, worked with partners instead of corporations, and sought vertical and horizontal integration. Although the entrepreneurs among them cooperated in efforts that benefitted everyone, such as river improvement, they also formed combinations that helped only themselves. They fixed prices and actively sought a monopolistic advantage; they hated unions and treated their workers paternalistically. They neither hesitated to cheat the government nor showed much interest in preserving the lands they acquired from that government. In short, these men influenced not only their industry, but the national economy as well (Douglass 1971).

BIBLIOGRAPHIC ANALYSIS

Anyone studying the lumber industry would quickly uncover extensive primary and secondary resources. But the archival sources and secondary literature are wanting; the most obvious shortcoming is the lack of a single, comprehensive history of the lumber industry in the United States. Furthermore, the historical studies are usually regional instead of national. Biographies and company histories are frequently dated and selective.

Primary Sources

There is a wealth of documentary and archival source material on the lumber industry in the United States. Federal depositories include the Library of Congress, the National Archives, the Franklin D. Roosevelt Library, and the Lyndon B. Johnson Library. Within these depositories, the papers of specific agencies and officials are important—for example, the U.S. Forest Service, the General Land Office, the U.S. Geological Survey, the Civilian Conservation Corps, the Secretary of Agriculture, and the Secretary of the Interior. E. N. Munn (1940) and Gerald Ogden (1976) provide excellent bibliographies along these lines. Richard C. Davis (1977) has put together a good bibliographic guide to archives and unpublished materials in the United States and Canada.

In addition to federal depositories there are state and university collections. The more important are the Michigan Historical Collections and those housed at the State Historical Society of Wisconsin, the Minnesota Historical Society, the University of California at Berkeley, the University of Washington, the University of Oregon, Cornell University, Harvard University, Yale University, and the University of Mississippi. These collections range from personal papers to company records.

The Forest History Society papers at Santa Cruz, California, are another source of valuable information. This depository includes the papers of the American Forestry Association and the National Lumber Manufacturers

Association. Business archives are accessible as well, for example, the Weyerhaeuser Company Archives in Tacoma, Washington (Pinkett 1983).

Professional and trade journals proliferate. The *Journal of Forestry, Home Center, Southern Lumberman, Forest Industries, Crossties,* and *Gulf Coast Lumbermen* are a few.

Secondary Sources

Secondary resource materials are even more extensive than primary resources. Important factors in assessing these works are the disjointed coverage of topics and the age of some of the studies.

Bibliographies. There are many general bibliographies in addition to standard works in American economic and business history. Ronald J. Fahl (1977) has a good bibliography on published materials. Edgar B. Nixon's (1957) edited volumes on Roosevelt and conservation, 1911–45, are a more specialized guide.

General Histories of the Industry. There is a need for an updated, comprehensive treatment of the lumber industry throughout American history. The best available is by James E. Defebaugh (1906–7). Considering the industry's importance in the development of the United States and in the history of American business, it is not surprising to find the lumber industry included in many general texts in American economic and business history. Among these are Victor S. Clark (1929), Lewis Cecil Gray (1933), Elisha P. Douglass (1971), and Herman Krooss and Charles Gilbert (1972). Harold Steen's (1976) study of the U.S. Forest Service naturally discusses the lumber industry.

Autobiographies/Biographies. There are many autobiographies and biographies available. The major entrepreneurs are covered, and the autobiographical sketches, such as I. Stephenson's (1915), are interesting. The following are of particular value: *American Lumbermen: The Personal History and Public and Business Achievements of One Hundred Eminent Lumbermen of the United States* (1905–6), John H. Moore (1967), Charles W. Crawford (1978), Richard N. Current (1950), F. McD. Dierks (1972), Robert E. Ficken (1979), Anita Goodstein (1962), Louis Haight (1948), Walter Johnson and Elwood Maunder (1974), Martin D. Lewis (1958), and Elwood Maunder (1977).

Company Histories. Although company records are becoming more readily accessible, there are few company histories available. Many are dated or were company-sponsored. Still, there are a few that are worthwhile, including Donald H. Clarke (1949), Edwin Coman and Helen M. Gibbs (1949), Ralph Hidy, Frank E. Hill, and Allan Nevins on Weyerhaeuser (1963), and Arthur Reynolds on the Daniel Shaw Lumber Company (1957).

Regional Development. Work on the regional development of the lumber industry is fairly extensive. Its primary weakness, however, is the unevenness of the coverage. Unquestionably, the Northeast and the South have received the most attention, although the work done on the Midwest and Far West is substantial.

Some of the studies for the Northeast are quite good, namely, Robert G. Albion (1926) on the colonies and the Royal Navy; Charles Carroll (1973) on the timber economy of colonial New England; Joseph Malone (1964) on the colonial economy and trade in naval stores with England; Richard Wood (1935) on lumbering in Maine in the antebellum period; and Gary Walton and James Shepherd (1979) on the colonial economy. The Midwest has received some excellent coverage: Robert Fries (1951) on lumbering in Wisconsin; George Hotchkiss (1898) on lumbering in the Northwest; James W. Hurst (1964) on the legal history of lumbering in Wisconsin, 1836–1915; Agnes Larson (1949) on the white pine industry in Minnesota; Marx Swanholm (1978) on lumbering in Minnesota, the last of the white pine states; and S. K. Stephens (1952) and Lewis E. Theiss (1952) on the lumber industry in Pennsylvania. The Far West has received the least coverage. Nevertheless, there are two outstanding studies on the Pacific Coast: Thomas R. Cox (1975) on lumbering on the Pacific Coast to 1900, and Walter Mead (1966) on the Douglas fir lumber industry.

The South has been analyzed in detail. A mere listing of important studies would be long. The following are particularly worthwhile: Ruth Alice Allen (1961) on lumber workers in East Texas; Thomas D. Clark's (1984) overview of the South; Michael Curtis (1973) on the Great Southern Lumber Company; Richard Douglas (1966) on logging in the Big Hatchie bottoms; John A. Eisterhold (1971, 1972, 1973) on southern ports; James Silver (1957) on hardwood production; James Fickle (1980) on the southern pine industry since the late nineteenth century; Nollie Hickman (1962) on lumbering the longleaf pine belt, 1840–1915; Calvin Hoover and Ben U. Ratchford (1951) on economic development in the South in the 1940s; Robert Maxwell and Robert Baker (1983) on the Texas lumber industry to 1940; Rachel Norgress (1947) on lumbering cypress in Louisiana; and Kenneth Smith (1986) on cutting the last virgin lumber east of the Rockies.

Land Law, Forestry, and Conservation. The lumber industry is tied to developments in land law, forestry, and conservation. On the issue of public land law and distribution, two important works are an edited volume on public lands by Vernon R. Carstensen (1963) and a bibliography compiled by the U.S. Department of Interior (1962). Valuable articles and books include Marion Clawson (1968) on land use and tenure; Ivan Doig (1970) on public timber laws; Paul Gates and Robert W. Swenson (1968) on public land law; Daniel Mandell (1982) on public timberlands policy; William Robbins (1982) on law and lumber; and Malcolm Rohrbough (1968) on the Land Office.

Richard C. Davis edited the outstanding *Encyclopedia of American Forest and Conservation History* (1983). The articles are short and factual, and cover a wide variety of topics affecting lumber and related areas. Nelson McGeary (1960) and Harold Pinkett (1970) offer biographies of Pinchot. Other important studies in forestry and conservation include Roderick Nash (1972) on environmental history; William Wyant (1982) on public lands and conservation; Samuel P. Hays (1959) on the Progressive conservation movement; Elmo Richardson (1980) on managing O and C lands; John Ise (1920) on federal forest policies; Gary Libecap and Ronald Johnson (1979) on property rights, federal timber policies, and conservation in the nineteenth century; Sherry Olson (1971) on the railroads' use of timber; and Donald Pisani (1985) on forests and conservation, 1865–1890.

Lumber as a Business Enterprise. The following works are valuable: William Rector (1953) on log transportation; Nelson C. Brown (1936) on logging practices; Michael Koch (1979) on railroads and timber; Ellis Lucia (1981) on the chain saw; Nathan Rosenberg (1972) on technology and economic growth; Vernon Jensen (1945) on labor; Melvyn Dubofsky (1969) on the IWW; Jacob and Rex Dye (1975) on life in a lumber camp; and Fred Kohlmeyer (1983a, 1983b) on marketing lumber products.

BIBLIOGRAPHY

Albion, Robert G. *Forests and Sea Power: The Timber Problem of the Royal Navy, 1652–1862.* Cambridge, MA: Harvard University Press, 1926.

Allen, Ruth Alice. *East Texas Lumber Workers: An Economic and Social Picture, 1870–1950.* Austin: University of Texas Press, 1961.

American Lumbermen: The Personal History and Public and Business Achievements of One Hundred Eminent Lumbermen of the United States. 3 vols. Chicago: American Lumberman, 1905–6.

Brown, Nelson C. *Logging—Transportation: The Principles and Methods of Log Transportation in the United States and Canada.* New York: John Wiley & Sons, 1936.

Carroll, Charles. *The Timber Economy of Puritan New England.* Providence: Brown University Press, 1973.

Carstensen, Vernon R., ed. *The Public Lands: Studies in the History of the Public Domain.* Madison: University of Wisconsin Press, 1963.

Clark, Thomas D. "Lumber Industry: Southern States." In *Encyclopedia of American Forest and Conservation History,* edited by Richard C. Davis, vol. 1. New York: Macmillan, 1983.

———. *The Greening of the South: The Recovery of Land and Forest.* Lexington: University Press of Kentucky, 1984.

Clark, Victor S. *History of Manufactures in the United States.* 3 vols. New York: McGraw-Hill, 1929.

Clarke, Donald H. *Eighteen Men and a Horse.* Seattle: Metropolitan Press, 1949.

Clawson, Marion. *The Land System of the United States: An Introduction to the History and Practice of Land Use and Land Tenure.* Lincoln: University of Nebraska Press, 1968.

Coman, Edwin, and Helen M. Gibbs. *Time, Tide, and Timber.* Stanford: Stanford University Press, 1949.

Cox, Thomas R. *Mills and Markets: A History of the Pacific Coast Lumber Industry to 1900.* Seattle: University of Washington Press, 1975.

——. "Lumber Industry: Pacific Coast." In *Encyclopedia of American Forest and Conservation History,* edited by Richard C. Davis, vol. 1. New York: Macmillan, 1983a.

——. "Lumberman's Frontier." In *Encyclopedia of American Forest and Conservation History,* edited by Richard C. Davis, vol. 1. New York: Macmillan, 1983b.

Crawford, Charles W. *Stanley F. Horn, Editor and Publisher.* Santa Cruz, CA: Forest History Society, 1978.

Current, Richard N. *Pine Logs and Politics: A Life of Philetus Sawyer, 1816–1900.* Madison: State Historical Society of Wisconsin, 1950.

Curtis, Michael. "Early Development and Operations of the Great Southern Lumber Company." *Louisiana History* 14 (Fall 1973): 347–68.

Davis, Richard C. *North American Forest History: A Guide to Archives and Manuscripts in the United States and Canada.* Santa Barbara, CA: ABC-Clio Press, 1977.

——, ed. *Encyclopedia of American Forest and Conservation History.* 2 vols. New York: Macmillan, 1983.

Defebaugh, James E. *History of the Lumber Industry in America.* 2 vols. Chicago: American Lumberman, 1906–7.

Dierks, F. McD. *The Legacy of Peter Henry Dierks, 1824–1972.* Tacoma, WA: Mercury Press, 1972.

Doig, Ivan. "John T. Gilvra and Timber Trespass." *Forest History* 13 (January 1970): 7–17.

Douglas, Richard. "Logging in the Big Hatchie Bottoms." *Tennessee Historical Quarterly* 25 (Spring 1966): 32–49.

Douglass, Elisha P. *The Coming of Age of American Business: Three Centuries of Enterprise, 1600–1900.* Chapel Hill: University of North Carolina Press, 1971.

Dubofsky, Melvyn. *We Shall Be All: A History of the Industrial Workers of the World.* Chicago: Quadrangle, 1969.

Dye, Jacob, and Rex Dye. *Lumber Camp Life in Michigan.* Hicksville, NY: Exposition Press, 1975.

Eisterhold, John A. "Colonial Beginnings in the South's Lumber Industry, 1607–1800." *Southern Lumberman* 223 (December 15, 1971): 150–53.

——. "Lumber and Trade in the Lower Mississippi Valley and New Orleans, 1800–1860." *Louisiana History* 13 (Winter 1972): 71–91.

——. "Mobile: Lumber Center of the Gulf Coast." *Alabama Review* 26 (April 1973): 83–104.

Fahl, Ronald J. *North American Forest and Conservation History: A Bibliography.* Santa Barbara, CA: ABC-Clio Press, 1977.

Ficken, Robert E. *Lumber and Politics: The Career of Mark E. Reed.* Santa Cruz, CA: Forest History Society, 1979.

Fickle, James. *The New South and the "New Competition": Trade Association*

Development in the Southern Pine Industry. Urbana: University of Illinois Press, 1980.

Fries, Robert. *Empire in Pine: The Story of Lumbering in Wisconsin, 1830–1900.* Madison: State Historical Society of Wisconsin, 1951.

Gates, Paul, and Robert W. Swenson. *History of Public Land Law Development.* Washington, DC: U.S. Government Printing Office, 1968.

Goodstein, Anita. *Biography of a Businessman: Henry W. Sage, 1814–1897.* Ithaca: Cornell University Press, 1962.

Goodyear, C. W. *Bogalusa Story.* Buffalo: Privately printed, 1950.

Gray, Lewis Cecil. *History of Agriculture in the Southern United States to 1860.* 2 vols. Washington, DC: Carnegie Institution of Washington, 1933.

Haight, Louis. *The Life of Charles Henry Hackley.* Muskegon, MI: Dana Print Co., 1948.

Hammond, Jay. "Lumber Industry: Rocky Mountain Region." In *Encyclopedia of American Forest and Conservation History,* edited by Richard C. Davis, vol. 1. New York: Macmillan, 1983.

Hays, Samuel P. *Conservation and the Gospel of Efficiency: The Progressive Conservation Movement, 1890–1920.* Cambridge, MA: Harvard University Press, 1959.

Hempstead, Alfred. *The Penobscot Boom and the Development of the West Branch of the Penobscot River for Log Driving.* Orono: University of Maine Press, 1931.

Hickman, Nollie. *Mississippi Harvest: Lumbering in the Longleaf Pine Belt, 1840–1915.* University: University Press of Mississippi, 1962.

Hidy, Ralph, Frank E. Hill, and Allan Nevins. *Timber and Men: The Weyerhaeuser Story.* New York: Macmillan, 1963.

Hoover, Calvin, and Ben U. Ratchford. *Economic Resources and Policies of the South.* New York: Macmillan, 1951.

Horn, Stanley F. *This Fascinating Lumber Business.* New York: Bobbs-Merrill, 1943.

Hotchkiss, George W. *History of the Lumber and Forest Industry of the Northwest.* Chicago: G. W. Hotchkiss, 1898.

Howard, John. *The Negro in the Lumber Industry.* Philadelphia: University of Pennsylvania Press, 1970.

Hurst, James W. *Law and Economic Growth: The Legal History of the Lumber Industry in Wisconsin, 1836–1915.* Madison: University of Wisconsin Press, 1964.

Ise, John. *The United States Forest Policy.* New Haven: Yale University Press, 1920.

Jensen, Vernon. *Lumber and Labor.* New York: Farrar & Rinehart, 1945.

Johnson, Walter, and Elwood Maunder. *Twentieth-Century Businessmen.* Santa Cruz, CA: Forest History Society, 1974.

Kilar, Jeremy. "Law and Order in Lumber Camps and Towns." In *Encyclopedia of American Forest and Conservation History,* edited by Richard C. Davis, vol. 1. New York: Macmillan, 1983.

Koch, Michael. *Steam and Thunder in the Timber.* Denver: World Press, 1979.

Kohlmeyer, Fred. *Timber Roots: The Laird, Norton Story, 1855–1905.* Winona, MN: Winona County Historical Society, 1972.

———. "Lumber Distribution and Marketing." In *Encyclopedia of American Forest and Conservation History*, edited by Richard C. Davis, vol. 1. New York: Macmillan, 1983a.

———. "Lumber Distribution and Marketing in the United States." *Forest History* 27 (April 1983b): 86–91.

Krooss, Herman, and Charles Gilbert. *American Business History*. Englewood Cliffs, NJ: Prentice-Hall, 1972.

Larson, Agnes. *History of the White Pine Industry in Minnesota*. Minneapolis: University of Minnesota Press, 1949.

Lewis, Martin D. *Lumberman from Flint: The Michigan Career of Henry H. Crapo, 1835–1869*. Detroit: Wayne State University Press, 1958.

Libecap, Gary, and Ronald Johnson. "Property Rights, Nineteenth-Century Federal Timber Policy and the Conservation Movement." *Journal of Economic History* 39 (March 1979): 129–42.

Lower, A. M. *The North American Assault on the Canadian Forest: A History of the Lumber Trade Between Canada and the United States*. Toronto: Ryerson Press, 1938.

Lucia, Ellis. "A Lesson from Nature: Joe Cox and His Revolutionary Chain Saw." *Journal of Forest History* 25 (July 1981): 158–65.

McGeary, Nelson. *Gifford Pinchot: Forester*. Princeton: Princeton University Press, 1960.

Malone, Joseph. *Pine Trees and Politics: The Naval Stores and Forest Policy in Colonial New England, 1691–1775*. Seattle: University of Washington Press, 1964.

Mandell, Daniel. "Compelling a Public Timberlands Policy." *Forest History* 26 (July 1982): 140–47.

Maunder, Elwood. *James Greeley McGowin—South Alabama Lumberman: The Recollections of His Family*. Santa Cruz, CA: Forest History Society, 1977.

Maxwell, Robert, and Robert Baker. *Sawdust Empire: The Texas Lumber Industry, 1830–1940*. College Station: Texas A&M University Press, 1983.

Mead, Walter. *Competition and Oligopsony in the Douglas Fir Lumber Industry*. Berkeley: University of California Press, 1966.

Moore, John H. *Andrew Brown and Cypress Lumbering in the Old Southwest*. Baton Rouge: Louisiana State University Press, 1967.

———. "Lumber Industry." In *Encyclopedia of Southern History*, edited by David Roller and Robert Twyman. Baton Rouge: Louisiana State University Press, 1979.

Munn, E. N. *A Selected Bibliography of North American Forestry*. 2 vols. U.S. Department of Agriculture Miscellaneous Publication 364. Washington, DC: 1940.

Nash, Roderick. "American Environmental History: A New Teaching Frontier." *Pacific Historical Review* 41 (1972): 363–72.

Nixon, Edgar B., ed. *Franklin D. Roosevelt and Conservation, 1911–1945*. 2 vols. Hyde Park, NY: Franklin D. Roosevelt Library, 1957.

Norgress, Rachel. "The History of the Cypress Lumber Industry in Louisiana." *Louisiana Historical Quarterly* 30 (July 1947): 979–1059.

Ogden, Gerald. *The United States Forest Service: A Historical Bibliography, 1876–1972*. Davis, CA: Agricultural History Center, University of California, 1976.

Olson, Sherry. *The Depletion Myth: A History of Railroad Use of Timber*. Cambridge, MA: Harvard University Press, 1971.

Ottoson, Howard, ed. *Land Use Policy and Problems in the United States*. Lincoln: University of Nebraska Press, 1963.

Pinkett, Harold. *Gifford Pinchot, Private and Public Forester*. Champaign: University of Illinois Press, 1970.

———. "Historical Sources." In *Encyclopedia of American Forest and Conservation History*, edited by Richard C. Davis, vol. 1. New York: Macmillan, 1983.

Pisani, Donald. "Forests and Conservation, 1865–1890." *Journal of American History* 72 (September 1985): 340–59.

Primack, M. L. "Land Clearing Under Nineteenth-Century Techniques: Some Preliminary Calculations." *Journal of Economic History* 22 (1962): 484–97.

Rector, William. *Log Transportation in the Lake States Lumber Industry, 1840–1918*. Glendale, CA: Arthur Clark, 1953.

———. "Log Transportation." In *Encyclopedia of American Forest and Conservation History*, edited by Richard C. Davis, vol. 1. New York: Macmillan, 1983.

Reynolds, Arthur. *The Daniel Shaw Lumber Company: A Case Study of the Wisconsin Lumbering Frontier*. New York: New York University Press, 1957.

Richardson, Elmo. *BLM's Billion-Dollar Checkerboard: Managing the O and C Lands*. Santa Cruz, CA: Forest History Society, 1980.

Robbins, William. *Lumberjacks and Legislators: Political Economy of the U.S. Lumber Industry, 1890–1941*. College Station: Texas A&M University Press, 1982.

Rohrbough, Malcolm. *The Land Office Business: The Settlement and Administration of the Public Lands, 1789–1837*. New York: Oxford University Press, 1968.

Rosenberg, Nathan. *Technology and American Economic Growth*. New York: Harper & Row, 1972.

Schurr, Sam, and B. C. Netschert. *Energy in the American Economy, 1850–1975*. Baltimore: Johns Hopkins University Press, 1960.

Shepherd, Jack. *The Forest Killers: The Destruction of the American Wilderness*. New York: Weybright & Talley, 1975.

Silver, James. "The Hardwood Producers Come of Age." *Journal of Southern History* 23 (November 1957): 427–53.

Smith, David. "Lumber Industry: Northeast." In *Encyclopedia of American Forest and Conservation History*, edited by Richard C. Davis, vol. 1. New York: Macmillan, 1983.

Smith, Kenneth. *Sawmill: The Story of Cutting the Last Great Virgin Forest East of the Rockies*. Fayetteville: University of Arkansas Press, 1986.

Smith, Walker. *The Everett Massacre: A History of Class Struggle in the Lumber Industry*. Chicago: IWW Publishing Bureau, 1920.

Southern Lumberman 193 (December 1956).

Steen, Harold. *The U.S. Forest Service: A History*. Seattle: University of Washington Press, 1976.

Stephens, S. K. "When Timber Was King in Pennsylvania." *Pennsylvania History* 19 (1952): 391–96.

Stephenson, I. *Recollections of a Long Life, 1829–1915*. Chicago: Privately printed, 1915.

Swanholm, Marx. *Lumbering in the Last of the White Pine States*. St. Paul: Minnesota Historical Society, 1978.

Theiss, Lewis E. "Lumbering in Penn's Woods." *Pennsylvania History* 19 (1952): 397–412.

Twining, Charles. "Plunder and Progress: The Lumbering Industry in Perspective." *Wisconsin Magazine of History* 47 (1963–64): 116–24.

———. "Lumber Industry: Lake States." In *Encyclopedia of American Forest and Conservation History*, edited by Richard C. Davis, vol. 1. New York: Macmillan, 1983.

Tyler, Robert. *Rebels of the Woods: The I.W.W. in the Pacific Northwest*. Eugene: University of Oregon Press, 1967.

U.S. Department of Commerce. *U.S. Industrial Outlook 1987*. Washington, DC: U.S. Government Printing Office, 1986.

U.S. Department of Interior. *Public Lands Bibliography*. Washington, DC: Bureau of Land Management, 1962.

Walton, Gary, and James Shepherd. *The Economic Rise of Early America*. New York: Cambridge University Press, 1979.

Williams, Michael. "Lumber Industry: Central States." In *Encyclopedia of American Forest and Conservation History*, edited by Richard C. Davis, vol. 1. New York: Macmillan, 1983.

Wood, Richard. *A History of Lumbering in Maine, 1820–1861*. Orono: University of Maine Press, 1935.

Wyant, William. *Westward in Eden: The Public Lands and the Conservation Movement*. Berkeley: University of California Press, 1982.

Part V

Chemicals and Drugs
ESIC 28.0

CHAPTER 7

INDUSTRIAL CHEMICALS AND SYNTHETICS, 28.1

AMY L. WALTON

The Industrial Chemicals and Synthetics sector has the distinction of producing goods that are both ubiquitous and anonymous. Industrial chemicals are part of nearly every consumer product, chiefly as intermediate goods to other production processes.

SECTOR COMPOSITION

Three Standard Industrial Classification (SIC) product categories are currently a part of the Industrial Chemicals and Synthetics sector: Industrial Inorganic Chemicals (SIC 281), Plastics Materials and Synthetics (SIC 282), and Industrial Organic Chemicals (SIC 286).

As new chemical products and processes have been introduced, the industry groupings within SIC codes have changed. For example, both inorganic and organic chemicals were part of SIC 281 in 1957 (*Standard Industrial Classification Manual* 1957). SIC 286 included only gum and wood chemicals until 1972, when coal tar crudes and intermediates (now SIC 2865) and industrial organic chemicals (now SIC 2869) were reclassified from SIC 281 to SIC 286 (*Standard Industrial Classification Manual* 1972). Jules Backman (1964, 1970) and Arnold Thackray and his coauthors (1985) have traced changes in industry definition and economic indicators from 1899 to the 1980s.

Organic Chemicals

Organic chemicals are defined as "compounds containing carbon atoms in a form similar to those in plant and animal matter" (Manufacturing

Chemists' Association 1962, 11). The Industrial Organic Chemicals category (SIC code 286) has three components:

- Gum and Wood Chemicals (SIC 2861)
- Cyclic (Coal Tar) Crudes and Intermediates, Dyes and Organic Pigments (SIC 2865)
- Industrial Organic Chemicals, Not Elsewhere Classified (SIC 2869)

Until the mid–1800s, organic chemistry was an empirical science. The middle of the nineteenth century brought a substantial increase in the understanding of organic chemistry, especially in Europe. A series of theoretical advances were combined with empirical information to produce insights into atomic relationships. The new knowledge allowed chemists to design methods for synthesizing organic compounds. This new field grew rapidly, and so did its associated industries.

Chapter 1 of *Chemistry in the Economy*, a study by the American Chemical Society (1973), discusses organic chemicals and their influence on the American economy. A history of organic chemistry research and the organic chemical industry may be found in chapters 7, 8, 12, 13, 17, 23, 25, and 26 of Aaron J. Ihde's *Development of Modern Chemistry* (1964). Because much of the early work in organic chemistry was done outside the United States, earlier chapters tend to focus on European research.

Miscellaneous works of interest include a *Science* article by James F. Norris (1932) discussing the linkage between research and organic chemistry, and an article by Charles M. A. Stine (1940) on the growth of organic chemistry and the organic chemical industry in the United States. In a study of the scientific communication process, Fletcher S. Boig and Paul W. Howerton (1952) trace the development of organic chemical periodicals.

Inorganic Chemicals

Inorganic chemistry has been defined to include "all studies that deal with the preparation and properties of compounds other than the hydrocarbons and their derivatives" (Ihde 1964, 363).

The Industrial Inorganic Chemicals SIC category contains four industry groupings:

- Alkalies and Chlorine (SIC 2812)
- Industrial Gases (SIC 2813)
- Inorganic Pigments (SIC 2816)
- Industrial Inorganic Chemicals, Not Elsewhere Classified (SIC 2819)

Unlike organics, inorganics were a relatively small and miscellaneous portion of the chemical industry until well into the twentieth century. Although a wide range of chemicals may be classified as inorganics, research efforts were hampered by a lack of knowledge about molecular structure. Production efforts were specialized and based on empirical knowledge. In this century, theoretical and instrumentation developments have changed inorganic chemistry. New approaches to structural and bonding problems (Werner's theory of ionization, use of quantum mechanical principles) have allowed chemists to apply organic chemistry structural theory to inorganic chemistry. New tools have enhanced the understanding of inorganic substances: X-ray diffraction techniques have facilitated the study of crystal structure, and high-speed computers have allowed rapid analysis of the spectra of complex compounds. These developments have made the search for new elements easier.

Chapters 14, 17, 22, 25, and 26 of *Development of Modern Chemistry* (Ihde 1964) contain a history of inorganic chemistry research and the inorganic chemistry industry. Inorganic chemicals and their influence on the American economy are discussed in chapter 2 of *Chemistry in the Economy* (American Chemical Society 1973).

Synthetics

The twentieth century has seen a disappearance of the traditional boundary between organic chemistry and inorganic chemistry, as a tremendous variety of new compounds have been developed. The Plastics Materials and Synthetics category comprises four industrial groupings:

- Plastics Materials, Synthetic Resins, and Nonvulcanizable Elastomers (SIC 2821)
- Synthetic Rubber (Vulcanizable Elastomers) (SIC 2822)
- Cellulosic Man-Made Fibers (SIC 2823)
- Synthetic Organic Fibers, Except Cellulosic (SIC 2824)

In *This Chemical Age: The Miracle of Man-Made Materials*, Williams Haynes (1942) provides a popular account of many of the key synthetic chemical developments. Synthetics are also discussed in chapters 3–5 of *Chemistry in the Economy* (American Chemical Society 1973). Histories of individual innovations include Robert D. Friedel's (1983) study of celluloid.

SOURCES OF INFORMATION

Pertinent literature for the industry is drawn from three distinct sources. Many references focus on the science of the chemical industry, emphasizing major technical advances, the chemists who made these advances, and chemistry as a discipline. A second body of literature emphasizes business and organization—growth of the industry, development of production processes and product lines, and contributions by entrepreneurs. A third source of information is quantitative and recurrent, providing indicators of scientific advancement and business activity.

Chemists and Chemistry

In the last century, the expansion of consumer products has been critically dependent on extensive research and development (R&D) by chemical companies. Unlike most other scientists, chemists are largely employed by industry, not academe. This collaboration has generated a range of scientific discoveries and consumer products. Thus, one of the major sources of literature has been scientific: studies of chemistry as a discipline, major research results, and consequent technical advances.

The study by Thackray et al. (1985) focuses on chemistry as a discipline and an occupation. It evaluates the growth of chemistry as a profession, the differentiation of chemistry as a research field, and the development of chemistry education and employment trends in the United States.

A similar focus is taken in reports from the American Chemical Society. *A Century of Chemistry* (Skolnik and Reese 1976) is a historical documentation of the growth of the American Chemical Society and its influence on chemical education and research.

Ihde (1964) offers a thorough analysis of the growth of chemistry and the chemical industry. He discusses early scientific developments, including chemical innovations by European as well as American chemists. F. J. Moore's *History of Chemistry* (1931) also concentrates on early European developments; a single chapter (chapter 22) covers chemistry in the United States.

A history of chemistry and chemists that is specific to America has been written by Edgar F. Smith (1972). *Chemistry in America* contains letters, addresses, and published excerpts by and about early American chemists such as James Woodhouse, Joseph Priestley, Thomas Cooper, and John Maclean. Smith's book was originally published in 1914, so the material only includes chemistry investigations through about 1900. The volume by Harrison Hale (1928) also focuses on American chemistry, but emphasizes product categories (acids, dyes, paints, metals, etc.) rather than particular scientists.

Other studies of the history of chemistry appear as articles, monographs, and essays. A monograph by Edward H. Beardsley (1964) details the slow, often painful development of American chemistry during the last half of the nineteenth century. A selection of articles reprinted from the 1933–63 volumes of the *Journal of Chemical Education* has been compiled by Ihde and William F. Kieffer (1965). The articles discuss scientists and discoveries from a number of chemistry subfields (organic and inorganic chemistry, analytical and physical chemistry, industrial chemistry), but, like those in

Ihde's 1964 volume, are often about European scholars and developments. Recent essays appear in a volume edited by John Parascandola and James C. Whorton (1983), although many treat pharmaceutical chemicals rather than industrial chemicals.

In this century, chemical engineering has become a field of research separate from chemistry. Histories of chemical engineering include edited volumes by William F. Furter (1980, 1982) and the book by Terry S. Reynolds (1983) commemorating the seventy-fifth anniversary of the American Institute of Chemical Engineers. While Reynolds's text is specific to the United States, articles edited by Furter (1980) include histories of chemical engineering in many nations—the United States, Germany, India, Italy, Japan, Canada—as well as studies of particular individuals and institutions.

The Chemical Industry

Chemical production in colonial America was a decentralized, home-based activity. Materials such as soap, bleaches, dyes, and salt were part of a cottage industry.

It was not until the Industrial Revolution that chemicals were produced on a large scale. The rapidly expanding steel industry produced coal tar as a by-product; coal tar was an important input to the organic chemical industry. Many new chemical products and processes were developed, and organizations such as the American Chemical Society and the Manufacturing Chemists' Association appeared.

Before World War I, the American chemical industry relied on processes and products developed in Europe, and the international chemical industry was dominated by Germany. The sudden loss of German chemical sources and the U.S. government's seizure of thousands of German chemical patents spurred the development of an American chemical industry. The momentum generated during that development allowed the United States to become a leading chemical producer, a position it maintained for the next half century.

In the 1920s mass markets for automobiles, radios, and other consumer products generated huge demand for industrial chemicals. That demand accounts for the better-than-average performance by the chemical industry during Depression years. Chemical laboratories were making research breakthroughs in synthetic materials, and synthetics such as rayon and nylon were cheaper than alternatives. Synthetic rubber was also developed at this time, and would become important during World War II.

Recently, contradictory forces have influenced the industrial chemical industry. Demand for consumer products has guaranteed a strong market in intermediate inputs, but the manufacture of those products has put pressure on environmental resources. Improvements in processing techniques have allowed the chemical industry to take advantage of alternative inputs such as petroleum, but that same ease of usage has lured petroleum companies into chemical production and blurred the definition of the chemical industry.

Between 1945 and 1954 Haynes compiled a six-volume history of the American chemical industry (1945, 1948, 1949, 1954a, 1954b). More recent information may be found in *Chemistry in the Economy* (American Chemical Society 1973) and in the *Kline Guide to the Chemical Industry* (Curry and Rich 1980). Studies by L. F. Haber (1958, 1971) trace the application of chemistry during the nineteenth and early twentieth centuries: both European and American data are included.

A good summary of progress in the U.S. chemical industry appears in a survey article by Kenneth L. Taylor (1976). The development of the American chemical industry and its significance for the economy was also discussed in chapters by M. Queeney and Richard M. Lawrence (1951), Malcolm J. Harkins and Charles E. Wallace (1959), and Alfred E. Kahn (1961). An article by Howard C. E. Johnson (1968) in *Chemical Week* provides a succinct history of U.S. industrial chemicals.

Several studies of individual firms and innovations have been published. The Goodyear Chemical Division was studied by David Dietz (1943, 1955), a history of the Dow Chemical Company was written by Don Whitehead (1968), and the first seventy-five years of Monsanto history are included in a book by Dan J. Forrestal (1977). Du Pont history was chronicled by Dorian (1962), although that volume contains more family history than business history. Willard F. Mueller (1962) studied particular research efforts at Du Pont. A new volume on research and development at Du Pont is *Science and Corporate Strategy: Du Pont R & D, 1902–1980* by David A. Hounshell and John Kenly Smith, Jr. (1988). Charles W. Cheape's history (1985) of the Norton Company is a fine study of a New England firm that became a multinational corporation.

Business and Historical Indicators

Chemical indicators are drawn from both scientific and industrial sources. Listed in the bibliography are the best summaries of information in each area.

The study by Thackray et al. (1985) emphasizes scientific indicators— measures of the quantity and quality of scientific research and related trends in employment, education, and industrial output. The bibliography contains a good overview of available federal and industrial data.

A summary of statistical, technical, and trade sources of information is available in *Chemical Industries Information Sources* (Peck 1979) and in section 6 of *The Kline Guide* (Curry and Rich 1980).

Updates on selected production, output, and employment figures may be obtained annually from *Chemical and Engineering News*, published by the American Chemical Society.

BIBLIOGRAPHY

American Chemical Society. *Chemistry in the Economy*. Washington, DC: American Chemical Society, 1973.

————. "Facts and Figures for the Chemical Process Industries." *Chemical and Engineering News*. Washington, DC: American Chemical Society. Annual.

Backman, Jules. *Competition in the Chemical Industry*. Washington, DC: Manufacturing Chemists' Association, 1964.

————. *The Economics of the Chemical Industry*. Washington, DC: Manufacturing Chemists' Association, 1970.

Beardsley, Edward H. *The Rise of the American Chemistry Profession, 1850–1900*. University of Florida Monographs, Social Sciences, No. 23 (Summer 1964). Gainesville: University of Florida Press, 1964.

Boig, Fletcher S., and Paul W. Howerton. "History and Development of Chemical Periodicals in the Field of Organic Chemistry: 1877–1949." *Science* 115 (1952): 25–31.

Cheape, Charles W. *Family Firm to Modern Multinational: Norton Company, a New England Enterprise*. Cambridge, MA: Harvard University Press, 1985.

Curry, Susan, and Susan Rich, eds. *The Kline Guide to the Chemical Industry*. 4th ed. Fairfield, NJ: Charles H. Kline, 1980.

Dietz, David. *The Goodyear Research Laboratory*. Akron, OH: Goodyear Tire & Rubber Co., 1943.

————. *Harvest of Research: The Story of the Goodyear Chemical Division*. Akron, OH: Goodyear Tire & Rubber Co., 1955.

Dorian, Max. *The du Ponts: From Gunpowder to Nylon*. Boston: Little, Brown, 1962.

Forrestal, Dan J. *Faith, Hope and $5000: The Story of Monsanto*. New York: Simon & Schuster, 1977.

Friedel, Robert D. *Pioneer Plastic: The Making and Selling of Celluloid*. Madison: University of Wisconsin Press, 1983.

Furter, William F., ed. *History of Chemical Engineering*. Advances in Chemistry Series, No. 190. Washington, DC: American Chemical Society, 1980.

————, ed. *A Century of Chemical Engineering*. New York: Plenum, 1982.

Haber, L. F. *The Chemical Industry During the Nineteenth Century: A Study of the Economic Aspect of Applied Chemistry in Europe and North America*. Oxford: Clarendon Press, 1958.

————. *The Chemical Industry, 1900–1930: International Growth and Technological Change*. Oxford: Clarendon Press, 1971.

Hale, Harrison. *American Chemistry*. 2d ed. New York: D. Van Nostrand, 1928.

Harkins, Malcolm, J., and Charles E. Wallace. "The Chemical Industry." In *The Development of American Industries: Their Economic Significance*, edited by John G. Glover and Rudolph L. Lagai, 4th ed., 297–331. New York: Simmons-Boardman, 1959.

Haynes, Williams. *Men, Money and Molecules*. New York: Doubleday, Doran, 1936.

————. *This Chemical Age: The Miracle of Man-Made Materials*. New York: Alfred A. Knopf, 1942.

———. *American Chemical Industry: The World War I Period, 1912–1922.* Vols. 2 and 3 of *American Chemical Industry: A History.* New York: D. Van Nostrand, 1945.

———. *American Chemical Industry: The Merger Era, 1923–1929.* Vol. 4 of *American Chemical Industry: A History.* New York: D. Van Nostrand, 1948.

———. *American Chemical Industry: The Chemical Companies.* Vol. 6 of *American Chemical Industry: A History.* New York: D. Van Nostrand, 1949.

———. *American Chemical Industry: Background and Beginnings.* Vol. 1 of *American Chemical Industry: A History.* New York: D. Van Nostrand, 1954a.

———. *American Chemical Industry: Decade of New Products, 1930–1939.* Vol. 5 of *American Chemical Industry: A History.* New York: D. Van Nostrand, 1954b.

Hounshell, David A., and John Kenly Smith, Jr. *Science and Corporate Strategy: Du Pont R & D, 1902–1980.* Cambridge, Eng.: Cambridge University Press, 1988.

Ihde, Aaron J. *The Development of Modern Chemistry.* New York: Harper & Row, 1964.

Ihde, Aaron J., and William F. Kieffer. *Selected Readings in the History of Chemistry.* Easton, PA: American Chemical Society, 1965.

Johnson, Howard C. E. "The Rise of the United States Chemical Industry, 1918–1968." *Chemical Week* 103 (November 16, 1968): 104–45.

Kahn, Alfred E. "The Chemical Industry." In *The Structure of American Industry: Some Case Studies,* edited by Walter Adams, 3d ed., 233–76. New York: Macmillan, 1961.

Manufacturing Chemists' Association. *The Chemical Industry Facts Book.* Washington, DC: Manufacturing Chemists' Association, 1962.

Moore, F. J. *A History of Chemistry.* New York: McGraw-Hill, 1931.

Mueller, Willard F. "The Origins of the Basic Inventions Underlying DuPont's Major Product and Process Innovations, 1920 to 1950." In *The Rate and Direction of Inventive Activity: Economic and Social Factors,* 323–46. National Bureau of Economic Research, Special Conference Series, No. 12. Princeton, NJ: Princeton University Press, 1962.

Norris, James F. "Research and Industrial Organic Chemistry." *Science* 75 (1932): 5–10.

Parascandola, John, and James C. Whorton, eds. *Chemistry and Modern Society: Historical Essays in Honor of Aaron J. Ihde.* ACS Symposium Series, No. 228. Washington, DC: American Chemical Society, 1983.

Peck, Theodore P., ed. *Chemical Industries Information Sources.* Management Information Guide Series, No. 29. Detroit: Gale Research, 1979.

Queeney, M., and Richard M. Lawrence. "The Chemical Industry." In *The Development of American Industries,* edited by John George Glover and William Bouck Cornell, 419–58. New York: Prentice-Hall, 1951.

Reynolds, Terry S. *Seventy-five Years of Progress—A History of the American Institute of Chemical Engineers, 1908–1983.* New York: American Institute of Chemical Engineers, 1983.

Skolnik, Herman, and Kenneth M. Reese, eds. *A Century of Chemistry.* Washington, DC: American Chemical Society, 1976.

Smith, Edgar F. *Chemistry in America.* 1914. Reprint. New York: Arno Press, 1972.

Standard Industrial Classification Manual. Executive Office of the President, Bureau of the Budget, Office of Statistical Standards, Technical Committee on Industrial Classification. Washington, DC: U.S. Government Printing Office, 1957.

Standard Industrial Classification Manual. Office of Management and Budget, Statistical Policy Division. Washington, DC: U.S. Government Printing Office, 1972.

Stine, Charles M. A. "The Rise of the Organic Chemical Industry in the United States." In *Smithsonian Institution Annual Report*, 177–92. Smithsonian Publication No. 3606. Washington, DC: Smithsonian Institution, 1940.

Taylor, Kenneth L. "Two Centuries of Chemistry." In *Issues and Ideas in America*, edited by Benjamin J. Taylor and Thurman J. White, 267–84. Norman: University of Oklahoma Press, 1976.

Thackray, Arnold, Jeffrey L. Sturchio, P. Thomas Carroll, and Robert Bud. *Chemistry in America, 1876–1976*. Dordrecht, Holland: D. Reidel, 1985.

Whitehead, Don. *The Dow Story: The History of the Dow Chemical Company.* New York: McGraw-Hill, 1968.

CHAPTER 8

DRUGS, 28.3

Marvin N. Fischbaum

The production of drugs to counteract illness is both one of the oldest and one of the newest industries. The *materia medica* of the colonial apothecary, and the system of medicine underlying its use, had strong ties to classical antiquity. In contrast, the therapeutic revolution of the past fifty years has all but overturned the contents of the U.S. pharmacopoeia (Temin 1980) and has led to rapid and dramatic change in the structure of the drug industry.

Few areas of human endeavor are tied as directly to the distant past as the healing professions, including pharmacy. Many of the symbols, and much of the language, can be traced to ancient Roman and Greek civilizations and beyond. Recipes for preparing medications can be found in Sumerian cuneiform tablets from 3,000 B.C. Surviving Egyptian records, particularly the Ebers papyrus, point to a surprisingly sophisticated *Ph Ar Maki* (that which brings safety). Quantified instructions for preparing medicines included indications for use and dosages (Boussel, Bonnemain, and Bove 1983). But it was the Greeks and their *Pharmakon* that set the tone and tenor of medicine for nearly two millennia. From Hippocrates in the fifth century B.C. to Galen, physician to Roman emperors in the second century A.D., there arose a variety of approaches to medicine. Galen believed the source of disease to be an imbalance in the four humors: blood, phlegm, yellow bile, and black bile. Each humor combined the characteristics hot or cold with wet or dry. A fever might therefore indicate a surplus of blood, which is hot and wet, or a deficiency of black bile, which is cold and dry. Treatment consisted of bleeding or medicating with simples that induce dryness or cold (Sonnedecker 1976). Galen often combined a large number of simples in the belief that the body would seek out and use the appropriate ones. If all else failed, he prescribed a *theriaca Andromachi*. This panacea contained no fewer than sixty-four ingredients, including opium, but the most potent was believed to be boiled, powdered viper.

Only fragments of Greek work survived in European monasteries, but the Arabic-speaking world preserved a substantial body of Greek material. The Persian Avicenna and other physicians introduced the practice of ingesting gold, ground-up semiprecious stones, and dissolved pearls; still, they came to look upon Galen as the master of medicine. Through the Crusades, trade, and the migration of Jewish physicians, Europe absorbed Arabic (and with it, Greek) medicine. By the fifteenth century, the Galenic system dominated European medicine as it had never dominated Rome (Ackerknecht 1973).

The Renaissance brought changes. A Swiss physician of the sixteenth century, Paracelsus, rejected Galen's philosophical system, emphasizing instead the impact of drugs on specific diseases. Paracelsus, however, used a comparable regime of medication, substituting for botanicals inorganic chemicals that produced similar effects. Paracelsus also revived primitive signatures—the idea that the shape or color of a substance would reveal its curative properties. In the course of the seventeenth and eighteenth centuries other tenets of Galenic medicine were challenged. The discovery that Peruvian chinchona bark (containing quinine) acted on intermittent fevers (malaria) but not on others raised doubt that a humoral imbalance was the source of all fever. Nonetheless, for the period of North American colonization it is useful to divide the medical world into two camps: the followers of Galen, who medicated with botanicals, and the followers of Paracelsus, who preferred chemicals (Ackerknecht 1973).

Migrants to colonial America came from a world where health services were provided by practitioners from three guilds. A physician was in charge; an apothecary and a surgeon assisted. As university graduates, and thereby gentlemen, physicians were unsullied by physical labor. Instead they observed and prescribed while surgeons and apothecaries, trained by apprenticeship, ministered to the sick. Surgeons bled patients and tended wounds. Apothecaries gathered raw materials, made medicines, compounded prescriptions, and advised patients on their use. But only the rich or powerful could afford a physician, and outside large cities the roles of surgeon and apothecary were often combined (Gill 1972).

The Virginia Company imported English theory to the New World. A surgeon sailed on the first ship to Jamestown in 1607, and a physician and two apothecaries arrived with the second ship in 1608. Subsidization of medicine ended, however, with the dissolution of the Virginia Company in 1624, and trained medical practitioners were no longer sent to the colonies. For most of the colonial period, those pursuing the healing trades were often part-time practitioners, serving as apothecaries and surgeons while farming or preaching as well. Practitioners were self-taught or had completed informal, uncertified apprenticeships. By the end of the seventeenth century, any health practitioner was called doctor (Gill 1972).

During the colonial period patients were attended at bedside, but medications were dispensed at a physician's office. Even university-trained physicians could not forgo the income from an apothecary shop, and few shops could profit without the physicians' custom. The *materia medica* remained essentially European, and most chemicals and many botanicals were imported. Notable among the few botanicals exported was ginseng root, prized in the Orient for its signature—its resemblance to the human body (Sonnedecker 1976). In the eighteenth century, apothecaries increasingly imported English patent medicines, liquids or pills, that were galenical mixtures of as many as twenty-seven ingredients. Many of these products had been sold in England since the early seventeenth century, but it was the container, not the contents, that was patented (Young 1961).

Specialization and professionalism in the healing arts increased during the eighteenth century. In addition to apothecaries who treated the sick, there were druggists and chemists (the terms were interchangeable) who acted principally as importers and wholesalers but who also sold medications if neither treatment nor advice was required. The colonists marketed English patent medicines by importing empty vials and bottles and filling them locally (Christianson 1987; Gill 1972). Many physicians received better training, and perhaps 5 percent earned university degrees (Starr 1982).

The American Revolution stimulated medical development. The collection of drugs and the compounding of medications were centralized at the shop of Apothecary General Andrew Craigie in Carlisle, Pennsylvania. Shortages stimulated the manufacture of purging salts, probably the first large-scale production of pharmaceutical chemicals in North America (Sonnedecker 1976). Such developments set the stage for growth in the nineteenth century, but hardly presaged the rapid changes that would occur, first, in the science of medicine and, later, in pharmacology and drug manufacture. But in the immediate postwar period medical science took a strange turn.

Benjamin Rush, signer of the Declaration of Independence, was the most prominent American physician in the last years of the eighteenth century. At the Philadelphia College of Medicine Rush taught the most current European doctrine, heroic medicine. He believed that hypertension of the blood vessels was the single cause of disease and that the cure was bleeding patients to the point of fainting. The bleeding treatment was combined with thorough purging with calomel. Patients might lose up to four-fifths of their blood and ingest so much salt of mercury that their teeth and jaws would decay (Gill 1972; Starr 1982).

Heroic medicine gained currency with physicians, but less-educated elements of society doubted its efficacy and safety. Revulsion against official medicine encouraged medical sects and reliance on folk remedies, and ensured the popularity of American patent medicines.

The most popular of the medical sects was founded by Samuel Thomson, a New England farmer. Thomson began his practice of medicine about 1800, and his influence peaked about the time of his death in 1843. In the spirit of the Age of Jackson, Thomson glorified the common man and common sense, and disparaged the aristocracy and education. To him, doctors were worse than useless; with his twenty-dollar book and his medicines, any household could care for its own sick. Thomson had no formal education, but he propounded a system of medicine with a distinctly classical flavor: disease was caused by an imbalance in the four elements—earth, air, fire, and water—which led to an excess of cold or a dearth of heat. Botanical medications, especially purgatives, were the cure (Young 1961).

Of the various sects that came into prominence after the decline of Thomsonism, homeopathy was the most influential. Founded in the eighteenth century by the German physician Samuel Hahnemann, homeopaths administered minute doses of highly diluted medications. They theorized that, like vaccines, minute dosages of drugs could induce weak versions of disease that could be cured by natural body defenses. Unlike vaccines, these drugs were administered to the sick in the hope that somehow the weak disease would displace the original (Starr 1982).

So-called patent medicines thrived on the public's distrust of orthodox treatment. No longer content just to fill or refill English bottles, Americans introduced a proliferation of brand-name medicines. Most were produced locally on a small scale, but promoters observed that aggressive use of newspaper advertisements broadened the area of distribution. Before the patent laws were tightened in 1836, a few of these nostrums were actually patented; but patents required disclosure, and most promoters preferred to keep their ingredients secret. A far larger number patented the shape of the bottle or some other part of the package (Young 1961).

A hierarchy of respectability developed among the patent, or more accurately, proprietary, medicines. Some, mostly liniments and plasters, made limited claims. Most nostrums to be ingested were strongly alcoholic, but were supposed to cure a wide range of infirmities. Others advertised as panaceas contained opium or cocaine, or were little but colored water.

The proprietary drug industry grew and prospered until reined in by the Pure Food and Drug Act of 1906. In the 1830s Thomas Dyatt, a proprietary medicine entrepreneur, lived lavishly on an annual income of $25,000 and an accumulated fortune of $250,000. Dyatt manufactured his own bottles and employed 100 apprentices. By mid-century the manufacturer of Swaim's Panacea was worth $500,000. By the end of the century, the annual advertising budget for leading nostrums, such as Scott's Emulsion or Lydia E. Pinkham's Vegetable Compound, exceeded a million dollars (Young 1961). But these were marketing, not manufacturing, enterprises. Pinkham spent as much as 80 percent of gross revenue on advertising and, during a decade of sustained growth, 1880–89, kept advertising expenses at 44 percent of gross revenue (Stage 1979). Proprietary drug sellers pioneered medicine shows, outdoor advertising, and lavish shops. Indeed, the sharp, inviolate distinction between proprietary drug sellers and ethical drug sellers was the marketing target: patent drugs were advertised to the public, ethical drugs to physicians and pharmacists.

While the public was voting with its purse for popular rather than official medicine, medical science was undergoing a transformation. It began in Paris in the aftermath of the French Revolution. With class and privilege out of fashion, physicians no longer just observed; they examined, touched, probed, and measured with instruments. They attended patients in the hospital, not the rich at their bedsides. They evaluated therapies using "the science of numbers" (Ackerknecht 1970). Doctors observed that disease was often self-limiting and that patients frequently recovered despite rather than because of medical intervention (Temkin 1964). The transformation continued apace in England and the United States. Anesthesia induced by ether and nitrous oxide made the pain of surgery bearable; Joseph Lister's work on antiseptics made the risks of surgery tolerable (Starr 1982). Thus in the course of the nineteenth century medicine progressed from a craft steeped in mystery to a modern science. The surgeon advanced from physician's assistant to principal. The stage shifted from the bedchamber to the voluntary hospital. Progress in the manufacture of ethical drugs was modest, but accelerating.

Most of the major pharmaceutical manufacturers can trace their roots back to the nineteenth century. One, Merck, dates from a 1654 apothecary shop. In 1827 Merck & Co. found a reason to build a factory: alkaloids, the therapeutically active crystalline substances found in a variety of plants. In the first three decades of the nineteenth century Parisian chemists discovered such alkaloids as morphine, strychnine, quinine, caffeine, and codeine. The morphine content will vary substantially in a given quantity of opium or in a fluidextract of opium, such as laudanum; so will the caffeine content of a cup of coffee. In many drugs the margin between a therapeutic and a toxic dose is quite narrow, so alkaloids are both safer and more potent than the botanicals they are extracted from. These alkaloids could not be isolated using the ordinary equipment of a neighborhood pharmacy, hence the factory (Ackerknecht 1973; Cowen 1970).

In Philadelphia, Pennsylvania, the home of the first college of pharmacy, two firms manufactured alkaloids. Farr and Kunzi, founded in 1818, produced quinine by 1822. Rosengarten and Sons, founded in 1822, produced morphine, piperine, strychnine, veratrine, and codeine by 1836. Both were eventually absorbed by Merck. But few American operations were that sophisticated, and most chemicals requiring complex processing were imported.

Two other early Philadelphia factories followed a more typical pattern. The Marshall Pharmacy, established in 1786, and Samuel P. Wetherall and

Co. produced traditional chemicals, utilizing scale economies (Sonnedecker 1976). But scale economies in drug manufacturing were not large; drugs were processed in batches, essentially by hand, with equipment larger but similar in design to that found in a retail pharmacy. Not until 1900 was drug manufacture mechanized, and even then much of the equipment was adapted from bakeries and other industries. In 1900 the typical manufacturing pharmacy employed fewer than twenty persons (Sonnedecker 1965).

Success and growth were the rewards for manufacturers who could market a specialty, improve the dosage form of their medications, or assure high quality. Specialties bore a certain resemblance to patent medicines. Parke Davis could pay its first dividend after it marketed a laxative, Cascara Sagrada (Mahoney 1959). With the introduction of Succus Alterans in 1883, Eli Lilly became more than a moderately successful regional concern. Promoted primarily as a treatment for syphilis, the product was used for a variety of purposes (Kahn 1976). Warner introduced the sugar-coated pill in 1886. Upjohn got its start with the friable pill, and Abbott introduced dosimetric granules to the American scene. Several firms produced compressed tablets, and Parke Davis and Eli Lilly manufactured gelatin capsules.

Improvements, real or imagined, in the quality of drugs yielded the greatest rewards. Squibb pointed the way. While a medical officer in the navy, E. R. Squibb was distressed over the unnecessary hazards of using adulterated or impure drugs. The purity of the ether used as an anesthetic was particularly critical. Eventually Squibb was put in charge of the navy drug manufacturing laboratory, where he designed and implemented a process for producing highly purified ether. In 1857, partly on the promise of custom from the army, Squibb resigned his commission and started his own manufacturing enterprise. By the end of the century Squibb ether and Squibb chloroform had become dominant brands, and the firm produced many other products as well. By the standards of the day the firm was not only well respected but large, with annual sales near $400,000 (Mahoney 1959).

Although Cascara Sagrada gave Parke Davis its initial lift, the firm made its reputation on quality control. Beginning in 1879, the company marketed a line of fluidextracts of supposed uniform potency that were dubbed "normal liquids" (Cowen 1970). In the 1890s Parke Davis and Smith Kline and French were among the first American drug companies to support research laboratories. The main function of the labs was to assay the quality of inputs, but they also tested finished products, giving their firms a major marketing tool (Liebenau 1984). By the end of the nineteenth century Parke Davis claimed to be the largest pharmaceutical manufacturer in the world, with estimated annual sales of $3 million (Mahoney 1959).

Change in the drug industry accelerated and, after 1935, exploded into what is called the therapeutic revolution. The seeds of this revolution had been planted by 1900 in Germany and Switzerland, not the United States. In the 1860s in Germany, and somewhat later in Basle, Switzerland, a number of firms were organized to produce aniline dyes from coal tar. It is not clear why, but in the 1880s the German companies branched out into pharmaceutical production; Jonathan Liebenau (1984) suggests a temporary dip in what had been a very profitable industry. Whatever the reason, the dye business had been research-driven, and these firms conducted their pharmaceutical business in much the same way. From the beginning they sought close ties with academic scientists and quickly committed substantial resources to in-house research facilities. Bayer produced phenacetin in the 1880s and aspirin, the first important synthesized drug, in the 1890s. Somewhat afield of dye chemistry, Hoechst developed diphtheria antitoxin (Davis 1984). Soon the Swiss companies Ciba, Sandoz, and Roche followed the German lead (Mahoney 1959).

The most significant discovery of this period was made by Paul Ehrlich, who is considered the father of chemotherapy. A coal-tar dye may be colorfast with one fiber but not with another, indicating that it can bond selectively. As a medical student Ehrlich experimented with the effect of various dyes on different tissues. When he injected methylene blue into a living rabbit, the dye spread only through the nervous system. Ehrlich theorized that a similar compound containing a poison could act as a "magic bullet," bonding with and destroying only disease-bearing cells (Davis 1984). Ehrlich systematically tested hundreds of compounds on various microorganisms. In 1906 he published a discouraging account of his work, but in 1910 he announced that compound 606, an arsenical he later named Salversan, was effective against syphilis. Hoechst marketed Salversan and, with other dye makers, frantically searched for similar drugs, but without apparent success (Temin 1980).

World War I stimulated the U.S. drug manufacturing industry. The British blockade of German shipping caused the price of pharmaceuticals to skyrocket. The price of saccharin, for instance, rose from $0.85 to $20 per pound (Bobst 1973). After the United States entered the war, German property and German patent rights were seized. The U.S. branch of Merck split from its German parent. Sterling Drug purchased Bayer property and the U.S. rights to Bayer trademarks and patents (Mahoney 1959). Other American firms undertook for the first time the production of complex pharmaceutical chemicals. (Sonnedecker 1976).

With peace came a startling development. In 1921 Frederick Grant Banting and Charles Herbert Best, working in the laboratories of the University of Toronto, isolated from the pancreas of animals a hormone that controlled the level of blood sugar in human diabetics. Scaling up production from laboratory levels while maintaining adequate purity proved to be beyond the university's resources. Eli Lilly received the license to help develop the manufacturing process and to manufacture and distribute insulin. Insulin was the first pharmaceutical product that could keep alive patients who would otherwise inevitably die. Insulin was the first product of modern pharmaceutical research to come from a North American laboratory and the first to be commercially introduced by a U.S. drug firm (Temin 1980).

The 1920s and early 1930s brought the introduction of other new drug products, including vitamins and biologicals—toxins, antitoxins, and serums (Temin 1980). Most discoveries continued to emanate from Europe, but American drug manufacturers began to invest in modern research facilities (Cowen 1970). None of the products had the dramatic impact of insulin or held the promise for future development that had once been associated with Salversan.

Then, in 1935, Gerhard Domagk, working in the laboratories of I. G. Farben—the gigantic combine of Bayer, Hoechst, and BASF—discovered that a red dye, Prontosil, had powerful antimicrobial properties. French scientists quickly determined that the active agent in Prontosil was sulfanilamide, a chemical that had been discovered in 1908. Drug companies quickly developed a broad family of sulfa drugs that improved on the safety or efficacy of sulfanilamide (Temin 1980).

Sulfanilamide was the first major discovery that marked the therapeutic revolution; penicillin was the second. In 1929 Alexander Fleming published his observations on the germicidal effect of penicilium mold. There was no immediate follow-through, however, on his suggestion that chemists try to isolate the active agent in the mold. In 1941 a team of Oxford University scientists, headed by Howard Florey and Ernest B. Chain, isolated penicillin and established its antibacterial properties; but they could produce only miniscule quantities. It required a massive wartime cooperative effort between government agencies and pharmaceutical companies in Great Britain and the United States to engineer production in quantity (Temin 1980; Schwartzman 1976).

Near the end of World War II, Selman Waksman of Rutgers University developed a method for screening soil samples to find penicillin-like substances that he named antibiotics. His discovery of streptomycin demonstrated the value of his method. The profit potential of antibiotics became clear when the patent office ruled that streptomycin was a new substance and thus eligible for a product patent as well as process patents. A new era had begun (Temin 1980; Mahoney 1959).

Before World War II there had been considerable diversity among drug houses; some marketed locally, others nationally or worldwide. A few firms, like Lilly and Parke Davis, distributed a full line of products. Most, though, fit neatly into the three-way SIC classification. Merck and Pfizer produced *medicinals and botanicals*; their products were sold in bulk to other drug firms. Most firms manufactured *pharmaceutical preparations*, either ethical or proprietary; they repackaged bulk chemicals for distribution to wholesalers. A few, such as Lederle, manufactured biological products; their vaccines, serums, antitoxins, and other blood products were sold to hospitals and physicians (Walker 1971). By modern standards, no firm was very large;

many were family owned or family controlled. Although proprietary drug manufacturers might have important brands, the ethical drug firms sold commodities. Each firm sold hundreds or thousands of products. Each product was available from a number of sources. Competition reigned.

The postwar drug industry was divided between firms that were research-driven and firms that were not. To take full advantage of patents and to pursue basic research, the large drug firms integrated comprehensive manufacturing facilities for both ethical and proprietary divisions. The flood of new products after World War II confirmed mankind's ancient faith in the efficacy of drugs. A plethora of antibiotics issued from the laboratories, capable collectively of destroying any microbe larger than a virus. The sulfa family proved to be large, leading to diuretics to control hypertension and oral antidiabetic drugs. Methylene blue yielded antihistamines that led to tranquilizers. In these developments and many more, American drug firms led the world (Temin 1980).

Pharmacological research proceeds by trial and error. Typically 10,000 chemicals are screened for each commercial success (Wardell 1979). Drug sales expand rapidly, especially for ethical drug preparations. No longer is the drug business geared to a large catalogue of stable commodities. Most revenue, and virtually all profits, comes from typically three and no more than eight products. The commercial life of a drug can be quite short. New products are heavily promoted, and advertising expenditures exceed those for research. Demand is inelastic, so new drugs can be priced well above direct costs to cover expenditures on research and advertising. When patents are about to expire, or when substitute products appear, prices can fall drastically. When patents expire, a generic drug may sell for a tenth of the price of the branded drug (Walker 1971).

The pricing behavior of drug firms, their advertising expenditures, and their licensing arrangements attracted the attention of the Senate Subcommittee on Antitrust and Monopoly, headed by Estes Kefauver. These hearings dealt generally with monopoly power in the United States. The ethical drug industry was a central concern. Kefauver wanted legislation that would reduce the value to drug firms of patents and brands. The opposition had the votes until the thalidomide story broke. The resulting 1962 Kefauver-Harris Amendments to the Food and Drug Act of 1938 seriously affected the drug industry and were a source of continuing controversy for the next quarter century. The 1962 act completed a series of earlier laws aimed at regulating the conduct of the drug industry (Temin 1980).

In the nineteenth century several states enacted laws to eliminate adulteration of food and to regulate drugs (Okun 1986). Persistent efforts to enact similar legislation at the federal level failed until the muckrakers stimulated public interest. *The Jungle*, Upton Sinclair's novel on the meat-packing industry, had the greatest impact, but a series of articles on patent medicines in *Colliers* by Samuel Hopkins Adams also attracted attention.

The 1906 law prohibited fraudulent labeling. The makers of patent medicines bitterly opposed the law; ethical drug manufacturers were divided (Temin 1980). The Sherley Amendment, enacted in 1912, clarified that the law applied to therapeutic claims. The Food and Drug Administration (FDA) was not concerned with ethical drugs until the 1920s. Under Walter Campbell's leadership, the agency enforced regulations requiring pharmacopoeial standards of purity and strength (Young 1970).

Campbell found the 1906 law inadequate to control false advertising; furthermore it provided no recourse against unsafe medications. From 1933, he pressured Congress for legislation that would expand his agency's powers. United opposition from the drug industry and hostility from the press were obstacles until scandal broke—this time over Elixir Sulfanilamide.

It had been common in the South to take medications in liquid form, so Massengill, a Tennessee company, sought a solvent for sulfanilamide. Neither water nor alcohol worked, but diethylene glycol did. Unfortunately the new dosage form was not tested on animals, and the literature check that would have disclosed its known toxicity was not made. Before the product could be withdrawn, there were 100 deaths. The law did not protect against Elixir Sulfanilamide. By calling the product an elixir, however, Massengill had illegally implied that the solvent was alcohol. Massengill was fined $21,100.

The Food and Drug Act of 1938 did not give Campbell the jurisdiction over advertising that he sought, but did substantially strengthen the powers of the FDA. Henceforth, a New Drug Application (NDA) would be submitted for any new drug. If the FDA approved, or if sixty day passed without action, the drug could be marketed. Labels on new and existing drugs must list all ingredients, directions for use, and possible dangers (Temin 1980).

The legislative history of the Kefauver-Harris Amendments of 1962 shares parallels with the past. Kefauver was concerned above all with the monopoly power that drug firms derived from product patents, and the proposed legislative remedy was mandatory licensing. Opposition from the drug industry and organized medicine threatened any chance of his bill becoming law. Then thalidomide was discredited. The drug, considered a safe sedative, had been introduced in Germany in 1958. Frances Kelsey of the FDA probably exceeded her authority when she delayed its marketing in the United States by repeatedly returning the NDA. Babies were born with congenital deformities of the extremities, and in November, 1961, the link was made to ingestion of thalidomide during pregnancy. The drug had been distributed for clinical trials in the United States, leading to about 100 cases of phocomelia out of about 10,000 worldwide (Silverman and Lee 1974). The legislation that followed retained little of the antimonopoly flavor of the original Kefauver bill. Instead it sought to assure the safety of new drugs. Before a drug can even be tested, an Investigational New Drug (IND) application must be approved. Clinical testing proceeds through three phases:

first the drug is tested on animals, then on healthy humans, and finally on patients requiring therapy. After successful clinical trials a New Drug Application (NDA) can be submitted, but the FDA has no fixed time constraint for approval (Silverman and Lee 1974).

A Senate committee, under the chairmanship of Gaylord Nelson, conducted a second set of hearings in the late 1960s. Again the focus was excessive monopoly power from product patents combined with exclusive licenses. No legislation ensued. Increasingly the drug industry became the focus of both popular and scholarly debate. Initially, the point of departure was testimony before the Kefauver Committee, and the framework of analysis was the traditional one of industrial organization, to wit, structure, conduct, performance. The studies were predominantly critical of the drug industry. After 1962, although the profits of the drug industry remained high, the rate at which new drugs were introduced dropped precipitously, and U.S. firms lost ground to foreign competitors. Furthermore, expenditures on drugs continued to rise rapidly, but inflated hospital costs were more pronounced. New drugs were increasingly viewed as a vehicle to contain costs while improving health. Scholarly work in the 1970s focused on dynamic rather than static conditions and was critical, not of the drug companies, but of the FDA and its administration of the 1962 amendments. In the 1980s the debate became less acerbic and attempted to synthesize rather than polarize the goals of the drug companies and the FDA. While the 1962 amendments certainly did not stimulate drug research, other forces at work also pushed the drug industry away from research (Comanor 1986).

BIBLIOGRAPHIC ESSAY

For an overview of the history of health care in the United States, see the Pulitzer Prize–winning *Social Transformation of American Medicine*, by Paul Starr (1982). Three books trace the use of drugs from ancient times to the present, but each presents problems for the general reader. Erwin H. Ackerknecht (1973) addressed his history to young physicians starting practice. Glenn Sonnedecker's (1976) textbook is designed to be part of the curriculum for a degree in pharmacy. The history by Patrice Boussel, Henri Bonnemain, and Frank J. Bove (1983) was written in French, and the translation suffers from numerous typographical errors.

Liebenau (1987) looks at the transformation to modern drug manufacturing in the United States. His 1984 article is a fine scholarly treatment of the critical years for industrial laboratories. Sonnedecker (1965) also presents a short but useful account of technical change in the drug industry at the turn of the century.

The colonial apothecary cultivated or gathered raw materials, manufactured the medicines, and treated the patient. Harold B. Gill, Jr. (1972), chronicles the apothecary's role in Virginia, and the volume edited by Ronald

I. Numbers (1987) covers medicine on much of the rest of the continent. Of particular interest is the chapter on New England by Eric H. Christianson. Letters relating the dealings of a London druggist with colonial apothecaries have been edited by I. K. Steele (1977).

Drug manufacturing as a separate industry began in the nineteenth century, but the legal distinction between prescription and nonprescription drugs would wait until 1951. From the start, the industry divided between patent drug manufacturers, who advertised to the general public, and ethical drug manufacturers, who advertised to physicians. *The Toadstool Millionaires*, by James Harvey Young (1961), presents a lively yet scholarly account of patent medicines in the nineteenth century. Sarah Stage (1979) investigates more closely, and from a sociological perspective, the story behind Lydia E. Pinkham's Vegetable Compound.

Perhaps because their roots often trace back well into the nineteenth century, many ethical drug companies have authorized company histories. Possibly in response to pervasive regulation of the industry, these accounts tend to be sanitized. In *The Merchants of Life: An Account of the American Pharmaceutical Industry*, Tom Mahoney (1959) recounts a fascinating tale of the rise and development of many drug firms. His account, though, is uncritical and appears to rely on company histories. Collections of company histories can also be found (Boussel, Bonnemain, and Bove 1983; Nelson 1983).

Elmer Holmes Bobst headed the American branch of Hoffman-La Roche and then became chief executive officer of Warner-Lambert. His autobiography (1973) chronicles a fascinating life and is more candid than most company histories. More remarkable yet is the life of Philip Musica, alias Dr. F. Donald Coster. This hoodlum took a small, respected drug wholesaler, added an *interesting* manufacturing operation, and turned McKesson and Robbins into a major corporation (Keats 1964).

Taking Your Medicine: Drug Regulation in the United States (Temin 1980) does much more than trace the history of drug regulation in the United States. Peter Temin analyzes the dynamic interaction between a rapidly changing drug industry, the medical profession, and government. Two conference reports provide further insight into the social and medical rationale for regulating the pharmaceutical industry (Blake 1970; Talalay 1964). Milton Silverman and Philip R. Lee (1974) review drugs and the drug industry from a different perspective, having been practitioners, pharmacologists, and regulators.

Monographs provide more detailed accounts of the political process in the passage of particular pieces of drug regulation: the state laws in the nineteenth century (Okun 1986), the Pure Food and Drug Act of 1906 (Wood 1986), the Food and Drug Act of 1938 (Jackson 1970), and the Drug Abuse Control Amendments of 1965 (Pekkanen 1973).

Hearings before the Kefauver Committee (U.S. Senate, Committee on the

Judiciary, Subcommittee on Antitrust and Monopoly 1959) and the Nelson Committee (U.S. Senate, Select Committee on Small Business 1967–68) have provided primary source material for a number of dissertations, but nuggets remain to be mined. Another government document (U.S. Department of Commerce, International Trade Administration 1984) presents a brief description of the contemporary drug industry.

The literature on the economic impact of the 1962 amendments to the Food and Drug Act is immense and has been reviewed elsewhere (Comanor 1986; Sevigny 1977).

BIBLIOGRAPHY

Ackerknecht, Erwin H. "Short Survey of Drug Therapy Prior to 1900." In *Safeguarding the Public: Historical Aspects of Medicinal Drug Control*, edited by John B. Blake, 52–58. Baltimore: Johns Hopkins University Press, 1970.

———. *Therapeutics from the Primitives to the Twentieth Century*. New York: Hafner Press, 1973.

Blake, John B., ed. *Safeguarding the Public: Historical Aspects of Medicinal Drug Control*. Baltimore: Johns Hopkins University Press, 1970.

Bobst, Elmer Holmes. *Bobst: The Autobiography of a Pharmaceutical Pioneer*. New York: David McKay, 1973.

Boussel, Patrice, Henri Bonnemain, and Frank J. Bove. *History of Pharmacy and the Pharmaceutical Industry*. Translated by Desmond Newell and Frank J. Bove. Paris: Asklepios Press, 1983.

Christianson, Eric H. "Medicine in New England." In *Medicine in the New World: New Spain, New France and New England*, edited by Ronald I. Numbers. Knoxville: University of Tennessee Press, 1987.

Comanor, W. S. "Research and Competitive Product Differentiation in the Pharmaceutical Industry in the United States." *Economica* 31 (November 1964): 372–384.

———. "The Drug Industry and Medical Research: The Economics of the Kefauver Committee Investigations." *Journal of Business* 39 (January 1966): 12–18.

———. "The Political Economy of the Pharmaceutical Industry." *Journal of Economic Literature* 24 (September 1986): 1178–1217.

Cowen, David L. "The Role of the Pharmaceutical Industry." In *Safeguarding the Public: Historical Aspects of Medicinal Drug Control*, edited by John B. Blake, 72–93. Baltimore: Johns Hopkins University Press, 1970.

Davis, Lee Niedringhaus. *The Corporate Alchemists: Profit Takers and Problem Makers in the Chemical Industry*. New York: William Morrow, 1984.

Gill, Harold B., Jr. *The Apothecary in Colonial Virginia*. Williamsburg, VA: Colonial Williamsburg Foundation, 1972.

Jackson, Charles O. *Food and Drug Legislation in the New Deal*. Princeton: Princeton University Press, 1970.

Kahn, E. J. *All in a Century: The First 100 Years of Eli Lilly and Company*. Indianapolis: Lilly, 1976.

Keats, Charles. *Magnificent Masquerade: The Strange Case of Dr. Coster and Mr. Musica*. New York: Funk & Wagnalls, 1964.

Liebenau, Jonathan. "Industrial R and D in Pharmaceutical Firms in the Early Twentieth Century." *Business History* 26 (November 1984): 327–46.

———. *Medical Science and Medical Industry: The Formation of the American Pharmaceutical Industry.* Baltimore: Johns Hopkins University Press, 1987.

Mahoney, Tom. *The Merchants of Life: An Account of the American Pharmaceutical Industry.* New York: Harper & Row, 1959.

Mann, H. M. "Seller Concentration, Barriers to Entry, and Rates of Return in Thirty Industries, 1950–1960." *Review of Economics and Statistics* 48 (August 1966): 296–307.

Nelson, Gary L., ed. *Pharmaceutical Company Histories.* Vol. 1. Bismarck, ND: Woodbine, 1983.

Numbers, Ronald I., ed. *Medicine in the New World: New Spain, New France and New England.* Knoxville: University of Tennessee Press, 1987.

Okun, Mitchell. *Fair Play in the Marketplace.* DeKalb: Northern Illinois Press, 1986.

Pekkanen, John. *The American Connection: Profiteering and Politicking in the "Ethical" Drug Industry.* Chicago: Follett, 1973.

Schifrin, L. G. "Thalidomide and Beyond: Some Recommendations Regarding Public Policies Toward the Ethical Drug Industry." *International Journal of Health Services* 4 (January 1974): 147–55.

Schwartzman, David. *Innovation in the Pharmaceutical Industry.* Baltimore: Johns Hopkins University Press, 1976.

Sevigny, David C. *The Ethical Pharmaceutical Industry and Some of Its Economic Aspects: An Annotated Bibliography.* Bibliographic Series, edited by R. J. Hall, vol. 13. Toronto: Addiction Research Foundation, 1977.

Silverman, Milton, and Philip R. Lee. *Pills, Profits, and Politics.* Berkeley: University of California Press, 1974.

Sonnedecker, Glenn. "The Rise of Drug Manufacture in America." *Emory University Quarterly* 21 (Summer 1965): 73–87.

———, rev. *Kremers and Urdang's History of Pharmacy.* 4th ed. Philadelphia: Lippincott, 1976.

Stage, Sarah. *Female Complaints: Lydia E. Pinkham and the Business of Women's Medicine.* New York: Norton, 1979.

Starr, Paul. *The Social Transformation of American Medicine.* New York: Basic Books, 1982.

Steele, I. K., ed. *Atlantic Merchant-Apothecary: Letters of Joseph Cruttenden 1710–1717.* Toronto: University of Toronto Press, 1977.

Talalay, Paul, ed. *Drugs in Our Society.* Baltimore: Johns Hopkins University Press, 1964.

Temin, Peter. *Taking Your Medicine: Drug Regulation in the United States.* Cambridge, MA: Harvard University Press, 1980.

Temkin, Owsei. "Historical Aspects of Drug Therapy." In *Drugs in Our Society,* edited by Paul Talalay, 3–16. Baltimore: Johns Hopkins University Press, 1964.

U.S. Department of Commerce. International Trade Administration. *A Competitive Assessment of the U.S. Pharmaceutical Industry.* Washington, DC: U.S. Government Printing Office, 1984.

U.S. Senate. Committee on the Judiciary. Subcommittee on Antitrust and Monopoly. *Hearings on Administered Prices.* 86th Cong., 1st sess., 1959.

————. Select Committee on Small Business. *Hearings on Present Status of Competition in the Pharmaceutical Industry*. 90th Cong., 1st and 2d sess., 1967–68.

Walker, Hugh D. *Market Power and Price Levels in the Ethical Drug Industry*. Bloomington: Indiana University Press, 1971.

Wardell, William M. "The History of Drug Discovery, Development, and Regulation." In *Issues in Pharmaceutical Economics*, edited by Robert I. Chien. Lexington, MA: D. C. Heath, Lexington Books, 1979.

Wood, Donna J. *Strategic Uses of Public Policy: Business and Government in the Progressive Era*. Marshfield, MA: Pitman, 1986.

Young, James Harvey. *The Toadstool Millionaires*. Princeton: Princeton University Press, 1961.

————. "Drugs and the 1906 Law." In *Safeguarding the Public: Historical Aspects of Medicinal Drug Control*, edited by John B. Blake, 147–54. Baltimore: Johns Hopkins University Press, 1970.

CHAPTER 9 ———————————————————————————

AGRICULTURAL CHEMICALS, 28.7

————————————————— DAVID M. WISHART

BACKGROUND

The agricultural chemicals industry comprises firms that manufacture phosphates, potash, nitrogen, mixed fertilizers, and pesticides. The industry originated in England in the late eighteenth century when bone fertilizers were first produced commercially. Bones are an excellent source of phosphorus, an essential plant nutrient. After 1780 crushing bones for fertilizer was transformed from a task done on the farm with axes and hammers to a manufacturing process pursued by merchant grinders with power mills.

By 1815 Great Britain was importing some 20,000 tons of bones per year from the Continent to support the bone fertilizer industry. The size of their imports prompted a German chemist, Justus von Liebig, to criticize the British for robbing graves and scouring battlefields for bones (Jacob 1964a).

Von Liebig treated bones with acid to produce superphosphates. His idea for applying organic chemistry to agriculture was not new, but was the first to appear in the scientific literature (Jacob 1964a). In England, J. B. Lawes patented a procedure for manufacturing superphosphates in 1842 (Parrish et al. 1939).

The first American to enter the superphosphate industry was James Jay Mapes, who established a plant in Newark, New Jersey, in 1852. Mapes's formula for his product, Improved Super-phosphate of Lime, included bones dissolved in sulfuric acid mixed with "pure Peruvian guano" and sulfate of ammonia. Guano, the accumulated droppings from sea fowl, was imported from South American islands as a second source of phosphate. Both bones and guano were replaced as a source of phosphate in manufacturing by phosphate rock discovered in South Carolina in 1867 (Jacob 1964a).

The first potash mine and muriate of potash plant were established in 1861 in Strassfurt, Germany. Under the direction of syndicates that controlled price and output, potash production was concentrated in Germany and France throughout the 1920s. The United States was the primary export market for potash (Lamer 1957).

Only one U.S. firm, the American Trona Corporation, had entered the potash industry by 1924. Later entrants included the United States Potash Company and the Potash Company of America (closely related to Diamond Match Company, which used potassium found in potash for match manufacture). Potash production did not take off until World War II, when the United States became a net exporter of fertilizer (Lamer 1957).

Until the twentieth century, the conventional wisdom in agricultural science held that sufficient nitrogen was available to crops from natural sources and crop rotation so that applications of nitrogen fertilizer were unnecessary. In response to the growing world population and the need for increased agricultural productivity, processes were developed for fixing atmospheric nitrogen as a fertilizer. An ammonia industry first developed in Germany after the introduction on a commercial scale of the Haber-Bosch process for fixing atmospheric nitrogen in 1913. Until 1960 nitrogen production was concentrated in the developed countries; production in the United States was dominated by many small plants operating close to fertilizer markets in the East and Midwest. Leading producers in the United States through the 1950s were Allied Chemical and Dye Corporation and E. I. du Pont de Nemours and Company (Markham 1958; Sheldrick 1987).

Before World War II, most farmers bought fertilizers as mixtures of nitrogen, phosphate, and potassium (potash). Some 1,000 grades of mixed fertilizers had been available, but wartime regulation reduced that number to 271 (Lamer 1957). Mixed fertilizers continue to be produced by small plants located close to the fertilizer market; however, single-nutrient fertilizers have chiefly replaced mixed fertilizers in American agriculture (Sittig 1979).

Before the war, farmers made limited use of crude pesticides—mercury, strychnine, and arsenic. Today, sophisticated organic compounds play a key role in agricultural production. The Nobel Prize–winning agronomist Norman Borlaug has estimated that if pesticide use in the United States were halted, crop losses to pests would reach 50 percent and food prices would increase four to five times (Kenyon 1977). By the mid–1980s, 130 producers in the United States manufactured 50,000 pesticide products to combat some 2,500 registered pest species (Aspelin 1983).

THE AGRICULTURAL CHEMICALS INDUSTRY DURING WORLD WAR II

The U.S. fertilizer industry exploded during World War II. The United States, Canada, and Great Britain—the "fertilizer triangle"—coordinated fertilizer production and trade to increase supplies of food for the Allied military and civilian populations (Lamer 1957).

The capacity for producing synthetic nitrogen in the United States increased threefold during the war. Nitrogen is necessary for explosives production, so much of the increase in capacity was related to military production, but considerable amounts of nitrogen fertilizer, especially ammonium nitrate, were produced as well (Lamer 1957).

Mining of phosphate rock and potash increased markedly during the war. Production of superphosphate in the United States doubled from 1938 to 1945 and tripled from 1938 to 1950. Capacity expanded through additions to existing plants, construction of fourteen new plants between 1940 and 1945, and increases in phosphate rock mining. Most of this increased production was concentrated in the South Atlantic and South Central states (Lamer 1957).

During World War I a critical potash shortage in the United States had been a strategic disadvantage (Lamer 1957). The government and private industry worked together after the war to develop reserves that would ensure self-sufficiency. Potash deposits discovered in New Mexico were mined during the 1930s, and these new sources helped build up U.S. reserves. By the outbreak of World War II, the United States still imported much of the potash consumed in the New England and Middle Atlantic states from German, French, and Spanish mines, but by the war's end, producers in the western states were supplying the domestic market (Harline 1950).

THE AGRICULTURAL CHEMICALS INDUSTRY IN THE POSTWAR PERIOD

The population growth worldwide heightened concern that the fertilizer industry would be unable to supply fertilizer for the United States and developing countries, too. The Federal Trade Commission issued a report in 1950 charging the fertilizer industry with introducing and using monopolistic controls within a highly concentrated structure. The report called for an end to "cartel and other agreements by which prices were fixed and competition restrained both among foreign suppliers and in the domestic production and distribution of fertilizer materials and mixed fertilizers" (U.S. Federal Trade Commission 1950, 151). Also cited were the numerous antitrust suits brought against raw material suppliers in the fertilizer industry and the legislative efforts to distribute fertilizer to farmers at reduced costs.

Jesse W. Markham attempted to determine whether the relatively high cost of fertilizer to farmers in the United States during the 1950s was attributable to cartel-like agreements among raw material suppliers or to problems of distribution. He concluded that the high costs stemmed not so much from monopolistic practices in raw materials markets as from farmers' imperfect knowledge about the products they were purchasing. Markham's proposals for policy changes included coordinating existing government fertilizer programs, improving extension services, and updating state control laws to "reduce the social costs of unintelligent buying" (1958, 237–38).

Concern over fertilizer supplies during the 1950s led to excess production throughout the 1960s and surpluses of nitrogen, phosphorus, and potassium (Lyon 1975; Teleki 1975a, 1975b). By the late 1960s industry specialists questioned the adequacy of sulfur supplies for producing phosphate and mixed fertilizers (Hignett 1968).

The need to conserve sulfur supplies in fertilizer production paled in the early 1970s when the energy crisis turned fertilizer surpluses into shortages. Moreover, the demand for fertilizers of all types increased as agricultural development programs were set up in many underdeveloped countries. Production of nitrogen fertilizer was particularly susceptible to disruption by the 1973 oil crisis because it is largely based on petrochemical feedstocks (Stangel 1984). Phosphate shortages in the 1970s can be traced to low prices and the surplus in the 1960s, and to price controls and industry stagnation in the early 1970s. The potash shortage was apparently the result of an increase in demand for potassium (Teleki 1975b).

Higher prices for fertilizers during the mid–1970s were an impetus to worldwide expansion in the industry. The unexpected price increase emphasized the poor international coordination between fertilizer production and distribution (Stangel 1984). The Food and Agriculture Organization (FAO) of the United Nations intensified its efforts to collect information about fertilizers and disseminate it to development planners and authorities.

The FAO has chronicled international fertilizer production and consumption in annual reports since 1949 (FAO 1949). The early reports trace the gradual recovery of the world fertilizer industry from the dislocations of World War II through 1953–54. They report a substantial technological change in U.S. fertilizer production by 1952, when nitrogen fixation plants shifted from coke to natural gas as an energy source. The change in energy sources encouraged gas-rich Middle Eastern nations to enter the fertilizer production industry (FAO 1953–77).

Technology transfer continues to be a major theme in more recent United Nations literature. The 1985 United Nations Conference on Trade and Development held in Geneva produced a study by S. K. Mukherjee that strongly recommended expanding the capacity for domestic fertilizer production in developing countries to cut dependence on oligopolistic supply sources in the United States and other nations. Tying-agreements in aid programs to developing countries give monopoly power to fertilizer exporters in the developed countries. In 1973, 94 percent of the fertilizer aid from the United States was tied to purchases from the United States (Mukherjee 1985).

The United Nations' focus is not limited to increasing domestic fertilizer production in developing countries. The 1982 publication *Transnational*

Corporations in the Fertilizer Industry (see United Nations 1982) describes how developing countries can best negotiate with transnational agricultural chemical corporations.

The FAO's emphasis on technology transfer is evident in the 1978 publication *Fertilizer Marketing*. This volume explains fertilizer marketing for countries that import substantial quantities of fertilizer from the developed world or that manufacture fertilizers (Wierer and Abbott 1978).

In the 1980s the U.S. fertilizer industry has concentrated on adapting to rapidly changing tillage practices and an agricultural economic environment that is more hostile than it was in the 1970s. These subjects were addressed at the TVA conference Situation 84, which brought together government, farm, and fertilizer industry officials.

Tillage practices were a major topic at the Situation 84 conference. Higher energy costs in the early 1980s and soil losses from erosion encouraged farmers to shift from the traditional moldboard plow to reduced tillage and no-till farming. Purdue University conducted a survey in conjunction with the National Fertilizer Development Center of the Tennessee Valley Authority to study the "interactions between tillage and fertilization practices" (Fletcher 1985, 78). Their report predicted that although the overall demand for fertilizer would not be affected by changes in tillage, the timing of fertilizer applications and equipment needs would change, as would the services that fertilizer dealers provide (Fletcher 1985).

In response to deteriorating economic conditions farmers have begun to adopt the maximum economic yield concept in the use of fertilizers: produce to maximize profits, not output. A profit-maximizing market permits fertilizer dealers to promote customer satisfaction and loyalty by taking an active interest in crop production (Reetz 1985).

The strong positive correlation between crop prices and the prices paid for various fertilizers was demonstrated during the farm crisis in the United States in the early 1980s (Douglas and Harre 1985). Fertilizer is an input to crop production, and the value of inputs depends on the value of the commodity being produced. The correlation between crop prices and performance in the early 1980s was evidently weaker in the pesticides industry than in the fertilizer industry. Nevertheless, producers of agricultural chemical pesticides enjoyed "relatively good growth and profits—in contrast to the very sluggish markets for industrial chemicals and plastics" during the recession years of 1981–82 (Pliszka 1983, 125).

The economic environment has been stable for the pesticides industry in recent years, but the regulatory and technological environments are ever-changing. One authority on government regulation of pesticides has noted that "the essential, but controversial, property of pesticides is toxicity to living organisms" (Tait 1981, 219). The time lag between confirmation of a pesticide's effectiveness and actual marketing averages from seven to nine years under the intense regulatory scrutiny required for new products

(Pliszka 1983). Something of an adversarial relationship exists between pesticide manufacturers and the U.S. Environmental Protection Agency (Tait 1981).

Pesticide manufacturers make large commitments to research and development. These investments are risky because of uncertainties in licensing, the short product life cycles of pesticides, and the natural resistance that pest species develop to the compounds. A typical manufacturer allocates about 8 percent of its annual sales to research. Most products have a twenty-five-to-thirty-year life cycle (Pliszka 1983). Manufacturers have responded to these risks by showing considerable interest in developing safer methods of pest control through genetic engineering (Kellogg 1983).

STATISTICAL SERIES AND ANALYSIS ON THE AGRICULTURAL CHEMICALS INDUSTRY

Statistical series on U.S. fertilizer supplies are available from 1942 to the present in a U.S. Department of Agriculture (Production and Marketing Administration) publication titled *The Fertilizer Situation*. In addition to detailed statistics by states on the use of nitrogen, phosphorus, and potash, the more recent issues of this volume contain information on the role of the United States in the international fertilizer market. Unfortunately, issues from the 1950s contain limited statistical information and almost no descriptive analysis.

Another source of data on the U.S. fertilizer industry and U.S. imports and exports of fertilizers is *Nitrogen, Phosphate, Potash: The Fertilizer Supply*, published annually by the Agricultural Stabilization and Conservation Service of the U.S. Department of Agriculture. This series highlights the U.S. role in the international fertilizer trade, so domestic consumption patterns receive less attention than in *The Fertilizer Situation*.

Fertilizer Trends, a biennial publication of the National Fertilizer Development Center, contains substantial descriptive information on TVA fertilizer programs, the fertilizer market, trends in fertilizer use, and statistics on North American production and consumption. *Fertilizer Trends* has been published since 1956.

The availability of good statistical data for the fertilizer industry in the United States makes it a natural area for econometric analysis, but one that has not been thoroughly investigated. The first estimates of demand relationships for the three main fertilizer groups in the United States showed demands with variable elasticities between regions (Griliches 1958). In the mid–1970s, energy costs became a significant variable on both the demand and the supply sides of the fertilizer market. Reestimates of demands for fertilizer in the 1960–80 period show that demand is inelastic in all three fertilizer categories. One can conclude from these results that "increases in fertilizer prices lead to increases in total cost of food production" (Gyawu et al. 1984, 50). Furthermore, the demand for nitrogen was much more sensitive to the farm price of corn than was the demand for potash or phosphate, which suggests that government price supports for corn "induce greater demand for nitrogen than for phosphates or potash" (Gyawu et al. 1984, 51).

As noted in the preceding section, the FAO has published international fertilizer production and consumption statistics in annual reports since 1949 (FAO 1949). These provide production and consumption statistics by category (nitrogen, potassium, and phosphatic fertilizers) for continents and individual countries. From these statistics the FAO can isolate trends and offer suggestions for expanding fertilizer usage and production worldwide.

Beginning in 1978, the FAO publication *An Annual Review of World Production and Consumption of Fertilizers* appeared under the title *FAO Fertilizer Yearbook*. This series is a well-organized presentation of statistics by country and by continent, but it provides little descriptive analysis.

For statistical information on pesticides production in addition to fertilizer production, see the National Agricultural Chemicals Association, *Annual Industry Profile Study*.

BIBLIOGRAPHY

Agricultural Division, Food and Agriculture Organization of the United Nations. *Commercial Fertilizers.* FAO Bulletin No. 17. Rome: Food and Agriculture Organization of the United Nations, 1949.

———. *FAO Commodity Report, Fertilizers.* Rome: Food and Agriculture Organization of the United Nations, 1950.

———. *Fertilizers—A World Report on Production and Consumption.* Rome: Food and Agriculture Organization of the United Nations, 1951 and 1952.

———. *An Annual Review of World Production and Consumption of Fertilizers,* published annually, 1953–77. Rome: Food and Agriculture Organization of the United Nations.

———. *FAO Fertilizer Yearbook,* published annually, 1978–present. Rome: Food and Agriculture Organization of the United Nations.

Agricultural Stabilization and Conservation Service, USDA. *Nitrogen, Phosphate, Potash: The Fertilizer Supply,* published annually, 1975–76–present. Washington, DC: U.S. Department of Agriculture.

Aspelin, Arnold L. "Economic Aspects of Current Pesticide Regulatory Programs and Outlook for the Future." In *Feast or Famine? The Future of Chemicals in the Food Industry,* 93–121, papers presented at the February 1983 meeting of the Chemical Marketing Research Association. New York: Chemical Marketing Research Association, 1983.

Douglas, John R., Jr., and Edwin A. Harre. "National Fertilizer Outlook." In *Situation '84: TVA Fertilizer Conference,* 27–35. Muscle Shoals, AL: National Fertilizer Development Center, 1985.

FAO. See Agricultural Division.

Fletcher, Jerald. "Corn Belt Survey Results: Impact of Changing Tillage Practices on the Fertilizer Industry." In *Situation '84: TVA Fertilizer Conference*, 78–87. Muscle Shoals, AL: National Fertilizer Development Center, 1985.

Griliches, Zvi. "The Demand for Fertilizer: An Economic Interpretation of a Technological Change." *Journal of Farm Economics* 40 (1958): 591–606.

Gyawu, Emmanuel A., et al. *An Econometric Analysis of the U.S. Fertilizer Industry.* Lexington: University of Kentucky Agricultural Experiment Station, 1984.

Harline, Osmond. "Economic Factors Affecting the Development of the Intermountain Fertilizer Industry." *Utah Economic and Business Review* 10 (June 1950): 1–179.

Hignett, Travis P. *Characteristics of the World Fertilizer Industry—Phosphatic Fertilizers.* TVA Report No. S–422. Muscle Shoals, AL: Tennessee Valley Authority, 1968.

Jacob, K. D. "History and Status of the Superphosphate Industry." In *Superphosphate: Its History, Chemistry, and Manufacture*, edited by Louis B. Nelson and Cecil H. Wadleigh. Washington, DC: U.S. Department of Agriculture, Agricultural Research Service, 1964a.

———. "Predecessors of Superphosphate." In *Superphosphate: Its History, Chemistry, and Manufacture*, edited by Louis B. Nelson and Cecil H. Wadleigh. Washington, DC: U.S. Department of Agriculture, Agricultural Research Service, 1964b.

Kellogg, Scott T. "The Impact of Genetic Engineering on Pesticides." In *Feast or Famine? The Future of Chemicals in the Food Industry*, 122–24, papers presented at the February 1983 meeting of the Chemical Marketing Research Association. New York: Chemical Marketing Research Association, 1983.

Kenyon, Ron. "The Agricultural Chemical Industry: An Endangered Species?" *Agrologist* 6 (Summer 1977): 6–7, 9–10.

Lamer, Mirko. *The World Fertilizer Economy.* Stanford: Stanford University Press, 1957.

Lyon, Fred D. "Nitrogen Supplies with Respect to Current and Future World Needs." In *International and National Outlook—The Necessity for Efficient Nutrient Utilization*, edited by Matthias Stelly, 51–56. Madison, WI: American Society of Agronomy, Soil Science Society of America, 1975.

Markham, Jesse W. *The Fertilizer Industry: Study of an Imperfect Market.* Nashville: Vanderbilt University Press, 1958.

Mukherjee, S. K. *Fertilizer Supplies for Developing Countries: Issues in the Transfer Development of Technology.* New York: United Nations, 1985.

National Agricultural Chemicals Association. *Annual Industry Profile Study* (also called *Annual Surveys*), 1970–present. Washington, DC.

National Fertilizer Development Center, TVA. *Fertilizer Trends*, published biennially, 1956–present. Muscle Shoals, AL: Tennessee Valley Authority.

Parrish, P., et al. *Calcium Superphosphate and Compound Fertilizers: Their Chemistry and Manufacture.* Plymouth, UK: Mayflower Press, 1939.

Pliszka, George C. "Commercial Considerations in Research on Pesticides." In *Feast or Famine? The Future of Chemicals in the Food Industry*, 125–37, papers presented at the February 1983 meeting of the Chemical Marketing Research Association. New York: Chemical Marketing Research Association, 1983.

Production and Marketing Administration, USDA (later years, Commodity Stabilization Service and Economic Research Service, USDA). *The Fertilizer Sit-*

uation, published annually, 1942–43–present. Washington, DC: U.S. Department of Agriculture.

Reetz, Harold F., Jr. "Maximum Economic Yields—What's in It for the Dealer?" In *Situation '84: TVA Fertilizer Conference*, 70–72. Muscle Shoals, AL: National Fertilizer Development Center, 1985.

Sheldrick, William F. *World Nitrogen Survey*. World Bank Technical Paper No. 59, Industry and Finance Series. Washington, DC: World Bank, 1987.

Sittig, Marshall. *Fertilizer Industry: Processes, Pollution Control and Energy Conservation*. Park Ridge, NJ: Noyes Data Corp., 1979.

Stangel, Paul J. "World Nitrogen Situation—Trends, Outlook, and Requirements." In *Nitrogen in Crop Production*, edited by Roland D. Hauck, 23–54. Madison, WI: American Society of Agronomy, Crop Science Society of America, Soil Science Society of America, 1984.

Tait, Joyce. "The Flow of Pesticides: Industrial and Farming Perspectives." In *Progress in Resource Management and Environmental Planning*, edited by T. O'Riordan and R. Kerry Turner, vol. 3, 219–50. New York: John Wiley & Sons, 1981.

Teleki, Deneb. "Phosphorus Supplies with Respect to Current and Future World Needs." In *International and National Outlook—The Necessity for Efficient Nutrient Utilization*, edited by Matthias Stelly, 57–62. Madison, WI: American Society of Agronomy, Soil Science Society of America, 1975a.

———. "Potassium Supplies with Respect to Current and Future World Needs." In *International and National Outlook—The Necessity for Efficient Nutrient Utilization*, edited by Matthias Stelly, 63–66. Madison, WI: American Society of Agronomy, Soil Science Society of America, 1975b.

United Nations Centre on Transnational Corporation. *Transnational Corporations in the Fertilizer Industry*. New York: United Nations, 1982.

U.S. Federal Trade Commission. *Report of the Federal Trade Commission on the Fertilizer Industry*. Washington, DC: U.S. Government Printing Office, 1950.

Wierer, K., and J. C. Abbott. *Fertilizer Marketing*. FAO Marketing Guide No. 7. Rome: Food and Agriculture Organization of the United Nations, 1978.

Part VI

Petroleum
ESIC 29.0

CHAPTER 10

PETROLEUM, 29.0

K. V. NAGARAJAN

On August 27, 1859, "Colonel" Edwin L. Drake struck oil. His crude rig, built like those used for pumping brine, drilled through 30 feet of solid rock near Titusville, Pennsylvania, and hit oil at a depth of 69 1/2 feet. The first Drake well was an instant money-maker. Although it yielded only twenty barrels a day, its precious product was in such demand as a lamp-oil base and lubricant that a barrel commanded the royal sum of $20. The lure of quick profits immediately attracted investors, wildcatters, and speculators to those rolling hills of western Pennsylvania that came to be known as the Oil Region. Rigs went up everywhere. The area was a beehive of activity.

Within a few years of the Drake well, the oil industry had spread across the globe to central Europe, southern Russia, and Southeast Asia. Now, more than a century later, offshore sites around the world are being probed intensively for new sources of oil.

In the Age of Illumination petroleum derivatives were predominantly used for home lighting (Williamson and Daum 1959). The twentieth century saw the rise of the Age of Energy (Williamson et al. 1963). Motorized transportation and industrialization created a vast demand for fuel and road-surfacing material. After World War II, that demand included high-quality gasoline for surface transportation and jet fuel for the commercial aviation industry.

The petrochemical industry has added a new dimension to demand in the form of "feedstock." To meet the steadily rising demand for petroleum products, the oil industry vigorously expanded its activity around the globe. Vast new fields were developed in the Middle East, Latin America, Africa, Southeast Asia, Mexico, Alaska, and western Canada, and offshore drilling has yielded producing wells in the North Sea.

Production of oil, of course, is just the beginning. In the downstream stages, the crude oil is transported and refined. The finished products are then shipped to markets. In the early years of the oil industry, refineries were located near the oil fields. With the development of rail transportation, pipeline systems, and supertankers, refineries dispersed closer to their markets. Regardless of their location, refineries link oil producers and energy consumers.

The design of the early refineries reflected the industry's simple processing technology: upright stills, pipes, and fuel to heat up the crude were all that were needed. Their main product was kerosene, which was in high demand. Later, as demand shifted to gasoline and fuel oil, refining technology became more sophisticated. Refineries grew to exploit economies of scale. World War II imposed stringent requirements for high-quality fuel, especially for combat aviation, and the high-compression automobile engines introduced after the war demanded high-octane fuel. Refineries adjusted accordingly.

The most important energy-related development in the postwar years was the 1973–74 oil crisis. Crude oil prices quadrupled in that period, putting the industrialized world on notice that the era of "cheap energy" had come to an end. The second oil shock of 1979–80 converted the remaining skeptics. Those crises affected the refining industry worldwide. The rising price of oil altered the demand for finished products. Refiners with flexible facilities adjusted fastest.

The price increases that followed the second oil shock and the steady rise in energy efficiency dramatically reduced the demand for petroleum products; so refining capacity in the United States declined. The growing imports of low-cost refined products manufactured abroad in recently built, cost-effective refineries encouraged domestic refiners to lobby for tariffs and import quotas. Some invoked national security as justification.

A concern in recent years has been the environmental impact of burning fossil fuels. The emissions from leaded gasoline, for example, may be hazardous, and proposals to ban its use are frequently aired. These proposals have important implications for the refining industry.

EARLY REFINING TECHNOLOGY

Modern crude oil refining can be traced to the manufacture and processing of coal oil. Coal oil became available in commercial quantities in the 1850s and was promoted as an alternative to volatile spirits and the dwindling supply of animal fats. The basic processes of refining coal oil were developed by A. F. Selligue, James Young, and others. Successful commercial applications were developed by Samuel Downer and Joshua Merrill, who operated gas retorts (Williamson and Daum 1959). Coal oil was refined in several steps. Broken pieces of coal were fed into gas retorts—temperatures below 800°F yielded crude coal oil. The oil was transferred to tanks, purified, and pumped into cast-iron stills. Distillation yielded illumination oil and paraffin-oil lubricants that were chemically treated to enhance their properties before they were marketed. With minor modifications, coal oil stills could be used to refine petroleum.

The usefulness of petroleum crude as a base for distillation was publicized by the landmark Silliman report of 1855. Professor Benjamin Silliman, Jr., a Yale University chemist, estimated that half the crude oil could be distilled to yield illuminant oil and the remainder, a variety of potentially useful by-products. His report encouraged New York investors George H. Bissell and Jonathan B. Eveleth to commission Drake to prospect for oil on the properties they had leased in Titusville. In the wake of Drake's success, oil flowed in sufficient quantities for refiners to shift from coal oil to petroleum crude oil.

THE CONVERSION FROM COAL CRUDE OIL TO PETROLEUM CRUDE OIL: 1860–62

The conversion from coal oil to petroleum oil refining began around 1860. Initially, economic conditions did not favor petroleum crude oil. Transporting crude from Pennsylvania's Oil Region to the refining facilities and markets on the Eastern Seaboard was expensive, cumbersome, unreliable, and hazardous. Without a dependable supply of petroleum, refiners were reluctant to convert from coal. There were two other considerations: the yield ratio and the price of petroleum. A 75 percent yield ratio and a price under $12 a barrel for petroleum were necessary to make the switch economically viable (Williamson and Daum 1959).

As petroleum crude supplies became steady and abundant, many large East Coast refiners began to convert. By 1861 several gushers in the Oil Region had lowered the price of crude oil. The world's first petroleum refinery is said to have been constructed near Titusville in 1861 for $15,000 (*New York Times*, May 31, 1959, sec. 11, p. 2). Many small refineries were established in the Oil Region. Pittsburgh, Erie, and Cleveland emerged as major refining centers.

The early 1860s were characterized by steady improvements in handling, processing, and transporting the crude oil and finished products. Standard nomenclature and measurement systems were adopted by the petroleum operators, but the industry was unstable. Crude oil prices, prices of refined products, and the refiners' profit margins all fluctuated widely (McLean and Haigh 1954).

Refining was a wide-open field. Just as there were many small producers of oil, there were innumerable refinery operators in the Oil Region. Many of the refineries were "teakettle" operations processing as little as five to ten barrels a day. In an atmosphere of instability, small operators were swamped by forces beyond their control. Low crude prices and rising demand for refined products led to frenzied refinery building. The Civil War was another impetus. The post–Civil War period, however, was disastrous for refiners with overbuilt capacity. The depression of 1866–67 shut down numerous refineries in the Oil Region.

Aside from the unstable economic environment, the small refiners' problems derived from the primitiveness of their equipment and the scale of their operations. The teakettle refineries were mostly direct-fire, upright stills carried over from the coal oil era. Their processing efficiency was so low that their economic viability depended on low crude oil prices and high prices for refined products. If these prices moved in the wrong direction, the small refineries were caught in a cost-price squeeze. Without process flexibility or a financial cushion, they fell by the wayside.

Large operators attempted to overcome technical limitations and maintain profit margins by adopting advanced refining techniques. The 1860s brought several improvements in distillation: one was the use of steam, ordinary or superheated, rather than direct-fire; another was vacuum distillation. These were especially suitable for processing the heavier crude components.

Fractional distillation can be supplemented by destructive distillation, or cracking. Cracking breaks down large hydrocarbon molecules into smaller ones, thereby increasing the yield of the desired product. Destructive distillation was known to coal oil refiners and was subsequently applied to petroleum refining. Initially, temperatures during cracking were uncontrolled; later, thermal cracking and catalytic cracking were introduced. Thermal cracking increases the yield of lighter products and is commonly used on asphaltic fractions to produce coke. A variety of catalysts is used to produce gasoline of a desired quality. Cracking improved yields, but also increased sulphur and other undesirable compounds in the product, necessitating treatment with acid and alkali. Many advanced refiners adopted these methods and produced the high-quality kerosene that was in great demand.

By the mid–1860s, the nation's refining capacity was concentrated in the Oil Region, Pittsburgh, Cleveland, New York, and Boston. Small operations were disappearing, but those that replaced them were not large by modern standards. Cracking and treating were widespread. Batch processing was giving way to continuous distillation. The output of crude and the demand for refined products continued to grow, even though the industry was unstable. Under these circumstances, John D. Rockefeller entered the oil business and brought far-reaching changes to the industry.

THE EARLY ROCKEFELLER YEARS: 1863–82

Before entering the oil business in 1862, John D. Rockefeller was a successful produce shipper. In that year, he and his partner, Maurice B. Clark, were asked by Samuel Andrews to finance a refinery venture. The threesome built and operated the Excelsior Works. By 1865 Rockefeller had quit the produce business to concentrate on his refinery properties. He shed his old partners, built new refineries, and began to expand his operations to the Eastern Seaboard and abroad. In 1870 the Standard Oil Company of Ohio was incorporated with Rockefeller at its head. Within a few years, the Standard organization became the dominant force in the oil industry, a history that is well documented (Tarbell [1904] 1925; Nevins 1940).

In the early stages of Standard's growth, Rockefeller pursued a policy of horizontally integrating refinery operations that is often called the Great Plan (Frankel 1969). When Rockefeller settled on this plan is unclear; the first phase, however, was implemented in the Cleveland area soon after he formed the Standard Oil Company. His strategy was based on a shrewd understanding of the crucial role of refineries and a desire to protect the interests of Standard Oil by stabilizing the industry. Furthermore, there were advantages to be gained in transportation costs by combining refineries and offering bulk freight to the competing railroad companies.

Crude oil in those days moved by gathering lines to shipping points and on to refineries by tank cars. Refined products moved to eastern markets by water or rail. There were no common carrier regulations to prevent railroads from procuring traffic by secretly offering favored shippers rebates at the time of shipment or discounting rates on quantities shipped over a period of time. When making deals, large shippers were in a position to demand special treatment. And those who were served by more than one system could play off one railroad company against the other. The Cleveland-based Standard organization was in such a favorable position. Rockefeller pressed his advantage.

In the mid–1860s, refineries were concentrated (in descending order of importance) in four major centers: Pittsburgh, New York-New Jersey, the Oil Region, and Cleveland. The fortunes of these centers were tied to decisions made by the railroads. As competition heated up between Thomas A. Scott's Pennsylvania Railroad, Jay Gould's Erie system, and Cornelius Vanderbilt's New York Central system, Pittsburgh found itself in a poor bargaining position. Pittsburgh refiners, dependent on the Pennsylvania for access to the eastern market, paid the local traffic rate rather than the lower through-traffic rate. With two competing railroad systems and the cheap alternative of water transportation through the Great Lakes and Erie Canal, Cleveland refiners were in a position to extract rate concessions. If the refining operations in Cleveland could pool their interests, the advantage could be compounded. These conditions impelled Rockefeller to initiate his Great Plan.

Standard officials entered into special deals with transportation companies for shipping crude oil into Cleveland and refined products out to the markets. Concessional agreements like Standard's 1870 deal with the Lake Shore Railroad contributed to the growth of its refining capacity. The railroad secretly agreed to a rate of $1.30 per barrel for shipping Standard's refined products to New York; the going rate was $2.00. The arrangement proved timely for Standard. Over the subsequent two years, the refining industry underwent a cycle of overbuilding, falling profit margins, and shutdowns. Standard not only survived the shakeout, but thrived on it. The transportation-cost advantage enabled Rockefeller to hold his own in the oil industry and expand refinery holdings.

The secret deals benefitted the shippers at the expense of the railroads. The leaders in the railroad industry wearied of rate wars and sought cooperative alternatives; one was to pool shipments. A pool was worked out between the Pennsylvania Railroad and the Lake Shore-New York Central. Their vehicle was the South Improvement Company. Using their influence in the Pennsylvania Legislature, the railroad companies obtained a charter to form South Improvement. Although the charter ensured freedom of action to the officers of the company, the pool's success depended on the cooperation of the refiners. Rockefeller was interested and cajoled his fellows to join. The railroads' plan was straightforward: raise the overall shipping rates. Members of the South Improvement Company, however, would ship at concessional rates. While those in the Rockefeller orbit joined the pool, most refiners in the Oil Region did not. When news of the agreement broke in the form of a rate hike for crude oil deliveries to New York, the excluded Oil Region producers howled in protest. They launched a campaign to break the pool. An embargo on crude shipments to refiners in the South Improvement Company was put into effect. Producers pressured the Pennsylvania Legislature to revoke the charter. The campaign was successful. The embargo dried up crude supplies to Cleveland and Pittsburgh. Rail yards were idled. Unable to withstand further loss of business, the railroads conceded defeat and cancelled their contracts with the South Improvement Company. Its charter was revoked in April, 1872.

The pool experiment ended in disaster, but it may have been a boon for Standard. Throughout the episode, Rockefeller quietly acquired other refineries. According to some accounts, he used the device of the South Improvement Company to threaten his competitors with bankruptcy, persuading them to sell out on his terms. Rockefeller himself denied applying such tactics, holding that he was simply buying distressed property from rivals only too willing to sell off their refinery holdings to Standard and enter the organization as officers (Williamson and Daum 1959). By the time the South Improvement Company collapsed, not a single Cleveland refiner operated outside the Standard organization.

The demise of the South Improvement Company did not end the efforts to unite refiners. In April, 1872, William G. Warden and Charles Lockhart launched the so-called Pittsburgh Plan (Williamson and Daum 1959), a proposal to form an association of refiners governed by a central board that would handle the refinery business. It was a proposal to form a cartel. The proposal was not initiated by Rockefeller, but once approached, he readily endorsed it and moved vigorously to promote the idea. The National Refiners' Association, a cartel of refiners, was organized in August, 1872, with Rockefeller as its head.

A cartel of refiners was a threat to the interests of crude oil producers. In an attempt to restrict crude output, the producers revived the moribund Petroleum Producers' Association. Their efforts bore no fruit, however. Having failed to restrict production or drilling, they later formed the Producers' Agency and authorized it to run a buffer stock operation, or a similar scheme, designed to maintain a fixed price for crude oil. Rockefeller did not oppose the agency; instead, he concluded an agreement with the producers on December 19, 1872, that established a base price of $4 per barrel of crude.

This "Treaty of Titusville" (Williamson and Daum 1959) failed. Within a few months it became apparent that the $4 per barrel price would not hold. The producers could neither stop new drilling nor control the level of output from existing wells; the price of crude sagged. The terms of the agreement were routinely ignored. The refiners were unwilling to be bound by their own rules. The National Refiners' Association had no choice but to disband in June, 1873.

The collapse of the National Refiners' Association may have convinced Rockefeller that the best way to preserve Standard's position was to acquire refinery operations beyond Cleveland. So began the last phase of the Great Plan. Rockefeller continued to play off one railroad against another. In addition, Standard entered the growing pipeline systems and used the advantage in transportation thus obtained to persuade rivals to sell out. During 1874 several major refiners in Pittsburgh, New York, and Philadelphia were brought into the Standard organization.

Complete control of the refineries eluded Rockefeller. Standard held a powerful position in the industry, but refiners outside Cleveland could still forge alliances with railroads and cut into Standard's market share. Many independent refiners and railroad officials relished the challenge. A serious threat was posed by the Pennsylvania Railroad through its Empire Transportation Company affiliate. Empire set about building an independent system of gathering lines and refineries in an attempt to undercut Standard. Rockefeller's response was to forge an alliance with the Erie and the New York Central and withhold shipments from the Pennsylvania Railroad system. The Pennsylvania Railroad could do little against such a massive display of power. The railroad strike of 1877 added to its problems. Later that year Empire was dissolved, and its refineries and other assets sold to Standard Oil, Empire's intended target. That year Standard also acquired a few remaining refineries in Pittsburgh and Buffalo. Over the next two years, many large refineries in New York were brought into the Standard organization. By early 1880 the Standard Oil Company could boast 80–90 percent control over refining capacity in the United States (Williamson and Daum 1959; Nevins 1953). Rockefeller's Great Plan had been largely achieved.

Although Rockefeller's strategy and Standard's power inspired awe, crude oil producers and independent refiners refused to be dominated. They continued to resist with embargoes, competing facilities, and political lobbying. Standard withstood such pressures, but its position as a virtual monopolist in the refining industry gradually eroded in the expanding market for petroleum products. Small independent refiners found a niche in the growing market for lubricants, which were becoming increasingly important in the 1880s. Many entered the specialty by-product market by refining the abundant, paraffin-rich Bradford crude. The competing trunk line between Bradford and Buffalo also promoted their interests.

As the refinery business was changing, the Standard Oil Company was itself in the throes of organizational change. Rockefeller sought to centralize control of his enterprises, but Ohio corporations were prohibited from owning out-of-state properties. That legality led to the development of an innovative corporate control device: the trust.

THE STANDARD OIL TRUST AND REFINERY OPERATIONS: 1882–98

On January 2, 1882, the Standard Oil Trust Agreement was signed. Trustees were delegated to guard the interests of the Standard Oil stockholders. The agreement authorized them to assume supervisory powers over routine operations and, if warranted, to elect themselves to management positions in any of Standard's affiliates. The original agreement provided for naming nine trustees and creating companies that would bear the names of the states where Standard operated. Having centralized control through the trust device, Standard's managers immediately moved to consolidate and reorganize the company's far-flung operations.

In trust, Standard's refinery operations underwent drastic changes. Starting around 1883, many refineries were closed; those that remained were closer to the markets. As a result, Standard's refining capacity was concentrated in fewer, but larger, plants. As Table 1 indicates, Standard's post-trust redeployment of refining capacity reduced the number of plants in Pittsburgh by 90 percent and in the Oil Region by 93 percent.

These moves improved Standard's profit position in refining. The falling prices for processing materials, economies of scale, and the capacity of the refineries combined to lower costs and increase profits. By mid–1885, however, there were signs that crude oil production in western Pennsylvania might be tapering off. If new oil fields were not developed, the refinery industry would be idled. Prospects improved in 1885 with the development of the Lima-Indiana fields, oil deposits that extended from Lima, Ohio, into

Table 1
Standard Refining Plants, 1882–86

	Number of Plants		
Location	1882	1886	% Reduction
Baltimore	2	2	0
Buffalo	1	1	0
Cleveland	4	1	75
New York	14	10	29
Oil Region	15	5	93
Philadelphia	6	2	67
Pittsburgh	11	1	90
Total	53	22	59

Source: Adapted from Harold F. Williamson and Arnold R. Daum. The
American Petroleum Industry: The Age of Illumination 1859-1899.
Evanston, IL: Northwestern University Press, 1959, p. 474.

parts of Indiana. But Lima crude had a high sulphur content, and there was
no technology for refining it out. Nonetheless, Standard moved into the
area with its own pipeline system and a refinery. Full-scale operations could
not commence, however, until refining techniques were perfected. Anxious
for a breakthrough, Standard hired Herman Frasch, an experienced research
chemist, and established him in Cleveland to work on Lima crude.

Frasch succeeded. Patented in 1887, the Frasch process spurred Standard
toward vertical integration. Beginning in 1888, Standard acquired producing
properties in the Lima-Indiana fields. By 1889 work on a large-scale refinery
had begun in Whiting, Indiana, a site strategically located south of Chicago.
Lima crude began to arrive there in 1890, and, over the next several years,
Standard drew on the Lima-Indiana fields for most of its refinery operations.

American industry came of age during the last two decades of the nineteenth century. For refiners that meant a tremendous spurt in the demand
for lubricants, in addition to the strong demand for kerosene. Accordingly,
Standard and other refiners adjusted their production runs. Small refiners
found room for growth in the expanding lubricant market.

As the century came to a close, output from the Lima-Indiana fields was
dwindling. Oil flows from the Far East and southern Russia were offering
stiff competition to Standard's operations abroad.

TRANSITION FROM THE AGE OF ILLUMINATION TO THE AGE OF ENERGY: 1899–1919

The early years of the twentieth century brought changes in international economics and politics that had ramifications for the petroleum industry. New oil fields on the Gulf coast and in Kansas, Oklahoma, Illinois, and California made up for the falling output in the East. The composition of demand for refined products shifted. The Age of Illumination was giving way to the Age of Energy (Williamson et al. 1963), but the Standard Oil Trust was broken up by court action in 1911. The separated units resumed their growth by mergers and acquisitions and continued to play a major role in the oil industry. World War I created pressures to produce fuel oil for the British Navy, a requirement that pushed Great Britain to launch the state-owned Anglo-Persian Oil Company (later Anglo-Iranian and now British Petroleum). There was an incipient demand for aviation fuel. Russia dropped out of the European markets, its petroleum industry crippled by war and revolution. Western Europe, however, introduced new challengers to Standard Oil, the most important of which was Royal Dutch Shell. The internal combustion engine in general and the Model-T Ford in particular (1916) revolutionized transportation first in the United States and then in other countries. Gasoline and oil to run those automobiles and paved roads to drive them on were in great demand.

Technological innovations developed in response to changing market conditions enabled the petroleum industry to meet the new demands. The introduction of the Livingston continuous distillation process in 1906, the Van Dyke tower stills in 1908, and the Trumble pipe stills in 1912 (Williamson et al. 1963) considerably reduced refining costs.

The major challenge, however, was raising the gasoline yield of the refining process to meet the rapidly growing demand for motor fuel. Initially, several ad hoc procedures were followed. Then, in 1912, Indiana Standard's William M. Burton developed the famous thermal pressure cracking process. After improvements, the Burton process was widely licensed and earned enormous revenues for Indiana Standard (Williamson et al. 1963).

The first two decades of the twentieth century saw tremendous growth in the demand for petroleum products. The demand for kerosene and lubricants continued to rise, but the most dramatic increase was in the demand for gasoline and fuel oil. Table 2 shows the relevant output figures.

Refining capacity increased in tandem with the rising demand for petroleum products, and many of the new refineries belonged to new firms. Standard's control of the market declined. At the time of the 1911 breakup, for instance, the Standard organization owned only 64 percent of refining capacity in the United States (Williamson et al. 1963).

The 1911 court order divided Standard Oil along geographic lines, not by operations. Refinery facilities were simply apportioned among the severed

Table 2
Refined Petroleum Product Outputs
Census Years, 1899–1921

Year	Gasoline	Kerosene (billion gal.)	Fuel Oil	Lubricating Oils (million gal.)
1899	0.281	1.26	0.305	170
1904	0.291	1.36	0.360	315
1909	0.540	1.67	1.700	537
1914	1.460	1.94	3.730	518
1919	4.110	2.31	7.770	822
1921	5.350	1.94	9.750	949

Source: U.S. Bureau of the Census. Historical Statistics of the United States, 1789-1945. Washington, DC: U.S. Government Printing Office, 1949, p. 186.

companies. The new Standard units continued to grow, and several dominated their geographical areas. For example, in 1920 the top three refiners were Standard Oil of New Jersey, Standard of California, and Indiana Standard (Williamson et al. 1963). For that same year, however, the combined refining capacity of the Standard family was only 50 percent of the industry total.

Independent oil companies formed at the beginning of the twentieth century eroded Standard's market share. The discovery of oil in the Texas-Oklahoma region and California enabled the independents to gain a foothold in the oil industry. One such successful independent operation was founded by the Pittsburgh-based Mellon family. Their venture illustrates the opportunities that opened up in the beginning of the century and is worth recounting briefly.

The Mellons entered the oil business in 1889. They acquired producing properties in the Oil Region and laid pipeline from outside Pittsburgh to Carlisle, Pennsylvania. At Carlisle their system joined the Philadelphia and Reading Railroad, giving the Mellons access to eastern markets. Later, they built a huge refinery complex in Marcus Hook, Pennsylvania. In 1893 the Mellons abandoned oil to pursue other business interests, and Standard Oil acquired their assets. The Mellons eventually came back to oil through a financing deal. A Mellon National Bank loan financed the construction of the rotary drill that opened up the famous "Spindletop" gusher (officially,

Table 3
Input to Refiners
(million bbl)

Year	U.S.	Imported
1918	328	1
1919	364	34
1920	437	61
1921	446	75
1922	504	75
1923	586	43
1924	656	46
1925	760	41
1926	807	45
1927	861	50
1928	949	78
1929	1034	76

Source: U.S. Bureau of the Census. Historical Statistics of the
United States, Colonial Times to 1970. Washington, DC: U.S.
Government Printing Office, 1971, p. 596.

Lucas No. 1) near Beaumont, Texas, on January 10, 1901. Other gushers
followed. There was plenty of oil, but not enough refining and transportation
facilities. Refining the Texas crude also posed some technical problems.
Unlike the Pennsylvania crude, which was high in paraffin, the Texas crude
was high in asphalt. It was heavy, black, and sulphurous. The Mellons
acquired producing properties and built a succession of refineries in Port
Arthur, Texas. Later, they acquired wells near Tulsa, Oklahoma, and transported their crude by pipeline to Port Arthur for refining. On February 13,
1907, the Mellon operations were reorganized as the Gulf Oil Corporation.

THE ERA OF EXPANSION: 1919–29

The Roaring Twenties saw continued expansion of demand for gasoline
and fuel oil, and concern over the adequacy of domestic crude. The search
for crude oil was taken abroad, and successful fields were developed in

Table 4
Refining Capacity
(million bbl, Jan. 1)

Year	Capacity
1918	434
1919	473
1920	559
1921	689
1922	770
1923	N/A
1924	1027
1925	1032
1926	1041
1927	1117
1928	1190
1929	1281

Source: U.S. Bureau of the Census. Historical Statistics of the United States, Colonial Times to 1970. Washington, DC: U.S. Government Printing Office, 1971, p. 698.

South America. Foreign crude was delivered to East Coast refiners at a competitive price. Instead of running out of domestic oil, output rose throughout the 1920s. Nevertheless, conservation emerged as a public policy issue, especially after the Teapot Dome scandal of 1921–23.

Table 3 shows crude petroleum inputs to refiners from domestic and foreign sources.

Table 4 shows that refining capacity registered a steady upward climb through 1918–29. During those years, capacity almost tripled.

Table 5 presents the composition of refinery output for the 1918–29 period. The output of gasoline increased more than fivefold, and kerosene output remained steady. Distillate and residual oil output more than doubled during the same period.

A steadily rising demand for gasoline pressured refiners to increase yields from crude. Although the Burton process of thermal pressure cracking im-

Table 5
Refinery Output
(million bbl)

Year	Gasoline	Kerosene	Distillate and Residual Fuel Oils	Lubricants
1918	85	43	174	20
1919	94	56	182	20
1920	116	55	211	25
1921	123	46	230	21
1922	148	55	255	23
1923	180	56	287	26
1924	213	60	320	27
1925	260	60	365	31
1926	300	62	365	32
1927	330	56	393	32
1928	377	59	427	35
1929	435	56	449	34

Source: U.S. Bureau of the Census. Historical Statistics of the United States, Colonial Times to 1970. Washington, DC: U.S. Government Printing Office, 1971, p. 596.

proved yields, it employed a slow batch mode of production. Texas Company's Holmes-Manley process put thermal cracking on a continuous basis (Williamson et al. 1963), but adoption of the improved processes was slowed by a tangle of lawsuits. In July, 1920, Texas Company sued Indiana Standard for patent infringement. A flurry of lawsuits by owners of other refining processes followed. In 1923 the parties to the disputes attempted to forge an agreement among themselves and formed the so-called Patent Club (Williamson et al. 1963). The Justice Department challenged the formation of the patent pool on antitrust grounds. In 1931 the Supreme Court dismissed such charges, clearing the way for a widespread sharing of the improved processes among the companies through private arrangements. Following this "Peace of 1931" (Williamson et al. 1963), thermal cracking processes were widely adopted by the refining industry.

During this period, the Dubbs process under the control of Universal Oil Products Company became a major addition to thermal cracking processes. It was especially suited for refining heavy, asphalt-laden crude like that found in California. Advances were also made in fractionation, heat exchange, and gasoline treatment techniques. Perhaps the most important technical innovation sprang from the discovery by a General Motors research team headed by Charles F. Kettering that tetraethyl lead was a good antiknock compound. This finding paved the way for developing the high-octane fuels that were to prove especially valuable for aviation.

The refining industry tripled capacity between 1919 and 1929, although it was in a transition phase. Technological advances forced firms to replace plants and equipment regularly; facilities built in the late 1920s used thermal cracking technology and produced gasoline with antiknock properties. These were not good times for small refiners. Thermal cracking technology demanded a high-minimum-size establishment. Most small refiners found such a scale out of their reach and were forced to shut down or sell out.

THE GREAT DEPRESSION, RECOVERY, AND WORLD WAR II: 1930–45

The oil industry fared poorly during the early years of the Depression: there was a sharp decline in all phases of the business, and uncertain demand and crude oil prices discouraged refinery construction. Soon, however, it became clear that automobile travel would continue to be popular. Accordingly, gasoline production resumed its upward path. Tables 6 and 7 capture the trends in refining capacity, inputs to refineries, and output composition of refineries during 1930–45.

The 1930–45 period brought technological improvements to cope with the rising demand for gasoline. Combination units that used heat generated from internal processes for refinery operations were brought into service. These units allowed the use of such new thermal cracking processes as delayed coking, thermal reforming, and thermal polymerization. Coking is a process that upgrades the higher boiling material found in crude oil. Reforming alters the molecular structure of hydrocarbons. High-octane gasoline components can be obtained by thermal reforming naphtha derived from distilling low-grade crude. Polymerization combines or blends lighter molecules of gaseous by-products to yield gasoline of desired quality. This process arrives at motor fuel from the opposite direction of cracking.

While thermal cracking and other processes greatly increased gasoline yield and the quality of the fuel, their impact on the industry was not revolutionary. That label is reserved for the catalytic cracking process introduced in the 1930s by Eugene J. Houdry. The Houdry process relied on catalysts to crack the hydrocarbons and produced high-octane fuel without the use of tetraethyl lead. Socony Mobil and Sun Oil Company opened

Table 6
Capacity and Inputs to Refineries
(million bbl)

Year	Capacity Crude	Domestic Crude	Imported Crude
1930	1374	970	61
1931	1439	930	47
1932	1469	846	42
1933	1420	887	35
1934	1430	924	35
1935	1481	997	32
1936	1507	1103	34
1937	1568	1223	26
1938	1588	1205	26
1939	1646	1277	34
1940	1694	1334	42
1941	1722	1457	51
1942	1809	1391	15
1943	1789	1491	12
1944	1864	1733	43
1945	1935	1790	74

Source: U.S. Bureau of the Census. Historical Statistics of the
United States, Colonial Times to 1970. Washington, DC: U.S.
Government Printing Office, 1971, pp. 596, 698.

refineries based on the Houdry process and began the "cat cracking" revolution. Improved versions based on the use of catalysts included thermofor catalytic cracking, fluid catalytic cracking, catalytic reforming, and catalytic polymerization.

These technical developments proved immensely valuable in meeting the wartime requirements for high-quality aviation fuel. On May 28, 1941, President Franklin D. Roosevelt appointed Harold Ickes Petroleum Coordi-

Table 7
Refinery Outputs
(million bbl)

Year	Gasoline	Kerosene	Distillate and Residual Fuel Oils	Lubricants
1930	432	49	372	34
1931	432	42	337	27
1932	392	44	295	22
1933	402	49	316	24
1934	417	54	335	26
1935	458	56	360	28
1936	505	57	414	31
1937	559	65	459	35
1938	556	65	447	31
1939	597	69	468	35
1940	597	74	500	37
1941	671	73	531	40
1942	587	67	556	39
1943	592	72	629	39
1944	723	78	701	41
1945	774	81	719	42

Source: U.S. Bureau of the Census. Historical Statistics of the United States, Colonial Times to 1970. Washington, DC: U.S. Government Printing Office, 1971, p. 596.

nator for National Defense. Ickes took on Ralph K. Davis of SOCAL as his deputy and immediately ordered a study to determine the fuel needs for defense and the country's production capabilities. The study showed that although the nation had adequate refining capacity, there was a potential shortfall in aviation fuel supplies. Following the attack on Pearl Harbor, the United States formally entered the war and the aviation fuel supply problem became a matter of great urgency. In December, 1942, President Roosevelt created by executive order the Petroleum Administration for War, with Ickes as its administrator (Nash 1968). The "Quick 100–Octane" program was launched to encourage production of large quantities of aviation-grade fuel in the shortest possible time. The refining industry geared up to respond. Within a year, production of 100–octane fuel increased fourfold. Refiners also produced butadiene for the manufacture of synthetic rubber to replace the disrupted supplies of natural rubber from Southeast Asia.

The Great Depression, World War II, and the cracking revolution hurt small refiners. In the early years of the Depression overproduction in Texas led to a surplus of crude. The price of crude dropped. Many small refiners took advantage of the low price and set up operations near the wells, only to be squeezed out as prorationing took effect in 1935 and prices stabilized, then rose (de Chazeau and Kahn 1959). The cracking process required large capital investments beyond the resources of many small refiners. The gap between large and small refiners widened. During World War II, small refiners without cracking capacity were at a disadvantage in manufacturing the urgently needed high-octane fuels. The federal government preempted private refiners by building a string of refining plants.

THE UNCERTAIN YEARS: 1946–50

On August 15, 1945, World War II ended with the surrender of Japan. Demobilization got under way immediately. The federal government disposed of many refining facilities. Wartime price controls and other restrictions were lifted, clearing the way for a peacetime economy. Prospects, however, were uncertain. Many economists and business leaders speculated that depression would return. Nevertheless, the economy rebounded vigorously, and the petroleum industry enjoyed a boom.

In response to the rising demand for petroleum products, additional refining investments were made. Most of the new capacity was in catalytic cracking and reforming. Small refiners were left out of this building boom because they could not meet the high capital cost of new facilities (Marshall 1979). By 1949 the top six oil companies controlled 47 percent of the cracking capacity in the United States (U.S. Federal Trade Commission 1952). Tables 8 and 9 summarize developments during the immediate postwar years.

THE BOOM YEARS: 1951–72

The 1950s and 1960s brought steady growth in the worldwide demand for petroleum products. Postwar decolonization and the spread of industrialization added an important dimension to the oil industry. As production in the United States leveled off, new wells were developed in the Middle East and Latin America. American companies joined European giants to

Table 8
Capacity and Input to Refineries
(million bbl)

Year	Capacity	Domestic Crude	Imported Crude
1946	1940	1793	84
1947	2033	1923	97
1948	2209	2125	124
1949	2350	2030	154
1950	2444	2190	176

Source: U.S. Bureau of the Census. Historical Statistics of the
United States, Colonial Times to 1970. Washington, DC: U.S.
Government Printing Office, 1971, pp. 596, 698.

Table 9
Refinery Output
(million bbl)

Year	Gasoline	Kerosene	Distillate and Residual Fuel Oils	Lubricants
1946	748	104	719	46
1947	815	110	760	52
1948	896	122	859	51
1949	939	102	766	45
1950	998	119	824	52

Source: U.S. Bureau of the Census. Historical Statistics of the
United States, Colonial Times to 1970. Washington DC: U.S.
Government Printing Office, 1971, p. 698.

form the seven companies known variously as the Big Seven, the Seven
Sisters (R. O. Anderson 1984), or simply the majors: EXXON, SOCAL,
Mobil, Gulf, Texaco, British Petroleum, and Royal Dutch Shell. They dom-
inated the international oil industry during the boom years that followed
World War II. Over 60 percent of the crude worldwide was processed by
the majors (Adelman 1972).

The most noteworthy technical development in the beginning of the postwar boom was the introduction of catalytic reforming by the Universal Oil

Products Company. Because the process uses platinum as a catalyst, it is popularly referred to as platforming. This and similar processes developed by competing companies improved the quality of gasoline and the yield rate. High-quality gasoline was required for cars with high compression ratios. From an average of five-to-one, the compression ratio went up to eight-to-one by the 1950s. The quality of fuel had to improve accordingly. The octane race was on. In 1954 refining companies spent $500 million for catalytic reforming units to produce high-quality gasoline (*New York Times*, April 18, 1954, sec. 3, p. 1).

In the postwar years refiners increased capacity and modernized their plants. Increased automation and computerized controls were part of the modernization program. These developments gave refineries greater flexibility to adjust to changing market conditions (*New York Times*, April 3, 1959, p. 37). Flexibility was further improved in 1961 by the introduction of hydrocracking—cracking in the presence of hydrogen. Universal Oil Products Company and the California Research Corporation developed such processes and were licensing them jointly under the Isomax trade label (*New York Times*, November 15, 1961, p. 63). Hydrocracking allows refiners to adjust the ratio of gasoline to fuel oil from a given input. Another process with high gasoline yield is isomerization—low-grade gasoline hydrocarbon molecules are altered into isotope hydrocarbons to produce a good quality unleaded gas.

In the boom years petroleum became a global enterprise, and refineries were built in many parts of the world. North America's refining capacity continued to increase, but its share of worldwide capacity declined dramatically. Western Europe and Japan took an increasing share of the international total and, as the output of oil from the Middle East and North Africa increased, many refineries were built there. Table 10 captures these developments.

In the United States, it became clear early in the 1951–72 period that domestic output would not satisfy the growing demand for refined products at a reasonable price. Domestic crude prices were influenced by state prorationing regulations designed to restrict output and keep prices high enough to encourage drilling activity. Oil from Middle Eastern sources was selling at a relatively low price; tension built between integrated oil companies that imported large quantities of oil from the Middle East and companies that advocated reliance on domestic sources. Import quotas were advocated on economic and national security grounds. During the Eisenhower administration, quotas were implemented on the basis of the Trade Agreements Extension Act of 1955. From 1955 to 1958, a system of voluntary import controls was in place, but failed. Consequently, in March, 1959, the Office of the Secretary of the Interior imposed mandatory restrictions that continued in various forms until 1973. The quota system failed (Burrows and Domenich 1970), and U.S. refineries increasingly relied on imported crude

Table 10
Crude Distillation Capacity, 1950 and 1970
(million metric tons per year)

	1950		1970	
	Amount	%	Amount	%
North America	348.8	62.7	697.5	28.4
Central and South America	25.1	4.5	139.6	5.7
Caribbean	46.4	8.3	88.7	3.6
Western Europe	42.3	7.6	707.5	28.8
Eastern Europe	42.7	7.7	363.5	14.8
East Africa	00.0	0.0	16.3	0.7
West Africa	00.0	0.0	8.3	0.3
Middle East and North Africa	47.5	8.5	128.5	5.2
South Asia	0.7	0.1	31.0	1.3
East Asia (excl. China)	0.0	0.0	56.3	2.3
Oceania	0.7	0.1	32.9	1.4
Japan	1.7	0.3	156.4	6.4
China	0.9	0.2	27.6	1.1

Source: Adapted from Lakdasa Wijetilleke and Anthony J. Ody. World Refinery Industry: Need for Restructuring. World Bank Technical Paper no. 32. Washington, DC: The World Bank, 1984, p. 20.

oil. Table 11 provides data on crude oil inputs to refineries and refining capacity in the United States for the 1951–72 period. Gasoline production continued its upward trend, and kerosene output continued to decline. Distillate and residual oils as well as lubricants held their own. Table 12 presents the relevant output data.

For small refiners the postwar years were the best of times and the worst of times. They benefitted from liberal licensing arrangements for cracking process equipment. The Universal Oil Products Company's platforming process, for example, made it possible for small firms to produce high-octane gasoline at competitive costs. Aside from catalytic cracking and reforming processes, there were many blending methods available in the manufacture

Table 11
Refining Capacity and Inputs
(million bbl)

		Input to Refiners	
Year	Capacity	Domestic	Imported
1951	2542	2470	181
1952	2684	2545	206
1953	2788	2666	233
1954	2923	2657	239
1955	3074	2857	283
1956	3159	3040	341
1957	3330	3041	361
1958	3434	2927	345
1959	3584	3071	352
1960	3624	3119	371
1961	3654	3157	383
1962	3682	3252	410
1963	3693	3361	412
1964	3801	3437	437
1965	3933	3526	453
1966	3830	3683	446
1967	3927	3827	409
1968	4221	4037	466
1969	4285	3880	516
1970	4388	3968	482
1971	4694	4088	613
1972	4865	4281	811

Source: U.S. Bureau of the Census. Historical Statistics of the United States, Colonial Times to 1970. Washington, DC: U.S. Government Printing Office, 1971, pp. 596, 698.

of high-octane gasoline. Small refiners also had opportunities in specialized markets. Countering these favorable factors was the high cost of entering the refinery market under the new octane regime. Table 13 shows the cost for 25,000 barrels per day (bpd) capacity refineries of different vintages from 1910 to 1950. These figures show that new technology promoted overall efficiency and created a barrier to entry.

High capital requirements made it difficult for companies to enter and thrive in refining. Small refiners were especially vulnerable to the octane squeeze (McLean and Haigh 1954) and the profit squeeze that accompanies adverse market developments (de Chazeau and Kahn 1959). Nevertheless, many independent refiners survived by improving their management practices and strategic advantages through integration (de Chazeau and Kahn

Table 12
Refinery Output
(million bbl)

Year	Gasoline	Kerosene	Distillate and Residual Fuel Oils	Lubricants
1951	1109	136	945	61
1952	1141	129	972	56
1953	1234	123	978	53
1954	1233	122	959	53
1955	1332	117	1023	56
1956	1397	123	1092	59
1957	1415	109	1084	56
1958	1412	110	995	51
1959	1473	111	1027	56
1960	1510	136	999	59
1961	1512	141	1012	59
1962	1570	156	1015	61
1963	1604	165	1041	63
1964	1676	93	1009	64
1965	1722	93	1034	63
1966	1813	101	1049	65
1967	1865	99	1080	65
1968	1961	101	1115	66
1969	2050	102	1113	65
1970	2130	96	1154	66
1971	2213	88	1187	66
1972	2320	86	1256	65

Source: U.S. Bureau of the Census. Historical Statistics of the United States, Colonial Times to 1970. Washington, DC: U.S. Government Printing Office, 1971, p. 596.

1959). They also formed lobby groups to influence legislation. The refineries owned by the large, integrated oil companies known as the majors formed the National Petroleum Refiners Association. Small, independent refiners without their own supply of crude lobbied through their Independent Refiners Association. Both were active during the energy crisis.

THE OIL SHOCKS: 1973–85

In the summer of 1972 experts noted a need for additional refining capacity to meet the growing demand for energy (*New York Times*, April 26, 1972, p. 65). They argued for a comprehensive national energy policy to cope with shortages and conflicting interests. Middle Eastern sources were becoming important to the Western industrial machine, and political factors influenced the international oil business.

Table 13
Total Investment Cost of Refineries
(capacity = 25,000 bpd)

	Total Cost	
Year	Current Dollars (millions)	1950 Dollars (millions)
1910	4.4	15.3
1915	5.37	19.3
1927	6.0	12.2
1935	8.1	18.9
1946	17.1	22.6
1950 (conventional)	24.5	24.5
1950 (combination unit)	16.0	16.0

Source: Adapted from John G. McLean and Robert Wm. Haigh. The Growth of Integrated Oil Companies. Boston: Harvard University, 1954, p. 554.

Shortages began to appear in 1973. On May 1, the Nixon administration announced a voluntary oil and gasoline allocation program—the "Share the Shortage" plan—to ensure that the majors did not deny independent refiners access to crude oil. Accordingly, import quotas were abandoned. Meanwhile, the Federal Trade Commission (FTC) and various politicians began charging the majors with attempting to run independents out of business to monopolize refining and other downstream operations. The majors, it was said, held profits from selling crude artificially high and profits from refining operations artificially low, so that entry into refining was difficult and unattractive. There was talk by the FTC of "significant divestiture of refinery operations" (New York Times, July 19, 1973, p. 49) even as other analysts traced the gasoline shortage to failure to build up refining capacity (New York Times, July 29, 1973, sec. 3, p. 12).

Members of the Organization of Arab Petroleum Exporting Countries (OAPEC) met in Kuwait on October 17, 1973—after conflict broke out between Egypt and Israel—and imposed oil export restrictions on countries considered unfriendly to the Arab combatants (Shwadran 1986). The embargo ended in less than five months, but not before making the American public aware of its dependence on imported oil. When the Organization of

Petroleum Exporting Countries (OPEC) quadrupled the price of crude oil in 1974, there remained little doubt about the reality of an energy crisis. Lingering doubts were eliminated in 1979–80 when OPEC doubled the price of crude oil as President Jimmy Carter conferred with his colleagues at the Economic Summit in Tokyo. Then, as the adjustment process took its course, demand dropped and supply increased, giving way to the third oil shock—oil glut—in the 1980s and softening oil process.

The crisis decade changed the refinery industry. Independent refiners persuaded political authorities to allow them favored access to crude oil. When mandatory allocation was imposed by President Richard M. Nixon, the Federal Energy Administration allowed small refiners a $3 advantage in crude oil price through its entitlement program. With the end of oil import quotas, the majors announced large-scale refinery expansion programs. The Arab oil export controls did not deter these companies from undertaking ambitious construction programs. By the time these refineries came on stream, however, demand had fallen. Moreover, foreign firms entered U.S. markets with refined products to compete directly with domestic sources. Foreign competition led to underutilization of domestic capacity and massive shutdowns. When President Ronald Reagan announced the end of price controls on oil early in 1981, small refiners lost their $3 advantage and faced business conditions on the same terms as the majors. The shakeout of refineries that followed the drop in demand adversely affected both the majors and the independent refiners. Those who remained in the business had to adjust their fuel mix to cope with changing demand (Dahl and Laumas 1981). Adjusting was difficult for European firms with relatively small ratios of cracking capacity (Dahl 1981); they ended up with more than 30 percent surplus capacity (*New York Times*, May 1, 1984, sec. 4, p. 1). A World Bank document called for worldwide restructuring of refining capacity (Wijetilleke and Ody 1984).

There is little doubt that the refiners' woes owed to the shifts in demand made in response to the two oil shocks of the 1970s. Table 14 illustrates the across-the-board response to the energy crisis. Table 15 shows petroleum fuel consumption by end use. Table 16 shows that energy efficiency improved remarkably.

In Table 17, figures for refining capacity, the number of refineries, and their capacity utilization rates are presented. The delayed impact of the oil shocks can be seen in these numbers. Between 1973 and 1981 capacity went up, followed by a precipitous fall. The number of refineries also declined sharply after 1981. The fall in demand was so steep that even those who remained in the business suffered severe capacity utilization problems. The rate, however, began to creep up following the 1983–84 recovery. The refinery slump also affected Europe, as Table 18 illustrates.

During this period, members of OPEC built large refining capacities within their borders (Razavi and Fesharaki 1984; Sinclair 1984). But demand had

Table 14
Petroleum Use
(million bbl)

Year	Total	Fuel	Non-fuel
1975	5958	5299	659
1976	6391	5689	702
1977	6727	N/A	N/A
1978	6879	N/A	N/A
1979	6757	5916	841
1980	6242	5455	788
1981	5861	5109	752
1982	5583	4889	694
1983	5559	4871	688
1984	5756	5057	699
1985	5729	5045	684

Source: U.S. Bureau of the Census. Statistical Abstract of the United
States. Washington, DC: U.S. Government Printing Office. Various
years.

slumped so far that even the disruption of supplies from refineries in Abadan, caught in the cross fire of the Iran-Iraq war, did not improve the OPEC refinery prospects. Many refinery projects within OPEC were postponed or cancelled.

In the United States, inputs to refineries followed an upward trend until 1978 and a downward trend afterwards. Imported crude inputs followed a similar pattern, as Table 19 shows. Table 20 presents the composition of refinery output during the 1973–85 period.

Through the volatile years of the oil shocks, importation of refined products made up for domestic production shortfalls. Table 21 presents the figures for imported refined products.

Between 1970 and 1973 there was a steady increase in the demand for petroleum products that was not met by domestic refinery output: imports made up the difference. Between 1973 and 1974—the period of the first oil shock—domestic gasoline production actually went down, giving rise to complaints of conspiracy by the majors (*New York Times*, July 29, 1974, p. 33). Over the next four years gasoline production increased and imports of refined products gradually decreased. After the second oil

Table 15
Fuel Consumption by End Use
(million bbl)

Year	Residential	Industrial	Transportation	Electricity
1975	710	1475	3266	506
1976	1094	1243	3501	553
1977	1244	1288	3549	647
1978	1251	1309	3707	612
1979	888	1761	3565	543
1980	555	1772	3494	421
1981	487	1563	3460	352
1982	454	1482	3396	251
1983	473	1407	3433	247
1984	491	1501	3558	206
1985	495	1471	3589	175

Source: U.S. Bureau of the Census. Statistical Abstract of the United States. Washington, DC: U.S. Government Printing Office. Various years.

shock of 1979–80, demand dropped off and so did production. The wave of refinery closings in 1982–83 combined with rising imports of refined products to spur demands from domestic refiners for protection from "cheap" imported refined products (New York Times, February 22, 1985, sec. 4, p. 6; May 10, 1985, p. D2; May 18, 1985, sec. 1, p. 24; July 8, 1985, sec. 1, p. 16; June 23, 1985, Business section, p. 2). The Reagan administration, however, did not heed the lobbyists' calls for import quotas and tariffs on refined products.

RECENT DEVELOPMENTS AND FUTURE PROSPECTS

As 1985 came to a close, the price of crude oil was sliding, so profit margins for refiners were improving. Accordingly, in early 1986 stock market analysts were upgrading refinery investments (New York Times, February 23, 1986, sec. 4, p. 4; May 19, 1986, sec. 4, p. 8). But the euphoria was short-lived. OPEC's attempt to keep the crude oil price around $18 a barrel combined with the continuation of the slide in the refined product price to put refiners through the squeeze again (Wall Street Journal, April

Table 16
Energy Consumption per GNP Dollar
(thousands of BTUs per 1972 dollar GNP)

Year	Energy Consumption per GNP Dollar	Petroleum and Natural Gas Consumption per GNP Dollar
1972	60.0	46.9
1973	59.2	45.7
1974	58.2	44.3
1975	57.2	42.8
1976	57.2	42.8
1977	55.6	41.6
1978	54.2	40.3
1979	53.3	39.1
1980	51.5	37.0
1981	48.8	34.3
1982	47.8	32.8
1983	46.0	31.0
1984	45.4	30.4
1985	45.0	29.7

Note: The figure for 1984 is an estimate;   for 1985, a forecast made
by the Department of Energy.

Source: U.S. Department of Commerce.   U.S. Industrial Outlook
1985.   Washington, DC: U.S.   Government Printing Office, 1984, p.
9.4.

4, 1986, p. 2). Many refineries, including those owned by the majors, were
put on the auction block. An unusual development was the purchase of
these facilities by foreign oil interests looking for a foothold in the U.S.
market. ARCO, for example, sold its 125,000 bpd Philadelphia refinery
along with a chain of retail outlets to John Deuss, a controversial Dutch
oil trader with connections to Oman (*New York Times*, February 23, 1986,
sec. 4, p. 4). Kuwaitis, Venezuelans, and others were acquiring refining
interests as well. Often the firms involved were national oil companies owned

Table 17
Number of Refiners, Capacity, and Utilization Rate

Year	Number	Capacity (million bbl, Jan. 1)	Utilization Rate (%)
1973	284	4979	89.8
1974	290	5242	83.9
1975	287	5461	84.2
1976	291	5577	87.0
1977	302	5985	89.1
1978	311	6222	86.9
1979	308	6366	84.4
1980	319	6584	75.4
1981	324	6589	68.6
1982	301	6530	69.9
1983	258	6154	71.7
1984	247	5906	76.2
1985	223	5715	77.6

Source: U.S. Bureau of the Census. Statistical Abstract of the United States. Washington, DC: U.S. Government Printing Office. Various years.

by the governments of the respective countries. Integration across national boundaries evokes déjà vu: it was precisely the strategy pursued by the majors in their heyday. The activities of the foreign-owned refineries in the United States are likely to become a public policy issue.

In addition to the public/private ownership issue, environmental considerations are likely to remain prominent in public discussions of refinery operations. Locating refineries near populated areas continues to be controversial. Another important problem is the production and use of leaded gasoline. The Environmental Protection Agency has established output goals for unleaded gasoline, and in the future refiners may be required to produce it at reasonable prices. Processes like isomerization and alkylation can increase the production of high-octane unleaded gasoline, but they are expensive. Researchers are challenged to reduce production costs in manufacturing high-octane unleaded gasoline.

Table 18
Possible Capacity Shutdowns in European Refining
1982–84
(1,000 bpd)

Country	Capacity	Shutdown	% Shutdown
U.K.	2,482	619	25
W. Germany	2,937	514	18
France	3,291	506	15
Italy	4,003	483	12
Netherlands	1,707	320	19
Sweden	471	45	10

Source: Adapted from Stuart Sinclair. The World Petroleum Industry: The Market for Petroleum and Petroleum Products in the 1980s. New York: Facts on File Publications, 1984, p. 46.

BIBLIOGRAPHICAL ESSAY

There is no single source to consult on the refining segment of the petroleum industry. Refinery engineering, however, is covered in textbooks. Detailed accounts of the evolution of the petroleum industry and refining are included. An indispensable general work is the two-volume study by Harold Williamson and associates (Williamson and Daum 1959; Williamson et al. 1963). This monumental work was sponsored by the American Petroleum Institute, but the authors were given editorial freedom to write a nonpartisan account. A more recent one-volume work on the petroleum industry is R. O. Anderson (1984), written by the chairman of ARCO and sprinkled with the author's policy views and interpretations.

Those interested in the technology of refining will find Mouzon (1966) a useful work. R. O. Anderson (1984) offers a short account of refining technology. A combined discussion of the technology and economics of petroleum refining is to be found in Abdel-aal and Schmelzlee (1976). A short account of the techno-economics of refining can be found in LeBel (1982).

The economics of the petroleum industry, including refining, are covered in a number of outstanding publications, such as McLean and Haigh (1954), de Chazeau and Kahn (1959), Frankel (1969), and Adelman (1972). In general, these authors are concerned with industrial organizational structures, and they examine such issues as vertical and horizontal integration,

Table 19
Inputs to Refiners
(million bbl)

Year	Domestic Crude	Imported Crude
1973	4537	1184
1974	4632	1269
1975	4709	1498
1976	5081	1935
1977	5468	2414
1978	5501	2320
1979	5459	2380
1980	5049	1926
1981	4657	1605
1982	4443	1273
1983	4361	1215
1984	4471	1245
1985	4381	1168

Source: U.S. Bureau of the Census. Statistical Abstract of the United States. Washington, DC: U.S. Government Printing Office. Various years.

competition, and barriers to entry. These works, however, cover the pre-OPEC era.

The history of the petroleum industry is covered in a variety of writings, both academic and popular. Biographies of prominent oil industry leaders and companies are among the available sources. The activities of Rockefeller and the Standard Oil Company, of course, are the most widely documented. The Tarbell ([1904] 1925) investigative report is the most famous study on the early history of Standard Oil. An exhaustive and more even-handed study, however, is Nevins (1940). An updated version of Nevins (1953) is also available. A good study of the government antitrust case against Standard Oil is Bringhurst (1979). Studies of other oil companies and personalities, however, are not so exhaustive. See McLean and Haigh (1954) for a short account of the Mellons' oil business. The role of Royal Dutch Shell is covered in the autobiography of Henri Deterding (1934). The rise of the

Table 20
Composition of Refinery Output
(million bbl)

Year	Gasoline	Kerosene	Distillate and Residual Oils	Lubricants	Jet Fuel
1973	2399	79	1383	69	314
1974	2336	56	1364	71	305
1975	2393	55	1419	56	318
1976	2516	56	1574	62	336
1977	2566	62	1836	65	355
1978	2630	56	1765	70	354
1979	2508	67	1767	71	369
1980	2388	50	1552	65	366
1981	2336	44	1436	61	353
1982	2313	42	1341	52	357
1983	2313	40	1208	54	373
1984	2362	42	1307	58	414
1985	2343	34	1302	61	434

Source: U.S. Bureau of the Census. Statistical Abstract of the United States. Washington, DC: U.S. Government Printing Office. Various years.

Seven Sisters is well documented in *The International Petroleum Cartel* (U.S. Federal Trade Commission 1952). Popular accounts of the same phenomenon are Sampson (1975) and Blair (1976).

Early government involvement in policy making for the petroleum industry can be traced to the Teapot Dome scandal, which is discussed in Bates (1963). A fallout from the scandal was the rising concern about conversation that led to the 1930s prorationing movement. During World War II national security considerations impelled the federal government to take a more active role in petroleum policy making. A good discussion of these issues can be found in Nash (1968). The ineffectiveness of the Eisenhower-era oil import quota system is discussed in Burrows and Domenich (1970). The

Table 21
Refined Petroleum Product Imports
(million bbl)

Year	Imported Refined Products
1970	765
1971	819
1972	924
1973	1099
1974	962
1975	712
1976	741
1977	800
1978	733
1979	707
1980	582
1981	584
1982	593
1983	629
1984	724

Source: U.S. Bureau of the Census. Statistical Abstract of the United States. Washington, DC: U.S. Government Printing Office. Various years.

post–World War II policy issues are discussed in Goodwin (1981). An updated analytical discussion of policy issues can be found in LeBel (1982).

Coverage of recent developments in the refining industry can be found in the *New York Times*. There are occasional articles in the *Wall Street Journal* as well. The world refinery status as of 1984 is covered by Sinclair (1984).

Data on the refining industry are available from a variety of private and government sources. The American Petroleum Institute is the foremost private source. The institute is supported by private oil companies, however, and some view their publications with skepticism. Recently, the Department of Energy has established its own data-gathering system, the results of which are available in a variety of publications including the *Monthly Energy Review* and *Petroleum Refineries*. The three editions of the *Historical Statistics of the United States* and the annual *Statistical Abstract of the United States* are handy sources of relevant data. And there is always the *Oil & Gas Journal*.

The prolific literature on American oil companies abroad is an important part of American business history. All the volumes in the Standard Oil Company (New Jersey) history deal with that enterprise's vast international business, including the latest publication in the series by Bennett H. Wall (1988). Likewise, foreign-owned oil companies operate in the United States, and there is a history of Shell Oil Company in this country (Beaton 1957). Mira Wilkins (1976) did an overview of multinational oil companies. Also useful is Edith Penrose's study of the international oil companies (1968). In addition, there are a number of excellent histories of individual American oil enterprises overseas, including two studies by Irvine H. Anderson, Jr. (1975, 1981), the first on Standard-Vacuum Oil Company in East Asia and the second on Aramco in Saudi Arabia. Jonathan C. Brown (1985) deals with the shift of foreign, particularly American, oil companies from Mexico to Venezuela. Mira Wilkins, "Multinational Oil Companies in South America in the 1920s: Argentina, Bolivia, Brazil, Chile, Colombia, Ecuador and Peru" (1974b), details U.S. oil enterprise in South America, showing what can be obtained from U.S. State Department files (and the limitations of such evidence). The 1945 U.S. Senate hearings on American petroleum interests in foreign countries are particularly useful.

Diplomatic historians have often plunged into business history when considering oil and politics. There is a long tradition of such works; for contributions made in the last decade, see, for example, Stoff (1980) and, for a more general discussion, Randall (1985). No industry has greater international associations than oil; its business history is deeply involved in international politics. The bibliography and text of Wilkins (1970, 1974a) give substantial material on the growth of multinational enterprise in oil, including some of the diplomatic relationships.

BIBLIOGRAPHY

Books, Journal Articles, and Government Documents

Abdel-aal, Hussein K., and Robert Schmelzlee. *Petroleum Economics and Engineering: An Introduction*. New York: Marcel Dekker, 1976.

Adelman, M. A. *The World Petroleum Market*. Baltimore: Johns Hopkins University Press, 1972.

Anderson, Irvine H., Jr. *The Standard-Vacuum Oil Company and United States East Asian Policy, 1933–1941*. Princeton: Princeton University Press, 1975.

———. *Aramco, the United States, and Saudi Arabia: A Study of the Dynamics of Foreign Oil Policy, 1933–1950*. Princeton: Princeton University Press, 1981.

Anderson, Robert O. *Fundamentals of the Petroleum Industry*. Norman: University of Oklahoma Press, 1984.

Bates, James L. *The Origins of Teapot Dome: Progressives, Parties, and Petroleum, 1909–1921*. Urbana: University of Illinois Press, 1963.

Beaton, Kendall. *Enterprise in Oil: A History of Shell in the United States*. New York: Appleton-Century-Crofts, 1957.

Blair, John M. *The Control of Oil*. New York: Pantheon Books, 1976.

Bringhurst, Bruce. *Antitrust and Oil Monopoly: The Standard Oil Cases, 1890–1911*. Westport, CT: Greenwood Press, 1979.

Brown, Jonathan C. "Foreign Oil Companies and the Shift from Mexico to Venezuela." *American Historical Review* 90 (April 1985): 362–85.

Burrows, James C., and Thomas A. Domenich. *An Analysis of the United States Oil Import Quota*. Lexington, MA: Lexington Books, D. C. Heath, 1970.

Dahl, Carol A. "Refinery Mix in the U.S., Canada, and the E.E.C." *European Economic Review* 16 (1981): 233–46.

Dahl, Carol A., and G. S. Laumas. "Stability of US Petroleum Refinery Response to Relative Product Prices." *Energy Economics* 6 (January 1981): 30–35.

de Chazeau, Melvin G., and Alfred E. Kahn. *Integration and Competition in the Petroleum Industry*. New Haven: Yale University Press, 1959.

Deterding, Henri. *Henri Deterding: An International Oil Man, as Told to Stanley Naylor*. London: Harper, 1934.

Frankel, P. H. *Essentials of Petroleum: A Key to Oil Economics*. London: Frank Cass, 1969.

Goodwin, Craufurd D., ed. *Energy Policy in Perspective*. Washington, DC: Brookings Institution, 1981.

LeBel, Phillip B. *Energy Economics and Technology*. Baltimore: Johns Hopkins University Press, 1982.

McLean, John G., and Robert Wm. Haigh. *The Growth of Integrated Oil Companies*. Boston: Harvard University, 1954.

Marshall, Chapman H. *The Marketing of Petroleum Products*. Ph.D. diss., Cornell University, 1951. New York: Arno Press, 1979.

Mouzon, Olin T. *Resources and Industries of the United States*. New York: Appleton-Century-Crofts, 1966.

Nash, Gerald D. *United States Oil Policy, 1890–1964*. Pittsburgh: University of Pittsburgh Press, 1968.

Nevins, Allan. *John D. Rockefeller: The Heroic Age of American Enterprise*. New York: Scribner's, 1940.

———. *Study in Power: John D. Rockefeller, Industrialist and Philanthropist*. 2 vols. New York: Scribner's, 1953.

Oil & Gas Journal. Tulsa, OK: Petroleum Publishing, 1910– .

Penrose, Edith. *The Large International Firm in Developing Countries: The International Petroleum Industry*. Cambridge, MA: MIT Press, 1968.

Randall, Stephen J. *United States Foreign Oil Policy 1919–1948: For Profits and Security*. Kingston and Montreal: McGill-Queen's University Press, 1985.

Razavi, Hossein, and Fereidun Fesharaki. "OPEC's Push into Refining." *Energy Policy* 12 (June 1984): 125–34.

Sampson, Anthony. *The Seven Sisters*. New York: Viking Press, 1975.

Shwadran, Benjamin. *Middle East Oil Crises Since 1973*. Boulder, CO: Westview Press, 1986.

Silliman, Benjamin, Jr. *Report on the Rock Oil, or Petroleum, from Venango Co., Pennsylvania, with Special Reference to Its Use for Illumination and Other Purposes*. New Haven: J. H. Benham's Steam Power Press, 1855.

Sinclair, Stuart. *The World Petroleum Industry: The Market for Petroleum and Petroleum Products in the 1980s*. New York: Facts on File Publications, 1984.

Stoff, Michael B. *Oil, War and American Security: The Search for a National Policy on Foreign Oil, 1941–1947*. New Haven: Yale University Press, 1980.

Tarbell, Ida M. *History of the Standard Oil Company*. New York: McClure, 1904. Reprint. New York: Macmillan, 1925.

U.S. Bureau of the Census. *Historical Statistics of the United States, 1789–1945*. Washington, DC: U.S. Government Printing Office, 1949.

———. *Historical Statistics of the United States, Colonial Times to 1970*. Washington, DC: U.S. Government Printing Office, 1971.

———. *Statistical Abstract of the United States*. Washington, DC: U.S. Government Printing Office. Annual.

U.S. Congress. Senate. Special Committee Investigating Petroleum Resources. *American Petroleum Interests in Foreign Countries*. 79th Cong., 1st sess., 1945.

U.S. Department of Commerce. *U.S. Industrial Outlook 1985*. Washington, DC: U.S. Government Printing Office, 1984.

U.S. Department of Energy. *Petroleum Refineries*. Washington, DC: Energy Information Administration, 1920– .

———. *Monthly Energy Review*. Washington, DC: Energy Information Administration, 1977– .

U.S. Federal Trade Commission. *The International Petroleum Cartel*. Staff Report to the F.T.C. Subcommittee on Monopoly of the Select Committee on Small Business. 82d Cong. August 22, 1952. Washington, DC: U.S. Government Printing Office, 1952.

Wall, Bennett H. *Growth in a Changing Environment: A History of Standard Oil Company (New Jersey), 1950–1972 and Exxon Corporation, 1972–1975*. New York: McGraw-Hill, 1988.

Wijetilleke, Lakdasa, and Anthony J. Ody. *World Refinery Industry: Need for Restructuring*. World Bank Technical Paper No. 32. Washington, DC: World Bank, 1984.

Wilkins, Mira. *The Emergence of Multinational Enterprise: American Business Abroad from the Colonial Era to 1914*. Cambridge, MA: Harvard University Press, 1970.

———. *The Maturing of Multinational Enterprise: American Business Abroad from 1914 to 1970*. Cambridge, MA: Harvard University Press, 1974a.

———. "Multinational Oil Companies in South America in the 1920s: Argentina, Bolivia, Brazil, Chile, Colombia, Ecuador and Peru." *Business History Review* 48 (Autumn 1974b): 414–46.

———. "The Oil Companies in Perspective." In *The Oil Crisis*, edited by Raymond Vernon, 159–78. New York: Norton, 1976.

Williamson, Harold F., and Arnold R. Daum. *The American Petroleum Industry:*

The Age of Illumination 1859–1899. Evanston, IL: Northwestern University Press, 1959.

Williamson, Harold F., et al. *The American Petroleum Industry: The Age of Energy 1899–1959*. Evanston, IL: Northwestern University Press, 1963.

Newspaper Stories and Articles (Arranged Chronologically)

Carmical, J. H. "Big Oil Companies Offer Better Gas." *New York Times*, April 18, 1954, sec. 3, p. 1.

"Computer Controls Big New Facility for Texaco." *New York Times*, April 3, 1959, p. 37.

"First Oil Refinery Completed Near Titusville at Cost of $15,000." *New York Times*, May 31, 1959, sec. 11, p. 2.

"The Refiner's Task Is to Get the Most out of a Barrel." *New York Times*, May 31, 1959, sec. 11, p. 7.

"Oil Refining Process: Two Companies Sign Pact to License Cracking Method." *New York Times*, November 15, 1961, p. 63.

Silk, Leonard. "Nation's Energy Crisis: A Coordinated Approach Is Essential for Tackling Soaring Need for Power." *New York Times*, April 26, 1972, p. 65.

Smith, William D. "Add Oil Refineries, Experts Urge U.S." *New York Times*, November 10, 1972, p. 53.

Cowan, Edward. "Nixon Sets Voluntary Curbs in Oil and Gas Shortage." *New York Times*, May 11, 1973, p. 23.

———. "Big Oil Concerns Cited in Shortage: F.T.C. Official Says They Add to Supply Problems." *New York Times*, May 12, 1973, p. 66.

———. "The Gasoline Shortage: Real or Contrived?" *New York Times*, July 8, 1973, p. 51.

Shanahan, Eileen. "Price Conspiracy by Eight Oil Concerns Charged by F.T.C." *New York Times*, July 18, 1973, p. 1.

"F.T.C. Weighs Divestiture in Oil Case." *New York Times*, July 19, 1973, p. 49.

Lichtblau, John. "Needed: More Refineries." *New York Times*, July 29, 1973, sec. 3, p. 12.

Savage, Ania. "Three Refineries in State Push Plans to Expand." *New York Times*, December 16, 1973, p. 99.

Salpukas, Agis. "Exxon Chief Admits Industry Mistakes." *New York Times*, January 29, 1974, p. 39.

Jensen, Michael C. "Major Concerns Reduce Output of Gasoline Despite Oil in Plenty." *New York Times*, July 29, 1974, p. 33.

"A Fight over Refined Oil Imports." *New York Times*, December 8, 1977, sec. 4, p. 1.

Lave, Charles A., and Lester B. Lave. "Curbing Lead Poisoning by Drivers." *New York Times*, February 2, 1979, p. A25.

"Gas Crunch from Refinery to Pump." *New York Times*, May 13, 1979, sec. 3, p. 1.

Friedman, Thomas L. "Cost Squeeze on Oil Refiners." *New York Times*, March 18, 1982, p. D1.

Tagliabue, John. "Europe's Worried Refiners: Overcapacity Put at 30–40%." *New York Times*, May 1, 1984, sec. 4, p. 1.

Reinhold, Robert. "Oil Glut Has Dulled the Gilt on Golden Triangle in Texas."
    New York Times, October 6, 1984, p. 1.

" 'Disastrous' Time for U.S. Refiners." *New York Times*, October 8, 1984, sec. 4,
    p. 6.

Diamond, Stuart. "U.S. Oil Refiners in Squeeze." *New York Times*, November 12,
    1984, sec. 4, p. 1.

"Refiners Ask Gas Quotas." *New York Times*, February 22, 1985, sec. 4, p. 6.

Hershey, Robert D., Jr. "Refiners' Bid for Protection." *New York Times*, May 10,
    1985, p. D2.

"The Refiners Are Coming" (Editorial). *New York Times*, May 18, 1985, sec. 1,
    p. 24.

Hall, John R. "Imports Could Kill the Refining Industry." *New York Times*, June
    23, 1985, Business section, p. 2.

Rothschild, Edwin. "Refiners' Problems Lie in U.S. Market." *New York Times*, June
    23, 1985, Business section, p. 2.

"Oil Refiners Need Sure Relief" (Letter). *New York Times*, July 8, 1985, sec. 1,
    p. 16.

"A Shakeout in East's Refineries." *New York Times*, October 9, 1985, sec. 4, p. 1.

Williams, Winston. "Refiners Breathe a Sigh of Relief: Cheaper Crude Oil Has
    Revived the Nation's Independents." *New York Times*, February 23, 1986,
    sec. 4, p. 4.

Tanner, James. "Refiners Again Cut Postings for Crude, but Price Plunge Appears
    Near Bottom." *Wall Street Journal*, March 12, 1986, p. 4.

Frazier, Steve. "Refiner Profits Start to Sag as Turmoil of Oil-Price Fall Registers at
    Gas Pump." *Wall Street Journal*, April 4, 1986, p. 2.

Sciolino, Elaine. "Saudis Tighten Belt, a Notch." *New York Times*, April 18, 1986,
    Business Day section, p. 1.

Vartan, Vartanig G. "Oil Industry's Brighter Side." *New York Times*, May 19,
    1986, sec. 4, p. 8.

Part VII

Leather
ESIC 31.0

CHAPTER 11

LEATHER AND LEATHER PRODUCTS, 31.0

JAMES L. WILES

Leather and its finished products constitute one of the most ancient industries. Tanning, boot and shoe making, harness making, saddlery, luggage, and gloves have occupied a prominent place in American industry from colonial times into the twentieth century. Alexander Hamilton noted their importance early in the nineteenth century, and in the mid–1800s industry employment figures were close to the top of all U.S. manufactures. At the turn of the century, leather industry value-added amounted to 4 percent of the U.S. manufacturing total, ninth among American industries. The 250,000 workers represented 6 percent of U.S. manufacturing employment. Since World War II, in the wake of serious import competition, the industry has declined in absolute terms and relative to other manufacturing sectors. Currently, leather and its products account for 1 percent or less of U.S. manufacturing employment and value-added. Tanning and finishing, and footwear account for about three-quarters of the leather industry's employment and value-added.

LEATHER TANNING AND FINISHING

Colonial America tanned leather to preserve it and to lengthen its life. The demand for leather arose naturally in an agrarian society. Colonial authorities were quick to note that demand and, because they had little faith in the efficacy of market forces, took steps to ensure the production of an adequate supply of leather. As early as 1642, Massachusetts law regulated leather production and fixed prices on hides and finished leather. New York granted a monopoly to its tanners and leather workers in 1676, limiting entry into the trade. In 1680 Virginia required that each county provide a tanhouse as well as the skilled workers needed for the several tasks involved. By 1700 Pennsylvania and New York had passed laws regulating the quality of leather as well as its price (Welsh 1964). Other laws discouraged the export of hides and leather in an attempt to develop domestic processing industries. Environmental concerns arose early: Massachusetts and Connecticut attempted to control the disposal of waste products, and records of the latter colony criticize the indiscriminate felling of trees whose bark was used in tanning.

This pattern of regulation persisted throughout the colonial period. After the Revolutionary War the national government also demonstrated its interest in the industry. Peter C. Welsh cites Hamilton's views on the status of tanning and his opinion that there were few manufactories of greater importance (1964). Earlier views on the persistence of old tanning techniques are questionable; important technological changes were in evidence by the 1840s (Ellsworth 1975). Still, at mid-century the industry remained one of small-scale firms, largely unaffected by machines (Welsh 1964).

The Tanbark Period

The history of the American leather industry, and of the shoe industry as well, readily breaks into stages, or periods. In the leather industry the years before 1880 are characterized as the tanbark period (Hoover 1937).

In addition to hides, bark from hemlock or oak trees (tanbark) and an adequate supply of running water were the prime requirements for the industry. Some of the settlers brought tanning skills with them from Europe. For the rest, technical manuals of varying quality were available toward the end of the eighteenth century. In any case, the tanning process followed a pattern. Skins were washed and soaked to remove hair. The hides were tanned in a vat with water and bark to soften and preserve them. Drying and finishing the leather was the last step. In the early nineteenth century the process took from twelve to eighteen months. Clearly, the challenge was to reduce the processing time without impairing the quality and appearance of the leather (Welsh 1964). Although lack of water could rule out a particular site, access to tanbark generally determined where tanneries would be located. One ton of tanbark was required to tan 200 pounds of leather; building tanneries on streams in close proximity to oak or hemlock forests reduced transportation costs (Hoover 1937).

Tanbark was widely available in great quantities; the supply of hides, however, was less certain. Domestic hides were attainable in the scattered farming communities, but their supply was tied to the demand for meat. The demand for hides did not determine the quantity of hides available to the tanners. Under these conditions the early leather industry concentrated near population centers and ports where domestic and imported hides and skins could be procured. Boston, New York City, and Philadelphia became prime producing areas. In 1879 firms in Massachusetts, New York, and Pennsylvania tanned 60 percent of the hides produced in the United States and 80 percent of the calf, goat, and sheep hides. The balance of the national output was distributed throughout the country. Despite the concentration of activity on the East Coast, tanning was still a local industry, one found in most sizable communities (Hoover 1937).

1880 to World War II

Prior to the 1880s, technological advances in the leather industry were not as radical as those associated with textiles and metals. Steam, for example, was used to power old methods of grinding and washing (Welsh 1964). From 1880 to World War II, however, was an era of far-reaching changes.

A series of developments in the 1880s significantly reduced the locational pull of tanbark supplies. First, a tanbark extract was developed that contained the active ingredients needed for tanning, but was one-tenth the weight of bark with the equivalent tanning value. Widespread use of the extract changed locational patterns: tanneries now operated profitably near the source of their hides. The new agent was particularly suited for tanning heavy cattle hides.

The second development, the railroad refrigerator car, had an indirect effect on tanning. Transporting fresh meat by refrigerator car freed packers to locate some distance from their markets. A number of them soon concentrated in Chicago, St. Louis, and Milwaukee. The ready supply of hides induced many tanners to relocate (Hoover 1937).

Finally, inorganic tanning agents were introduced. Although chemical tanning was known as early as the 1850s, it was not economically feasible until the 1880s. The process was first used in treating lighter skins, but by World War I, was widely applied to heavy leather (Clark 1929). Although this development reinforced the movement toward the meat-packing centers and the supply of hides, a migration was already under way in the mid–1880s, prompted by diminishing supplies of tanbark in some of the older tanning areas. To some extent, the extracts and chemicals halted the movement of firms from the depleted areas; but the new processes provided an added incentive to relocate in the meat-packing centers (Hoover 1937).

These geographic movements led to a decline in the percentage of value-of-product attributable to the three major leather producing states: Pennsylvania, Massachusetts, and New York. In 1889 their combined share amounted to about 60 percent of the U.S. total for the industry. In 1899 the figure stood at 52 percent; in 1909, at 44 percent. In the interim, Illinois and Wisconsin had registered gains.

Changes in the structure of the leather industry reflected a common practice at the turn of the century: large combinations of firms were formed in both heavy and light leather manufacturing. The United States Leather Company was organized by the principal sole leather manufacturers in 1893 and reorganized as the Central Leather Company in 1905. Overall, the company accounted for only about one-third of the U.S. sole leather production. The major meat packers, who had entered the tanning industry on a large scale, were the dominant force in the industry. The combination's counterpart in light, or upper, leathers was the American Hide and Leather Company (1899). This group of twenty-three firms probably controlled about one-third of the total U.S. output of lighter leathers (Clark 1929).

At least in the sole leather factories, these combinations emphasized power machinery to improve technical efficiency (Clark 1929). Flaying, shaving, and embossing machines became commonplace in the fifty years preceding World War II.

In the heavy leather sector particularly, the increased use of power machinery encouraged the construction of larger factories to attain economies of scale. Census data show that in 1889 the average leather factory employed twenty-four workers. By 1899 that figure had increased to forty and by 1914 to seventy-five. Factories making lighter leather in the older tanning areas employed numbers close to the national average. States that specialized in the heavier product supported larger plants. In 1899 average employment in Wisconsin firms was 126; in 1914, 219. On the eve of World War II, the typical plant employed 126. Firms in Massachusetts and New York averaged about 100 workers, and plants in Pennsylvania, Illinois, and Wisconsin employed from 150 to 250.

The geographical pattern established in the tanbark period was modified by the technological developments of the 1880s and 1890s. Yet in the early twentieth century, the tanneries of Pennsylvania, New York, and Massachusetts still produced about one-half of the industry's employment and value-added. Up to World War II neither Wisconsin nor Illinois held a permanent place among the top three producers.

The availability of hides and skins continued to fluctuate. Although the United States had become the world's most important source of hides and skins, the supply was inadequate in the interwar period to meet domestic manufacturing requirements. To close the gap, cattle hides were imported from Argentina, Brazil, and other Latin American countries. The lighter goat and sheep hides came from around the globe: Australia, India, Europe, and Latin America.

The U.S. tanning industry gained important markets abroad. Exports of leather increased in the 1870s as the obvious quality of the product overcame European misgivings about the hemlock tanning agent used in this country. The export boom two decades later reflected a growing respect for the industry's technology. Indeed, expert American tanners were sought by British and German firms (Clark 1929).

During the Depression of the 1930s tanning fared somewhat better than American manufacturing as a whole. Production and employment fell by less than the U.S. average, and by 1936 exceeded 1929 levels. The overall manufacturing sector remained 10 percent below its pre-Crash figures.

The Post–World War II Period

The tanning industry in the United States has never relinquished the technical lead it established at the end of the nineteenth century; in the 1980s it remains the world's most cost competitive and productive. Yet the industry is beset by major problems: the dramatic decline in domestic leather manufacturing and the increased use of substitute materials. The fall in domestic demand for leather has forced the U.S. tanning industry to seek wider export markets. On occasion, high prices for domestic hides have hampered this effort, as have trade restrictions imposed by foreign countries.

These problems posed no serious threat until the 1960s, when shoe imports began to rise. Nor were synthetic substitutes for leather a major concern. The failure of Du Pont's highly touted Corfam to win acceptance as a leather substitute indicated leather's strong position in medium- to higher-priced products. But a number of other synthetic materials were marketed in the late 1960s. Nonetheless, tradespeople and industry analysts argued that moderate leather prices would encourage consumers to maintain their preference for leather products.

Leather prices did increase significantly in 1966, however, when Argentina banned the export of hides. The U.S. government restricted exports for eight months as an anti-inflationary device. As predicted, substitutes once again came into greater use in the lower-priced lines, and the trend continued in 1967. By the end of the decade about 70 percent of shoes had leather uppers (a drop of about 10 percentage points in a few years), and only 20 percent had leather soles. The decline continued as leather prices soared, and in 1984 only about 55 percent of American-made shoes had leather uppers.

The impact of declining American shoe production and the increased use of substitute materials is reflected in tanning industry statistics. From 1972 to 1984, shoe shipments decreased by 45 percent. Leather tanning and finishing employment fell from 22,000 to 14,000, and industry shipments dropped from 25 million hides to 17 million.

In addition to changing economic conditions, the tanning and finishing industry encountered environmental problems. The industry maintained a laboratory at the University of Cincinnati to explore pollution control practices and to conduct research on product quality. By 1971, 35 to 40 percent of tanneries had pollution control systems. But small tanneries in areas without adequate sewerage systems found the installation and operation of control devices costly. When the Environmental Protection Agency tightened standards in 1979, the industry complained that the regulations put them at a competitive disadvantage in international trade.

In the meantime, the industry renewed its emphasis on technological progress. Plants were enlarged and increasingly mechanized. The twenty-firm concentration ratio has risen from 49 to 56 percent of shipments since 1967, but the four-firm figure has fallen from 20 to 16 percent.

Technological changes included a concrete-mixer type of tanning vat that replaced the conventional tanning drum. The new technique reduced the water and chemicals used, cutting both production costs and sewage disposal problems. A complementary development was an improvement in the chrome tanning system that used less of the costly chemicals and reduced the tanning process to three and one-half hours.

The post–World War II period saw significant changes in locational patterns in the tanning and finishing industry. The share of employment and value-added accounted for by Massachusetts, New York, and Pennsylvania continued to fall. In the years just after the war it remained at about 50 percent. By the mid–1960s their share was down to one-third and has remained at that level. The industry has become even more dispersed. Maine and New Hampshire are now important producers. In 1982 Wisconsin led all states in tanning value-added and was a close second in employment, whereas California had moved ahead of Pennsylvania and Illinois in those categories. In addition, Tennessee emerged as a major producer. Proximity to the populous markets of the South and West has become a locational factor. All told, in 1982 the states named accounted for about three-quarters of the industry's employment and two-thirds of its value-added.

Current Status and Industry Outlook

Despite continuing technological advances and productivity gains, the economic status of the American leather tanning and finishing industry is largely beyond its control. Until the decline in the domestic leather products industry is halted or reversed, tanners must look to export markets for their growth. Without open access to raw materials and foreign leather markets, the industry's prospects remain clouded (U.S. Department of Commerce 1967).

BOOTS AND SHOES

Boots and shoes have always been closely associated with the tanning and finishing industry. Makers of footwear have consistently been the principal purchasers of American leather. Despite the association, the two industries were not necessarily linked geographically as supplier and consumer; nonetheless, they often located in the same regions. Historically,

Massachusetts, New York, and Pennsylvania are among the most important shoe-producing states (Hoover 1937).

Blanche Evans Hazard (1921) and Edgar M. Hoover, Jr. (1937), agree, for the most part, on the periods and stages in the developing boot and shoe industry: (1) a home and handicraft stage, ending just before the Revolutionary War; (2) the domestic, or home-worker, stage, ending at about the Civil War; and (3) the factory stage, beginning about 1860.

Prefactory Period

Handicraft production characterized the colonial period. Shoemaking was simple and unmechanized, following a time-honored pattern. The worker first cut leather for the sole and the upper part of the shoe, then sewed together, or fitted, the several parts of the upper. To complete the shoe, the worker placed the upper over a form, or last, and affixed the inner and outer soles.

Farmers usually made boots and shoes for their families in the early part of the prefactory period, but itinerate cobblers also turned out shoes. Their products were generally better made and better fitting, and provided the wearer a bit of prestige as well. Gradually, these cobblers remained in their own shops, producing shoes to order. Competition for customers increased, and they began making shoes for the general market. Boston received the surplus output from its hinterland, becoming the industry's first major distribution center (Hazard 1921).

The domestic, or home-work stage, grew naturally out of the handicraft stage. Specialization in shoe production had already arrived with the settled cobbler in place of the farmer-shoemaker. The next step was to divide the process into its component parts and to parcel out the work accordingly. This stage was well under way by the Revolutionary War. As early as 1760, producers in Massachusetts, New York, and Pennsylvania were selling their shoes elsewhere. Tariff protection enacted in 1789 boosted production. Custom manufacturing became less common, although it was not distinguished from factory production until the Census of 1880 (Hoover 1937).

Proximity to populous markets and a dependable labor supply gave the Northeast major advantages in this prefactory period. Normally, a central shop organized production and distribution, but low-paid workers completed most of the work in their homes. Except in isolated frontier areas, people bought ready-made shoes from Massachusetts, New York, New Jersey, or Pennsylvania (Hoover 1937).

The development of the railroad threatened to undermine the Northeast's leading position: transportation costs fell, and new population centers grew in the West. Nonetheless, the older area's lead declined only gradually because of its advantages in labor skills and credit facilities. With the coming of shoe machinery, however, the pool of skilled labor became a less decisive factor.

The Factory Period: 1860–World War II

The factory stage overlapped the domestic, or putting-out, stage. In the 1850s, the need to retain markets against competitors encouraged some manufacturers to produce shoes in large, central locations. Closer supervision helped control the quality of the product as well as its processing time (Hazard 1921). The central shop became a genuine factory with the coming of the McKay sewing machine in 1860. The McKay attached the sole to the upper part of the shoe, the most time-consuming task of the entire process. As the machines were improved, labor costs fell from 75 cents per pair, hand-sewn, to 3 cents per pair sewn on the McKay (Clark 1929).

The successful introduction of the sewing machine made shoes cheaper, but neither improved their quality nor made them more comfortable. The McKay system left an exposed rough seam inside the shoe, a source of complaints by the wearers. Although the output of McKay-stitched shoes soared during the Civil War, the search continued for a better bottoming machine. The Goodyear Welt process came into use in the 1870s and was improved in 1880. The insole, upper, and welt were sewed together and the welt stitched to the outsole, leaving the upper surface of the insole free of tacks and stitches. The Goodyear process was at first more expensive than the McKay, but was widely adopted after improvements. The two systems dominated the bottoming process until the "Compo" adhesive method was applied to women's shoe production in the 1920s (Hoover 1937).

Although a number of other machines were developed in this period, the industry was difficult to mechanize. Many of the machine operations were quite intricate, and leather varies in grain and texture from piece to piece, requiring adjustments by the operator. And as style changes became more frequent, the cost of making the many dies reduced the advantages of some machines.

With the introduction of machinery, the demand for power increased. Steam was first used about 1860, but because of start and stop operations, electricity ultimately proved to be the most suitable substitute for prefactory hand and foot power (Hoover 1937).

Because American shoe production more than doubled between 1878 and 1895, exports also increased. Here, too, color and style played a part as American manufacturers heeded European tastes. American merchandizing practices improved in another direction: three major manufacturers of men's shoes, Endicott Johnson of New York State and W. L. Douglas and George E. Keith of Brockton, Massachusetts, opened their own retail stores. The latter two firms maintained stores abroad as well.

The locational pattern of boot and shoe manufacturing changed during the factory period. At the outset, about 1860, Massachusetts, New York, and Pennsylvania produced almost three-quarters of the industry's value-of-product. By the turn of the century, their share had fallen to about 60 percent. Massachusetts remained the industry leader, although its share was down from 60 to 45 percent of total value. In the intervening years Ohio, Missouri, and New Hampshire emerged as significant producers: in 1899 their output represented some 20 percent of industry value-of-product.

Hoover suggests that two forces began to influence the boot and shoe industry during the early years of this century: style changes and union activity. Labor organizations and the proliferation of shoe styles took on added significance after 1900. Better tanning processes meant that a greater variety of leather finishes and colors were available to shoe manufacturers. Women's shoes were particularly affected by these developments, but throughout the industry shoe design became an art. The shoe industry in the early 1900s embodied one of the few artistic phases of manufacturing in which America led the world (Clark 1929).

The emphasis on styling placed a premium on the rapid filling of orders and quick delivery to market areas. New England's shoe industry suffered another setback as these considerations grew in importance. In addition, frequent style changes meant that plants making women's shoes would remain small. Long production runs with attendant scale economies were rare.

New England manufacturers, particularly those producing men's shoes in Brockton, recovered some of the sales lost at home by expanding exports. Their success was short-lived, however; World War I and protectionism effectively closed foreign markets to American shoes. Massachusetts's position as the leading producer of shoes eroded still further during the interwar years. In 1919 its factories accounted for 40 percent of the industry's value-added and 38 percent of its employment. In 1937 Massachusetts still led the nation, but the figures had fallen to 20 and 22 percent. New York and Missouri were the other major producers just before World War II.

Labor's increasing prominence at the turn of the century is the second factor cited by Hoover (1937) in marking out this stage. Shoemakers enjoyed a reputation as superior craftsmen and members of the community. This opinion, whether accurate or not, apparently carried over into the factory period, because shoe workers were considered more skilled than their counterparts in woolen mills (Hazard 1921).

Societies of shoe craftsmen in Boston and Philadelphia predated organized labor in the factory period; indeed, those workers were among the first to unionize. In 1868 skilled shoe workers in the eastern United States formed the Knights of St. Crispin, the industry's first large labor organization. The Knights did not oppose mechanization, but sought a closed shop to counteract cheap labor trained to operate the McKay machine.

The Knights claimed 50,000 members by 1870, but the organization's weak financial base precluded adequate strike benefits. Despite successful strikes in Lynn, Massachusetts, in 1869 and 1870, the Knights were seriously weakened in the depression that followed the Panic of 1873.

A better-known group, the Knights of Labor, was also active in the shoe industry during the 1870s and 1880s. But this organization proved incapable of reconciling local autonomy with the prerogatives of a strong central body. In the 1890s, a quasi-industrial union made up of local craft unions and general workers under the direction of the central body grew out of the Knights of Labor and became the industry's principal labor organization. The Boot and Shoe Worker's Union affiliated in turn with the American Federation of Labor (Norton 1932).

The Boot and Shoe Worker's Union followed conservative policies: closed shop agreements, a "union stamp" for employers, and steadfast adherence to contracts. Throughout this period the union consistently enrolled more members than its more aggressive rivals did. Its main strength was in Massachusetts, particularly in Brockton, the center of men's shoe production.

Organized labor affected the shoe industry's location to a limited extent. Some firms left the older New England shoe centers, not for other regions, but for nonunion towns within the same region.

In addition to styling and organized labor, a third major change confronted the industry at the turn of the century. The United Shoe Machinery Company (later Corporation) (USMC) brought together in 1899 the major manufacturers of sewing, welting, and lasting equipment. The latter companies had already absorbed scores of smaller machinery firms, so that shoe producers were now effectively tied to USMC, which controlled at least 70 percent of machinery output (Kaysen 1956).

United Shoe Machinery policies generated antitrust questions. The principal issue was tying contracts: requiring a shoe manufacturer to accept a full line of company machines as a condition for obtaining any United Shoe Machinery equipment. The controversial policy of leasing, rather than selling, machines to the shoe factories originated at the McKay Company in the 1860s. Leasing permitted easy entrance to and exit from the industry and was generally favored by small producers. Under USMC guidelines, the smaller firms received the same quality equipment and service as their larger competitors. This nondiscriminatory policy extended to royalties. The per unit royalty did not vary by the factory's location or the extent of the machine's use (Hoover 1937). Major shoe producers and the U.S. government periodically battled USMC and its policies, registering some success in modifying the leasing arrangements (Kaysen 1956). Antitrust charges arose again in the 1940s.

Overall, the industry output of men's and women's shoes grew from 133 million pairs in 1899 to 254 million pairs in 1940, a 90 percent increase. Women's shoes registered the largest gain: output more than doubled, while production of men's shoes increased by 50 percent between 1899 and 1937. The influence of style is discernible in these figures. In turn, the changing composition of industry output affected the method of shoe construction. The welted process continued to be used in about one-third of the shoes produced, but the McKay method fell from 41 percent to 20 percent. By 1937 the newer cementing and stitchdown methods for making women's shoes were used in 35 percent of all shoes produced (Fabricant 1939).

The industry's output growth was far below the 276 percent gain registered by U.S. manufacturing as a whole. Boot and shoe employment rose from 142,000 to 218,000, a 54 percent increase. Here, too, the industry fell below the 90 percent gain in employment registered in the manufacturing sector (Fabricant 1940).

During the Depression, the boot and shoe industry's output fell to 84 percent of its 1929 level, but by 1935 the industry had exceeded its 1929 output. Industry employment recovered its pre-Depression level by 1937.

World War II and the Postwar Period

Military requirements stimulated production of men's shoes after 1940: output increased from 102 million pairs that year to 143 million in 1942. Production declined to 129 million pairs in 1943 and returned to prewar levels in 1946. Meanwhile, the output of women's shoes decreased during the war, but reached new highs in the early postwar years. Employment remained around 220,000 in 1947.

The geographic distribution of shoe firms changed little during the war years. Massachusetts was still the leader in 1947, although its share of industry employment and value-added continued to fall.

The 1947 employment figure of 220,000 proved a high-water mark for the boot and shoe industry. Except for a 1953 estimate, all subsequent years have shown declines in industry employment. The 1982 Census of Manufactures reported 107,000 boot and shoe production workers; 1987 estimates were 66,000. Despite the growing importance of the service sector, overall U.S. manufacturing employment has increased by some 4 percent.

Two antitrust cases in the 1950 and 1960s influenced the shoe industry. In the United Shoe Machinery case of 1954, the court ruled against United, citing the firm's overwhelming strength in the shoe machinery market. As a result, United had to sell as well as lease its machines to shoe manufacturers. The long-standing practice of leasing was frequently associated with easy entry into and exit from the shoe industry. In the Brown Shoe case of 1962, the court overruled a merger between Brown and Kinney, another major producer. The two firms owned retail outlets and shoe factories. The court found that their combined market share tended toward a concentration of power that should be curbed. The ruling is a landmark in the area of close-knit combinations.

For two decades after the war, U.S. production of boots and shoes increased. Total output of nonrubber shoes and slippers was 462 million pairs in 1948, 585 million in 1955, and 626 million in 1965. But the industry's growth in output and value-added was well below the averages in those years for U.S. manufacturing as a whole.

By the late 1960s, a steady decline in the production of footwear had set in. Output fell from 611 million pairs in 1967 to 431 million in 1977 to 235 million in 1987. This decline adversely affected the tanning and finishing industry. From 1974 to 1982, employment in the entire leather and leather products group declined annually by 2.7 percent and output by 0.7 percent.

These developments were, of course, closely related to a phenomenon that dates to the 1960s, the remarkable increase in imported footwear. Shipments of shoes from abroad coincided with a shift in American preferences for lower-priced canvas and rubber footwear. The import/new supply ratio rose from 0.037 in 1963 to 0.07 in 1967 to 0.16 in 1970 (new supply is the sum of the value of U.S. shoe shipments plus imports). By 1984 the ratio had climbed to 0.504; that is, imports made up one-half of the shoe supply in the United States that year. Shipments of leather shoes originated mainly in Italy, Taiwan, South Korea, and Brazil. Most plastic and children's shoes came from Taiwan, and South Korea supplied athletic and work shoes.

American producers reacted to their loss of market share by introducing new manufacturing techniques and lobbying for government protection against imports. The new processes use plastics, synthetics, and fabrics in volume-line shoes. These materials can be worked with conventional shoe machinery, which reduces training costs and outlays for equipment. Moreover, the materials are generally less expensive than leather and are easier to work up. Shoe manufacturers also adopted new methods of bottoming shoes. By using forms that allow soles and heels to be attached in one operation, injection molding and direct vulcanization greatly simplify this labor-intensive phase of shoemaking.

Although these innovations were timely and welcome, the Department of Commerce noted in the mid–1960s that only a few shoe manufacturers were engaged in research and development activities. Most research was conducted by shoe machinery manufacturers and suppliers of materials or shoe components. The department suggested that shoe manufacturers cooperate in setting up a comprehensive research program (U.S. Department of Commerce 1967). A 1975 grant from the department encouraged the industry to increase productivity and sales by conducting consumer research and reexamining methods of production. To improve technical and managerial competence, the industry established in 1979 the American Shoe Center in Philadelphia. Its fifteen-member board included nine shoe manufacturers as well as suppliers and retailers. A year earlier, the U.S. government had launched a two-year, $56 million revitalization program aimed at shoe firms injured by import competition. Some 150 firms employing about 80,000 people were judged to be eligible to participate. Specialists in production, management, finance, and marketing were to analyze particular cases and make recommendations. Three-quarters of the funds were directed at new investment.

Perhaps the principal breakthrough sought in these efforts was automation—linking machines to allow a smooth, uninterrupted flow of work from one process to the next. Automated machinery would effect the greatest cost reductions in pattern making and in cutting the stitching uppers. Attempts to automate these labor-intensive tasks were hindered by a familiar difficulty: a firm must make long production runs of one style to recover the cost of the equipment. Once again, styling changes and nonstandard sizing hampered the introduction of new techniques. Still, a number of larger firms have installed computer-aided design and computer-aided manufacturing equipment. Modular production techniques are sometimes used that combine four or more operations or machines and require fewer operators. It is difficult to assess postwar productivity gains in the shoe industry. Productivity increased at a compound rate of 2.1 percent for the leather group as a whole. This rate exceeded the ones registered by all manufacturing (1.7 percent) and nondurable manufactures (1.9 percent). Improved tanning processes probably account for a large portion of the group's gain.

In addition to combatting imports through technology, American shoe manufacturers periodically petitioned the government for trade protection after World War II. Following the Civil War, little protection had been sought because American shoes had won an important share of world markets, and imports took only a small share of the American market. When the import/new supply ratio exceeded 0.2 (20 percent) in the mid–1970s, however, the U.S. International Trade Commission noted the impact of imports on the domestic industry. Orderly marketing arrangements were concluded with Taiwan and South Korea in 1977. These take the form of quantitative restraints on imports, monitored by the United States (Hufbauer, Berliner, and Elliott 1986). Those arrangements remained in effect during the Carter administration but were ended by the Reagan administration in 1981. The import/new supply ratio stabilized at about 0.33 from 1978 to 1981, but has since increased dramatically. Although supported by the International Trade Commission under the Trade Act of 1974, appeals by the industry have not been effective. While acknowledging the impact of imported footwear, President Ronald Reagan cited shoe industry statistics to argue that the injury is not widespread. Employment had stabilized by 1984, productive capacity had increased, and profit margins exceeded those in all manufacturing. The industry sought relief from Congress, which passed legislation calling for quotas in late 1985. President Reagan vetoed this action in December of that year.

Current Status and Industry Outlook

The downward trend in shoe industry employment continued into 1987. Output fell in 1987 as well, the tenth consecutive year of decline. The pace of factory closings slowed, but from 1982 through 1986, 307 plants shut down. The Department of Commerce estimated that in 1985, 210 shoe factories employed ten or more workers; in 1977, 648 factories; and in 1982, over 500. From 1972 to 1982, concentration increased slightly in women's footwear, but decreased in men's. In 1982 the four largest manufacturers of women's shoes produced 36 percent of the sector's value of shipments; the four largest manufacturers of men's shoes, 27 percent.

The geographic distribution of the shoe industry has changed considerably since the end of World War II. In 1982 Massachusetts accounted for about 7 percent of employment in the industry and 8 percent of the value-added. The longtime leader now ranks fifth in employment behind Maine, Missouri, Pennsylvania, and Tennessee.

Imports have pushed the leather and footwear industry close to extinction (Eckstein et al. 1984). Yet the footwear industry's long-term prospects might be termed fair. Production has begun to stabilize in the late 1980s. Many weaker firms have already closed, and others will fail or will be absorbed by larger companies. The remaining plants will be better able to afford the advanced equipment on which so much depends. One industry analyst predicts that the long period of industry contraction is over (U.S. Department of Commerce 1987).

BIBLIOGRAPHIC ANALYSIS

Biography and Company History

Despite its long-standing importance in American industry, the leather group has not promoted a voluminous literature in biography and company history. One reason lies, perhaps, in the structure of the industry itself. Unlike some industries, leather is made up of relatively small firms, with few recognizable company names. Indeed, because of the diversity of its products, the shoe industry can be considered a collection of subindustries (Jacks 1971). Industry innovation has been attributed to shoe machinery manufacturers rather than to the shoe companies themselves. Entrepreneurs were less likely to be noticed in such a setting.

Nevertheless, a few companies are singled out. Arthur S. Dewing (1911) recounts the troubles of the U.S. Leather Company ("the leather trust") and its financial reorganization. By the late nineteenth century several shoe firms had managed to differentiate their products and warranted special attention. Two Brockton manufacturers, W. L. Douglas and George E. Keith, established well-known retail outlets in the United States and abroad. The Keith

Company (the "Walk-Over" shoe) published *The Story of the George E. Keith Company* (n.d.) as well as a journal, *Walk-Over Shoe Prints*. The journal ran from 1906 until 1931 and emphasized the firm's marketing activities.

Charles W. Chatfield (1950) provides a brief history of the W. L. Douglas Company as background to the merger that ended the company's independence. Once again, merchandizing is emphasized. Another major shoe company, Rice and Hutchins (1916), published its own fifty-year retrospective. Ernest A. Bragg (1950) sketches the history of a number of companies in two of the smaller Massachusetts shoe towns.

The history of one of the largest producers, Endicott Johnson, is related in two brief works. G. Ralph Smith (1956) outlines the company's history from its inception in the 1890s, emphasizing personnel policies and labor relations. Eli G. White (1967) traces the origins and development of the firm while concentrating on its reorganization in the 1960s. In a more recent work, Gerald Zahavi (1987) deals with "the welfare capitalism" espoused by company president George Johnson, whom Eli White characterized as "a labor relations genius."

Several general works on the industry examine firms and prominent businessmen. Frank A. Norcross's book on the New York leather district (1901) deals with the "kings of the tanning trade" from early times to late nineteenth century. There is a street by street, family by family depiction of the trade's growth in that important center. Added items of interest include a section on the U.S. Leather Company and an account of an 1859 trade banquet in New York, which featured speakers who offered remarkably accurate predictions on the course of the industry. Fred A. Gannon (1912) provides some information on the inventors of the stitching and lasting machines that came into service after the Civil War. In addition to providing a sweeping history of the shoe and leather group, Charles H. McDermott (1918) devotes over 100 pages to biographical sketches of the industry's past and current leaders. As former editors of major trade journals, McDermott and Norcross were familiar with the inner workings of their industry.

Industrial History

A more complete chronicle of the leather group's history can be found in industrial histories. While particular firms or individual entrepreneurs have not attracted much attention, other considerations have stimulated scholarly interest in the industry. Leather and shoes provided excellent case studies for location theorists, and the rise of shoemaking from a craft to a national industry has been explored. Technological development was especially prominent in tanning and shoe manufacturing. Labor organizations have had a long and colorful history within the industry. The leather group's post–World War II problems have brought forth a considerable, if narrowly focused, body of material.

Pre–Civil War Period

Malcolm Keir (1928) and Clark (1929) include early tanning and shoe-making in their general histories of U.S. manufactures. These histories serve as helpful introductions by providing details on key figures, the geographic location of activity, and contemporary trade practices. The same can be said of still earlier works by J. Leander Bishop (1866) and Albert S. Bolles ([1881] 1966). They are particularly useful in placing tanning and shoes in the context of American manufacturing as a whole. Ellsworth (1969) is meant for school use, but it is an expert brief history.

Hoover's classic work (1937) remains indispensable as a source for both tanning and shoe manufacturing. Although his book is primarily concerned with location of industry, it gives a clear picture of all facets of the shoe and leather industries. Hoover's discussion of the tanbark period extends to the Civil War era.

More recently, Welsh (1964) has published a useful short work on tanning up to 1850. He concentrates on tanning in Delaware, outlining the status of the industry in that period as well as explaining and illustrating the techniques employed. The book also cites several specialized works of that era. Tanning in New Jersey is covered in short works by the Newark Museum Association (1926) and Harry B. and Grace M. Weiss (1959).

Lucius F. Ellsworth (1975) details the tanning industry in New York State. He shows how, by the Civil War, changes in institutional arrangements and technology had transformed once localized activity into a national industry.

The antebellum boot and shoe industry has received greater coverage than leather tanning and finishing. Hoover (1937) and Hazard (1921) treat the industry's prefactory stage in considerable detail. Hazard illustrates shoe-making techniques and marketing practices in Massachusetts before 1875. To fill out this picture, Winifred B. Rothenberg (1985) shows that a regional capital market was developing in the rural areas that made up Boston's hinterland.

John R. Commons (1909) discusses at length workers' attempts to organize in the prefactory era. His article also details the changing methods of making shoes. A more personal account of these changes can be found in David N. Johnson's ([1880] 1970) memoirs of a shoemaker's life and work in Lynn, Massachusetts. Bishop (1866) shows the transition to the factory system in his brief sketches of a number of shoemaking towns.

Lynn, Massachusetts, figures in several works on the shoe industry. Paul G. Faler (1974, 1981) focuses on the cultural and social aspects of Lynn's industrialization up to 1860. He provides material on the industry itself and on some of the city's manufacturers. Alan Dawley (1976) deals in part with the pre–Civil War years in Lynn, but he also examines the impact of the factory system on Lynn shoe workers in the latter part of the nineteenth century. His book explores the forms of unionism that emerged from the sustained opposition to industrial capitalism in Lynn.

An interesting, authoritative account of manufacturing practices in the 1850s is contained in Wallis (1969). Nathan Rosenberg contributes an editor's introduction to the body of the work: a chronicle of the 1854 travels of two Englishmen as they inspected American factories, including leather and shoemaking establishments. The visitors were impressed with the quality of the materials and the work they observed. Their comments show that they saw quite clearly the emerging factory system.

Fred Bateman and Thomas Weiss (1975) examine the regional development of American manufacturing in the mid-nineteenth century. The largest leather-producing firm in the western states accounted for a greater percentage of its state's leather production than did the largest firms in the East and South. The same was true for boot and shoe firms by 1860. Jeremy Atack (1986) looks at firm size in the middle decades of the last century. The average size of plants producing boots and shoes declined by 16 percent between 1820 and 1870. The largest shoe firm accounted for less than 1 percent of industry output in 1870.

For an earlier period, Kenneth L. Sokoloff (1984) estimated that tanning lagged well behind cotton in the percentage of total capital invested in machinery and tools. In 1832 boot and shoe producers held a smaller percentage of fixed capital than tanners did. On a related topic, Atack (1985) holds that despite the relatively small size of shoe plants, economies of scale were exploited in the industry during the antebellum period.

1860 to World War II

Between 1860 and World War II technological changes aided mechanization in both tanning and shoe manufacture. Hoover (1937) shows the implications of these changes for both industries; Clark (1929) and Keir (1928) survey these years as well. Frederick J. Allen (1922) provides a wealth of information on the machines employed in shoe factories and shows how a plant of that period was organized. Solomon Fabricant (1939, 1940) examines employment and output trends in the industry from the turn of the century to the late 1930s.

Works on labor history often yield insights into the problems and prospects of the leather industries. Leo C. Brown (1947) describes tanning and finishing processes and summarizes the industry's performance in the pre–World War II years. He traces earlier attempts to unionize the industry and concentrates on labor movements after the Civil War. Augusta E. Galster (1924) reviews the several stages of shoemaking history while focusing on labor organizations in post–Civil War Philadelphia. She reproduces the texts of several union constitutions and agreements. Irwin Yellowitz (1977) discusses the lasters' union and the reaction of these skilled workers to mechanization in the 1890s. Thomas L. Norton (1932) examines union activities in the Massachusetts shoe industry in the 1920s. Here, too, is a brief history of shoe manufacture as well as a careful analysis of the economic conditions facing the industry in the twenties.

American shoe exports expanded during the pre–World War I years. Clark (1929) deals with the growing foreign markets for U.S. shoes, while William H. Becker (1973) argues that the American export boom of that time was a sign of U.S. economic strength, not weakness. R. A. Church (1968) cautions against overstating the impact of U.S. shipments on the British shoe industry.

Hoover and Clark show how a new emphasis on style affected the shoe industry after 1890. Dwight E. Robinson (1963) offers a more general explanation of the impact fashion has on manufacturers' production and marketing activities.

A National Recovery Administration study (1935) was halted short of completion by the Supreme Court decision that invalidated portions of the National Industrial Recovery Act. Nonetheless, the report contains interesting testimony from hearings devoted to developing a shoe industry code in the Depression years. Two works by Ernest S. Bradford (1931, 1936) also deal with the industry's experiences in the Depression. The earlier study surveys the 1920s; the 1936 update offers an analysis of the industry's recovery in the middle of the decade.

Ruth P. Mack (1954, 1956) examines business fluctuations in the shoe and leather industry for the interwar period. In the course of her detailed work she presents a concise description of the work and structure of the various leather industry stages. Kalman J. Cohen (1960) builds upon Mack's data, but uses the computer to model the aggregate behavior of the leather group's several sectors.

World War II and the Postwar Years

In his study of wage setting in Brockton, George P. Shultz (1951) provides an industry-wide review of the interwar and World War II periods. He succinctly states the shoe industry's economic characteristics as background for a discussion of wage movements and negotiations, particularly in Brockton.

A British productivity team's report on the American shoe industry for the Anglo-American Council on Productivity (1951) is comprehensive and instructive. It details manufacturing materials, methods, and practices in the war and earlier postwar years, concluding that production in America was higher than in Britain.

Despite this vote of confidence, there were trouble spots in the shoe industry during the 1950s. Carl Kaysen's (1956) analysis of the 1947 United Shoe Machinery case shows the effect of the government's victory on

United's leasing and royalty practices. Shoe manufacturers overwhelmingly supported United's position in the case, arguing that its leasing policy allowed easy entry and exit for small shoe firms. Kaysen disputes this view, but argues that the managerial services offered by United undoubtedly helped small as well as new shoe firms. He adds, however, that this service probably inhibited the development of managerial talent in shoe manufacturing.

Harry L. Hansen (1959) identifies some of the industry's weaknesses: many obsolete plants, lax management and industrial engineering, and inadequate marketing operations. Marguerite I. Coughlin (1959) saw U.S. income and population trends as the major determinants of the New England shoe industry's health, although imported shoes were beginning to stir some concern. Alluding to the fact that shoe imports caught the Americans by surprise, Charles J. Colazzo, Jr. (1970), calls for a center for research and information on the industry. A Department of Commerce study carried out by the Battelle Memorial Institute (1967) made a similar, but more ambitious, recommendation: a technological center and cooperative shoe research programs among manufacturers. Stanley M. Jacks (1971) argues that the industry's low productivity would have placed it in jeopardy even without import competition. Bruce R. Kalisch (1980) shows that output per production worker in the late 1970s remained at approximately the 1959 level. He attributes this stagnation to imports and smaller production runs, as well as to the need for operator guidance at almost every stage of production. Albert J. Niemi (1970) ascribes postwar regional growth differentials in the United States to the decline in New England's traditional strengths: leather and textiles.

The import phenomenon is amply documented in an annual publication by the U.S. Department of Commerce. *U.S. Industrial Outlook* contains analyses and statistics for all facets of the entire leather group. In addition, the U.S. International Trade Commission (1976, 1977, 1981, 1984) carried out a number of investigations of the footwear industry.

Several works assess the efficacy of policies adopted to cope with the import problem. Michael Szenberg, John W. Lombardi, and Eric Y. Lee (1977) point out that, although shoe industry growth in less developed countries reduces international income inequality, the injury to U.S. firms is considerable. They examine demand and supply conditions in the shoe industry and carry out a cost-benefit analysis of protection for domestic producers. The authors conclude that, in the mid–1970s, tariff removal could result in a consumer welfare gain approximately twice the dollar loss in earnings that would be experienced by displaced employees. Gary C. Hufbauer and Howard F. Rosen (1986) present a more recent digest of the footwear industry's adjustment to import competition. Hufbauer, Diane T. Berliner, and Kimberly Ann Elliott (1986) summarize the import problem and the trade adjustment assistance programs put into effect in 1977, as well as provide estimates from various studies on demand elasticities for footwear and the costs and benefits of trade restriction. They conclude that, although the United States could find a worse approach to special protection, it could surely find a better one.

BIBLIOGRAPHY

Allen, Frederick J. *The Shoe Industry*. New York: Henry Holt, 1922.

Anglo-American Council on Productivity. *Productivity Team Report on the Footwear Industry*. New York: Anglo-American Council on Productivity, 1951.

Atack, Jeremy. *Estimation of Economies of Scale in Nineteenth Century United States Manufacturing*. New York: Garland, 1985.

———. "Firm Size and Industrial Structure in the United States During the Nineteenth Century." *Journal of Economic History* 46 (June 1986): 463–75.

Bateman, Fred, and Thomas Weiss. "Comparative Regional Development in Antebellum Manufacturing." *Journal of Economic History* 35 (March 1975): 182–208.

Becker, William H. "American Manufacturers and Foreign Markets, 1870–1900." *Business History Review* 47 (Winter 1973): 467–81.

Bishop, John Leander. *A History of American Manufactures from 1608 to 1860*. 3 vols. Philadelphia: Edward Young, 1866.

Bolles, Albert S. *Industrial History of the United States*. Norwich, CT: Henry Hill, 1881. Reprint. New York: Augustus M. Kelley, 1966.

Bradford, Ernest S. *Economic Forces Affecting Shoe Marketing: A Study of Some Problems of the Shoe Manufacturer*. Research Report, Marketing, ser. 1, vol. 5. New York: College of the City of New York, Bureau of Business Research, 1931.

———. *Economic Forces Affecting Shoe Marketing: A Study of Some Problems of the Shoe Manufacturer*. New York: College of the City of New York, Bureau of Business Research, 1936.

Bragg, Ernest A. *The Origin and Growth of the Boot and Shoe Industry in Holliston and Milford, Massachusetts, 1793–1950*. Boston: Recording & Statistical Corp., 1950.

Brooke, Iris. *Footwear: A Short History of European and American Shoes*. New York: Theatre Arts Books, 1971.

Brown, Leo C. *Union Policies in the Leather Industry*. Cambridge, MA: Harvard University Press, 1947.

Cahn, Miles, and Jeremy Lezin. *The Factory: Portrait of a Leathergoods Factory in Downtown New York City*. New York: Rapoport, 1977.

Chatfield, Charles W. "A Brief History of the W. L. Douglas Company." *Bulletin of the Business Historical Society* 24 (December 1950): 159–83.

Church, R. A. "The Effect of the American Export Invasion on the British Boot and Shoe Industry 1885–1914." *Journal of Economic History* 28 (June 1968): 223–54.

Clark, Victor S. *History of Manufactures in the United States*. 3 vols. New York: Peter Smith, 1929.

Cohen, Kalman J. *Computer Models of the Shoe, Leather, Hide Sequence.* Englewood Cliffs, NJ: Prentice-Hall, 1960.

Colazzo, Charles J., Jr. *The Development of Research Activities in the Footwear Industry.* Lowell, MA: Merrimack Valley Industrial Information Center, 1970.

Commons, John R. "American Shoemakers, 1648–1895." *Quarterly Journal of Economics* 24 (November 1909): 39–84.

Coughlin, Marguerite I. *Federal Reserve Bank of Boston 1970 Projection No. 14: Outlook for New England's Shoe Industry to 1970.* Boston: Federal Reserve Bank of Boston, December 1959.

Dawley, Alan. *Class and Community.* Cambridge, MA: Harvard University Press, 1976.

Dewing, Arthur S. "The United States Leather Company and Its Reorganization." *Quarterly Journal of Economics* 26 (November 1911): 68–104.

Eckstein, Otto, Christopher Caton, Roger Brinner, and Peter Duprey. *The DRI Report on U.S. Manufacturing Industries.* New York: McGraw-Hill, 1984.

Ellsworth, Lucius F. *The American Leather Industry.* Chicago: Rand McNally, 1969.

———. *Craft to National Industry in the Nineteenth Century: A Case Study of the Transformation of the New York State Tanning Industry.* New York: Arno Press, 1975.

Fabricant, Solomon. *Output of Manufacturing Industries 1899–1937.* New York: National Bureau of Economic Research, 1939.

———. *Employment in Manufacturing 1899–1939.* New York: National Bureau of Economic Research, 1940.

Faler, Paul G. "Cultural Aspects of the Industrial Revolution: Lynn, Mass., Shoemakers and Industrial Morality 1826–1860." *Labor History* 15 (Summer 1974): 367–94.

———. *Mechanics and Manufacturers in the Early Industrial Revolution: Lynn, Massachusetts 1780–1860.* Albany: State University of New York Press, 1981.

Galster, Augusta E. *The Labor Movement in the Shoe Industry.* New York: Ronald Press, 1924.

Gannon, Fred A. *A Short History of American Shoemaking.* Salem, MA: Newcomb & Gause, 1912.

Hansen, Harry L. *A Study of Competition and Management in the Shoe Manufacturing Industry.* New York: National Shoe Manufacturers Association, 1959.

Hazard, Blanche Evans. *The Organization of the Boot and Shoe Industry in Massachusetts Before 1875.* Cambridge, MA: Harvard University Press, 1921.

Hoover, Edgar M., Jr. *Location Theory and the Shoe and Leather Industries.* Cambridge, MA: Harvard University Press, 1937.

Hufbauer, Gary C., Diane T. Berliner, and Kimberly Ann Elliott. *Trade Protection in the United States: Thirty-one Case Studies.* Washington, DC: Institute for International Economics, 1986.

Hufbauer, Gary Clyd, and Howard F. Rosen. *Trade Policy for Troubled Industries.* Washington, DC: Institute for International Economics, 1986.

Jacks, Stanley M. *Productivity Issues in the Domestic Shoe Industry.* Washington, DC: National Commission on Productivity, 1971.

Johnson, David N. *Sketches of Lynn, or the Changes of Fifty Years.* 1880. Reprint. Westport, CT: Greenwood Press, 1970.

Kalisch, Bruce R. "Shoe Manufacturing." In *The Improvement of Productivity: Myths and Realities,* edited by John E. Ullmann, 146–57. New York: Praeger, 1980.

Kaysen, Carl. *United States v. United Shoe Machinery Corporation: An Economic Analysis of an Anti-trust Case.* Cambridge, MA: Harvard University Press, 1956.

Keir, Malcolm. *Manufacturing.* New York: Ronald Press, 1928.

McCarthy, James E. *Trade Adjustment Assistance: A Case Study of the Shoe Industry in Massachusetts.* Research Report 58. Boston: Federal Reserve Bank of Boston, 1975.

McDermott, Charles H. *A History of the Shoe and Leather Industries in the United States.* Boston: John W. Denehy, 1918.

Mack, Ruth P. *Factors Influencing Consumption: An Experimental Analysis of Shoe Buying.* New York: National Bureau of Economic Research, 1954.

————. *Consumption and Business Fluctuations: A Case Study of the Shoe, Leather, Hide Sequence.* New York: National Bureau of Economic Research, 1956.

Martin, David D. "The Brown Shoe Case and the New Antimerger Policy." *American Economic Review* 53 (June 1963): 340–58.

National Recovery Administration. *Report of the Survey Committee on the Operation of the Code for the Boot and Shoe Manufacturing Industry.* Washington, DC: NRA, 1935.

Newark Museum Association. *Nothing Takes the Place of Leather.* Newark: Museum Association, 1926.

Niemi, Albert J. "The Development of Industrial Structure in Southern New England." *Journal of Economic History* 30 (September 1970): 657–62.

Norcross, Frank A. *A History of the New York Swamp.* New York: Chiswick Press, 1901.

Norton, Thomas L. *Trade Union Policies in the Massachusetts Shoe Industry 1919–1929.* New York: Columbia University Press, 1932.

OECD (Organization for Economic Cooperation and Development). *The Footwear Industry: Structure and Governmental Policies.* Paris: OECD, 1976.

Porter, Glenn, and Harold C. Livesay. *Merchants and Manufacturers: Studies in the Changing Structure of Nineteenth-Century Marketing.* Baltimore: Johns Hopkins University Press, 1971.

Rice & Hutchins, Inc. *A Retrospect: 1866–1916.* Cambridge, MA: University Press, 1916.

Robinson, Dwight E. "The Importance of Fashions in Taste to Business History." *Business History Review* 37 (Spring–Summer 1963): 5–37.

Rothenberg, Winifred B. "The Emergence of a Capital Market in Rural Massachusetts, 1730–1838." *Journal of Economic History* 45 (December 1985): 781–808.

Shultz, George P. *Pressures on Wage Decisions: A Case Study in the Shoe Industry.* Cambridge, MA: MIT Press, 1951.

Smith, G. Ralph. *The Endicott Johnson Corporation.* New Orleans: Loyola University, College of Business Administration, 1956.

Sokoloff, Kenneth L. "Investment in Fixed and Working Capital During Early Industrialization." *Journal of Economic History* 44 (June 1984): 545–56.

The Story of the George E. Keith Company. Brockton, MA: George E. Keith Co., n.d.

Szenberg, Michael, John W. Lombardi, and Eric Y. Lee. *Welfare Effects of Trade Restrictions: A Case Study of the U.S. Footwear Industry*. New York: Academic Press, 1977.

United Nations Conference on Trade and Development. *Leather and Leather Products*. New York: United Nations, 1971.

U.S. Department of Commerce. Economic Development Administration. *Opportunities for Increasing Markets and Employment in the Shoe Industry*. Washington, DC: U.S. Government Printing Office, 1967.

———. International Trade Administration. *U.S. Industrial Outlook*. Washington, DC: U.S. Government Printing Office, 1960– .

U.S. International Trade Commission. USITC 758. Washington, DC: U.S. Government Printing Office, 1976.

———. USITC 799. Washington, DC: U.S. Government Printing Office, 1977.

———. USITC 1139. Washington, DC: U.S. Government Printing Office, 1981.

———. USITC 1545. Washington, DC: U.S. Government Printing Office, 1984.

Walk-Over Shoe Prints. Brockton, MA: George E. Keith Co., 1906–31.

Wallis, George. "Special Report: Leather and Wearing Apparel." In *The American System of Manufactures*, edited by Nathan Rosenberg, 235–36, 254–57. Edinburgh: Edinburgh University Press, 1969.

Watson, Merrill A. *Economics of Cattlehide Leather Tanning*. Chicago: Rumpf, 1950.

Weiss, Harry B., and Grace M. Weiss. *Early Tanning and Currying in New Jersey*. Trenton: New Jersey Agricultural Society, 1959.

Welsh, Peter C. *Tanning in the United States to 1850*. Washington, DC: Smithsonian Institution, 1964.

White, Eli G. *The Awakening of a Company: The Story of Endicott Johnson Corporation*. New York: Newcomen Society in North America, 1967.

Yellowitz, Irwin. "Skilled Workers and Mechanization: The Lasters in the 1890s." *Labor History* 18 (Spring 1977): 197–213.

Zahavi, Gerald. *Workers, Managers, and Welfare Capitalism: The Shoemakers and Tanners of Endicott Johnson*. Urbana: University of Illinois Press, 1987.

Part VIII

Furnaces
ESIC 33.1

BLAST FURNACES AND STEEL MILLS, 33.1

_____ SPIRO G. PATTON

THE PRIMACY OF IRON

Before 1880 the ferrous metals industry in the United States was almost exclusively identified with the production of iron. It was, according to Victor S. Clark, comprised of two complementary yet autonomous segments: the refining and smelting of iron (furnaces and bloomeries) and rolling mills. The separation was determined by technology and logistics. Refining and smelting iron required a furnace or bloomery located close to both iron ore deposits and a fuel source—charcoal or coal—because the cost of transporting ore and fuel was high. Rolling mills were located close to their customers: machine tool establishments and railroads. Because they could use imported iron just as easily as domestic, rolling mills could be established without regard to the availability of furnaces.

The furnace segment of the industry dates from colonial times, with little growth before 1820. Backyard charcoal furnaces, an ancient technology, served local needs. If available figures are correct, furnace output in the United States rose from a colonial period level of 66,000 tons in 1820 to 600,000 tons by 1840. Growth of output was steady but slow between 1840 and 1860, rapid from 1860 to 1873, and depressed from 1873 to 1880 (Clark 1929).

Technological constraints caused the spurt and sputter pattern of iron furnace production. Until the introduction of coal as a fuel in the 1840s, the furnace burned charcoal, a fuel that produced a high-quality product, but kept furnaces small-scale operations. Impurities were refined from the molten metal by hand, a second constraint on size. The British used coke for fuel and mechanically puddled out impurities to produce iron inferior to charcoal iron. Puddled iron could be produced in large quantities at costs below charcoal methods. The availability of British iron during the American railroad boom of 1840–60 turned rolling mills to imported iron; a source of transformation for the furnace segment of the domestic industry was thus lost and its growth retarded (Temin 1964).

During the 1840s both hard coal (anthracite) and soft coal (bituminous, or coking, coal) were introduced into blast furnaces. Furthermore, the introduction of British puddling techniques enabled blast furnaces in the United States to challenge the British mills. It was not, however, until the extraordinary demands of the Civil War and the disruption of British trade that the American furnaces were able to displace British imports substantially. The years between 1860 and 1880 brought a rapid transformation in the iron furnace industry. Growth was concentrated in coke furnaces and centered in those states west of the Alleghenies where soft coal and iron ore from Lake Superior combined to make that region best suited for large-scale production of iron for architectural use. Only the largest anthracite furnaces remained competitive.

As a national industry, rolling mills closely mirrored the development of their major customer—the railroads. Imported iron was the material used by the rolling mill; its primary output was rails. By 1860 the Census listed 256 rolling mills with a total product of over 500,000 tons, nearly half of which was rails. This figure is impressive, because virtually no rolling mills existed in the United States before 1825. Rolling mills employed large-scale production and state of the art techniques. American mills displayed two key trends in this period. One was a tendency to integrate refining and smelting operations into the rolling mill companies to insure a more stable and uniform supply of metal. A second was to capitalize on technical advancements, especially the "three-high" rolling process developed by John Fritz in 1857 (Clark 1929).

A note about steel must be offered here. The technology for mass producing steel, known as a fine metal for cutlery, was being developed in several countries during the mid-nineteenth century, but it was not until the Civil War, and its demand for mass-produced bayonets, swords, and the like, that the United States took an active interest in developing a steel industry. Producers immediately recognized that its superior qualities would elevate steel to the primary position among ferric metals. It had, however, but partially displaced iron by 1880: of the ferric metal produced that year, roughly 10 percent was steel. Only ten large-scale steel mills were then in operation, and they employed a modified Bessemer process (a pneumatic process of decarbonizing iron to produce steel) that had been developed in Britain. Steelmaking was protected by a stiff tariff on British imports and a patent pooling arrangement among the major steel companies (Temin 1964).

THE TRANSFORMATION TO CORPORATE STEEL

After 1880 all segments of this industry changed dramatically. The combination of a tariff on British imports and rapid economic growth provided a favorable long-term market for the industry. Technical advances in steel-making accelerated the conversion of primary metal production from iron to steel. Large-scale enterprises were synonymous with efficiency and market success. Patents for key innovations were controlled by a few major producers, so concentration of economic power became characteristic of the industry. Geographic concentration of production at key centers like Pittsburgh and Chicago became the norm, but the developing rail system enabled centers of production to emerge in more remote locales in Alabama and Colorado. By the end of the nineteenth century the industry, once mainly backyard furnaces and proprietorships, was largely integrated corporate entities, led by United States Steel (Clark 1929).

The average capacity of iron blast furnaces increased eighteenfold between 1865 and 1914 (5,000 tons to 90,000 tons), but fewer than half the furnaces operating in 1865 remained in 1914. The development of furnaces reflected the growing use of coke as fuel. The depressed conditions of the 1870s provided the initial impetus for consolidation and integration of furnace operations and eliminated the pre-industrial furnaces. From the 1880s, the expanding market for steel led to the expansion of furnaces. The demand for rails, the major source of market expansion since the 1840s, was now complemented by a rapidly growing demand for structural and ornamental steel. Because these uses appeared more stable than rail demand, producers were ambitious in their expansion plans. Output increased over eight times between 1870 and 1913 (3.7 million tons to 31 million tons).

The control of a Bessemer process patent for steel production appeared to be a key condition for an enterprise planning to convert from iron to steel. Other conditions were a willingness to merge and integrate operations and access to large deposits of iron and coal. Regional complexes integrated into corporate structures after 1880, led by the Pennsylvania Steel Company of Steelton, Pennsylvania; Bethlehem Iron and Steel of Bethlehem, Pennsylvania; Carnegie Iron and Steel of Pittsburgh; and Illinois Steel Company of Chicago. These corporations integrated all operations, including mining, refining, smelting, foundry, and distribution. Such consolidations not only improved profits and provided a guaranteed and continuous flow of product, but also exploited the inherent scale economies of the Bessemer process (Temin 1964).

The average capacity of steelworks rose from 3,000 tons in 1869 to 23,000 tons in 1899. From a handful of small-scale Bessemer producers in 1865, the number of full-fledged steelworks had risen to twenty-one by 1885. The increase was relatively small, and the so-called patent pool maintained by original producers apparently discouraged potential competitors, especially iron companies wishing to convert to steel production. The patent pool disappeared with the expiration of most of the patents in 1886, and eighteen new plants appeared by 1890. From an output of 151,000 tons in 1872, steel output had reached 31 million tons by 1914. While steel output continued to lag behind iron output, it was inevitable that steel would overtake iron.

The years 1898–1901 witnessed no less than a dozen major consolidations of iron and steel companies. Not all production was in the hands of these new corporate giants, but the concentration of production along geographic and organizational lines did reflect the increasing dominance of corporate iron and steel. Two types of organizational arrangements were prevalent. The horizontal organization merged several companies, usually geographically dispersed, under the umbrella of a financial holding company, a structure best exemplified by U.S. Steel. The vertical merge, as noted above, grouped the various stages of production under one corporate organization, and most of the giants displayed this type of integration as well.

The consolidation movement was designed to reduce the damaging effects of price competition on capital value and profit rates and yet permit a greater degree of competition based on technical efficiency and product differentiation. Smaller companies could survive by consolidating or by exploiting specialized lines untouched by the giants. The greatest of the consolidated corporations was U.S. Steel, based in Pittsburgh and Chicago and organized under the financial umbrella of J. P. Morgan. U.S. Steel became the nation's first billion-dollar corporation in terms of capital value. The corporation was highly integrated vertically, and when formed in 1901, controlled 65 percent of the valuable Lake Superior iron ore deposits; operated the largest fleet of ships in the nation; owned half of the coke furnace capacity in the industry; and, among its various product lines, controlled 60–90 percent of the market.

Predictably, the federal government, in the contemporary spirit of trust-busting, challenged the perceived monopoly of U.S. Steel. Immediately, the corporation was taken to court in an attempt to dissolve its organization, a case lost by the government after more than two decades of litigation. During that time the competitive pressures of other corporate giants began to erode U.S. Steel's power in most product lines by at least 10 percent. The corporation's holdings in iron ore and coal, however, remained formidable.

Given the atmosphere of wide price swings, the conversion from iron to steel, and the consolidation movement, the industry's economic performance was predictably unstable. The year 1894 was the nadir for the industry, with all production indicators at historic lows. It was not until the consolidation period that the industry was able to surpass its peak of 1892. The corporate giants were able to restore some order to the market, at least in terms of prices, but other factors in the industry remained unstable. The year 1901 marked a major downturn in the United States economy. The industry was forced into a retreat from which it would not fully recover until World War I (Clark 1929).

By 1914 the United States had become the world's leading producer of both iron and steel products. The nation that had imported most of its metal in the antebellum period was now the world's third leading exporter. The corporate giants of the industry represented the greatest business organizations in the world and were leaders in the refinement of new techniques, including the development of alloy steel and the open-hearth furnace. The industry was on the road to maturity.

THE PRIMACY OF STEEL

With the advent of World War I the fortunes of the industry dramatically changed. The demand for steel was accelerated by the war, as was the growing dominance of the United States in world production of essential products—most notably alloy steels for armaments, armor plate, and barbed wire. Although overall production reached new highs, expansion was effected through the utilization of existing capacity. Earnings were abnormally high owing to the belated imposition of price controls by the government, controls that appeared only after prices had risen substantially.

An industrial board was convened after the Armistice to return steel to "normalcy." Prices were forcibly reduced, and output was reduced by 20 percent. A series of labor problems that began in 1919 crippled the industry until 1922, when the growing demand for machinery and a concerted effort to increase exports brought more prosperous times, at least until the Great Depression (Clark 1929).

The war and its aftermath did not interrupt the fundamental trends of conversion, consolidation, and innovation. In 1904 five of the top ten ferric metals firms were iron and steel companies. By 1926 only one of the top ten companies retained any overt association with iron (Colorado Fuel & Iron). By 1930 the top companies accounted for 80 percent of the steel-making capacity of the United States. It had become difficult to separate the activities of steelmaking from the support functions of mining, coking, rolling, and so on. Certainly the largest companies had fully integrated the production and distribution processes. The various phases of production, once separate industries, were managed as departments within the corporate hierarchy. Although mining could perhaps maintain its identity, no other operation associated with steelmaking remained a separate industrial entity. While smaller firms continued to provide the specialty and more innovative products, the fate of the industry rested with the largest of the giants: U.S. Steel, Bethlehem Steel, Republic Steel, and Jones & Laughlin (Schroeder 1953).

The devastative effects of the Great Depression were a bitter contrast to the prosperity of 1915–29. The initial contraction of the Depression produced the sharpest decline in output yet experienced by the industry. By 1932 production levels had retreated to those of three decades previous, about one-fourth of the peak level of 1929. Only the needs of warring Europe at the end of the decade enabled the industry to recover, and recover it did. By 1940 steel output had reached a record level of 67 million tons.

The Depression stifled technical progress. Marginal companies disappeared, but this time they were not absorbed by the giants. Existing companies began modifying their capital structure to take advantage of lower-cost resources. For example, heavy fuel oil residues were used as a heat source with satisfactory results for the first time. The product mix had been directed toward sheet steel for autos and appliances during the 1920s, but profit margins did not encourage discovery of lower-cost techniques for its production. Conditions changed with the Depression. The Bessemer process now proved antiquated. The open-hearth process, a marginal technique for the past half century, became the best method for the production of sheet steel. Alloy steel, once the primary output of the open-hearth, was now produced in the electric furnace, which had become the futuristic process. Efficiency of existing capacity replaced expansion in the Depression period (Rosegger 1984).

The Depression also broke the apparent labor-management peace that had followed the 1919 uprisings. From 1920 to 1935 unionization in the steel industry had been stymied by the courts and by management's attempt to create a scientifically controlled optimal work environment, led by the pioneering studies of Frederick W. Taylor at Bethlehem Steel (from which the concept of scientific management emerged). The Depression signalled a new call for association. The passage of the National Labor Relations Act in 1935 gave the newly formed Congress of Industrial Organization the green light to organize the steelworkers. U.S. Steel quickly capitulated, signing an agreement with the Steel Workers Organizing Committee in 1937. Other companies proved less accommodating, but the war intervened, bringing a moratorium on organizing (Perlman 1984).

World War II, although a brief period by historical standards, has merited special attention by contemporary historians of the steel industry. Competitive pressures and labor problems dissipated in response to the war effort. The objective was simple: expand output by any means, at any cost. Government control at each stage of the production process forced costs up. There was no time for experimentation, no time for rational calculation. Even marginal plants and equipment became useful, regardless of their obsolescence. The newest capital came on-line immediately without being fully tested. New product lines, especially in alloy steels, became major outputs, even if the alloys had enjoyed little use in the past. Despite the potential problems posed by such a dramatic change in policy, the effort was successful. Levels of production and efficiency soared. Output rose from 67 million tons in 1940 to 95 million tons in 1945.

Since World War II, the history of the industry has developed on three fronts: technological improvement, government regulation of prices and labor conditions, and international competition. Technological change has evolved around the concurrent needs of expanding capacity and reducing unit costs to maintain at least a constant level of average total cost. Before World War II the largest furnaces handled 300 tons; by 1960, 600–ton furnaces had become the norm. A notable change was the injection of oxygen into the open-hearth furnaces. The introduction of the basic-oxygen process (BOP) was facilitated by a dramatic reduction in the cost of refining oxygen, from $12 per unit in 1920 to $3 in 1950. Although still a minority process, electric furnaces have become more popular, particularly in the production of alloy steel. The Bessemer process has all but disappeared. Since 1960 new capacity has been provided by either the BOP or the electric furnace, especially in the so-called mini-mills that produce specialty products (Rosegger 1984).

When the war ended, government contracts were cancelled, but price controls remained. In January, 1946, workers struck for higher wages, and the industry was forced to seek permission from the federal government to raise prices. Although the controls were subsequently lifted, the government has continued to monitor steel prices. During the 1950s and 1960s "jawboning" became the strategy, with the President and other high officials attempting to persuade the industry to minimize price increases. Because of growing competition from foreign producers, the government has designed a trigger price mechanism to protect domestic steel prices against foreign steel dumped into this country at low prices that are supported by foreign government subsidies (Crandall 1981).

The strike of 1946 touched off a period of turmoil in the labor relations of the steel industry. As the United Steel Workers organized each producer, it exerted its influence to raise the incomes of members. The atmosphere of antagonism that prevailed before World War II returned. Major strikes occurred in 1949, 1955, and 1959, each contributing to a major economic downturn. Consequently, labor relations in the steel industry forced government supervision and even intervention. The 1959 strike was especially traumatic and compelled the government's direct participation in its resolution. By mutual consent the union and the producers chose to end the strike pattern in the next agreement. Drafted in 1962, the Experimental Negotiating Agreement (ENA) has served as the basis for labor-management relations in the industry and has been a model for other industries. Its no-strike agreement and use of binding arbitration to settle impasses has stabilized the industry. Although antagonisms remain, especially over job security and income adjustments, both sides have cooperated on such issues as trade protection and federal support for recovery (Perlman 1984).

The first post–World War II decade saw a concomitant increase in steel industry wages and prices at an average annual rate of almost 7 percent. Little resistance was offered by the federal government because the burgeoning demand for steel, coupled with the loss of capacity in Europe and Japan, created a nearly total domination of the world steel market (outside the Communist bloc) by the United States. The industry experienced perhaps its most prosperous times during the 1940–60 period.

More than the face of labor relations was altered with the disastrous strike of 1959. In response to the strike, the producers and consumers of steel turned to imported sources of raw materials and products. A rapid increase in iron ore imports was the first noticeable effect, as users other than the big steel companies required supplies to maintain operations, and "big steel's" hold over iron ore supplies disappeared. Consumers of steel products likewise turned to imported sources as the strike persisted (it lasted seven months).

Figures now show that the internationalization of the United States steel market has steadily developed since 1959. The U.S. share of world steel production, as high as 30 percent in the boom period 1940–60, is now less than 10 percent and falling. Imported steel was a miniscule 2 percent or less of all steel used until 1958. The latest figures show that imported steel products average 25–30 percent in most product lines. Comparative advantages of foreign producers, coupled with foreign governments' support of their steel industries, have propelled nations such as West Germany and Japan and industrializing countries such as South Korea and Brazil into favorable competitive positions relative to American industry. These industries enjoy low unit costs of production, the most modern techniques, and the support of their governments.

The United States steel industry has developed a close relationship with the federal government. Its fortunes over the past forty-five years have been closely tied to the demands of the military and the system of surface highways provided by the government, which in turn has supported the development of the motor vehicle industry. But, although the industry's pricing policies and its labor conflicts have come under federal scrutiny, no policy designed to support the steel industry against international competition has been forthcoming, either as support for capital improvements or as import restrictions. Through most of the 1960s and 1970s, government and industry refused to take the foreign challenge seriously. Most market shares were preserved and, more important, steel producers continued to perform well financially. Yet, in terms of technical dynamism, the domestic industry has apparently lost its vitality (Crandall 1981).

In 1977 world steel demand dropped noticeably and has not recovered. The problem can be traced in part to the relatively sluggish growth of the world economy, and in part to the emergence of substitute metals—most notably aluminum—and plastics for use in cars, construction, and appliances. Steel-exporting nations have been forced to revamp their sales strategy and to encourage public support of their steel industries. Without public support in America, the United States steel industry has been forced into retreat. Major producers have curtailed many operations and, occasionally, turned away from steel entirely. Marginal plants have shut down, and the economies of many smaller steel towns and cities have become depressed. While there is some protection based on the Solomon plan of trigger prices, trade adjustment assistance to displaced workers, and jawboning with exporting countries, the philosophy of free trade prevails over that of protection.

The industry stands at a crossroads: to regain its earlier dominance appears impossible; to implement the latest techniques will cost billions of dollars and force thousands of steelworkers from the production process. Specialty steel producers, especially the so-called mini-mills, have managed to hold their own, but in the long run, imported products will compete successfully with these producers as well. An industry that has been identified with American industrial might has been thrust back into a pre-industrial, or at best early industrial, level of existence.

BIBLIOGRAPHIC ANALYSIS

Biography

Perhaps no field of business history presents as formidable a challenge as biography. In modern corporate structure notable figures are difficult to locate, and in the steel industry corporatization was complete by 1920. Biography requires research into personal memorabilia. Corporations and family descendants become reticent when the biographer intends to disclose the subject's business practices, especially when that information could leak present corporate strategies or prove embarrassing to the family. Consequently, little work in the field has been produced in the past twenty years, leaving the interested student to seek vintage work.

A signal biography of recent years is that of the man most closely associated with iron and steel—Andrew Carnegie (Wall 1970). Joseph Frazier Wall's study is a general presentation, not a purely business biography. The work must be examined, however, because the vintage biography of Carnegie (Alderson 1908) and the autobiography (Carnegie 1920) are dated. Bernard Alderson's biography is written from the labor viewpoint and is a more critical evaluation than Wall's. Reading all three biographical works, while time-consuming, will provide the student with a triad of perspectives on this captain of industry.

A number of Carnegie's contemporaries attracted the biographer's interest in the years before 1940. The oldest contribution, ignored by previous bibliographies, is John Fritz's (1912) autobiography. Fritz focuses on his industrial career, especially his years at Cambria Iron Works, where he perfected the three-high rolling process, and at Bethlehem Steel, where he served many years as general superintendent. Other vintage works, in chronological order, include Ida M. Tarbell's (1925) biography of Chicago steel magnate Elbert H. Gary; George Harvey's (1928) biography of Carnegie's superintendent Henry Clay Frick; Allan Nevins's (1935) biography of iron pioneer Abram Hewitt; Christy Borth's (1941) biography of George Matthew Verity, founder of ARMCO; and Henry Oliver Evans's (1942) tribute to Henry W. Oliver.

During the past twenty years, after a hiatus of twenty-five years, a small number of works in addition to Wall's biography noted earlier have appeared. Two are book length. Robert Hessen's (1975) biography of Charles M. Schwab, Carnegie associate and later president of U.S. Steel, is an important piece in the puzzle of the formation and operation of the giant steel company (now history in light of the corporate name change to USX). Jeanne McHugh (1980) has written a semi-biographical account of Alexander Holley and his contemporaries who brought the Bessemer process to the American steel industry. McHugh's work would prove an excellent complement to the Fritz autobiography cited earlier.

Journal articles explore limited periods in the lives of four men critical to the development of regional iron and steel production. George C. Crout and Wilfred D. Vorhis (1967) deal with John Butler Tytus, inventor of the continuous process steel mill and a figure in the development of the industry in Ohio. Robert H. McKenzie (1973) presents a brief sketch of Horace Ware, a key figure in the industry of Alabama, a region that has generated little interest, although it is a center of steel production. John D. Ubinger's (1975) work is a two-part study of Ernest Tener Weir—a name associated with Weirton Steel and its town, Weirton, West Virginia, part of the Ohio Valley complex. A recent contribution notable for its subject is Craig Bartholomew's (1986) presentation of William M. Weaver of the Lehigh Valley, the only biographical analysis available of a merchant pig iron producer.

As a final note to this section, students are urged to read two surveys of biographies. Jonathan R. T. Hughes's *The Vital Few* (1966) is a standard student text that provides biographies of key business leaders, including Andrew Carnegie and J. P. Morgan, the financier who masterminded the formation of U.S. Steel. Fritz Redlich's classic work of business biography also contains sketches of a number of industry figures in Volume 1 (1940).

Company History

Historians seeking to chronicle iron and steel companies face challenges as formidable as those of the biographers. Many companies are still active and are often unwilling to share even the most dated records for fear of their interpretation by the market. For those companies extinct and not simply absorbed by an existing concern, historians must deal with the proprietors' descendants or face the simple reality that records have been destroyed. The past decade, however, has witnessed a limited but steady flow of company history as companies cease operations and data become accessible.

Of the classic works, two are worth noting, and, not surprisingly, both deal with U.S. Steel and Carnegie Steel. Abraham Berglund (1907), a pioneer in the economic history of the steel industry, offers a contemporary account of the tumultuous first decade of U.S. Steel. Likewise, Ayer Reprint of Salem, New Hampshire, offers a history of the Carnegie Steel Company written soon after its absorption into U.S. Steel (Bridge 1972). Interestingly, only two major articles on U.S. Steel have been published in the past fifteen years. Donald O. Parsons and Edward John Ray (1975) evaluate the impact of its formation on the steel market, using the relatively new approach of the Chicago school of industrial organization. For a unique contribution to the literature, consider Richard Vangermeersch's (1971) examination of the accounting methods employed by U.S. Steel to measure depreciation. Accounting history remains one of the relatively unexplored facets of business history, yet it is one of the most vital for understanding any corporate entity.

The remaining contributions cover a variety of companies and yield broadening perspectives. A vintage work is Ernest Dale's (1960) comparative analysis of National Steel and Weirton Steel. Dale's work could be read in tandem with Ubinger's biographical sketch of the founder of Weirton Steel noted in the previous section. Other book-length presentations include H. Lee Scamehorn's (1976) analysis of the Colorado Fuel and Iron Company at the turn of the century. Of the top ten companies (in terms of value-added) producing iron and steel after 1920, CF&I was the one company whose sole product was iron. Henry Richard Kuriansky (1976) presents the history of an eastern steel power, the Atlantic Steel Company. Mansel G. Blackford (1982) integrates business history and urban history as he weighs the impact of Buckeye International on Columbus, Ohio, during the past century. Two noteworthy monographs are Ralph D. Gray's (1974) study of the Haynes Stellite Corporation, a company that processed a form of iron ore for use in the manufacture of steel, and Bernice Shield Hassinger's (1978) story of Henderson Steel, the first major Birmingham, Alabama, steelmaker.

Several articles that deal with limited periods in company histories should be examined because of the scholarship they entail. A brief article relates the Depression era labor-management policies of Republic Steel and its then leader Tom Girdler (Cook 1967). William R. Braisted (1968) contributes an interesting piece on Bethlehem Steel, investigating its military connection and that connection's impact on Sino-American relations during the second decade of the twentieth century. Histories of nineteenth-century companies are sorely missed in the field, but two contributions have appeared in article form. W. David Lewis (1972) presents an analysis of the Lackawanna Coal and Iron Company's conversion to anthracite technology. Data on the anthracite iron industry and its major players have become more accessible in recent years at such locations as Eleutherian-Mills Library in Wilmington, Delaware, and the Center for Canal History and Technology in Easton, Pennsylvania. James E. Fell, Jr. (1984), deals with two Pittsburgh area iron companies in his article. Two articles on specialty products companies should be cited. Joseph M. McFadden (1978) develops the barbed wire industry group in his article on the American Steel and Wire Company. And Donald Sayenga (1986) has edited the diary of one Charles Stewart, a diary that is not so much biography as a sketch of the Stewart Company of Easton and Stewart's role in the perfection of wire rope and steel wire technology.

Industrial History

Pre-Industrial History

Although this reference work is essentially concerned with industries, the production of ferric metals is based upon an ancient technology. Certainly, the ferric metal industry in the United States, while retaining a revolutionary flavor, emanated from that ancient base. The student of this industry's history should therefore be at least familiar with a handful of works that specialize in the prehistory of the industry, a period that spans colonial times until about 1840.

Two of the recommended works are nineteenth-century classics on the national dimensions of pre-industrial iron production. John B. Pearse's (1876) treatise is the seminal work on iron manufacture in colonial America. The book has apparently not been reprinted, so the student will have to search carefully for copies. The second work is Benjamin F. French's pioneering study in economic history, which covered the iron industry from the beginnings of our colonial existence to 1857, with special attention to trade flows. Written over a century ago, this history was reprinted in 1968.

Beyond those by Pearse and French, studies on the pre-industrial period have dealt with either regional production or the output of specific furnaces, forges, or plantations. The studies of individual units are not very useful to business historians; but three regional studies supply information needed in tracing the antecedents of the iron industry. Two of these are vintage studies recently reprinted. Arthur Cecil Bining's (1973) definitive study of iron manufacture in eighteenth-century Pennsylvania has been revised by the author and reprinted.

Kathleen Bruce's (1967) equally authoritative study of iron plantations in Virginia has spawned a number of articles on individual plantations. She reveals that Virginia was a center of iron manufacturing and that slaves were indeed engaged in industrial work. One recent work in this field is worth noting. Paul Paskoff has extended Bining's study of the Pennsylvania iron industry by identifying the forces that shaped iron manufacture into a recognizable industry. Paskoff's (1983) work is one of several that have been authored on the transformation of the Middle Atlantic region into an industrial center, and perhaps is the most useful of the studies cited here for the industrial historian who seeks an analytic approach.

Nineteenth-Century Iron Industry

Until twenty years ago little of substance had been written on the nineteenth-century iron industry. James Moore Swank's (1892) classic tome on the iron industry devoted space to the developing industry, as did Clark's (1929) volumes on manufacturing, but no study has exclusively detailed the iron industry after 1840. Several reasons can be suggested for the lack of research on this period. The ferric industry's concentration on iron was relatively short-lived (1840–1900). Given the spectacular development of the steel industry, the iron industry was viewed as a transition from the ancient charcoal furnaces to the modern steelworks, a view analogous to the role ascribed to canals in our transportation revolution. But it cannot be denied that many of the key technological advances that facilitated the development of steel technology were originally based in iron production— the use of coal as a fuel, the techniques of puddling and rolling iron to fashion beams and rails, and the development of such specialty products as wire, wire rope, and nails, so critical to the construction industry. As with biographical and company history, the inaccessibility of data explains the dearth of work on nineteenth-century iron production. Because of the recency of the data now available, works cited in this section are twenty years old or less.

Research on nineteenth-century iron has primarily set out the technological development of iron production, particularly the sources of technological progress and the diffusion of innovation. W. Ross Yeates (1974) gives an account of the discovery of anthracite, its adaptation as a furnace fuel, and the development of the iron industry in eastern Pennsylvania, the initial center of the industry. William D. Walsh (1975) likewise examines this innovation and others that propelled the Pennsylvania pig iron industry into prominence. Walsh surveys the bituminous iron industry of western Pennsylvania as well as the eastern anthracite segment. His work in particular complements the studies by Bining and by Paskoff cited in the previous section. Combined, they offer a trio of monographs that relate the history of the Pennsylvania iron industry from colonial times to 1900. Another regional study is Robert B. Gordon's (1984) investigation of the Connecticut iron industry, a story of limited response to change in a region of marginal production potential. Richard H. Schallenberg in two contributions (one coauthored) traces the general decline of the charcoal iron industry in the nineteenth century (Schallenberg 1975; Schallenberg and Ault 1977). Peter Berck (1978) offers a cliometric approach to the iron industry in the spirit of Robert Fogel's study of the railroads. He takes a cross section of the industry circa 1890 and infers his conclusions from this historical snapshot.

Output, or production, analysis is used to study technological change and to determine what was produced and in what amount, not how production was carried out. John Ward Wilson Loose and John B. Ryan each offer regional studies of iron output. Loose (1982a) concentrates on the anthracite iron industry of Lancaster County, Pennsylvania, one of the smaller pockets of eastern Pennsylvania iron, and Ryan (1971) investigates the industry in Tecumseh, Alabama, an unlikely area for iron production. Robert A. Jewett (1969) solves the puzzle behind the development of the structural rail beam by studying the companies that pioneered its production. Harold Livesay (1971) makes a singular contribution to the literature by establishing the marketing patterns of the antebellum iron industry. Two pioneers of the new economic history, Robert W. Fogel and Stanley L. Engerman, do for iron production what they did for slavery. They estimate sources of output change with relatively little data in a work free of the controversy generated by their infamous study of slavery, although their methodology did elicit comment from cliometricians (1969).

Two studies of labor relations in the iron industry deserve mention. Charles B. Dew (1974) records the discipline of slave workers on the iron plantations and in the iron mills of the antebellum South. Although slave labor and the iron plantations received considerable attention in the pre-industrial literature, Dew is the only historian to concentrate on the iron mills themselves, and he provides perhaps the most useful of the slave iron contributions. Loose, cited above, offers a labor-oriented piece. He sets out labor-management relations in the anthracite mills of Lancaster County and, like Dew, helps to complete the literature. His is the only major study to treat labor relations in the early years of the iron industry (Loose 1982b).

The "Transition" Period: Iron and Steel

The latter half of the nineteenth century was a transition period for the ferric metals industry. The iron industry began to decline as progressive iron producers included a growing proportion of steel in their production plans and as companies whose output was exclusively steel formed the early steel industry. Although all the contemporary literature for this period is readable, there are three standards. Swank's (1892) history of the iron and steel industry is valuable for its contemporary account of developments during this transition phase of the industry's history. He was associated with the American Iron and Steel Association (AISA). Clark's magnum opus on American manufacturing history devotes relatively little space to earlier periods, but the study of the industry from 1860 to 1893 is almost book length (180 pages) and provides a worthy revision of Swank's work (Clark

1929, vol. 2). The serious economic historian will already be familiar with Peter Temin's analysis of the nineteenth-century iron and steel industry. Temin (1964) applies basic economics to the Clark and Swank presentations without falling into the cliometric abyss.

Within the contemporary literature two topics stand out, tariff policy and labor relations. The tariff on iron and steel was a major article in United States protectionist policy during the nineteenth century, and has long been a topic for economic historians, especially cliometricians. One of the latter, V. Sundarajan, gauges the impact of the tariff on a number of specific product lines (1970), and Bennett D. Baack and Edward John Ray (1973) assay the tariff vis-à-vis the industry's international comparative advantage. In one of a series of articles, Robert C. Allen (1979) includes the tariff in his general analysis of international competition in iron and steel during this period. Paul H. Tedesco (1985) presents a political economy perspective on the tariff issue and details the personal involvement of Swank and the AISA.

Labor relations is allotted a substantial amount of space in the contemporary literature. One classic reprint must be acknowledged. A century ago George McNeil edited an account of the labor movement, including commentaries on labor relations in specific industries. John Jarrett's (1971) contribution on the ironworkers (no steelworkers' labor group then existed) provides interesting reading today, despite an informal literary style. Peter Doeringer is recognized as one of the leading experts on labor market dynamics and is widely known for his work with Michael Piore on the segmented labor market model. One of his earlier contributions breaks down the piece rate structure of Pittsburgh area producers in the late nineteenth century (Doeringer 1968). Andrea Graziosi (1981), in a more radical vein, focuses on the conditions of unskilled workers in the large mills.

Three noteworthy contributions deal with other segments of the iron and steel industry in transition. Melvin I. Urofsky (1968) combines biographic and industrial history as he relates the development of the armorplate trust and Josephus Daniels's role in organizing and maintaining it. Allen, cited earlier in this section, offers another distinctive contribution. In a cliometric work, Allen (1977) appraises the productivity trend of blast furnaces. Jeremy Atack and Jan K. Brueckner (1982), in a quantitative study, document the demand from domestic railroads for American-produced steel rails.

One general work from the contemporary literature should be perused. William T. Hogan (1971) sets out a general history of iron and steel with special emphasis on the nineteenth century. While the work does not represent a true revision of Clark, Swank, or Temin, it does update some of Temin's work.

Early History of Steelmaking

The literature on the early years of the steel industry (1880–1920) is surprisingly sparse. The basic reference work, Clark's *History of Manufac-*

tures in the United States, is itself somewhat sketchy (1929, vol. 3). All of the notable work is of recent vintage, but the most recent is dated 1982. Some work may have appeared since, but it has yet to reach the general academic community. Undoubtedly, this field is ripe for scholarly cultivation.

The most dominant theme of research in early steel has been the formation of U.S. Steel and its impact on the industry. This literature was reviewed in the company history section. Second in terms of research emphasis has been labor relations. Three excellent books on labor relations in this period are available. One of the key works in labor history is David Brody's (1965) account of the steel strike of 1919, one of the major incidents during the so-called Red Scare in a summer of rioting throughout the industrial belt. Gerald G. Eggert (1981) investigates the steel capitalists' movement to improve industrial relations. An interesting contrast to Eggert's managerial perspective is Michael Nash's (1982) documentation of the evolution of class identity among the workers in two industries—steelmaking and coal mining.

On a smaller scale are three articles on industrial relations worth noting. Charles Hill (1974) makes a close study of the movement during the 1890s to eliminate the twelve-hour shift in the steel mills, a major factor underlying labor unrest during that decade. Katherine Stone (1974) has written a history of the job structure in the industry—the so-called internal labor market. Lastly, James Holt's (1977) work is an interesting comparison of the union movement in the steel industries in the United States and Great Britain.

Two contributions examine the behavior of steel prices. Allen, cited twice in the previous section, rounds out his contribution to the literature by particularizing the sources of price changes for domestic steel rails during this period (1981). Robert D. Cuff and Melvin I. Urofsky (the latter also cited in the previous section) examine the industry's price-fixing arrangements during World War I. They used original company and government documentations for their research (Cuff and Urofsky 1970).

Ann K. Harper provides an analysis of the spatial evolution of the steel industry in its early years. Harper's (1977) work is an extension of Clark's study of the geography of steel production and should be of interest to regional historians.

The crucible steel sector is rarely dealt with in any depth in studies of the American steel industry. Geoffrey Tweedale (1987) claims that this is a grave omission, and he fills the gap when he considers the profound impact of the Sheffield (England) steel industry on American developments. His is an important work in American business history.

Twentieth-Century Steel: 1900–1960

Contemporary historians of the American steel industry have seemingly chosen 1960 as the benchmark that divides the current from the historic account. Only a small group of works covers the period 1900–1960; these include virtually nothing on the iron industry. About half the literature is vintage, some of it reprinted, some readily available. Only a handful of works have appeared in this area; the recent literature includes contemporary analysis and will be covered in the final section.

Each of the classics covers a different subject matter, setting out a variety of source material. The earliest of these works is Abraham Berglund and Phillip G. Wright's exhaustive study of the impact of the tariff on the iron and steel industry during the 1920s, a work recently reprinted by its sponsor, the Brookings Institution. Not only does it represent one of the earliest Brookings studies, studies well respected among economists, but it also stands as a prototype of modern quantitative economic analysis, valuable to students to cliometrics. The work is a necessary complement to studies of the tariff in the nineteenth century (Berglund and Wright 1929). From labor's perspective comes Robert R. Brooks's 1940 account of the history of the steelworkers' union, then newly formalized. Brooks (1970) complements the nineteenth-century literature, carrying the saga through the implementation of the Wagner Act (National Labor Relations Act of 1935) and the formation of the CIO (Congress of Industrial Organizations), the umbrella organizing body of the steelworkers' union that was also formed in 1935. Charles R. Walker's (1970) study of the development of a steel company town provides a social history of the steel industry during this period. An essential reference for every steel industry historian is Gertrude G. Schroeder's (1953) study on the evolution of the organization of producers in the steel industry during the first half of the twentieth century. Labor historians of a more analytic bent will find Lloyd G. Reynolds and Cynthia H. Taft's (1956) presentation of the wage structure of the steel industry invaluable. Theirs was a pioneering study in labor market analysis.

Recent works are likewise varied. Book-length presentations include K. Warren's sweeping study of the geographic development of the steel industry. Warren's work covers more ground than Harper's study cited in the previous section; in fact, Warren (1973) follows the nascent industry from 1850 to its decline in 1970. His greatest contribution is a discussion of the 1900–1960 period and its tremendous geographic shifts in steel production. Eldon S. Hendricksen (1978) discusses the capital expenditures of the steel industry during the first half of the twentieth century, nicely paralleling Schroeder's study. Richard A. Lauderbaugh (1980) sets out the strategies of the big steel companies during the years previous to World War II. Amos J. Loveday, Jr. (1983), offers one of those truly rare studies on a product line other than basic steel by dealing with the cut nail industry.

Three articles are noteworthy. Philip E. Stebbins, a political historian, traces the actions taken by President Truman against the steel industry during the strike of 1949, one of the more damaging labor disruptions for the industry and a testing ground for the Taft-Hartley Act (1971). Donald S. McPherson (1972) offers an account of the "little steel" strike of 1937 in Johnstown, Pennsylvania, and Paul A. Tiffany (1984) surveys the industry's relationship with the federal government, a love-hate union at best, during the period 1945–60.

Contemporary Accounts with Historical Content

It is naive to argue that the present situation in the ferric metals industry suddenly appeared during the 1970s; any historic account should acknowledge trends. A starting point in this literature is Robert W. Crandall's economic analysis of the steel industry from 1946 to the advent of the trigger-price protective strategy in 1978. It is too brief to be a comprehensive study, but strong enough to provide the student with a perfunctory understanding of the industry's recent history; however, the work demands at least a background in economics (Crandall 1981). The AISI's assessment of the industry's condition also merits reading (American Iron and Steel Institute 1980). Granted the assessment is biased, it is nonetheless appropriate for business history (Swank's classic work was an AISI publication).

There is a handful of general articles to consider. In one of the trade publications, *Iron and Steel Engineer*, Darwin I. Brown's (1975) presentation of the so-called mini-mills is worth perusing as one of the earliest references to that concept. The mini-mill, hailed as one of industry's bright stars, is reminiscent of the merchant pig iron producers popular in the last century. For another perspective, see the Robert G. Vambery survey (1971), notable because it was written when international competition in the industry was just gaining significance. William Scheuerman (1975) depicts the industry's present state as an example of monopoly power abused. Edward Greer (1977) presents an analysis of the trend in steel prices after World War II. And Elisabeth K. Rabitsch (1974) studies the relationship between energy consumption and economic performance in the steel industry.

The topic that has captured the most attention in the contemporary literature has been technological change, a natural for historical analysis. Two monographs to read are Myles G. Boylan's (1975) study of the economic effects of increasing blast furnace size, an interesting application of the scale economies concept, and Hans Muller and Kiyoshi Kawahito's (1978) comparative, but somewhat biased, analysis of the technological performance of the U.S. and Japanese steel industries. Among the articles worth considering is the seminal work of Walter Adams and J. B. Dirlam (1966). They explore the relationship between industrial organization and innovation in the steel industry, testing whether monopoly power causes industrial stagnation by stifling the urge to innovate. In a federal government study on technology in the economy, an analysis of technological change in primary steel from 1947 to 1965 by William Haller, Jr. (1966), will prove a valuable reference. Bela Gold and Gerhard Rosegger have devoted most of their careers to the study of technological change and have specialized to an extent in steel. To follow their progress, begin with their survey of the diffusion of major technological innovations in steel (Gold, Rosegger, and Pierce 1970). Next consider Rosegger's (1974) record of the environmental impact of technological change in the industry. Gold (1976) compares the relationship between the expected results of innovation and the actual results, using steel as a case study. The most recent of their contributions is Rosegger's (1984) follow-up survey of technological change and economic performance, part of a longer multi-industrial study.

The international environment has proved somewhat difficult to place in historic perspective, but three references attempt to do so. A reference that would be considered historic today is Hogan's (1965) commentary on the steel import problem of the early 1960s, a valuable reference in analyzing more recent trends. The U.S. Federal Trade Commission's 1978 assessment of the steel industry's international position contains a wealth of data on the industry since World War II and is considered a key reference source by economic analysts. Jacqueline M. Nolan-Haley's (1980) survey of the trigger-price mechanism sets out its evolution as policy.

Two articles on labor-management relations should be cited. Mark Perlman (1984) writes a general survey of labor-management relations in the twentieth century, and Richard Betheil (1978) addresses the impact of the Experimental Negotiating Agreement of 1962, a landmark in industrial relations throughout industry. The agreement was shattered in 1986 by the lockout-strike at USX.

BIBLIOGRAPHY

Adams, Walter, and J. B. Dirlam. "Big Steel, Invention and Innovation." *Quarterly Journal of Economics* 80 (May 1966): 167–89.

Alderson, Bernard. *Andrew Carnegie: The Man and His Work*. New York: Doubleday, Page, 1908.

Allen, Robert C. "The Peculiar Productivity History of American Blast Furnaces, 1840–1913." *Journal of Economic History* 37 (September 1977): 605–33.

———. "International Competition in Iron and Steel, 1850–1913." *Journal of Economic History* 39 (December 1979): 911–37.

———. "Accounting for Price Changes: American Steel Rails, 1879–1910." *Journal of Political Economy* 89 (June 1981): 512–28.

American Iron and Steel Institute. *Steel at the Crossroads: The American Steel Industry in the 1980s*. Washington, DC: American Iron and Steel Institute, 1980.

Atack, Jeremy, and Jan K. Brueckner. "Steel Rails and American Railroads, 1867–1880." *Explorations in Economic History* 19 (October 1982): 339–59.

Baack, Bennett D., and Edward John Ray. "Tariff Policy and Comparative Advantage in the Iron and Steel Industry, 1870–1929." *Explorations in Economic History* 11 (Fall 1973): 3–23.

Bartholomew, Craig. "William M. Weaver: Superintendent of the Macungie Furnace." *Proceedings of the Canal History and Technology Symposium* 6 (1986): 109–64.

Berck, Peter. "Hard Driving and Efficiency: Iron Production in 1890." *Journal of Economic History* 38 (December 1978): 879–900.

Berglund, Abraham. *The United States Steel Corporation: A Study of the Growth and Influence of Combination in the Iron and Steel Industry.* New York: Columbia University Press, 1907.

Berglund, Abraham, and Philip G. Wright. *Tariff on Iron and Steel.* Washington, DC: Brookings Institution Reprint Series, 1929.

Betheil, Richard. "The ENA in Perspective: The Transformation of Collective Bargaining in the Basic Steel Industry." *Review of Radical Political Economy* 10 (Summer 1978): 1–24.

Bining, Arthur Cecil. *Pennsylvania Iron Manufacture in the Eighteenth Century.* Rev. ed. Harrisburg: Pennsylvania Historical and Museum Commission, 1973.

Blackford, Mansel G. *A Portrait Cast in Steel: Buckeye International and Columbus, Ohio, 1887–1980.* Westport, CT: Greenwood Press, 1982.

Borth, Christy. *True Steel: The Story of George Matthew Verity and His Associates.* Indianapolis: Bobbs-Merrill, 1941.

Boylan, Myles G. *Economic Effects of Scale Increases in the Steel Industry: The Case of U.S. Blast Furnaces.* New York: Praeger, 1975.

Braisted, William R. "China, the United States Navy, and the Bethlehem Steel Company, 1909–20." *Business History Review* 42 (Winter 1968): 50–60.

Bridge, James Howard. *The Inside History of the Carnegie Steel Company: A Romance of Millions.* Salem, NH: Ayer Reprint, 1972.

Brody, David. *Labor in Crisis: The Steel Strike of 1919.* Philadelphia: Lippincott, 1965.

Brooks, Robert R. *As Steel Goes: Unionism in a Basic Industry.* History of American Economy Series. New York: Johnson Reprints, 1970.

Brown, Darwin I. "Mini and Medium Steel Plants of North America." *Iron and Steel Engineer* 52 (November 1975): 1–29.

Bruce, Kathleen. *Virginia Iron Manufacture in the Slave Era.* New York: Augustus C. Kelley, 1967.

Carnegie, Andrew. *Autobiography of Andrew Carnegie.* Boston: Houghton Mifflin, 1920.

Clark, Victor S. *History of Manufactures in the United States.* 3 vols. New York: McGraw-Hill, 1929.

Cook, Philip L. "Tom M. Girdler and the Labor Policies of Republic Steel Corporation." *Social Science* 42 (January 1967): 21–30.

Crandall, Robert W. *The U.S. Steel Industry in Recurrent Crisis.* Washington, DC: Brookings Institution, 1981.

Crout, George C., and Wilfred D. Vorhis. "John Butler Tytus: Inventor of the Continuous Steel Mill." *Ohio History* 76 (1967): 132–45.

Cuff, Robert D., and Melvin I. Urofsky. "The Steel Industry and Price-Fixing During World War I." *Business History Review* 44 (Autumn 1970): 291–300.

Dale, Ernest. *The Great Organizers.* New York: McGraw-Hill, 1960.

Dew, Charles B. "Disciplining Slave Ironworkers in the Antebellum South: Coercion, Conciliation and Accommodation." *American Historical Review* 79 (April 1974): 393–418.

Doeringer, Peter. "Piece Wage Rate Structures in the Pittsburgh Iron and Steel Industry, 1880–1900." *Labor History* 9 (Summer 1968): 262–74.

Eggert, Gerald G. *Steelmasters and Labor Reform, 1886–1923.* Pittsburgh: University of Pittsburgh Press, 1981.

Evans, Henry Oliver. *Iron Pioneer: Henry W. Oliver, 1840–1904.* New York: Dutton, 1942.

Fell, James E., Jr. "Iron from the 'Bend': The Great Western and Brady's Bend Iron Companies." *Western Pennsylvania Historical Magazine* 67 (1984): 323–45.

Fogel, Robert W., and Stanley L. Engerman. "A Model for the Explanation of Industrial Expansion During the Nineteenth Century: With an Application to the American Iron Industry." *Journal of Political Economy* 77 (May-June 1969): 306–28.

French, Benjamin F. *History of the Rise and Progress of the Iron Trade of the United States, 1621–1857.* New York: Augustus C. Kelley, 1968.

Fritz, John. *Autobiography of John Fritz.* New York: John Wiley & Sons, 1912.

Gold, Bela. "Tracing Gaps Between Expectations and Results of Technological Innovations: The Case of Iron and Steel." *Journal of Industrial Economics* 25 (September 1976): 1–28.

Gold, Bela, Gerhard Rosegger, and William S. Pierce. "Diffusion of Technological Innovations in U.S. Iron and Steel Manufacturing." *Journal of Industrial Economics* 18 (July 1970): 218–42.

Gordon, Robert B. "Materials for Manufacturing: The Response of the Connecticut Iron Industry to Technological Change and Limited Resources." *Technology and Culture* 24 (1984): 602–34.

Gray, Ralph D. *Stellite: A History of the Haynes Stellite Corporation.* Kokomo, IN: Cabott, 1974.

Graziosi, Andrea. "Common Laborers, Unskilled Workers, 1880–1915." *Labor History* 22 (Fall 1981): 512–44.

Greer, Edward. "The Political Economy of U.S. Steel Prices in the Postwar Period." In *Research in Political Economy: An Annual Compilation of Research,* edited by Paul Zarembka, vol. 1, 59–86. Greenwich, CT: JAI Press, 1977.

Haller, William, Jr. "Technological Change in Primary Steel-Making in the United States, 1947–65." In National Commission on Technology, Automation and Economic Progress, *Technology and the American Economy,* vol. 2 Appendix, *Employment Impact of Technology Change.* Washington, DC: U.S. Government Printing Office, 1966.

Harper, Ann K. *The Location of the U.S. Steel Industry, 1879–1919.* Salem, NH: Ayer, 1977.

Harvey, George. *Henry Clay Frick: The Man.* New York: Scribner's, 1928.

Hassinger, Bernice Shield. *Henderson Steel: Birmingham's First Steel.* Birmingham, AL: Jefferson County Historical Society, 1978.

Hendricksen, Eldon S. *Capital Expenditures in the Steel Industry, 1900–1953.* New York: Arno Press, 1978.

Hessen, Robert. *Steel Titan: The Life of Charles M. Schwab.* New York: Oxford University Press, 1975.

Hill, Charles. "Fighting the Twelve-Hour Day in the American Steel Industry." *Labor History* 15 (Winter 1974): 19–35.

Hogan, William T. "The Steel Import Problem: A Question of Quality and Price." *Thought* 40 (Winter 1965): 567–94.

———. *Economic History of the Iron and Steel Industry of the United States.* Lexington, MA: D. C. Heath, 1971.

Holt, James. "Trade Unionism in the British and U.S. Steel Industries, 1888–1912: A Comparative Study." *Labor History* 18 (Winter 1977): 5–35.

Hughes, Jonathan R. T. *The Vital Few: American Economic Progress and Its Protagonists.* Boston: Houghton Mifflin, 1966.

Jarrett, John. "The Story of the Iron Workers." In *The Labor Movement: The Problem of Today,* edited by George E. McNeil, 268–311. Clifton, NJ: Kelley Reprints, 1971.

Jewett, Robert A. "Solving the Puzzle of the First American Structural Rail Beam." *Technology and Culture* 10 (1969): 371–91.

Kuriansky, Henry Richard. *A Business History of the Atlantic Steel Company.* New York: Arno Press, 1976.

Lauderbaugh, Richard A. *American Steel Makers and the Coming of the Second World War.* Ann Arbor: UMI, 1980.

Lewis, W. David. "The Early History of the Lackawanna Coal and Iron Co.: A Study in Technological Adaptation." *Pennsylvania Magazine of History and Biography* 96 (October 1972): 424–68.

Livesay, Harold. "Marketing Patterns in the Antebellum American Iron Industry." *Business History Review* 45 (Autumn 1971): 269–95.

Loose, John Ward Wilson. "The Anthracite Iron Industry of Lancaster County: Rolling Mills, 1850–1900." *Journal of the Lancaster County Historical Society* 86 (1982a): 78–117, 129–44.

———. "Protectionism, Wages and Strikes in the Anthracite Iron Industry of Lancaster County, 1840–1900." *Journal of the Lancaster County Historical Society* 86 (1982b): 2–23.

Loveday, Amos J., Jr. *The Rise and Decline of the American Cut Nail Industry: A Study of the Interrelationships of Technology, Business Organization and Management Techniques.* Westport, CT: Greenwood Press, 1983.

McFadden, Joseph M. "Monopoly in Barbed Wire: The Formation of the American Steel and Wire Company." *Business History Review* 52 (Winter 1978): 465–89.

McHugh, Jeanne. *Alexander Holley and the Makers of Steel.* New Series of the Johns Hopkins Studies in the History of Technology. Baltimore: Johns Hopkins University Press, 1980.

McKenzie, Robert H. "Horace Ware: Alabama Iron Pioneer." *Alabama Review* 26 (1973): 157–72.

McPherson, Donald S. "The 'Little Steel' Strike of 1937 in Johnstown, PA." *Pennsylvania History* 39 (April 1972): 219–38.

Muller, Hans, and Kiyoshi Kawahito. *Steel Industry Economies: A Comparative Analysis of Structure, Conduct and Performance.* New York: Japanese Steel Information Center, 1978.

Nash, Michael. *Conflict and Accommodation: Coal Miners, Steel Workers and Socialism, 1890–1920.* Westport, CT: Greenwood Press, 1982.

Nevins, Allan. *Abram S. Hewitt, with Some Account of Peter Cooper.* New York: Harper, 1935.

Nolan-Haley, Jacqueline M. "The Trigger Price Mechanism: Protecting Competition of Competitors." *NYU Journal of International Law and Politics* 13 (1980): 1–25.

Parsons, Donald O., and Edward John Ray. "The United States Steel Consolidation: The Creation of Market Control." *Journal of Law and Economics* 18 (April 1975): 181–219.

Paskoff, Paul F. *Industrial Revolution: Organization, Structure and Growth of the Pennsylvania Iron Industry, 1750–1860*. Baltimore: Johns Hopkins University Press, 1983.

Pearse, John B. *A Concise History of the Iron Manufacture of the American Colonies*. Philadelphia: Allen, Lane & Scott, 1876.

Perlman, Mark. "Governmental Intervention and the Socioeconomic Climate." In *Technological Progress and Industrial Leadership*, edited by Bela Gold et al., 609–31. Lexington, MA: D. C. Heath, 1984.

Rabitsch, Elisabeth K. "Blast Furnaces and Steel Mills—SIC 3312." In Conference Board, *Energy Consumption in Manufacturing: A Report to the Energy Policy Project of the Ford Foundation*, 415–55. Cambridge, MA: Lippincott, Ballinger, 1974.

Redlich, Fritz. *History of American Business Leaders: A Series of Studies*. Vol. 1. Ann Arbor: Edwards Brothers, 1940.

Reynolds, Lloyd G., and Cynthia H. Taft. *The Evolution of Wage Structure*. New Haven: Yale University Press, 1956.

Rosegger, Gerhard. "Technological Change and Materials Consumption in U.S. Iron and Steel Manufacturing: An Assessment of Some Environmental Impacts." *Human Ecology* 2 (January 1974): 13–30.

———. "Technological Progress and Economic Effects in Iron and Steel Production." In *Technological Progress and Industrial Leadership*, edited by Bela Gold et al., 447–606. Lexington, MA: D. C. Heath, 1984.

Ryan, John B. "Willard Warner and the Rise and Fall of the Iron Industry in Tecumseh, Alabama." *Alabama Review* 24 (1971): 261–79.

Sayenga, Donald. "The Stewart Company." *Proceedings of the Canal History and Technology Symposium* 6 (1986): 3–46.

Scamehorn, H. Lee. *Pioneer Steel Maker in the West: The Colorado Fuel and Iron Company, 1892–1903*. New York: Arno Press, 1976.

Schallenberg, Richard H. "Evolution, Adaptation and Survival: The Very Slow Death of the American Charcoal Iron Industry." *Annals of Science* (U.K.) 32 (1975): 341–58.

Schallenberg, Richard H., and David A. Ault. "Raw Materials Supply and Technological Change in the American Charcoal Iron Industry." *Technology and Culture* 18 (1977): 436–66.

Scheuerman, William. "Economic Power in the United States: The Case of Steel." *Politics and Society* 5 (1975): 337–66.

Schroeder, Gertrude G. *The Growth of Major Steel Companies, 1900–1950*. Baltimore: Johns Hopkins University Press, 1953.

Stebbins, Philip E. "Truman and the Seizure of Steel: A Failure in Communication." *Historian* 34 (1971): 1–21.

Stone, Katherine. "The Origins of Job Structures in the Steel Industry." *Review of Radical Political Economy* 6 (Summer 1974): 113–73.

Sundarajan, V. "The Impact of the Tariff on Some Selected Products of the U.S. Iron and Steel Industry, 1870–1914." *Quarterly Journal of Economics* 84 (November 1970): 590–610.

Swank, James M. *History of the Manufacture of Iron in All Ages, and Particularly in the United States from Colonial Times to 1891.* Philadelphia: American Iron & Steel Association, 1892.

Tarbell, Ida M. *The Life of Elbert H. Gary: The Story of Steel.* New York: Appleton, 1925.

Tedesco, Paul H. *Patriotism, Protection and Prosperity: James Moore Swank, the American Iron and Steel Association and the Tariff, 1873–1913.* American Economic History Series. New York: Garland, 1985.

Temin, Peter. *Iron and Steel in Nineteenth Century America: An Economic Inquiry.* Cambridge, MA: MIT Press, 1964.

Tiffany, Paul A. "The Roots of Decline: Business-Government Relations in the American Steel Industry, 1945–60." *Journal of Economic History* 44 (June 1984): 407–19.

Tweedale, Geoffrey. *Sheffield Steel and America: A Century of Commercial and Technological Interdependence, 1830–1930.* Cambridge, Eng.: Cambridge University Press, 1987.

Ubinger, John D. "Ernest Tener Weir: Last of the Great Steelmasters." *Western Pennsylvania Historical Magazine* 58 (1975): 287–306, 486–507.

U.S. Federal Trade Commission. *The United States Steel Industry and Its International Rivals: Trends and Factors Determining Competition.* Washington, DC: U.S. Government Printing Office, 1978.

Urofsky, Melvin I. "Josephus Daniels and the Armor Trust." *North Carolina Historical Review* 45 (1968): 237–63.

Vambery, Robert G. "The American Steel Industry." *Journal of World Trade Law* 5 (1971): 5–28.

Vangermeersch, Richard. "A Historical View of Depreciation: U.S. Steel 1902–70." *Mississippi Valley Journal of Business and Economics* 7 Winter (1971–72): 56–74.

Walker, Charles R. *Steeltown: An Industrial Case History of the Conflict Between Progress and Security.* New York: Russell Reprints, 1970.

Wall, Joseph Frazier. *Andrew Carnegie.* New York: Oxford University Press, 1970.

Walsh, William D. *The Diffusion of Technological Change in the Pennsylvania Pig Iron Industry.* Salem, NH: Ayer, 1975.

Warren, K. *The American Steel Industry, 1850–1970: A Geographic Interpretation.* Oxford: Clarendon Press, 1973.

Yeates, W. Ross. "Discovery of the Process for Making Anthracite Iron." *Pennsylvania Magazine of History and Biography* 98 (April 1974): 206–23.

Part IX

Industrial and Commercial Machinery and Computer Equipment
ESIC 35.0

CHAPTER 13

FARM AND GARDEN MACHINERY, 35.2

ROBERT CHARLES GRAHAM

A BRIEF HISTORY OF THE AGRICULTURAL MACHINERY INDUSTRY

Early American agricultural implements were produced on farms and by local blacksmiths. By the beginning of the nineteenth century, however, regional markets were served by manufacturers of agricultural implements. The Lagona Agricultural Works of Springfield, Ohio, for example, produced a wide variety of hand tools (Mills 1986). The modern agricultural machinery industry is rooted in the manufacture of the plow, the thresher, and the reaper.

The first patent for an iron plow was issued to Charles Newbold in 1797. Jethro Wood received a patent in 1814 for an iron plow made from several castings (Mills 1986). The establishment of large-scale firms to manufacture plows, however, followed John Deere's 1837 invention of the steel plow. Both the Grand Detour Plow Company (later merged with J. I. Case Company) and Deere and Company trace their origins to this refinement.

The invention of the reaper encouraged the founding of a large number of agricultural machinery manufacturers. The building of the McCormick Reaper Works in Chicago accelerated the production and diffusion of the reaper. In response to the strong demand for reapers, many others like the John H. Murray Company and the Marsh Harvester Company undertook their production.

In 1837 Hiram and John Pitts patented the first successful threshing machine. Shortly thereafter, Jerome Case established the J. I. Case Threshing Machine Company in Racine, Wisconsin (Mills 1986). By 1860 several firms were producing threshers. Indeed, many of the better known agricultural machinery firms were established in the 1840s and 1850s. In addition to those already mentioned, the Oliver Chilled Plow Company (the forerunner of Oliver Farm Equipment), the Rumley and the E. P. Allis Companies (forerunners of Allis Chalmers), and the Massey and the Harris Companies (forerunners of Massey, Harris, Ferguson) were established before 1860.

By 1860 the farm implement industry was in place, but the application of mechanical power to farm operations had hardly begun. Mechanical power in farming was first used in threshing and plowing. Although his thresher was initially horsepowered, Case explored the feasibility of applying portable steam power to farm operations. The first of the approximately 36,000 steam tractors he produced came out in 1869, about the same time as the company's popular Eclipse thresher (Holbrook 1955). In 1861 the M. Rumley Company added stationary steam engines to its line of farm equipment. The growing interest in applying steam power to farm work continued after the Civil War, and by the late 1870s farmers were purchasing self-propelled steam engines in considerable numbers. At the turn of the century, more than thirty firms were manufacturing 5,000 steam tractors annually for plowing and threshing (Gray 1974). These large, heavy tractors, however, were primarily used on farms in the Great Plains states. There remained a substantial demand for a lightweight, portable source of farm power.

The solution to the farm power problem was embodied in the internal combustion engine tractor. In 1892 John Froelich built a prototype gasoline-powered tractor and used it with a Case thresher for fifty days (Gray 1974). Several firms subsequently produced gasoline-powered tractors. These early internal combustion engine tractors had many of the same problems as steam tractors. Their primary uses were plowing and threshing, and they were heavy, sometimes weighing over ten tons.

Introduced by Henry Ford in 1917, the Fordson tractor represented a breakthrough in design. Its small size and low price helped the Fordson capture nearly 75 percent of the market in the mid–1920s (M. Williams 1974). Ford's dominance of the market was short-lived, however; in 1924 International Harvester introduced the McCormick-Deering Farmall.

The Farmall met the long-standing need for a general-purpose tractor that could cultivate row crops. Its triangle design, high ground clearance for cultivating, power takeoff, maneuverability, and differential brakes for close turning made it a versatile source of farm power. Subsequent improvements in design, including pneumatic-rubber tires and diesel engines, continued to improve the efficiency of the tractor as a source of low-cost farm power.

The development and widespread diffusion of the tractor encouraged mergers that eventually produced corporate giants in the agricultural machinery industry. The combination of the severe national economic contraction in 1896 and the intense competition between harvester manufacturers—the "Harvester Wars"—fostered three important mergers. In 1901 Allis Chalmers was formed from a merger of four companies; at the end of 1902, International Harvester, from five major manufacturers of harvesting equipment; and in 1911, Deere and Company, from its branch houses and other companies (Mills 1986). By these mergers, most of the large agricultural equipment manufacturers had a full line of implements. The farmers' adoption of the tractor reinforced the merger trend because it created a market for implements that were compatible with a tractor. Ford's lack of a supporting line of farm implements was one reason production of the Fordson tractor was discontinued in the United States in 1928. Ford resumed tractor production in the United States in 1939 because a link with the Ferguson System mitigated that limitation.

By 1930 the giants of the agricultural machinery industry had been established. Both the Oliver Farm Equipment Company and the Minneapolis Moline Power Implement Company had been organized in 1929. For manufacturers, 1929 was the most profitable year since 1920, but the prosperity of the late 1920s gave way dramatically to the Great Depression of the 1930s. The fall in farm income sharply curtailed machinery purchases. By 1936 conditions were improving. The combination of higher farm incomes and long-delayed purchases meant increased sales for many manufacturers. Recovery was complicated, however, by the United States' involvement in World War II. Farm equipment production was regulated by the government, and shortages developed in a number of areas.

After World War II industry growth returned. The continuing rural to urban movement and the accelerating mechanization of southern farms supported a steady demand for farm equipment. Despite periods of fierce competition, general conditions for manufacturers were good through the 1970s, at least in part because of an increase in the international market for American farm equipment.

Postwar prosperity ended in 1981. As worldwide production of agricultural commodities increased, the American share of the export market declined. In addition, American agricultural commodity prices, high compared to international prices, were lower than during the 1970s. The recession in agriculture and the resultant decline in equipment purchases led to retrenchment in the industry. International Harvester filed for bankruptcy and sold its farm equipment assets to Tenneco, Inc., the parent company of J. I. Case, and Allis Chalmers was sold to Deutz Corporation (Mills 1986).

By the end of the 1980s, prospects for the agricultural machinery industry had improved. The need for farm equipment is continual, but the industry growth of the last 150 years cannot be duplicated. The decline in rural population, from more than 30 million in 1940 to less than 6 million in the 1980s, created a market for farm machinery to replace farm labor—a one-time market. Growth in the industry will depend on improving existing equipment and developing more specialized equipment for specific crops.

BIBLIOGRAPHIC ESSAY

There is ample literature on agricultural development, but little on agricultural machinery. This review is limited to literature addressing the production and use of agricultural machinery in the United States and is divided into two major sections: the agricultural machinery industry in the United States and specific pieces of equipment.

The Agricultural Machinery Industry

Several books examine the early history of International Harvester. Herbert N. Casson, in *The Romance of the Reaper* (1908), summarizes the roles of Cyrus Hall McCormick and William Deering in building two of the major companies that merged as International Harvester in 1902. In *The Century of the Reaper* (1931), Cyrus McCormick provides an insider's look at the invention of the reaper and the evolution of International Harvester. Although McCormick is the son of one of the inventors of the reaper, his writing shows little bias. A company publication, *Roots in Chicago One Hundred Years Deep, 1847–1947* (1948), provides a brief history of International Harvester. Of particular interest are the diagrams and photographs of production facilities. Of interest to the historian examining the development of International Harvester is Robert Ozanne's volume on the company's relations with its labor force. Entitled *Wages in Practice and Theory: McCormick and International Harvester, 1860–1960* (1968), the work examines the firm's wage patterns and managerial decisions. In addition, earnings are compared with those at other agricultural machinery firms and in other areas of U.S. manufacturing.

Although the historical coverage of International Harvester is probably the best on any agricultural machinery manufacturer, a recent work has improved the coverage of another firm. Wayne G. Broehl's *John Deere's Company* (1984) is an excellent history of Deere. In addition to presenting the history of the founder and the company, Broehl details how economic conditions influenced the company. McCormick and then International Harvester were very active in world markets; Fred V. Carstensen (1984) documents the activities of International Harvester and its predecessor in Imperial Russia.

Other books that deal with the evolution of an agricultural machinery firm include Stewart H. Holbrook's *Machines of Plenty* (1955) and Merrill Denison's *Harvest Triumphant: The Story of Massey-Harris* (1949). Holbrook examines the development of the J. I. Case Company from Case's introduction of a thresher in 1842 through the 1950s. Similarly, Denison summarizes the history of Massey-Harris from the early activities of its founders, Daniel Massey and Alanson Harris, to 1947. Both books are excellent narratives, but contain little historical data. *Fifty Years on Tracks* (1954), published by the Caterpillar Tractor Company, is a brief company history. Of primary interest are the sections on the Holt and Best combines and the use of steam power.

Biographies of founders are an additional source of company history. William T. Hutchinson's (1930, 1935) two-volume biography of Mc-Cormick is an outstanding example. Hutchinson relates McCormick's invention of the reaper, the establishment of McCormick Company in Chicago, and the legal battles over patents. He also devotes numerous sections to McCormick's social, political, and religious activities. Another work on McCormick is Casson's *Cyrus Hall McCormick: His Life and Work* ([1909] 1971). But Casson is favorably biased toward McCormick and generally lacks Hutchinson's thoroughness.

Biographies of other company founders include *John Deere: He Gave to the World the Steel Plow* (1937) by Neil M. Clark and *Benjamin Holt and Caterpillar: Tracks and Combines* (1984) by Reynold M. Wik. Clark romanticizes Deere, but Wik's work on Holt concentrates more on the historical record. Less thorough coverage that focuses on individuals rather than their inventions is found in Edward Jerome Dies's *Titans of the Soil* (1949), which contains chapters on Eli Whitney, Deere, and McCormick.

A number of publications address the agricultural implement industry in general. An outstanding book examining the development of the industry in the United States during the nineteenth century is Robert L. Ardrey's *American Agricultural Implements: A Review of Invention and Development in the Agricultural Implement Industry of the United States* ([1894] 1972). An excellent complement for Ardrey's book is Harvey Schwartz's 1966 Ph.D. dissertation, "The Changes in the Location of the American Agricultural Implement Industry, 1850 to 1960," which describes the growth of the industry and summarizes and analyzes its changing locational pattern. A comparable book on the Canadian agricultural implement industry is *The Agricultural Implement Industry in Canada* (1956) by W. G. Phillips. Included is a useful foldout that summarizes mergers in both the Canadian and the U.S. agricultural machinery industry from 1830 to 1940. Examining the development of the agricultural implement industry from a different perspective is *Implement and Tractor: Reflections on 100 Years of Farm Equipment* (1986). Editor Robert K. Mills has collected reproductions of stories, illustrations, and advertisements that appeared in *Implement and Tractor* magazine. Coverage begins with McCormick's reaper and Deere's plow.

Two volumes focus on the role of the tractor in the development of the agricultural machinery industry. In *The Tractor and Its Influence upon the*

Agricultural Implement Industry (1916) Barton W. Currie studies the early (pre–1920) impact of the tractor on sales methods and the farmer's purchase decision. *Agricultural Tractors: A World Industry Study* (1975) by Robert T. Kudrle focuses on the production and distribution of tractors since World War II as the basis for explaining the worldwide industry of the 1970s.

Additional sources that focus on the agricultural implement industry are U.S. government publications. Examples include three reports of the U.S. Federal Trade Commission: *Report on the Causes of High Prices of Farm Implements* (1920), *Report on the Agricultural Implement and Machinery Business, Part 2, Cost, Prices and Profits* (1938), and *Report on Manufacture and Distribution of Farm Implements* (1948).

Agricultural Implements

Without a doubt, the tractor is the agricultural machine whose history has received the greatest attention. Even today the internal combustion engine tractor is the primary source of farm power. Early attempts to provide a mechanized source of farm power, however, were based on the steam engine. Two interesting and complementary books examine the application of steam power on American farms. Wik's *Steam Power on the American Farm (1953)* is an excellent historical account of the rise and fall of the use of steam power in American agriculture. Jack Norbeck's *Encyclopedia of American Steam Traction Engines* (1976) provides 1,250 illustrations or photographs and brief descriptions of steam traction engines. Together, these works provide a comprehensive written and pictorial history of the use of steam power on farms in the United States.

R. B. Gray's *The Agricultural Tractor, 1855–1950* (1974) also covers the early use of steam power in agriculture, but is better known as the definitive source of information on tractors used in the United States during the first half of the twentieth century. In an excellent chronological presentation, Gray summarizes the evolution of tractor design with descriptions, diagrams, and photographs. Two studies complement Gray's. Michael William's *Farm Tractors in Color* (1974) is a brief history of tractor development accompanied by color photographs of vintage tractors. C. H. Wendel's *Encyclopedia of American Farm Tractors* (1979) is part of a series that includes Norbeck's encyclopedia. Wendel's pictorial history of the tractor amasses approximately 1,500 illustrations and photographs along with brief histories of various tractors and the firms that produced them.

Numerous other publications focus on the history of the tractor. Included is a promotional brochure written by Will McCracken and published by Deere and Company: *John Deere Tractors, 1918–1976* (1976). John Strohm's "Farm Power: From Muscle to Motor" appeared in the January 11, 1941, issue of the *Prairie Farmer*. Although brief, it contains several interesting anecdotes on the early use of steam and gasoline tractors. In addition to these works, an examination of contemporary sources, such as *Implement and Tractor* magazine, *National Farm Tractor and Implement Blue Book*, and *Official Guide: Tractors and Farm Equipment*, will provide a wealth of information on the tractor and related implements.

Second only to the tractor in the attention it has attracted is the reaper. Several works have focused on its development. An excellent book by John F. Steward is entitled *The Reaper: A History of the Efforts of Those Who Justly May Be Said to Have Made Bread Cheap* (1931). Steward, who headed the Department of Patents, wrote this work in response to Casson's *Romance of the Reaper*, which he viewed as long on romance and short on facts. Steward focused on the patent history of the reaper and, in the process, included many comments on less well known reaper manufacturers. The *Official Retrospective Exhibition of the Development of Harvesting Machinery for the Paris Exposition of 1900* (1900), which was published by Deering Harvester Company (later to become part of International Harvester), contains a brief history of the evolution in reaper design. The accompanying photographs and illustrations demonstrate these improvements.

In addition to unbiased histories, a number of pamphlets were published in conjunction with patent disputes between Cyrus McCormick and Obed Hussey. Two pamphlets are biased toward Hussey: *Overlooked Pages of Reaper History* (1897), by J. Russell Parsons et al., and *Obed Hussey: Who, of All Inventors, Made Bread Cheap* (1912), edited by Follett Greeno. In contrast, *Who Invented the Reaper?* (1897) by R. B. Swift is sympathetic to McCormick's position. Together, these pamphlets show the bitterness associated with one of the most noteworthy patent disputes.

Additional studies summarize the evolution in design for other implements. Lillian Church's *History of the Plow* (1935) reviews the development of the plow. In a more general work, *Farm Inventions in the Making of America* (1976), Paul C. Johnson provides a brief history of various implements and their inventors. Also included are diagrams, pictures, and reproductions of old advertisements. *Power to Produce* (Alfred Stefferud, editor), which is the title of the *Yearbook of Agriculture, 1960*, is an overview of the agricultural implements available in 1960.

The agricultural implement publications just summarized focus on the evolution of implement designs. The authors of a number of publications include that information, along with various economic data, and analyze the adoption decision that underlies the diffusion process for agricultural implements. The most interesting of these articles is Wayne Rasmussen's "Advances in American Agriculture: The Mechanical Tomato Harvester as a Case Study" (1968), in which he uses a systems approach to analyze the development and diffusion of the mechanical tomato harvester. The package associated with this innovation included the development of a tomato that could withstand mechanized harvesting.

Another method used to study the diffusion of agricultural implements is based on a threshold level defined as the acreage at which the total cost associated with two alternative production techniques is equal. In his article "The Mechanization of Reaping in the Antebellum Midwest" (1966), Paul David used this method to explain the pattern of reaper diffusion during the 1840s and 1850s. In a subsequent comment entitled "The Mechanization of Reaping and Mowing in American Agriculture, 1833–1870" (1975), Alan L. Olmstead argues that the slow diffusion of the reaper was primarily attributable to the need for design improvements. In a second article, "The Landscape and the Machine: Technical Interrelatedness, Land Tenure and the Mechanization of the Corn Harvest in Victorian Britain" (1971), David recognizes the constraints on the application of the threshold model in studying reaper diffusion in nineteenth-century Britain. Therefore, although the theoretical validity of the threshold level is firmly established, its application to diffusion is complicated by the large number of additional factors that influence that process.

The diffusion of the tractor has received considerable attention, and the threshold model has been applied to it. Robert Eugene Ankli's article "Horses vs. Tractors on the Corn Belt" (1980) estimates the threshold level for tractor adoption on midwestern farms. Ankli's analysis yields the somewhat surprising result that two thresholds existed: one between small teams of horses and tractors and another between large teams of horses and tractors. Ankli and Olmstead coauthored a second article on tractor diffusion entitled "The Adoption of the Gasoline Tractor in California" (1981), in which they examined the impact of crop rotation on the threshold level. A third study on tractor diffusion, "Tractorization" in the United States and Its Relevance for the Developing Countries (1979) by Nicholas Peter Sargen, examines the adoption of steam and internal combustion engine tractors on the Great Plains and assesses the relevance of this process for developing countries.

Tractor diffusion in the South has also been examined. Moses S. Musoke concludes that the delayed diffusion of the tractor in the South can largely be explained by unsuitable designs and low farm incomes during the 1930s— "Mechanizing Cotton Production in the American South: The Tractor, 1915–1960" (1981). Other studies of the mechanization of southern agriculture have focused on the delays associated with the institutional structure. The landmark work in this area is James H. Street's The New Revolution in the Cotton Economy: Mechanization and Its Consequences (1957). Two more recent articles by Warren Whatley, "A History of Mechanization in the Cotton South: The Institutional Hypothesis" (1985) and "Southern Agrarian Labor Contracts as Impediments to Cotton Mechanization" (1987), reveal how labor contracts delayed mechanization. Other articles on the mechanization of the South include Gilbert Fite's "Mechanization of Cotton Production Since World War II" (1980) and Clarence A. Wiley's "The Rust Mechanical Cotton Picker and Probable Land-Use Adjustments" (1939).

More publications examine the impact of agricultural mechanization than the diffusion process. Included are many contemporary sources from agricultural research stations, the U.S. Department of Agriculture, and farm magazines like the *Prairie Farmer* and the *Country Gentleman*. Particularly noteworthy titles are mentioned below.

Many of the publications that address the impact of agricultural mechanization focus on labor displacement. A series of publications funded under the Works Progress Administration examines displacement from 1910 to the mid–1930s. Those of particular interest are listed in the bibliography. Another excellent source for the same period is *American Agriculture, 1899–1939: A Study of Output, Employment and Productivity* (1942) by Harold Barger and Hans H. Landsberg. Barger and Landsberg provide a general examination of agricultural development and include an excellent section on the impact of farm machinery. Another brief description of the impact of farm mechanization before World War II is Allan G. Bogue's "Changes in Mechanical and Plant Technology: The Corn Belt, 1910–1940" (1983). Given as the presidential address to the Economic History Association in 1982, this paper discusses the development of tractors and mechanical picker-huskers and the cost of using them on midwestern farms. In addition, Bogue discusses the introduction of hybrid corn seed.

Two outstanding books examine the impact of the tractor during the first part of the twentieth century. *Research Methods on Farm Use of Tractors* (1938) by Naum Jasny includes an essay on the validity of contemporary (1930) research, primarily performed by agricultural experiment stations, on the cost of tractor usage. Any researcher making use of these cost studies must read Jasny's caveats. In a more historical treatment, Robert C. Williams's *Fordson, Farmall and Poppin' Johnny: A History of the Farm Tractor and Its Impact on America* (1987) examines the role of the tractor in American agriculture. A quite different and interesting perspective on the tractor can be found in Wik's "The American Farm Tractor as Father of the Military Tank" (1980). Wik argues that the tractor is an example of how progressive American farmers are in adopting innovations.

Leo Rogin's *The Introduction of Farm Machinery in Its Relation to the Productivity of Labor in the Agriculture of the United States During the Nineteenth Century* (1931) has long been considered a standard for evaluating other works. Rogin focuses on various mechanical innovations and the resultant changes in labor requirements for crop production. *Change in Agriculture: The Northern United States, 1820–1870* (1969) by Clarence H. Danhof examines agricultural development in general, but two chapters are devoted to agricultural mechanization.

BIBLIOGRAPHY

Ankli, Robert Eugene. "Horses vs. Tractors on the Corn Belt." *Agricultural History* 54 (January 1980): 134–48.

Ankli, Robert Eugene, and Alan L. Olmstead. "The Adoption of the Gasoline Tractor in California." *Agricultural History* 55 (July 1981): 213–30.

Ardrey, Robert L. *American Agricultural Implements: A Review of Invention and Development in the Agricultural Implement Industry of the United States.* 1894. Reprint. New York: Arno Press, 1972.

Barger, Harold, and Hans H. Landsberg. *American Agriculture, 1899–1939: A Study of Output, Employment and Productivity.* New York: National Bureau of Economic Research, 1942.

Bogue, Allan G. "Changes in Mechanical and Plant Technology: The Corn-Belt, 1910–1940." *Journal of Economic History* 43 (March 1983): 1–25.

Broehl, Wayne G. *John Deere's Company.* New York: Doubleday, 1984.

Carstensen, Fred V. *American Enterprise in Foreign Markets.* Chapel Hill: University of North Carolina Press, 1984.

Casson, Herbert N. *The Romance of the Reaper.* New York: Doubleday, Page, 1908.

———. *Cyrus Hall McCormick: His Life and Work.* 1909. Reprint. Freeport, NY: Books for Libraries Press, 1971.

Church, Lillian. *History of the Plow.* Information Series No. 48. Washington, DC: U.S. Department of Agriculture, Bureau of Agricultural Engineering, Division of Mechanical Equipment, October 1935.

Clark, Neil M. *John Deere: He Gave to the World the Steel Plow.* Moline, IL: Desaulniers, 1937.

Collier, George W. *The Husker-Shredder on Eastern Corn Belt Farms.* Farmer's Bulletin No. 1589. Washington, DC: U.S. Department of Agriculture, December 1928.

Cooper, Martin R., Glen T. Barton, and Albert P. Brodell. *Progress of Farm Mechanization.* Miscellaneous Publication No. 630. Washington, DC: U.S. Department of Agriculture, October 1947.

Country Gentleman. Albany, NY: 1853–1955.

Currie, Barton W. *The Tractor and Its Influence upon the Agricultural Implement Industry.* Philadelphia: Curtis, 1916.

Danhof, Clarence H. *Change in Agriculture: The Northern United States, 1820–1870.* Cambridge, MA: Harvard University Press, 1969.

David, Paul. "The Mechanization of Reaping in the Antebellum Midwest." In *Industrialization in Two Systems: Essays in Honor of Alexander Gerschenkron,* edited by Henry Rosovsky. New York: Wiley, 1966.

———. "The Landscape and the Machine: Technical Interrelatedness, Land Tenure and the Mechanization of the Corn Harvest in Victorian Britain." In *Essays on a Mature Economy: Britain After 1840,* edited by Donald McCloskey. Princeton: Princeton University Press, 1971.

Denison, Merrill. *Harvest Triumphant: The Story of Massey-Harris.* New York: Dodd, Mead, 1949.

Dies, Edward Jerome. *Titans of the Soil.* Chapel Hill: University of North Carolina Press, 1949.

Elwood, Robert B., Lloyd E. Arnold, Clarence D. Schmutz, and Eugene G. Mc-Kibben. *Changes in Technology and Labor Requirements in Crop Production: Wheat and Oats*. National Research Project Report No. A–10. Philadelphia: Works Progress Administration, April 1939.

Elwood, Robert B., Arthur A. Lewis, and Ronald A. Struble. *Changes in Technology and Labor Requirements in Livestock Production: Dairying*. National Research Project No. A–14. Washington, DC: Works Progress Administration, June 1941.

Fifty Years on Tracks. Peoria, IL: Caterpillar Tractor Co., 1954.

Fite, Gilbert. "Mechanization of Cotton Production Since World War II." *Agricultural History* 55 (January 1980): 190–207.

Gray, Ray Burton. *The Agricultural Tractor, 1855–1950*. St. Joseph, MI: American Society of Agricultural Engineers, 1974.

Greeno, Follett, ed. *Obed Hussey: Who, of All Inventors, Made Bread Cheap*. Rochester, NY: Rochester Herald Publishing Company, 1912.

Holbrook, Stewart H. *Machines of Plenty*. New York: Macmillan, 1955.

Holley, William C., and Lloyd E. Arnold. *Changes in Technology and Labor Requirements in Crop Production: Cotton*. National Research Project on Studies of Changing Techniques and Employment in Agriculture, Report No. A–7. Philadelphia: Works Progress Administration, September 1938.

Horne, Roman L., and Eugene G. McKibben. *Changes in Farm Power and Equipment: Mechanical Cotton Picker*. Studies of Changing Techniques and Employment in Agriculture, Report No. A–2. Philadelphia: Works Progress Administration, August 1937.

Hurst, William, and Lillian Church. *Power Machinery in Agriculture*. Miscellaneous Publication No. 157. Washington, DC: U.S. Department of Agriculture, 1933.

Hutchinson, William T. *Cyrus Hall McCormick: Seedtime, 1809–1856*. New York: Century, 1930.

———. *Cyrus Hall McCormick: Harvest, 1856–1884*. New York: Century, 1935.

Implement & Tractor. Kansas City, MO: Implement Trade Journal Co., 1982– .

Jasny, Naum. *Research Methods on Farm Use of Tractors*. New York: Columbia University Press, 1938.

Johnson, Paul C. *Farm Inventions in the Making of America*. Des Moines, IA: Wallace-Homestead, 1976.

Kinsman, D. C. *An Appraisal of Power Used on Farms in the United States*. Dept. Bulletin 1348. Washington, DC: U.S. Department of Agriculture, 1925.

Knowlton, Harry E., Robert B. Elwood, and Eugene G. McKibben. *Changes in Technology and Labor Requirements in Crop Production: Potatoes*. Studies of Changing Techniques and Employment in Agriculture, Report No. A–4. Philadelphia: Works Progress Administration, March 1938.

Kudrle, Robert T. *Agricultural Tractors: A World Industry Study*. Cambridge, MA: Ballinger, 1975.

Lane, C. S., and W. A. Stocking. *The Milking Machine as a Factor in Dairying: A Preliminary Report*. Bureau of Animal Industry Bulletin 92. Washington, DC: U.S. Department of Agriculture, 1907.

McCormick, Cyrus. *The Century of the Reaper*. Boston: Houghton Mifflin, 1931.

McCracken, Will. *John Deere Tractors, 1918–1976*. Moline, IL: John Deere, 1976.

McKibben, Eugene G., and R. Austin Griffin. *Changes in Farm Power and Equip-

ment: Tractors, Trucks and Automobiles. National Research Project Report No. A–9. Philadelphia: Works Progress Administration, December 1938.

McKibben, Eugene G., John A. Hopkins, and R. Austin Griffin. *Changes in Farm Power and Equipment: Field Implements.* National Research Project Report No. A–11. Philadelphia: Works Progress Administration, August 1939.

Macy, Loring K., Lloyd E. Arnold, and Eugene G. McKibben. *Changes in Technology and Labor Requirements in Crop Production: Corn.* National Research Project Report No. A–5. Philadelphia: Works Progress Administration, June 1938.

Macy, Loring K., Lloyd E. Arnold, Eugene G. McKibben, and Edmund J. Stone. *Changes in Technology and Labor Requirements in Crop Production: Sugar Beets.* Studies of Changing Techniques and Employment in Agriculture, Report No. A–1. Philadelphia: Works Progress Administration, August 1937.

Mills, Robert K., ed. *Implement and Tractor: Reflections on 100 Years of Farm Equipment.* Overland Park, KS: Intertel, 1986.

Musoke, Moses S. "Mechanizing Cotton Production in the American South: The Tractor, 1915–1960." *Explorations in Economic History* 18 (June 1981): 347–75.

National Farm Tractor and Implement Blue Book. Chicago: National Market Reports, annually 1939– .

Norbeck, Jack. *Encyclopedia of American Steam Traction Engines.* Glen Ellyn, IL: Crestline, 1976.

Official Guide: Tractors and Farm Equipment. St. Louis: National Farm and Power Services, Fall 1960–Fall 1968.

Official Retrospective Exhibition of the Development of Harvesting Machinery for the Paris Exposition of 1900. Chicago: Deering Harvester, 1900.

Olmstead, Alan L. "The Mechanization of Reaping and Mowing in American Agriculture, 1833–1870." *Journal of Economic History* 35 (June 1975): 327–52.

Ozanne, Robert. *Wages in Practice and Theory: McCormick and International Harvester, 1860–1960.* Madison: University of Wisconsin Press, 1968.

Parsons, J. Russell, Lewis Miller, and John F. Steward. *Overlooked Pages of Reaper History.* Chicago: W. B. Conkey, 1897.

Peck, H. W. "The Influence of Agricultural Machinery and the Automobile on Farming Operations." *Quarterly Journal of Economics* 41 (August 1927): 534–44.

Peterson, Willis, and Yoav Kislev. "The Cotton Harvester in Retrospect: Labor Displacement or Replacement?" *Journal of Economic History* 46 (March 1986): 199–216.

Phillips, W. G. *The Agricultural Implement Industry in Canada.* Toronto: University of Toronto Press, 1956.

Prairie Farmer. Chicago, 1840– .

Quaintance, Hadly Winfield. "The Influence of Farm Machinery on Production and Labor." Ph.D. diss., University of Wisconsin, 1904.

Rasmussen, Wayne. "Advances in American Agriculture: The Mechanical Tomato Harvester as a Case Study." *Technology and Culture* 9 (October 1968): 531–43.

Reynoldson, L. A. *The Combined Harvester-Thresher in the Great Plains*. Technical Bulletin 70. Washington, DC: U.S. Department of Agriculture, 1928.

Rogin, Leo. *The Introduction of Farm Machinery in Its Relation to the Productivity of Labor in the Agriculture of the United States During the Nineteenth Century*. Berkeley: University of California Press, 1931.

Roots in Chicago One Hundred Years Deep, 1847–1947. Chicago: International Harvester, 1948.

Sargen, Nicholas Peter. *"Tractorization" in the United States and Its Relevance for the Developing Countries*. New York: Garland, 1979.

Schilletter, J. C., Robert B. Elwood, and Harry E. Knowlton. *Changes in Technology and Labor Requirements in Crop Production: Vegetables*. National Research Project Report No. A–12. Philadelphia: Works Progress Administration, September 1939.

Schwartz, Harvey. "The Changes in the Location of the American Agricultural Implement Industry, 1850 to 1960." Ph.D. diss., University of Illinois, 1966.

Stefferud, Alfred, ed. *Power to Produce: The Yearbook of Agriculture, 1960*. Washington, DC: U.S. Department of Agriculture, 1960.

Steward, John F. *The Reaper: A History of the Efforts of Those Who Justly May Be Said to Have Made Bread Cheap*. New York: Greenberg, 1931.

Street, James H. *The New Revolution in the Cotton Economy: Mechanization and Its Consequences*. Chapel Hill: University of North Carolina Press, 1957.

Strohm, John. "Farm Power: From Muscle to Motor." *Prairie Farmer* 113 (January 11, 1941): 30–36.

Swift, R. B. *Who Invented the Reaper?* Chicago: n. p., 1897.

Taylor, Paul S. "Power Farming and Labor Displacement in the Cotton Belt." *Monthly Labor Review* 46 (March 1938): 595–607.

U.S. Federal Trade Commission. *Report on the Causes of High Prices of Farm Implements*. Washington, DC: U.S. Government Printing Office, 1920.

———. *Report on the Agricultural Implement and Machinery Business, Part 2, Cost, Prices and Profits*. Washington, DC: U.S. Government Printing Office, 1938.

———. *Report on Manufacture and Distribution of Farm Implements*. Washington, DC: U.S. Government Printing Office, 1948.

Wendel, C. H. *Encyclopedia of American Farm Tractors*. Sarasota, FL: Crestline, 1979.

Whatley, Warren C. "A History of Mechanization in the Cotton South: The Institutional Hypothesis." *Quarterly Journal of Economics* 100 (November 1985): 1191–1215.

———. "Southern Agrarian Labor Contracts as Impediments to Cotton Mechanization." *Journal of Economic History* 47 (March 1987): 45–70.

Wik, Reynold M. *Steam Power on the American Farm*. Philadelphia: University of Pennsylvania Press, 1953.

———. "The American Farm Tractor as Father of the Military Tank." *Agricultural History* 55 (January 1980): 126–33.

———. *Benjamin Holt and Caterpillar: Tracks and Combines*. St. Joseph, MI: American Society of Agricultural Engineers, 1984.

Wiley, Clarence A. "The Rust Mechanical Cotton Picker and Probable Land-Use

Adjustments." *Journal of Land and Public Utility Economics* 15 (February 1939): 155–66.

Williams, Michael. *Farm Tractors in Color.* New York: Macmillan, 1974.

Williams, Robert C. *Fordson, Farmall and Poppin' Johnny: A History of the Farm Tractor and Its Impact on America.* Champaign: University of Illinois Press, 1987.

CHAPTER 14

ELECTRONIC COMPUTING
EQUIPMENT, 35.71

EMIL E. FRIBERG, JR.

The U.S. electronic computer industry originated in World War II military programs and has been characterized by steady technical advance, rapid growth, and a diffusion of computer use throughout government and industry. The modern electronic computer industry includes mainframe computers, minicomputers, printers, and all other peripheral equipment. Although a product of wartime development, the computer industry has prewar roots in office machine manufacturing for data processing and demand by scientific users for computational power. The manufacturing roots are manifest in the continuing role played by office machine manufacturers in the computer industry (Beniger 1986). Prewar office machine producers who succeeded in making the transition from mechanical data processing technology to electronic control technologies include International Business Machines (IBM), Sperry Corporation (formerly Sperry Rand, but now Unisys following the 1986 merger with Burroughs Corporation), National Cash Register (NCR), and Burroughs Corporation (now Unisys). These firms successfully bridged the technological gap between mechanical and electronic technologies, met the growing demand for data processing in government and business, and catered to scientific and engineering requirements.

The continuity of office machine producers in computer development reflects the increasing demand by users for data processing capability (Beniger 1986). Among these users, government played a crucial role in the generation of mechanical as well as electronic data processing technology. The demand for tabulating resources at the U.S. Bureau of the Census spawned two corporations that dominate much of computer industry history: IBM and Remington Rand (later the Sperry Corporation) (Austrian 1982).

In the late nineteenth century, Census engineer Herman Hollerith left government employment to form a tabulating machine business and won a contest to supply equipment for the 1890 and 1900 censuses. A 1911 merger with other machine firms under the direction of Charles Flint led to the formation of the Calculating-Recording-Tabulating Corporation, now better known as IBM, the world's dominant computer firm (Engelbourg [1954] 1976). Another Census employee, James Powers, with bureau encouragement, left federal employment to develop a machine competitive with Hollerith's, and was awarded the 1910 census contract. His firm, Powers Accounting Machines Corporation, was later merged into Remington Rand (Sobel 1981).[1] The machines developed by Hollerith and Powers were capable of simple arithmetic and repetitive data sorting; thus, they were ideal for manipulating collected data.

A second strand of computer development derived from the scientific and engineering demand for computation power, a need that during World War II led to army funding of the ENIAC computer at the University of Pennsylvania's Moore School of Electrical Engineering. The growing postwar demands for computing power from the nuclear and aerospace industries, combined with generous federal support, provided the organizational impetus and market for the computer industry's initial decade.

The commercial computer industry was launched on March 3, 1946, when J. Presper Eckert and John Mauchly, the inventors of the first electronic digital computer, the ENIAC, resigned their positions at the Moore School to form the Electronic Control Company and began commercial production of the UNIVAC computer.[2] Their first machine was turned over to the Census Bureau on March 30, 1951, and their first non-government installation was at General Electric (GE) in 1954 (Sharpe 1969). IBM produced its first electronic computer in 1953, the Defense Calculator, to support the Korean War effort. With the proven success of these installations, the mid and late 1950s saw a rapid increase in the number of firms involved and in machine placements.

INDUSTRY GROWTH

The computer industry is only one of several science-based industries that grew from wartime roots to play an important role in the postwar economy. The other industries that benefitted from military support include aviation and electronics (Nelson 1982). Although the computer industry is not large, it has contributed a distinctive character to post–World War II economic growth. The efforts of Marc Uri Porat (1977) to measure the input of this industry into the "information sector"—he estimated that this sector accounts for 46 percent of GNP—gives some indication of the important role that the computer industry is widely believed to have played in recent decades.

The growth of computing as measured by value of shipments increased from $480 million in 1952 to $4.5 billion in 1967, and to $38.2 billion in 1982 (*Census of Manufactures*).[3] The importance of the industry can easily be overstated, since in 1981 shipments of electronic computing equipment were only slightly greater than 1 percent of GNP. However, if we measure the increase in computing power in real terms, that is, by holding the "quality" measured constant, the growth is truly impressive. Investigators have found that due to technological advance, the retail price for an "identical computer" fell by 29 percent annually between 1958 and 1965, by 32 percent annually between 1966 and 1972, and by 18.2 percent per year from 1973 to 1978 (Flamm 1987). A price index for a constant technological quality can be calculated and the current dollar value of shipments deflated to estimate the *real* value of computer stocks with the qualitative change included. The annual estimates imply an annual average rate of growth in user capabilities of 78 percent for the period 1954–65, a remarkable rate of expansion and technological advance (Chow 1967).

Fluctuations in the rate of expansion correspond to the product cycle of different machine "generations" (Gropelli 1970). These generations are based on changes in machine components, as the basis of machine technology evolved from electromechanical relays, to vacuum tubes, to transistors, and most recently to integrated circuits (Braun and MacDonald 1982). Each generation represents the development of possibilities inherent in machines with improved basic components. During the first twenty years these generations also coincided with changes in the corporate composition of the industry. The rapidly improving technology and expanding computer market enabled many corporations to enter the industry, particularly when new components were introduced. Rapid change also drove many firms to merge or exit if they were slow to adopt new components in their product line.

PRECOMMERCIAL MACHINES

During the 1930s several different university research projects designed to expand scientific computational capability were initiated. MIT, Harvard, Columbia, and the University of Pennsylvania had a variety of calculators and analyzers in operation or under construction. During World War II, a unit of women working at the Moore School computed artillery ballistic tables for the Army Ordnance office. With the wartime bottleneck in calculating firing tables, the army agreed to fund Eckert and Mauchly's design for the ENIAC computer (Stern 1981). The ENIAC was tested in December, 1945, and was used to model equations for the hydrogen bomb. The army continued its support and funded a second machine, the EDVAC, with an internally stored program. But the inventors, Eckert and Mauchly, became involved in a patent assignment dispute with the University of Pennsylvania and resigned their positions before the EDVAC was completed and put into commercial production. Organized as a partnership, they sought federal support for machine development and signed contracts to deliver three computers to the federal government. Out of a planned six-machine production run, the Census Bureau, the Air Force Comptroller's Office, and the Army Map Service were to receive one each, and the now incorporated Eckert-Mauchly Computer Company (EMCC) was under contract to deliver the other machines to the Prudential Insurance Company and A. C. Nielson.

EMCC experienced serious financial difficulties as their costs escalated above their fixed-price contracts, and, after their first backer died in a 1949 plane crash, they sought a buyer. They approached Hughes Aircraft, NCR, Philco, Burroughs, IBM, and Remington Rand. IBM was interested in hiring Eckert and Mauchly, but not in buying their firm. Thomas J. Watson, Sr., dropped the contact, presumably because antitrust considerations restricted IBM's action. Remington Rand, already a diversified office machine and office supplies manufacturer, acquired the firm in 1950 and immediately sought to renegotiate the six machine contracts, with mixed success. Prudential and Nielson cancelled their contracts, and the federal government agreed to buy the remaining three machines from the first production run.

Remington Rand consolidated its lead in the computing field by acquiring the St. Paul–based Engineering Research Associates (ERA) in 1952 for $1.7 million, a figure established by multiplying $5,000 times the number of engineers in the firm (Tomash 1980). Like Eckert-Mauchly, ERA also had explicit origins in military research and government contracts. ERA's organizational core came from a World War II navy intelligence unit that developed code-breaking machines. At the end of the war the navy helped establish the for-profit firm and granted it a series of cost-plus contracts for classified machine development. Bolstered by these contracts, ERA expanded rapidly but lacked the capital necessary to enter civilian markets. ERA president John Parker had the difficult task of seeking buyers or financial backers for a firm whose work was classified. Remington Rand's purchase in 1952 came two years after ERA's first machine was installed for the navy in Washington, D.C.

Simultaneous with East Coast computer development at the University of Pennsylvania and MIT and Midwest development at ERA, employees of West Coast military aerospace contractors resigned their positions to form their own companies. Concentrated in the Los Angeles area, the West Coast developments were applications of computer capabilities for military uses (Ceruzzi 1985; Smithsonian Computer History Project 1969–73). For example, Northrop Aircraft had an impact on both East and West Coast computing through its development work on the SNARK long-range guided missile. They contracted with Eckert-Mauchly for a special airborne computer, the BINAC, while simultaneously developing their own machine. Fourteen different firms can be traced to Northrop employees who worked on the SNARK project. Northrop sold its computer division, which in turn spun off other firms (Ceruzzi 1985). There were similar spin-offs at Hughes Aircraft, North American Aviation, Bendix, and Lockheed. Two West Coast computer firms provided entry for office machine firms into the computer industry. Computer Research Corporation, one of Northrop's employee spin-offs, was acquired by NCR in 1953, as the office machine manufacturer sought entry to the computer industry. Likewise, Burroughs acquired the West Coast firm of ElectroData in its 1956 bid for an industry foothold.

The growth of firms across the country, and the replacement of IBM card tabulating equipment by the UNIVAC at the Census Bureau, prompted IBM to enter the market. IBM's president from 1914 to 1956, Thomas J. Watson, Sr., had failed to recognize growing scientific and engineering demand for high-speed computing and visualized only a small market for the new electronic machines. Only under the patriotic cover of IBM's support for the Korean War effort and through the leadership of Thomas J. Watson, Jr., did the firm manufacture its first computer, the Defense Calculator—IBM Model 701. The eighteen machines produced were oriented toward scientific use, with limited input/output equipment, and were all placed at government installations or with defense contractors. The successful delivery of the IBM 701 and the demonstrated demand for Remington Rand's first UNIVAC were eventually to move both firms into mass production.

MASS PRODUCTION: FIRST GENERATION

IBM easily entered the commercial market, mainly by replacing IBM punched card machine installations with IBM computers—all on lease. From 1953, rivalry was intense in the computer market. IBM dominated the industry. Remington Rand's alleged market share of computers fell from 100 percent in 1953 to 16 percent by 1957; IBM's share rose from zero to 78.5 percent (Brock 1975). This market reversal reestablished the precomputer era punched card and tabulating machine industry structure. Managerial problems at Remington Rand and IBM's successful change in leadership from Watson, Sr., to Watson, Jr., contributed to the reversal. Remington Rand failed to capitalize on its acquisition of ERA and EMCC and functioned as an uncoordinated holding company, with its Philadelphia group competing against the St. Paul organization and both in turn against a smaller Norwalk, Connecticut, machine lab. James Rand showed foresight in acquiring ERA and EMCC, but failed to merge these antagonistic divisions or to invest in product development. Rand found that the firm lacked the necessary capital for expansion and merged with Sperry in 1955. Even with new centralized management, problems persisted, and in 1957 Vice-President William C. Norris of the newly unified UNIVAC Division led a core of the most ambitious engineers and top managers out of UNIVAC to form Control Data Corporation (CDC). Many of this group, including

Seymour Cray and Norris, had been with ERA before Remington Rand's acquisition and were asserting their independence.

IBM did not suffer any important defections of talent. It successfully reorganized and reoriented itself for computer marketing and manufacturing, and began hiring engineers experienced in the new technologies. This successful transition was facilitated by the transfer of corporate power from Watson, Sr., to Watson, Jr., and by Watson, Jr.'s, settlement of a Justice Department antitrust lawsuit. IBM accepted the 1956 consent decree, which primarily concerned technologies of the precomputer era and unresolved issues from a 1932 antitrust suit. The consent decree required that IBM offer its equipment for sale as well as for rent and separate the service bureau from manufacturing sales. With no restriction on its entry into computer technology, IBM continued successfully to introduce machines for business and scientific processing, beginning in 1954 with the delivery of the IBM 650, a machine for data processing. The structure of the computer industry was ensured in 1952 when the computer contract for Project SAGE—a nationwide air defense interception system under development at MIT and its Lincoln Laboratories—was awarded to IBM. Lincoln Labs based its noncompetitive contract award on IBM's "purposefulness, integration and esprit de corps" (Pugh 1984). Although only forty-eight machines were built, the project earned IBM $500 million in revenue. More important, IBM learned valuable state-of-the-art techniques and trained an entire generation of engineers. Core memory developed during Project SAGE remained the main memory for the next decade, even while transistors pushed computing into the second generation.

During the same decade in which IBM overtook competitor Sperry Rand, other firms, some of them very large, made minor inroads into the computing field. After filling military contracts, General Electric (GE), Philco, NCR, Honeywell, and Radio Corporation of America (RCA) marketed commercial product lines, but failed to challenge seriously IBM's position. The growth of the less important competitors transformed the market from a duopoly of IBM and Sperry Rand into a market of small firms dominated by IBM. In describing market power within the industry, analysts characterized IBM and its competitors as Big Brother and the Seven Dwarfs (Fishman 1981).

MASS PRODUCTION: SECOND GENERATION

With the arrival of transistor-based second generation machines and the decline of vacuum tubes, computer reliability increased while electrical power and cooling requirements fell. The first push into the new and initially expensive transistor technology came from two Atomic Energy Commission (AEC) projects to develop advanced high-speed computers. In 1954 the AEC's Lawrence Livermore Laboratory at the University of California solicited bids from IBM and Sperry Rand to build a state-of-the-art computer. Sperry Rand was awarded the bid based on cost, design criteria, and an earlier delivery date. The LARC was produced according to specifications but was completed twenty-seven months late (Fisher, McKie, and Mancke 1983). IBM hunted for a buyer for its proposed computer and negotiated a contract with the AEC's Los Alamos Laboratory. Completed in 1961, twelve months behind schedule, the STRETCH failed to achieve its required performance gain of 100 times IBM's most powerful commercial machine, the 704 (Bashe et al. 1986). The contracting firms suffered heavy losses on both projects, but gained experience with manufacturing and designing transistor-based machines. By 1960 the transition between machine generations was complete, and IBM, Sperry Rand, NCR, Philco, CDC, Honeywell, and GE had transistorized products on the market.

The 1960s saw a substantial turnover in the composition of the industry, as new firms took up the competitive challenge and old rivals exited the market. IBM's dominance continued, and in 1964 the firm established a new operating standard for the industry by introducing a unified product line—System/360. Prior to the introduction of the 360 series, IBM offered a chaotic mix of incompatible machines that were difficult to upgrade and expand. Before System/360, machine development was incremental, and scientific and business machines followed separate lines of evolution. System/360 unified these machine types and allowed modular installation, letting customer requirements dictate machine organization and permitting easy expansion. Labeled by *Fortune* as "IBM's $5,000,000,000 Gamble," the new product line was extraordinarily successful and insured IBM's rapid expansion over the years 1964 to 1970 (Wise 1966a, 1966b).

The continuing success of IBM in the late 1960s was accompanied by the withdrawal of GE and RCA from the commercial computer market. GE, listed among the top six firms of the *Fortune* 500 and larger than IBM, devoted limited attention to the computer market and drew only 3.5 percent of its revenues from electronic data processing sources. It sold its computer operations to Honeywell in 1969 (Fisher, McKie, and Mancke 1983). RCA's computer division experienced moderate success through much of the 1960s, and in 1968 the division expanded under the direction of former IBM executives brought in to develop a new line of computers. The new strategy failed, and, facing current and predicted losses, RCA left the industry. In 1971 it sold its computer division to Sperry Rand. As GE and RCA retreated from the industry, Sperry Rand, Honeywell, NCR, Burroughs, and CDC, all with successful machine lines, enjoyed profits and rapid growth in the still expanding market.

Startup firms of the 1960s also prospered in their selected market niches. Scientific Data Systems started in 1961 with $80,000 capitalization and was acquired by Xerox Corporation in 1969 for $980 million worth of stock, an ill-advised move, because Xerox dropped out of the mainframe computer market in 1975. MIT researchers from Project SAGE left academic life to establish Digital Equipment Corporation (DEC) in 1957. DEC, with $70,000 in initial capital, was able to establish a broad base of minicomputer installations. By 1970 DEC ranked third behind IBM and Sperry Rand in number of machines installed and by 1984 was second to IBM in data processing revenues (Fisher, McKie, and Mancke 1983).

In summary, a long period of explosive growth culminated in the 1960s. U.S. electronic data processing revenue grew from $39.2 million in 1952, to $1.3 billion in 1960, to $6.4 billion in 1964, to $12.8 billion in 1972— a compound growth rate of 33.5 percent (Fisher, McKie, and Mancke 1983). That growth represented an expansion of computing demand by existing users and an increased number of users, as new applications were written and data processing technology permeated government and business operations. Small firms entered the service, leasing, maintenance, and peripheral manufacturing markets, and industry competition increased. IBM's commitment to a modular system in the architecture of its mainframe equipment allowed plug-compatible suppliers to expand their market.

While the 1960s were characterized by rapid growth and major technological breakthroughs, the next decade brought legal rivalry as industry firms filed lawsuits against each other for violations of trade secrets and patent infringements as well as antitrust violations. Moreover, IBM again found itself under federal antitrust prosecution.

THE COURTS AND THE COMPUTER INDUSTRY

The legal conflict between Honeywell and Sperry Rand involved basic and essential patents for the industry. At stake was the validity of the ENIAC patent, under which all computers manufactured would be subject to royalty payments. Eckert and Mauchly's patent on the ENIAC belonged to Sperry Rand following the purchase of EMCC and the patent's award to the firm in 1964. Following its award, Sperry Rand proceeded to collect royalties from industry firms and to file claims of infringement against those that refused to cooperate. Because IBM and Sperry Rand had cross-licensed their patents in 1956, IBM was protected against claims of patent infringement, but the smaller and uncooperative Honeywell became party to a 1967 lawsuit. A countersuit filed by Honeywell alleged that the ENIAC patent was invalid and that the IBM/Sperry Rand agreement was conspiracy under antitrust statutes. A 1973 decision judged the patent invalid, because the ENIAC was in public use a year before the patent was filed and because Mauchly had derived some of his ideas from an earlier, uncredited inventor. The 1956 cross-licensing agreement was held to be a conspiracy in constraint of trade, but IBM and Sperry Rand were protected by the statute of limitations and thus not subject to treble damages. The lawsuit did little to change industry structure, but rewrote some of the industry's history.

IBM's antitrust problems began when CDC, unable to interest the Justice Department in its grievances, filed an antitrust suit against IBM's marketing practices and sought treble damages. Following CDC's 1968 filing, Attorney General Ramsey Clark filed a similar suit in the waning hours of the Johnson administration. Discovery proceedings for the CDC suit lasted several years, and in January, 1973, before going to trial, CDC and IBM settled out of court. CDC acquired IBM's Service Bureau Corporation and cash payment for a total gain, net of legal expenses, of $75 million; IBM obtained the destruction of CDC's computerized index to IBM documents, which the Justice Department had planned to use in its proceedings.

Other lawsuits were filed by injured peripheral equipment manufacturers and leasing companies, but the outcomes of these were more favorable to IBM. In those cases in which IBM lost the initial trial, the verdict was overturned on appeal; otherwise IBM won outright or made a small out-of-court settlement. The Reagan administration's Justice Department dropped the antitrust suit against IBM in early 1982 when Assistant Attorney General William Baxter found the case to be "without merit" (DeLamarter 1986).

These legal proceedings in the 1970s occurred during a period of reduced rate of growth in mainframe placements, a change that reflected the growing importance of other segments of the computer industry. Expanding computer use during the 1970s created specialized markets for new suppliers of supercomputers, minicomputers, communication services, and software. Minicomputer producers accepted the entrepreneurial mantle of the industry and experienced the rapid advance previously associated with mainframe producers. Data General, a 1968 spin-off of DEC employees, began operation from its Massachusetts base producing minicomputers. Hewlett-Packard, a long-established instrument and electronics firm, entered the computer industry to provide complementary products for its measuring instruments and then branched out into computer construction. Former IBM engineer Gene Amdahl, who had worked on the Defense Calculator and System/360, began producing his own large-scale computer, as did Seymour Cray, CDC's most famous engineer. Both Amdahl and Cray were in direct competition with IBM and CDC in the high-speed scientific computer market. Wang Laboratories successfully marketed office automation equipment and established a market later invaded by IBM. The potential for industrial reorganization also appeared large when the Federal Communications Commission decided to allow AT&T to compete on an unregulated basis in all areas of electronic data processing (Fisher, McKie, and Mancke 1983).

THE 1980s

With the growth of office automation, minicomputers, and time-sharing systems, the organization of centralized IBM processing centers was undermined as users decentralized their computing activities. IBM responded by marketing a desktop computer in 1975 and then, as hobbyist machines began entering the market for home and office use, introduced the IBM Personal Computer (PC) in 1981. Apple Computer's successful market domination prior to IBM's 1981 entry shifted the geographical focus of computer design and manufacturing to the high technology firms of California's Silicon Valley (Freiberger and Swaine 1984; Moritz 1984). Once again, as users moved to a new technology, IBM's use of its existing market power enabled it to maintain its control (Levering, Katz, and Moskowitz 1984; McClellan 1984). The rise of software and hardware manufacturers has dominated the public view of the industry since then.

BIBLIOGRAPHIC ANALYSIS

Because electronic computing is a young industry, business and economic historians have not substantially contributed to its records. Most of the history has been written by the individuals and firms that have led the industry in the postwar period, a written record that has rapidly expanded since 1980. The dearth of works by business historians does not imply that corporate history is inaccessible; rather, many of the existing works have been written for nonhistorical purposes. As the industry's pioneers and founders approach retirement, there is a broad-based interest in preserving the industry's history—orally, in corporate and institutional archives, and through the preservation of artifacts. This work is augmented by a growing number of historians of science and technology who now address industry topics. Not surprisingly, almost all these works and collections refer to successful, surviving firms and products.

Existing works of interest to business historians include a few books by academic historians, biographies and memoirs, corporate and institutional histories, and a large volume of primary source material. Contemporary industry historical material is presented in commercial publications such as *Datamation, Computer World, Computers and Automation, Infoworld,* and the proceedings of several trade and professional organizations. Successful firms and promoters of computers are proud of their commercial accomplishments and sponsor "Pioneer Days" to commemorate various anniversaries, which are reported in the industry press.

The most important resource for business or technological history is the quarterly journal *Annals of the History of Computing.* Started in 1979 by the American Federation of Information Processing Societies (AFIPS), *Annals* publishes memoir-style articles by participants, reprints important historical documents, and reviews work published elsewhere. Although its emphasis on participant history may be changing, the journal is a better source of technological history interpreted by associated engineers than it is of institutional history. AFIPS also sponsored an oral history project, the transcripts of which are at the Smithsonian Institution in Washington, D.C. (Smithsonian Computer History Project 1969–73; Tropp 1980).

The Charles Babbage Institute (CBI) has published two guides to primary historical material for researchers. One, an annotated bibliography of software history, appeared in the fall 1987 issue of *Annals*, and includes citations of interest to business historians. The other is a guide to archival material for the history of computing at sites throughout the United States (Bruemmer 1987). The work is oriented toward the industry's technological development, but includes information on corporate archives as well as government and university sources.

In addition to the research guides produced by CBI, there is a series of useful books by James W. Cortada published by Greenwood Press. The first of these is *An Annotated Bibliography on the History of Data Processing* (1983). Another is an edited collection of descriptive essays by twelve archivists describing their institution's collections (forthcoming 1990). This guide to major collections covers far fewer collections than the CBI report, but offers a more detailed statement of what is available at each location. Cortada has completed a three-volume dictionary of the data processing industry covering people, organizations, and technology (1987a, 1987b, 1987c). These works provide a good starting place for any detailed investigation of the industry. Another bibliographic source for technological history is Brian Randell's "The Origins of Digital Computers: Supplementary Bibliography" (1980), which is less institutionally oriented than Cortada's.

Industry Overview

Several books written for public audiences provide a general introduction to the computer industry. *Bit by Bit: An Illustrated History of Computers* (1984) by Stan Augarten, a Silicon Valley journalist, is a well-illustrated survey of the technologies and individuals that have advanced the computer industry. A survey of the early technological history of computing and the main individuals involved is also provided in Jeremy Bernstein's *The Analytical Engine: Computers—Past, Present and Future* (1963). Bernstein's chapters, originally published in the *New Yorker* magazine, provide a broad overview of the philosophical and conceptual origins of the modern industry. In contrast to these broad-ranging accounts of technology and invention, Katharine Davis Fishman examines the computer establishment (1981), the firms, and their management.

Works for popular audiences should be read in company with a dry, scholarly tome, such as *IBM and the U.S. Data Processing Industry: An Economic History* (1983) by Franklin M. Fisher, James W. McKie, and Richard B. Mancke. This book, while a comprehensive study of the business and economic aspects of the industry's development, is difficult to evaluate.

It was prepared as a "historical exhibit" by IBM's legal/economic defense team during the 1969–81 IBM antitrust lawsuit. The book is based solely on trial evidence—depositions, exhibits, and testimony. As a scholarly reference it is disappointing. The citations cannot be independently accessed, and much historical work is ignored. It is, however, a solid piece of research that carefully outlines the industry's evolution around IBM, from IBM's perspective.

Two books oriented toward engineering and technological history provide an overview of the industry's development from an academic and scientific perspective. *The Computer from Pascal to von Neumann* (1972), by Herman H. Goldstine, combines historical investigation with a memoir. Goldstine outlines a scientific basis for computing and details the role of science in its evolution. To a large extent his work is a student and colleague's tribute to John von Neumann's conceptualization of computer design. A collection of essays, *A History of Computing in the Twentieth Century* (1980), edited by N. Metropolis, J. Howlett, and Gian-Carlo Roto, includes essays by inventors, producers, buyers, and users of computer equipment. These technical accounts exhibit the breadth of the computer industry's technological development.

Economic Studies

Economists have investigated the computer industry in dissertations, and in research for antitrust lawsuits and industrial organization studies. Several interesting dissertations are available through university interlibrary loan, including those by Angelico A. Gropelli (1970), Mohammed Khalil Hamid (1966), Kenneth E. Knight (1963), E. G. Shuster (1969), and John Wells (1978). Gerald W. Brock and John T. Soma have both published economic studies originating from their theses. Brock's work, *The U.S. Computer Industry: A Study of Market Power* (1975), documents the structure of industry concentration and advocates the breakup of IBM. Soma's (1976) work emphasizes the legal aspects of the industry and makes a technological forecast.

A large collection of industry data has been compiled by Montgomery Phister, Jr., for the mid–1960s to the early 1970s. The republished data collected by industry analysts are a good source of research materials (Phister 1979). Fisher and colleagues have, in addition to their economic history of the computer industry, published the economic analysis they prepared in IBM's antitrust defense (Fisher, McGowan, and Greenwood 1983).

These broad industry studies are not as interested in the forces of industry evolution as they are in the structure and performance of the industry—traditional fare for economists. Nancy S. Dorfman (1987) has explored the conditions under which small, new firms innovate and enter the computer industry. A small but growing body of literature specifically addresses the effect of government industrial policy on the development and growth of the computer industry. An essay, "The Computer Industry" (1982) by Barbara Goody Katz and Almarin Phillips, argues convincingly that the evolution of the computer industry is wholly tied up with the role of the government as regulator of industry and procurer of advanced products. This essay is one of several appearing in Richard Nelson's edited volume, *Government and Technical Progress: A Cross Industry Analysis* (1982), which helps place the computer industry's growth and history in a broader postwar perspective. A pair of recently published volumes by Kenneth Flamm expands on the work of Katz and Phillips. In *Creating the Computer: Government, Industry, and High Technology* (1988), Flamm carefully reviews the industry's historical origins, as well as the ways in which government policy affected industry growth. Flamm's historical volume is matched with *Targeting the Computer: Government Support and International Competition* (1987), which, though not institutional history, is a current assessment and international comparison of government promotion of technological projects in Japan and Europe.

Biography: People, Projects, and Firms

IBM

As the industry's dominant and most visible firm, a target of antitrust enforcement, and an often-praised example of successful management, IBM has been the subject of a large volume of research and writing. The firm's history and development prior to the mass production of computers are ably documented in Saul Engelbourg's 1954 dissertation, *International Business Machines: A Business History*, reprinted in 1976. This book provides a scholarly basis for any subsequent understanding of the success and dominance of IBM through the postwar period.

IBM has operated under the leadership of the father and son team of Thomas J. Watson, Sr., and Thomas J. Watson, Jr., so many of the histories are biographical as well as institutional. Watson, Sr., is the subject of an authorized biography, *The Lengthening Shadow: The Life of Thomas J. Watson* (1962), by Thomas Graham Belden and Marva Robins Belden, which uses company archives, personal papers, and interviews to provide a history of IBM until 1956. According to William Rodgers, the book was not well received by the firm or the Watsons, and IBM has since restricted access to its archives. The Beldens' book was followed by Rodgers's study of IBM's organization and history through 1969, *Think: A Biography of the Watsons and IBM* (1969).

A historian of many corporations, Robert Sobel has authored two books on IBM's history and prospects. The first, *IBM: The Colossus in Transition* (1981), reviews the firm's history through 1980. The second, *IBM vs. Japan:*

The Struggle for the Future (1986a), replicates much of his earlier book, but does cover the entry of personal computers and IBM's competition with Japan. These books are generally fair in their portrayal of the industry, but have been criticized for factual errors.[4] IBM's international operations have been addressed by Nancy Foy in *The Sun Never Sets on IBM* (1975), a valuable and unique book. Rex Malik, in *And Tomorrow the World?: Inside IBM* (1975), assaults IBM's power, image, and corporate culture from a European perspective. International operations are also examined industry-wide in economic works by Alvin J. Harmon (1971) and Wayne J. Lee (1971).

The sales policy that many of these authors disparage is clearly outlined in *A Business and Its Beliefs: The Ideas that Helped Build IBM* (1963) by IBM president Thomas J. Watson, Jr., and recently eulogized in *The IBM Way* (1986) by retired Vice-President F. G. "Buck" Rodgers. These books deal mainly with the attitudes, personalities, and crises in the firm and are less concerned with organizational and technological history.

The 1969 antitrust lawsuit and subsequent legal proceedings against IBM led to the two previously mentioned volumes coauthored by Fisher, which record IBM's history of marketing, sales efforts, and technological advance. These presentations made on the firm's behalf are counterbalanced by Richard Thomas DeLamarter's analysis of the antitrust issues and the firm's history in *Big Blue: IBM's Use and Abuse of Power* (1986). DeLamarter served as an economist for the Justice Department's legal team that brought the suit. He views IBM's actions as conspiratorial throughout the firm's history, a position contrary to Fisher's, but consistent with Malik's.

Recent books about IBM are devoted to technological history as articulated by project engineers. *Memories that Shaped an Industry: Decisions Leading to IBM System/360* (Pugh 1984) is a highly readable account of IBM's biggest gamble and most successful product line, System/360. A detailed and technical account of IBM's product line development from punched card days to System/360 is found in *IBM's Early Computers* (1986) by Charles J. Bashe, Lyle R. Johnson, John H. Palmer, and Emerson W. Pugh. These engineering accounts, plus articles in *Annals*, record the firm's technological history. As pointed out by Bashe et al., histories of IBM's manufacturing, field service, and marketing remain to be written.

Sperry Rand

The strand of computer history leading from ERA and EMCC through Remington Rand and ultimately to Sperry Rand has not been presented in a unified historical work. In fact, the emphasis to date has been on technological developments and projects seen through the eyes of engineers. Computer historian Nancy Stern, in *From ENIAC to UNIVAC: An Appraisal of the Eckert-Mauchly Computers* (1981), has explored the origins of the Eckert-Mauchly Computer Corporation from the World War II

ENIAC project through their acquisition by Remington Rand in 1950. Using interviews and archival documents collected for the *Honeywell v. Sperry Rand* lawsuit, Stern carefully outlines the interaction of the private and public sectors that led to UNIVAC production.

Numerous articles in the *Annals* by ENIAC and UNIVAC design participants discuss technological development. The absorption of EMCC into Remington Rand and then into Sperry is indirectly covered in Herman Lukoff's autobiography *From Dits to Bits: A Personal History of the Electronic Computer* (1979). As an engineering student working on the ENIAC and later as an engineering manager for Sperry Rand in charge of the LARC's manufacture, he was present at the transformation of the industry from academic and science-based enterprise into corporate manufacturing. Firm veteran Erwin Tomash has recorded the history of ERA in two articles (Tomash and Cohen 1979; Tomash 1980). Additional material may be found in books on William Norris, the founder of CDC.

RCA

A number of authors have examined the history of RCA and its longtime head, David Sarnoff. A recent biography, *The General: David Sarnoff and the Rise of the Communications Industry* (1986), published fifteen years after Sarnoff's death by close associate and friend Kenneth Bilby, is a well-written, detailed account of the firm's history of technological triumphs and disasters. Unfortunately, Bilby ignores the firm's computing activities and concentrates on its more important product lines. But he does use IBM as a benchmark for RCA's postwar growth and earnings—a strategy also used by Sobel in *RCA* (1986b).

Sobel, having previously studied IBM, devotes most of his effort to recording RCA's experience as a computer manufacturer. His narrative spans RCA's entry into computer production in the late 1950s, its efforts to achieve a 3 percent market share in the late 1960s, and the sale of its computer division to Sperry Rand in 1970.

The Minis

As the Watsons are the focus of IBM histories, so are the founders of minicomputer firms the subject of biographies. William Norris's broad-ranging career as a founder of ERA, vice-president at Remington Rand, and the founder of CDC is the basis of CDC's history. Because the firm's archives are closed to outside researchers, the only available history is a biography of Norris by CDC Board of Directors member James C. Worthy (1987). Using internal company documents and interviews, Worthy discusses the firm's origins and history of acquisitions, but concentrates on defending Norris's strategy of "addressing unmet societal needs as profitable business opportunities." A similar view of Norris and CDC emerges in a chapter in

Ralph Nader and William Taylor's *The Big Boys: Power and Position in American Business* (1986).

In an address to the Newcomen Society, Kenneth H. Olsen (1983), the founder of DEC, tells how the firm arose from an MIT research group and produced transistorized minicomputers. Although Olsen's address lacks detail, it is a well-crafted story of DEC's growth and business strategy. The "minicomputer wars" between DEC and smaller offspring Data General are treated in Tracy Kidder's *The Soul of a New Machine* (1981). Written for popular audiences as an adventure saga of innovation and invention, this book is of limited use to a business historian.

In another founder's autobiography, An Wang (*Lessons: An Autobiography* 1986) traces his personal and professional life from the Harvard Computational Laboratory, through patent licensing negotiations with IBM, to the manufacture of minicomputers and office automation equipment. Wang's history is the most complete of those on the smaller firms specializing in computer manufacturing.

West Coast Computing

The rise of computing in the aerospace industry on the West Coast is a neglected area in the technological and corporate history of the computer industry. Histories of computer development or manufacturing at Hughes Aircraft and its offspring TRW, Litton Industries, North American Aviation, and Northrop Aircraft have yet to be written. Two office machine manufacturers who entered the computer industry by acquiring computer spin-off firms of the aerospace industry are NCR and Burroughs. Although NCR's early history is extensively covered by corporate historian and executive Isaac F. Marcosson in *Wherever Men Trade: The Romance of the Cash Register* ([1945, 1948] 1972), NCR's computer division has not been investigated. Burroughs's experience in the computer industry is outlined in Chairman and CEO Ray W. MacDonald's 1978 address to the Newcomen Society, similar to that given by DEC's Olsen. A company publication, *Total to Date: The Evolution of the Adding Machine, the Story of Burroughs* (Morgan 1953), describes Burroughs's history as an adding machine manufacturer; Burroughs's transition from office equipment to military contracts is an interesting replay, albeit on a smaller scale, of IBM's experience. Burroughs's considerable technological expertise is documented in a special issue of *Annals* (Volume 9, Number 1, 1987) that is devoted to its B 5000 machine line.

Industrial giant GE entered the computer industry twice—in 1958 as the manufacturer of a statewide bank automation system for Bank of America and in 1963 with a commercial computer line. Although firm histories such as *A Century of Progress: The General Electric Story, 1876–1978* (1981) are available, none have documented the firm's computer manufacturing.

The same is true for Philco, which manufactured many military computers before its acquisition by Ford Motor Company in 1961.

Other Institutions

Government sponsorship of Project SAGE at MIT led to the establishment of two air force–sponsored nonprofit corporations and has been the subject of several histories as well. MIT's role in developing computer technology is one subject in faculty members Karl L. Wildes and Nilo A. Lindgren's (1985) 100–year appraisal of MIT's electrical engineering and computing department. SAGE's predecessor, Project Whirlwind, is investigated in Kent C. Redmond and Thomas M. Smith's *Project Whirlwind* (1980), a scholarly account of how computer technology arising from a World War II project to build a flight simulator ultimately evolved into Project SAGE at MIT's Lincoln Labs. The size and duration of Project SAGE led Lincoln Labs to spin off a nonprofit firm, MITRE, which has recorded its own story in *MITRE: The First Twenty Years. A History of the MITRE Corporation (1958–1978)* (1979).

More interesting is System Development Corporation's (SDC) transition from a sponsored, nonprofit spin-off of Rand Corporation to an independent profit-seeking firm. Rand Corporation, itself a nonprofit air force–sponsored organization, was contracted to do the system programming for Project SAGE. When Rand's System Research Lab grew from 6 employees to 1,000, the air force approved SDC's separation from Rand (Baum 1981). Following years of uncertain growth as a nonprofit firm, SDC became a commercial firm in 1969 and was acquired by Burroughs in 1981.

Government policy has played a significant role in the industry's technological advance through research and development grants and procurement contracts; therefore, agency and project histories are relevant to corporate history (Gilchrist and Wessel 1972). Although shrouded in secrecy, the National Security Agency and its military predecessors have long promoted important developments in technology, according to Samuel S. Snyder (1980). The Office of Naval Research (ONR) has also promoted development projects at many corporations and universities, for example, Project Whirlwind at MIT (Rees 1982, 1985).

The National Bureau of Standards (NBS) worked with the ONR and administered the Census Bureau, army, and air force contracts for the first three UNIVACs. The technological accomplishments of NBS have been documented in *Measures for Progress: A History of the National Bureau of Standards* (Cochrane 1966). The Census Bureau was the progenitor of IBM and Remington Rand, as each was built around patents from and leases at the bureau (Eckler 1972). In addition to fathering mechanized data processing and the largest firms in the office machine industry, the Census Bureau also spawned the use of computers for data processing by acquiring UNIVAC serial #1.

NOTES

The author is indebted to Robert Gallman and Kathleen Brown (University of North Carolina-Chapel Hill), Anne Mayhew and Walter C. Neale (University of Tennessee), Paul Ceruzzi (Smithsonian Institution), and Jim Cortada (IBM) for their comments, criticisms, and suggestions. The research for this chapter was carried out with the support of a Smithsonian Graduate Fellowship.

1. Remington Rand subsequently merged with the Sperry Corporation in 1955, and Sperry merged with Burroughs to form Unisys in 1986.

2. The question of ENIAC patent priority was the focus of the *Honeywell v. Sperry Rand* lawsuit and a monograph by Nancy Stern that chronicles the development of the ENIAC. The court ruled that John Atanasoff was the neglected inventor of some of the basic ideas from which the ENIAC patent claims were derived. For this essay, I have accepted Stern's assertion that Eckert and Mauchly developed the first practical electronic computer.

3. Shipments for 1952 and 1967 are for SIC code 3571 (Computing Machines and Cash Registers). In 1967, SIC 3571 was divided between SIC 3573 (Electronic Computers) and SIC 3574 (Calculating and Accounting Machines). In 1982 shipments for SIC 3573 were $36.7 billion and for SIC 3574, $1.48 billion.

4. See the review in *Annals 9*, no. 1 (1987).

BIBLIOGRAPHY

American Federation of Information Processing Societies. *Annals of the History of Computing*, 1979–88.

Augarten, Stan. *Bit by Bit: An Illustrated History of Computers*. New York: Ticknor & Fields, 1984.

Austrian, Geoffrey. *Herman Hollerith: Forgotten Giant of Information Processing*. New York: Columbia University Press, 1982.

Bashe, Charles J., Lyle R. Johnson, John H. Palmer, and Emerson W. Pugh. *IBM's Early Computers*. Cambridge, MA: MIT Press, 1986.

Baum, Claude. *The System Builders: The Story of SDC*. Santa Monica, CA: System Development Corporation, 1981.

Belden, Thomas Graham, and Marva Robins Belden. *The Lengthening Shadow: The Life of Thomas J. Watson*. Boston: Little, Brown, 1962.

Beniger, James R. *The Control Revolution: Technological and Economic Origins of the Information Society*. Cambridge, MA: Harvard University Press, 1986.

Bernstein, Jeremy. *The Analytical Engine: Computers—Past, Present and Future*. New York: Random House, 1963.

Bilby, Kenneth. *The General: David Sarnoff and the Rise of the Communications Industry*. New York: Harper & Row, 1986.

Braun, Ernest, and Stuart MacDonald. *Revolution in Miniature: The History and Impact of Semiconductor Electronics*. 2d ed. London: Cambridge University Press, 1982.

Brock, Gerald W. *The U.S. Computer Industry: A Study of Market Power*. Cambridge, MA: Ballinger, 1975.

Bruemmer, Bruce H. *Resources for the History of Computing*. Minneapolis: University of Minnesota, Charles Babbage Institute, Center for the History of Information Processing, 1987.

Ceruzzi, Paul. "The First Generation of Computers and the Aerospace Industry." In *National Air and Space Museum Research Report 1985*, 75–89. Washington, DC: Smithsonian Institution Press, 1985.

Chow, Gregory C. "Technological Change and the Demand for Computers." *American Economic Review* 57 (December 1967): 1117–30.

Cochrane, Rexmond. *Measures for Progress: A History of the National Bureau of Standards*. Washington, DC: National Bureau of Standards, 1966.

Cortada, James. *An Annotated Bibliography on the History of Data Processing*. Westport, CT: Greenwood Press, 1983.

———. *Historical Dictionary of Data Processing: Biographies*. Westport, CT: Greenwood Press, 1987a.

———. *Historical Dictionary of Data Processing: Organizations*. Westport, CT: Greenwood Press, 1987b.

———. *Historical Dictionary of Data Processing: Technology*. Westport, CT: Greenwood Press, 1987c.

———. *Archives of Data-Processing History: A Guide to Major U.S. Collections*. Westport, CT: Greenwood Press, forthcoming (1990).

DeLamarter, Richard Thomas. *Big Blue: IBM's Use and Abuse of Power*. New York: Dodd, Mead, 1986.

Dorfman, Nancy S. *Innovation and Market Structure: Lessons from the Computer and Semiconductor Industries*. Cambridge, MA: Ballinger, 1987.

Eckler, A. Ross. *The Bureau of the Census*. Praeger Library of U.S. Government Departments and Agencies. New York: Praeger, 1972.

Engelbourg, Saul. *International Business Machines: A Business History*. Ph.D. diss., Columbia University, 1954. Reprint. New York: Arno Press, 1976.

Fisher, Franklin M., John J. McGowan, and Joen E. Greenwood. *Folded, Spindled, and Mutilated: Economic Analysis and U.S. v. IBM*. Cambridge, MA: MIT Press, 1983.

Fisher, Franklin M., James W. McKie, and Richard B. Mancke. *IBM and the U.S. Data Processing Industry: An Economic History*. New York: Praeger, 1983.

Fishman, Katharine Davis. *The Computer Establishment*. New York: Harper & Row, 1981.

Flamm, Kenneth. *Targeting the Computer: Government Support and International Competition*. Washington, DC: Brookings Institution, 1987.

———. *Creating the Computer: Government, Industry, and High Technology*. Washington, DC: Brookings Institution, 1988.

Foy, Nancy. *The Sun Never Sets on IBM*. New York: William Morrow, 1975.

Freiberger, Paul, and Michael Swaine. *Fire in the Valley: The Making of the Personal Computer*. Berkeley, CA: Osborne/McGraw-Hill, 1984.

General Electric. *A Century of Progress: The General Electric Story, 1876–1978*. Schenectady, NY: Hall of History, 1981.

Gilchrist, Bruce, and Milton R. Wessel. *Government Regulation of the Computer Industry*. Montvale, NJ: Association for Information Processing Societies, February 1972.

Goldstine, Herman H. *The Computer from Pascal to von Neumann*. Princeton, NJ: Princeton University Press, 1972.

Gropelli, Angelico A. "The Growth Process in the Computer Industry." Ph.D. diss., New York University, June 1970.

Hamid, Mohammed Kahlil. "Price and Output Decisions in the Computer Industry." Ph.D. diss., University of Iowa, February 1966.

Harmon, Alvin J. *The International Computer Industry: Innovation and Comparative Advantage.* Cambridge, MA: Harvard University Press, 1971.

Katz, Barbara Goody, and Almarin Phillips. "The Computer Industry." In *Government and Technical Progress*, edited by R. Nelson, 162–232. New York: Pergamon Press, 1982.

Kidder, Tracy. *The Soul of a New Machine.* Boston: Little, Brown, 1981.

Knight, Kenneth E. "A Study of Technological Innovation: The Evolution of Digital Computers." Ph.D. diss., Carnegie Institute of Technology, November 1963.

Lee, Wayne J., ed. *The International Computer Industry.* Washington, DC: Applied Resources, 1971.

Levering, Robert, Michael Katz, and Milton Moskowitz. *The Computer Entrepreneurs: Who's Making It Big and How in America's Upstart Industry.* New York: New American Library, 1984.

Lukoff, Herman. *From Dits to Bits: A Personal History of the Electronic Computer.* Portland, OR: Robotics Press, 1979.

Lundstrom, David E. *A Few Good Men from UNIVAC.* Cambridge, MA: MIT Press, 1987.

McClellan, Stephen T. *The Coming Computer Industry Shakeout: Winners, Losers, and Survivors.* New York: John Wiley & Sons, 1984.

MacDonald, Ray W. *Strategy for Growth: The Story of Burroughs Corporation.* New York: Newcomen Society in North America, 1978.

Malik, Rex. *And Tomorrow the World?: Inside IBM.* London: Millington, 1975.

Malone, Michael S. *The Big Score: The Billion-Dollar Story of Silicon Valley.* Garden City, NY: Doubleday, 1985.

Marcosson, Isaac F. *Wherever Men Trade: The Romance of the Cash Register.* 1945, 1948. Reprint. New York: Arno Press, 1972.

Metropolis, N., J. Howlett, and Gian-Carlo Roto, eds. *A History of Computing in the Twentieth Century.* New York: Academic Press, 1980.

MITRE Corporation. *MITRE: The First Twenty Years. A History of the MITRE Corporation (1958–1978).* Bedford, MA: MITRE, 1979.

Moreau, Rene. *The Computer Comes of Age: The People, the Hardware, and the Software.* Translated by J. Howlett. Cambridge, MA: MIT Press, 1984.

Morgan, Bryan. *Total to Date: The Evolution of the Adding Machine, the Story of Burroughs.* London: Burroughs Adding Machine, 1953.

Moritz, Michael. *The Little Kingdom: The Private Story of Apple Computer.* New York: William Morrow, 1984.

Nader, Ralph, and William Taylor. *The Big Boys: Power and Position in American Business.* New York: Pantheon Books, 1986.

Nelson, Richard. *Government and Technical Progress: A Cross Industry Analysis.* New York: Pergamon Press, 1982.

Norris, William C. *New Frontiers for Business Leadership.* Minneapolis: Dorn Books, 1983.

Olsen, Kenneth H. *Digital Equipment Corporation: The First Twenty-five Years.* New York: Newcomen Society in North America, 1983.

Phister, Montgomery, Jr. *Data Processing Technology and Economics*. 2d ed. Bedford, MA: Digital Press, 1979.

———. "Computer Industry." In *Encyclopedia of Computer Science and Engineering—Second Edition*, edited by Anthony Ralston and Edwin D. Reilly, Jr., 333–50. New York: Van Nostrand Reinhold, 1983.

Porat, Marc Uri. *The Information Economy: Definition and Measurement*. Washington, DC: U.S. Department of Commerce, Office of Telecommunications, 1977.

Pugh, Emerson W. *Memories that Shaped an Industry: Decisions Leading to IBM System/360*. Cambridge, MA: MIT Press, 1984.

Randell, Brian. "The Origins of Digital Computers: Supplementary Bibliography." In *A History of Computing in the Twentieth Century*, edited by N. Metropolis, J. Howlett, and Gian-Carlo Roto, 629–53. New York: Academic Press, 1980.

———, ed. *The Origins of Digital Computers: Selected Papers*. 3d ed. New York: Springer-Verlag, 1982.

Redmond, Kent C., and Thomas M. Smith. *Project Whirlwind: The History of a Pioneer Computer*. Bedford, MA: Digital Press, 1980.

Rees, Mina. "The Computing Program of the Office of Naval Research, 1946–1953." *Annals of the History of Computing* 4 (April 1982): 102–20.

———. "The Federal Computing Program." *Annals of the History of Computing* 7 (April 1985): 156–63.

Rodgers, F. G. "Buck," with Robert L. Shook. *The IBM Way*. New York: Harper & Row, 1986.

Rodgers, William. *Think: A Biography of the Watsons and IBM*. New York: Stein & Day, 1969.

Rogers, Everett M., and Judith K. Larsen. *Silicon Valley Fever: Growth of High-Technology Culture*. New York: Basic Books, 1984.

Sharpe, William F. *The Economics of Computers*. New York: Columbia University Press, 1969.

Shuster, E. G. "Selective Demand Determinants in the Computer Acquisition Process." Ph.D. diss., American University, May 1969.

Smithsonian Computer History Project [transcripts of interviews]. Collection 196. Archives Center. National Museum of American History. Smithsonian Institution. Washington, DC, 1969–73.

Snyder, Samuel S. "Computer Advances Pioneered by Cryptologic Organizations." *Annals of the History of Computing* 2 (January 1980): 60–70.

Sobel, Robert. *IBM: The Colossus in Transition*. New York: Times Books, 1981.

———. Review of *Folded, Spindled, and Mutilated: Economic Analysis and U.S. v. IBM*, by Fisher et al. *Business History Review* 58 (Summer 1984): 287–89.

———. *IBM vs. Japan: The Struggle for the Future*. New York: Stein & Day, 1986a.

———. *RCA*. New York: Stein & Day, 1986b.

Soma, John T. *The Computer Industry: An Economic-Legal Analysis of Its Technology and Growth*. Lexington, MA: Lexington Books, 1976.

Stern, Nancy. *From ENIAC to UNIVAC: An Appraisal of the Eckert-Mauchly Computers*. Bedford, MA: Digital Press, 1981.

Tomash, Erwin. "The Start of an ERA: Engineering Research Associates, Inc., 1946–

1955." In *A History of Computing in the Twentieth Century*, edited by N. Metropolis, J. Howlett, and Gian-Carlo Roto, 485–95. New York: Academic Press, 1980.

Tomash, Erwin, and Arnold A. Cohen. "The Birth of an ERA: Engineering Research Associates, Inc., 1946–1955." *Annals of the History of Computing* 1 (October 1979): 83–97.

Tropp, Henry S. "The Smithsonian Computer History Project and Some Personal Recollections." In *A History of Computing in the Twentieth Century*, edited by N. Metropolis, J. Howlett, and Gian-Carlo Roto, 115–22. New York: Academic Press, 1980.

U.S. Bureau of the Census. *Census of Manufactures*. Washington, DC: U.S. Government Printing Office, 1905– .

Wang, An, with Eugene Linden. *Lessons: An Autobiography*. Reading, MA: Addison-Wesley, 1986.

Watson, Thomas J., Jr. *A Business and Its Beliefs: The Ideas that Helped Build IBM*. New York: McGraw-Hill, 1963.

Wells, John. "The Origins of the Computer Industry: A Case Study in Radical Technological Change." Ph.D. diss., Yale University, 1978.

Wildes, Karl L., and Nilo A. Lindgren. *A Century of Electrical Engineering and Computer Science at MIT, 1882–1982*. Cambridge, MA: MIT Press, 1985.

Wise, T. A. "I.B.M.'s $5,000,000,000 Gamble." *Fortune* (September 1966a): 118.

———. "The Rocky Road to the Marketplace." *Fortune* (October 1966b): 138.

Worthy, James C. *William C. Norris: Portrait of a Maverick*. Cambridge, MA: Ballinger, 1987.

Wulforst, Harry. *Breakthrough to the Computer Age*. New York: Scribner's, 1982.

Part X

Electrical Equipment
ESIC 36.0

HOUSEHOLD APPLIANCES, 36.3

_____ SUSAN B. CARTER

This category includes household cooking equipment; refrigerators and home and farm freezers; household laundry equipment; small electric housewares, such as electric blankets, toasters, waffle irons, and fans; household vacuum cleaners; sewing machines; and miscellaneous appliances, such as dishwashing machines, floor waxers, garbage disposal units, trash compactors, and water heaters. The development and diffusion of these devices awaited the establishment of electrical generation plants and the electrification of households (Beard 1927; T. Martin and Coles 1922; MacLaren 1943; Passer 1953; Sharlin 1963; Rose and Clark 1979; Hughes 1979, 1983). However, hand- and foot-driven sewing machines, washers, vacuum cleaners, and cooking equipment were the precursors of the electric models. Sigfried Giedion (1948) uses patent records and *Scientific American* articles to survey the mechanization of cooking, home laundering, ironing, dishwashing, garbage disposing, cleaning, and refrigeration from classical times to the 1940s. Victor S. Clark (1929) and Earl Lifshey (1973) provide additional evidence. Elizabeth Mickle Bacon (1942), Edgar W. Martin (1942), Heidi I. Hartmann (1974), Susan Strasser (1977, 1982), and Ruth Schwartz Cowan (1976a, 1976b, 1983) examine the effect of these devices on the organization of housework in the nineteenth century.

Histories of several industries have been written for the nineteenth century. The manufacture of sewing machines is described by Frederick G. Bourne (1895), Grace Rogers Cooper (1976), and David A. Hounshell (1984). Bacon (1946), Robert Bruce Davies (1976), and Alfred D. Chandler, Jr. (1977), discuss the marketing strategy that was critical to Singer's dominance. The development of refrigeration in the nineteenth century is recounted by Oscar Edward Anderson, Jr. (1953).

For the twentieth century, the most detailed discussions of household appliances are contained in analyses of women's work in the home (Hartmann 1974; Oakley 1974; Strasser 1977, 1982; Cowan 1976a, 1976b, 1983). These studies develop evidence on the availability of various appliances using popular magazines, such as the *Ladies Home Journal* (Cowan 1983), and trade journals, such as *Air Conditioning and Refrigeration News*, *American Gas Journal*, *Electrical Merchandising Week*, *Gas Age*, *Hardware Age*, *Ice and Refrigeration*, *Merchant Plumber and Fitter*, and *Sewing Machine Advance*. Hartmann, Strasser, and Cowan also make imaginative use of the *Journal of Home Economics* and of home economics texts, such as Allen (1922) and the various editions of Peet and Thyre.

Sketches of consumption patterns provide some insight into the diffusion of household appliances (Lynd and Lynd 1929; E. W. Martin 1942; Handlin 1979). Data on consumer expenditures, sometimes including household appliances, were collected by a number of state agencies beginning in the 1870s. Jeffrey G. Williamson (1967), Martha May (1984), and Clair Brown (1987) survey these sources and assess their usefulness. The U.S. Bureau of the Census (1975) lists some of these sources, together with data collected by other agencies. Raymond S. Goldsmith (1955) provides estimates of consumer spending disaggregated into ten categories (one of which is household appliances) for the years 1930 to 1950. Martha L. Olney (1985) extends the series back to 1900.

Home economics in the 1920s and 1930s predicted enormous savings in time and gains in efficiency from the use of electrical appliances (Whitton 1927; Gilbreth 1930; Reid 1934; Bent 1938). Theoretical work on labor force participation suggests that the greater availability and lower price of household appliances may have been responsible for the enormous increase in the number of married women that worked outside the home in the post–World War II era (Becker 1965; Bowen and Finegan 1969). More recent analyses argue that although appliances may have lightened the requirements for individual tasks, standards rose, suburbanization created new tasks, and certain essential tasks did not lend themselves to mechanization; so the overall time requirements of housework were not noticeably reduced (Brown 1985; Bose, Bereano, and Malloy 1984; Cowan 1976a, 1976b, 1983; Hayden 1981, 1984; Hartmann 1974; Oakley 1974; Strasser 1977, 1982; Thrall 1982). Myra H. Strober (1977) finds purchase of household appliances unrelated to the wife's labor force status when family income is held constant.

Advertising and the availability of consumer credit were critical to the commercial success of household appliance manufacturers. These products therefore receive attention in general discussions of the growth of advertising and shifts in consumer behavior over time (Marchand 1985; Ewen 1976; Horowitz 1985; Brown 1987). The effect of consumer credit on purchases of household appliances and other consumer durables is analyzed in Harberger (1960); Hardy (1938); Hendricks, Youmans, and Keller (1973); Houthaker and Taylor (1966); Juster (1966); Lippitt (1959); Michelman (1966); Olney (1985); and Vatter (1967).

BIBLIOGRAPHY

Air Conditioning and Refrigeration News. Detroit, 1926–58.

Allen, Edith. *Mechanical Devices in the Home.* Peoria, IL: Manual Arts Press, 1922.

American Gas Journal. East Stroudsburg, PA, 1859– .

Anderson, Oscar Edward, Jr. *Refrigeration in America: A History of a New Technology and Its Impact.* Princeton: Princeton University Press, 1953.

Bacon, Elizabeth Mickle. "The Growth of Household Conveniences in the United States from 1865 to 1900." Ph.D. diss., Radcliffe College, 1942.

———. "Marketing Sewing Machines in the Post–Civil War Years." *Bulletin of the Business History Society* 20 (1946): 90–94.

Beard, Belle Boone. *Electricity in the Home.* New York: Workers Education Bureau Press, 1927.

Becker, Gary. "A Theory of the Allocation of Time." *Economic Journal* 75 (September 1965): 493–517.

Bent, Silas. *Slaves by the Billion: The Story of Mechanical Progress in the Home.* New York: Longmans, Green, 1938.

Bose, Christine E., Philip L. Bereano, and Mary Malloy. "Household Technology and the Social Construction of Housework." *Technology and Culture* 25 (1984): 53–82.

Bourne, Frederick G. "American Sewing-Machines." In *One Hundred Years of American Commerce,* edited by Chauncey M. Depew, vol. 2, 524–39. New York: D. O. Haines, 1895.

Bowen, William, and T. Aldrich Finegan. *The Economics of Labor Force Participation.* Princeton: Princeton University Press, 1969.

Brown, Clair. "An Institutional Model of Wives' Work Decisions." *Industrial Relations* 24 (Spring 1985): 182–204.

———. "Consumption Norms, Work Roles, and Economic Growth, 1918–80." In *Gender in the Workplace,* edited by Clair Brown and Joseph Pechman, 13–48. Washington, DC: Brookings Institution, 1987.

Chandler, Alfred D., Jr. *The Visible Hand: The Managerial Revolution in American Business.* Cambridge, MA: Harvard University Press, 1977.

Clark, Victor S. *History of Manufactures in the United States.* 3 vols. New York: McGraw-Hill, 1929.

Cooper, Grace Rogers. *The Sewing Machine: Its Invention and Development.* Washington, DC: Smithsonian Institution Press, 1976.

Cowan, Ruth Schwartz. "The 'Industrial Revolution' in the Home: Household Technology and Social Change in the Twentieth Century." *Technology and Culture* 17 (January 1976a): 1–23.

———. "Two Washes in the Morning and a Bridge Party at Night: The American Housewife Between the Wars." *Women's Studies* 3 (1976b): 147–71.

———. *More Work for Mother: The Ironies of Household Technology from the Open Hearth to the Microwave.* New York: Basic Books, 1983.

Davies, Robert Bruce. *Peacefully Working to Conquer the World: Singer Sewing Machines in Foreign Markets, 1854–1920*. New York: Arno Press, 1976.

Ehrenreich, Barbara, and Deirdre English. *For Her Own Good: 150 Years of the Experts' Advice to Women*. New York: Doubleday, 1978.

Electrical Merchandising Week. Newark, NJ, 1907– .

Ewen, Stuart. *Captains of Consciousness: Advertising and the Social Roots of the Consumer Culture*. New York: McGraw-Hill, 1976.

Gas Age. Philadelphia, 1888– .

Giedion, Sigfried. *Mechanization Takes Command: A Contribution to Anonymous History*. New York: W. W. Norton, 1948.

Gilbreth, Lillian M. *The Homemaker and Her Job*. New York: D. Appleton, 1930.

Goldsmith, Raymond S. *A Study of Saving in the United States*. 3 vols. Princeton: Princeton University Press, 1955.

Handlin, David. *The American Home: Architecture and Society, 1815–1915*. Boston: Little, Brown, 1979.

Harberger, Arnold C., ed. *The Demand for Durable Goods*. Chicago: University of Chicago Press, 1960.

Hardware Age. New York, 1913– .

Hardy, Charles O., ed. *Consumer Credit and Its Uses*. New York: Prentice-Hall, 1938.

Hartmann, Heidi I. "Capitalism and Women's Work in the Home, 1900–1930." Ph.D. diss., Yale University, 1974.

Hayden, Dolores. *The Grand Domestic Revolution*. Cambridge, MA: MIT Press, 1981.

——. *Redesigning the American Dream*. New York: W. W. Norton, 1984.

Hendricks, Gary, Kenwood C. Youmans, and Janet Keller. *Consumer Durables and Installment Debt: A Study of American Households*. Ann Arbor, MI: Institute for Social Research, University of Michigan, 1973.

Horowitz, Daniel. *The Morality of Spending: Attitudes Toward the Consumer Society in America, 1875–1940*. Baltimore: Johns Hopkins University Press, 1985.

Hounshell, David A. *From the American System to Mass Production 1800–1932: The Development of Manufacturing Technology in the United States*. Baltimore: Johns Hopkins University Press, 1984.

Houthaker, H. S., and Lester D. Taylor. *Consumer Demand in the United States, 1929–1970*. Cambridge, MA: Harvard University Press, 1966.

Hughes, Thomas P. "The Electrification of America: The System Builders." *Technology and Culture* 20 (January 1979): 124–61.

——. *Networks of Power: Electrification in Western Society, 1880–1930*. Baltimore: Johns Hopkins University Press, 1983.

Ice and Refrigeration. Chicago, 1891– .

Journal of Home Economics. Baltimore, 1909– .

Juster, F. Thomas. *Household Capital Formation and Financing: 1897–1962*. New York: National Bureau of Economic Research, 1966.

Ladies Home Journal. Philadelphia, 1883– .

Lifshey, Earl. *The Housewares Story: A History of the American Housewares Industry*. Chicago: National Housewares Manufacturers Association, 1973.

Lippitt, Vernon G. *Determinants of Consumer Demand for House Furnishings and Equipment.* Cambridge, MA: Harvard University Press, 1959.

Lynd, Robert S., and Helen Merrell Lynd. *Middletown: A Study in Modern American Culture.* New York: Harcourt, Brace & World, 1929.

MacLaren, Malcolm. *The Rise of the Electrical Industry During the Nineteenth Century.* Princeton: Princeton University Press, 1943.

Marchand, Roland. *Advertising the American Dream: Making Way for Modernity, 1920–1940.* Berkeley: University of California Press, 1985.

Martin, Edgar W. *American Consumption Levels on the Eve of the Civil War.* Chicago: University of Chicago Press, 1942.

Martin, Thomas C., and Stephen L. Coles, eds. *The Story of Electricity.* New York: M. M. Marcy, 1922.

May, Martha. "The 'Good Managers': Married Working Class Women and Family Budget Studies, 1895–1915." *Labor History* 25 (Summer 1984): 351–72.

Merchant Plumber and Fitter. New York, 1911– .

Michelman, Irving S. *Consumer Finance: A Case History in American Business.* New York: Frederick Fell, 1966.

Noble, David M. *America by Design: Science, Technology, and the Rise of Corporate Capitalism.* New York: Oxford University Press, 1977.

Oakley, Ann. *Women's Work: The Housewife, Past and Present.* New York: Pantheon Books, 1974.

Olney, Martha L. "Advertising, Consumer Credit, and the 'Consumer Durables Revolution' of the 1920s." Ph.D. diss., University of California, Berkeley, 1985.

Passer, Harold C. *The Electrical Manufacturers, 1875–1900.* Cambridge, MA: Harvard University Press, 1953.

Peet, Louise J., and Lenore Sater Thyre. *Household Equipment.* New York: John Wiley & Sons, 1934, 1940, 1949, 1955.

Reid, Margaret G. *Economics of Household Production.* New York: John Wiley & Sons, 1934.

Rose, Mark H., and John Clark. "Light, Heat, and Power: Energy Choices in Kansas City, Wichita, and Denver, 1900–1935." *Journal of Urban History* 5 (May 1979): 340–64.

Scientific American. New York, 1845– .

Scott, John. *Genius Rewarded; or The Story of the Sewing Machine.* New York: John J. Caulon, 1880.

Sewing Machine Advance. Chicago, 1879– .

Sharlin, Harold. *The Making of the Electrical Age.* New York: Abelard-Schuman, 1963.

Snyder, Edna B. *A Study of Washing Machines.* Research Bulletin No. 56. Lincoln: Nebraska Agricultural Experiment Station, 1931.

Strasser, Susan. "Never Done: The Ideology and Technology of Household Work, 1850–1930." Ph.D. diss., State University of New York, Stony Brook, 1977.

———. *Never Done: A History of American Housework.* New York: Pantheon Books, 1982.

Strober, Myra H. "Wives' Labor Force Behavior and Family Consumption Patterns." *American Economic Review* 67 (February 1977): 410–17.

Thrall, Charles A. "The Conservative Use of Household Technology." *Technology and Culture* 23 (1982): 175–94.

U.S. Bureau of the Census. *Historical Statistics of the United States, Colonial Times to 1970.* Bicentennial Edition. Washington, DC: U.S. Government Printing Office, 1975.

Vatter, Harold G. "Has There Been a Twentieth-Century Consumer Durables Revolution?" *Journal of Economic History* 27 (March 1967): 1–16.

Whitton, Mary Ormsbee. *The New Servant: Electricity in the Home.* Garden City, NY: Doubleday, Page, 1927.

Williamson, Jeffrey G. "Consumer Behavior in the Nineteenth Century: Carroll D. Wright's Massachusetts Workers in 1875." *Explorations in Entrepreneurial History,* 2d ser., 4 (Winter 1967): 98–135.

CHAPTER 16

ELECTRIC LIGHTING AND WIRING EQUIPMENT, 36.4

WILLIAM J. HAUSMAN

Electric lighting and wiring equipment is a somewhat peculiar industry. Its foundation is the electric light bulb, a product barely 100 years old but so common and important to everyday life that it would be difficult to imagine living without it. The industry includes the often mundane but sometimes elegant, even artistic, lighting fixture. In addition, there are such prosaic products as bus bars, electrical conduits, wall plugs, insulators, and junction boxes—necessary items for enjoying the convenience of lighting, but about which only aficionados are likely to get excited. It may likewise be difficult to generate excitement about the companies that produce these products. The industry is comprised of a large number of rather anonymous companies about which we have little information. The firms responsible for most of the initial developments in the industry are no longer part of the same SIC code, and the histories of most of the remaining firms have yet to be written. Still, the industry has had an important social and economic impact and is worthy of more consideration than it has received.

EVOLUTION OF SIC CODE AND GROWTH OF THE INDUSTRY

For a historian interested in tracing the quantitative importance of the electric lighting and wiring equipment industry, data in the various issues of the *Census of Manufactures* are invaluable. Tracing is complicated, however, by the periodic revisions that have been made in the SIC code. It will be helpful to track these changes, beginning with the present and moving backwards. The current four-digit classifications for this industry date from 1972, the year of the last major change in the SIC system. Evaluating the

Table 1
Evolution of SIC Code

1982 1977 1972	3641	3643	3644	3645	3646	3647	3648
1967 1963 1958	3641	3643	3644		3642		
1954 1947	3651	3611 3661(part)			3571 3693(part)		
1939	(1650)→	(1611)→			(1580)→		

Source: U.S. Bureau of the Census, <u>Census of Manufactures</u>, issues indicated in first column.

growth of the industry at the four-digit level over the past fifteen years is thus relatively simple. In 1972 the code number 3642 (lighting fixtures) was eliminated, and the establishments under it were broken into four new categories: 3645 (residential electric lighting fixtures), 3646 (commercial, industrial, and institutional electric lighting fixtures), 3647 (vehicular lighting equipment), and 3648 (lighting equipment, not elsewhere classified). No changes were made in 1967 and only a minor change was made in 1963: electronic connectors were moved out of 3643 and into 3679. Major adjustments to the system were made in 1958. The most confusing changes took establishments formerly classified in 3651 (electric lamps) and moved them to 3641. Establishments already in 3641 (engine electrical equipment) were shifted into code 3694. In addition, establishments formerly found in 3471 (lighting fixtures), plus ultraviolet and infrared lamps (a small part of 3693), were moved into 3642; part of 3611 (wiring devices and supplies) and a few establishments from 3661 (radios and related products) were merged to form 3643 (current-carrying wiring devices); finally, the remaining establishments of 3611 were moved into 3644 (noncurrent-carrying wiring devices). Thus the unified three-digit industry (36.4) dates from 1958. No changes were made in 1954. The 1947 *Census of Manufactures* was the first to use the formal SIC code. Electric lamps (industry 1650 under the pre-SIC system) became 3651, wiring devices and supplies (1611) became 3611, and lighting fixtures (1580) became 3471. Taking account of the above changes, I have traced the electric lighting and wiring equipment industry to the 1939 *Census of Manufactures*. Table 1 contains a summary of these changes.

Prior to establishment of the SIC code, firms were listed under industry

Table 2
Electric Lamps (3641)*

	Value of Shipments (mil$)	Number of Establishments	Number of Employees (000s)
1985	$2,702	-	-
1982	2,037	149	22.4
1977	1,651	167	28.7
1972	1,096	143	31.5
1967	782	106	29.5
1963	574	81	23.4
1958	417	66	21.5
1954	331	66	22.0
1947	203	62	23.8
1937	83	41	-
1933	50	-	-
1929	85	-	-
1919	61	-	8.0
1909	16	-	-
1900	4	-	-

* This category does not include arc lights, which would have been relatively more important in the early years of the industry and are now listed under 3648.

Sources: U.S. Bureau of the Census, Annual Survey of Manufactures, 1985 and U.S. Bureau of the Census, Census of Manufactures, various issues.

groups. A substantial part of the electric lighting and wiring equipment industry can be found in the various issues of the *Census of Manufactures* under "Electrical Machinery, Apparatus, and Supplies," and parts can be found under "Lamps and Reflectors" (which in the early days included gas and kerosene lamps), "Auto Lamps," and "Lighting Fixtures." Despite the difficulty of precisely integrating this earlier information into the current classifications, I have attempted to trace several dimensions of the industry back to the beginning of the twentieth century for historical perspective on its quantitative evolution.

Tables 2 through 4 present figures for value of shipments, number of establishments, and number of employees for the major industry subsectors. The growth of the industry is evident from these tables. Total shipments increased from approximately $74 million in 1909 (0.36 percent of total manufacturing shipments) to over $15 billion in 1985 (0.67 percent of total manufacturing shipments, representing an 86 percent increase in the industry's share of total manufacturing shipments). The impact of the Great Depression of the 1930s is visible in these figures: the value of shipments fell by roughly 60 percent between 1929 and 1933, and employment in the lighting fixture business declined similarly. Employment in the industry

Table 3
Lighting Fixtures (3645, 3646, 3647, 3648)

	Value of Shipments (mil$)	Number of Establishments	Number of Employees (000s)
1985	$6,414	-	-
1982	5,066	1,203	66.2
1977	3,489	1,226	66.6
1972	2,452	1,174	71.6
1967	1,594	1,213	64.6
1963	1,159	1,239	53.9
1958	827	1,181	47.3
1954	660	1,228	45.1
1947	465	1,202	46.9
1937	115	466	25.6
1933	46	357	12.5
1929	145	614	28.3
1919	80	512	21.8
1909	45	619	22.5
1899	20	370	12.5

Sources: See Table 2.

Table 4
Current- and Noncurrent-Carrying Wiring Devices (3643, 3644)

	Value of Shipments (mil$)	Number of Establishments	Number of Employees (000s)
1985	$5,998	-	-
1982	4,910	641	70.8
1977	3,217	615	69.7
1972	2,142	580	76.1
1967	1,475	549	63.0
1963	1,140	631	55.7
1958	915	556	50.7
1954	584	395	43.2
1947	384	344	39.1
1937*	102	124	-
1933*	42	-	-
1929*	108	-	-
1919**	63	-	-
1909**	13	-	-

* Includes conduits and fittings, fuses and fuse blockers, wiring
devices and supplies.

** Includes conduits, fuses and cutouts, fuse plugs, insulators,
wiring devices, and lightning arresters.

Sources: See Table 2.

reached a peak in 1972. Over the next decade total employment fell from 179,000 to 159,000, a drop of just over 10 percent, while nominal sales more than doubled (although there was little change in the sales adjusted for inflation).

COMPANIES ENGAGED IN THE INDUSTRY

To begin my study of the history of electric lighting and wiring equipment, I will identify the firms engaged in the industry. One of the most useful sources for this purpose is *Ward's Business Directory* (1987). *Ward's* is a two-volume manual that gives the names and addresses of firms engaged in industries (conveniently listed by SIC code) along with other pertinent information, such as sales, employment, assets, and, useful for historical purposes, the year the firm was founded. The first volume includes public and private firms with sales of at least $11 million. A study of the data reveals 27 public firms and 247 subsidiaries and private firms whose primary interests were within the electric lighting and wiring equipment industry and whose combined sales in 1986 were approximately $20 billion. The second volume lists an additional 286 subsidiaries and private firms with sales between $.5 and $11 million (with total sales of $1.6 billion). The firms within the industry and their relative sizes can thus be readily identified.

The nature of the industry is revealed by an examination of its major firms, as identified in the first volume of *Ward's*. Of the twenty-seven public firms primarily engaged in this industry, the ten largest had sales of at least $100 million each in 1986. Two firms had sales of over a billion dollars: AMP Inc. ($1.6 billion) and National Service Industries ($1.2 billion). The remaining firms in the top ten included Bairnco, Hubbell, Atcor, Thomas & Betts, Thomas Industries, KDI, Joslyn, and Cherry Electric Products. Although five of these firms are also listed among the *Fortune 500*, theirs are not household names (although some of their subsidiaries, such as Lightolier, may be familiar to consumers). With the exception of Thomas & Betts, which is the subject of a forthcoming volume by Louis Cain (also see Cain 1986), none of these companies has been the subject of a corporate history.

In addition to the companies mentioned above, several large private firms are primarily engaged in this industry. The largest is Allied Tube and Conduit (sales of $680 million in 1986), followed by Leviton Manufacturing Company ($275 million) and Eagle Electrical Manufacturing Company ($125 million). Both Electrical Sciences and Carlton-Aurora, two subsidiaries of the privately held Dutch firm Thyssen-Bornemisza, had sales of over $100 million. Again, these firms are relatively unfamiliar.

Another major sector of this industry is composed of subsidiaries and divisions of publicly held firms whose major line of business is not in the 36.4 SIC code, and these tend to be familiar companies. The largest single entity in the business was the GTE Electrical Products Division (formerly the Sylvania division) of the GTE Corporation, with sales of $1.9 billion in 1986, or nearly 10 percent of the total sales of the top 270 firms. In fact, fourteen divisions of GTE were among the top 270 firms in the industry. The combined sales of these fourteen subsidiaries, however, comprised only 25 percent of GTE's total sales (listed under SIC 48.1). Another major firm engaged in the industry, and one whose roots stretch back to its beginning in the late nineteenth century, is General Electric. Seventeen divisions of General Electric were among the top 270 firms. But the combined sales of these divisions contributed a mere 2 percent to the company's total sales (listed under SIC 36.2). A third company with a substantial number of subsidiaries in the industry was the Dutch firm Philips Gloeilampen, which had eight subsidiaries in the top 270 firms, the largest being North American Philips Lighting with sales of $620 million. The first volume of a projected three-volume history of Philips Gloeilampen has recently been published (Heerding 1986). Other companies whose subsidiaries had sales over $100 million include Kidde, Honeywell, Cooper Industries, and Ford Motor Company. Finally, because Westinghouse Electric (SIC 36.2) has been engaged in the industry from the beginning, it should be noted that two of its subsidiaries with combined sales of $99 million are on the list of the top 270 firms.

THE EARLY HISTORY OF THE INDUSTRY

A number of companies that played a major role in the evolution of this industry (particularly General Electric and Westinghouse) are no longer included in SIC 36.4. It is impossible to discuss the history of the industry without mentioning them, so this section focuses on the early development of the electric light and its accoutrements.

Until the development of the electric light, man relied on open flames to provide artificial illumination. Although illumination progressed from camp fires through torches and oil lamps to culminate in the gas lights of the early nineteenth century, the technology remained inherently dangerous and inefficient. The electric lamp truly revolutionized the production of artificial illumination.

Although the English chemist Humphry Davy was in the first decade of the nineteenth century the first to produce both arc and incandescent light, a long heritage of scientific experimentation preceded Davy's success, and it was sixty years after his work that the electric light became commercially feasible. Discussion of these early developments can be found in Norris (1909), Howell and Schroeder (1927), Keating (1954), Hughes (1983), and Friedel and Israel (1986).

The development of commercial arc lighting preceded that of incandescent lighting. Following Davy's successful demonstrations in the early nineteenth century, various arc lights were gradually perfected. The first use of electricity to light urban streets was probably that by Paul Jablochkoff in Paris in the early 1860s. One factor early experiments had in common was that uneconomical batteries were used as a source of power. It was not until the development of the dynamo for producing current that arc lighting became practical. In 1870 Z. T. Gramme, a Belgian residing in Paris, patented a dynamo capable of operating an arc light (for use in a lighthouse).

Inventive activity in the United States accelerated in the last third of the nineteenth century, and a number of arc lighting companies were formed to capitalize on the developments. Charles F. Brush was the first to install commercial systems of arc lighting in the United States. Although systems were installed in Philadelphia in 1877 and Cleveland in 1879, the first commercial central station operating a system of arc lights was that in San Francisco in 1879. At about the same time, William Wallace and Moses G. Farmer developed a competing system, as did Edward Weston (whose company was later taken over by Westinghouse), Charles Van Depoele, and Elihu Thomson and Edwin J. Houston. The Brush and Thomson-Houston companies eventually merged. These developments are discussed fully in U.S. Bureau of the Census, *Central Electric Light and Power Stations 1902* (1905); U.S. Senate, *Supply of Electrical Equipment and Competitive Conditions* (1928); and Neil (1942). Technical improvements in arc lights to the end of the nineteenth century are described in detail in Martin (1900).

Because of its importance and its impact on the growth of large electric utilities, historians have devoted considerable attention to the development of the incandescent light. The fundamental problem with arc lighting was its intensity, which relegated it to use outdoors and in large open spaces. The success of the arc light, however, stimulated the search for a workable incandescent lamp.

As for the incandescent light, developments had proceeded after Davy's early experimentation. The first patent on an incandescent lamp was granted in Britain to Frederick De Moleyns in 1841. Lamps were also invented by J. W. Starr, W. E. Staite, Edward C. Shepard, M. J. Roberts, J. De Changy, Moses G. Farmer, Joseph W. Swan, and others. With the exception of Swan's, none of these lamps were commercially feasible because of their great expense and short life. Indeed, Swan has a claim equal to Edison's for inventing a successful incandescent lamp.

Had Thomas Alva Edison stopped with the invention of the high-resistance, carbon-filament incandescent lamp, many more years might have passed before practical indoor lighting was developed. Edison did much more, however, than invent the light bulb. It was clear from the beginning that he was thinking in terms of a system for delivering light. His system was composed of a steam engine, jumbo generator, network of mains and feeders, parallel distribution system, and, at the end of all this apparatus, the incandescent lamp. Although Edison illuminated his Menlo Park laboratory with incandescent lights, the first commercial installation was made on the steamship Columbia in 1880. In the following years numerous isolated installations were completed, but Edison's goal was to install a large central station to supply light to numerous buildings. After two years of intense development, on September 4, 1882, Edison's Pearl Street Station began supplying current to 1,200 lamps in a one-sixth square mile area of Wall Street. Within a year, Pearl Street was supplying over 7,000 lights with current. The system was an immediate and resounding success. By 1886, 410 central stations were operating in the United States; the electric utility industry was born. A number of excellent studies of this process of early development exist, including classics such as Howell and Schroeder (1927), Bright (1949), and Keating (1954). In addition there are interesting accounts in Martin (1900), U.S. Bureau of the Census, *Central Electric Light and Power Stations 1902* (1905), and U.S. Senate, *Supply of Electrical Equipment and Competitive Conditions* (1928). Also helpful are biographies of Edison, including Josephson (1959), Silverberg (1967), Clark (1977), Conot (1979), and Wachhorst (1982), which contains a comprehensive bibliography of writing on Edison. Additional citations can be found in Larson ([1948] 1964) and Lovett (1971). The recent works of Thomas P. Hughes (1983) and Robert Friedel and Paul Israel (1986) contain excellent treatments that focus on the process of invention and early commercialization.

To exploit his inventions, Edison established a number of commercial enterprises. The Edison Electric Light Company was formed in October, 1878, to fund development and to hold and license patents worldwide. The Edison Electric Illuminating Company of New York was formed in December, 1880, to build and operate the Pearl Street Station. Numerous operating companies were subsequently established. During 1880–81 the Edison Machine Works, Edison Electric Tube Company, Edison Lamp Works, and Bergmann and Company were formed to produce components of the system. The Edison Company for Isolated Lighting was formed in 1881 to capture the noncentral station business. Most of these companies merged in 1886 to form the Edison Electric Light Company, which was succeeded in 1889 by the Edison General Electric Company. In 1892 the Edison company merged with one of its chief competitors, the Thomson-Houston Electric Company, to form the General Electric Company. Alfred D. Chandler, Jr. (1977), regards this merger as particularly important to the development of modern industrial management in the United States.

During these dynamic years a second major company was being organized. In 1882 George Westinghouse established the Union Switch and Signal Company. The name was changed to Westinghouse Electric Company in 1886. Two companies formerly controlled by Thomson-Houston, the Consolidated Electric Light Company and Sawyer-Man, along with the United States Electric Lighting Company and Waterhouse Electric and Manufacturing Company, were purchased in 1888 and the name of the company was changed to the Westinghouse Electric and Manufacturing Company. Thus was formed the second of the two rivals that would dominate the business well into the twentieth century. By 1923, for example, General Electric alone was producing approximately 50 percent of the incandescent lamps in the United States. For a discussion of the formation of these companies, see U.S. Senate, *Supply of Electrical Equipment and Competitive Conditions* (1928), Passer (1953), Keating (1954), and Hughes (1983).

Although historians have exhibited considerable interest in exploring the early days of the industry, much less attention has been devoted to subsequent developments, including the entry of rivals. Paul W. Keating (1954), for example, discusses subsequent innovations in the light bulb, including the adoption of fluorescent lighting in the late 1930s, but there has been little work on later periods. The industry is a candidate for a study that will update the history of the electric light and the companies that produce it.

This industry, of course, comprises more than the electric light, and some work has been done on its more prosaic components. The work by Thomas Commerford Martin (1900) contains brief discussions of the development of switchboards, electric light fixtures, electrical conduits, and fuses. A first-rate study of the electrical plug and the companies involved in its early development is Schroeder (1986). Two recent pieces on industrial research during the early period are Wise (1980) and Reich (1985). On the failure of one incandescent electric lighting company in the early days of the industry, see Wrege and Greenwood (1984). On the development of fluorescent lighting and its technical characteristics, see Amick (1942). I was unable to find a comprehensive history of the lighting fixture, but for anyone interested in pursuing this topic, several sources are available. The Illuminating Engineering Society was formed in 1906 for the purpose of disseminating information on technical aspects of lighting. *Illuminating Engineering Society Transactions*, as well as the *Magazine of Light*, published by General Electric, could prove to be valuable starting points for such research. Fashbender (1947) would also be helpful.

PROSPECTS FOR FURTHER RESEARCH

To determine if the large firms in the industry had any interest in their historical antecedents, I wrote to twenty-five firms listed in *Ward's* (including the parent companies of firms in other lines of business, but with large subsidiaries in this industry). I inquired if a business history had been published or was in progress, or if there was any interest in having one produced. The response from the half who replied to the inquiry was decidedly mixed. Cooper Industries responded by sending a copy of a recent book by David N. Kellner (1983), commissioned to celebrate their 150th year in business.

Although uncritical, the work is informative and includes an interesting chapter on Crouse-Hinds, a subsidiary founded in 1897 that produces various electrical products including sockets, fuses, insulators, traffic signals, trolley lights, and floodlights. Several firms supplied ten- to twenty-page brochures (probably intended for stockholders) highlighting the historical development of the firm, often with an emphasis on acquisitions. The majority of the respondents reported that they had not produced a business history. One firm indicated that it would cooperate with a historian interested in writing a company history, but the majority of the responses were less encouraging, ranging from "casual" interest through "no immediate interest" to "little to no interest." A recently retired chief executive responded that he "would not wish to meet with a potential writer to discuss such a project." One vice-president responded that "we feel corporate histories, while a useful reference tool, have little reading appeal. Our centennial offered us another opportunity to write a formal account of our history, but we decided not to pursue it for this reason." These responses are likely to be disconcerting to business historians. They indicate that history is not fully understood by many business executives, which is an argument for some vigorous "missionary" work by the profession. The industry has had a tremendous social and economic impact and deserves further attention from historians.

BIBLIOGRAPHY

Amick, Charles L. *Fluorescent Illumination*. New York: McGraw-Hill, 1942.

Bright, Arthur A., Jr. *The Electric-Lamp Industry: Technical Change and Economic Development, 1800–1947*. New York: Macmillan, 1949.

Cain, Louis P. "How Public Works Saved Private Enterprise: The Thomas & Betts Company in the Great Depression." *Business and Economic History*, 2d ser., 15 (1986): 29–40.

Chandler, Alfred D., Jr. *The Visible Hand: The Managerial Revolution in American Business*. Cambridge, MA: Harvard University Press, 1977.

Clark, Ronald W. *Edison: The Man Who Made the Future*. New York: G. P. Putnam's Sons, 1977.

Conot, Robert. *A Streak of Luck*. New York: Bantam, 1979.

Fashbender, Myrtle. *Residential Lighting*. New York: D. Van Nostrand, 1947.

Friedel, Robert, and Paul Israel. *Edison's Electric Light: Biography of an Invention*. New Brunswick, NJ: Rutgers University Press, 1986.

Heerding, A. *The History of N. V. Philips' Gloeilampenfabrieken. Volume 1. The Origin of the Dutch Incandescent Lamp Industry*. Translated by Derek S. Jordan. Cambridge, Eng.: Cambridge University Press, 1986.

Howell, John W., and Henry Schroeder. *History of the Incandescent Lamp*. Schenectady: Maqua Co., 1927.

Hughes, Thomas P. *Networks of Power: Electrification in Western Society, 1880–1930*. Baltimore: Johns Hopkins University Press, 1983.

Illuminating Engineering Society Transactions. Illuminating Engineering Society, 1906– .

Josephson, Matthew. *Edison.* New York: McGraw-Hill, 1959.

Keating, Paul W. *Lamps for a Brighter America: A History of the General Electric Lamp Business.* New York: McGraw-Hill, 1954.

Kellner, David Neal. *Cooper Industries, 1833–1983.* Athens: Ohio University Press, 1983.

Larson, Henrietta M. *Guide to Business History.* 1948. Reprint. Boston: J. S. Canner, 1964.

Lovett, Robert W. *American Economic and Business History Information Sources.* Detroit: Gale Research Co., 1971.

Magazine of Light. Cleveland: General Electric Co., 1930–73.

Martin, Thomas Commerford. "Electrical Apparatus and Supplies." In U.S. Bureau of the Census, *Twelfth Census, 1900, Census Reports,* vol. 10, 151–205.

Neil, C. E. *Entering the Seventh Decade of Electric Power.* New York: Edison Electric Institute, 1942.

Norris, Henry H. *An Introduction to the Study of Electrical Engineering.* New York: John Wiley, 1909.

Passer, Harold C. *The Electrical Manufacturers 1875–1900.* Cambridge, MA: Harvard University Press, 1953.

Reich, Leonard S. *The Making of American Industrial Research: Science and Business at GE and Bell, 1876–1926.* Cambridge, Eng.: Cambridge University Press, 1985.

Schroeder, Fred E. H. "More 'Small Things Forgotten': Domestic Electrical Plugs and Receptacles, 1881–1931." *Technology and Culture* 27 (July 1986): 525–43.

Silverberg, Robert. *Light for the World: Edison and the Power Industry.* Princeton: D. Van Nostrand, 1967.

U.S. Bureau of the Census. *Census of Manufactures.* Washington, DC: U.S. Government Printing Office, 1905– .

———. *Central Electric Light and Power Stations, 1902.* Washington, DC: U.S. Government Printing Office, 1905.

———. *Annual Survey of Manufactures.* Washington, DC: U.S. Government Printing Office, 1974– .

U.S. Congress. Senate. *Supply of Electrical Equipment and Competitive Conditions.* 70th Cong., 1st sess., 1928. Document No. 46.

Wachhorst, Wyn. *Thomas Alva Edison.* Cambridge, MA: MIT Press, 1982.

Ward's Business Directory. 2 vols. Belmont, CA: Information Access Co., 1987.

Wise, George. "A New Role for Professional Scientists in Industry: Industrial Research at General Electric, 1900–1916." *Technology and Culture* 21 (July 1980): 405–29.

Wrege, Charles D., and Ronald G. Greenwood. "William E. Sawyer and the Rise and Fall of America's First Electric Light Company, 1878–1881." *Business and Economic History,* 2d ser., 13 (1984): 31–48.

CHAPTER 17

RADIO, TV, AND COMMUNICATION EQUIPMENT, 36.6

Robert M. Aduddell and Louis P. Cain

The literature on radio, TV, and the communication equipment industry can be divided into three sections: general, telephone and telegraph, and radio and television. The telephone and the telegraph were among the first commercial applications of electricity, and a great deal has been written about the production of the equipment. Although little has been written about the production of radio and television equipment, there is a vast literature on programming. Much of the information on the production of communication equipment is contained in general histories of the electrical and electronics industry. And the broadcasting industry has a large trade press that often publishes articles about equipment production. Anyone researching this industry would be well advised to consult that literature.

GENERAL

The first section of the bibliography lists eight items of general interest. Thomas P. Hughes (1979) and Harold Passer (1952) concentrate on the development of the electrical industry; Ernest Braun and Stuart Macdonald (1978) and the editors of *Electronics* (1981) concentrate on the development of the electronics industry. All discuss how improvements in component parts contributed to the evolution of communication equipment. Gerald W. Brock (1981) and John R. Meyer et al. (1980) present economists' views of the telecommunications industry just prior to the dissolution of AT&T. These works provide the necessary context for more detailed exploration in the telephone and telegraph industries and the radio and TV industry.

TELEPHONE AND TELEGRAPH

The most important recent addition to the historiography of the telephone industry is a series of studies produced by the combined efforts of AT&T and the telephone history group at Johns Hopkins. These include the volumes by Robert Garnet (1985), George David Smith (1985), and Neil H. Wasserman (1985b), the article by Kenneth Lipartito (1985), and Garnet's (1984) and Lipartito's (1987) dissertations. Other recent works evoked by the dissolution of the Bell system include MacAvoy and Robinson (1983), Shooshan (1984), Temin and Peters (1985), and Temin (1987). Robert W. Crandall and Kenneth Flamm examine the aftermath of the dissolution (Crandall 1988, 1989; Crandall and Flamm 1989; Flamm 1989). M. R. Irwin's (1969) article clarifies some of the issues involved in the dissolution.

Among recent works on the telephone industry that do not focus on dissolution are Brooks (1975), de Sola Pool (1977), Wiesner (1977), and Young (1983). Kempster B. Miller's (1905) earlier study emphasizes the technology of the industry at the turn of the twentieth century. Telephone research—Bell Labs—is the focus of the recent work by Leonard S. Reich (1980, 1985) and an interesting internal review edited by M. D. Fagan (1975). W. H. Doherty (1968) offers a corporate autobiography. Richard Balzer's volume (1976) is a study of Western Electric, the producing arm of the Bell system, and its Hawthorne plant, the site of several historical managerial studies. John Sheahan's (1956) article is a study of the economic impact of the telephone equipment industry. John N. Schacht (1985) focuses on unionization in the telephone industry in the interwar period.

Both the telephone and the telegraph industries have been the subject of governmental inquiries. The most important of these are included in the bibliography. Particularly useful is the seventy-seven-volume report of the U.S. Federal Communications Commission's (1939) investigation of the telephone industry. The evolution of the industries in their early years can be seen in various bulletins produced by the U.S. Bureau of the Census.

Modern research on the telegraph has emphasized its role in market integration. Included in this research are the works of Richard B. DuBoff (1980, 1983) and JoAnne Yates (1986). Robert L. Thompson (1947) emphasizes the initial implementation of telegraph technology; his is the most comprehensive recent work. Alvin F. Harlow's (1936) earlier study discusses the evolution of the telephone and telegraph and radio as well. His bibliography includes several commonly cited nineteenth-century works on the telegraph and its impact on society. Alexander Jones (1852), Marshall Lefferts (1856), G. B. Prescott (1860, 1877), John D. Reid (1879), and Alfred Vail (1845) cover much the same ground as Thompson. Walter P. Marshall (1951) has written a biography of Ezra Cornell, one of the early leaders of the telegraph industry.

RADIO AND TELEVISION

A few historical works focus directly on the production of radio and television equipment. Some on radio equipment are Aitken (1985), Archer (1938), and MacLaurin (1949). Those on TV equipment include Long (1977), Shiers (1975), Swift (1950), and Udelson (1982). Graham (1986) is an interesting study of RCA's development of the video disc. Page (1962) and Watson-Watt (1959) are two studies on the development of radar; the latter is an autobiography.

Biographical studies of entrepreneurs and accounts of companies are more common than historical discussions of the equipment. Among the many biographies of Thomas A. Edison are Bryan (1926), Clark (1977), Hughes (1987), and Josephson (1961). Histories of General Electric include Hammond (1941), Miller (1947), and Nye (1985). Broderick (1929) and Cordiner (1956) are written by former executives of General Electric. Biographies of George Westinghouse include those by the American Society of Mechanical Engineers (1937) and Henry G. Prout (1922). Case and Case (1982) is a biography of Owen D. Young, who created RCA as a corporate entity from his position in the legal department of GE. Carl Dreher (1977) writes about David Sarnoff, the longtime chief executive officer of RCA. Geoffrey Jones (1985) examines the Gramophone Company, an English company with ties to the United States.

Harry Mark Petrakis (1965) focuses on Paul Galvin, founder of Motorola. Sterling Quinlan (1979) offers an insider's view of the ABC television network. C. Joseph Pusateri's (1980a, 1980b) business history of station WWL in New Orleans emphasizes its operations.

In a 1977 article, Leonard S. Reich emphasizes radio research; his aforementioned 1985 work deals with electrical research at GE and Bell. Kendall Birr (1957) and George Wise (1985) also discuss the research program at GE. Ronald W. Schatz (1983) examines labor relations at both GE and Westinghouse.

The interrelations between the industry and the government are discussed in Baughman (1985), Kittross (1959), Reeves and Baughman (1983), Rosen (1980), and Webbink (1968). Several Senate documents relating to the history of the industry and regulation are also available. Frank W. Peers (1968, 1979) discusses politics in the Canadian broadcasting industry, whose primary network is owned by the government.

BIBLIOGRAPHY

General

Braun, Ernest, and Stuart Macdonald. *Revolution in Miniature: The History and Impact of Semiconductor Electronics.* New York: Cambridge University Press, 1978.

Brock, Gerald W. *The Telecommunications Industry: The Dynamics of Market Structure.* Cambridge, MA: Harvard University Press, 1981.

The Editors of *Electronics. An Age of Electronics: The World of Electronics, 1930–2000.* New York: McGraw-Hill, 1981.

Hughes, Thomas P. "The Electrification of America: The System Builders." *Technology and Culture* (January 1979): 124–61.

————. *Networks of Power: Electrification in Western Society, 1880–1930.* Baltimore: Johns Hopkins University Press, 1983.

Meyer, John R., Robert W. Wilson, M. Alan Baughcum, Ellen Burton, and Louis Caovette. *The Economics of Competition in the Telecommunications Industry.* Cambridge, MA: Oelgeschlager, Gunn & Hain, 1980.

Passer, Harold. "Electrical Manufacturing Around 1900." *Journal of Economic History* (1952): 378–95.

————. *The Electrical Manufacturers, 1875–1900.* Cambridge, MA: Harvard University Press, 1953.

Telephone and Telegraph

Balzer, Richard. *Clockwork: Life in and Outside an American Factory.* Garden City, NY: Doubleday, 1976.

Brooks, John. *Telephone: The First Hundred Years.* New York: Harper & Row, 1975.

Crandall, Robert W. "Surprises from Telephone Deregulation and the AT&T Divestiture." *American Economic Review* 78 (May 1988): 323–27.

————. "Structural Separations and the Role of the Telephone Operating Companies." In *Changing the Rules: Technological Change, International Competition, and Regulation in Communications,* edited by Robert W. Crandall and Kenneth Flamm. Washington, DC: Brookings Institution, 1989.

Crandall, Robert W., and Kenneth Flamm, eds. *Changing the Rules: Technological Change, International Competition, and Regulation in Communications.* Washington, DC: Brookings Institution, 1989.

de Sola Pool, Ithiel, ed. *The Social Impact of the Telephone.* Cambridge, MA: MIT Press, 1977.

Doherty, W. H. *The Bell System and the People Who Made It.* New York: Bell Telephone Laboratories, 1968.

DuBoff, Richard B. *Electric Power in American Manufacturing: 1889–1958.* New York: Arno Press, 1979.

————. "Business Demand and the Development of the Telegraph in the United States, 1844–1860." *Business History Review* 54 (Winter 1980): 459–79.

————. "The Telegraph and the Structure of Markets in the United States, 1845–1890." In *Research in Economic History,* edited by Paul J. Uselding, vol. 8. Greenwich, CT: JAI Press, 1983.

Fagan, M. D., ed. *A History of Engineering and Science in the Bell System: The Early Years (1875–1925).* New York: Bell Laboratories, 1975.

Flamm, Kenneth. "Economic Dimensions of Technological Advance in Communications: A Comparison with Computers." In *Changing the Rules: Tech-*

nological Change, International Competition, and Regulation in Communications, edited by Robert W. Crandall and Kenneth Flamm. Washington, DC: Brookings Institution, 1989.

Garnet, Robert. "The Telephone Enterprise: The Evolution of the Bell System's Horizontal Structure." Ph.D. diss., Johns Hopkins University, 1984.

————. *The Telephone Enterprise: The Evolution of the Bell System's Horizontal Structure, 1876–1909*. Baltimore: Johns Hopkins University Press, 1985.

Green, Norvin. "The Government and the Telegraph." *North American Review* 137 (November 1883): 422–32.

Harlow, Alvin F. *Old Wires and New Waves: The History of the Telegraph, Telephone, and Wireless*. New York: D. Appleton-Century, 1936.

Hubbard, Gardiner G. "Government Control of the Telegraph." *North American Review* 137 (December 1883): 523, 529–30.

"Influence of the Telegraph." *Hunt's Merchants' Magazine* 59 (1868): 106–8.

Irwin, M. R. "Vertical Integration and the Communications Industry: Separation of Western Electric and AT&T?" *Antitrust Law and Economics Review* 3 (Fall 1969).

Jones, Alexander. *Historical Sketch of the Electric Telegraph: Including Its Rise and Progress in the United States*. New York: Putnam, 1852.

Lefferts, Marshall. "The Electric Telegraph: Its Influence and Geographical Distribution." *Bulletin of the American Geographical and Statistical Society* 2 (1856).

Lipartito, Kenneth. "A Comparative Analysis of the Early History of the Southern and Northern Telephone Systems." In *Business and Economic History*, edited by Jeremy Atack, vol. 14, 159–76. Champaign, IL: Bureau of Economic and Business Research, 1985.

————. "The Telephone in the South: A Comparative Analysis, 1877–1920." Ph.D. diss., Johns Hopkins University, 1987.

MacAvoy, Paul W., and Kenneth Robinson. "Winning by Losing: The AT&T Settlement and Its Impact on Telecommunications." *Yale Journal on Regulation* 1 (1983): 1–42.

Marshall, Walter P. *Ezra Cornell, 1807–1874: His Contributions to Western Union and to Cornell University*. New York: Newcomen Society in North America, 1951.

Miller, Kempster B. *Telephone Theory and Practice*. New York: McGraw, 1905.

Orton, William. *Government Telegraphs, Argument of William Orton, President of the Western Union Telegraph Company on the Bill to Establish Postal Telegraph Lines*. New York: Russells' American Steam Printing House, 1870.

————. *Argument of Wm. Orton on the Postal Telegraph Bill, Delivered Before the [U.S. Senate] Committee on Post-Offices and Post-Roads, January 20–23, 1874*. New York: Western Union Telegraph Co., 1874.

Parsons, Frank. *The Telegraph Monopoly*. Philadelphia: C. F. Taylor, 1899.

Prescott, G. B. *History, Theory, and Practice of the Electric Telegraph*. Boston: Ticknor & Fields, 1860.

————. *Electricity and the Electric Telegraph*. New York: Appleton, 1877.

Reich, Leonard S. "Industrial Research and the Pursuit of Corporate Security: The Early Years of Bell Labs." *Business History Review* 54 (Winter 1980): 504–29.

————. *The Making of American Industrial Research: Science and Business at GE and Bell, 1876–1926.* New York: Cambridge University Press, 1985.

Reid, John D. *The Telegraph in America: Its Founders, Promoters and Noted Men.* New York: Derby Brothers, 1879.

Schacht, John N. *The Making of Telephone Unionism, 1920–1947.* New Brunswick, NJ: Rutgers University Press, 1985.

Sheahan, John. "Integration and Exclusion in the Telephone Equipment Industry." *Quarterly Journal of Economics* 70 (1956):249–69.

Shooshan, Harry M. III, ed. *Disconnecting Bell: The Impact of the AT&T Divestiture.* New York: Pergamon Press, 1984.

Sivowitch, Elliot N., ed. *The Development of Wireless to 1920.* New York: Arno Press, 1977.

Smith, George David. *Anatomy of a Business Strategy: Bell, Western Electric, and the Origins of the American Telephone Industry.* Baltimore: Johns Hopkins University Press, 1985.

"The Telegraph." *DeBow's Review* 16 (1854): 167–71.

Temin, Peter. *The Fall of the Bell System: A Study in Politics, Prices, and Power.* New York: Cambridge University Press, 1987.

Temin, Peter, and Geoffrey Peters. "Is History Stranger Than Theory? The Origin of Telephone Separations." *American Economic Review* 75 (May 1985): 324–27.

Thompson, Robert L. *Wiring a Continent: The History of the Telegraph Industry in the United States 1832–1866.* Princeton: Princeton University Press, 1947.

Turnbull, Laurence. *The Electro-Magnetic Telegraph: With an Historical Account of Its Rise, Progress, and Present Condition.* 2d ed. Philadelphia: A. Hart, 1853.

U.S. Bureau of the Census. *Bulletin 17. Telephones and Telegraphs, 1902.* Washington, DC: U.S. Government Printing Office, 1905.

————. *Bulletin 102. Telegraph Systems, 1907.* Washington, DC: U.S. Government Printing Office, 1909.

————. *Bulletin 123. Telephones and Telegraphs, 1912.* Washington, DC: U.S. Government Printing Office, 1914.

————. *Telephones and Telegraphs and Municipal Electric and Fire-Alarm and Police-Patrol Signaling Systems, 1912.* Washington, DC: U.S. Government Printing Office, 1915.

————. *Census of Electrical Industries, Telegraphs, 1927.* Washington, DC: U.S. Government Printing Office, 1930.

U.S. Congress. Senate. Committee on Post-Offices and Post-Roads. *To Provide for the Establishment of a Postal Telegraph.* 1884. Report No. 577, pt. 2.

————. *Letter from the Postmaster General Relative to the Establishment of a Telegraph in Connection with the Postal System.* June 2, 1866. Executive Document No. 49.

————. *Investigation of Western Union and Postal Telegraph-Cable Companies.* February 16, 1909. Document No. 725.

U.S. Federal Communications Commission. *Investigation of the Telephone Industry.* 77 vols. Washington, DC: U.S. Government Printing Office, 1939.

Vail, Alfred. *The American Electro-Magnetic Telegraph with the Reports of Con-*

gress, and a Description of All Telegraphs Known. Philadelphia: Lea & Blanchard, 1845.

Wasserman, Neil H. "The Changing Technological Culture at AT&T." *Research Management* 28 (September-October 1985a): 35–45.

———. *From Invention to Innovation: Long Distance Transmission at the Turn of the Century*. Baltimore: Johns Hopkins University Press, 1985b.

Wiesner, Jerome B. *The Telephone's First Century and Beyond*. New York: Crowell, 1977.

Yates, JoAnne. "The Telegraph's Effect on Nineteenth Century Markets and Firms." In *Business and Economic History*, edited by Jeremy Atack, vol. 15, 149–64. Champaign, IL: Bureau of Economic and Business Research, 1986.

Young, Peter. *Power of Speech: A History of Standard Telephones and Cables, 1883–1983*. London: George Allen & Unwin, 1983.

Radio and Television

Aitken, Hugh G. J. *The Continuous Wave: Technology and American Radio: 1900–1932*. Princeton: Princeton University Press, 1985.

American Society of Mechanical Engineers. *George Westinghouse Commemoration: A Forum Presenting the Career and Achievements of George Westinghouse on the Ninetieth Anniversary of His Birth*. New York: American Society of Mechanical Engineers, 1937.

Archer, Gleason L. *History of Radio to 1926*. New York: American Historical Society, 1938.

Baughman, James L. *Television's Guardians: The FCC and the Politics of Programming, 1958–1967*. Knoxville: University of Tennessee Press, 1985.

Birr, Kendall. *Pioneering in Industrial Research: The Story of the General Electric Research Laboratory*. Washington, DC: Public Affairs Press, 1957.

Broderick, John T. *Forty Years with General Electric*. Albany: Fort Orange Press, 1929.

Bryan, George. *Edison: The Man and His Work*. Garden City, NY: Garden City Publishing, 1926.

Case, Josephine Young, and Everett Needham Case. *Owen D. Young and American Enterprise: A Biography*. Boston: David R. Godine, 1982.

Clark, Ronald W. *Edison: The Man Who Made the Future*. New York: Putnam, 1977.

Cordiner, Ralph J. *New Frontiers for Professional Managers*. New York: McGraw-Hill, 1956.

Dreher, Carl. *Sarnoff: An American Success*. New York: New York Times Book Co., 1977.

Erickson, Don B. *Armstrong's Fight for FM Broadcasting*. University: University of Alabama Press, 1973.

Graham, Margaret B. W. *RCA and the Video Disc: The Business of Research*. New York: Cambridge University Press, 1986.

Gross, Lynne S. *The New Television Technologies*. Dubuque, IA: W. C. Brown, 1983.

Hammond, John W. *Men and Volts: The Story of General Electric*. Philadelphia: Lippincott, 1941.

Head, Sidney W. *Broadcasting in America*. Boston: Houghton Mifflin, 1972.

Hughes, Jonathan R. T. *The Vital Few*. New York: Oxford University Press, 1987.

Jones, Geoffrey. "The Gramophone Company: An Anglo-American Multinational, 1898–1931." *Business History Review* 59 (Spring 1985): 76–100.

Josephson, Matthew. *Edison: A Biography*. London: Eyre & Spottiswood, 1961.

Kittross, John M. "Television Frequency Allocation Policy in the United States." Ph.D. diss., University of Illinois, 1959.

Lichty, Lawrence W., and Malachi C. Topping, eds. *American Broadcasting: A Source Book on the History of Radio and Television*. New York: Hastings House, 1975.

Long, Stewart L. "Television Network Development: The Early Years." In *Business and Economic History*, edited by Paul J. Uselding, 69–83. Champaign, IL: Bureau of Business and Economic Research, 1977.

MacLaurin, W. Rupert. *Invention and Innovation in the Radio Industry*. New York: Macmillan, 1949.

Miller, John A. *Men and Volts at Work: The Story of General Electric in World War II*. New York: McGraw-Hill, 1947.

Nye, David E. *Image Worlds: Corporate Identities at General Electric, 1890–1930*. Cambridge, MA: MIT Press, 1985.

Page, Robert M. *The Origin of Radar*. Garden City, NY: Anchor Books, 1962.

Peers, Frank W. *The Politics of Canadian Broadcasting, 1920–1951*. Buffalo: University of Toronto Press, 1968.

———. *The Public Eye: Television and the Politics of Canadian Broadcasting, 1952–1968*. Buffalo: University of Toronto Press, 1979.

Petrakis, Harry Mark. *The Founder's Touch: The Life of Paul Galvin of Motorola*. New York: McGraw-Hill, 1965.

Prout, Henry G. *A Life of George Westinghouse*. New York: C. Scribner, 1922.

Pusateri, C. Joseph. *Enterprise in Radio: WWL and the Business of Broadcasting in America*. Lanham, MD: University Press of America, 1980a.

———. "Radio Broadcasters and the Challenge of Television: A New Orleans Case." *Business History Review* 54 (Autumn 1980b): 303–30.

Quinlan, Sterling. *Inside ABC: American Broadcasting Company's Rise to Power*. New York: Hastings House, 1979.

Reeves, Byron, and James L. Baughman. " 'Fraught with Such Great Possibilities': The Historical Relationship of Communication Research to Mass Media Regulation." In *Telecommunications Policy Research Conference: Proceedings of the Tenth Annual Telecommunications Research Conference*, edited by Oscar H. Gandy, Jr., et al. Norwood, NJ: ABLEX, 1983.

Reich, Leonard S. "Research, Patents, and the Struggle to Control Radio: Big Business and the Uses of Industrial Research." *Business History Review* 51 (Summer 1977).

———. *The Making of American Industrial Research: Science and Business at GE and Bell, 1876–1926*. New York: Cambridge University Press, 1985.

Rosen, Philip T. *The Modern Stentors: Radio Broadcasting and the Federal Government, 1920–1934*. Westport, CT: Greenwood Press, 1980.

Schatz, Ronald W. *The Electrical Workers: A History of Labor at General Electric and Westinghouse, 1923–1960*. Urbana: University of Illinois Press, 1983.

Shiers, George. "Television Fifty Years Ago." *Journal of Broadcasting* 19 (Fall 1975): 387–400.

Swift, John. *Adventures in Vision: The First Twenty-Five Years of Television*. London: J. Lehmann, 1950.

Taylor, John P. *What Broadcasters Should Know About Satellites*. New York: Television/Radio Age, 1981.

Udelson, Joseph H. *The Great Television Race: A History of the American Television Industry, 1925–1941*. University: University of Alabama Press, 1982.

U.S. Congress. Senate. Committee on Interstate and Foreign Commerce. *Investigation of Television Networks and the UHF and VHF Problem—Progress Report Prepared by Robert J. Jones, Special Counsel*. 84th Cong., 1st sess., 1955.

————. *Allocation of T.V. Channels—Report of the Ad Hoc Advisory Committee on Allocations*. 85th Cong., 2d sess., 1958.

————. Subcommittee on Communications. *Hearings on Status of T.V. Stations and S. 3095*. 83d Cong., 2d sess., 1954.

U.S. Federal Radio Commission. *Annual Report*. Washington, DC: U.S. Government Printing Office, 1927.

Watson-Watt, Robert A. *The Pulse of Radar: The Autobiography of Sir Robert Watson-Watt*. New York: Dial Press, 1959.

Webbink, Douglas William. "The All-Channel Receiver Law and the Future of Ultra-High Frequency Television." Ph.D. diss., Duke University, 1968.

Wise, George. *Willis R. Whitney, General Electric, and the Origins of U.S. Industrial Research*. New York: Columbia University Press, 1985.

Part XI

Transportation Equipment
ESIC 37.0

CHAPTER 18

MOTOR VEHICLES AND EQUIPMENT, 37.1

ROBERT M. ADUDDELL AND LOUIS P. CAIN

The principal historian of the American automobile industry is John B. Rae, who dominates the historiography of automobiles to an extent unmatched by the scholars of other industries. Rae has published several general studies, each of which includes an extensive bibliography (1959, 1965, 1971, 1984).

Inventors from several countries contributed to the development of the automobile. In the early years of the twentieth century the industry became an American phenomenon, largely because Henry Ford made the automobile available to the middle class. In Europe automobiles remained a toy for the upper classes. Nevertheless, the European industry continued to add technological improvements.

In the years since World War II the automobile industry has been internationalized. Any bibliography that focused exclusively on America would miss an important dimension of the industry, one that affects American consumers. Public policy toward the automobile industry is increasingly complex, especially in treating the international dimensions of the industry and the safety and environmental issues of the domestic economy. The energy crisis of the 1970s changed policy and the composition of industry output.

The bibliography is divided into five sections. The first emphasizes the history of the American automobile industry and the second, histories of individual companies within that industry. The third section contains biographies and autobiographies of industry leaders and is followed by a listing of recent books dealing with the international industry. The fifth section provides a broad view of public policy on the automobile industry, including such issues as mileage, pollution, safety, quotas, and the effect of interna-

tional trends in the industry. The following discussion provides a short guide
to the important entries in each section.

INDUSTRY STUDIES

In addition to Rae's books mentioned above, the most widely cited industry overviews are Chandler's (1964) and White's (1971). Alfred D. Chandler, Jr., offers a collection of source materials and readings on the industry
in general, and on Ford and General Motors in particular. L. J. White
presents a comprehensive view of the postwar industry, but his analysis
does not encompass the current period of increasing regulatory control and
international competition. The National Academy of Engineering (1982)
provides an excellent overview of the industry from the end of White's
coverage and is particularly suited to the technologically oriented researcher.
J. A. Hunker (1983) discusses that same period from a more technical economic viewpoint. Hunker emphasizes joint ventures as a response to what
he describes as the U.S. failure to maintain technological leadership. In a
widely cited study of the early industry, Ralph C. Epstein (1928) emphasizes
the emergence of the three largest U.S. producers: Chrysler, Ford, and General Motors. One of the best and most accessible studies of the contemporary
industry, which also contains an exceptional bibliography, is a paper by
Walter Adams and James W. Brock (1986) published in a volume edited
by Adams. Most of the other entries deal with narrower aspects of industry
development and performance. Of these, Seltzer's (1928) is an early financial
history of the industry, and Pashigian's (1961) is a classic study of the
industry's dealership network. Robert Paul Thomas (1973) explains how
annual model changes contributed to concentration in the industry.

COMPANY HISTORY

Although the history of the automobile industry has been dominated by
a single scholar, John B. Rae, many others have written important studies
of individual firms. The most famous of these studies is Allan Nevins and
Frank E. Hill's three-volume history of the Ford Motor Company. The initial
volume concentrates on Henry Ford as an individual and is included in the
biography section of the bibliography. The other two volumes, *Ford: Expansion and Challenge, 1915–1932* (Nevins and Hill 1957) and *Ford: Decline and Rebirth, 1933–1962* (Nevins and Hill 1962), are perhaps the most
widely cited histories of an automobile firm. Ford dominated the early
industry, so there are many studies of the company and specific aspects of
its history. Among the most important is Meyer (1981) on the infamous
"five-dollar day," a topic that has also been the subject of an interesting
study by Daniel Raff (1988). Arthur J. Kuhn (1986) presents an analysis of
the decline of Ford relative to General Motors.

In his justly famous *Strategy and Structure*, Alfred D. Chandler, Jr. (1962), includes a detailed case study of the evolution of managerial structures at General Motors. H. Thomas Johnson (1978) in turn describes how GM's multidivisional structure precipitated important developments in managerial accounting. An early work by Peter F. Drucker (1946), a popular writer on management, makes extensive use of individual company histories. R. B. Reich and J. D. Donahue (1985) examine the recent travails of Chrysler, as do two congressional studies (U.S. Congress 1980a, 1980b). A U.S. Department of Transportation (1981) publication focuses on how the Iranian crisis of 1979 affected major American firms.

BIOGRAPHY

Biographical and autobiographical accounts of key American automobile producers are even more plentiful than company histories, although it is difficult to separate the contributions of Henry Ford, William C. Durant, Alfred P. Sloan, Jr., and Walter Chrysler from the companies they headed. As noted, *Ford: The Times, the Man, the Company* (Nevins and Hill 1954) is volume 1 of a three-volume history of the company and focuses on the entrepreneur. *My Life and Work* (Ford 1922), written with the assistance of Samuel Crowther, is perhaps Ford's most important account of his enterprise. An eminently readable short biography of Ford can be found in *The Vital Few* (Hughes 1986). In 1948 Charles E. Sorensen published an autobiographical account of his forty years at Ford. Among the more important studies on Durant are Gustin (1973), Rae (1958), and Weisberger (1979). Sloan (1941) and (1964) are two autobiographical accounts by Durant's successor at General Motors. Beasley (1945), Boyd (1957), Leslie (1983), May (1977), and Niemeyer (1963) are biographies of individuals whose primary contribution to the industry was through General Motors. *Life of an American Workman* (1938) is an autobiography by Chrysler, an early pioneer whose company became the third largest American producer. *Iacocca* (1984) is a popular autobiography of that company's current chief executive officer. Frank Cormier and William J. Eaton (1970) and Victor G. Reuther (1976) contributed studies of the industry's most prominent labor leader.

INTERNATIONAL STUDIES

This section lists a variety of studies, including histories of the industry in particular countries, company histories, and biographies. Of particular interest is Wilkins and Hill (1964), which was written to complement Nevins' three-volume history of Ford. Bennett and Sharpe (1985), Cusumano (1985), Dunnett (1980), and Kronish and Mericle (1984) are examples of recent studies of national industries. Laux (1976) is a study of the French

industry in the years before World War I. Healey (1978), Rae (1982), and
Sedgwick (1974) are recent corporate histories of important international
companies. Bentley (1976), Church (1979), and Kamiya (1976) are interesting biographical studies. Tetsuo Abo (1981) discusses American automobile companies abroad in the interwar years. American automobile
companies' operations in Japan have been studied by Masaru Udagawa
(1985) and Mira Wilkins (1989).

PUBLIC POLICY

Before the mid–1950s road building and labor relations were the focus
of what little public policy there was toward the automobile industry. The
public sector generally supported the industry until the publication of *Unsafe
at Any Speed*, Ralph Nader's (1965) polemic on the industry's technology.
By then pollution and safety were developing as policy issues. More than
any other single event, the revelation that the industry had in turn investigated Nader altered the regulatory environment in which the industry
operated. Almost overnight the supportive public posture was replaced by
an adversarial relationship in which congressional committees mandated
change. The bibliography includes congressional and departmental documents that either investigate suggested changes or support the need for
change. The energy crisis emerging in the early 1970s forced the industry's
regulatory agencies to formulate fuel conservation policies. As the American
automobile industry's dominant position in the world market began to
erode, government addressed the question of the impact of its regulations
on the competitiveness of the domestic industry and thus added a new
dimension and direction to regulation. Most of the important studies on
public policy toward the American automobile industry are of recent vintage.

As noted, Nader's (1965) is the seminal work on the need for modern
public policy. The later studies of automobile safety include Eastman (1984),
which emphasizes the impact of safety concerns on style, and Halpern
(1972), which discusses the corporate response to safety regulation. Peltzman (1975) and Robertson (1977) present opposing views of the economics
of safety regulation and White (1982) writes about the regulation of automobile pollution.

Studies on engine efficiency and mileage include Ginsburg and Abernathy
(1980), Hanson (1980), John et al. (1980), and Ronan and Abernathy (1978).
The development of international quotas is the subject of two U.S. International Trade Commission publications (1983, 1985), and Wells (1980).

Miscellaneous policy studies include Fine (1963), a study of the industry
under the NIRA; Fisher, Griliches, and Kaysen (1962) and Thomas (1973),
both on the impact of annual style changes; Macaulay (1966) and Marx
(1985), studies of the relationship of the manufacturers to their dealers; and

Guest (1973, 1979) and MacDonald (1963) on labor relations in the industry.

BIBLIOGRAPHY

Industry Studies

Abernathy, William J. *The Productivity Dilemma: Roadblock to Innovation in the Automobile Industry.* Baltimore: Johns Hopkins University Press, 1978.

Adams, Walter, and James W. Brock. "The Automobile Industry." In *The Structure of American Industry,* edited by W. Adams, 7th ed., 126–71. New York: Macmillan, 1986.

Anderson, Rudolph E. *The Story of the American Automobile.* Washington, DC: Public Affairs Press, 1950.

Automobile Manufacturers Association. *Freedom's Arsenal.* Detroit: AMA, 1950.

———. *Automobiles of America.* Detroit: Wayne State University Press, 1968.

Boyle, S. E., and T. F. Hogarty. "Pricing Behavior in the American Automobile Industry, 1957–71." *Journal of Industrial Economics* 24 (December 1975): 81–95.

Bruckberger, R. L. *Image of America.* New York: Charles Scribner's Sons, 1949.

Burlingame, Roger. *Backgrounds of Power.* New York: Charles Scribner's Sons, 1949.

Chandler, Alfred D., Jr. *Strategy and Structure: Chapters in the History of the Industrial Enterprise.* Cambridge, MA: MIT Press, 1962.

———. *Giant Enterprise: Ford, General Motors, and the Automobile Industry.* New York: Harcourt, Brace & World, 1964.

Chinoy, Gilbert. *Automobile Workers and the American Dream.* Garden City, NY: Doubleday, 1955.

Crandall, R. W. "Vertical Integration in the Automobile Industry." Ph.D. diss., Northwestern University, 1968.

Cray, E. *Chrome Colossus.* New York: McGraw-Hill, 1980.

Davison, C. St. C. B. *History of Steam Road Vehicles.* London: Science Museum, 1953.

Denison, Merrill. *The Power to Go.* Garden City, NY: Doubleday, 1956.

Diesel, Eugen, Gustav Goldbeck, and Friedrich Schildberger. *From Engines to Autos.* Chicago: Henry Regnery, 1960.

Douglass, Paul F. *Six upon the World.* Boston: Little, Brown, 1954.

Edwards, Charles E. *Dynamics of the United States Automobile Industry.* Columbia: University of South Carolina Press, 1965.

Epstein, Ralph C. *The Automobile Industry.* Chicago: A. W. Shaw, 1928.

Flink, James J. *America Adopts the Automobile.* Cambridge, MA: MIT Press, 1970.

———. *The Car Culture.* Cambridge, MA: MIT Press, 1975.

Flugge, Eva. "Possibilities and Problems of Integration in the Automobile Industry." *Journal of Political Economy* 37 (1929): 150–74.

The Future of the Automobile. Report of MIT's International Automobile Program. Cambridge, MA: MIT Press, 1984.

Glasscock, C. B. *The Gasoline Age.* Indianapolis: Bobbs-Merrill, 1937.

Greenleaf, William C. *Monopoly on Wheels*. Detroit: Wayne State University Press, 1961.

Harbridge House, Inc. *Corporate Strategies of the Automotive Manufacturers*. Lexington, MA: D. C. Heath, 1979.

Hunker, J. A. *Structural Change in the U.S. Automobile Industry*. Lexington, MA: D. C. Heath, 1983.

Hurley, Neil P. "The Automotive Industry: A Study in Industrial Location." *Land Economics* 35 (1959): 1–14.

Irvine, F. O. "Demand Equations for Individual New Models Estimated Using Transactions Prices with Implications for Regulatory Issues." *Southern Economic Journal* 49 (January 1983): 764–82.

Jerome, J. *The Death of the Automobile*. New York: Norton, 1972.

Keats, J. *The Insolent Chariots*. New York: J. B. Lippincott, 1958.

Kennedy, E. D. *The Automobile Industry*. New York: Reynal & Hitchcock, 1941.

Kwoka, J. E. "Market Power and Market Change in the U.S. Automobile Industry." *Journal of Industrial Economics* 32 (June 1984).

Maxim, Hiram Percy. *Horseless Carriage Days*. New York: Harper, 1937.

May, George S. *A Most Unique Machine: The Michigan Origins of the American Automobile Industry*. Grand Rapids, MI: Wm. B. Eerdmans, 1975.

Melman, S. *Profits Without Production*. New York: Knopf, 1983.

National Academy of Engineering. *The Competitive Status of the U.S. Auto Industry*. Washington, DC: National Academy Press, 1982.

Pashigian, B. P. *The Distribution of Automobiles: An Economic Analysis of the Franchise System*. Cambridge, MA: MIT Press, 1961.

Rae, John B. *American Automobile Manufacturers: The First Forty Years*. Philadelphia: Chilton, 1959.

———. *The American Automobile: A Brief History*. Chicago: University of Chicago Press, 1965.

———. *The Road and the Car in American Life*. Cambridge, MA: MIT Press, 1971.

———. *The American Automobile Industry*. Boston: Twayne, 1984.

Rothschild, Emma. *Paradise Lost: The Decline of the Auto-Industrial Age*. New York: Random House, 1973.

Seltzer, Lawrence H. *A Financial History of the American Automobile Industry*. Boston: Houghton Mifflin, 1928.

Seltzer, Lawrence H., and Robert P. Thomas. *An Analysis of the Pattern of Growth of the Automobile Industry, 1895–1929*. New York: Arno Press, 1977.

Thomas, Robert Paul. "An Analysis of the Pattern of Growth of the Automobile Industry: 1895–1929." Ph.D. diss., Northwestern University, 1965.

———. "Style Change and the Automobile Industry During the Roaring Twenties." In *Business Enterprise and Economic Change: Essays in Honor of Harold F. Williamson*, edited by Louis P. Cain and Paul J. Uselding. Kent, OH: Kent State University Press, 1973.

Thompson, George V. "Intercompany Technical Standardization in the Early American Automobile Industry." *Journal of Economic History* 14 (1954).

U.S. Department of Transportation. *The U.S. Automobile Industry, 1980*. Washington, DC: U.S. Government Printing Office, 1981.

———. *The U.S. Automobile Industry, 1981*. Washington, DC: U.S. Government Printing Office, 1982.

Vatter, Harold G. "Closure of Entry in the American Automobile Industry." *Oxford Economic Papers* 4 (October 1952): 213–34.

White, L. J. *The Automobile Industry Since 1945*. Cambridge, MA: Harvard University Press, 1971.

———. "The American Automobile Industry and the Small Car, 1945–70." *Journal of Industrial Economics* 20 (April 1972): 179–92.

Company History

Arnold, Horace, and Fay Faurote. *Ford Methods and the Ford Shops*. 1915. Reprint. New York: Arno Press, 1973.

Borth, Christy. *Masters of Mass Production*. Indianapolis: Bobbs-Merrill, 1945.

Chandler, Alfred D., Jr. *Strategy and Structure: Chapters in the History of the Industrial Enterprise*. Cambridge, MA: MIT Press, 1962.

Drucker, Peter F. *The Concept of the Corporation*. New York: John Day, 1946.

Fine, Sidney. *Sit-Down! The General Motors Strike in 1936–1937*. Ann Arbor: University of Michigan Press, 1969.

Johnson, H. Thomas. "Management Accounting in an Early Multi-divisional Organization: General Motors in the 1920s." *Business History Review* 52 (Winter 1978): 490–517.

Kuhn, Arthur J. *GM Passes Ford, 1918–1938: Designing the General Motors Performance-Control System*. University Park: Pennsylvania State University Press, 1986.

Longstreet, Stephen D. *A Century on Wheels: The Story of Studebaker*. New York: Henry Holt, 1952.

McLaughlin, Charles C. "The Stanley Steamer: A Study in Unsuccessful Innovation." *Explorations in Entrepreneurial History* 7 (October 1954): 37–47.

Meyer, Stephen III. *The Five Dollar Day: Labor Management and Social Control in the Ford Motor Company, 1908–1921*. Albany: State University of New York Press, 1981.

Nevins, Allan, and Frank E. Hill. *Ford: Expansion and Challenge, 1915–1932*. New York: Charles Scribner's Sons, 1957.

———. *Ford: Decline and Rebirth, 1933–1962*. New York: Charles Scribner's Sons, 1962.

Pound, Arthur. *The Turning Wheel: The Story of General Motors Through Twenty-Five Years, 1908–1933*. Garden City, NY: Doubleday, Doran, 1934.

Raff, Daniel. "Wage Determination Theory and the Five-Dollar Day at Ford." *Journal of Economic History* 48 (June 1988): 387–400.

Reich, R. B., and J. D. Donahue. *New Deals: The Chrysler Revival and the American System*. New York: Times Books, 1985.

U.S. Congress. House. Committee on Banking, Finance, and Urban Affairs. Subcommittee on Economic Stabilization. *Findings of the Chrysler Corporation Loan Guarantee Board*, parts 1 and 2. 96th Cong., 1st sess., 1980a.

———. *Findings of the Chrysler Corporation Loan Guarantee Board*. 96th Cong., 2d sess., 1980b.

———. *To Determine the Impact of Foreign Sourcing on Industry and Communities, Hearing*. 97th Cong., 1st sess., 1981.

U.S. Congress. Senate. Committee on the Judiciary. Subcommittee on Antitrust and

Monopoly. *Bigness and Concentration of Economic Power—A Case Study of General Motors Corporation, Report.* 84th Cong., 2d sess., 1956.

U.S. Department of Labor. "The General Motors Corporation Strike." *Monthly Labor Review* (March 1937): 666–70.

U.S. Department of Transportation. *The U.S. Automobile Industry, 1980.* Washington, DC: U.S. Government Printing Office, 1981.

————. Transportation Systems Center. *U.S. Department of Transportation, Transportation Systems Center, Analysis of American Motors Corporation's Financial Status.* Cambridge, MA: Transportation Systems Center, February 1977.

Wright, J. P. *On a Clear Day You Can See General Motors.* Grosse Point, MI: Wright Enterprises, 1979.

Biography

Beasley, Norman. *Knudsen: A Biography.* New York: McGraw-Hill, 1945.

Boyd, Thomas A. *Professional Amateur: The Biography of Charles F. Kettering.* New York: Dutton, 1957.

Chrysler, Walter, with Boyden Sparks. *Life of an American Workman.* Philadelphia: Curtiss, 1938.

Cormier, Frank, and William J. Eaton. *Reuther.* Englewood Cliffs, NJ: Prentice-Hall, 1970.

Ford, Henry, with Samuel Crowther. *My Life and Work.* New York: Doubleday, 1922.

Gustin, Lawrence R. *Billy Durant: Creator of General Motors.* Grand Rapids, MI: Wm. B. Eerdmans, 1973.

Herndon, Booton. *Ford: An Unconventional Biography of the Men and Their Times.* New York: Weybright & Talley, 1969.

Hughes, Jonathan R. T. *The Vital Few.* New York: Oxford University Press, 1986.

Iacocca, Lee. *Iacocca.* New York: Bantam Books, 1984.

Jardin, Anne. *The First Henry Ford: A Study in Personality and Business Leadership.* Cambridge, MA: MIT Press, 1970.

Leland, Ottilie M., and M. D. Millbrook. *Master of Precision: Henry M. Leland.* Detroit: Wayne State University Press, 1966.

Leslie, Stuart W. "Thomas Midgeley and the Politics of Industrial Research." *Business History Review* 54 (Winter 1980): 480–503.

————. *Boss Kettering: Wizard of General Motors.* New York: Columbia University Press, 1983.

Lewis, David L. *The Public Image of Henry Ford.* Detroit: Wayne State University Press, 1976.

May, George S. *R. E. Olds: Auto Industry Pioneer.* Grand Rapids, MI: Wm. B. Eerdmans, 1977.

Nevins, Allan, and Frank E. Hill. *Ford: The Times, the Man, the Company.* New York: Charles Scribner's Sons, 1954.

Niemeyer, Glenn E. *The Automotive Career of Ransom E. Olds.* East Lansing: Michigan State University Press, 1963.

Rae, John B. "The Fabulous Billy Durant." *Business History Review* 32 (Fall 1958): 225–71.

Reuther, Victor G. *The Brothers Reuther and the Story of the UAW: A Memoir.* Boston: Houghton Mifflin, 1976.

Sloan, Alfred P., Jr., with Boyden Sparks. *Adventures of a White Collar Man.* New York: Doubleday, Doran, 1941.

————. *My Years with General Motors.* New York: Doubleday, 1964.

Sorensen, Charles E. *My Forty Years with Ford.* New York: Rinehart, 1948.

Sward, Keith. *The Legend of Henry Ford.* New York: Rinehart, 1948.

Thomas, Robert P. "The Automobile Industry and Its Tycoon." *Explorations in Entrepreneurial History.* 2d ser., 6 (Winter 1969): 139–57.

Weisberger, Bernard A. *The Dream Maker: William C. Durant, Founder of General Motors.* Boston: Little, Brown, 1979.

Wik, Reynold M. *Henry Ford and Grass Roots America.* Ann Arbor: University of Michigan Press, 1972.

International Studies

Abernathy, William J., James E. Harbour, and Jay M. Henn. *Productivity and Comparative Cost Advantage: Some Estimates for Major Automotive Producers.* Report to the Transportation Systems Center, U.S. Department of Transportation. Cambridge, MA: Transportation Systems Center, December 1980.

Abo, Tetsuo. "American Automobile Enterprises Abroad in the Interwar Period." *Annals of the Institute of Social Science* 22 (1981): 183–224.

Ankli, Robert E., and Fred Frederiksen. "The Influence of American Manufacturers on the Canadian Automobile Industry." In *Business and Economic History*, edited by Jeremy Atack, vol. 10, 101–13. Champaign, IL: Bureau of Economic and Business Research, 1981.

Bennett, Douglass C., and Kenneth E. Sharpe. *Transnational Corporations Versus the State: The Political Economy of the Mexican Auto Industry.* Princeton: Princeton University Press, 1985.

Bentley, John. *We at Porsche: The Autobiography of Dr. Ing. h.c. Ferry Porsche.* Garden City, NY: Doubleday, 1976.

Bergsten, C. Fred. "On the Non-equivalence of Import Quotas and 'Voluntary' Export Restraints." In *Toward a New World Trade Policy: The Maidenhead Papers*, edited by C. Fred Bergsten. Lexington, MA: Lexington Books, D. C. Heath, 1975.

Bhaskar, Krish N. *The Future of the World Motor Industry.* New York: Nichols Publishing, 1980.

Bloomfield, Gerald T. *The World Automotive Industry.* Newton Abbott, Eng.: David & Charles, 1978.

British Central Policy Review Staff. *The Future of the British Car Industry.* London: Her Majesty's Stationery Office, 1974.

Church, Roy. *Herbert Austin: The British Motor Car Industry to 1941.* London: Europa Publications, 1979.

Cusumano, Michael A. *The Japanese Automobile Industry: Technology and Management at Nissan and Toyota.* Cambridge, MA: Harvard University Press, 1985.

Duncan, W. *U.S.-Japan Automobile Diplomacy.* Cambridge, MA: Ballinger, 1973.

Dunnett, Peter J. S. *The Decline of the British Motor Industry: The Effects of Government Policy, 1945–1975.* Totowa, NJ: Croom Helm, 1980.

Fuller, Mark B. *Government Intervention in the Auto Industry: Japan.* Boston: Harvard Business School, 1980.

Giedion, Sigfried. *Mechanization Takes Command.* New York: Oxford University Press, 1948.

Hayes, Robert H. "Why Japanese Factories Work." *Harvard Business Review* 59 (July-August 1981): 56–66.

Healey, Geoffrey. *Austin Healey: The Study of the Big Healeys.* New York: Dodd, Mead, 1978.

Heywood, John, and John Wilkes. "Is There a Better Automobile Engine?" *Technology Review* (November-December 1980): 18–29.

Hurter, Donald A. *The Changing World Automotive Industry Through 2000.* Cambridge, MA: Arthur D. Little, 1980.

Kamiya, Shotaro. *My Life with Toyota.* Translated by Thomas I. Elliott. Tokyo, Japan: Toyota Motor Sales Co., 1976.

Katz, Abraham. Statement of Abraham Katz, Assistant Secretary of Commerce for International Economic Policy, before the Subcommittee on Trade of the House Ways and Means Committee. March 18, 1980.

Kraar, L. "Detroit's New Asian Car Strategy." *Fortune* 110 (December 10, 1984): 172–78.

Kronish, Rich, and Kenneth S. Mericle, eds. *The Political Economy of the Latin American Motor Vehicle Industry.* Cambridge, MA: MIT Press, 1984.

Laux, James M. *In First Gear: The French Automobile Industry to 1914.* Montreal: McGill-Queen's University Press, 1976.

Laux, James M., Jean-Pierre Bardou, Jean-Jacques Chanaron, and Patrick Fridenson. *The Automobile Revolution: The Impact of an Industry.* Translated by James M. Laux. Chapel Hill: University of North Carolina Press, 1982.

Monden, Yasuhiro. "What Makes the Toyota Production System Really Tick?" *Industrial Engineering* 13 (January 1981): 37–46.

Office of Technology Assessment. *U.S. Industrial Competitiveness: A Comparison of Steel, Electronics, and Automobiles.* Washington, DC: U.S. Government Printing Office, 1981.

Rae, John B. *Nissan/Datsun: A History of Nissan Motor Corporation in the U.S.A., 1960–1980.* New York: McGraw-Hill, 1982.

Ronan, Lawrence, and William J. Abernathy. "The Honda Motor Company's CVCC Engine: A Case Study of Innovation." Harvard Business School Working Paper No. 78, 1978.

Sedgwick, Michael. *Fiat.* New York: Arco, 1974.

Stokes, H. S. "Honda, the Market Guzzler." *Fortune* 109 (February 20, 1984): 104–108.

Thomas, David, and Tom Donnelly. *The Motor Car Industry in Coventry Since the 1890s.* New York: St. Martin's Press, 1985.

Toder, Eric J., Nicholas S. Cardell, and Ellen Burton. *Trade Policy and the U.S. Automobile Industry.* New York: Praeger, 1978.

Udagawa, Masaru. "The Prewar Japanese Automobile Industry and American Manufacturers." *Japanese Yearbook on Business History* 2 (1985): 81–99.

U.S. Congress. House. Committee on Ways and Means. Subcommittee on Trade.

World Auto Trade: Current Trends and Structural Problems, Hearings. 96th Cong., 2d sess., 1980.

———. House. Committee on Banking, Finance, and Urban Affairs. Subcommittee on Economic Stabilization. *To Determine the Impact of Foreign Sourcing on Industry and Communities, Hearing.* 97th Cong., 1st sess., 1981.

———. Joint Economic Committee. *Japanese Voluntary Export Limits, Hearings.* 98th Cong., 1st sess., 1984.

White, L. J. *The Automobile Industry Since 1945.* Cambridge, MA: Harvard University Press, 1971.

Wilkins, Mira. "Multinational Automobile Enterprises and Regulation: An Historical Overview." In *Government, Technology and the Future of the Automobile,* edited by D. H. Ginsburg and William J. Abernathy, 221–58. New York: McGraw-Hill, 1980.

———. "The Contributions of Foreign Enterprises to Japanese Economic Development." In *Foreign Business in Japan,* edited by T. Yuzawa and M. Udagawa. Tokyo: University of Tokyo Press, forthcoming.

Wilkins, Mira, and Frank E. Hill. *American Business Abroad: Ford on Six Continents.* Detroit: Wayne State University Press, 1964.

Public Policy

Barrett, Paul. *The Automobile and Urban Transit: The Formation of Public Policy in Chicago, 1900–1930.* Philadelphia: Temple University Press, 1983.

Bradley, P. Stephen, and Annel G. Karnani. *Automotive Manufacturer Risk Analysis: Meeting the Automotive Fuel Economy Standards.* Report prepared for the U.S. Department of Transportation-Transportation Systems Center. Bedford, MA: HH Aerospace Design Co., 1978.

Committee on Motor Vehicle Emissions. National Research Council Consultants Report. *Manufacturability and Costs of Proposed Low Emissions Automotive Engine Systems.* Washington, DC: National Academy of Sciences, 1974.

Eastman, Joel W. *Styling vs. Safety: The American Automobile Industry and the Development of Automotive Safety, 1900–1966.* Lanham, MD: University Press of America, 1984.

Fine, Sidney. *The Automobile Under the Blue Eagle.* Ann Arbor: University of Michigan Press, 1963.

Fisher, F. M., Z. Griliches, and C. Kaysen. "The Costs of Automobile Model Changes Since 1949." *Journal of Political Economy* 70 (October 1962): 433–51.

Foster, Mark S. *From Streetcar to Superhighway.* Philadelphia: Temple University Press, 1981.

Ginsburg, D. H., and William J. Abernathy. *Government, Technology and the Future of the Automobile.* New York: McGraw-Hill, 1980.

Goodson, R. E. *Federal Regulation of Motor Vehicles: A Summary and Analysis.* Report to the U.S. Department of Transportation. Washington, DC: U.S. Department of Transportation, 1977.

Guest, Robert H. "The Man on the Assembly Line: A Generation Later." *Tuck Today* (May 1973): 1–8.

———. "Quality of Work Life—Learning from Tarrytown." *Harvard Business Review* 57 (July-August 1979): 76–87.

Halpern, Paul J. "Consumer Politics and Corporate Behavior: The Case of Automobile Safety." Ph.D. diss., Harvard University, 1972.

Hanson, Kirk O. "The Effect of Fuel Economy Standards on Corporate Strategy in the Automobile Industry." In *Government, Technology and the Future of the Automobile*, edited by D. H. Ginsburg and William J. Abernathy, 144–61. New York: McGraw-Hill, 1980.

Harbridge House, Inc. *Corporate Strategies of the Automotive Manufacturers: Vol. 1, Strategic Histories*. Prepared for the U.S. Department of Transportation, National Highway Traffic Safety Administration. Boston: Harbridge House, June 1978.

John, Richard, et al. "Mandated Fuel Economy Standards as a Strategy for Improving Motor Vehicle Fuel Economy." In *Government, Technology and the Future of the Automobile*, edited by D. H. Ginsburg and William J. Abernathy, 118–43. New York: McGraw-Hill, 1980.

Katz, Harold. *The Decline of Competition in the Automobile Industry, 1920–1940*. New York: Arno Press, 1977.

Leavitt, H. *Superhighway-Superhoax*. New York: Doubleday, 1970.

Macaulay, Stewart. *Law and the Balance of Power: The Automobile Manufacturers and Their Dealers*. New York: Russell Sage Foundation, 1966.

MacDonald, Robert. *Collective Bargaining in the Automobile Industry*. New Haven: Yale University Press, 1963.

Marx, Thomas G. "The Development of the Franchise Distribution System in the U.S. Automobile Industry." *Business History Review* 59 (Autumn 1985): 465–74.

Menge, John A. "Style Change Cost as a Market Weapon." *Quarterly Journal of Economics* 76 (November 1962):623–47.

Mills, D. Q. "The Techniques of Automotive Regulation: Performance Versus Design Standards." In *Government, Technology and the Future of the Automobile*, edited by D. H. Ginsburg and William J. Abernathy, 64–76. New York: McGraw-Hill, 1980.

Nader, R. *Unsafe at Any Speed*. New York: Grossman, 1965.

National Academy of Sciences. *Report by the Committee on Motor Vehicle Emissions*. *Congressional Record*, February 28, 1973, 5831–52, Senate edition.

Owen, W. *The Accessible City*. Washington, DC: Brookings Institution, 1972.

Peltzman, S. "The Effects of Automobile Safety Regulation." *Journal of Political Economy* 83 (August 1975): 677–725.

Robertson, L. "A Critical Analysis of Peltzman's 'The Effects of Automobile Safety Regulation.'" *Journal of Economic Issues* 11 (September 1977): 587–600.

Ronan, Lawrence, and William J. Abernathy. "The Development and Introduction of the Automobile Turbocharger." Harvard Business School Working Paper No. 78, 1978.

Rose, Mark H. *Interstate: Express Highway Politics, 1941–1956*. Lawrence: Regents Press of Kansas, 1979.

Smog-Control Antitrust Case. *Congressional Record*, May 18, 1971, 15626–37, House edition.

Stockman, David. "The Wrong War? The Case Against National Energy Policy." *Public Interest* 53 (Fall 1978): 3–44.

Thomas, Robert P. "Style Change and the Automobile Industry During the Roaring

Twenties." In *Business Enterprise and Economic Change: Essays in Honor of Harold F. Williamson,* edited by Louis P. Cain and Paul J. Uselding. Kent, OH: Kent State University Press, 1973.

U.S. Congress. House. Committee on Energy and Commerce. Subcommittee on Commerce, Transportation, and Tourism. *Fair Practices in Automotive Products Act, Hearings.* 97th Cong., 2d sess., 1982a.

———. House. Committee on Energy and Commerce. Subcommittee on Telecommunications, Consumer Protection, and Finance. *National Highway Traffic Safety Administration, Oversight Hearings.* 97th Cong., 2d sess., 1982b.

———. House. Committee on Science and Technology. Subcommittee on Transportation, Aviation, and Materials. *H.R. 5880: Automobile Research Competition Act, Hearings.* 97th Cong., 2d sess., 1982.

———. House. Committee on Ways and Means. Subcommittee on Trade. *Domestic Content Legislation and the U.S. Automobile Industry.* 97th Cong., 2d sess., 1982a.

———. House. Committee on Ways and Means. Subcommittee on Trade. *Fair Practices in Automotive Products Act, Hearings.* 97th Cong., 2d sess., 1982b.

———. House. Committee on Energy and Commerce. Subcommittee on Commerce, Transportation, and Tourism. *Future of the Automobile Industry, Hearings.* 98th Cong., 2d sess., 1984.

———. Senate. Committee on the Judiciary. *Administered Prices: Automobiles.* 85th Cong., 2d sess., 1958.

———. Senate. Committee on Government Operations. Subcommittee on Executive Reorganization. *Federal Role in Traffic Safety, Hearings.* 89th Cong., 1st and 2d sessions, 1965–66.

———. Senate. Committee on Small Business. Subcommittee on Retailing, Distribution, and Marketing Practices. *Planning, Regulation, and Competition: Automobile Industry, Hearings.* 90th Cong., 2d sess., 1968.

———. Senate. Committee on Commerce. *Automotive Research and Development and Fuel Economy, Hearings.* 93d Cong., 1st sess., 1973.

———. Senate. Committee on the Judiciary. Subcommittee on Antitrust and Monopoly. *The Industrial Reorganization Act, Hearings.* 93d Cong., 2d sess., 1974a.

———. Senate. Committee on the Judiciary. Subcommittee on Antitrust and Monopoly. *A Reorganization of the U.S. Automobile Industry.* 93d Cong., 2d sess., 1974b.

———. Senate. Committee on Banking, Housing, and Urban Affairs. Subcommittee on Economic Stabilization. *Government Regulation of the Automobile Industry, Hearings.* 96th Cong., 1st sess., 1979.

———. Senate. Committee on Finance. Subcommittee on International Trade. *Issues Relating to the Domestic Auto Industry, Hearings.* 97th Cong., 1st sess., 1981–82.

———. Senate. Committee on Commerce, Science, and Transportation. Subcommittee on Surface Transportation. *Motor Vehicle Safety and the Marketplace, Hearings.* 98th Cong., 1st sess., 1983.

U.S. Department of Transportation. *Automobile Fuel Economy Program: Fifth Annual Report to the Congress.* Washington, DC: U.S. Government Printing Office, 1981.

U.S. Federal Trade Commission. *Report on the Motor Vehicle Industry.* Washington, DC: U.S. Government Printing Office, 1939.

U.S. International Trade Commission. *Certain Motor Vehicles and Certain Chassis and Bodies Therefor.* USITC Pub. No. 1110. Washington, DC: USITC, 1980.

———. *The U.S. Auto Industry: U.S. Factory Sales, Retail Sales, Imports, Exports, Apparent Consumption, Suggested Retail Prices, and Trade Balances with Selected Countries for Motor Vehicles, 1964–82.* USITC Pub. No. 1419. Washington, DC: USITC, 1983.

———. *A Review of Recent Developments in the U.S. Automobile Industry. Including an Assessment of the Japanese Voluntary Restraint Agreements.* USITC Pub. No. 1648. Washington, DC: USITC, February 1985.

Wells, Louis T., Jr. "The International Product Life Cycle and United States Regulation of the Automobile Industry." In *Government, Technology and the Future of the Automobile,* edited by D. H. Ginsburg and William J. Abernathy, 270–305. New York: McGraw-Hill, 1980.

White, L. J. *The Regulation of Air-Pollutant Emissions from Motor Vehicles.* Washington, DC: American Enterprise Institute, 1982.

CHAPTER 19

SHIP AND BOAT BUILDING AND REPAIRING, 37.3

TIMOTHY E. SULLIVAN

SHIPBUILDING—GENERAL

Water transportation has always been important to the U.S. economy. Americans enjoy an extensive system of navigable rivers, coastal waters, lakes, and, of course, access to oceans. They know the necessity of building and maintaining a variety of boats and ships. Their shipwrights constructed vessels of wood, iron, steel, aluminum, and composite materials and propelled them with wind, human and animal muscle, and machinery fueled by wood, coal, oil, and nuclear power.

The importance of waterborne commerce throughout the eighteenth and early nineteenth centuries made shipbuilding, boatbuilding, and repair a leading industry whose significance was magnified by its unique standing in both input and output markets. The ownership of vessels was widely dispersed, although a few investors held many titles. Diversified ownership has long been used to decrease financial risk in maritime societies (Bailyn and Bailyn 1959).

Shipbuilding declined in the second half of the nineteenth century, but remained an important industry well into the twentieth. After a half century of neglect and decline, from 1850 to 1914, U.S. shipbuilding was reinvigorated by the Shipping Act of 1916. Nevertheless, the prodigious production of wartime ships was followed by a shipping depression that began in the early 1920s and continued into the 1930s. During World War II, U.S. shipyards mass produced ships, especially the Liberty class merchant vessels. After 1945 U.S. shipbuilders found it increasingly difficult to meet foreign competition, and by the 1980s two-thirds of the gross new tonnage was built in Japan, South Korea, and China. Japan dominates shipbuilding, although it is domination of a declining industry (Whitehurst 1986).

Several general histories of transportation analyze the regional and national impact of ships, shipbuilding, and related industries. Chief among these is George Rogers Taylor's study of the transportation revolution. Although he limited his investigation to 1815–1860, his book is a standard on the importance and impact of transportation (Taylor [1951] 1968). Another early comprehensive study of pre–Civil War transportation emphasizes lake and river vessels and the development and improvements of inland water routes (Meyer [1917] 1948).

The early history of the American shipbuilding industry was outlined in impressive detail by the U.S. Bureau of the Census (Hall 1884). Data and descriptions were collected from primary and secondary sources from 1880 to 1882 on fishing vessels, merchant sailing vessels, ship design and construction, steam vessels, iron vessels, canal boats, the U.S. Navy yards, and shipbuilding timber. Henry Hall's report includes not only scaled diagrams and illustrations of ship design but also the estimated costs of outfitting a typical voyage. The report describes the state of shipbuilding and repair by the nation's centennial and serves as a history of shipping since the colonial era.

An overview of the modern history of the U.S. shipbuilding industry can be garnered from contemporary figures published by the U.S. Bureau of the Census (1975) as well as the annual report on shipbuilding and repair published by the U.S. Navy. Among the useful comprehensive guides to the history of shipbuilding is a study by Clinton Whitehurst, Jr. (1986).

COLONIAL SHIPBUILDING

Shipbuilding and repair was an essential industry in colonial America, where domestic shipbuilders followed European techniques. Despite their importance, shipwrights were generally not awarded the esteem that their skills and economic contributions warranted (Goldenberg 1976). Difficulties persist in determining the size and tonnage of colonial ships, but evidence indicates that cargo tonnage averaged more than twice registered tonnage. Since most of the data on colonial ships are expressed in registered tonnage, both the size of ships and the size of the industry can be easily understated (McCusker 1981). Estimates of the industry's impact on colonial exports suggest that shipbuilding contributed to colonial export earnings (Price 1976).

Technical advances in colonial shipbuilding were obstructed by institutional factors, such as the guild system, that affected the free movement of capital and labor (Walton 1970). Techniques of production varied by shipyard. Several regional histories describe the methods and evolution of colonial shipbuilding and illustrate how the industry differed from New England to Virginia (Huffington and Nelson 1939; Minchinton 1961; Kelso 1973).

MERCHANT SHIPPING

The rise of merchant shipping from the colonial period through the Golden Age of the mid-nineteenth century, the decline in the postbellum period, and the maritime activity surrounding the world wars is reflected in ship design and the number of ships constructed (Kilmarx 1979; MacGregor 1984). Ships are usually built for business or warfare. In Baltimore during the early national period the majority of maritime vessels were registered to merchants (Gilbert 1984). Modern commercial fleets comprise some 25,000 oceangoing vessels that accommodate diverse needs, business practices, and economic organization (Kendall 1986).

Maritime economics is the application of economic principles to sea transport, optimal ship design, seaport construction, and the movements of ships in seaports (Goss 1968). The economics of flag discrimination, estimations of the cost of a ship's time, the costs of maritime congestion, and the economies of size for merchant ships are other maritime economics issues (Goss 1977).

Commercial ships and merchant shipping have been important to U.S. domestic as well as international trade. The rapid expansion of Great Lakes shipping during the late nineteenth century would have been impossible without improvements in the design and capacity of merchant vessels (Williamson 1977). Nevertheless, the American merchant marine languished during a period of rapid industrial and agricultural development. The years from 1865 to 1914 are often referred to as the era of neglect and decline. Neglect ended with the federal government's establishing inducements for linking commerce with defense. In many ways these links still govern U.S. maritime policy (Safford 1985).

SHIP DESIGN, CONSTRUCTION, AND TECHNOLOGY

For most of recorded history ships were the largest and most elaborate machines that people constructed. The complexities of shipbuilding technology notwithstanding, the hulls of wooden ships were constructed without formal plans; so there was little uniformity among ships. Several business histories describe, often in great detail, the boats and ships manufactured in America. They also offer a social history of the industry (Briggs [1889] 1970; Wright 1969).

Technological change is usually cited as the primary factor behind economic growth and improvements in productivity. From 1600 to 1850, however, the decline in maritime piracy and improved economic organization appear to have contributed more to productivity than did technological change in ship design (North 1968).

The importance of U.S. wooden sailing ships can be traced to their low cost of construction. Their decline is tied to the technical and practical improvements in British steamship production (Graham 1956). In the years after 1820, the American shipping industry dominated world maritime trade because American shipyards built clipper ships renowned for speed (Howe and Matthews 1986). Speed gave Americans an edge on the China trade route, a passage for speculators bound for the gold strikes of California and Australia. But the clippers could not compete with British steamships. The second half of the nineteenth century witnessed the decline of the sleek clipper and the ascendency of the steam-powered scow. The steamship's large cargo capacity overwhelmed its romantic competitor.

The decline of U.S. shipbuilding in the late nineteenth century was linked to American reluctance to replace wooden hulls with metal hulls and to the falling prices of British iron (Harley 1973). Unfortunately this was neither the first, nor the last, time the industry was slow to adopt new technology. In the early twentieth century British shipbuilders hesitated to replace coal with oil and thereby contributed to the decline of British shipping (Fletcher 1975).

Newer technologies do not always drive out older ones. American flat-boats—wooden barges—remained a viable form of transportation long after the adoption of steamboats, because they were an inexpensive way to move cargo downriver (Mak and Walton 1973). A variety of technological, economic, and political factors have created the modern shipping industry, but increased specialization may be one of its few constants (Gubbins 1986).

STEAMBOATING ON THE WESTERN RIVERS

The development and diffusion of technological change and the resulting improvements in productivity in shipping during the early nineteenth century can be gauged by the emergence of steamboats and the decline of keelboats (Hunter 1949; Mak and Walton 1972). Keelboats—barges pushed upstream with poles—were displaced by the more efficient steamboat, but flatboats—barges that flowed downstream with the current—remained a part of river traffic. Steamboats were more cost-effective than keelboats but not as cost-effective as flatboats (Smith 1957; Haites and Mak 1970, 1973; Haites, Mak, and Walton 1975). Variations in the rate of profitability of steamboating reflect risks of capital losses. After 1850 steamboats remained economically viable on tributary rivers but were declining in importance on trunk river routes (Atack, Haites, Mak, and Walton 1975). They were eventually replaced by railroads, but the rise and decline of steamboating provide insights into contemporary technological and economic change (Brown 1918; Shepard 1948).

The romance of steamboating is an integral part of American social history, and it has economic links as well. The diaries, recollections, and interpretations of steamboat captains and commercial operators provide insight into the impact that shipping had on the pace and pattern of business activity as well as on the design, construction, operation, and maintenance of vessels (Chittenden 1903; Hoopes 1936; Lass 1962; Petersen 1968; Merrick [1909] 1987).

SHIPPING POLICIES, PRACTICES, AND REGULATIONS

The organization, management, and operation of American shipping parallels shifting political and economic power (Branch 1975, 1982; Frankel 1982a, 1982b). Modern shipping benefitted from favorable public policy and an expanded perspective of American commerce in the world economy (Hutchins 1941, 1954). However, transportation costs may well be a more imposing trade barrier than administered prices and a tariff structure (Yeats 1981).

Shipbuilding techniques and methods of debt financing are developed and managerial decisions made within an economic system that is defined by rules and regulations (Roukis 1983). The precise impact of these is debatable, but it would be impossible to describe modern shipbuilding without considering the regulations imposed on shipping and alternative forms of transportation (Taylor 1970).

American shipbuilding was often dependent upon the fortunes of war (Heine 1980). During a national crisis, the commitment to shipbuilding is analogous to a feast; but once the crisis abates, famine returns.

The most obvious form of government involvement in shipbuilding is the construction of naval forces. Since the late eighteenth century, the federal government has funded the development and deployment of vessels from sailing ships, to steamships, to oil and diesel ships, and ultimately to nuclear-powered vessels (Hougaard 1978; Beach 1986). The debate continues on the relative costs and efficiencies of developing and deploying alternative vessels (Kaufmann 1987).

SHIPPING, INTERNAL IMPROVEMENTS, AND PORT CITIES

The location of economic activity and the efforts to improve the productivity of specific places offer insights into the history of the American shipbuilding industry. Shipping is primarily a commercial activity, so the growth of seaport cities can be traced to both ship design and port facilities (Gilchrist 1967; Clark 1970). Public works projects to improve port facilities often receive top priority (Krenkel 1965). Commercial activity dominates the twenty-four leading American ports of the modern era, but the composition of that activity is changing (Barsness 1974).

Improvements were not restricted to maritime trade or port cities. Over the years the shipping industry and the American economy have been dramatically influenced by internal improvements on rivers and canals (Taylor

[1951] 1968; Segal 1962; Goodrich 1970; Ransom 1975). The construction and use of canal boats, settlements along improved water routes, and the types of products transported demonstrate changes in the American shipping industry (Garrity 1977).

SHIPWRECKS, SHIPPING ACCIDENTS, AND MARITIME ARCHAEOLOGY

Shipwrecks and accounts of shipping accidents provide information not only on the design and construction of various vessels but also on the cargo they carried. Bruce D. Berman's (1972) *Encyclopedia of American Shipwrecks* lists more than 13,000 vessels, all over fifty tons, lost in U.S. territorial waters. He provides the names of the vessels, types, sizes, dates built, dates wrecked, causes and locations of the wrecks, and comments on the wrecks. For example, on the Chesapeake Bay from 1608 to 1978 the causes of shipwrecks included ice, fire, collision, explosion, war loss, stranding, and scuttling (Shomette 1982). Among other things the cause of a shipwreck provides a measure of technical progress and safety.

Many of the earlier histories of shipwrecks and accidents are sensational (Howland 1843). Others concentrate more on the facts and circumstances of the shipping disasters—useful information for an industry that requires large initial capital investments (Lloyd 1856).

The discovery, excavation, and reconstruction of lost vessels allows modern researchers to examine the design of various ships as well as the contents of the holds (Petsche 1974; Muckelroy 1978).

BIBLIOGRAPHY

Shipbuilding—General

Bailyn, Bernard, and Lotte Bailyn. *Massachusetts Shipping 1697–1914: A Statistical Study*. Cambridge, MA: Harvard University Press, 1959.

Hall, Henry. "Report on the Ship-building Industry in the United States." *Tenth Census of the United States, 1880*. Vol. 8, 1–265. Washington, DC: U.S. Government Printing Office, 1884.

Meyer, Balthasar Henry. *History of Transportation in the United States Before 1860*. Washington, DC: Carnegie Institution, 1917. Reprint. Gloucester, MA: Peter Smith, 1948.

Taylor, George Rogers. *The Transportation Revolution 1815–1860*. New York: Holt, Rinehart & Winston, 1951. Reprint. New York: Harper & Row, 1968.

U.S. Bureau of the Census. *Historical Statistics of the United States: Colonial Times to 1970*, ser. Q 413–564. Washington, DC: U.S. Government Printing Office, 1975.

U.S. Department of Navy. *Annual Report of the Secretary of the Navy*. Washington,

DC: Various publishers, 1836 to present. For reports prior to 1836, see *American State Papers*.

Whitehurst, Clinton H., Jr. *The U.S. Shipbuilding Industry: Past, Present, and Future*. Annapolis: Naval Institute Press, 1986.

Colonial Shipbuilding

Goldenbérg, Joseph A. *Shipbuilding in Colonial America*. Charlottesville: University Press of Virginia, 1976.

Huffington, Paul, and J. Nelson. "Evolution of Shipbuilding in Southeastern Massachusetts." *Economic Geography* 15 (October 1939): 362–78.

Kelso, William M. "Shipbuilding in Virginia, 1763–1774." In *Records of the Columbia Historical Society of Washington, D.C., 1971–1972*, 1–14. Baltimore: Waverly Press, 1973.

McCusker, John J. "The Tonnage of Ships Engaged in British Colonial Trade During the Eighteenth Century." In *Research in Economic History*, edited by Paul Uselding, vol. 6, 73–105. Greenwich, CT: JAI Press, 1981.

Minchinton, William E. "Shipbuilding in Colonial Rhode Island." *Rhode Island History* 20 (October 1961): 119–24.

Price, Jacob M. "A Note on the Value of Colonial Exports of Shipping." *Journal of Economic History* 36 (September 1976): 704–24.

Shepherd, James, and Gary Walton. *Shipping, Maritime Trade, and the Economic Development of Colonial North America*. New York: Cambridge University Press, 1972.

Walton, Gary. "Obstacles to Technical Diffusion in Ocean Shipping, 1675–1775." *Explorations in Economic History* 8 (Winter 1970): 123–40.

Merchant Shipping

Gilbert, Geoffrey. "Maritime Enterprise in the New Republic: Investment in Baltimore Shipping, 1789–1793." *Business History Review* 58 (Spring 1984): 14–29.

Goss, R. O. *Studies in Maritime Economics*. Cambridge, Eng.: Cambridge University Press, 1968.

———, ed. *Advances in Maritime Economics*. Cambridge, Eng.: Cambridge University Press, 1977.

Kendall, Lane. *The Business of Shipping*. Centerville, MD: Maritime Press, 1986.

Kilmarx, Robert A., ed. *America's Maritime Legacy: A History of the U.S. Merchant Marine and Shipbuilding Industry Since Colonial Times*. Boulder: Westview Press, 1979.

MacGregor, David R. *Merchant Sailing Ships 1775–1875*. 3 vols. Annapolis: Naval Institute Press, 1984.

Safford, Jeffrey. "The United States Merchant Marine in Foreign Trade, 1800–1939." In *Business History of Shipping: Strategy and Structure*, edited by Tsunehiko Yui and Keiichiro Nakagawa, 91–122. Tokyo: University of Tokyo Press, 1985.

Williamson, Samuel H. "The Growth of the Great Lakes as a Major Transportation

Resource, 1870–1911." In *Research in Economic History*, edited by Paul Uselding, vol. 2, 173–248. Greenwich, CT: JAI Press, 1977.

Ship Design, Construction, and Technology

Briggs, L. Vernon. *History of Shipbuilding on North River, Plymouth County, Massachusetts: With Genealogies of the Shipbuilders, and Accounts of the Industries upon Its Tributaries*. Boston: Coburn Brothers, 1889. Reprint. New York: Research Reprints, 1970.

Fletcher, Max E. "From Coal to Oil in British Shipping." *Journal of Transport History* n.s. 3 (February 1975): 1–19.

Graham, Gerald S. "The Ascendency of the Sailing Ship, 1850–85." *Economic History Review* 2d ser., 9 (August 1956): 74–88.

Gubbins, Edmund J. *The Shipping Industry: The Technology and Economics of Specialization*. New York: Gordon & Breach Science Publishers, 1986.

Harley, C. K. "On the Persistence of Old Technologies: The Case of North American Wooden Shipbuilding." *Journal of Economic History* 33 (June 1973): 372–98.

Howe, Octavius T., and Frederick C. Matthews. *American Clipper Ships 1833–1858*. 2 vols. New York: Dover Publications, 1986.

Mak, James, and Gary Walton. "The Persistence of Old Technologies: The Case of Flatboats." *Journal of Economic History* 33 (June 1973): 444–51.

North, Douglass C. "Sources of Productivity Change in Ocean Shipping." *Journal of Political Economy* 76 (September/October 1968): 953–70.

Wright, Richard J. *Freshwater Whales: A History of the American Ship Building Company and Its Predecessors*. Kent, OH: Kent State University Press, 1969.

Steamboating on the Western Rivers

Atack, Jeremy, Erik Haites, James Mak, and Gary Walton. "The Profitability of Steamboating on Western Rivers: 1850." *Business History Review* 49 (Autumn 1975): 346–54.

Brown, Paul W. "The Collapse of the Steamboat Traffic upon the Mississippi: An Inquiry into Causes." *Proceedings of the Mississippi Valley Historical Association* 9 (1918): 422–28.

Chittenden, Hiram M. *History of Early Steamboat Navigation on the Missouri River: Life and Adventures of Joseph La Barge*. 2 vols. New York: Francis P. Harper, 1903.

Haites, Erik, and James Mak. "Ohio and Mississippi River Transportation 1810–1860." *Explorations in Economic History* 8 (Winter 1970): 153–80.

———. "The Decline of Steamboating on the Antebellum Western Rivers: Some New Evidence and an Alternative Hypothesis." *Explorations in Economic History* 11 (Fall 1973): 25–36.

Haites, Erik, James Mak, and Gary Walton. *Western River Transportation: The Era of Early Internal Development, 1810–1860*. Baltimore: Johns Hopkins University Press, 1975.

Hoopes, Penrose Robinson. "Connecticut's Contribution to the Development of the

Steamboat." In *Tercentenary Commission of the State of Connecticut: Committee on Historical Publications*, No. 53. New Haven: Yale University Press, 1936.

Hunter, Louis C. *Steamboats on the Western Rivers: An Economic and Technological History.* Cambridge, MA: Harvard University Press, 1949.

Lass, William. *A History of Steamboating on the Upper Missouri River.* Lincoln: University of Nebraska Press, 1962.

Mak, James, and Gary Walton. "Steamboats and the Great Productivity Surge in River Transportation." *Journal of Economic History* 32 (September 1972): 619–40.

Merrick, George B. *Old Times on the Upper Mississippi: The Recollections of a Steamboat Pilot from 1854 to 1863.* Cleveland: Arthur C. Clark, 1909. Reprint. St. Paul, MN: Minnesota Historical Society Press, 1987.

Petersen, William J. *Steamboating on the Upper Mississippi.* Iowa City: State Historical Society of Iowa, 1968.

Shepard, Lee. "Early Steamboat Building at Cincinnati." *Bulletin of the Historical and Philosophical Society of Ohio* 6 (April 1948): 16–18.

Smith, Ophia D. "Cincinnati: From Keelboat to Steamboat." *Bulletin of the Historical and Philosophical Society of Ohio* 15 (October 1957): 259–89.

Shipping Policies, Practices, and Regulations

Beach, Edward L. *The United States Navy: 200 Years.* New York: H. Holt, 1986.

Branch, Alan E. *The Elements of Shipping.* London: Chapman & Hall, 1975.

———. *Economics of Shipping Practice and Management.* London: Chapman & Hall, 1982.

Frankel, Ernst G. *Management and Operations of American Shipping.* Boston: Auburn House, 1982a.

———. *Regulation and Policies of American Shipping.* Boston: Auburn House, 1982b.

Heine, Irwin M. *The U.S. Maritime Industry: In the National Interest.* Washington, DC: National Maritime Council, 1980.

Hougaard, William. *Modern History of Warships: Comprising a Discussion of Present Standpoint and Recent War Experiences.* London: Conway Maritime Press, 1978.

Hutchins, John. *The American Maritime Industries and Public Policy, 1789–1914: An Economic History.* Cambridge, MA: Harvard University Press, 1941.

———. "The American Shipping Industry Since 1914." *Business History Review* 28 (June 1954): 105–27.

Kaufmann, William W. *A Thoroughly Efficient Navy: Studies in Defense Policy.* Washington, DC: Brookings Institution, 1987.

Roukis, George S., ed. *The American Maritime Industry: Problems and Prospects.* 2 vols. Hempstead, NY: Hofstra University Yearbook of Business, 1983.

Taylor, William L. *A Productive Monopoly: The Effect of Railroad Control on New England Coastal Steamship Lines, 1870–1916.* Providence, RI: Brown University Press, 1970.

Yeats, Alexander J. *Shipping and Development Policy: An Integrated Assessment.* New York: Praeger, 1981.

Shipping, Internal Improvements, and Port Cities

Barsness, Richard W. "Maritime Activity and Port Development in the United States Since 1900: A Survey." *Journal of Transport History* n.s. 2 (February 1974): 167–84.

Clark, John G. *New Orleans, 1718–1812: An Economic History.* Baton Rouge: Louisiana State University Press, 1970.

Garrity, Richard. *Canal Boatman: My Life on Upstate Waterways.* Syracuse: Syracuse University Press, 1977.

Gilchrist, David, ed. *The Growth of Seaport Cities, 1790–1825.* Charlottesville: University Press of Virginia, 1967.

Goodrich, Carter. "Internal Improvements Reconsidered." *Journal of Economic History* 30 (June 1970): 289–311.

Krenkel, John H. "The Development of the Port of Los Angeles." *Journal of Transport History* 7 (May 1965): 24–33.

Ransom, Roger. "Public Canal Investment and the Opening of the Old North-West." In *Essays in Nineteenth Century Economic History: The Old Northwest,* edited by David Klingaman and Richard Vedder, 246–68. Athens: Ohio University Press, 1975.

Segal, Harvey. "Canals and Economic Development." In *Canals and Economic Development,* edited by Carter Goodrich, 216–48. New York: Columbia University Press, 1962.

Taylor, George Rogers. *The Transportation Revolution 1815–1860.* New York: Holt, Rinehart & Winston, 1951. Reprint. New York: Harper & Row, 1968.

Shipwrecks, Shipping Accidents, and Maritime Archaeology

Berman, Bruce D., ed. *Encyclopedia of American Shipwrecks.* Boston: Mariners Press, 1972.

Howland, S. A. *Steamboat Disasters and Railroad Accidents in the United States: to which are appended accounts of recent shipwrecks, fires at sea, thrilling incidents, etc.* Worcester, MA: Dorr, Howland, 1843.

Lloyd, James T. *Lloyd's Steamboat Directory and Disasters on the Western Rivers.* Cincinnati: James T. Lloyd, 1856.

Muckelroy, Keith. *Maritime Archaeology.* Cambridge, Eng.: Cambridge University Press, 1978.

Petsche, Jerome E. *The Steamboat Bertrand: History, Excavation, and Architecture.* Washington, DC: U.S. Government Printing Office, 1974.

Shomette, Donald. *Shipwrecks on the Chesapeake: Maritime Disasters on the Chesapeake Bay and Its Tributaries, 1608–1978.* Centreville, MD: Tidewater Publishers, 1982.

Part XII

Instruments and Related Products
ESIC 38.0

CHAPTER 20

SCIENTIFIC AND MEASURING INSTRUMENTS, 38.1

Thomas A. McGahagan

The scientific instrument industry has not received attention commensurate with its strategic role in the development of science and industry. Understanding its linkages with science and technology requires a familiarity with basic bibliographies in those fields. Paul Durbin (1980) provides a good set of background bibliographic essays, and Marc Rothenberg (1982), an exceptionally well-annotated selection of works on the history of American science and technology. Magda Whitrow (1971) and Eugene S. Ferguson (1968) present comprehensive bibliographies that are supplemented by the thorough bibliographies in issues of *Isis* since 1965 and in *Technology and Culture*.

P. H. Sydenham's (1979) work provides perhaps the best general survey in tandem with a good bibliography. Its concentration on pre–nineteenth-century European instruments reflects the emphasis of research in this field. Sydenham takes a broad approach; other general surveys are often antiquarian.

The Korean ruler Sejong declared in 1437 that "the making of celestial globes and armillary spheres is a high and ancient practice" (Needham et al. 1987, 18). Only in recent times, however, has the practice supported large numbers of craftsmen. Before the seventeenth century, those who used scientific instruments often manufactured them also. Surveying and navigation equipment was simple and required no specialization in manufacture. But the emphasis on measurement in early modern science and the complexity of constructing optical instruments demanded specialization in the expanding craft. The Dutch and the English offered prizes for applying the new techniques in instrumentation to navigation. The market for navigational instruments was the economic foundation for instrument makers throughout the eighteenth century.

During the eighteenth century the economic status of instrument makers improved considerably. Advances in instrumentation are evident in the standard handbooks of Nicholas Bion (1723) and George Adams (1813). The changing status of instrument makers in England is documented in the works of Joyce Brown (1979a, 1979b) and Eva G. R. Taylor (1966). The most famous English craftsman was Jesse Ramsden, whose dividing engine calibrated instruments with far greater accuracy and speeded production (Howe 1847). Ramsden's workshop employed sixty men; pre–1800 mass production methods in an industry demanding far more precision than firearms manufacturing are surely worth more notice than they have yet received. Ramsden was not unique: Benjamin Martin was another large-scale English manufacturer (Millburn 1986); and the firm of Spencer, Browning and Rust sold navigational instruments wholesale to dealers in England and America, some of whom relabeled those instruments for resale (Brewington 1963).

More attention has been devoted to instrumentation in the colonial period than in any other period. The works of Silvio Bedini are fundamental, in particular his account of colonial instrument makers (1964; for criticisms, see Anthony Garvan's 1965 review) and his biographies of Anthony Lamb (1954) and Benjamin Banneker (1971). Brooke Hindle (1964) has written a splendid biography of David Rittenhouse, the greatest early American instrument maker. For background on early American science, Hindle (1956), Bedini (1975a, 1975b), and Stearns (1970) are recommended. For bibliographies of science and technology in the early period, with suggestions for further work, see Bell (1955) and Hindle (1966).

The smaller, unspecialized American industry produced instruments that were largely inferior to British instruments. Bedini lists 131 individuals in the industry (some of whom had apprentices), but defines the industry broadly enough to include clockmakers who occasionally sold surveying instruments. Isaac Doolittle, who advertised that he sold surveying instruments as well as "clocks, watches, bar iron and chocolate" (Bedini 1964, 45), or Daniel Burnap, whose shop records have been published by Hoopes (1958), may have been more typical figures than Lamb. The colonial industry was concentrated in three cities. Bedini (1964) lists twenty-seven instrument makers in Boston, twenty-six in Philadelphia, and fifteen in New York; no other city boasted more than five. Sixty instrument makers provided surveying instruments, the most common measuring devices made in America, and thirty provided nautical instruments. Doubtless many of the eighteen listed only as "mathematical instrument makers" would have been happy to provide either. Surveying instruments and techniques were generally less sophisticated than in England (Adams 1813; Richeson 1966). In America, surveyors' instruments were homemade wooden devices as often as they were products of skilled craftsmen (Bedini 1975a).

Nautical instruments depended on precision. Improved quadrants developed independently by Thomas Godfrey in Philadelphia (manufactured by Lamb) and John Hadley in England represented the most important advances in instrumentation during the eighteenth century (Adams 1813). The manufacture and careful recalibration of the new quadrants demanded great skill. After Ramsden's dividing machine carried the precision of manufacture to almost microscopic levels, the American trade seems to have been limited to relabeling and resale of English instruments and to repair and recalibration (Brewington 1963).

A review of the many catalogues of American university collections attests that scientific instruments were largely imported from and often returned to England for repair (Wheatland 1968). Important exceptions include the work of Rittenhouse, Joseph Pope, and John Prince and the electrical equipment produced for Benjamin Franklin's experiments. Ebenezer Kinnersley, a co-worker of Franklin, has been studied by Joseph Lemay (1964). Benjamin Silliman, Jr., of Yale had a low opinion of the ability of a Connecticut instrument maker, but noted that "the same blunder would probably not have been made in Philadelphia or Boston" (Kuslan 1978, 30). Even in the 1830s, Charles Wilkes equipped an expedition in London, noting that the required instruments could not be obtained in the United States (Borthwick 1965).

The instrument industry in the nineteenth century has not been intensively studied. General works include Peter R. de Clercq's *Nineteenth Century Scientific Instruments and Their Makers* (1985) and Gerard L'Estrange Turner's *Nineteenth Century Scientific Instruments* (1983); both focus on the industry of Europe. The current impression of a relative decline in the American instrument industry in the early nineteenth century may not hold up under close examination. Richard Shyrock's (1948–49) thesis of American indifference to pure science in the early 1800s dissolved under the examinations of George H. Daniels (1968), Nathan Reingold (1972), Alexandra Oleson and Sanborn C. Brown (1976), and John C. Greene (1984).

Problems in the mature English industry of the early nineteenth century included an oversupply of craftsmen and specialization, compounded by the instrument makers' belief that their status had fallen from researcher to mechanic. The American industry did not have the same problems. Not only did scientists such as Joseph Henry, Alexander Bache, and Robert Hare contribute to the development of instrumentation, but industry practitioners such as William Bond, Edmund and George Blunt, James Green (Middleton 1964), and Isaiah Lukens (Sinclair 1974) were important members of the American scientific community.

The records of international exhibitions from 1851 on are an important indicator of growth in the industry and the improving quality of American-made instruments. An unexploited source for mass-market data in the industry is the trade catalogue. Deborah Jean Warner ([1856] 1984) has edited Benjamin Pike's 1856 catalogue and added a useful preface; the Smithsonian Institution has a particularly impressive collection, but it is not fully covered in Lawrence E. Romaine's (1960) guide. The industry did not expand dramatically in the first half of the century, however. John Leander Bishop (1861) noted thirty establishments in Philadelphia and eighteen in New York City, each averaging four or five workmen. Navigation and surveying (Smart 1962) remained the mainstay of the industry.

Nineteenth-century steam engines and the interchangeable parts produced in the American System of Manufactures created a demand for precision instruments in industry and laboratory. Problems with steam engines led to the development of feedback controls—Charles Porter of New York improved James Watt's governor in the 1850s (Bennett 1979). Paul Uselding (1981) stresses the importance of precise measurement in the American System of Manufactures; the firm of Brown and Sharpe led the way (H. F. Brown 1971).

The transformation of American science at mid-century is treated by Robert V. Bruce (1987). Science and industry grew closer later in the century (Pursell 1972; Rae 1979): photography depended on optical instruments (Jenkins 1975), petroleum on chemical instruments (Sturchio 1981; Child 1940), and electrical industries on a wide range of new instruments. The American optical industry attained respectability with the microscopes of J. L. Ridell, Robert B. Tolles, and Charles A. Spencer (Padgitt 1975; Bradbury 1967; Cassedy 1976) and the telescopes of Alvan Clark, Worcester Reed Warner, and Ambrose Swazey (Warner 1968, 1979; Roe 1916). Spectroscopy became especially important at the turn of the century; Henry Augustus Rowland and Albert A. Michelson, two leading figures of American science, owed their fame to precise instrumental work (Mendenhall, 1966; Hughes 1976). Chemistry labs were established in the steel industry—Cambria Iron in Johnstown, 1860, and the Pennsylvania Railroad, 1875—and the oil industry. The electrical and telecommunications industries took the lead in creating research laboratories that added to the steady flow of innovative instruments (Birr 1957; Reich 1985; White 1961).

Growth in the measuring instruments industry during the twentieth century has been fueled by research labs, some 10,000 industrial labs, manufacturers using instrument-dependent process-control techniques, and government funding of research and military needs. Government involvement in the industry began informally with the Coast Survey under Friedrich Hassler and Bache, but was institutionalized only with the establishment of the National Bureau of Standards in 1901 (Cochrane 1966). A comprehensive account of the government's role to 1940 is furnished by A. Hunter

Dupree (1957). The crucial role of scientific and measuring instruments in World War I is apparent from the career of Elmer Sperry (Hughes 1971, ch. 8), the fortunes of firms like Perkin-Elmer (White 1961), and employment statistics that show the industry doubled in size to meet war needs. The war also limited foreign competition for the American industry. Adjustment problems after the war explain why the Scientific Apparatus Makers' Association (SAMA) made tariff protection one of their key goals.

The formation of SAMA was a sign that the industry had come of age; another was the publication of the first American periodical devoted entirely to instrumentation, the *Review of Scientific Instruments* (1930). The industry weathered the Depression. Renewed government interest during World War II and the Cold War assured continued support for research. A glance at the funding sources listed in any recent issue of the *Review of Scientific Instruments* will show that government purchases account for over a third of the sales of a typical firm (OECD 1968).

Histories of specific firms within the industry are mostly company-sponsored. The works of William P. Vogel on Leeds and Northrup (1949), Arch Merrill on Taylor Instrument Companies (1951), and Harrison Stephens on Beckman Instruments (1985) are above average for this genre. There is, however, no study of an American firm comparable to M. J. G. Cattermole and A. F. Wolfe's study of the Cambridge Scientific Instrument Company (1987). Leeds and Northrup would be an attractive target for further study; company archives were donated to Eleutherian Mills and its founder's papers to Haverford College.

There are no comprehensive studies of the scientific and measuring instruments industry in the twentieth century. The annual industry survey in *U.S. Industrial Outlook* includes a list of trade publications; the U.S. Department of Commerce has published global market surveys. Norman McLennan and Caleb Hathaway's (1976) is particularly interesting. The OECD study (1968) of the industry is also worth special mention, as is the Stanford Research Institute's (1968–69) five-volume study, which is based on extensive interviews with industry executives.

Despite recent mergers, the industry remains open to entry and innovation. Nearly half of all sales revenues were derived from instruments less than five years old (OECD 1968), and the pace of innovation has not slackened. Integrating computing intelligence with laboratory instruments amounts to a major revolution that is far from over (see Hirschfield 1985 for a survey of expected developments). The increased dependence of industry on process-control instrumentation is strikingly illustrated by the favorable sales projections made by a leading manufacturer in the wake of the Bhopal calamity (Graff 1985). Although world competition has made the American industry dependent on the fortunes of the dollar and comparative advantage, the industry and interest in its history continue to grow.

BIBLIOGRAPHY

Adams, George. *Geometrical and Graphical Essays*. 4th ed. London: Baldwin, 1813.

Bedini, Silvio. *At the Sign of the Compass and Quadrant: The Life and Times of Anthony Lamb*. Philadelphia: American Philosophical Society, 1954.

————. *Early American Scientific Instruments and Their Makers*. Washington, DC: Smithsonian Institution, 1964.

————. "The Evolution of Science Museums." *Technology and Culture* 6 (Winter 1965): 1–29.

————. *The Life of Benjamin Banneker*. New York: Scribner, 1971.

————. "Artisans in Wood: The Mathematical Instrument Makers." In *America's Wooden Age: Aspects of Its Early Technology*, edited by Brooke Hindle. Tarrytown, NJ: Sleepy Hollow Restorations, 1975a.

————. *Thinkers and Tinkers: Early American Men of Science*. New York: Scribner, 1975b.

Bell, Whitfield. *Early American Science: Needs and Opportunities for Study*. Williamsburg, VA: Institute of Early American History and Culture, 1955.

Bennett, Stuart. *A History of Control Engineering 1800–1930*. New York: Peregrinus, 1979.

Bion, Nicholas. *The Construction and Principal Uses of Mathematical Instruments*. London: Senex, 1723.

Birr, Kendall. *Pioneering in Industrial Research*. Washington, DC: Public Affairs Press, 1957.

Bishop, John Leander. *A History of American Manufactures from 1608 to 1860*. Philadelphia: Young, 1861.

Borthwick, Doris Esch. "Outfitting the United States Exploring Expedition: Lieutenant Charles Wilkes' European Assignment, August-November 1836." *Proceedings of the American Philosophical Society* 109 (June 1965): 159–72.

Bradbury, Savile. *The Evolution of the Microscope*. New York: Pergamon Press, 1967.

Brewington, Marion. *The Peabody Museum Collection of Navigating Instruments*. Salem, MA: Peabody Museum, 1963.

Brown, Harold Francis. "The Saga of Brown and Sharpe." Master's thesis, University of Rhode Island, 1971.

Brown, Joyce. "Guild Organization of the Instrument Making Trade, 1550–1830." *Annals of Science* 36 (1979a): 1–34.

————. *Mathematical Instrument Makers in the Grocers' Company, 1688–1800*. London: Science Museum, 1979b.

Bruce, Robert V. *The Launching of Modern American Science, 1846–1876*. New York: Knopf, 1987.

Cassedy, James H. "The Microscope in American Medical Science, 1840–1860." *Isis* 67 (1976): 76–97.

Cattermole, M. J. G., and A. F. Wolfe. *Horace Darwin's Shop: A History of the Cambridge Scientific Instrument Company, 1878 to 1968*. Bristol, Eng.: Hilger, 1987.

Child, Ernest. *The Tools of the Chemist: Their Ancestry and American Evolution*. New York: Reinhold, 1940.

Cochrane, Rexmond C. *Measures for Progress: A History of the National Bureau of Standards.* Washington, DC: National Bureau of Standards, 1966.

Cohen, I. Bernard. *Some Early Tools of American Science.* Cambridge, MA: Harvard University Press, 1950.

Daniels, George H. *American Science in the Age of Jackson.* New York: Columbia University Press, 1968.

———, ed. *Nineteenth Century American Science: A Reappraisal.* Evanston, IL: Northwestern University Press, 1972.

de Clercq, Peter R., ed. *Nineteenth Century Scientific Instruments and Their Makers.* Leiden, Holland: Museum Boerhaave, 1985.

Dupree, A. Hunter. *Science in the Federal Government.* Cambridge, MA: Harvard University Press, Belknap Press, 1957.

Durbin, Paul, ed. *A Guide to the Culture of Science, Technology and Medicine.* New York: Free Press, 1980.

Ferguson, Eugene S. *Bibliography of the History of Technology.* Cambridge, MA: MIT Press, 1968.

Garvan, Anthony. "Review of Bedini 1964." *Technology and Culture* 6 (Summer 1965): 464–65.

Graff, Gordon. "Beyond Bhopal." *High Technology* 5 (April 1985): 55–61.

Greene, John C. *American Science in the Age of Jefferson.* Ames: Iowa State University Press, 1984.

Hindle, Brooke. *The Pursuit of Science in Revolutionary America.* Chapel Hill: University of North Carolina Press, 1956.

———. *David Rittenhouse.* Princeton: Princeton University Press, 1964.

———. *Technology in Early America: Needs and Opportunities for Study.* Chapel Hill: University of North Carolina Press, 1966.

———, ed. *America's Wooden Age: Aspects of Its Early Technology.* Tarrytown, NY: Sleepy Hollow Restorations, 1975.

Hirschfield, Tomas. "Instrumentation in the Next Decade." *Science* 230 (October 18, 1985): 286–91.

Hoopes, Penrose. *Shop Records of Daniel Burnap, Clockmaker.* Hartford, CT: Historical Society, 1958.

Howe, Henry. *Memoirs of the Most Distinguished American Mechanics: Also, Distinguished European Mechanics.* New York: Harper, 1847.

Hughes, Thomas Parke. *Elmer Sperry: Inventor and Engineer.* Baltimore: Johns Hopkins University Press, 1971.

———. *Science and the Instrument Maker: Michelson, Sperry and the Speed of Light.* Washington, DC: Smithsonian Institution, 1976.

Isis. Philadelphia, 1913– .

Jaffe, B. *Michelson and the Speed of Light.* London: Heinemann, 1961.

Jenkins, Reese V. *Images and Enterprise: Technology and the American Photographic Industry, 1839–1925.* Baltimore: Johns Hopkins University Press, 1975.

Jones, Bessie, ed. *The Golden Age of Science.* New York: Simon & Schuster, 1966.

Kuslan, Louis I., ed. *Connecticut Science, Technology and Medicine in the Era of the American Revolution.* Hartford, CT: American Revolution Bicentennial Commission, 1978.

Lemay, Joseph. *Ebenezer Kinnersley, Franklin's Friend*. Philadelphia: University of Pennsylvania Press, 1964.

McGucken, William. *Nineteenth Century Spectroscopy*. Baltimore: Johns Hopkins University Press, 1969.

McLennan, Norman, and Caleb Hathaway. *Export Trends for United States Measuring, Analyzing and Controlling Instruments*. Washington, DC: U.S. Department of Commerce, 1976.

Mayr, Otto, and Robert Post, eds. *Yankee Enterprise: The Rise of the American System of Manufactures*. Washington, DC: Smithsonian Institution Press, 1981.

Mendenhall, Thomas Corwin. "Henry Augustus Rowland, 1848–1901." In *The Golden Age of Science*, edited by Bessie Jones, 564–80. New York: Simon & Schuster, 1966.

Merrill, Arch. *Graduated by Years from One to One Hundred (1851–1951)*. Rochester, NY: Taylor Instrument Companies, 1951.

Middleton, W. E. Knowles. *The History of the Barometer*. Baltimore: Johns Hopkins University Press, 1964.

Millburn, John R. *Retailer of the Sciences: Benjamin Martin's Scientific Instrument Company*. London: Vade Mecum, 1986.

Multhauf, David P. *A Catalogue of Instruments and Models in the Possession of the American Philosophical Society*. Philadelphia: American Philosophical Society, 1961.

Needham, Joseph, et al. *The Hall of Heavenly Records*. Cambridge, Eng.: Cambridge University Press, 1987.

OECD (Organization for Economic Cooperation and Development). *Scientific Instruments: Gaps in Technology*. Paris: OECD, 1968.

Oleson, Alexandra, and Sanborn C. Brown, eds. *The Pursuit of Knowledge in the Early Republic: American Scientific and Learned Societies*. Baltimore: Johns Hopkins University Press, 1976.

Oleson, Alexandra, and John Voss, eds. *The Organization of Knowledge in Modern America, 1860–1920*. Baltimore: Johns Hopkins University Press, 1979.

Padgitt, Donald. *A Short History of the Early American Microscopes*. Chicago: Microscope Publications, 1975.

Pursell, Caroll. "Science and Industry." In *Nineteenth Century American Science: A Reappraisal*, edited by George H. Daniels. Evanston, IL: Northwestern University Press, 1972.

Rae, John. "The Application of Science to Industry." In *The Organization of Knowledge in Modern America, 1860–1920*, edited by Alexandra Oleson and John Voss. Baltimore: Johns Hopkins University Press, 1979.

Reich, Leonard S. *The Making of American Industrial Research: Science and Business at General Electric and Bell, 1876–1926*. Cambridge, Eng.: Cambridge University Press, 1985.

Reingold, Nathan. "American Indifference to Basic Research: A Reappraisal." In *Nineteenth Century American Science: A Reappraisal*, edited by George H. Daniels. Evanston, IL: Northwestern University Press, 1972.

———, ed. *The Sciences in the American Context: New Perspectives*. Washington, DC: Smithsonian Institution, 1979.

The Review of Scientific Instruments. New York, 1930– .

Richeson, A. W. *English Land Measuring to 1800: Instruments and Practices.* Cambridge, MA: MIT Press, 1966.

Roe, Joseph Wickham. *English and American Tool Builders.* New Haven, CT: Yale University Press, 1916.

Romaine, Lawrence E. *A Guide to American Trade Catalogs, 1744–1900.* New York: Bowker, 1960.

Rothenberg, Marc. *The History of Science and Technology in the United States.* New York: Garland, 1982.

Shyrock, Richard. "American Indifference to Basic Research in the Nineteenth Century." *Archives Internationales d'Histoire des Sciences* 28 (1948–49): 50–65.

Sinclair, Bruce. *Philadelphia's Philosopher Mechanics: A History of the Franklin Institute, 1824–1865.* Baltimore: Johns Hopkins University Press, 1974.

Smart, Charles E. *The Makers of Surveying Instruments in America Since 1700.* Troy, NY: Regal Art Press, 1962.

Stanford Research Institute. *Diversification Opportunities in Instrumentation.* 5 vols. Menlo Park, CA: Stanford Research Institute, 1968–69.

Stearns, Raymond P. *Science in the British Colonies of North America.* Urbana: University of Illinois Press, 1970.

Stephens, Harrison. *Golden Past, Golden Future: The First Fifty Years of Beckman Instruments, Incorporated.* Claremont, CA: Claremont University Press, 1985.

Sturchio, Jeffrey. "Chemists and Industry in Modern America." Ph.D diss., University of Pennsylvania, 1981.

Sydenham, P. H. *Measuring Instruments: Tools of Knowledge and Control.* New York: Peregrinus, 1979.

Taylor, Eva G. R. *The Mathematical Practitioners of Hanoverian England.* Cambridge, Eng.: Cambridge University Press, 1966.

Technology and Culture. Chicago: University of Chicago Press, 1959.

Tucker, Wallace. *The Cosmic Inquirers: Modern Telescopes and Their Makers.* Cambridge, MA: Harvard University Press, 1986.

Turner, Gerard L'Estrange. *Nineteenth Century Scientific Instruments.* Berkeley: University of California Press, 1983.

U.S. Department of Commerce. Bureau of Industrial Economics. *U.S. Industrial Outlook.* Washington, DC: U.S. Government Printing Office, 1960– .

Uselding, Paul. "Measuring Techniques and Manufacturing Practice." In *Yankee Enterprise: The Rise of the America System of Manufactures,* edited by Otto Mayr and Robert Post. Washington, DC: Smithsonian Institution Press, 1981.

Vogel, William P. *Precision, People and Progress.* Philadelphia: Leeds & Northrup, 1949.

Warner, Deborah Jean. *Alvan Clark and Sons, Artists in Optics.* Washington, DC: Smithsonian Institution Press, 1968.

———. *Graceanna Lewis: Scientist and Humanitarian.* Washington, DC: Smithsonian Institution Press, 1979.

———, ed. *Pike's Illustrated Catalogue of Scientific and Medical Instruments.* 1856. Reprint. Dracut, MA: Antiquarian Scientist, 1984.

Wheatland, David P. *The Apparatus of Science at Harvard, 1765–1800.* Cambridge, MA: Harvard University Press, 1968.

White, Frederick Andrew. *American Industrial Research Laboratories.* Washington,
     DC: Public Affairs Press, 1961.
Whitrow, Magda. *The Isis Cumulative Bibliography 1913–1965.* 2 vols. London:
     Mansell, 1971.
Woodbury, Robert S. *Studies in the History of Machine Tools.* Cambridge, MA:
     MIT Press, 1972.

CHAPTER 21

PHOTOGRAPHIC EQUIPMENT AND SUPPLIES, 38.6

_____ LUTZ ALT

BACKGROUND AND ANTECEDENTS

The photographic industry exploits the physical phenomenon that certain silver halides darken when exposed to light. Spreading silver salts suspended in a carrying agent over metal, glass, paper and its derivatives, and plastics sensitizes these materials. A camera envelopes such sensitized material in darkness, concentrates the light reflected by the object to be photographed, and exposes the sensitized material to this light.

A viable process for producing photographic images was first demonstrated in Paris by the Frenchman L.J.M. Daguerre in the year 1839. From there, knowledge of the process spread quickly to other countries, including the United States. During the next four decades, the practice of photography was marked by a number of technological and economic fits and starts. The base materials used to capture photographic images were changed from silver-plated metal to glass plates. The carrying agents for the compounds used to sensitize glass plates progressed from collodion to gelatin; the agents for the compounds used to sensitize paper, from egg whites to gelatin. These advances expanded photography and made it less complicated and expensive.

Until this evolution, photography remained the domain of individual artisans who sensitized materials shortly before taking or developing a photograph. Manufacturers had no opportunity to sensitize materials and were limited to producing unsensitized materials, chemicals, and apparatus. But the production of even these was limited in America. During the middle decades of the nineteenth century, the technical knowledge required to make such products was more highly developed in Europe.

The business activity associated with photography during the decades 1840–80 was thus confined to commerce in photographic equipment and supplies. In the United States, the field depended on imports from Europe, and thus created opportunities for middlemen, whose functions were to buy, stock, and distribute these goods to photographers.

Given these conditions, it may be more appropriate to describe the related business activities as those of the U.S. photographic trade. Nevertheless, modest efforts were made to supply photographers from local production. J.M.L. & W. H. Scovill Company, a Connecticut producer of copper and brass hardware, was one of the early entrants whose successors' involvement with the manufacture of photographic supplies would last well into the latter part of the twentieth century. Scovill began silvering copper plates used in Daguerre's process and was the leading U.S. producer of such plates until newer photographic processes using other materials eclipsed daguerreotypy in the 1850s. The Scovills established a New York store in 1846 to distribute their products. This outlet soon expanded its offerings to include other photographic supplies, many of which were imported. As the business grew, Scovill became a wholesale supplier to stockists outside New York and supplied local practitioners at retail. Scovill was soon a leading supply house; the profits generated by that service eventually exceeded those earned from its manufacturing operations. However, to lessen its dependence on unreliable independent producers, in 1867 Scovill acquired American Optical Company, a producer of stereoscopic viewers and related apparatus.

Edward Anthony also founded a prominent supply house. A New York daguerreotypist in 1842, he branched out five years later as a retailer and wholesaler of photographic goods. By the early 1850s his enterprise was producing camera boxes and cases to hold photographic supplies and chemicals. Later in the decade, Anthony manufactured and published stereoscopic view cards, using his extensive marketing network to distribute them. About the same time, the firm acquired the camera business of William Lewis, a small New York apparatus manufacturer. From Lewis's base as an importer of German albumenized papers, the Anthony enterprise began in the 1860s to albumenize its imported raw paper.

Despite initial forays into the manufacturing sector that served to strengthen their positions in the market for photographic goods, suppliers maintained mercantile attitudes toward their economic functions well into the 1880s. Although their close contact with the market enabled them to appreciate the role of technical innovation as a sales stimulant, they left the financial risks of generating novelties to the innovators. Once a novelty had proved itself, suppliers would seek exclusive distribution rights. This strategy served them well so long as fundamental processes used by photographers were changing, if at all, in small increments. They could supply a growing market in a stable environment, the requirements of which were well known.

The strategy failed when new technologies emerged and brought with them new service requirements that suppliers could not fulfill because of their commitment to established ways of doing business.

In summary, industry encompasses the collective business activity of a particular branch of enterprise as well as factory production of goods. An embryonic U.S. photographic industry sprang to life within months of the 1839 introduction of photography, but there was little large-scale factory production of photographic goods before 1880.

GELATIN

The technical innovation that reduced the influence of the leading supply houses and provided the basis for an American photographic industry was the adoption of gelatin as the carrier for photosensitive silver salts. In 1871 the Englishman R. L. Maddox reported his successful experiments with the dispersal of silver salts in gelatin. Gelatin emulsions retain their sensitivity to light for some time after they dry, and can be sensitized well before exposure and at a remote location.

Preparing gelatin emulsions and applying them to glass spawned dozens of factory enterprises. Although these operations began as cottage industries, ambitious entrants produced more even coating and larger output with mechanical aids. Among the entrepreneurs who saw the potential benefits of mechanization was George Eastman, who established a dry-plate factory in Rochester, New York, in 1880. The enterprise he founded became inextricably bound to the photographic industry in the United States and eventually in much of the rest of the world, and in large measure became synonymous with it.

Gelatin dry plates were a radical departure from previous photographic products, but were not a technically mature product in those early years. An evolution that extended into the twentieth century followed their introduction in the early 1880s. Each step required that photographers change their methods. Photographic suppliers purchased, sold, and distributed tangible goods, but they offered no directions for their use. Manufacturers recognized the need for instruction and began to assume responsibility for it as part of their marketing. Although gelatin dry plates had sufficient shelf life to make remote factory sensitization feasible, the perishability of the gelatin encouraged producers to control the distribution of their wares. Improved methods of communication and transportation made it feasible for manufacturers to control their own distribution as an alternative to relying on independent middlemen, who consequently lost much of their marketing power.

Manufacturers began coating photographic printing papers with photosensitive gelatin emulsions about five years after the gelatin had been adopted for negative plates. Presensitized papers brought new technical problems, however, and were not widely used until the 1890s. Numerous paper-sensitizing firms emerged, each specializing in one or a few emulsions of unique chemical makeup. A few of these firms—Eastman's was paramount among them—also coated and marketed papers.

As the initial difficulties incident to gelatin emulsions were gradually overcome during the 1880s and more photographers adopted them, a small market of amateur photographers began to develop. Advances in manufacturing photographic paper permitted enlarging prints from small negatives and led to the progressive miniaturization of cameras. The late 1880s brought a number of designs generically labeled as detective cameras. Moreover, as gelatin-coated plates became increasingly sensitive to light, various mechanical shutter mechanisms were incorporated in cameras.

EASTMAN KODAK AND THE RISE OF THE LARGE-SCALE PHOTOGRAPHIC INDUSTRY

Coating printing papers with photosensitive gelatin emulsions radically transformed photography into an important industry. The flexibility of paper permitted sensitizing long rolls in a continuous mechanical process; the roles could then be cut into small sheets. Such manufacturing promised economies in production cost and predictably uniform output.

Among the American pioneers who saw these potentialities was George Eastman. Working with William H. Walker, a hitherto unsuccessful inventor and producer of cameras, Eastman modified the designs of several English and American coating mechanisms and built a machine that successfully coated paper with gelatin emulsions. In 1884 the same collaboration devised a paper-based roll film and a roll holder that included a mechanism to roll the film inside the camera. After the film was exposed, the sensitized gelatin layer had to be stripped from its paper base before it could be developed and printed.

Paper was an unsatisfactory film base. In 1886 Eastman engaged a University of Rochester chemist to develop a base that combined the lightness and flexibility of paper with the transparency of glass. Three years of work produced celluloid. The first Eastman-Walker roll system was a commercial failure, so in 1887 Eastman devised a small, hand-held camera to use the paper-based film. He called this camera the Kodak and introduced it under that registered trademark the following year. The celluloid base replaced paper in Kodak cameras one year later. These developments brought changes in the practice and business of photography.

Eastman had keen insight into his potential market. The slogan for the first Kodak system—"You Press the Button. We Do the Rest"—conveys the strategy that guided the company during the succeeding century. The photographer was to be relieved of all technical difficulties. Eastman precisely delineated that user by distinguishing the true photographic amateur as a picture maker and the ordinary snapshooter as a picture taker. He estimated the picture takers to outnumber the picture makers by ten to one, and he saw his company's market among the picture takers.

Having defined his market, Eastman set out to tap it by the most direct means feasible and to widen the channels of distribution. The company opened or bought hundreds of photographic retail shops during Eastman's lifetime. These retailers either carried Kodak products exclusively or concentrated on selling those products. Although they performed normal retailing functions, their main purpose may well have been publicizing the product and making customers comfortable with it. The company pioneered the distribution of photographic goods to opticians, stationers, jewelers, hardware merchants, druggists, and other high-traffic sellers.

Retailers of Kodak products who remained nominally independent of the company agreed to restrictive terms. A dealer buying from Kodak stocked no goods made by competing manufacturers and sold photographic goods at prices fixed by Kodak.

Eastman exploited communications media to draw public attention to Kodak products. Starting in the late 1880s, the company exhibited at every international fair or exposition of consequence. It was among the first firms to display illuminated billboards, omnibus posters, and full-page advertisements in mass circulation newspapers and magazines.

From the outset Eastman patented his inventions and those of his associates. As large-scale commercial photography became increasingly feasible, he knew that inventors would be attracted to the field. Realizing that his company could not anticipate every development or invention, he undertook to buy or control patents he thought potentially important.

In the initial Kodak process for making film, syrupy nitrocellulose was spread over 200-foot glass-topped tables. When the celluloid dried, it was coated with photosensitive emulsion from a hopper on side rails traveling the length of the tables. After the emulsion dried, the film was stripped from the table, slit, and packaged. Eastman replaced this manual batch manufacturing process in 1899 with a continuous flow process of casting and drying the celluloid base that, in turn, enabled continuous emulsion coating, a system the company had adopted for sensitizing papers fifteen years earlier. The changes dramatically increased production capacity, reduced labor costs, and lowered the price of Kodak film. The continuous flow processes ensured a consistency of film thickness impossible with earlier methods and allowed the company to exploit the extraordinary opportunity provided by the explosive growth of the cinema early in the twentieth century.

Paper used for photographic prints must be free of metallic traces that might react chemically with the silver salts in the emulsion. Papermaking in the nineteenth century employed naturally flowing water, so the metallic content of the streams where paper mills were established determined whether their output was suitable for photographic use. Two European mills enjoyed renown for the purity of their papers. In 1898 the owners of these decided to exploit their position by forming a cartel. They created the General Paper Company and awarded it their exclusive sales right. Eastman secured exclusive North American purchase and distribution rights from General Paper under a nine-year contract. He then acquired five of the largest U.S. paper sensitizers, which he dissolved or merged into Eastman Kodak.

Control of the U.S. photographic paper market was but one part of an overall business strategy. Between 1894 and 1909 Eastman Kodak acquired twenty-two competing American manufacturers in all segments of the business. Soon after most of these acquisitions, the firms were dissolved and their brands disappeared. Often the purchase agreement enjoined the officers and owners of the acquired firms from participating in the photographic industry for periods up to twenty years.

In a 1913 petition charging the company with numerous violations of the Sherman Act, the federal government asserted that illegal methods had given Eastman Kodak market shares of 86 percent in film cameras, 88 percent in film, and 67 percent in photographic papers. The legal proceedings following the indictment consumed more than two years. The court found that Eastman Kodak's practices furthered an intention to form an illegal monopoly and to erect perpetual barriers to the entry of others into the business. After more than five years of appeals by the company, it reached an understanding with the government in 1921. The company withdrew its appeal to the Supreme Court and acquiesced in a consent decree calling for Eastman Kodak to divest itself of seven earlier acquisitions and enjoining it in perpetuity from acquiring any competing U.S. plant or business. Three of the enterprises to be divested were camera or parts suppliers; three were dry-plate producers; and one was a sensitized papers producer. None was essential to the company's business. Eastman Kodak's hegemony over the U.S. photographic industry remained undiminished.

The second decade of the twentieth century marked other noteworthy developments in the history of Eastman Kodak. Among these was the firm's entrance into the manufacture of raw paper, lenses, gelatin, and fine chemicals. These steps on the road to vertical integration freed Kodak from its dependence on European suppliers for several major product components.

Another key advance at Kodak was the institutionalization of research and development. Eastman initiated a policy of continuous product innovation during the 1890s, and had engaged experimenters and inventors a decade earlier. But much of the research was ad hoc and the knowledge gained empirical. Eastman's policy changed in 1912 when he engaged C.E.K. Mees, an English photographic scientist, to organize the Kodak research laboratories. Under Mees's direction, which spanned more than four decades, the laboratories systematically explored photographic phenomena and materials to elevate the company's knowledge to a scientific basis. This thorough but necessarily plodding approach produced tangible results only after many years, but it served the company well in the long run by reinforcing its technical leadership in the industry.

OTHER PARTICIPANTS

Beyond dominant Eastman Kodak the photographic industry supported a few minor firms, most of which held specialized niches. The explosive growth of the cinema as a medium of mass entertainment during the first two decades of the new century attracted inventors of movie cameras and projection apparatus. They refined the equipment devised by Thomas A. Edison, his associate W.K.L. Dickson, and other inventors on both sides of the Atlantic. American innovators saw potential profit in producing and exhibiting motion pictures. So they concentrated their efforts in those fields and left the manufacture of equipment to Edison's company and other members of a patent pooling arrangement that was eventually declared illegal.

Established at the end of the nineteenth century, the Defender Photo Supply Company was a marginal supplier of photosensitive materials for nearly fifty years. Relying on a variety of sources, it sold products under its brand names and marketed them through its wholesale supply houses. Among Defender's sources in the early years of the century were European suppliers; the Keystone Dry Plate Company, which it acquired; and Eastman Kodak, which for a time supplied Defender branded films from its own factory. Defender was the temporary and limited beneficiary of the 1921 consent decree calling for Kodak's divestiture of three dry-plate producers. As there were no separate production facilities to divest, Defender acquired only the original brand names of those producers. The plates carrying these brand labels were coated, as before, by Eastman Kodak. Defender had one distinction, the production of X-ray plates. In an effort to develop a special niche, it turned increasingly during the 1920s to this and other professional applications of photography. The need for a suitable sheet film base for such applications brought Defender into a close working relationship with E. I. Du Pont de Nemours & Co., which acquired the company in 1945.

The aforementioned houses of Anthony and Scovill, largely traders in photographic supplies with periodic marginal involvements in manufacturing, had by the end of the nineteenth century run out of energy and leadership. They joined forces in 1901, and six years later abbreviated their company and brand names to Ansco. Under a new generation of management during the early years of the century, Ansco produced a diversified line of photographic goods including cameras, paper, and film. The firm held one intangible asset of potentially enormous value, the right to exploit the Goodwin patent, under which it began to produce roll film in 1902. The patent covered the ingredients used in making a celluloid base for photographic emulsions. Hannibal Goodwin, an impecunious inventor, had applied for a patent in 1887, two years before Kodak commercialized a celluloid roll film. Bizarre circumstances slowed the Patent Office, which issued the patent to Goodwin in 1898. Goodwin formed a company to exploit the patent, but he died soon thereafter. His executors' efforts to interest established photographic firms in using the patent led them to the Anthony and Scovill companies and may well have precipitated the 1901 merger of those firms.

Whether the Goodwin patent constituted a valid prior claim was joined in an infringement suit entered by Ansco against Eastman Kodak in 1906. In 1913–14 the courts ruled that the Goodwin patent had indeed been infringed. In an out-of-court settlement, Ansco accepted a $5 million payment from Eastman Kodak. It dissipated the proceeds by distributing a large dividend to its common shareholders, retiring several preferred stock and bond issues, and constructing an unworkable cellulose nitration plant.

Lacking adequate capital, distinctive technical competence, or a strategy for profitable participation in the rapidly growing market for photographic goods, Ansco remained a weak producer in the shadow of Eastman Kodak for the next decade and a half. Ansco did, however, develop a distribution network and production facilities operating behind the high tariff barrier that the United States had erected in 1922. These assets attracted the Agfa Division of I. G. Farbenindustrie AG (hereafter I. G. Farben), formed in 1925 to consolidate most of the German chemical industry. By the 1920s Agfa was operating the second largest photographic enterprise in the world, but entry of its products into the United States was foreclosed by the tariff. I. G. Farben took over Ansco in 1927 through the formation of Agfa-Ansco Photo Products Company. The new entity's product was sold under the Ansco label, and in acknowledgment of the political sensitivities of the postwar era, every effort was made to maintain an American face toward the public. Marketing and general administration were headed by Americans; production, technical support, and finance by Germans. A new film factory was built, and the paper and camera plants were extensively modernized. The quality of Ansco products began to show remarkable improvement, the product offerings were extended, and by 1935 Agfa-Ansco was reporting reasonable profits.

PRODUCT DEVELOPMENTS DURING THE INTERWAR PERIOD

The dominant position Eastman Kodak had achieved in nearly every sphere of photography by the 1920s made it a magnet for new ideas in the field. Ideas flowed into the company from outside, and technicians in the research laboratories developed them into viable commercial products. During the interwar years, new products proliferated and existing technologies were adapted to new uses. In the 1920s Kodak apparatus and film suitable for amateur use broadened cinematography. The 16mm film used in this amateur equipment soon found a variety of noncinematic business uses. Prominent among these was a system introduced in 1928 for photographing checks passing through the nation's banks. Within eight years, virtually all commercial banks in the United States had installed the system. Success in recording bank documents led to a variety of other microfilm and microfiche applications. Photographic applications that came into massive use included dry presensitized lithographic printing plates and radiographic materials. The latter found their way into a variety of industrial applications beyond the traditional use of X rays in medical diagnosis.

Although color photography was not the preeminent medium until the mid–1960s, it was perhaps the most significant innovation introduced during the 1930s. A few color processes were marketed as early as the first decade of the century, but they were technically or commercially infeasible. Included was a short-lived process introduced by Kodak in 1928 for its 16mm amateur motion picture system. Technicolor, an awkward system for use in professional cinema, was offered by an independent enterprise in the early 1930s. In the final processing step a different dye layer was added to three rolls of monochrome film and the rolls projected simultaneously. The small number of motion picture projectors needed for theaters in the nation's larger cities enabled the Technicolor system to enjoy a vogue for some years, but it was too cumbersome for other photographic uses.

Viable color processes were introduced by Agfa and Kodak in 1935. The initial Kodachrome product was a negative that was in the course of processing reversed into a positive. It was suitable only for projection, either as still transparencies or amateur cinefilm. Kodacolor, which produced a negative, was developed in 1939. Through its Agfa-Ansco subsidiary, I. G. Farben had a four-year lead on Kodak in this field. However, the lingering effects of economic depression and the subsequent demands of the war economy precluded widespread commercialization of color photography by either company until much later.

POSTWAR DEVELOPMENTS AND PARTICIPANTS IN CONVENTIONAL PHOTOGRAPHY

Ansco was only one of several investments made in the United States by I. G. Farben. These were consolidated into one holding entity, and in an effort to camouflage its German ownership as World War II approached, the name was changed to General Aniline and Film Corporation (hereafter GAF). The tactic did not deceive the U.S. government, and early in 1942 GAF was expropriated. Following extended litigation and political pressure, GAF shares were sold to the public in 1965. Ansco products were manufactured throughout the period of government custody and were for some years marketed under the GAF label. But the company specialized in other sectors of the chemical industry and terminated its production of photographic goods in the late 1970s.

E. I. Du Pont de Nemours & Co. began its involvement with photosensitive materials in the 1920s. It has, however, maintained a modest profile in the industry and has confined itself to a limited number of radiological and industrial application niches.

In a sharp departure from its corporate traditions, Minnesota Mining & Manufacturing Company (hereafter 3M) bought its way into the photographic industry during the early 1960s by acquiring several minor manufacturers. Among these was Ferrania, an Italian producer of sensitized materials that had been in operation since 1920. Ferrania's modest capability in producing color film was the result of the expropriation and freeing for common use of all Agfa patents by the Allied powers in the aftermath of World War II. Combining the knowledge acquired from Ferrania with its own competence in a variety of coating technologies, 3M developed a commercially viable color film. The company was eager to exploit the growing popularity of color photography, but reluctant to incur the heavy costs of a direct brand confrontation with Eastman Kodak. It chose to operate as a private-label film supplier to chain retailers.

In the 1950s the groundwork was prepared for exploiting technologies that would make photography a mass consumption industry. Color processes were refined by the few industry participants that commanded the requisite financial and intellectual capital. Celluloid was replaced by polyester as a film base. Injection molding of plastics presented an enormous potential for producing photographic equipment and supplies.

In 1957 Eastman Kodak initiated the design, engineering, production, and marketing plans for a product that would secure its position as the industry's predominant supplier of consumer goods. Introduced with enormous fanfare in 1963, the Kodak Instamatic system quickly swept the world of consumer photography. Before the decade was out, some 50 million Instamatic cameras had been sold. The system included several features to attract consumers, photofinishers, and manufacturers alike, but its heart was the new film transport mechanism. A roll of 35mm film was packaged in a plastic cartridge designed to eliminate the treading and rewinding of the film in the camera. The user opened the camera, inserted the cartridge, and closed the camera. A lever in the camera advanced the film and cocked the shutter. Although the cartridges were initially notched to identify several different types of film—including the more sensitive contemporary monochrome films—the overwhelming success of color film packaged in this convenient, inexpensive format drove black and white film from the mass consumer market. Departing from company tradition, Kodak licensed the cartridge to other film producers and private-label packagers around the world.

Twice since the Instamatic's debut, Kodak has introduced new mass consumption systems that further miniaturized both the camera and the amount of negative material required for taking a photograph.

INSTANT PHOTOGRAPHY

The only serious challenge to Eastman Kodak's dominant position in the photographic industry came from the Polaroid Corporation. During the late 1930s researchers at Gevaert in Belgium and Agfa in Germany independently discovered the phenomenon of image diffusion transfer reversal—the migration of silver salts from negative to positive image layers when both are immersed in a developer and brought into contact. The rapid formation of the positive image by this process considerably shortens the conventional sequence of developing, fixing, washing, and drying a photographic print. Polaroid founder Edwin H. Land and his associates adapted this process to create a system capable of producing a finished print within a minute of exposure. A sealed pod containing a viscous reagent was coupled to the negative and positive sheets. A pair of precision rollers was fitted to a camera. After exposure, the materials were pulled through the rollers and out of the camera. The pressure of the rollers ruptured the pod and spread the reagent evenly over the inner surfaces of the sheets. After a very short processing interval the two sheets were peeled apart.

The Polaroid Land system of instant photography was a popular and commercial success. Within eight years of its introduction in 1948, 1 million Polaroid Land cameras had been sold. The company invested its resources heavily in research and development that brought forth a stream of ever more sophisticated film and camera products. By 1963 the company had mastered the application of its basic process to color film. During the same year it reconfigured the packaging of its film products from rolls to flat sheets. These developments laid the groundwork for diversifying uses for Polaroid processes. The steady, high volume of industrial, commercial, and professional applications sustained Polaroid for two decades as it suffered the vicissitudes of the rapid technological development it undertook in consumer photography.

Throughout the first quarter-century of its involvement with photography, Polaroid was to a far greater extent a research and marketing enterprise than a manufacturer. Its cameras were manufactured to its specifications by outside suppliers, as were the negative and print paper used in its film products. Its own production during this period was confined to assembling and packaging the components of its film product. A key supplier was Eastman Kodak, which produced the negative incorporated in Polaroid's color films.

In the early 1970s Polaroid took quantum leaps into new technologies in photographic chemistry, optics, and electronics. To bring out its SX–70 system, the company became an integrated manufacturer of cameras and color negative. The move into spheres of activity in which the company had inadequate expertise and no experience reversed the exponential earnings growth it had enjoyed during the previous decade.

The SX–70 system, and its modifications, included a film unit in which the color negative, transparent plastic positive sheet, and reagent pod were integrated into one unit, thereby obviating the need to separate positive and negative after development. Ten such units were packed together with a flat battery to power the camera's electronic components, flash array, and the small motor that drove the film through the rollers and ejected it from the camera. In 1978 the technical sophistication of the camera was enhanced by an automatic focusing device based on ultrasonic echo ranging. The light sensitivity of the film was increased in 1981. For a time it was the fastest amateur color print film on the market. To exploit the film's high sensitivity, Polaroid modified the camera's exposure control system to mix ambient light with electronic flash that was built into the camera. In 1986 new high-saturation dyes were added to the film, and the picture format was enlarged.

The beginning of in-house production of its principal products and their major components was one of several reasons for Polaroid's erratic earnings. Another was the entry of direct competition into the domain in which it had been the sole occupant for nearly three decades. As the supplier of Polaroid's color negative during the 1960s and early 1970s, Eastman Kodak had ample firsthand evidence of the extent to which instant photography was invading the industry it had long dominated. In 1976 Eastman Kodak brought to market its instant system. Its chemistry differed somewhat from Polaroid's, but the products were nearly identical from the consumer's point of view. Polaroid initiated legal action charging Kodak with infringement of several key Polaroid patents. The litigation was protracted over nearly a decade, but the court ruled in favor of Polaroid and enjoined Kodak from further infringement from the beginning of 1986. Kodak obeyed this injunction and ceased its commercialization of instant photographic products. The initial court judgment, however, left pending a number of unresolved issues, including the determination of damages to compensate Polaroid for Kodak's infringement.

THE PHOTOGRAPHIC INDUSTRY IN HISTORICAL PERSPECTIVE

The manufacture of photosensitive materials has become capital intensive. The consumer market for cameras, film, and associated equipment is built on product differentiation by brand names established through intensive advertising. The industry has prospered by process and product innovation generated by institutionalized research and development. The photographic goods industry, then, is characterized by high fixed costs.

The photographic industry is oligopolistic. Furthermore, the internation-alization of American enterprises manufacturing and selling photographic goods was nearly contemporaneous with the emergence of the mass pro-duction industry. The forerunner of Eastman Kodak set up its first per-manent establishment abroad as early as 1885, and a century later every major industry participant was a multinational enterprise.

Because human beings rely on their eyes for information and pleasure, photographic images satisfy a fundamental need. The market for equipment and supplies to produce artificial images is probably permanent. Neverthe-less, it is unlikely that the market will always be satisfied by the photo-chemical means in use for a century and a half. Research conducted during the 1980s inside and outside the photographic industry suggests a future in which images will be captured and displayed by electronic technologies.

BIBLIOGRAPHIC ESSAY

Photography and its history have spawned a vast literature. With rare exceptions, however, the standard approach to the subject is to recite either technical progress or the development of photography as a medium of artistic expression. The business and economic history of the field has been largely ignored by serious scholars.

Among the exceptions is the work of Reese V. Jenkins. His *Images and Enterprise: Technology and the American Photographic Industry 1839–1925* is the definitive history of the American photographic industry (Jenkins 1975a). Although most of this work is based on the author's primary source research, it includes an encyclopedic collection of secondary source citations. Owing to space limitations, few of the latter are repeated here.

It is possible for the well-informed to attribute a significance to the events reported by Jenkins other than that which his interpretive framework gives them. Nevertheless, it is advisable to heed Jenkins if the goal is to understand the history of the American photographic industry. Jenkins has also written several shorter pieces that illuminate individual aspects of the industry's history (Jenkins 1975b, 1981).

One of the primary themes in Lutz Alt's dissertation (1986) is the exten-sion of this industry's business across national frontiers. He attempts to summarize the strategic factors responsible for the long-term survival of the world's leading photochemical producers. Alt includes a long chapter on the development of Eastman Kodak and a section of a chapter on Agfa's involvement in the United States. An extended summary of this work has been published (Alt 1987).

The history of American photography from the time it became an im-portant industry is largely the history of the Eastman Kodak Company. Kodak's management rarely opens its archives to historians; thus few serious works about the company or its founder have been published.

The only published full-length biography of George Eastman is that by Carl W. Ackerman (1930). In addition to the highlights of Eastman's life, this work offers factual material about the enterprise he founded and led for nearly five decades. Perhaps characteristic of a biography sponsored by the subject, its sins are those of omission. The unsavory side of Eastman and his company is either ignored or glossed over in this fawning portrait.

A more balanced Eastman biography and company history was written in the early 1970s by Lawrence P. Bachmann. Two unpublished draft manuscripts (Bachmann Papers, ca. 1973) are held by the University of Rochester and are accessible to scholars.

Most of the popular press works can be ignored. An exception is an extended article published by *Life* to celebrate the centennial of Eastman's birth (Butterfield 1954). This piece is quite possibly the best starting point for any study of Eastman's role in the history of the photographic industry.

Roger Butterfield did not complete his book-length Eastman biography. He did, however, assemble a comprehensive collection of correspondence and memorabilia that constitutes a primary information source (Eastman-Butterfield Collection). This collection is held by the University of Rochester and is open to scholars. In it Eastman reveals himself and his business ideas in voluminous correspondence.

The editors of *Fortune* published an overview of Eastman Kodak operations and management in the year of its founder's death. The article includes background information on Ansco ("Sunlight and Shadow" 1932).

A tendentious and angry little tract covers some of the developments of the first Kodak camera (Hammer 1940). Written in a style so stilted as to be ludicrous, it nevertheless offers useful glimpses of the business climate in which Eastman's company bought the rights to a key patent.

Institutionalized research and development distinguishes the photographic industry. Eastman Kodak was a pioneer in this institutionalization. An insight into the policies guiding the work of the Kodak Laboratories is provided by C.E.K. Mees, who headed the labs from their foundation in 1912 until his retirement in 1955 (Mees and Leermakers 1950). The same theme is taken up by Jenkins (1981).

Scholars seeking additional background on George Eastman and his work may wish to consult a bibliographic essay published by the University of Rochester (Kabelac 1971–72).

Photographic business enterprise is bound up with and dependent on the exploitation of materials, processes, and the possibilities offered by the economic infrastructure. Anyone seeking an appreciation of photography's business history needs some background about the field's technical progress and the environment in which it was made. The following highly selective list of works should help.

Among the photographic histories that have stood the test of time is the Gernsheims' (1969). It traces the field from its origins to roughly the beginning of World War I, offering individual chapters on specific business and professional uses of photography that emerged during the nineteenth century.

Jenkins's dissertation (1967) is an indispensable guide to nineteenth-century knowledge of the physical and chemical phenomena exploited by photography.

A work by Beaumont Newhall (1964) covers the major developments from an aesthetician's point of view. The "present day" in this book's title is the early post–World War II period.

A penetrating background work examines the conditions and changes in American market practices and institutions during the nineteenth century. These practices and institutions gave rise to Eastman Kodak, which in turn accelerated their influence on business life (Porter and Livesay 1971).

A work that has become a classic of its genre is Robert Taft's social history of photography (1938). He describes the various photographic processes and materials used in the United States during photography's first five decades and relates these to the country's history.

BIBLIOGRAPHY

Ackerman, Carl W. *George Eastman*. Boston: Houghton Mifflin, 1930.

Alt, Lutz. "The Photochemical Industry: Historical Essays in Business Strategy and Internationalization." Ph.D diss., Massachusetts Institute of Technology, 1986.

———. "The Photochemical Industry: Historical Essays in Business Strategy and Internationalization." *Business and Economic History* 16 (1987): 183–88.

Bachmann, Lawrence P. Papers. University of Rochester Library, Rochester, NY.

Butterfield, Roger. "The Prodigious Life of George Eastman." *Life* 36 (April 26, 1954): 154–56.

Eastman-Butterfield Collection. University of Rochester Library, Rochester, NY.

Gernsheim, Helmut, in collaboration with Alison Gernsheim. *The History of Photography from the Camera Obscura to the Beginning of the Modern Era*. New York: McGraw-Hill, 1969.

Hammer, Mina Fisher. *History of Kodak and Its Continuations*. New York: House of Little Books, 1940.

Jenkins, Reese V. "Some Interrelations of Science, Technology and the Photographic Industry." Ph.D. diss., University of Wisconsin, 1966. Ann Arbor, MI: University Microfilms, 1967.

———. *Images and Enterprise: Technology and the American Photographic Industry 1839–1925*. Baltimore: Johns Hopkins University Press, 1975a.

———. "Technology and the Market: George Eastman and the Origins of Mass Amateur Photography." *Technology and Culture* 16 (January 1975b): 1–19.

———. "George Eastman and the Coming of Industrial Research in America." In *Technology in America*, edited by Carroll W. Pursell, Jr. Cambridge, MA: MIT Press, 1981.

Kabelac, Karl Sanford. "George Eastman: A Bibliographical Essay of Selected References." *University of Rochester Library Bulletin* 27 (Winter 1971–72): 33–38.

Mees, C.E.K., and John A. Leermakers. *The Organization of Industrial Scientific Research.* 2d ed. New York: McGraw-Hill, 1950.

Newhall, Beaumont. *The History of Photography from 1839 to the Present Day.* Rev. and enlarged ed. New York: Museum of Modern Art, 1964.

Porter, Glenn, and Harold C. Livesay. *Merchants and Manufacturers: Studies in the Changing Structure of Nineteenth-Century Marketing.* Baltimore: Johns Hopkins University Press, 1971.

"Sunlight and Shadow." *Fortune* 5 (May 1932): 50–59.

Taft, Robert. *Photography and the American Scene: A Social History.* New York: Macmillan, 1938.

Part XIII

Musical Instruments, Toys, and Sporting Goods
ESIC 39.0

_____

CHAPTER 22

MUSICAL INSTRUMENTS, 39.3

_____ ROBERT M. ADUDDELL AND LOUIS P. CAIN

The production of musical instruments is primarily a handicraft industry. The few large-scale producers have well-known names, but they have been little studied. Two recent historical works emphasizing the business affairs of piano manufacturing are Kornblith (1985) and Singer (1986).

Small-scale producers are the subject of a literature aimed at collectors. It often explores the commercial functions of a particular craftsman or craft, but business is a secondary interest at best. At the center of this literature are the Gilpin Society in Great Britain and the American Musical Instrument Society in the United States. The latter publishes a newsletter and an annual journal. Almost every issue of the A.M.I.S. journal has at least one article on a handicraft producer. In addition, the book reviews and lists of newly published books are excellent sources for materials on handicraft production.

Among reference works, the standard source is *The New Grove Dictionary of Musical Instruments*, edited by Stanley Sadie (1984). The three volumes include summations of important producers, both large and small, listed alphabetically by company. Other reference works—for example, Baines (1976) and Marcuse (1975)—emphasize the evolution of each instrument, but they add little to what can be found in *Grove*.

Another source that focuses on the evolution of the instruments, but that contains a little information on important producers, is a series entitled "Instruments of the Orchestra." With few exceptions, the volumes discuss a single instrument—for example, Bate (1979), Morley-Pegge (1973), and Nelson (1972). This series was published jointly in Great Britain by E. Benn and in the United States by W. W. Norton; second editions of most of the books appeared in the 1970s. The following bibliography includes a few titles from the series. The authors' formats are similar; consult the cited examples to see what the series offers.

Finally, several interesting, widely cited books on specific instruments are included here even though their primary focus is not business history—for example, Loesser (1954) and Good (1982).

BIBLIOGRAPHY

Ayars, Christine Merrick. *Contributions to the Art of Music in America by the Music Industries of Boston 1640 to 1936.* New York: W. W. Wilson, 1937.

Baines, Anthony, ed. *Musical Instruments Through the Ages.* New York: Walker, 1976, for the Gilpin Society.

Bate, Philip. *The Oboe.* New York: W. W. Norton, 1975.

———. *The Trumpet and Trombone.* New York: W. W. Norton, 1978.

———. *The Flute.* New York: W. W. Norton, 1979.

Bellson, Julius. *The Gibson Story.* Kalamazoo, MI: Gibson, 1973.

Bowers, Q. David. *Encyclopaedia of Automatic Musical Instruments.* Vestal, NY: Vestal Press, 1972.

Dolge, Alfred. *Pianos and Their Makers.* Covina, CA: Covina Publishing, 1911.

Ehrlich, Cyril. *The Piano: A History.* London: Dent, 1976.

Eliason, Robert E. *Keyed Bugles in the United States.* Washington, DC: Smithsonian Institution Press, 1972.

———. *Graves & Company: Musical Instrument Makers.* Dearborn, MI: Greenfield Village-Henry Ford Museum, 1975.

———. *Early American Brass Makers.* Brass Research Series No. 10. Nashville: The Brass Press, 1979a.

———. "The Meachams, Musical Instrument Makers of Hartford and Albany." *Journal of the American Musical Instrument Society* 5 (1979b): 54–73.

———. "George Catlin, Hartford Musical Instrument Maker." *Journal of the American Musical Instrument Society* 8 (1982): 16–37; 9 (1983): 21–52.

Farrell, Susan Caust. *Directory of Contemporary American Musical Instrument Makers.* Columbia: University of Missouri Press, 1981.

Ferguson, John Allen. *Walter Holtkamp: American Organ Builder.* Kent, OH: Kent State University Press, 1979.

Geiringer, Karl. *Instruments in the History of Western Music.* New York: Oxford University Press, 1978.

Gellerman, Robert F. *The American Reed Organ.* Vestal, NY: Vestal Press, 1973.

General History of the Music Trades of America. New York: Bill & Bill, 1891.

Good, Edwin M. *Giraffes, Black Dragons, and Other Pianos: A Technological History from Cristofori to the Modern Concert Grand.* Stanford: Stanford University Press, 1982.

Grafing, Keith G. "Alpheus Babcock: American Pianoforte Maker (1785–1842): His Life, Instruments, and Patents." D.M.A. diss., University of Missouri, Kansas City, 1972.

Groce, Nancy Jane. "Musical Instrument Making in New York City During the Eighteenth and Nineteenth Centuries." Ph.D. diss., University of Michigan, 1982.

Harding, Rosamond E. M. *The Piano-forte: Its History Traced to the Great Exhibition of 1851.* 2d ed. Old Woking, UK: Gresham Books, 1978.

Hemke, Frederick L. "The Early History of the Saxophone." D.M.A. diss., University of Wisconsin, Madison, 1975.

Heron-Allen, Edward. *Violin-Making: As It Was and Is.* 2d ed. New York: C. Fisher, 1985.

Hoover, Cynthia Adams. "The Steinways and Their Pianos in the Nineteenth Century." *Journal of the American Musical Instrument Society* 7 (1981): 47–89.

Hume, Paul, and Ruth Hume. "The Great Chicago Piano War." *American Heritage* 21 (October 1970): 16–21.

Kaufman, Charles H. "Musical-Instrument Makers in New Jersey, 1796–1860." *Journal of the American Musical Instrument Society* 3 (1976): 5–33.

Kornblith, Gary J. "The Craftsman as Industrialist: Jonas Chickering and the Transformation of American Piano Making." *Business History Review* 59 (Autumn 1985): 349–68.

Loesser, Arthur. *Men, Women and Pianos: A Social History.* New York: Simon & Schuster, 1954.

Longworth, Mike. *Martin Guitars: A History.* Nazareth, PA: M. Longworth, 1980.

Majeski, John F., Jr. "Steinway: A Century of Distinguished Family Enterprise." *The Music Trades* (October 1953): 23–34, 63.

Marcuse, Sybil. *A Survey of Musical Instruments.* New York: Harper & Row, 1975.

Morley-Pegge, R. *The French Horn.* New York: W. W. Norton, 1973.

Nelson, Sheila M. *The Violin and Viola.* New York: W. W. Norton, 1972.

Ochse, Orpha. *The History of the Organ in the United States.* Bloomington: Indiana University Press, 1975.

Ogasapian, John. *Organ Building in New York City: 1700–1900.* Braintree, MA: Organ Literature Foundation, 1977.

———. *Henry Erben: Portrait of a Nineteenth-Century American Organ Builder.* Braintree, MA: Organ Literature Foundation, 1980.

Owen, Barbara. *The Organ in New England: An Account of Its Use and Manufacture to the End of the Nineteenth Century.* Raleigh, NC: Sunbury Press, 1979.

Riley, Maurice W. *The History of the Viola.* Ypsilanti, MI: Maurice Riley, 1980.

Sachs, Curt. *History of Musical Instruments.* New York: W. W. Norton, 1940.

Sadie, Stanley, ed. *The New Grove Dictionary of Musical Instruments.* 3 vols. New York: Grove's Dictionaries of Music, 1984.

Singer, Aaron. *Labor Management Relations at Steinway & Sons, 1853–1896.* New York: Garland, 1986.

Skei, Allen B. *Woodwind, Brass, and Percussion Instruments of the Orchestra: A Bibliographic Guide.* New York: Garland, 1984.

Spillane, Daniel. *History of the American Pianoforte: Its Technical Development and the Trade.* New York: D. Spillane, 1890.

Steinway, Theodore. *People and Pianos.* New York: Steinway & Sons, 1961.

Steinway, William. "American Musical Instruments." *The Music Trades* 29 (March 1896): 8–11.

Summer, William Leslie. *The Pianoforte.* New York: St. Martin's Press, 1971.

Waller, Robert J. "American Guitar Manufacturing: Oligopoly and the Economics of a Craft Industry." D.B.A. diss., Indiana University, 1968.

Webb, Robert Lloyd. *Ring the Banjo! The Banjo in America from Folklore to Factory.* Cambridge, MA: MIT Press, 1984.

Wells, Grant J. "Kimball International: Playing a Sound Tune." *Ball State Business Review* 11, no. 2 (1982): 7–14.

Wheeler, Tom. *American Guitars: An Illustrated History.* New York: Harper & Row, 1982.

CHAPTER 23

TOYS AND SPORTING GOODS, 39.4

⸻ JOHN S. BOWDIDGE

As archaeologists have plumbed the mysteries of the most primitive societies they have found little or no evidence of toys. Perhaps our earliest ancestors were too engrossed in the struggle to survive to craft playthings. The traces left by advanced, sophisticated civilizations, however, contain numerous toylike objects. In ancient Egypt, Greece, and Rome, there was leisure time to devote to the making, collecting, and cherishing of tiny artifacts.

Just how many of these miniature items were indeed children's playthings? Many were religious icons, others were precious works of art designed to bring pleasure to mature adults. Probably some were for children's play. Even today, confusion surrounds toys and dolls manufactured within the last two centuries. Toy and doll collections in mint condition generate the suspicion that items in such a treasure have never known the sweaty grasp of a child, or been cuddled or used as missiles in a childhood spat. Regardless of their purposes or audiences, toys, dolls, and games are a part of Western tradition. The United States has shared that tradition.

TOYS

In the early days of the American colonies, children's toys were usually homemade. Parents fashioned small playthings from wood and metal scraps left over from vocational activities. Some firms used their industrial scraps to make toys, an early example of diversification. But the finest toys were produced in Europe; and as American imports grew in the eighteenth century, toys took up their share of space in the holds of westbound merchant ships. Until well after the presidency of George Washington, toys purchased for American children came largely from abroad. Germany had the best reputation in toys, and the center of the industry was Nuremberg.

Only after 1820 was there any appreciable toy manufacturing in the United States. The Crandall family—Asa, Jesse, Charles, and Benjamin—started it all in that year. The 1830s witnessed the opening of the first complete factory dedicated to the production of toys, the Tower Toy Company of South Higham, Massachusetts. In the 1840s the Turners in Meriden, Connecticut, were among the first to use tin scraps for making toys. The idea soon spread to companies in New York and Philadelphia.

In 1860 Milton Bradley moved a lithographic press from Providence, Rhode Island, to Springfield, Massachusetts, and opened for business. His first important project was the printing of hundreds of thousands of copies of a photograph of a promising American politician, Abraham Lincoln. The press run was doomed; Lincoln was growing a beard while the posters were in production. Bradley later moved into educational books and materials, games, and toys. Playskool, Incorporated, for example, belongs to the Milton Bradley Company.

Following Bradley closely was the toys and games firm founded by George S. Parker in 1888 at Salem, Massachusetts. Parker Brothers' first nationwide hit was Ping Pong, introduced toward the end of the nineteenth century.

Toy soldiers made of cardboard, paper, tin, or lead have long been popular in Europe. Sales flourish during times of nationalistic fervor. Because Europe was the scene of many wars in the nineteenth century, the miniature militias were always in demand. The demand spread to America. The first native American toy soldiers can be credited to C. W. Beiser in 1898. Calling his company Eureka American, he catered to a market that was enthusiastic when the United States was on the verge of war. Since the mid–1960s, a most effective representative of the toy soldier mania has been G. I. Joe from Hassenfeld Brothers (Hasbro).

Shortly after Beiser's success, Morris Michtom created a novelty of lasting popularity. In 1902 President Theodore Roosevelt was in the South settling a border dispute between Louisiana and Mississippi. As a break from negotiations, the President spent an afternoon hunting with friends. When a bear cub appeared in the sights of his rifle, TR refused to shoot. Cartoonist Clifford Berryman of the *Washington Post* elevated the incident to a national event. Michtom proposed to manufacture stuffed cloth bears and secured the President's permission to call them Teddy Bears. The cubs were an instant success. The Teddies marked the birth of Michtom's new firm, Ideal Novelty and Toy Company.

As steam locomotives became commercially feasible in Britain and the United States in the 1830s, miniaturized models quickly appeared. There were two methods for moving these diminutive locomotives (whether on a track or free running): steam and clockwork. The former used a wick to heat water in a tiny boiler, and steam moved the wheels. Clockwork engines were wound like a mechanical clock, and they rolled until the spring ran down. Early leaders in the American toy train industry were Merriam Manufacturing; Hull and Stafford; Francis, Field and Francis; and Ives, Blakeslee and Company.

Americans were wiring their homes for electricity, and miniature trains could be powered by that energy source. Progressing from battery-operated locomotives before World War I, Joshua Lionel Cowen and his Lionel Corporation expanded their electric line as electricity became more common throughout the land. After a period of fierce postwar competition with the Ives locomotives, Lionel bought them out in 1928. The Lionel trains are now produced by Model Products Company. They enjoy a small but loyal following. The fading of passenger trains from the American scene has dimmed the appeal of electric trains for today's children.

When creativity and constructive tendencies can be integrated into children's play, so much the better. Several firms have responded to this notion by offering building or construction toys. In 1901 an Englishman, Frank Hornby, a genius with toys, developed the Meccano system of small metal pieces that could be assembled with nuts and bolts to form myriad structures. American Olympic pole-vaulter A. C. Gilbert decided in 1912 to add a similar toy to the product mix of his magician's equipment firm, Mysto Manufacturing Company. His brainchild was the Erector set, marketed today by the Gilbert Division of Gabriel Industries.

While Gilbert was promoting sales of his Erector sets, a tombstone cutter in Evanston, Illinois, was working in his garage on a set of small wooden pieces that children could assemble as they chose. The cutter, Charles H. Pajeau, called his creation Tinkertoy, and it is made today by Questor Education Products Company.

During the 1930s a Danish carpenter, Ole Kirk-Christiansen, kept food on his family's table by hand carving toys and selling them in the village of Billund. When his four sons were grown, they joined the business. One of the sons, Godtfred, discovered a way to attach one plastic block to another. His innovation allowed kids to pile their blocks high and to enlarge their scope of construction. In 1954 the Christiansens marketed their Lego blocks. They were quickly accepted in Europe and are manufactured in the United States under a license held by Samsonite Corporation.

Toy soldiers, Teddy Bears, train sets, and construction toys, once they arrived, never left the American scene. Although their popularity has waxed and waned through the years, they have remained available to the public. Many ideas for toys, like brilliant comets, have blazed briefly across the sky, then disappeared. Some reappear at a later date; others hover in the background. The procession defies complete listing, but worthy of remembering are airplanes (assembled and to-be-assembled), army helmets, badges of every description, Bingo Bear, castles, Charlie McCarthy, cowboy six-shooters, crickets, the Duncan Yo-Yo, fire engines, gasoline stations,

GoBots, Howdy Doody, the Hula Hoop, laser guns, mechanical banks, the Pet Rock, plastic Sherman tanks, Pip Squeak, police cars, police pistols, Pound Puppies, rubber knives, Rubik's Cube, space pistols, space ships, suction-cup arrows, Teddy Ruxpin, Tommy guns, Transformers, Trolls, Wrestling Superstars, and the numerous toys derived from Walt Disney productions.

Matchbox cars and Silly Putty gave every appearance of briefly glowing fads. Nevertheless, they have exhibited amazing staying power. To mark the 1953 coronation of Queen Elizabeth II of England, John W. Odell and Leslie C. Smith made and sold 1 million five-inch miniatures of the royal coronation coach. Their firm, Lesney Products and Company, Ltd., capitalized on its first success by manufacturing tiny replicas of motor vehicles and packaging them in containers the size of matchboxes. Despite the reluctance of toy dealers to carry these items, the public—adults and children alike—was enthralled by Matchbox cars. Although rivaled for a time by Mattel's Hot Wheels, the Lesney line has adapted, expanded, and remained.

Silly Putty was an accident. In 1945 an engineer in a General Electric laboratory mixed boric acid with silicone oil to produce a rubbery substance. The laboratory was trying to develop a synthetic rubber compound to aid the American war effort. But the boric-silicone glob was hardly a material from which army truck tires could be made. Marketing specialist Peter Hodgson called the mixture Silly Putty—a toy for kids and a relaxer for tense and hurried adults. Set back temporarily by a silicone shortage during the Korean War and by the viscosity of the product, Hodgson in 1960 introduced nonsticky Silly Putty. The product has since been a regular in America's repertory of toys.

A new firm that entered the industry in 1985, Worlds of Wonder, Incorporated, created a stir with two of their products, Teddy Ruxpin, the singing bear, and Lazer Tag, an electronic game. By 1987 several older toy companies were perfecting toys powered by signals sent from television cartoon shows. Mattel's Captain Power and Axlon's Tech Force led the way in this latest electronic caper.

Several sources in the literature on toys indicate that "knocking off," copying or the alleged copying of toy ideas, is commonplace in the industry. For example, in early 1987 Mattel filed suit against Hasbro in a federal court in California, claiming the latter was making use of the name of a Mattel product, Slime. Mattel's Slime is a green gelatinous, putty-like substance. Hasbro has allegedly infringed on Mattel's copyright by introducing a line of watches known as Slime Time.

DOLLS

Credit for inaugurating the manufacture of dolls, toys, and games in the United States has been given to various branches and generations of the

Crandall family. In the 1830s Benjamin Potter Crandall made a name for himself by offering and frequently updating an array of baby carriages for dolls—two wheels, four wheels, collapsible, and so on. The dolls that rode in Crandall's carriages were largely European-made.

Except for rag dolls, most of a doll's body was made of cotton or other soft material stuffed into a form, with head and limbs of papier-mâché, wax, porcelain, or china. Rubber, celluloid, composition, and Parian were later used. In more recent times, the entire anatomy has been made of durable plastics.

As with many toys, dolls in early America were collectibles for adults. Most early dolls were representations of full-grown adults, some famous. A big seller during the 1850s and 1860s was the Jenny Lind, honoring the "Swedish Nightingale" of the concert stage. Dolls of President and Mrs. Washington were also in demand.

That a doll should represent a newborn baby is a relatively recent idea. The Montanari family produced the first "baby dolls" in Europe in 1825. Their infant was displayed at the Crystal Palace Exhibition in London in 1851. Although a "baby" made in 1730 may be found in the Victoria and Albert Museum, such dolls were not commonplace in the United States until the latter years of the nineteenth century.

Johnny Gruelle brought some standardization to American dolls, beginning in 1918, and his influence is felt to this day. Gruelle was a cartoonist who depicted details of the escapades of Raggedy Ann and her pal Raggedy Andy. Cashing in on the popularity of the cartoons and books, Knickerbocker Toy Company made rag dolls to match. Millions of children have loved these dolls, and Knickerbocker continues to manufacture them under a license granted by the Gruelle family.

America has witnessed many doll crazes. The Kewpie Doll was one of many that captured public attention for a time and then faded. Rose O'Neill was a skilled illustrator whose elfish, cupid-like figures—Kewpies—began appearing in 1909 in *Ladies Home Journal, Women's Home Companion,* and *Good Housekeeping.* By 1923, 5,000 Kewpie stories had appeared. For a year, her cartoon Kewpie Korner was carried by a newspaper syndicate. Fan mail expressed a longing for dolls to match, so O'Neill commissioned German firms to manufacture them. The bisque dolls were created at the Kestner factory in Walterhausen and, beginning in 1913, were produced in nine sizes and distributed by Borgfeldt Doll Company. The Kewpies were shipped to the United States and around the globe, causing one O'Neill biographer to declare the dolls a universal toy. Five million sold quickly.

World War I was a sad time for O'Neill. She revealed to a friend that she had lost many loved ones on a German ship torpedoed in the English Channel. The friend wondered if they were all close relatives. "Relatives? They were my Kewpies," O'Neill replied. After the torpedo incident, Kewpies were made in the United States by Fulper Pottery of New Jersey and other firms on this side of the Atlantic.

The child actress Shirley Temple appeared in her first Hollywood film in 1933. A year later, Morris Michtom (the creator of Teddy Bear) obtained the rights to a doll emulating the star. So captivating was Miss Temple's screen persona for Twentieth Century-Fox that by Christmas, 1936, the Shirley Temple was the best-selling doll in history. Along with sons Ben and Joseph and son-in-law David Rosenstein, Michtom offered a quality product. Made of composition, the blonde, curly-haired beauty required 400 manufacturing steps. Michtom's firm was Ideal Novelty and Toy Company, but imitators of Michtom's doll were legion.

In 1977 a junior college student in Georgia set the toy and doll world on its ear. Xavier Roberts made some soft, cuddly dolls with unique features that he called Little People. In 1978 he established Original Appalachian Artworks. The firm's outlet in Cleveland, Georgia, was known as Babyland General Hospital; there, "parents" could "adopt" Roberts's "children," all of whom came with birth certificates and adoption papers. These were custom-made dolls, and some sold for as much as $1,000. Roberts had a winner. A license to mass distribute a smaller, less expensive version was granted to Coleco; actual production took place in eight plants in the Far East. The Coleco product was called Cabbage Patch Kids.

As Christmas, 1983, approached, it became clear that Coleco had not produced Kids enough to meet the national demand. Across America, when the word was out that a given store had forty Cabbage Patch Kids on hand, hundreds of customers would be waiting at the front door when the store opened for business. As of July, 1986, *Toy and Hobby World* reported that Cabbage Patch Kids had been on the top-ten toys list for thirty-seven months.

Dolls continue to come and go. But a love affair of nearly thirty years has endured between American children and a coterie of beautiful creatures. It all began when Ruth and Elliott Handler, the guiding forces at Mattel, Incorporated, decided in 1959 to give a mature fashion-model doll a spin in the marketplace. They named the beauty after their daughter Barbie, and an American obsession was launched. This 11½-inch doll was a glamorous adult with an infinite wardrobe of stunning garments for dancing, skiing, swimming, performing, studying, and working. Along with Barbie, children could acquire her boyfriend, Ken, and several other friends. Barbie's troupe has adapted through the years; all are as chic today as when they first appeared.

Even the most successful dolls have competition. In 1986 Hasbro brought out Jem and the Holograms to compete directly with Mattel's Barbie. Indications are that Jem and entourage are catching on. Topps Chewing Gum, Incorporated, long-lived purveyor of baseball cards in bubble gum packages, introduced a new series of cards called "Garbage Pail Kids"—whose characterizations are alleged to parody Cabbage Patch Kids. The Cabbage Patch creators filed suit against Topps in federal court, charging copyright infringement. In a quiet settlement in 1987, Topps agreed to make a cash payment to Original Appalachian Artworks and to make design changes in the Garbage Pail series.

GAMES

Some authors point out that the earliest board games introduced in the United States stressed moral values. That was not true, however, of a spate of enduring games introduced in Great Britain. In 1649 Oliver Cromwell took the reins of English government and, until his death nine years later, imposed puritanism on one and all. With the restoration of the monarchy in 1660, citizens (including King Charles II himself) began importing games of chance. The sudden popularity of such pastimes was a reaction to Cromwell's era of forced morality. These games were not wholesome family entertainment; they were, rather, vehicles by which men and women of means wagered money. Among the games were ombre, basset, whist, billiards, chess, cribbage, and backgammon. Most made their way to the New World.

As a rule, early Americans played games with equipment and pieces that were made in Europe. Large game-manufacturing concerns did not appear in the United States until well into the nineteenth century. Leading the parade were the Milton Bradley Company (founded 1860) and Parker Brothers (1888). In the closing years of the twentieth century, these two firms are still industry leaders. Popular nineteenth-century American-made games were The Checkered Game of Life from Milton Bradley and Pigs in Clover from Charles M. Crandall of the famous toymaking family.

Both Milton Bradley and Parker Brothers played a part in a curious tale attached to one of the most dominant board games extant. The Landlord's Game was patented in 1904 by Lizzie J. Magie. It was a real estate game involving the purchase of properties. In the early 1930s, Charles B. Darrow designed a similar game for the amusement of family and friends. Having fond memories of a vacation spent some years earlier in Atlantic City, Darrow gave locations on his board Atlantic City designations. Friends were so taken with the game that Darrow found himself making numerous copies out of linoleum and wood scraps. Eventually, he used the services of a printer; but the time had come to turn the project over to a national marketing operation.

In the Great Depression, the Milton Bradley Company was, like many American firms, in financial doldrums. The company could have used the reviving effect that the Darrow game might provide. But Bradley officials ruled the game too difficult and time-consuming. Darrow went to Parker Brothers. The latter firm was also reluctant, but at least agreed to try to sell the games Darrow had already printed. They disappeared quickly from store shelves at Christmastime, 1934. With demands pouring in for more Monopoly games, Parker Brothers took on the game permanently in early 1935. The Brothers have never been sorry.

In the years between Magie's Landlord's Game and Darrow's Monopoly, a traveling salesman stumbled upon a great American game idea. One evening in the 1920s, Edwin S. Lowe watched while carnival-goers feverishly competed in a game of chance in which a game master called out numbers, and players filled in corresponding spots on a card. The players lingered over Beano into the wee hours of the morning. Lowe developed a comparable game and tried it out on friends; they were as eager as the carnival crowd. According to legend, one player became so excited when her card filled up (and she was eligible for a prize) that instead of shouting Beano, she blurted out "bingo." Now Lowe had a name for his game, and Bingo swept the country during the Depression.

Lightning struck a second time for E. S. Lowe Company, Incorporated. One day in the early 1950s, a well-to-do Canadian came to company headquarters with an unusual request. While their yacht was docked in Bermuda each winter, the woman and her husband entertained guests on deck with a dice diversion they called the Yacht Game. Would E. S. Lowe Company produce a thousand copies of the game so that the couple could present them to friends as gifts? When Lowe discovered that the couple wanted no payment for their surrender of rights to the game, he printed 1,000 sets for them at no charge and marketed the game worldwide as Yahtzee. Sales were slow initially, but after 1956 Yahtzee sold 40 million sets in fifteen years.

Popular games rarely catch fire overnight. In 1931 Alfred Mosher Butts began devising a board game in which players formed words with letters printed on small wooden pieces. When the scheme was complete (1948), Butts and friend James Brunot received clearance from a patent attorney to call the game Scrabble. Operating in a former schoolhouse in Connecticut, the new firm, Production and Marketing Corporation, made and sold some 2,500 sets of Scrabble in 1949. For 1954, the company produced 4.5 million games, triggering a surge in sales that is still largely unexplained. To meet the demand, Butts and Brunot arranged a license agreement (and in 1971 manufacturing rights) with Selchow and Righter of Bay Shore, New York. That veteran game firm, long a competitor with Milton Bradley and Parker Brothers, is now a unit of Coleco.

In 1979 two Canadian journalists, Scott Abbott and Chris Haney, hatched a game. The idea was that movement around a flat board would be powered by the roll of a die; this was nothing new. Rewards and victory would accrue to players answering questions in six categories of trivia. For help in amassing thousands of questions, Haney added his brother John to the team. On their own, the three manufactured and sold 20,000 sets of Trivial Pursuit.

To press for more expansive distribution would require an arrangement with a large game manufacturer. The three gamesters approached both Milton Bradley and Parker Brothers and were turned down. In 1982 Selchow and Righter adroitly stepped into the picture. There is some poetic justice in their hopping on the trivia bandwagon: Selchow and Righter (along with Milton Bradley) had rejected Monopoly in 1934. Late in 1984, the firm was making 1 million games per week, and total retail sales of Trivial Pursuit in 1984 were $750 million. The first set of questions was called the Genus Edition. Following swiftly were editions labeled Genus II, Silver Screen, Baby Boomer, and All-Star Sports. Claims and counterclaims will be made for the most popular board game in America. Trivial Pursuit will certainly be a candidate for that honor.

SPORTING GOODS

Of the major team sports played by professional teams today, the first was baseball. Any synopsis of the sporting goods industry must begin with the development of professional baseball.

Four founders of lasting baseball equipment firms were originally baseball players themselves. In 1864 the Philadelphia Athletics lured a star from a baseball club in the New York metropolitan area, the Brooklyn Eckfords. As an added inducement, the A's paid the player, A. J. Reach, the sum of $1,000. Reach has been designated the first professional baseball player in America. Harry Wright was the playing manager of the Boston Red Stockings in 1871, and his brother George was the Boston shortstop. Harry went to Rockford, Illinois, to recruit a pitcher of some renown, Albert Goodwill Spalding.

In the 1880s Reach bought the Philadelphia Phillies, and then opened a sporting goods firm in Philadelphia. The Wright Brothers set up their equipment shop in New England. A. G. Spalding, now president of the Chicago White Stockings, was a steadying force in the early days of the National League and by 1876, chief executive of A. G. Spalding and Brothers, purveyors of sports equipment.

The Spalding organization soon dominated the industry, buying up Reach's firm and forming a partnership with the Wright Brothers (later known as Wright and Ditson). From the beginning, Spalding was responsible for the official National League baseball. For the one glorious 1884 season of the Union Association (which started with twelve franchises), the Wrights supplied the official ball. In 1901 Reach took over the manufacture of the official ball for the American League. Spalding, of course, was behind all of these balls, but zealously kept from the public the news of his mergers and acquisitions.

Despite expanding and diversifying his line (including designing James Naismith's first basketball), Spalding did not by any means have the industry to himself. Peter Browning saw to that. Browning was a consistently good hitter for the baseball club in Louisville. When his personal supply of bats ran low during the 1884 season, Browning requested that a wood-turning shop make him a new one. The craftsman assigned to that piece was J. F. Hillerich. The bat was so successful for Browning that the shop began specializing in the glossy clubs, and Hillerich and Bradsby was formed. The firm's best known product even today is the Louisville Slugger.

The Federal League was formed in 1915, thirty-one years after the Union Association had fielded its teams. In the interim, the National League and the American Association (later called the American League) were often squabbling. The shortened season of 1918 and the Black Sox scandal of 1919 presaged sterner regulation of the game: Judge Kenesaw Mountain Landis was installed as the first commissioner of baseball in time for the 1920 season. Major league baseball settled in with two leagues of eight teams each, a configuration that endured for forty-one years. Thus began "the golden age of sports"—the 1920s.

Giants inhabited the realm of spectator sports in that day. Bobby Jones was a headliner in golf. Tennis fans marveled at Big Bill Tilden. Babe Ruth and Lou Gehrig made the Yankees the favorite team of many a youngster. Jack Dempsey, heavyweight boxing champion, epitomized American masculinity. Knute Rockne and Amos Alonzo Stagg were the premier college football coaches, and Red Grange, the "Galloping Ghost of the Gridiron," was an electrifying player. Athletic prowess was chronicled in epic style by skilled sportswriters intent on prolonging short-lived fame. Grantland Rice was such a wordsmith. On October 18, 1924, Rice was in the pressbox at the Polo Grounds in New York for a football game between Army and Notre Dame. He was impressed by the performance of the four players in the Notre Dame backfield. Rice's dispatch from the Polo Grounds that day immortalized those youngsters as "the Four Horsemen of Notre Dame." In this setting, the popularity of both team and individual sports thrived, and America's boom economy swept along the sporting goods industry.

Although interest in sports has been, for many, a route of escape from the harsh realities of life, the sporting goods industry itself has been unable to escape world conditions. The economic austerity of the Great Depression limited average citizens' participation in sports, both as players and as spectators. Colleges cut appropriations for athletic equipment, and professional baseball teams often operated at a deficit because of reduced gate receipts. In 1929 the number of habitual golfers in the United States was close to 3 million; by 1932 they numbered 600,000. Total value of golf balls at the factory in 1929 was $7,460,000; according to *Business Week*, for 1935 that figure was down to $3,863,000. Likewise, the factory value of golf bags had dropped from $1,908,000 in 1929 to only $455,000 in 1935.

By 1936 the economy began to rally, and so did the sporting goods industry. Boat manufacturers Gar Wood, Incorporated, and Chris-Craft

Corporation reported record sales that year—far surpassing their sales in 1929. And Hacker Boat Company bragged that its sales were 800 percent better than in 1935. The 205,543 fans who attended opening day of 1936 in major league ballparks constituted the largest opening day crowd in five years. As the Works Progress Administration (WPA) completed many of the 600 golf courses on its agenda, golf equipment firms such as Burke Golf Company and Hagen Products anticipated more players and greater sales. Certainly, prospects were improving for particular golf ball manufacturers. The Professional Golfers' Association had endorsed the products of the leading ball producers—Spalding, John Wannamaker, L. A. Young, Worthington Ball Company, U. S. Rubber, Dunlop, and Acushnet Process Corporation. Also on this list was a new firm. In 1935 the Chicago meatpacking firm of Wilson and Company had acquired General Sports Company and changed its name to Wilson Sporting Goods Company.

Even as America began its slow recovery from the Depression, it found itself drawn into a world conflict. The supply of sporting goods for citizens at home was greatly curtailed during World War II. *Business Week* reported that sixty-five materials used in sports equipment manufacture were under the control of the War Production Board (WPB), including copper, cotton, leather, rubber, silk, and zinc. In addition to the raw materials shortages, most sporting goods produced were being sent to the armed forces: the equipment made the leisure hours more bearable for servicemen overseas. But at home, the shortages were felt at the factory as well as on the playing fields. The production of fishing rods, for example, was 5 percent of normal by 1945. And retailers were receiving only 5 percent of the normal supply of baseball bats. With the supply of baseballs running about 40 percent of normal, major and minor league teams encouraged their fans to return foul balls and home runs hit into the stands.

By the late 1960s, retail sales in the sporting goods industry were nearly $4 billion. Accounting for a respectable portion of this amount was the trimming down of America. Exercycle Corporation of New York had sold around 150,000 stationary bikes by 1969, and Battle Creek Manufacturing Company of Michigan could claim that 86 percent of the treadmills Americans were walking on came from their factory. The industry was learning anew that endorsement by major sports stars could move merchandise— and at a higher price. AMF put the name of Dick Weber, pro bowler, on a $20–$25 ball, and it sold for $32.95.

In 1972 the Japanese were discovering bowling, and a boom in the sport ensued. Both AMF and Brunswick (American firms) joined forces with Japanese companies to provide the needed equipment. AMF teamed with C. Itoh Bowling Company and Brunswick with Mitsui and Company. Sales for AMF-C. Itoh peaked at $258 million in 1972, sagging to $3 million by 1975 as the sales spree ended.

Conglomerate mergers were endemic from the 1960s through the 1980s, and the sporting goods industry was not immune. Brunswick acquired MacGregor Golf Club Company, Beatrice Foods bought Hart Ski Manufacturing Company, and the Rawlings Division of Spalding was sold to an organization known today as Figgie International Holdings, Incorporated. The Questor Corporation took over A. G. Spalding; PepsiCo purchased Wilson Sporting Goods from LTV Corporation; and AMF acquired Ben Hogan Golf Clubs, Head Skis, Voit Balls, Hatteras Yachts, Harley-Davidson Motorcycles, and Roadmaster Bicycles. Acushnet Process Corporation announced in 1973 that it was reducing the number of dimples on its industry-leading golf ball from 336 to 324; this would cause the ball to fly farther. At the same time, Acushnet expressed its intent to remain independent; however, in 1976 the firm was acquired by American Brands, whose flagship firm is American Tobacco Company. In 1977 Hart Ski became independent again, and AMF sold Harley-Davidson and Head Skis in 1981. The year 1985 saw PepsiCo sell Wilson Sporting Goods to Wesray Capital Corporation.

When the 1977 major league baseball season opened, a staple of the national pastime was missing: A. G. Spalding was no longer furnishing the balls for the big leagues. The honor of providing the official ball had become too expensive. It cost Spalding two dollars to produce a ball, and the venerable firm was selling each to the majors at $1.50. Supplying the leagues with 250,000 balls each season was creating a considerable loss for Spalding.

Just about the time citizens of many nations were learning the benefits of running, jogging was swiftly adopted as an American fad, and smart runners sought special shoes for comfort as well as protection. A well-established German manufacturer for soccer shoes, Adidas, moved to the front of the pack in the scramble to provide equipment for runners. In 1982 Adidas sales for all its lines worldwide were $1 billion. Moving into the second spot was an American company, Nike. Another German firm, Puma, lagged far to the rear. Good fortune, however, was about to smile on Puma.

Adidas had for years promoted its products—especially soccer shoes—with celebrity endorsements; many stars of European soccer wore Adidas. Puma employed no comparable contingent, but had attempted to sign up a few well-known athletes. It executives sensed fabulous potential in a teenage tennis player. For his endorsement, Puma paid the lad $600,000. Shortly thereafter, the player, Boris Becker, won the Wimbledon tournament—twice. The company has estimated that signing Becker brought an additional $50 million in sales for 1985. Becker's latest contract with Puma is a multimillion dollar, six-year pact.

Product liability has become a critical concern for the sporting goods industry in the closing years of the twentieth century. Where does a firm stand when a consumer files suit over faulty equipment? A focal point is the football helmet. Putting these helmets on the market is a risky venture, because it makes a firm vulnerable to damage suits. In 1972 Spalding ceased manufacturing helmets. In the next decade and a half, *Fortune* reported, another half-dozen firms suspended helmet production. Two dominant companies remain: Bike Athletic Company (of Colgate-Palmolive) and Riddell (of MacGregor Sports Goods). After a high school player broke his neck in practice, a judge awarded a $12 million settlement against Riddell. According to *Fortune*, some equipment firms have estimated that, with insurance premiums rising, liability insurance costs for a helmet manufacturer could exceed manufacturing costs.

The sporting goods saga is not merely one of megafirms and their rapid responses to American tastes. It is also the story of astute retailers. One retail store, located in New York City, has billed itself as "The Greatest Sporting Goods Store in the World." At the start of the twentieth century, David T. Abercrombie was operating a camping gear emporium on South Street in Manhattan. In 1902 attorney Ezra M. Fitch bought an interest in the business. He led the firm through a vigorous expansion phase that included relocating to Madison Avenue in 1917. For years, the company featured a broad assortment of merchandise for the well-to-do sportsman— baseballs, boxing gloves, running shorts, and any piece of equipment necessary for an African safari, including a wide array of guns. In the autumn of 1976, when *Business Week* was bemoaning the dip in sporting goods sales across America, Abercrombie and Fitch went into reorganization under the bankruptcy laws. It was soon acquired by Oshman's Sporting Goods, a firm holding around 200 stores in the United States by the 1980s. No longer on Madison Avenue and no longer carrying firearms, A and F has stores on Fifth Avenue and on Water Street in Manhattan.

Catering to the clothing and equipment needs of the outdoorsman (hunters, fishermen, campers, hikers, backpackers) has been the hallmark of L. L. Bean's mail order catalogue firm. In 1907 Leon Leonwood Bean moved back to Freeport, Maine, to help his brother Ervin run a retail dry goods store. In 1911 L. L. invented a boot with leather top and rubber bottom: the Maine Hunting Shoe. Shortly afterward L. L. Bean began selling the shoe by mail, using a small catalogue. Expansion of the catalogue business was gradual and irregular; today, a grandson of L. L. Bean heads the firm, and annual sales exceed $250 million.

Nearly a century after A. G. Spalding entered the industry, a weightlifter's complaint spawned what is today a large manufacturer and distributor of sporting goods. The body builder, in a 1960 conversation with engineer Forrest Hood "Fob" James, Jr., lamented that cast-iron barbells rusted, were noisy, and tended to mar household floors. James agreed, and in 1961 set out to develop a high-density material that could be poured into a plastic mold. He called the concrete-like substance Orbatron and built a company around it, using $31,000 contributed by a cadre of East Alabama businessmen. His brother Calvin soon joined him in the firm, Diversified Products Corporation of Opelika, Alabama.

The new barbells were ready for market by 1964, and Fob James made a call to the manager of the Sears, Roebuck store in Mobile in an effort to procure a retail outlet for the innovative product. The local store did not carry weightlifting equipment, but the manager thought that the far-flung merchandising chain might be interested. His suggestion led to a commitment from Sears, and to this day Sears, Roebuck and Company is the lead customer of Diversified Products.

In 1972 Fob James sold his firm to the Liggett Group. The following year he was elected governor of Alabama. Management of Diversified Products Corporation fell to Calvin James. Under Calvin's leadership, Diversified Products has expanded its line of sporting goods to include hundreds of products, among them exercise bikes, hand exercisers, table tennis tables, sportswear, basketball goals and backboards, free-standing fitness systems, racquetball equipment, sports bags, golf accessories, rowing machines, and treadmills.

Customers (open line accounts) number over 8,000 and include, in addition to Sears, general merchandising firms such as K-Mart, Montgomery Ward, and J. C. Penney. Currently a division of Grand Metropolitan of London, the firm has facilities in the United States at Opelika, Alabama, Compton, California, and Hackensack, New Jersey, and abroad in Great Britain, West Germany, and Canada.

BIBLIOGRAPHIC ESSAY

Toys, Dolls, and Games

More of the history of toys, dolls, and games can be found in Marvin Kaye's *A Toy Is Born*, a compact yet comprehensive look at how some of our favorites were brought into production. A bibliography is provided. Despite no coverage beyond 1973 (Cabbage Patch Kids are not included) and no pictures, *A Toy Is Born* is an excellent indicator of directions to take in learning more about the toy industry. It is the best source of personal stories behind our most-loved toys, games, and dolls.

Providing plenty of pictures (both black-and-white and color) but little historical narrative is *A History Of Toys* (1966) by Antonia Fraser. It includes a list of works suitable for historical research. A similar volume is *The Golden Age of Toys* (1967) by Jac Remise and Jean Fondin.

Constance Eileen King's *The Encyclopedia of Toys* (1978) is liberally illustrated (including many color photos) and divides the history of the toy industry into six logical sections: miniature living; toys purely for pleasure; wheeled toys and children's transport; metal toys; board and table games; and educational toys and pastimes.

Well illustrated with some absorbing snatches of historical narrative on sturdy toys—no dolls—is *Collecting Antique Toys: A Practical Guide* (Dou-

cette and Collins 1981). The book is a guide for adults wishing to invest
in valuable toys of yesteryear. There is, for example, a helpful section entitled
"Ferreting Out the Flakes." Nevertheless, children will enjoy beautiful color
photos of toys like those their grandparents played with.

In Praise of Dollhouses: The Story of a Personal Collection (1978) by
Catherine Dorris Callicott and Lawson Holderness is billed as the documentation of a single dollhouse collection, but it is far more. The reader is
treated to an open-house day in a village of tiny houses, and learns of the
pleasure such dwellings have provided through the centuries.

King's *Dolls and Dolls' Houses* (1977) provides, along with the visuals,
detailed histories of famous dolls with ample mention of firm names and
creators. Robert Culff's *World of Toys* (1969) is a unique treatment of dolls
of antiquity and dolls outside the well-covered Euro-American sphere.

Articles in periodicals can also be helpful. The December, 1936, issue of
Fortune contains "Dolls—Made in America" (p. 103), which captures the
state of the doll-making industry when Dy-Dee and the Shirley Temple and
Dionne Quintuplet look-alikes were top sellers.

More recently, the October 24, 1983, issue of *Time* brought us "Let's
Get Trivial" (p. 88), an interesting account of the development of the Trivial
Pursuit game. The story begins on "a rainy Saturday afternoon in Montreal
in 1979 . . ." and ends with the mass manufacture of the game by Selchow
and Righter. In the December 26, 1983, issue of *Fortune* Steven Flax considers the toy industry at Christmas, emphasizing Roberts's creation of the
Cabbage Patch Kids. Edward C. Baig provided an insert on Roberts. For
the April, 1989, issue of *Sky*—in-flight magazine of Delta Air Lines—Sally
Stich suitably marked a milestone birthday of a favorite American doll with
"Barbie at 30" (p. 32), a compact bio of the stunning blonde, her origins,
her collectors, and her continuing grasp on popularity.

Narratives developed by firms themselves are another historical source.
Kaye (in *A Toy Is Born*) lists several such works in his bibliography. One
example (not found in Kaye) of this form is *The Milton Bradley Story*,
published by the Newcomen Society from a speech in 1972 by James J.
Shea, Jr., then president and chairman of the board of Milton Bradley.

Sporting Goods

Books in Print 1986–1987—Subject Index lists no histories of sporting
goods. The *Cumulative Book Index*, going back through 1967, is equally
silent. If such a narrative on the industry was written in 1966 or earlier, it
is missing a quarter century of change in a dynamic business. But the outlook
is not bleak for the person wishing to learn more about sporting goods.
Several books offer help.

Peter Levine has written *A. G. Spalding and the Rise of Baseball* (1985).
One chapter (starting on page 71) deals with Spalding as a purveyor of

sporting goods. His early association with major league baseball enabled him to dominate the industry for years; Spalding's story is almost synonymous with that of the early industry.

The Man Who Invented Baseball (1973) by Harold Peterson covers the early days of organized baseball in the United States. Scattered throughout the book are references to equipment manufacturers such as Reach, Wright, and Spalding. References to equipment are gathered in a single chapter in *A Baseball Century* (1976) by Roger Angell et al. The chapter on major league baseball equipment (p. 204) is written by Mercer Field and is a fascinating account of the development of gloves, catcher's masks, bats, batting helmets, and so on, through 100 years of the National League. Field freely credits individuals and firms involved in equipment production.

M. R. Montgomery's book, *In Search of L. L. Bean* (1984), captures the affability of this Maine entrepreneur whose catalogue of outdoor gear and wearing apparel has been a retailing success.

Much of the published history of the sporting equipment industry is in periodicals. The July, 1939, issue of *Fortune* sketches the history of a well-known New York retailer of sporting goods, Abercrombie and Fitch. The May 9, 1936, issue of *Business Week* depicted how the Depression had affected the industry but hailed signs of recovery in "Outdoor Fever Booms Business" (p. 13). "Ball and Bat Crisis" (p. 41) in the June 2, 1945, issue of *Business Week* explained how the war had drastically reduced sporting goods supplies here at home. Seven years later, *Business Week* described the postwar boom for sports retailers in "A New Trend: Everybody's Going Out for Sports" (June 7, 1952, p. 84). In 1969 *Business Week* reported on how this exciting industry stood in "The $4-Billion Market in Fun" (February 8, p. 82). Two *Fortune* pieces investigate the age of acquisitions and mergers. In "The Happy Divorce that Saved Hart Ski" (December 18, 1978, p. 86), Dick Griffin tells how that company was acquired by Beatrice Foods and then broke free. A study of AMF and its many sports divisions is found in "AMF Vrooms into Who Knows What" (Loomis, April 9, 1979, p. 76).

The impact of the fitness craze on the industry is revealed in at least three items. "The Affluent Activists" (p. 22) in *Forbes* for August 1, 1976, provides a status report on Americans' tendency to be energetic and on the go, and glances at the accompanying equipment needs. *Business Week*, July 18, 1983, analyzes sports shoe manufacturers and the sharp competition that has accompanied the jogging fad in "Two U.S. Rivals Give Adidas a Run for Its Money" (p. 69). Within a year, however, running products had saturated the market (Phalon 1984, p. 39).

A prime concern in the final years of the twentieth century is product liability. *Fortune*'s Michael Brody warns what can happen "When Products Turn into Liabilities" (March 3, 1986, p. 20); as evidence, he cites a $12 million judgment over a football helmet. But *Business Week* had happier news for the industry. In "Boris Becker May Be Puma's Ace in the U.S."

(July 21, 1986, p. 84), Frederick Miller and Rose Brady recount how Becker's endorsement has put a hump in Puma's sales.

BIBLIOGRAPHY

"Abercrombie and Fitch." *Fortune* 20 (July 1939): 124–234.

"The Affluent Activists." *Forbes* 118 (August 1, 1976): 22–25.

Angell, Roger, et al. *A Baseball Century*. New York: Rutledge Books, 1976.

"Ball and Bat Crisis." *Business Week* 822 (June 2, 1945): 41–42.

Brody, Michael. "When Products Turn into Liabilities." *Fortune* 113 (March 3, 1986): 20–24.

Callicott, Catherine Dorris, and Lawson Holderness. *In Praise of Dollhouses: The Story of a Personal Collection*. New York: William Morrow, 1978.

Culff, Robert. *The World of Toys*. New York: Hamlyn Publishing Group, 1969.

"Dolls—Made in America." *Fortune* 14 (December 1936): 103–200.

Doucette, Joseph, and C. L. Collins. *Collecting Antique Toys: A Practical Guide*. New York: Macmillan, 1981.

Flax, Steven. "The Christmas Zing in Zapless Toys." *Fortune* 108 (December 26, 1983): 98–108.

"The $4-Billion Market in Fun." *Business Week* 2058 (February 8, 1969): 82–84.

Fraser, Antonia. *A History of Toys*. London: Delacorte Press, 1966.

Griffin, Dick. "The Happy Divorce that Saved Hart Ski." *Fortune* 98 (December 18, 1978): 86–90.

Hartmann, Cyril Hughes. *Games and Gamesters of the Restoration*. 1930. Reprint. Port Washington, NY: Kennikat Press, 1971.

Kaye, Marvin. *A Toy Is Born*. New York: Stein & Day, 1973.

King, Constance Eileen. *Dolls and Dolls' Houses*. New York: Hamlyn Publishing Group, 1977.

———. *The Encyclopedia of Toys*. New York: Crown, 1978.

"Let's Get Trivial." *Time* 122 (October 24, 1983): 88.

Levine, Peter. *A. G. Spalding and the Rise of Baseball*. New York: Oxford University Press, 1985.

Loomis, Carol J. "AMF Vrooms into Who Knows What." *Fortune* 99 (April 9, 1979): 76–88.

Miller, Frederick A., and Rose Brady. "Boris Becker May Be Puma's Ace in the U.S." *Business Week* 2956 (July 21, 1986): 84.

Montgomery, M. R. *In Search of L. L. Bean*. Boston: Little, Brown, 1984.

"A New Trend: Everybody's Going Out for Sports." *Business Week* 1188 (June 7, 1952): 84–86.

"Outdoor Fever Booms Business." *Business Week* 349 (May 9, 1936): 13–14.

Peterson, Harold. *The Man Who Invented Baseball*. New York: Charles Scribner's Sons, 1973.

Phalon, Richard. "Out of Breath." *Forbes* 134 (October 22, 1984): 39–40.

Remise, Jac, and Jean Fondin. *The Golden Age of Toys*. Greenwich, CT: New York Graphic Society (Time-Life Books), 1967.

Shea, James J., Jr. *The Milton Bradley Story*. New York: Newcomen Society in
    North America, 1973.
Stich, Sally. "Barbie at 30." *Sky* 18 (April 1989): 32–40.
"Two U.S. Rivals Give Adidas a Run for Its Money." *Business Week* 2799 (July
    18, 1983): 69.

INDEX

ABOUT THE EDITORS AND CONTRIBUTORS

ROBERT M. ADUDDELL, associate professor of economics at Loyola University of Chicago, holds a B.A. in economics from Drake University and an M.A. and a Ph.D. in economics from Northwestern University. He is the author of several papers on the meat-packing industry, which have appeared in *Business Enterprise and Economic Change*, *Business History Review*, and *Business and Economic History*.

LUTZ ALT received a liberal arts education at C.C.N.Y. and a business education at the University of Chicago. He held a variety of executive positions at CBS, Inc., and Polaroid Corporation. He retired from Polaroid as vice president-international to pursue academic interests at M.I.T. (Ph.D., 1986). He has been professor at Queens College, C.U.N.Y., since 1987.

JACK BLICKSILVER is professor of economics at Georgia State University. He has been on the faculties of Northwestern University and the Harvard Business School. His major areas of interest and research include U.S. economic history, 1865–1900; southern economic development; and the business history of textiles, apparel, insurance, and railroads. He is the author of *Cotton Manufacturing in the Southeast: An Historical Analysis* (1959) and *Defenders and Defense of Big Business in the United States, 1880–1900* (1985), and the editor of *Views on U.S. Economic and Business History: Molding the Mixed Enterprise Economy* (1985).

JOHN S. BOWDIDGE is a professor of finance and general business at Southwest Missouri State University. A graduate of the University of Georgia, he received his doctorate from the University of Missouri-Kansas City.

He serves as an associate editor of the *Wall Street Review* and coauthors a weekly stock-market column for the *Springfield* (MO) *Business Journal*.

LOUIS P. CAIN, professor of economics at Loyola University of Chicago, holds an A.B. in economics from Princeton University and an M.A. and a Ph.D. in economics from Northwestern University. He is the author of *Sanitation Strategy for a Lakefront Metropolis* (1978) and the forthcoming *Wherever Electricity Goes*. His articles have appeared in *Journal of Economic History, Explorations in Economic History*, and *Business History Review*. He serves on the editorial board of *Business History Review*.

SUSAN B. CARTER, associate professor of economics at Smith College, received her Ph.D. in economics from Stanford University in 1981. She has published articles on women's educational history, women's work as teachers and department store employees, and women in manufacturing at the turn of the century. She has also written about gender differences in rural-urban migration.

MARVIN N. FISCHBAUM received his Ph.D. in economics from Columbia University in 1965. In 1966–67 he did postdoctoral work in history at the University of Pittsburgh. He is currently professor of economics at Indiana State University. He writes regularly for the *Indiana Business Review*.

EMIL E. FRIBERG, JR., is an economist with the National Security and International Affairs Division of the U.S. General Accounting Office. He received his Ph.D. from the University of North Carolina at Chapel Hill, where his dissertation, "The Federal Government and the History of the U.S. Computer Industry," was directed by Robert Gallman.

ROBERT CHARLES GRAHAM completed his Ph.D. in economics at the University of Illinois in 1985. He has served as an assistant professor of economics at the University of North Carolina at Charlotte. In addition, he was a visiting assistant professor at the University of North Carolina at Chapel Hill during the 1988–89 academic year. His dissertation, "Diffusion During Depression: The Adoption of the Tractor by Illinois Farmers," was one of three recognized by the Business History Conference in 1985. He is currently researching individual farm records from the 1920s and 1930s.

WILLIAM J. HAUSMAN is professor of economics at the College of William and Mary and Secretary-Treasurer of the Business History Conference. He received his Ph.D. from the University of Illinois in 1976. His current research interests include the history of the electric utility industry, and he has published with John Neufeld "Time of Day Pricing in the U.S.

Electric Power Industry at the Turn of the Century," *Rand Journal of Economics* 15 (Spring 1984).

K. AUSTIN KERR, professor of history at the Ohio State University, holds an A.B. degree from Oberlin College, an M.A. from the University of Iowa, and a Ph.D. from the University of Pittsburgh. He is the coauthor of *Business Enterprise in American History*, 2d ed. (forthcoming) and the author of *Organized for Prohibition: A New History of the Anti-Saloon League* (1985) as well as other books and articles. He serves as series editor of "Historical Perspectives on Business Enterprise" for the Ohio State University Press.

THOMAS A. McGAHAGAN holds the Ph.D. in intellectual history from the University of Pennsylvania. He taught the history of science at Shiraz University in Iran before turning to the study of economic history and the history of economic thought, subjects he currently teaches at the University of Pittsburgh at Johnstown.

CAROL J. MILLER, associate professor of business law and history at Southwest Missouri State University, earned a J.D., an M.B.A., and a B.A. in history from the University of Missouri-Columbia, and a B.S. in social science from Northwest Missouri State University. She was awarded the 1989 Best Article in the *Midwest Law Review* for a constitutional legal history article and was named the 1988 Bicentennial Lecturer at SMSU. Miller has published articles in numerous legal and professional journals and is the past president of the Midwest Business Law Association.

K. V. NAGARAJAN is an assistant professor at the School of Commerce and Administration, Laurentian University, Sudbury, Ontario, Canada. His articles have appeared in the *Journal of Post Keynesian Economics* and other journals. He is a contributor to *Asiaweek*.

MICHAEL V. NAMORATO is associate professor of history at the University of Mississippi. His areas of specialization are southern United States economic and business history and twentieth-century American history. He has edited two books, one on the New Deal and the South and the other on civil rights since the *Brown* decision. His biography of Rexford G. Tugwell was published by Praeger in 1988. He has also published in the *Wall Street Review of Books*, the *Journal of Economic History*, and the *Journal of Mississippi History*.

SPIRO G. PATTON, a private economic consultant, holds a B.A. in economics from Pennsylvania State University and a Ph.D. in economics from the University of Pittsburgh. He is the author of *Economics: Cases and Applications* (1989). His articles have appeared in *Business Economics,* the *Christian Science Monitor,* and other journals.

DONALD R. STABILE, associate professor of economics at St. Mary's College of Maryland, has a B.S. in business administration from the University of Florida and an M.S. and a Ph.D. in economics from the University of Massachusetts at Amherst. He is the author of *Prophets of Order* (1984) and of several articles on the ideas of Thorstein Veblen.

TIMOTHY E. SULLIVAN, assistant professor of economics at Elon College, North Carolina, previously served as visiting assistant professor at Wellesley College. He graduated from the University of Illinois at Urbana-Champaign and wrote his dissertation on the industrial development of the American Midwest from 1850 to 1880.

AMY L. WALTON is a senior economist with the Jet Propulsion Laboratory, California Institute of Technology. She received a Ph.D. degree in economics from Princeton University and has taught economics at Princeton University and the California Institute of Technology. While a member of the Division of Industrial Science and Technological Innovation at the National Science Foundation, Walton conducted a study of research practices at the top 100 universities in the United States. The results of the study are summarized in "Research Management at the University Department," *Science and Technology Studies* 4 (Fall/Winter 1986): 35–38. Other publications include *The Solar Alternative: An Economic Perspective* (1982).

BESSIE E. WHITTEN is the supervisor of the Manuscript Preparation Division of the College of Business at Auburn University. She has served as copy editor for the *University of Florida Law Review* and the *Journal of Management.* She is the assistant editor of the *Wall Street Review.*

DAVID O. WHITTEN holds a B.S. from the College of Charleston (SC), an M.A. from the University of South Carolina, and a Ph.D. from Tulane University of Louisiana. He is professor of economics at Auburn University and editor of the *Wall Street Review.* He is the author of *Andrew Durnford: A Black Sugar Planter in Antebellum Louisiana* (1981), *The Emergence of Giant Enterprise, 1860–1914: American Commercial Enterprise and Extractive Industries* (1983), and articles in *Business History Review, Agricultural History,* and the *Journal of Southern Studies.*

JAMES L. WILES is a professor of economics at Stonehill College in North Easton, Massachusetts. He also serves as co-director of the Bridgewater State College-Stonehill College Regional Research Institute. Wiles received his Ph.D. in economics from Harvard University. His teaching and research interests are economic history, regional studies, and the history of economic theory.

MIRA WILKINS, professor of economics, Florida International University, holds an A.B. degree from Radcliffe College and a Ph.D. from the University of Cambridge. She is the author of many scholarly books and articles. Among her books are *The Emergence of Multinational Enterprise: American Business Abroad from the Colonial Era to 1914* (1970); *The Maturing of Multinational Enterprise: American Business Abroad from 1914 to 1970* (1974), nominated for a National Book Award; and *The History of Foreign Investment in the United States to 1914* (1989). Wilkins was president of the Business History Conference, the professional society of business historians, 1987–88.

DAVID M. WISHART, assistant professor of economics at Wittenberg University, holds the A.B., M.S., and Ph.D. degrees from the University of Illinois, Urbana-Champaign. His research interests include natural resource economics and American economic history.